Frommer's®

The Carolinas & Georgia

10th Edition

by Darwin Porter & Danforth Prince

D0062650

WILEY
Wiley Publishing, Inc.

ABOUT THE AUTHORS

As a team of veteran travel writers, **Darwin Porter** and **Danforth Prince** have produced dozens of previous titles for Frommer's, including many of their guides to Europe, the Caribbean, Bermuda, The Bahamas, and parts of America's Deep South. A film critic, columnist, and radio broadcaster, Porter is also a noted biographer of Hollywood celebrities, garnering critical acclaim for overviews of the life and times of, among others, Marlon Brando, Katharine Hepburn, Humphrey Bogart, Howard Hughes, and Michael Jackson. Prince was formerly employed by the Paris bureau of the *New York Times* and is today the president of Blood Moon Productions and other media-related firms. In 2008, Porter and Prince released *Hollywood Babylon,* their newest book about Hollywood, sexuality, and sin as filtered through 85 years of celebrity excess.

Published by:

WILEY PUBLISHING, INC.

111 River St.
Hoboken, NJ 07030-5774

ISBN 978-0-470-88730-1 (paper); ISBN 978-1-118-03339-5 (ebk); ISBN 978-1-118-03340-1 (ebk); ISBN 978-1-118-03341-8 (ebk)

Editor: Alexia Travaglini
Production Editor: Jana M. Stefanciosa
Cartographer: Roberta Stockwell
Production by Wiley Indianapolis Composition Services
Front Cover Photo: North Carolina's Cape Lookout National Seashor
Back Cover Photo: Wright Brothers National Memorial on the Outer
Vehse / Alamy Images

For information on our other products and services or to obtain tec
Customer Care Department within the U.S. at 877/762-2974, outside
317/572-4002.

Wiley also publishes its books in a variety of electronic formats. Sor
not be available in electronic formats.

Manufactured in the United States of America

5 4 3 2 1

CONTENTS

10 GREAT SMOKY MOUNTAINS NATIONAL PARK 220

11 CHARLESTON 239

12 HILTON HEAD & THE LOW COUNTRY 280

13 MYRTLE BEACH & THE GRAND STRAND 303

14 COLUMBIA & THE HEARTLAND 330

LIST OF MAPS

AN INVITATION TO THE READER

In researching this book, we discovered many wonderful places—hotels, restaurants, shops, and more. We're sure you'll find others. Please tell us about them, so we can share the information with your fellow travelers in upcoming editions. If you were disappointed with a recommendation, we'd love to know that, too. Please write to:

Frommer's The Carolinas & Georgia, 10th Edition
Wiley Publishing, Inc. • 111 River St. • Hoboken, NJ 07030-5774
frommersfeedback@wiley.com

AN ADDITIONAL NOTE

Please be advised that travel information is subject to change at any time—and this is especially true of prices. We therefore suggest that you write or call ahead for confirmation when making your travel plans. The authors, editors, and publisher cannot be held responsible for the experiences of readers while traveling. Your safety is important to us, however, so we encourage you to stay alert and be aware of your surroundings. Keep a close eye on cameras, purses, and wallets, all favorite targets of thieves and pickpockets.

FROMMER'S STAR RATINGS, ICONS & ABBREVIATIONS

Every hotel, restaurant, and attraction listing in this guide has been ranked for quality, value, service, amenities, and special features using a **star-rating system.** In country, state, and regional guides, we also rate towns and regions to help you narrow down your choices and budget your time accordingly. Hotels and restaurants are rated on a scale of zero (recommended) to three stars (exceptional). Attractions, shopping, nightlife, towns, and regions are rated according to the following scale: zero stars (recommended), one star (highly recommended), two stars (very highly recommended), and three stars (must-see).

In addition to the star-rating system, we also use **seven feature icons** that point you to the great deals, in-the-know advice, and unique experiences that separate travelers from tourists. Throughout the book, look for:

special finds—those places only insiders know about

fun facts—details that make travelers more informed and their trips more fun

kids—best bets for kids and advice for the whole family

special moments—those experiences that memories are made of

overrated—places or experiences not worth your time or money

insider tips—great ways to save time and money

great values—where to get the best deals

The following **abbreviations** are used for credit cards:

AE American Express	DISC Discover	V Visa
DC Diners Club	MC MasterCard	

TRAVEL RESOURCES AT FROMMERS.COM

Frommer's travel resources don't end with this guide. Frommer's website, **www.frommers. com**, has travel information on more than 4,000 destinations. We update features regularly, giving you access to the most current trip-planning information and the best airfare, lodging, and car-rental bargains. You can also listen to podcasts, connect with other Frommers. com members through our active-reader forums, share your travel photos, read blogs from guidebook editors and fellow travelers, and much more.

THE BEST OF THE CAROLINAS & GEORGIA

Visitors won't have any trouble amusing themselves in the Carolinas and Georgia, with activities ranging from exploring the beaches along the Atlantic and taking scenic drives through farmland and forest, to visiting small historic towns, hitting world-class links, and dining at a wide variety of restaurants.

We've made it easier for you to narrow down your plans by compiling a list of some of our favorite experiences and discoveries and providing the kind of candid advice we'd give our close friends.

THE best SCENIC DRIVES

- **The Outer Banks** (North Carolina): If you can get past the overly crowded highways in summer and the strip-mall development, prepare yourself for one of the strangest and most beautiful natural geographical areas in North America. To explore this thin slip of land, drive N.C. 12, beginning at Corolla in the north and ending at the Ocracoke lighthouse in the south. Along the way, you'll pass the shifting shoals of Oregon Inlet, Pea Island National Wildlife Refuge, and pristine stretches of beach along Cape Hatteras National Seashore. See chapter 5.
- **The Blue Ridge Parkway** (North Carolina): This is the single most dramatic drive in the tri-state area and one of the grandest drives in the world. Beginning in Virginia, the parkway winds and twists along mountain crests for some 470 miles. It passes through most of western North Carolina before halting at Great Smoky Mountains National Park near the Tennessee border. See chapter 10.
- **Chattahoochee National Forest** (Georgia): U.S. Route 76 from Ellijay and past Blairsville to Clayton is one of the most scenic routes in Georgia, dating back to the 1920s and 1930s, when the federal government purchased much of the land here. That act alone helped preserve the fading culture of the southern Appalachians, which you can see today as you slowly make your way through this national forest. See chapter 18.

THE best FAMILY VACATIONS

- **Great Smoky Mountains National Park** (North Carolina): Sixteen peaks of the southern Appalachians soar skyward to approximately 6,000 feet. We're attracted not just by the mountains, but also by the surrounding theme parks and activities, ranging from water parks to valley railroads and offering countless opportunities for fun. See chapter 10.
- **Charleston** (South Carolina): If the tri-state area has a town that's designed for families, it's Charleston. The city has been called an 18th-century etching come to life. You can take boat rides to Fort Sumter, where the Civil War began; explore Magnolia Plantation, with its petting zoo and gardens; and visit several family-oriented nature parks, including one at Palmetto Islands. See chapter 11.
- **Hilton Head** (South Carolina): Much more upscale than Myrtle Beach, Hilton Head is filled with broad beaches. You can enjoy myriad activities, such as biking on the beaches, taking a dolphin-watching cruise, and exploring the 605-acre Sea Pines Forest Preserve, a public wilderness tract with walking trails. All major hotels offer summer activity centers for kids. See chapter 12.
- **The Golden Isles** (Georgia): This string of lush, subtropical barrier islands, located south of Savannah near the Florida border, is designed for family fun and adventure. Summer Waves, a 118-acre water park on Jekyll Island, is just one of the many attractions designed with children in mind. Nature still thrives in this setting, including Cumberland Island National Seashore, a 16×3-mile wildlife sanctuary. See chapter 21.

THE best OF THE OLD SOUTH

- **Beaufort** (North Carolina): Not to be confused with the town of the same name in South Carolina (see below), Beaufort is North Carolina's third-oldest settlement, dating from 1713. Its 200-year-old houses and narrow streets reflect the old way of life. The town is rich in Carolina tradition that predates the Civil War. See chapter 6.
- **Beaufort** (South Carolina): Straight from the screen in *The Big Chill* and *The Prince of Tides*, Beaufort is like a sleepy dream of long ago. Established in 1710, it grew fat from Sea Island cotton. Wealthy owners built lavish antebellum houses that still stand today, luring visitors with their faded charm. See chapter 12.
- **Georgetown** (South Carolina): A town with surprisingly well-preserved pre–Revolutionary War houses and churches, Georgetown invites you to enter a time capsule. In this small enclave of some 11,000 people, more than 50 historic homes still stand, dating back as far as 1737. See chapter 13.
- **Madison** (Georgia): Only an hour's drive east of Atlanta stands today's version of what antebellum travelers called "the wealthiest and most aristocratic village between Charleston and New Orleans." General Sherman was an acquaintance of a local U.S. senator from here and, for old times' sake, agreed not to burn down the town. Its oak-lined streets and historic homes still stand. See chapter 17.
- **Savannah** (Georgia): Because General Sherman was talked out of burning it, he gave Savannah to President Lincoln as a Christmas present instead. No city in all the South has Savannah's peculiar charm. Its very name suggests Spanish moss, hoop skirts, mint juleps on the veranda, *Midnight in the Garden of Good and Evil*, and lovely antebellum architecture. See chapter 20.

THE best SMALL TOWNS

○ **Edenton** (North Carolina): Edenton is the quintessential small port town along the Outer Banks. If colonial-style clapboard is your thing, this is the place to see it. You can wander past well-tended gardens on streets shaded by magnolia and pecan trees. Edenton has been here since 1722, and the National Register of Historic Places long ago gave the town its blessing. See chapter 5.

○ **Asheville** (North Carolina): The city might object to such a classification, but it's the "small town" of cities. One of the most desirable places to live in America, Asheville has attracted everybody from the Vanderbilts to the tragic feuding couple F. Scott and Zelda Fitzgerald. With its well-tended blocks and broad, tidy streets, it's the most stylish town of its size in the tri-state area, and locals are determined to keep it that way. See chapter 9.

○ **Thomasville** (Georgia): The plantation era never died here, and life still moves at a leisurely pace along Thomasville's shady, tree-lined streets. Over the years, the town's aristocratic elegance has attracted the wintering wealthy, including the Rockefellers and Goodriches. Jacqueline Kennedy fled here to recover from the assassination of her husband. See chapter 19.

○ **Macon** (Georgia): In the heart of the state, this sleepy town has a historic core of approximately 50 buildings listed on the National Register of Historic Places. Nearly 600 other structures here have been cited for their architectural significance. Macon long ago decided to let Atlanta race hysterically toward the millennium; it prefers to wander slowly along, content in its appealing charm, although its cherry-tree-lined downtown is undergoing revitalization. See chapter 19.

THE best GOLF COURSES

○ **The Pinehurst Resort Golf Courses** (1 Carolina Vista, Pinehurst, North Carolina): This is the only resort in the South that has eight signature courses. The original architect was the now-legendary Donald Ross. All the great names in golf—including Nelson, Jones, and Hogan—have played these courses. In all, there are 126 holes of golf, with modern holes designed by Tom Fazio and Rees Jones. See p. 182.

○ **Pine Needles Lodge & Golf Club** (Southern Pines, North Carolina): This 1927 Donald Ross masterpiece is a challenging par-71 course, attracting golfers of various skills. The course plays to 6,708 yards from the championship tees and has been immaculately restored to its original splendor. See p. 188.

○ **Palmetto Dunes Oceanfront Resort** (Hilton Head, South Carolina): This course, designed by George Fazio, is an 18-hole, 6,534-yard, par-70 course named by *Golf Digest* as one of the "75 Best American Resort Courses." It has been cited for its combined "length and keen accuracy." See p. 284.

○ **Old South Golf Links** (Bluffton, South Carolina): This 18-hole, 6,772-yard, par-72 course has been recognized as one of the "Top 10 Public Courses" by *Golf Digest*. It has panoramic views and a natural setting that ranges from an oak forest to tidal salt marshes. See p. 285.

○ **The Lodge at Sea Island Golf Club** (St. Simons Island, Georgia): Owned by the Cloister, the most exclusive resort in the South, this widely acclaimed golf course lies at the end of the Avenue of Oaks, the site of a former plantation. Opened in 1927, the club consists of several courses, such as the 18-hole Ocean

Forest (7,011 yd., par 72). It has been compared favorably to such golfing meccas as St. Andrews in Scotland and Pebble Beach in California. See p. 500.

THE best BEACHES

- **Cape Hatteras National Seashore** (North Carolina): Some 70 miles of relatively unspoiled beaches begin at Whalebone Junction in South Nags Head and stretch down through Hatteras and Ocracoke islands in the south; in fact, Ocracoke's beaches consistently show up on top-10 lists of the nation's finest. Ferocious tides, strong currents, and fickle winds constantly alter the most dramatic beaches along the Eastern Seaboard. See chapter 5.
- **Hilton Head** (South Carolina): *Travel + Leisure* has hailed these beaches as being among the most beautiful in the world, and we concur. The resort-studded island offers 12 miles of white-sand beaches; still others front the Calibogue and Port Royal sounds. The sand is extremely firm, providing a good surface for biking and many beach games. It's also ideal for walking and jogging—against a backdrop of natural dunes, live oaks, palmettos, and tall Carolina pines. See chapter 12.
- **Myrtle Beach & the Grand Strand** (South Carolina): This is the most popular sand strip along the Eastern Seaboard, attracting 12 million visitors a year—more than the state of Hawaii. Sure, it's overdeveloped and crowded in the summer, but what draws visitors to Myrtle Beach is 10 miles of sand, mostly hard packed and the color of brown sugar. See chapter 13.
- **Wrightsville Beach** (6 miles east of Wilmington, North Carolina): It's the widest beach on the Cape Fear coast: Wrightsville's beige sands stretch for a mile along the oceanfront, set against a backdrop of thick vegetation. It gets very crowded in summer, however. See chapter 6.

THE best LUXURY HOTELS & RESORTS

- **Grove Park Inn Resort & Spa** (Asheville, North Carolina; © 800/438-5800 or 828/252-2711; www.groveparkinn.com): The premier resort of the state has sheltered everybody from Thomas Edison to F. Scott Fitzgerald, and the big names still check in. The hotel is continually upgraded, and it is said to be just as grand as it was on the day it opened in 1913; it even boasts a $14-million, full-service spa. See p. 199.
- **The Sea Pines Resort** (Hilton Head, South Carolina; © 866/561-8802 or 843/785-3333; www.seapines.com): This is the oldest and most famous of the island's resort developments. Set on 4,500 thickly wooded acres, with a total of three golf courses, Sea Pines competes for the summer beach traffic as few resorts in the Caribbean ever could. Its focal point is Harbour Town, which is built around one of the most charming marinas in the Carolinas. Luxurious homes and villas open onto the ocean or golf courses. See p. 293.
- **Ritz-Carlton Buckhead** (Atlanta, Georgia; © 800/241-3333 or 404/237-2700; www.ritzcarlton.com): Often a discreet rendezvous for visiting celebrities, this hotel is the epitome of plushness and luxury. General Sherman wouldn't have burned it; he would have checked in and called for room service. European style and flair set the grace notes, evoked by Regency and Georgian antiques, white

marble floors, and French-crystal chandeliers. Exquisitely decorated guest rooms and one of Atlanta's premier deluxe restaurants add much allure. See p. 372.

o **The Mansion on Forsyth Park** (Savannah, Georgia; © **888/213-3671** or 912/238-5158; www.mansiononforsythpark.com): Almost from its first day, this has been hailed as the most opulent and spectacular boutique hotel in Savannah, a restored redbrick mansion dating from 1888. In addition to all the creature comforts, it is a showcase of art, home to some 400 paintings. See p. 465.

o **The Cloister** (Sea Island, Georgia; © **800/SEA-ISLAND** [732-4752] or 912/638-3611; www.seaisland.com): This hotel has been called the grande dame of all Southern resorts. The Cloister's clubby vibe means formal dinners by night and outdoor activities by day: Think along the lines of the best tennis in Georgia, riding, fishing, and swimming (at the beach or in two inviting pools). See p. 504.

THE best MODERATELY PRICED HOTELS

o **Cedar Crest Inn** (Asheville, North Carolina; © **877/251-1389** or 828/252-1389; www.cedarcrestvictorianinn.com): In a city famed for its B&Bs—the finest in North Carolina—this one rates at the top. A Queen Anne–style mansion built in 1894, Cedar Crest Inn is rich in Victorian trappings, including a captain's walk, projecting turrets, and various architectural follies. See p. 198.

o **Anchorage Inn** (Charleston, South Carolina; © **800/421-2952** or 843/723-8300; www.anchoragencharleston.com): Converted from an antebellum cotton warehouse, this inn, with its mock-Tudor facade, is a bastion of charm and grace, with canopied beds and individually decorated guest rooms. See p. 250.

o **Indigo** (Atlanta, Georgia; © **800/972-2404** or 404/874-9200; www.hotelindigo.com): This boutique hotel across from the famous Fox Theatre offers beautifully furnished guest rooms with hardwood floors and oversize beds. See p. 370.

o **The River Street Inn** (Savannah, Georgia; © **800/253-4229** or 912/234-6400; www.riverstreetinn.com): On Savannah's historic waterfront, this former warehouse has been converted into one of the best inns in town. Its guest rooms are bastions of style and comfort. See p. 464.

THE best BUDGET HOTELS

o **Archers Mountain Inn** (Banner Elk, North Carolina; © **888/827-6155** or 828/898-9004; www.archersmountaininn.com): On Beech Mountain in the Banner Elk area, this is Blue Ridge–mountain living at its best. You can even stay in a modernized log cabin if you choose. Rooms in the main lodge are well equipped, each with a fireplace. See p. 211.

o **Sugar Magnolia** (Atlanta, Georgia; © **404/222-0226;** www.sugarmagnoliabb.com): Situated in a historic district, this 1892 Victorian house of considerable charm rents individually styled and commodious guest rooms with Southern style and flair, each suitable to house a colonel in the Confederate army. The staircase alone is worthy of an entrance by Miss Scarlett. See p. 376.

o **Old Village Post House** (Mount Pleasant, outside Charleston, South Carolina; © **843/388-8935;** www.oldvillageposthouse.com): Across the bridge from downtown Charleston is one of the area's best B&Bs, still steeped in its traditional aura of long ago, though filled with modern conveniences. See p. 252.

- **Bed & Breakfast Inn** (Savannah, Georgia; © **888/238-0518** or 912/238-0518; www.savannahbnb.com): This little charmer is adjacent to the landmark Chatham Square in the oldest section of the Historic District. Built in 1853, just years before the Civil War, it has been restored with sensitivity and filled with antiques and reproductions. See p. 469.

THE best RESTAURANTS

- **Elliotts on Linden** (Pinehurst, North Carolina; © **910/215-0775;** www.elliots onlinden.com): Its fans deem this restaurant the best in North Carolina. Its chef is English-born Mark Elliott, who carefully prepares an inventive cuisine with market-fresh products. See p. 184.
- **Horizons** (in the Grove Park Inn Resort & Spa, Asheville, North Carolina; © **800/438-5800** or 828/252-2711; www.groveparkinn.com): This is the most formal restaurant in western North Carolina, as befits its location in the city's grandest resort. Horizons is consistently rated among the top restaurants in the nation. Patrons are served an excellent array of Continental dishes—including brook trout, bouillabaisse, and medallions of venison—prepared from the freshest ingredients on the market. See p. 201.
- **Anson** (Charleston, South Carolina; © **843/577-0551;** www.ansonrestaurant. com): Hip, stylish, and upscale, this is a favorite dining room of discriminating Charlestonians, who flock here for Low Country dishes with an original, modern twist. Anson compares with top-notch restaurants in New York and San Francisco, and offers the best service in the city. Try the fried cornmeal oysters with potato cakes or the cashew-crusted grouper with champagne sauce. See p. 254.
- **Charlie's L'Etoile Verte** (Hilton Head, South Carolina; © **843/785-9277;** www.charliesgreenstar.com): Like a whimsical Parisian bistro, this elegant yet unpretentious establishment packs them in every night in an area that has more restaurants than customers. The reason is the food. The cuisine borrows freely from almost everywhere. See p. 295.
- **Quinones** (Atlanta, Georgia; © **404/365-0410;** www.starprovisions.com): This gourmet citadel of just 36 seats offers discerning foodies an original take on modern Southern cuisine. It's pricey, but the ever-changing 10-course menu is among the best in Georgia. See p. 378.
- **The Lady & Sons** (Savannah, Georgia; © **912/233-2600;** www.ladyandsons. com): Launched with $200 in 1989, this restaurant has become one of the finest in eastern Georgia, turning out a Southern cuisine of taste and refinement. The buffets are reason enough to visit. And wait until you try Food Network star Paula Deen's chicken potpie. See p. 470.

THE CAROLINAS & GEORGIA IN DEPTH

From steep, sloping mountain forests to lush farmlands that evoke the English countryside, the Carolinas and Georgia offer a landscape as diverse and colorful as the region's residents are personable. Some achingly pastoral countryscapes seem to be torn right from the pages of books by Deep South authors such as Tennessee Williams, Eudora Welty, and William Faulkner.

Hollywood has been reluctant to let go of its love affair with this colorful Old South, and bestselling novels and Academy Award–winning screenplays continue to mine the mystique of a region clad in its own troublesome history. In fact, so many movies have been made in Wilmington, North Carolina, that it has been dubbed "Hollywood East."

Long burdened with a "Scarlett" reputation cluttered with pickup trucks and good ol' boys, these Southern states are actually aging gracefully with time, while maintaining an amiable drawl and such culinary traditions as hot buttered grits and fresh boiled peanuts. Yet they now also boast neon-lit cities with cutting-edge architecture, high-tech industry, exhilarating sports events, and intricately designed highways—not to mention big-city gridlock.

The voices of today's Carolinas and Georgia reflect the diversity of a population that not so long ago faced considerable racial inequality, issues that Georgia native son Martin Luther King, Jr., so eloquently challenged. Other key players in the New South include politicos clamoring to fill the shoes and Senate seat of the recently expired Strom Thurmond. And, of course, there's the dignified, soft-spoken peanut farmer who became president of the United States and is now an agent of world peace.

The Carolinas and Georgia rank among the top 10 states for residential travel and are major destinations for international travelers as well. Every year, Charleston and Savannah place in the top 10 U.S. cities in *Condé Nast Traveler*'s Readers' Choice Awards. From the Smoky Mountains to the sun-kissed Atlantic coastline, from Kitty Hawk's windswept dunes to Georgia's Suwannee River country and Okefenokee Swamp, the tri-state area attracts visitors to the tune of almost 140 million per year.

THE CAROLINAS & GEORGIA TODAY

The late historian C. Vann Woodward once labeled the New South "the Second Reconstruction." As the millennium deepens, he noted that Yankees were coming South, rural life was diminishing, and urbanization was ongoing. "Let's call it the 'Bulldozer Revolution,'" he said, adding that, nonetheless, "I don't think it has demolished the South."

This fast-growing region remains one of the most dynamic and versatile in the country, and yet it still evokes stereotypes, caricatures, and images, some of them still there to be seen: corrupt potbellied sheriffs, crooked Southern judges, country politicians, demure belles, and hell-raisin' preachers. Parts of the backward South are notorious for their "redneck juries," insanely awarding millions upon millions of dollars' worth of damages in civil cases if the defendants are perceived as coming from Yankeeland. But it would be wrong to confuse the South with its caricatures or to fail to understand how rapidly the states of North Carolina, South Carolina, and Georgia are evolving.

The New South is meeting resistance, however. In some respects, the battles of the South no longer center on the age-old conflicts between blacks and whites. As if establishing a last stand in the Old South, the hard-right wing of the Republican Party and the religious right are engaging in a cultural war. Homosexuality is often the issue today that provokes the most moral outrage, with some Southern preachers ranting against it as a "sin against God," whereas more progressive elements in the South (sometimes from the pulpit, but more often from the business world) preach tolerance and understanding, with respect for individual rights regardless of sexual preference.

A dramatic case highlighting this occurred in September 2000 when the Atlanta Gas Light Company, one of the biggest utilities in the South, announced it would offer domestic partner benefits as an option for its employees, including same-sex couples, in order to attract the brightest and best employees in the future. Georgia Equality Project, the statewide gay political group, immediately hailed the move as a major breakthrough.

GEP is continuing to target other major companies in the state to offer the same benefits, and some of these companies are responding. But in other cases, the proposal is met with a "wall of silence." For the GEP, it's an uphill fight.

The New South has prevailed in other areas as well. Witness the removal of the Confederate flag from the dome of the South Carolina State Capitol. It had been flying since 1962, when it was raised in honor of the 100-year anniversary of the Civil War; in the ensuing years, repeated calls to remove it were rejected. This time, it was a fight to the finish: Election-year presidential hopefuls and media pundits from all over the globe weighed in, and 50,000 protesters marched in Columbia on Martin Luther King, Jr.'s, birthday. In the glare of the national spotlight, the opposition agreed to a compromise. On July 1, 2000, the flag was replaced by a shiny replica—said to be more "accurate" than the one that had flown for 38 years—hoisted on a 30-foot pole in front of the Capitol.

Cultural conflicts seem to be inevitable, given the rate of growth and the population shift. The South boasts the fastest-expanding economy in the industrialized world. Each day, the ever-changing population, attracted to the tri-state's industry and technology, grows larger, wealthier, and better educated. Today, instead of magnolia-lined plantations or outhouse-dotted backwoods, a soccer-mom subculture dominates the southern suburbs of Atlanta and Charlotte, complete with minivans, malls, glass office towers, well-manicured subdivisions, and traffic jams. Some tourist areas, such as Hilton Head, are filling up with Northern transplants.

By contrast, income and population in "Black Belt" counties are shrinking. Somewhat ironically, the South also contains some of America's poorest regions, the home of millions who are mired in ignorance and poverty. The *Tobacco Road* image lingers in remote counties where young people grow up but don't stick around. Problems are on the horizon, as automation and global trade promise to wipe out many of the remaining rural textile jobs, and welfare reform will eliminate the money needed to keep some small towns alive.

Yet, Southern tradition is being redefined, from elegant ballets to symphonies set in the refurbished concert halls of days gone by. Indeed, a slow-paced way of life still holds in many small towns, but the cities of the New South are on the move. People have flocked here from around the world—Northerners seeking a milder climate, rural Southerners bored with small-town life, African Americans overcoming years of segregation, Mexicans opening restaurants, Asian immigrants seeking a new life in America, and gays and lesbians, who finally can taste liberation in a region where they were once shunned—turning once-lethargic areas into fast-paced international business complexes.

Time simply can't take away from the true Southerner his small pleasures: fresh-picked butterbeans in the summer, iced sweet tea in the afternoon, a Saturday-morning golf game, sunset cocktails on the porch, church on Sunday, and an overall politeness and civility.

But from Savannah to Charlotte, Southern cities are sprucing up with colorful floral gardens, newly designed roadways, and world-class food markets and restaurants. Atlanta has grown into one of the strongest industrial capitals in the world. As the home of some of the best-known companies in the nation (including Coca-Cola, BellSouth, and Delta), the city has become a transportation hub and has been highly praised for its capability to adapt to a rapidly changing environment. The land of hospitality has opened its arms even wider. Even Scarlett O'Hara herself would be proud.

LOOKING BACK AT THE CAROLINAS & GEORGIA

The Carolinas and Georgia have much in common—a similar historical background, shared social traditions, and cherished culinary customs—and as movers and shakers of the New South, the states share a dynamic future.

Although they have their own political pasts, the Carolinas and Georgia began life as one British colony and, in many other respects, they have a common history. Their settlement by Europeans during the 17th and 18th centuries gave the three states a similar character, which has lasted to this day.

ONE BIG COLONY BECOMES THREE When the first English settlers arrived, they found the region inhabited by bands of American Indians, many of them part of the greater Iroquois and Sioux families. Some native tribes cooperated with the settlers; others were hostile. Whatever their reactions to the newcomers, Indian tribes were decimated by European diseases, and the whites pushed the survivors off their land, either through trumped-up sales or by force. Only the Cherokees, an Iroquoian people in the southern Appalachians, have survived as an organized Indian nation (see chapter 10).

The tribes in what is today South Carolina were the first to encounter the Europeans, in 1520, when a Spanish caravel explored St. Helena Sound. Six years later, Lucas Vázquez Ayllón tried to establish a Spanish colony, first near the mouth of the Cape Fear River in North Carolina and later on Winyah Bay, but disease, bad weather, and the Indians put an end to it after only a year.

In search of gold rather than colonies, Spanish conquistador Hernando de Soto explored the area's interior in 1540, crossing from Georgia through South Carolina to the mountains of western North Carolina. French Huguenots arrived in 1563 and built Fort Charles at South Carolina's Port Royal Sound, but they pulled up stakes when fire destroyed their supplies. A Spanish contingent from Florida came to the same site in 1566 and built Fort San Filipe; they stayed 20 years but abandoned the colony when English buccaneer Sir Francis Drake raided St. Augustine.

A COLONY LOST England fared no better in its first attempt to establish a colony. In 1584, Walter Raleigh, a soldier and courtier to Queen Elizabeth I, sent an expedition to search out a suitable site. The expedition returned with glorious tales of an island named Roanoke—part of what we now know as North Carolina's Outer Banks—and with two Indians named Manteo and Wanchese. A year later, Raleigh sent Manteo, Wanchese, and 108 Englishmen to colonize Roanoke Island. Rather than planting crops, they spent much of their time searching for gold and a passage to the Pacific Ocean. When Sir Francis Drake fortuitously showed up within the year, they hitched a ride with him back to England.

In June 1587, Raleigh's second attempt at colonization—this time with about 120 men, women, and children—arrived at Roanoke Island under the leadership of John White. It was too late in the year to plant crops, and White left for England at the

DATELINE

1520–26 Spanish arrive in South Carolina.	name the region "Carolina" in his honor.
1540 Spanish conquistador Hernando de Soto crosses Georgia and the Carolinas, bringing disease and death to the Cherokee Indians.	**1670** South Carolina's first permanent settlement is established on Ashley River.
1587 Sir Walter Raleigh sends English to settle Roanoke Island; the "Lost Colony" disappears.	**1710** Proprietors appoint Edward Hyde governor of North Carolina, separating its administration from that of South Carolina.
mid-1600s Planters from Virginia settle in the Albemarle Sound region in northeastern North Carolina.	**1718** British forces behead buccaneer Edward "Blackbeard" Teach during a bloody fight off Ocracoke Island, North Carolina.
1663 King Charles II of England grants land between Virginia and Florida to eight Lords Proprietors, who	

end of August to secure fresh stores. War was on with Spain, however, preventing White's return. When he did sail back 3 years later, he found only the word *Croatoan*—the name of a nearby Indian tribe—carved on a tree. The settlers had disappeared. Among them was White's granddaughter, Virginia Dare, the first child born in America of English parents. Not a trace of the legendary "Lost Colony" was ever found (see chapter 5).

THE LORDS PROPRIETORS GET THEIRS The English had better luck at Jamestown, Virginia, in 1607. By the mid-1600s, tobacco farmers had drifted south into the Albemarle Sound region of northeastern North Carolina, around Elizabeth City and Edenton. They were the first permanent European settlers in the Carolinas and Georgia.

But real colonization began after the restoration of King Charles II in England. In 1663, strapped for funds and owing financial and political debts to those who had supported his return to the throne, King Charles granted to eight Lords Proprietors all of North America between 31 degrees and 36 degrees North latitude—that's all of the Carolinas and Georgia. The grant was later extended north to 36½ degrees, to make sure that the Albemarle Sound area wasn't in Virginia, and south to 29 degrees. This southern extension infuriated the Spanish because it encompassed nearly half of their colony in Florida.

The proprietors named their possession Carolina, in the king's honor. You'll see these men's names throughout the Carolinas: George Monck, duke of Albemarle; Edward Hyde, earl of Clarendon; William Craven, earl of Craven; brothers Lord John Berkeley and Sir William Berkeley (the latter was then governor of Virginia); Sir George Carteret; Anthony Ashley-Cooper, later the first earl of Shaftesbury; and Sir John Colleton.

The proprietors soon recruited rice farmers from Barbados, who arrived on the banks of South Carolina's Ashley River in 1670. Within a decade, they had established Charles Town. With slaves producing bumper rice and indigo crops, and with one of the colonies' finest natural harbors, South Carolina soon became the wealthiest of

1729 Lords Proprietors sell Carolina to the English crown; the colony officially divides into North and South.

1730s Ulster Scots, Quakers, and Germans migrate south from Pennsylvania into the Piedmont regions of the Carolinas and Georgia.

1732 James Edward Oglethorpe founds Georgia in the southern part of the Lords Proprietors' grant.

1750 Slavery is introduced in Georgia, spurring production of rice, indigo, and cotton on large plantations.

1752 Moravians from Pennsylvania settle in northwestern North Carolina and found Salem (now part of Winston-Salem).

1774 Women in Edenton, North Carolina, protest the British tax on tea by refusing to brew English leaves.

1775 Patriots sign the Mecklenburg Declaration in Charlotte, declaring independence from Great Britain.

continues

England's American colonies. Charles Town (its name was changed to Charleston in 1783) was America's busiest port until well into the 19th century.

The proprietors appointed a colonial governor to sit in Charles Town, with authority to appoint a deputy for northern Carolina. The great distances involved made this plan unworkable, so in 1710, Edward Hyde (a cousin of Queen Anne, who was then on the throne) was named governor of the north. This arrangement lasted until the proprietors sold their possession to the British crown in 1729, whereupon North and South Carolina became separate British colonies.

CONVICTS & CATHOLICS NEED NOT APPLY   Partially to create a buffer between the Spanish in Florida and flourishing South Carolina, the British crown in 1731 granted a charter to a group of investors, headed by Gen. James Edward Oglethorpe, to establish a colony in the southern part of the original Lords Proprietors grant.

Oglethorpe's utopian goal was to create a microcosm of England—but without landownership, slaves, hard liquor, and Catholicism. Contrary to popular belief, he did not recruit convicts for this enterprise; instead, he sought industrious tradesmen, small-business owners, and laborers with promises of free passage, land to farm, and supplies. The first of the settlers arrived in the new colony of Georgia in 1732.

Without slaves (and also without liquor, some wags say), the settlers had a rough go of it initially. Only after Georgia's first African slaves arrived in 1750 did rice, indigo, and cotton make the colony economically viable. As in South Carolina, the owners of the large plantations dotting the coastal plain grew rich, as did their merchant friends in the ports of Charles Town and Savannah.

UP COUNTRY, LOW COUNTRY   The rich Easterners of the Carolinas and Georgia looked down on the poor, non-slave-owning farmers who settled the inland hills. In South Carolina, these farmers were called Up Country folk by the Low Country folk. In Georgia, the coastal crowd pejoratively referred to their country cousins as "crackers"—from the practice of cracking corn to make meal.

Beginning in the 1730s, another type of settler arrived in the Piedmont area of all three colonies: Scots-Irish, Germans, and other Europeans who migrated overland

1776 North Carolina revolutionaries pass the Halifax Resolves, authorizing their delegates to the Continental Congress to vote for independence. The British attack Charleston and are repulsed.

1779 Gold is discovered near Charlotte, North Carolina, setting off the nation's first gold rush.

1780–81 Lord Cornwallis occupies Charleston and is defeated at the Battle of Kings Mountain near Gaffney, South Carolina.

1782 The British evacuate Charleston, the last city that they held south of Canada.

1793 Eli Whitney's cotton gin leads to an explosion of cotton production throughout the South.

1800 The nation's second federal canal (after the Erie) is dug to move cotton from inland South Carolina to Charleston.

1819 Northern opposition to the admission of Missouri as a slave state stirs talk of secession below the Mason-Dixon Line.

1822 The slave Denmark Vesey leads an insurrection and attempts to capture Charleston. The revolt is put down, and Vesey and 36

from Pennsylvania by way of the great valleys of Virginia. Most of them were self-sufficient yeoman farmers. They had no use for slaves and even less for the rich folks down along the coast who didn't work with their hands. Instead of Anglican churches, they worshiped at Presbyterian, Quaker, and Moravian churches.

Although Piedmont industrial growth reversed the economic situation beginning in the 1880s, and more recent migration from other states has changed the equation somewhat, this division has survived to a large extent.

GIVING CORNWALLIS FITS   People in the Carolinas and Georgia had mixed feelings about independence from Great Britain. Being largely of Scots-Irish or other European origins, the hill folk weren't particularly enamored of the English crown, but they also hesitated to endorse a war. Down in the lowlands, the rich planters and merchants saw themselves as being English, but they also chafed at the British import and export taxes, which hurt their businesses.

There were enough go-for-it patriots around, however, to throw things toward the side of freedom. To protest the English tax on tea, the women of Edenton, North Carolina, held a tea party in 1774 and promised never again to brew leaves from England. In 1775, a group of revolutionaries met in Charlotte and passed the Mecklenburg Resolves, declaring themselves to be independent of Britain. The same year, a group of patriots tarred and feathered British Loyalists in Charleston, and shortly after the Battle of Bunker Hill in Massachusetts, patriots captured Fort Charlotte in South Carolina. In 1776, delegates from all three colonies endorsed the Declaration of Independence in Philadelphia.

When the British attacked Charleston in 1776, Revolutionary soldiers quickly built Fort Moultrie at the mouth of Charleston Harbor. They used palmetto logs, which proved to be impervious to cannon fire. The fort held out for 4 years, and the palmetto became the new state's symbol.

Lord Cornwallis, the British commander, decided in 1780 to launch a Southern strategy against George Washington's Continental army. His plan was to take Charleston; march overland through the Carolinas, picking up Loyalist volunteers as he went; and attack George Washington in Virginia. It took him 14 battles to finally capture

others are executed. Southern planters blame "outside agitators" and institute tighter controls on slaves.

1830s The abolitionist movement gains strength in the North. Extremists advocate the secession of the South from the North.

1830 The South Carolina legislature adopts the "Doctrine of Nullification" of federal laws by the states and threatens to leave the Union. Congress compromises by lowering the export tariff on cotton.

1833 Great Britain emancipates all slaves in its colonies.

1835 The federal government orders the Cherokee Indians west to Oklahoma Territory. Thousands die on the Trail of Tears; others hide in the mountains and later form the Eastern Band of the Cherokee Nation.

1839 A young slave accidentally overheats a North Carolina tobacco barn, baking the drying leaves golden and creating the smooth-tasting Bright Leaf used in cigarettes.

continues

Charleston, but Francis Marion (nicknamed "the Swamp Fox") escaped into the Low Country marshes and organized a series of successful guerrilla raids on the British forces.

The support of Loyalist hill folk, which Cornwallis had counted on, disappeared when his forces massacred a group of rebels trying to surrender near Lancaster, South Carolina. The locals then pitched in with the patriots to defeat the British army at the Battle of Kings Mountain, near Gaffney. Cornwallis was forced to send half his men back to Charleston, significantly weakening his forces.

Despite the defeat, Cornwallis marched north and captured Charlotte, where a 14-pound nugget had been discovered a year earlier, fueling America's first gold rush. Cornwallis found more patriots than gold, causing him to call the town a "hornet's nest."

Cornwallis advanced through North Carolina to meet defeat at Washington's hands at Yorktown in 1781. The troops he had sent back to Charleston held out for a year, but they evacuated when Gen. Nathanael Greene's army advanced to within 14 miles of the city. Charleston was the last British-held city south of Canada.

KING COTTON & THE "PECULIAR INSTITUTION" Along with rice, indigo, and tobacco, cotton was important in the region's early history. But growing and picking the crop was backbreaking work in itself; and after the fiber balls were harvested, someone had to tediously pick out the seeds by hand. Thanks to the South's "peculiar institution," slaves did most of the work.

Most slaves were confined to the large coastal plantations during colonial times. Then, in 1793, Eli Whitney invented the mechanical cotton gin on a Savannah River plantation in Georgia. That meant a small farmer could buy a slave or two, plant his land with cotton, and not have to worry about extracting the seeds. Life in the South would never be the same.

With people in Great Britain and elsewhere beginning to prefer cotton garments to those made of wool and linen, the price of the fluffy white fibers went through the roof. More and more land was devoted to cotton, and production soared. By 1850, cotton accounted for two-thirds of American exports.

1849 South Carolina objects to the admission of California as a free state. The legislature considers secession but backs off when other Southern states refuse.	**1859** John Brown's aborted raid at Harpers Ferry (then in Virginia) alarms the South.
1854 The Republican Party is formed, nominating John C. Fremont for president and adopting an antislavery platform. Democrat James Buchanan is elected president, however.	**1860** A split at the Democratic National Convention in Charleston over a pro-slavery platform plank helps elect Republican Abraham Lincoln. South Carolina secedes.
1858 Republicans gain the majority in Congress on a pro-business, antislavery platform.	**1861** Georgia secedes on January 19. North Carolina waits until South Carolina forces attack Fort Sumter on April 15, launching the Civil War.

Threatening clouds began to gather during the 1830s, with the growth of the abolitionist movement in the North. Some abolitionists were moderates, advocating that slave owners be compensated for the value of their freed slaves. Others were extremists, such as newspaper editor William Lloyd Garrison, who at one point advocated the secession of the North from the South.

JOHN C. CALHOUN & NULLIFICATION Secession wasn't a new idea, and soon its chief proponent would be a brilliant South Carolina lawyer named John C. Calhoun.

A chief spokesman for the Low Country planter class, Calhoun served as a U.S. senator, as secretary of war and secretary of state under President James Monroe, and as U.S. vice president under Andrew Jackson in 1828. As a senator, he joined with Kentuckian Henry Clay to advocate a system of national laws and the building of federal roads and canals to bind the states of the rapidly expanding new nation.

Beginning in 1816, Calhoun supported a series of tariffs designed to protect America's emerging industries from inexpensive manufactured goods imported from overseas. He and other South Carolinians reasoned that their state had both water power and cotton, so they could build textile mills to manufacture cloth rather than import it.

But mills in New England profited from the tariffs, which drove up the price of consumer goods. At the same time, expanding production depressed the price of Southern cotton. Compounding the problem, much of South Carolina's land became worn out from overplanting with a single crop, causing some of its best planters to move to the rich black soil of Alabama and Mississippi. Many South Carolinians believed that textile interests up North were getting rich at their expense, and they started blaming their problems on the federal government.

With the tariffs hurting his home state, and with the system of national laws that he had once advocated beginning to threaten slavery, Calhoun came up with the Doctrine of Nullification. According to this doctrine, because the U.S. Constitution was merely a contract among 13 sovereign nations, a single state could nullify laws

1864 Union Gen. William Tecumseh Sherman drives to the sea through Georgia, leaving a trail of destruction behind.

1865 The blockade-running port of Wilmington, North Carolina, falls to a Union amphibious assault in January. Sherman burns 80 square blocks of Columbia, South Carolina, in February. Confederate Gen. Joseph Johnston surrenders to Sherman in April at Durham, North Carolina.

1865–67 White-dominated state legislatures pass "Black Code" laws, giving newly freed slaves some rights, but not the vote.

1867 Congress passes the Reconstruction Act, dividing the South into five military districts.

1870s The Ku Klux Klan becomes active in the South.

1876 Reconstruction officially ends. Whites return to power and adopt "Jim Crow" laws to keep African Americans from voting.

continues

passed by the federal government. By implication, any state was as free to secede from the Union as it was to join.

When Congress passed another, higher tariff in 1830, the South Carolina legislature declared it to be "null, void, and no law," and promised to secede from the Union if the federal government attempted to use force to collect the money. President Jackson declared that the Union could not be dissolved and threatened to use federal force. South Carolina raised a voluntary military force but backed off when Congress reduced the levy.

Nullification was unpopular up in North Carolina, although the Tarheels didn't like Jackson's threat to use force against a "sovereign" state. Down in Georgia, the state legislature said that it "abhorred" the doctrine, but it also proposed a convention of the Southern states.

SAYING GOODBYE TO OLD GLORY The issue of secession next came up in 1849, when South Carolina objected to the admission of California as a nonslave state and called for a Southern convention, which met in Nashville, Tennessee, the following year. Congress prevented a showdown, however, by passing the Compromise of 1850, which admitted California as a free state but also enacted stringent fugitive-slave laws. The latter was a key point for Southerners, who wanted their escaped "property" to be returned, even from free states.

From the Southern slave-owning perspective, events in the North over the next decade were most unsettling—especially the creation of the Republican Party in 1854. Two years later, this new antislavery party nominated John C. Fremont for president, and in 1858, it won a majority in Congress. One of the party's prominent members was Abraham Lincoln, a lanky Illinois congressman.

The Democrats held their 1860 national convention in Charleston, South Carolina. When the delegates refused to adopt a proslavery platform plank, the eight cotton states walked out. The split helped elect Lincoln, the Republican nominee.

South Carolina called a convention that adopted an Ordinance of Secession on December 20, and the convention sent delegations to the other Southern states to beseech them to do likewise.

1880s Cotton, tobacco, and furniture factories in the Piedmont give the three states major industries for the first time.	**1911** A hurricane devastates the South Carolina coastal area, ending large-scale rice production.
1896 The U.S. Supreme Court's *Plessy v. Ferguson* decision legalizes separate-but-equal segregation laws.	**1915** The Ku Klux Klan is reborn in a huge cross-burning atop Stone Mountain, Georgia. A mob enters a Georgia state penitentiary at Milledgeville and lynches Leo Frank, a Northern-born Jew convicted of murdering 14-year-old Mary Phagan, a white girl, in an Atlanta pencil factory.
1901-04 North Carolina builds 1,100 schools, bringing public education to all Tarheels.	
1903 The Wright Brothers fly the first airplane at Kill Devil Hills on North Carolina's Outer Banks.	**1922** Georgian feminist Rebecca Lattimer Felton, then 87, is appointed as the first female U.S. senator.

Georgia wasted little time, seceding on January 19, 1861, but a majority of North Carolina voters rejected the idea. Only some 35,000 of the one million Tarheels owned slaves, and the rest weren't for what they saw as a "rich man's war and a poor man's fight." The North Carolinians didn't change their minds until April, when Lincoln requested that they send troops to fight against their neighbors.

THE WAR OF NORTHERN AGGRESSION   The American Civil War (which many Southerners still call the War of Northern Aggression) began at 4:30am on April 15, 1861, when South Carolinian forces opened fire on Fort Sumter in Charleston's harbor. Lincoln immediately called for volunteers to put down the rebellion. Within a few months, federal troops occupied much of the coastal lowlands of the Carolinas and Georgia, leaving only the port cities of Wilmington, Charleston, and Savannah in Confederate hands, albeit blockaded by the Union navy.

Except for a few skirmishes and the bombardment of Charleston in 1863, the Carolinas and Georgia escaped heavy fighting until May 1864, when Union general Ulysses S. Grant told Gen. William Tecumseh Sherman to "get into the interior of the enemy's country as far as you can, inflicting all the damage you can against their war resources." Thus began Sherman's famous March to the Sea, the world's first modern example of total war waged against a civilian population.

Sherman fought his way south from Chattanooga, Tennessee, to Atlanta, Georgia, a key railroad junction, which the Confederates evacuated on September 1. Leaving Atlanta burning, he departed for the sea on October 17, cutting a 60-mile path of destruction across central and eastern Georgia. Despite Sherman's orders to the contrary, looting and pillaging were rampant, especially by hangers-on and newly freed slaves.

Sherman arrived at Savannah on December 10, in time to make the port city a Christmas present to Lincoln. (Fortunately, he did not burn the city.) In January 1865, he turned his war machine northward into South Carolina. He torched 80 square blocks of Columbia in February. Confederate general Joseph E. Johnston made several attempts to slow Sherman's advance. One such attempt was the Battle of Rivers Bridge, between Allendale and Erhardt, South Carolina, in February; the

1934   Georgia Gov. Eugene Talmadge declares martial law and uses National Guard troops to break a statewide textile strike.

1940   Great Smoky Mountains National Park is dedicated by President Franklin D. Roosevelt.

1942   Military bases in the Carolinas and Georgia make the area one of the nation's primary troop-training centers during World War II.

1945   President Roosevelt dies of a cerebral hemorrhage at Warm Springs, Georgia.

1954   The U.S. Supreme Court declares segregated schools unconstitutional in *Brown v. Board of Education*.

1960   A lunch-counter sit-in at Greensboro, North Carolina, launches similar civil-rights protests across the South.

1964   Georgians cast the majority vote for Barry Goldwater as president—the first time that a Southern state goes Republican since Reconstruction.

continues

last was the Battle of Bentonville, near Durham in central North Carolina, in March. On April 26, 2 weeks after Gen. Robert E. Lee surrendered to Grant at Appomattox Courthouse in Virginia, Johnston met Sherman at Durham and handed over his sword. The war was over.

The conflict was monstrously costly to the region—particularly to North Carolina, which had joined the fray only reluctantly in the first place. Of the 125,000 Tarheels who served, 40,000 died in battle or of disease, more than from any other Southern state. Those who fought earned their "Tarheel" moniker because of their tenacious refusal to yield ground during battle.

SCALAWAGS, CARPETBAGGERS & JIM CROW
The Civil War survivors straggled home to face Reconstruction. At first, Confederate war veterans dominated the state legislatures in the Carolinas and Georgia. They enacted so-called Black Code laws, which gave some rights to the newly freed slaves but denied them the vote. This and other actions infuriated the radical Republicans who controlled the U.S. Congress and wanted to see the South punished for its rebellion. In 1867, Congress passed the Reconstruction Act, which gave blacks the right to vote and divided the South into five districts, each under a military governor who had near-dictatorial powers. Twenty thousand federal troops were sent to the South to enforce the act.

Recalcitrant white officials were removed from state office, and the ex-slaves helped elect Republican legislatures in all three states. Many blacks won seats for themselves. Despite doing some good work, these legislatures were corrupt and also enacted high taxes to pay for rebuilding and social programs, further alienating the struggling white population.

White Carolinians and Georgians also complained bitterly about "scalawags" (local whites who joined the Republican Party) and "carpetbaggers" (Northerners who came South looking to become wealthy landowners). The animosity led to the formation of two secret white organizations—the Knights of the Camilla and the Knights of the Ku Klux Klan—that undertook terrorism to keep blacks from voting or exercising their other new rights. The former slaves also were disappointed with the radical Republicans

1965 Congress passes the Voting Rights Act, enfranchising Southern African Americans for the first time since Reconstruction. Blacks are elected to Congress, local offices, and state legislatures.

1966 Segregationist restaurateur Lester "Ax Handle" Maddox is elected governor of Georgia.

1968 State police open fire during student protests at a bowling alley in Orangeburg, South Carolina, killing three and wounding 27.

1970 Courting Maddox voters, peanut farmer Jimmy Carter is elected governor of Georgia, promising to end racial discrimination.

1972 North Carolinians elect conservative Republican television commentator Jesse Helms to the U.S. Senate.

1973 U.S. Sen. Sam J. Ervin, Jr., of North Carolina leads the Senate Watergate hearings.

1976 Jimmy Carter becomes the first Southerner to be elected president of the United States since before the Civil War.

when it became obvious that they wouldn't receive their promised "40 acres and a mule." Those who did vote began to cast their votes for their former masters.

All this set the stage for whites to regain control of North Carolina and Georgia in 1871. By January 1877, only South Carolina still had a carpetbagger regime, and when the new president, Rutherford B. Hayes, a Republican, withdrew federal troops from Charleston in April, former Confederate general Wade Hampton became governor. Reconstruction was over.

During the next 20 years, white governments enacted Jim Crow laws, which imposed poll taxes, literacy tests, and other requirements intended to prevent African Americans from voting. Whites flocked to the Democratic Party, which restricted its primaries—tantamount to elections throughout the South—to white voters. Blacks who did try to vote faced action from the Ku Klux Klan.

Racial segregation became a legal fact of life in the region, from public drinking fountains to public schools. The U.S. Supreme Court ratified the scheme in its 1896 *Plessy v. Ferguson* decision, declaring "separate but equal" public schools to be constitutional. Black schools in the South were hardly equal, but they surely were separate.

LINTHEADS & BRIGHT LEAF Economically, the Carolinas and Georgia changed drastically during the 1880s. With slaves turned into sharecroppers and tenant farmers, the region went back to growing cotton after the Civil War—so much of it that the price dropped drastically. Taking advantage of the cheap raw material and free power provided by rushing rivers, enterprising industrialists soon built cotton mills throughout the Piedmont. Instead of scratching a living out of their hardscrabble land, the Piedmont's farmers flocked to the new factory jobs. These low-paid workers, who worked long hours and included many women and children, were derided as "lintheads." But at long last, the region had the textile industry that John C. Calhoun had dreamed of.

The Civil War ended for General Sherman's troops at Durham, the heart of North Carolina's tobacco-producing region, and the soldiers took home a taste for the smooth-tasting bright-leaf tobacco. The 1881 invention of the cigarette-rolling

1989 South Carolina legislators are charged with taking bribes to vote for legalized horse-race betting in the FBI sting "Operation Lost Trust."

1994 African American Ernest Finney is elected chief justice of the South Carolina Supreme Court.

1995 A federal court orders the Citadel in Charleston to admit the first female cadets.

1996 Atlanta hosts the Summer Olympic Games.

2000 The South experiences dramatic increases in population, largely in the suburbs. South Carolina's Confederate flag over the State Capitol stirs nationwide protest.

2003 After 48 years and 15,000 votes, South Carolina Sen. Strom Thurmond retires from the U.S. Senate and turns 100 years of age. He dies on June 26.

2004 U.S. Sen. John Edwards of North Carolina gives up his seat to run as the Democratic Party's nominee for vice president on a ticket with U.S. Sen. John Kerry. They lose to incumbent George W. Bush.

continues

machine meant that cigarette factories soon dotted central North Carolina, making fortunes for men such as James B. Duke and R. J. Reynolds.

The Piedmont rivers also powered new furniture factories, especially in North Carolina and northern Georgia.

SIT-INS AT LUNCH COUNTERS   For the first half of the 20th century, whites were firmly in control in the Carolinas and Georgia. The Democratic Party reigned supreme, and racial segregation was a way of life. For the most part, politics in the three states followed the old Low Country/Up Country split, but with the Piedmont's wealthy industrialists playing an increasingly important role.

From the beginning, the textile-mill owners fought any effort to unionize their predominately white workers, often threatening to replace them with blacks if they voted to join a union. In 1934, Georgia governor Eugene Talmadge went so far as to call out the state's National Guard to put down a strike. To this day, the Carolinas and Georgia are antiunion, "right to work" states.

The state legislatures tended to switch between progressive and conservative Democrats, often following hard-fought primary campaigns. The favorite progressive platform called for increased spending for public education. North Carolina built some 1,100 public schools between 1901 and 1904. But as late as 1942, conservative governor Talmadge of Georgia claimed that "education ain't never taught a man to plant cotton" (or to mill it, some would say). Accordingly, the three states lagged far behind the rest of the nation in education. (To their credit, however, the industrialists did contribute to the region's institutions of higher learning; tobacco interests turned little Trinity College in Durham, North Carolina, into prestigious Duke University.)

Even after the U.S. Supreme Court declared in its 1954 *Brown v. Board of Education* decision that segregated public schools were unconstitutional, division of the races continued. Nearly 10 years went by before the first black student enrolled in an integrated South Carolina public school.

But it all began to change with the advent of the civil rights movement. In 1960, black college students in Greensboro, North Carolina, held the first sit-in at a Woolworth's lunch counter. Unlike the violent scenes that erupted in Alabama and

2008   Survey shows gentrification has changed the face of the New Atlanta.

2010   Charleston joined with the rest of South Carolina in November of 2010, electing its first woman governor, a Tea Party backed Republican lawmaker who succeeded scandal-stained Gov. Mark Sanford. Nikki Haley became the nation's second Indian-American governor.
As predicted, Savannah joined with the Republicans in a sweep of Georgia in the elections of November, 2010. The race for governor was particularly tight, but former congressman Nathan Deal, a Republican, beat out former governor Roy Barnes, his Democratic opponent.

Mississippi, most civil rights demonstrations in the Carolinas and Georgia were peaceful. One exception was a 1962 rock-throwing incident in Albany, Georgia (a demonstration that set the precedent for the later protests of Dr. Martin Luther King, Jr.). Another occurred in 1968, when state police opened fire on black students at a bowling alley in Orangeburg, South Carolina.

Although the Voting Rights Act was strenuously opposed by powerful U.S. senators Richard B. Russell of Georgia, Strom Thurmond of South Carolina, and Sam J. Ervin, Jr., of North Carolina, Congress enacted it in 1965. No other result of the civil rights movement has changed the South more. Today blacks represent several Carolina and Georgia districts in the U.S. House of Representatives, others hold many seats in the state legislatures, and African-American local officials number in the hundreds. And, of course, on January 20, 2009, Barack Obama, the first African-American president of the United States, took up occupancy in the White House.

In 1966, Georgia Democrats nominated for governor a man named Lester Maddox, who had waved an ax handle to keep civil rights protesters out of his whites-only Atlanta restaurant. His Republican opponent actually won a plurality, but the Democratic legislature put Maddox in office. Four years later, a peanut farmer from Plains, Georgia, courted Maddox's segregationist voters, but at his inauguration as governor in 1971, Jimmy Carter promised to end the racial divide. In 1976, Carter became the first Georgian, and the first Southerner since before the Civil War, to be elected president of the United States.

The 1980s and 1990s saw many changes in the region. High-tech modern industries set up shop, especially in the Raleigh-Durham area in North Carolina, along the I-85 corridor in South Carolina, and in the burgeoning Atlanta suburbs. With them came a migration of Northerners, many bringing Republican leanings that made the old one-party South a thing of the past. Today's Carolinas and Georgia are politically competitive, usually voting Republican in presidential elections but splitting their votes at the statehouse level.

Senator Strom Thurmond (1902–2003) died on June 26, 2003. The longest-serving senator in American history, Ol' Strom was completely senile at the end of a notorious political career. A racist, segregationist, and homophobe, he was also the master Southern politician and a war hero. His political legacy today rests on his reshaping of the Republican Party and reestablishing a two-party system in the Southeast.

Atlanta has long been a symbol of black success and a lure to African Americans. But surveys have shown that for the first time since the 1920s, the white percentage of the city's population is on the rise. The black population reached an all-time high of 61% in 1990, but by 2008, it had fallen to just 53%.

ARCHITECTURE & ART

The grandest architecture of the antebellum South is centered around Charleston and Savannah, which survived the Civil War a lot better than Atlanta—which, of course, General Sherman burned to the ground.

The epitome of Southern graciousness, the plantation culture of Charleston, Savannah, and the surrounding Low Country spans 2 centuries that saw everything from a glorious antebellum past (for the landed gentry, not the slaves) to depression, decay, and the passing of a way of life.

The most remarkable buildings were constructed between 1686 and 1878 along the South Carolina coastal plain centered at Charleston.

Many of these once-elegant structures still stand today to enchant us, although they are in varying states of preservation, some no more than ruins. Only the camera has captured some of these stately Low Country manses for posterity. From churches to gardens, chapels to memorable homes, plantation houses to graceful frame structures, Charleston and Savannah have it all.

Charleston's Art & Architecture

All you need to do is walk down Broad Street in the center of Charleston to see three dozen ornately decorated and historic structures on the block between East Bay and Church streets. Much of what has been saved was because of an ordinance passed in 1931 that preserved whole sectors of town. Charleston was the first city in the world to adopt such a preservation law.

To many visitors today, the so-called historic core lies **south of Broad Street.** This sector is certainly one of the great districts of architecture in the Deep South. But the landed gentry in the heyday of the plantation era also built many superb homes and mansions in other sections of the city, such as **Harleston Village** and **Radcliffeborough.** Harleston Village lies west of the Historic District. Directly north of Harleston is the neighborhood of Radcliffeborough, beginning north of Calhoun Street. Some of the grandest Victorian manses stand around **Colonial Lake.** These neighborhoods deserve at least an hour of your time to walk around. Lacy iron gates, 19th-century ornaments, towering old trees, and private gardens make it worthwhile, even if you're not particularly interested in architecture.

The Georgian-Palladian style reigned supreme in historic Charleston, lasting over the centuries, and surely there are more columns in Charleston today than in a small Greek city in classical days. One of the finest Georgian mansions in America stands at **64 S. Battery St.,** dating from 1772 when it was built by William Gibbes, a successful ship owner and planter. He modeled it after English designs but was also inspired by Palladio. The house is not pure Georgian, however, as Adamesque features, such as wrought-iron railings, were added later.

The columned single house prevailed for 250 years—there are some 3,000 such houses standing in Charleston today. Its most defining feature is its single-room width, and it is also set at right angles to the street. One of the most evocative examples of a Charleston single house is the **Colonel Robert Brewton House** at 71 Church St. The domestic structure of the single house is one of Charleston's greatest contributions to city architecture in America.

Some were more lavish than others, but even less-expensive dwellings were adorned with wrought-iron balconies or two-columned porches. Although much great architecture is gone, what remains is nearly 75 buildings from the colonial period, approximately 135 from the 18th century, and more than 600 built during the antebellum heyday.

COLONIAL TO ADAMESQUE

In the beginning, roughly from 1690 to 1740, there was the colonial style, with such defining features as clapboard wooden siding, low foundations, and steeply pitched roofs. The **John Lining House** at 106 Broad St. is the most evocative building of that period. Coexisting for a certain time with colonial architecture was Georgian, a style that flourished between 1700 and 1800. Its defining features are box chimneys, hipped roofs, flattened columns, and raised basements. Nowhere is this style better exemplified than in the **Miles Brewton House** at 27 King St.

As colonial and Georgian faded, another style of architecture appeared, especially during a 3-decade span beginning in 1790. Although it was called Federalist architecture in the North, most Charlestonians referred to the structures of this era as "Adamesque" or "the Adam period," a reference to what Scottish brothers James and Robert Adam were creating in the British Isles. The best example of Federalist/Adamesque architecture in Charleston is the **Nathaniel Russell House** at 51 Meeting St., which is open to the public (see chapter 11).

Constructed around the same time as the Nathaniel Russell House, the **James Moultrie House,** at 20 Montagu St., is an Adamesque treasure of delicate proportions. Although it was built by a planter, Daniel Cobia, it became more famous as the address of the Moultrie family in 1834. Dr. Moultrie, related to the Revolutionary War hero Gen. William Moultrie, was one of South Carolina's early physicians, founding its first medical school.

A magnificent Adamesque mansion, built around 1802, was constructed at 60 Montagu St. The restored **Gaillard-Bennett House,** constructed by a rice planter, Theodore Gaillard, is famous for its fluted columns with "tower-of-the-winds" capitals, along with an elliptically shaped window in its portico gable and a modillion cornice, with other Palladian architectural motifs. In 1870, 5 years after the end of the Civil War, Robert E. Lee was a guest of the Bennett family, and he spoke to admiring well-wishers from the second-floor balcony.

Another stellar example of the Adamesque style is the **Jonathan Lucas House,** built around 1808, at 286 Calhoun St. Several generations of rice barons lived here, establishing rice milling as a big industry in the southeastern United States.

GREEK REVIVAL VERSUS GOTHIC REVIVAL

The Regency style came and went quickly in Charleston, filling in a transitional period between Adamesque and the Greek Revival style. The most evocative example of Regency is the **Edmondston-Alston House** at 21 E. Battery St., erected by Charles Edmondston in 1825. The purity of the original style was later altered by Charles Alston, a rice planter who added Greek Revival details. From its precincts, General Beauregard watched the attack on Fort Sumter in 1861, and Robert E. Lee once took refuge here when a fire threatened the Mills House Hotel where he was lodged. This historic home is open to the public (see chapter 11).

The Greek Revival period flourished roughly from 1820 to 1875. Its defining features are heavy columns and capitals (often Doric), along with a hipped or gabled roof and a wide band of trim. One of the most solid examples of this form of bold architecture is the **Beth Elohim Reform Temple** at 90 Hasell St., the oldest synagogue in continuous use in the United States, first organized in 1749.

However, the most spectacular example of the Greek Revival style is at **172 Tradd St.,** built in 1836 by Alexander Hext Chisolm, who made his fortune in rice. The lavish capitals are copies of those designed in Athens in 335 B.C. The architect is thought to be Charles F. Reichardt of New York.

At the turn of the 19th century, Gabriel Manigault, a French Huguenot, was the biggest name in Charleston architecture. His greatest buildings have been torn down, but one that remains is **City Hall,** at the corner of Broad and Meeting streets. Constructed in 1801, this stellar example of Adamesque-Palladian architecture was originally a bank before becoming City Hall in 1818.

THE GULLAH TONGUE MAKES IT TO BROADWAY

In the 1920s while he was living in Charleston, DuBose Heyward wrote *Porgy*, which in time became a Broadway play. Later, it became even more famous as a folk opera created by George Gershwin and retitled *Porgy and Bess*. Living for a time in Charleston, Gershwin incorporated sounds and rhythms he'd seen in black churches around the Low Country. Heyward was inspired by the city's rich heritage, even though the glorious mansions of old had fallen into disrepair and Charlestonians were going through hard times—"too poor to paint, too proud to whitewash." Heyward used not only the byways of Charleston for his setting, but also the Gullah language for his dialogues.

One of the few buildings that can be directly traced to the architectural drawing board of Manigault is the house at **350 Meeting St.** that the architect designed for his brother, Joseph, in 1803. Many critics hail it as one of the most impressive Adamesque homes in America. Manigault's father, also known as Gabriel Manigault, was in his day not only the richest man in Charleston but also one of the wealthiest in the country. The **Joseph Manigault House** is one of the few historic homes in Charleston open to the public (see chapter 11).

Another national landmark attributed to Manigault is at **18 Bull St.,** an Adamesque manse constructed at the turn of the 19th century by William Blacklock, a wine merchant. At its lowest point this mansion became a cheap boardinghouse and barely escaped bulldozers in 1958.

Robert Mills, who designed the Washington Monument, filled in when Manigault resettled in Philadelphia. But Mills was never as well received, although he left the monumental **First Baptist Church** (1819–22) on lower Church Street and the five-columned **Fireproof Building** (1822–26) at Chambers and Meeting streets.

When an 1838 fire destroyed a large part of antebellum Charleston, many districts were reconstructed in the Greek Revival style. Doric columns were particularly fashionable, along with rectangular shapes inspired by Greek temples, such as those found in Sicily.

A monumental "pillar" to Greek Revival is the columned **Centenary Methodist Church,** one of the grandest examples of a Greek Doric temple in America, at 60 Wentworth St., an 1842 structure by Edward Brickell White.

Along came Andrew Jackson Downing, the mid-19th-century arbiter of America's taste in architecture, who ridiculed Charleston's obsession with Greek Revival. The way was paved for the emergence of E. B. White, who brought in the Gothic Revival design, which prevailed from 1850 to 1885 and was characterized by pointed arches and buttressed stone tracery. The best example of Gothic Revival is the **French Protestant (Huguenot) Church,** at 136 Church St.

AFTER THE CIVIL WAR

Also dominating the 1850s, the decade before the Civil War, were the architects F. D. Lee and Edward C. Jones. Together and separately they began to change the cityscape of Charleston, creating, for example, the Moorish-style fish market, their most exotic invention—alas, now gone. They pioneered the use of cast iron, which became a dominant feature in city architecture and can still be seen at its most prolific on the western side of Meeting Street, stretching from Hasell to Market streets.

One of the most talented of all Charleston architects, Jones designed the **Trinity Methodist Church,** on Meeting Street, in 1850. This impressive edifice has a pedimented Palladian portico of Corinthian columns. In just 3 years he shifted his style to Italianate, which remained popular until the dawn of the 20th century. The architecture is defined by verandas, low-pitched roofs, and balustrades. An evocative example of the style is the **Colonel John Ashe House,** designed by Jones, at 26 S. Battery St.

In 1853, Jones designed his first commercial building in the Italianate Renaissance Revival style: a bank at **1 Broad St.** At one time this building was owned by George A. Trenholm, a cotton broker and blockade runner, one of several 19th-century power brokers in Charleston who were said to have inspired Margaret Mitchell's character of Rhett Butler in *Gone With the Wind.*

Still one of the city's most magnificent landmarks, the columned building at **200 E. Bay St.** is the most stellar example of the Italian Renaissance Revival style, built over a period of 26 years, from 1853 to 1879. This U.S. Custom House was the creation of Ammin Burnham, a Boston architect who'd created a similar building in his home city. Burnham was largely instrumental in launching the tradition of designing federal buildings, such as post offices, in a classical style. The Roman Corinthian portico of this splendid temple is much photographed.

About 20 years before Charleston got sucked up in the Civil War, all purism in architectural style vanished. Most architects and builders were more interested in a dramatic facade. This period saw the bastardization of a lot of Charleston's landscape. Architects reached out internationally for inspiration—to the Moors, to Persia, to the Norman style of church, or even Gothic Venice, if they were fanciful.

The best example of this bastardized, though architecturally beautiful, style is at **67 Rutledge Ave.,** the home (ca. 1851) that Col. James H. Taylor ordered built "in the style of a Persian villa," with Moorish arches as ornamentation. This was once a famous address, entertaining the likes of such distinguished guests as the 19th-century politician, tastemaker, and orator, Daniel Webster.

And then came the Civil War, when all building ceased except for fortifications. Much great architecture was destroyed during Union bombardments, especially in 1863.

After the war, the Victorian style arrived in Charleston and would prevail from 1870 until the coming of World War I. This style did not predominate as much as it

CHARLESTON: ART, ARCHITECTURE & GARDENS

The best and most helpful practical guide—virtually a street-by-street survey—is *Complete Charleston: A Guide to the Architecture, History and Gardens of Charleston,* by Margaret H. Moore, with photographs by Truman Moore. Sold all over Charleston, the book divides Charleston into 11 neighborhoods and takes you on a tour of each, a voyage of discovery of the city's world-class architecture and lush secret gardens.

Art and Landscape in Charleston and the Low Country, by John Beardsley, was published as part of the 21st season of the Spoleto Festival U.S.A. The color photographs of Charleston and the Low Country alone are reason enough to purchase this guide.

did in other American cities because many Charlestonians, wiped out economically from the effects of the Civil War, did not have money to build. Nonetheless, you'll see some fine Victorian manses in Charleston today, notably the **Sottile House,** with its wide verandas opening onto Green Street on the College of Charleston campus.

When Victorian architects did design buildings in Charleston, they often created "fantasies," as exemplified by the startling manse that stands at **40 Montagu St.** Built by food merchant Bernard Wohlers in 1891, the house was restored in 1963. Its unique style combines Charles Eastlake with Queen Anne motifs.

Not all Charlestonians during the latter Victorian Age were building in the Victorian style. Albert W. Todd, for example, an architect and state senator, constructed one of Charleston's most magnificent private residences at **40 Rutledge Ave.** in the Colonial Revival style at the turn of the 20th century. With its verandas and splendid columned portico, this house is worth a detour.

Rainbow Row (79–107 E. Bay St.) is one of the most celebrated blocks in the city. It got its name in the 1930s when the entire block was rejuvenated and then painted in colors used by the colonials. The architecture is mainly of the so-called British style, in that there was a store on the ground floor with the living accommodations on the floors above. Rainbow Row is the longest such Georgian block of buildings in America, and it inspired DuBose Heyward's "Catfish Row" in *Porgy and Bess.*

> ### Impressions
>
> *Come quickly, have found heaven.*
> —Artist Alfred Hutty, in a wire to his wife upon visiting Charleston

Although it's an arguable point, a Florida professor, Sigmund Heinz, once stated: "For all practical purposes, the Civil War brought an end to the grandeur of Charleston architecture. As for the 20th century, the kindest thing is not to mention it."

THE ART OF CHARLESTON

As might be expected, Charleston is far more distinguished by its architecture than by its art. But it's had some peaks and valleys over the years, and today boasts a creative core of artists whose works are displayed at the Spoleto Festival USA and in museums in the city—and often showcased in traveling exhibitions around the state.

In the colonial period, the art decorating the antebellum homes of England—most often landscapes or portraits of dogs and horses—was imported from London and brought over by British ships sailing into Charleston Harbor. When families grew rich from rice and indigo, portrait painters, many of them itinerant, did idealized portraits of the founding father of a dynasty and his wife (always made out to be prettier than she was), or else the whole brood gathered for an idealized family portrait.

Out of this lackluster mess, one artist rose to distinguish himself.

CHARLESTON'S RENAISSANCE MAN

Born in South Carolina of Scottish descent, Charles Fraser became the best-known artist in Charleston for his miniature portraits, many of which you can see in the **Gibbes Museum of Art** (see chapter 11). Although he was also a distinguished landscape painter, he is mainly known today for his miniatures.

When the Marquis de Lafayette came to Charleston in 1825, he sat for a portrait by Fraser. In turn the artist gave the marquis one of his miniatures as a gift. Lafayette later wrote that the portrait was a "very high specimen of the state of arts in America."

Fraser received his artistic training at the age of 13 when he studied with Thomas Coram. He was educated at the Classical Academy, which in time became the College of Charleston. For 11 years he was a lawyer before giving up his practice in 1818 to devote himself to art full time.

As a miniaturist, he captured the essence of many of the city's most distinguished citizens. His color was relatively flat, but his compositions were filled with linear detail, and he was known for his delicate, lyrical art.

Fraser had many other talents as well. He distinguished himself as a civil leader, and he was also a designer, having provided the plans for the steeple on St. John's Lutheran Church at 10 Archdale St. In 1854 he wrote a valuable history of the city, *Reminiscences of Charleston.*

THE CHARLESTON RENAISSANCE

The long, dreary years of the Reconstruction era, when much of Charleston was mired in poverty, did not encourage the growth of great art. In the early 20th century, however, the "Charleston Renaissance" was born. This cultural movement spanned the decades between 1915 and 1940 on the eve of the U.S. entry into World War II. Fostered by artists, musicians, architects, and poets, the Renaissance rescued Charleston from the physical devastations of the Civil War and later from the deep mire of the Depression.

Laura Bragg, the director of the Charleston Museum from 1920 to 1931, presided over a salon in her home at 38 Chambers St. In time this parlor became as famous in the South as the salon of Gertrude Stein and her longtime companion, Alice B. Toklas, became in Paris. Much of the Southern literary world, including the novelist and playwright Carson McCullers from Georgia, dropped by.

Elizabeth O'Neill Verner (1883–1979) has emerged as the towering figure of the Charleston Renaissance artists. Charleston-born-and-bred, she studied art in Philadelphia from 1901 to 1903 before returning to Charleston. When she found herself unexpectedly widowed, she turned to art to earn a living to support herself and her two small children.

Verner specialized in beautiful etchings and drawings of Charleston scenes, as exemplified by her *Avenue at the Oaks.* She chose such subjects as churches, beautiful homes, columns, porticos, and wrought-iron gates. But her forte was in depicting scenes of the vendors in the city market, none more evocative than her pastel on silk *Seated Flower Seller Smoking Pipe.* She was instrumental in reviving an interest in art in Charleston during the 1920s and 1930s. As she aged, she switched to pastels and worked almost until the time of her death at the age of 96.

Another major artist of the period was **Alice Ravenel Huger Smith** (1876–1958), a Charleston native who was intrigued by the Low Country landscape, with its acres of marshes, cypress swamps, palmettos, rice fields, egrets, herons, and lonely beaches. Her sketches were filled with imagery. After 1924 she worked mainly in watercolor, which she found best for depicting the hazy mist of the Low Country. One of her most evocative works is the 1919 *Mossy Tree.*

Another native of South Carolina, **Anna Heyward Taylor** (1879–1956) found her inspiration in Charleston, which she considered a city of "color and charm." Her paintings, in private collections and major galleries today, are steeped in the misty aura of the Low Country. Our favorite among her works is the 1930 *Fenwick Hall* in which she captures the rot, despair, and decay of this laconic plantation before its renovation.

Notable Michigan-born artist **Alfred Hutty** (1877–1954) began a lifelong love affair with Charleston when he was sent here to establish an art school for the Carolina Art Association. His greatest fame came as an etcher, although he was an accomplished painter as well. His works today are displayed in such institutions as the British Museum in London and the Metropolitan Museum in New York. His *White Azaleas-Magnolia Gardens,* done in 1925, captures the luxuriant vegetation of the Low Country that was evocative of the Ashley River plantations.

Savannah's Architecture & Art

Savannah's greatest collection of evocative architecture lies in the Historic District, where you can admire the old buildings, churches, and squares. Some structures are from the Colonial era; others were perhaps inspired by the Adam brothers or built in the Regency style. There are tons of ironwork and antique buildings in brick or clapboard. Even modest town houses from the 18th century have been restored to become coveted addresses.

Because many of its residents lacked money in the final decades of the 19th century and the beginning of the 20th, antique structures were allowed to stand, whereas many American cities destroyed their heritage and built modern buildings. When Savannahians started thinking about tearing down their old structures, a forceful preservation movement was launched—and just in time.

What you won't see, as you travel through the Low Country around Savannah, is a lot of plantations where cotton was king. Many of these have "gone with the wind."

THE FIRST CITY

In 1733, at the founding of Savannah, James Oglethorpe faced a daunting challenge. He not only had to secure homes for trustees and colonists, but he also had to construct forts around the new town of Savannah to fend off possible Indian raids, even though the local Native Americans were friendly.

Since they weren't well built and were later torn down to make way for grander structures, none of the founding fathers' little wooden homes remain today. But the town plan envisioned by Oglethorpe back in London still remains. He wanted an orderly grid composed of 24 squares. In case of rebellion he also wanted "mustering points" where troops could gather to squelch the problem.

Nine years after the colonists arrived in port, they had enough money and building materials to construct their first church, which quickly became the most elaborate structure in town. Called "the Orphan House," the church took its name from the Bethesda Orphanage founded by evangelist George Whitefield in 1738. Along with Oglethorpe, Whitefield believed that rum drinking caused a yellow fever–like disease but that beer drinking was acceptable. This philosophy was expounded to the congregation of Georgia's first church. Unfortunately, this landmark building no longer stands.

After the Revolutionary War, the port of Savannah began to grow rich on profits it made shipping sago powder, beef, pork, animal skins, tar, turpentine, and other exports. Money generated from this thriving trade with Europe, especially London, was poured into architecture. Grander homes began to sprout on the squares of Savannah. Still, none of these early structures equaled the glory of the rival city of Charleston. While visiting the family of Gen. Nathanael Greene, Eli Whitney invented the cotton gin in 1793, bringing even greater prosperity to the area, which led to grander building.

Little post-Revolutionary architecture survived a disastrous fire that struck in 1796, burning block after block of the city. Built by James Habersham, Jr., in a Georgian style, the remaining structure is a solid brick foundation covered in pink stucco. Today it is a well-recommended restaurant and bar, known as the Olde Pink House Restaurant (p. 472), open to the general public at 23 Abercorn St.

In 1820, another devastating fire swept over Savannah, destroying architectural gems that had been erected by builders from both Charleston and the North. The fire erupted just at the time an epidemic of yellow fever broke out. Thousands of slaves died from the fever, temporarily slowing down building efforts because they provided the hard labor on the construction projects. Work on rebuilding Savannah was further slowed by a cholera epidemic in 1834.

But through it all, Savannahians survived and prospered and continued to pour money into elaborate structures, many of which remain today, especially those constructed of brick. The Federalist style was very prevalent, as it was along the east coast of America. Some builders, perhaps those with Loyalist hearts, preferred the Georgian style. Locals continued to spend money on churches, notably the Independent Presbyterian Church of Savannah, whose architectural beauty competed with that of some of the finest churches of Charleston.

THE REGENCY STYLE SWEEPS SAVANNAH

The cotton planters with their newfound money invited William Jay of London to come to Savannah in 1817. He introduced the Regency style, which became all the rage in Savannah.

Some of his structures still stand today. His greatest achievement is the Owens-Thomas House, the best example of English Regency architecture in the United States. Inspired by classical buildings, the flourishing style was named for King George IV, who ruled as prince regent from 1811 to 1820. The house overlooks Oglethorpe Square and was standing in 1825 to welcome the Marquis de Lafayette when he was the guest of honor in Savannah. The French war hero addressed a crowd of Savannahians from the cast-iron veranda on the south facade of the building. This landmark building was constructed in the main from "tabby," a concrete mixture of oyster shells, sand, and lime. The Grecian-inspired veranda on the southern facade was the first major use of cast iron in Savannah. As an architectural device, cast iron later swept the city.

Jay also designed the Telfair Mansion in a neoclassical Regency style. It was constructed in 1818 for Alexander Telfair, the scion of Edward Telfair, a former Georgia governor and Revolutionary War hero. The mansion was bequeathed to the city for use as a museum, and it was formally opened in 1886. Many notables attended; most of the crowd's interest focused on Jefferson Davis, the former president of the Confederacy.

The Irish-born architect Charles B. Cluskey (1808–71) arrived in Savannah in 1838 and stayed for almost a decade, becoming known for his antebellum architecture influenced by the Greek Revival style. The elite of Savannah, prospering from neighboring plantations, hired him to design their town houses, including the Champion-McAlpin-Fowlkes house in 1844. He served as city surveyor of Savannah from 1845 to 1847, when he went to Washington with plans to renovate the White House and Capitol (few of his ideas were carried out, however).

Another antebellum architect, John Norris (1804–76), flourished in Savannah between 1846 and 1860. His most famous landmark is the Savannah Customs House, which was constructed between 1848 and 1852 in the Greek Revival style, with its mammoth portico. He also designed many more notable structures through-out the city in the same general style, including the Andrew Low House in 1849.

A competitor of his was John B. Hogg, who hailed from South Carolina. Hogg's most notable structure is the Trinity United Methodist Church at 225 W. President St. The church was built of the famous "Savannah grays," or stucco-covered gray brick. The building became known in Georgia as the "Mother Church of Method-ism."

As Georgia, along with South Carolina, moved closer to the horror of the Civil War, Savannah architecture stood at the peak of its beauty and charm. A visitor from Lon-don claimed, "Savannah puts on a hell of a good show. It's not London but not bad for a colony."

WAR, RECONSTRUCTION & PRESERVATION

Unlike Atlanta, Savannah was not burned to the ground. Even in 1864, after all the wartime deprivation suffered by the long blockade of its port, Savannah was a worthy "gift" when Sherman presented it as a Christmas present to Lincoln.

The Civil War introduced most Savannahians to poverty, and the decades of Reconstruction meant the end of opulence. Oglethorpe's original town plan had stretched from 6 to 24 city squares. Architects of renown avoided building in Savan-nah, going to richer cities instead.

The famous "Savannah grays" ceased production in the 1880s. Many buildings fell into ruin or decay. Modern structures outside the historic core were haphazardly constructed, although the Victorian era produced some notable architecture to grace the cityscape.

Just when it appeared that Savannah was going to rot away in the hot Georgia sun, the 1950s preservation movement arrived. Historic Savannah was subsequently saved and restored during the latter part of the 20th century.

THE ART OF SAVANNAH

In antebellum days, portraiture was the most common form of art. Any moderately well off family commissioned idealized portraits of its family members, at least the gentleman and lady of the house. Most were either in oil on canvas or in watercolor. In some rare instances, the portraits were done on ivory. The subjects of the portraits are attired in their "Sunday go-to-meeting" garb. Backdrops were romanticized—an elegant drapery, a Grecian column, a distant view of the ocean.

With the coming of the deprivations caused by the Civil War and the lean years of the Reconstruction era, Savannah was more in survivalist mode than in the mood for painting.

As time went on, a number of self-taught artists emerged in Savannah and the Low Country. Many of them were black, working in a folk-art medium. Sometimes they painted on unpainted clapboard from some abandoned barn or other structure. The Telfair Museum is the showcase for these self-taught artists, displaying Low Country art in various temporary exhibitions.

Among the other artists who have distinguished themselves in modern times is Leonora Quarterman (1911–79), who became one of the best-known watercolorists in the South. Her silk-screen prints of Savannah and Georgia coastal scenes are highly prized by collectors today.

Christopher P. H. Murphy (1902–69) was a native of the city who became known for drawings that captured both the cityscape of Savannah and the coastal landscape of the Low Country coastline. His originals and reproductions are as sought after as those of Ms. Quarterman.

THE REGION IN BOOKS, FILM & MUSIC

Books

This region is particularly identified with its great writers, especially **Thomas Wolfe** (1900–38) of Asheville, North Carolina, and **(Mary) Flannery O'Connor** (1925–64) of Savannah, Georgia. William Faulkner, the Nobel Prize–winning Mississippi novelist, once said about Wolfe, "He tried the hardest to say the most." Wolfe's four long, hauntingly beautiful novels bespeak his realism, lyricism, and brutal views of family life in the Deep South: *Look Homeward, Angel* (1929), *Of Time and the River* (1935), *The Web and the Rock* (1939), and *You Can't Go Home Again* (1940). O'Connor explored such themes as evil, sin, and the religious outlook of the Old South in *A Good Man Is Hard to Find* (1955), *Everything That Rises Must Converge* (1965), and *The Habit of Being* (1979).

No mention of Southern writers is complete without reference to Georgia's own **Carson McCullers,** whose *The Heart Is a Lonely Hunter* was cited in 1998 by Modern Library as being one of the 100 best novels of the 20th century. Her *Member of the Wedding* became a Broadway play, and Elizabeth Taylor portrayed the heroine in the film version of *Reflections in a Golden Eye.* McCullers wrote a strange, powerful kind of fiction—tender and grotesque at the same time, and peopled by characters who always bore some mark of psychic or environmental deformity.

The late **Charles Kuralt,** another famous North Carolinian, was an Emmy Award–winning journalist known for his insightful yet folksy *On the Road* books and TV reports about America's heritage, and for his nationally broadcast CBS News show *Sunday Morning with Charles Kuralt.* He made the bestseller list in 1996 with *Charles Kuralt's America.*

It goes without saying that there's no better introduction to the story of the antebellum South, the Civil War, and the early years of Reconstruction than **Margaret Mitchell**'s classic *Gone With the Wind.*

OTHER FICTION

Set in Greenville County, South Carolina, **Dorothy Allison**'s *Bastard Out of Carolina* (1993) is the tale of an illegitimate girl growing up in an abusive home. It evokes memories of Southern Gothic writing: hard hitting, effective, and written in tough, terse prose in the style of Carson McCullers and Truman Capote. Allison's later work, *Cavedweller* (1998) details the life of a woman determined to give her children the good life in spite of their deadbeat father. The book is set in Cairo, Georgia.

One of the major breakthroughs in African-American literature was the publication of *Ugly Ways* (1994) by St. Simons Island writer **Tina McElroy Ansa.** The novel challenged the stereotypical image of the African-American mother as a superwoman of unlimited compassion and wisdom. It was named Best Fiction of 1994 by the African-American Blackboard List.

Susan Dodd's *The Mourner's Bench* (1998) takes place on the Albemarle Sound and is very much in the genre of North Carolina's Reynolds Price. The story of a long-lost love, the book brings together the memories of two women who have different voices, the sharp New England Yankee accent contrasting with the molasses-thick Southern drawl.

Hailed as the best Civil War novel since Michael Shaara's *The Killer Angels, Cold Mountain* (1997) by **Charles Frazier** is spare and eloquent. It evokes a portrait of Inman, a soldier returning home from war across a devastated landscape. Based on local history and family stories passed down by the author's great-great grandfather, it is also an evocative love story. Frazier received the National Book Award in 1997.

In *The Promise of Rest* (1995), **Reynolds Price** tells the story of a young man with AIDS who has come home to his parents' house to die. The book concludes a trilogy about the Kendal-Mayfield clan that began 15 years ago. Price himself was diagnosed with spinal cancer in 1984 (confining him to a wheelchair), and this remarkable book is testament to his determined spirit.

Nicholas Sparks's *The Notebook* (1996) evokes the coastal Carolinas in a *Great Gatsby*–like tale of post–World War II love set in New Bern, just inland from the southern Outer Banks.

BIOGRAPHY

Citizen Turner: The Wild Rise of An American Tycoon (1995) is a controversial book written by a father-and-son team, **Robert Goldberg** and **Jay Gerald.** The title is a takeoff on the Orson Welles movie *Citizen Kane.* In it, we learn that launching the Cable News Network almost ruined Ted Turner financially and that he cheated on his first two wives. The book explodes some of Turner's favorite myths about himself—for example, that he was a poor underdog, when in fact he grew up rich.

The press hailed **Al Stump**'s 1994 work, *Cobb,* as the story of a "psychotic at the bat." According to this insider's biography, Ty Cobb viewed both his life and baseball as being a "blood sport." Cobb's 24-year major-league career began in 1905. The good ol' Georgia boy died of cancer in 1961, at the age of 74.

At 85, **"Miss Effie" Leland Wilder** published her first novel, *Out to Pasture (But Not Over the Hill)* in 1995, a lighthearted but poignant story of growing old in a Southern retirement home.

COOKBOOKS

In the cookbook *Paula Deen & Friends: Living It Up, Southern Style* (2005), the popular Food Network personality and owner of a Savannah restaurant shares 24 party menus, featuring recipes culled from her own family and friends.

As much a social historian as a celebrated cook, the late **Bill Neal** elevated such standards as shrimp and grits and fish muddle to culinary heights in *Southern Cooking* (1985) and *Biscuits, Spoonbread, and Sweet Potato Pie* (1990).

Southern-born eco-chef Bryant Terry has taken soul food to a new level: He introduces vegan cooking to the South's culinary lexicon in his books *Grub: Ideas for an Urban Organic Kitchen* (2006), cowritten with Anna Lappé, with a forward by Eric Schlosser of *Fast Food Nation* fame. Most recently he penned *Vegan Soul Kitchen: Fresh, Healthy, and Creative African-American Cuisine* (2009).

GENERAL

Midnight in the Garden of Good and Evil (1994) by **John Berendt** is the book that put Savannah on the map—with a little help from the movie *Forrest Gump.* Characters such as the Lady Chablis (a wickedly funny black drag queen) and Danny Hansford (a hustler) are introduced in this brilliantly conceived and seductive story of murder (or was it self-defense?) in the steamy Old South.

Bailey White's best-yet depiction of life in a small Georgia town, *Mama Makes Up Her Mind* (1994) made the *New York Times* bestseller list.

HISTORY

A tale of the region's rascals, **Lindley Butler**'s saga paints eight compelling sketches of the rogues and Confederate ship captains who operated in North Carolina's coastal waters in *Pirates, Privateers, and Rebel Raiders of the North Carolina Coast* (2000). Even Blackbeard springs to life along with 1812 commerce raiders and Confederate commerce raiders operating out of the port of Wilmington.

Gen. William Tecumseh Sherman pledged "to make a trail that would be visible for 50 years"—250 miles long and 60 miles wide, from Atlanta to Savannah. **Lee Kennett**'s *Marching Through Georgia* (1995) is the carefully researched story of how he did it.

In 3 decades, the state has become the 10th most populous in America, and **Milton Ready**'s tome titled *The Tar Heel State: A History of North Carolina* (2005) traces its storied past, a tale of pioneers, soldiers, tobacco tycoons, and farmers, including contributions of African Americans and women.

Jeff Shaara penned *Gods and Generals* (1998) as the sequel to the 1984 Pulitzer Prize–winning work *The Killer Angels,* written by his late father, Michael. The younger Shaara's book complements his father's work on the Battle of Gettysburg by turning back the clock and portraying the days leading up to the epic battle.

Films

Many critically acclaimed movies have used the South as a cultural backdrop, especially the tri-state area of the Carolinas and Georgia. The second-largest studio complex in America, EUE Screen Gems, is located in Wilmington, North Carolina, and Spoleto Festival USA, a world-class event for film and the arts, is held annually in Charleston.

No film to come out of the South is as famous around the world as *Gone With the Wind* (1939), adapted from Margaret Mitchell's sprawling 1936 epic that introduced Rhett Butler (Clark Gable) and Scarlett O'Hara (Vivien Leigh) to the world. The film, which tells the story of the Civil War from a white Southern point of view, was awarded 10 Oscars. The story opens in rural Georgia in 1861 and goes through Atlanta's Reconstruction era.

A feature produced by Walt Disney, *Song of the South* (1946) is based on the Uncle Remus cycle of stories by Joel Chandler Harris. It was Disney's first live-action film but it has never been released on home video in the U.S. because of a fear that it is racially insensitive to African Americans (though hundreds of copies have been smuggled into the U.S. from the U.K.). The film's hit song, "Zip-a-Dee-Doo-Dah," won the 1947 Oscar for Best Song.

Other than *Gone With the Wind,* one of the most famous films to come out of the South is *To Kill a Mockingbird,* directed by Robert Mulligan and based on the novel by Harper Lee. The 1962 film stars Gregory Peck as Atticus Finch, who has been hailed as a great hero in American cinema. Peck won an Oscar for Best Actor for the role.

A landmark drama, *Deliverance* (1972), set in rural backwoods Georgia, stars Jon Voight and Burt Reynolds. It's the story of four suburban professional men from Atlanta who set out on a highly disturbing weekend canoe and camping trip.

One of the highest-grossing films of the 1970s, *Smokey and the Bandit* stars Sally Field and Burt Reynolds. It's an action comedy that in its own silly way is a celebration of redneck culture, with Jackie Gleason cast as the potbellied Southern sheriff. This movie is a favorite of any fan who loves a good car chase.

The Big Chill (1983) is set in a posh South Carolina winter house. It tells the story of eight old friends searching for something they lost. They find that all they need is each other. Tom Berenger, Glenn Close, and William Hurt are among the stars.

A 1985 drama directed by Steven Spielberg, *The Color Purple,* based on the Pulitzer Prize–winning novel by Alice Walker, tells the story of a young African-American girl named Celie (Whoopi Goldberg). Oprah Winfrey also appears in the movie as Sofia, who delivers the line, "A girl child ain't safe in a family of men." Set in the Deep South in the early 20th century, the film follows Celie—pregnant at 14 by her father—through 30 years of a tough life.

Filmed on location in North Carolina, *Bull Durham* (1988) stars Kevin Costner. This is one of the most famous baseball pictures to come out of the 1980s, and its costars, Tim Robbins and Susan Sarandon, met on the set for the first time and later became a real-life couple.

Filmed in Atlanta, *Driving Miss Daisy* (1989) stars Morgan Freeman and Jessica Tandy. It dramatically tells the heartwarming story of an elderly Southern Jewish lady and her African-American chauffeur. Tandy won an Oscar for her role. At the age of 80, she was the oldest winner and the oldest nominee in history to win in the Best Actress category. The film also won the Oscar for Best Picture of the Year.

Set in Savannah, *Forrest Gump* (1994) was a huge worldwide commercial success, winning six Oscars, including Best Actor for Tom Hanks. The movie tells the story of a man with an IQ of 75 and his epic journey through life. The film received rave reviews, except for a dissent here and there—*Entertainment Weekly* called it "a baby boomer version of Disney's America."

Director Clint Eastwood's *Midnight in the Garden of Good and Evil* (1997) is based on John Berendt's spectacular bestseller. The Southern Gothic film depicts some fabulously eccentric personalities of Savannah, including drag queen Lady Chablis. The book is based on the actual killing of Danny Hansford, a local hustler, by art dealer Jim Williams, an event that resulted in four murder trials before a final acquittal.

With Savannah as a setting, *The Legend of Bagger Vance* (2000) was directed by Robert Redford. It stars Will Smith as Bagger Vance and Matt Damon as Rannulph Junuh, the best golfer in the city. Bagger teaches Rannulph the secret of an authentic golf stroke, which turns out to also be the secret to mastering any challenge and finding meaning in life.

Ray (2004) is a biopic that focuses on 30 years of the life of legendary rhythm and blues musician Ray Charles. Born in a small town in Georgia, he went blind at the age of eight. As Ray, Jamie Foxx delivers a tour de force performance, winning the Oscar for Best Actor.

Music

The music of the Deep South enjoys one of the richest heritages in the United States. Even before the Civil War, traditional folk music brought from Ireland and Britain rivaled the songs of African slaves. African Americans developed the blues at the beginning of the 20th century.

All three states have added richly to the repertoire of country music, soul music, gospel, spirituals, rock 'n' roll, blue grass, jazz, and beach music. With origins stretching back to colonial days, Appalachian folk music is still played and sung today.

Not only Elvis, but many Carolina and Georgia artists were pioneers of rock 'n' roll, including Little Richard, Otis Redding, Carl Perkins, and James Brown.

Arguably, the only major American music not started in the South is rap. However, the tri-state area, especially Atlanta, has given rise to a subgenre of rap called "dirty south." Atlanta has long been a center of hip-hop culture.

MUSIC OF NORTH CAROLINA

From the traditional rural blues called Piedmont blues—characterized by a unique finger-picking method on the guitar—to Chapel Hill rock, North Carolina has a long musical tradition. Performers such as the North Carolina Ramblers helped popularize the sound of country music nationwide.

Called "the Triangle," the Chapel Hill–Raleigh-Durham area is known for its indie rock from bands such as Superchunk and Archers of Loaf. Later punk rock bands from this section of the state have had such provocative names as Stillborn Christians or Oral Fixation.

Many notable jazz musicians, such as Thelonious Monk, also hail from North Carolina.

On the Chapel Hill rock scene, some of the more modern bands include Squirrel Nut Zippers and the Annuals; and Chris Daughtry from *American Idol* hails from McLeansville.

MUSIC OF SOUTH CAROLINA

The first musical society in North America, St. Cecilia Society, was founded in 1766 in Charleston. In the centuries that followed, the state would produce a number of artists who would enjoy world renown, including sultry Eartha Kitt, Dizzy Gillespie, and even Chubby Checker, who after all these years is still "twisting again like we did last summer."

The best-known rock band to hail from South Carolina is Hootie and the Blowfish, and James Brown also has roots in the state as well as ties to Georgia.

South Carolina "birthed" beach music, an offshoot of early R&B. Its shuffling beat spawned the dance called the Shag, which is still popular along the coast today, especially in the Myrtle Beach area. The state also produced two other celebrated dances, the Charleston and the Big Apple.

South Carolina is also known for groups singing spirituals, those sacred Christian songs originally developed by 19th-century African Americans. A country-based variety show, *Carolina Opry,* launched in 1986, has turned Myrtle Beach into the major showcase for East Coast country music, luring such artists as Dolly Parton and Alabama. Myrtle Beach is also the base for the South Carolina State Bluegrass Festival.

THE MUSIC OF GEORGIA

Getting their first break on the "Chitlin' Circuit," James Brown, a native of Augusta, and Little Richard, born in Macon, went on to greater glory. They fused gospel with blues and boogie-woogie, which paved the road for R&B and soul. An aging Little Richard still wows audiences with his famous "Tutti Frutti" and "Good Golly, Miss Molly."

In the 1960s Motown introduced Gladys Knight, who became one of its bestselling artists. Like Little Richard, Otis Redding grew up in Macon and helped define a gritty Southern soul sound.

Georgia has deep roots in folk music tradition, having been a player in every sound from Piedmont blues to African-American music. Mcintosh County is about the only place in American today that keeps alive "ring shout" music, featuring clapping and stick-beating percussion with call-and-response vocals.

Atlanta musicians spearheaded the rise of Southern rock, as exemplified by such bands as the Atlanta Rhythm Section. Lowrey Music became one of the world's major music publishers from its Atlanta base. Atlanta-based OutKast became one of the first major hip-hop groups to spring up outside New York or Los Angeles.

Guitarist Chet Atkins, reared in Hamilton, helped create a country music style known as the Nashville sound.

Athens, Georgia, has played an iconic role in the evolution of alternative rock and new wave, giving the world such artists as R.E.M. (with lead vocalist Michael Stipe) and the B-52s. One music critic called much of the music emerging from Athens as "quirky college rock."

EATING & DRINKING IN THE REGION

A Southern-style breakfast may consist of the following: homemade biscuits, country (very salty) ham, red-eye gravy, and grits swimming in butter. If a fellow were still hungry, he might cook up some Jimmy Dean sausage, toss a few buckwheat pancakes with cane syrup (or molasses), and fry a mess o' eggs with the yolk cooked hard. Healthful? Hardly. But it's easy to eat very well (and very nutritiously) in the South, given the region's bounty of local vegetables and fruits, farm-raised meats, and fresh-off-the-boat seafood.

Southern cuisine is a blend of the Old World (meaning Europe) and the New World (meaning North America). Necessity forced early settlers to find ways to integrate New World foods, like wild turkey and corn, into their bland diet of dumplings and boiled chicken. Many of the most important elements of the cuisine came from African slaves, who championed such exotica as okra and peanuts, and who turned the vitamin-rich black-eyed peas, used by plantation owners to fertilize fields, into a Southern classic. These influences came together to create Southern cuisine, an amalgam that embraces such favorites as sweet-potato pie, pecan pie, buttermilk biscuits, sweetened iced tea, long-cooked greens, sweet creek shrimp, fried green tomatoes, pan gravy, and peanuts (preferably boiled).

Virtual culinary wars have broken out over how to make **Southern fried chicken.** Even Colonel Sanders once denounced the way that his chain franchise fried chicken. One old-time cook who had a reputation for serving the best fried chicken in Georgia confided that her secret was bacon grease and a heavy black skillet that was 50 years old.

If you travel the hidden back roads of the tri-state area, you can still find a granny cooking country delicacies such as **chitlins** (chitterlings): Not for the fainthearted, this backwoods plate is pig intestines turned inside out and then braised, boiled, and deep-fried to a crispy brown. **Crackling bread** is corn bread with crispy leftovers from the renderings of pork fat at slaughter time. Traditional **collard greens** are long simmered and seasoned with ham hocks.

What lobster is to Maine, **catfish** is to the Southern palate. Fried catfish and **hush puppies** (fried cornmeal balls) reign supreme. With a sweet, mild flavor and a firm texture, catfish (now commercially raised in ponds) is one of the most delectable of freshwater fish, despite its ugly appearance. The traditional way to cook it is in grease, but cooks today have created more delicate preparations, serving it with such dainty fixings as lime-and-mustard sauce.

Low Country specialties in the Charleston area include such dishes as **shrimp 'n' grits** and **she-crab soup.** Outdoor **oyster roasts** are popular in the late fall, when the bivalves grow big and plump. **Confederate bean soup** is made with onion, celery, bacon, sausage, ham stock, brown sugar, baked beans, and heavy cream. "No wonder our boys in gray lost the war," one diner told us.

In a bow to Southern heritage, **wild game** is featured on many a menu. Around October or November, hunters in the South, dressed in blaze orange, set out in the forests to stalk deer. The venison may be eaten right away or frozen for later use in the winter, when a steak might appear on your plate with grits and gravy. In the Carolinas, quail sautéed in butter is a tasty delicacy. More modern cooks season it with wine or sherry. Wild duck—brought down by hunters in blinds on the scenic coastal marshes—may be roasted and stuffed with potato-and-apple dressing (winning such noted gourmands as former president Bill Clinton).

Eventually, all talk of Southern cooking comes down to **barbecue.** People in Georgia, for example, have strong opinions about the barbecue that they're served in North Carolina—and take our word for it, those views are never favorable. And what Carolinians think about Georgia barbecue is best left unprinted. Unlike Texans, who prefer beef-based barbecue, Southern barbecue artists prefer a slab of pork ribs or pork shoulders.

Some cooks slow roast the pork shoulder for 12 hours or so. Traditionalists prefer smoking it with hickory wood, although some use charcoal. No one agrees on the sauce. Will it be a pepper-and-vinegar sauce (eastern North Carolina); a pepper, vinegar, and catsup sauce (western North Carolina); or a sweet mustard sauce (South Carolina)? Surely barbecue—regardless of how it's made—has entered Dixie's Hall of Culinary Fame.

In summer, the fruit pickings are plenty, with local **strawberries, blueberries, cantaloupes,** and **plums** ripening at dusty farm stands. Georgia **peaches** are legendarily sweet and fragrant. The melon of choice is the **watermelon.** You'll find the best ones in your own garden or a farm stand.

Potlikker (also known as pot liquor) is the tasty water left in the pot after the greens, beans, or whatever have been long cooked, usually in the company of bacon grease, a ham hock, or fatback.

Many Southerners point with pride to the fact that you can get Continental dishes, French-influenced cuisine, and sushi throughout the South today. But visitors to the region deliberately seek out down-home Southern food. Though, unfortunately, it's harder than ever to come by.

PLANNING YOUR TRIP TO THE CAROLINAS & GEORGIA

3

Taken as a whole, the states of North Carolina, South Carolina, and Georgia would be tantamount to visiting a large European country. Many motorists, both foreign and domestic, prefer to visit the highlights of this grand trio. If you'd like to do this, see our suggested itineraries in chapter 4, which take in the highlights of this region.

Other vacationers will prefer to concentrate on cities such as Charleston or Savannah, or on particular scenic regions such as the Great Smoky Mountains National Park, and most definitely the beach communities found on Hilton Head or on the Outer Banks of North Carolina.

For additional help in planning your trip and for more on-the-ground resources in the Carolinas and Georgia, please turn to "Fast Facts: The Carolinas & Georgia" in chapter 22.

WHEN TO GO

North Carolina

CLIMATE

For the most part, North Carolina's climate is moderate, with average winter temperatures in the 60s along the southern coast and in the low 40s inland. Summer temperatures can rise to the high 90s in the state's interior, accompanied by some serious humidity. In the mountains or at the shore, temperatures can be in the mid-60s or high 70s.

So if you're thinking about a summer vacation in North Carolina, escape to Boone, which has an average temperature of 69°F (21°C). It's warm enough during the day to swim or hike, but you'll want a light blanket to sleep under at night. The Outer Banks is another great destination in summer; bring your beach gear, and enjoy the breezes.

Raleigh Average Temperatures & Rainfall

	JAN	FEB	MAR	APR	MAY	JUNE	JULY	AUG	SEPT	OCT	NOV	DEC
HIGH (°F)	50	52	61	72	78	85	88	87	81	71	61	52
HIGH (°C)	10	11	16	22	26	29	31	31	27	22	16	11
LOW (°F)	29	30	37	46	55	62	67	66	60	47	38	31
LOW (°C)	-2	-1	3	8	13	17	19	19	16	8	3	-1
RAIN (IN.)	3.5	3.7	3.8	2.6	3.9	3.7	4.0	4.0	3.2	2.9	3.0	3.2

Asheville Average Temperatures & Rainfall

	JAN	FEB	MAR	APR	MAY	JUNE	JULY	AUG	SEPT	OCT	NOV	DEC
HIGH (°F)	49	51	57	68	76	83	85	84	79	69	57	50
HIGH (°C)	9	11	14	20	24	28	29	29	26	21	14	10
LOW (°F)	30	30	36	44	52	60	64	63	57	46	36	30
LOW (°C)	-1	-1	2	7	11	16	18	17	14	8	2	-1
RAIN (IN.)	3.2	3.0	3.7	3.2	2.9	3.5	4.3	3.6	2.8	2.5	2.2	2.9

In late September or early October, fall colors are brilliant here. Thousands of monarch butterflies cluster in the mountains near Asheville, around Wagon Road Gap on the Blue Ridge Parkway, as part of their annual migration to South America. (Be prepared for incredible crowds along the parkway.)

Spring is also a spectacular time to visit. In March and April, the state bursts into bloom, with azaleas in vibrant hues everywhere and delicate dogwood blossoms in pink and white in the woodlands.

North Carolina Calendar of Events

JANUARY

Duke University Jazz Series, Durham. Formerly known as the NC International Jazz Festival, this event is in its 20th year. Internationally renowned jazz musicians are featured at various locations throughout the city. Call ℂ **919/660-3300** or go to www.duke.edu/music for more information. Throughout the year.

FEBRUARY

African American Arts Festival, Greensboro. Many cultural and artistic events highlight the achievements of the state's African-American population. Call ℂ **336/333-6885** or visit www.ncgov.com for more information. Early February to April.

Home, Garden & Flower Show, Raleigh. You can find everything from roses to garden fountains to furniture in this vast display in the Raleigh Convention Center, which attracts serious gardeners from all over the South. Call ℂ **919/996-8500** or visit www.raleighconvention.com for more information. Late February to early March.

MARCH

Annual Star Fiddlers Convention, Star. This event features performances by virtuoso bluegrass fiddlers from all over the South. Call ℂ **910/428-2171** for more information. First weekend in March.

APRIL

Stoneybrook Steeplechase, Southern Pines. This event features horse races and tailgate parties. Call ℂ **910/875-2074** or go to www.carolinahorsepark.com for more information. April (exact date varies).

North Carolina Azalea Festival, Wilmington. A parade, entertainment, and home and garden tours are all included in this annual festival. Call ℂ **910/794-4650** or visit www.ncazaleafestival.org for more information. Early April.

Full Frame Documentary Film Festival, the Carolina Theatre, Durham. The largest festival of its kind in North America, this event (formerly the DoubleTake Documentary Film Festival) has been hailed for its creative programming and exhibition of films rarely seen on screen. Call ℂ **919/687-4100** or visit www.fullframefest.org for more information. Early April.

Festival of Flowers, Biltmore Estate, Asheville. This festival celebrates a century of elegance at the Biltmore Estate. The gardens are brilliant with color for your viewing. Call ✆ **800/411-3812** or go to www.biltmore.com for more information. Early April to mid-May.

Spring Garden Tour, Winston-Salem. Each spring in historic Old Salem, people gather from everywhere to celebrate spring with a tour of the city's 18th-century gardens. Call ✆ **888/653-7253** or visit www.oldsalem.org for more information. Mid-April.

Easter Sunrise Service, Winston-Salem. Thousands of people come to see this Moravian religious service in "God's Acres," the cemetery where the early settlers are buried. Call ✆ **336/725-0651** or visit www.carolinamusicways.org for more information. Easter Sunday.

Spring Historic Homes & Gardens Tour, New Bern. Tour Tryon Palace and other area homes, gardens, and historic sites. Call ✆ **800/437-5767** or visit www.visitnewbern.com for more information. Late April.

MAY

Ole Time Fiddlers and Bluegrass Festival, Union Grove. Traditional musicians and the fans who love bluegrass make a yearly pilgrimage to what may be the most renowned fiddling competition in the country. PBS made an award-winning documentary on the festival, held in the Brushy Mountain foothills. Call ✆ **828/478-3735** or visit www.fiddlersgrove.com for more information. Memorial Day weekend.

Coca-Cola 600, Charlotte. This action-packed race, which is part of the NASCAR Winston Cup Series, takes place at Lowe's Motor Speedway. Enjoy the Food Lion Speed Street, 3 days of race-related festivities on Tryon Street in Charlotte. Call ✆ **704/455-5555** or go to www.600festival.com for more information. End of May.

JUNE

Herb Day, Durham. See displays of traditional herbal remedies and recipes from the mid–19th century. There are herb plants from an on-site garden, herbal crafts, and food available for purchase. Call ✆ **919/477-5498** for more information. First Saturday in June.

American Dance Festival, Durham. Considered to be the largest and most prestigious modern-dance event in the world, this festival has been held on the Duke University campus since 1978. Call ✆ **919/684-6402** or go to www.americandancefestival.org for more information. Early June to late July.

The Lost Colony, Roanoke Island. Paul Green's moving drama is presented in the Waterside Theater Monday through Saturday at 8:30pm. It's the country's oldest outdoor drama, running since 1937. Tickets cost $24 for adults; $19 for seniors, military personnel, and people with disabilities; and $12 for children 11 and under. Contact the Waterside Theater (✆ **252/473-3414;** www.thelostcolony.org) for tickets. Early June to late August.

75th Anniversary Weekend, Great Smoky Mountains National Park. The park staff offers programs and events honoring the region's Cherokee and Appalachian ties. Call ✆ **865/436-1200** or visit www.nps.gov/grsm/parknews for more information. Mid-June.

Hillsborough Hog Day, Hillsborough. Featured attractions include barbecue, potbellied-pig contests, entertainment, crafts, and a vintage car show. Call ✆ **919/732-8156** or visit www.hogdays.com for more information. Mid-June.

National Hollerin' Contest, Spivey's Corner. Immortalized by a visit from Charles Kuralt at its 1969 inaugural, this event celebrates hollerin' as a traditional form of communication. Drawing visitors from all over the country, the contest swells Spivey's Corner's usual population of 49. Call ✆ **910/567-2600** or visit www.hollerincontest.com for more information. Third Saturday in June.

Brevard Music Festival, Brevard. For more than half a century, this has been one of the major open-air events in western North Carolina, featuring opera, classic music, pops, and jazz. The center for information is at 100 Probart St. (© **888/384-8682** or 828/862-2105; www.brevardmusic.org). Mid-June to early August.

JULY

Shindig on the Green, Asheville. At the City/County Plaza (College and Spruce sts.), you'll find mountain musicians and dancers having an old-fashioned wingding. The event is free and lots of fun. For details, call © **828/258-6101** or go to www.folkheritage.org. Every Saturday night from early July to September.

Grandfather Mountain Highland Games and Gathering of the Scottish Clans, Linville. This event is complete with Scottish dance, music, and athletic competitions. Call © **828/733-1333** or go to www.gmhg.org for more information. Early July.

Festival of the Arts, Brevard. This week-long festival features a children's exhibit, creative and performing arts, and food, in venues throughout the city. Call © **828/884-2787** or go to www.tcarts.org for more information. Early July.

Coon Dog Day, Saluda. For more than 30 years, coon hunters and nature lovers have gathered for dog trials, arts and crafts shows, a parade, a pancake breakfast, a treeing contest, barbecue, bluegrass and Southern folk concerts, and a square dance. It's truly folkloric Carolina. Call © **828/749-2581** or visit www.saluda.com for more information. Saturday following the Fourth of July.

Folkmoot USA (North Carolina International Folk Festival), Waynesville and Maggie Valley. Folkmoot USA provides international music and dance, plus good old-fashioned North Carolina mountain music. Call © **877/365-5872** or 828/452-2997 or visit www.folkmootusa.org for more information. Mid-July.

National Black Theatre Festival, Winston-Salem. This festival includes performances, workshops, and seminars at various theaters around the city, produced and hosted by the city's own North Carolina Black Repertory Co. Call © **336/723-2266** or go to www.nbtf.org for more information. Late

July to early August. Held biannually in odd years.

Bele Chere, Asheville. Billed as the "largest outdoor street festival in the Southeast," this music, arts, and food festival has big-name bands and "Taste of Asheville" samplings from local restaurants. Contact the Department of Parks and Recreation (© **828/259-5800;** www.belecherefestval.com) for more information. Late July.

AUGUST

Mountain Dance & Folk Festival, Asheville. At the Diana Worth Theatre, 2 South Pack Square, the fiddlers, banjo pickers, dulcimer players, ballad singers, and clog dancers don't call it quits until nobody is interested in one more dance. This is the oldest such festival in the country, and you're encouraged to join in. For details, call © **828/258-6101** or go to www.folkheritage.org. First weekend in August.

SEPTEMBER

North Carolina Apple Festival, Hendersonville. Bring your favorite apple-pie recipe, and enjoy music, crafts, games, and a cooking contest. Call © **828/697-4557** or go to www.ncapplefestival.org for more information. Labor Day weekend.

Festival in the Park, Charlotte. A celebration of regional arts and crafts, with entertainment and good food as bonuses. Call © **704/338-1060** or visit www.festivalinthepark.org for more information. Late September.

Mayberry Days, Mount Airy. A celebration of *The Andy Griffith Show*, with entertainment, a golf tournament, walking tours, and a pig pickin'. Call © **800/948-0949** or visit www.visitmayberry.com or www.surryarts.org for more information. Last weekend in September.

OCTOBER

SAS Championship, Cary. This $2-million PGA Champions (Senior) Tour event is drawing such well-known golfers as Tom Kite, Lanny Wadkins, and Fuzzy Zoeller as it approaches its seventh tournament year. Call © **919/531-4653** or go to www.saschampionship.com for more information. Early October.

MUMfest, New Bern. Swiss Bear Downtown Development Corp. hosts a street festival loaded with food, fun, arts and crafts, and tours. Call ✆ 252/638-5781 or visit www. mumfest.com for more information. Early October.

North Carolina State Fair, Raleigh. This traditional gathering draws crowds from all over. Call ✆ 919/821-7400 or visit www. ncstatefair.org for more information. Mid-October.

NOVEMBER

Christmas at the Biltmore Estate, Asheville. The Biltmore Estate becomes a winter wonderland long before Christmas. Enjoy Christmas lights, trees, decorations, and music. Call ✆ 800/411-3812 or 828/225-1333, or go to www.biltmore.com for more information. Early November to early January.

Festival of Lights, Tanglewood Park, Winston-Salem. For 9 weeks, more than 750,000 lights are presented in more than five dozen displays. Enjoy storybook themes. Call ✆ 336/778-6300 or visit www.forsyth.cc/parks/tanglewood for more information. Mid-November to early January.

DECEMBER

Holiday Festival, Raleigh. The city hosts the Holiday Festival at the North Carolina Museum of Art. It's an old-fashioned yule-tide celebration. Call ✆ 919/839-6262 or visit http://ncartmuseum.org for more information. Early December.

Old Salem Christmas and Candle Teas, Winston-Salem. A re-creation of yuletide as it was celebrated 200 years ago in Old Salem. Enjoy making candles, tasting Moravian sugar cakes, and touring the 1788 Gemeinhaus by candlelight. Call ✆ 336/722-6171 or visit www.homemoravian.org for more information. First 2 weekends in December.

South Carolina

CLIMATE

Although parts of South Carolina can be very hot and steamy in summer, temperatures are never extreme the rest of the year.

Charleston Average Temperatures & Rainfall

	JAN	FEB	MAR	APR	MAY	JUNE	JULY	AUG	SEPT	OCT	NOV	DEC
HIGH (°F)	59	61	68	76	83	87	89	89	85	77	69	61
HIGH (°C)	15	16	20	24	28	31	32	32	29	25	21	16
LOW (°F)	40	41	48	56	64	70	74	74	69	49	49	42
LOW (°C)	4	5	9	13	18	21	23	23	21	9	9	6
RAIN (IN.)	3.5	3.3	4.3	2.7	4.0	6.4	6.8	7.2	4.7	2.9	2.5	3.2

Columbia Average Temperatures & Rainfall

	JAN	FEB	MAR	APR	MAY	JUNE	JULY	AUG	SEPT	OCT	NOV	DEC
HIGH (°F)	56	59	67	77	84	89	91	85	76	68	67	59
HIGH (°C)	13	15	19	25	29	32	33	29	24	20	19	15
LOW (°F)	33	35	42	50	59	66	70	69	64	50	41	35
LOW (°C)	12	6	10	15	19	21	21	18	10	5	2	
RAIN (IN.)	4.4	4.1	4.8	3.3	3.7	4.8	5.5	6.1	3.7	3.0	2.9	3.6

South Carolina Calendar of Events

JANUARY

Lowcountry Oyster Festival, Charleston. Steamed buckets of oysters greet visitors at Boone Hall Plantation. Enjoy live music, oyster-shucking contests, kids' events, and other activities. Contact the Greater Charleston Restaurant Association (✆ 843/452-6088; www.charlestonrestaurantassociation. com) for more information. End of January.

FEBRUARY

Southeastern Wildlife Exposition, Charleston. More than 150 of the finest artists and more than 500 exhibitors participate at 13 locations in the downtown area. Enjoy carvings, sculptures, paintings, live-animal exhibits, food, and much more. Call $\textcircled{C}$ **843/723-1748** or visit www.sewe.com for details. Mid-February.

Africa Alive, Rock Hill. Learn about African heritage by way of storytelling, craft activities, exhibits, music, and dance from the Museum of York County. Call $\textcircled{C}$ **803/329-2121** or visit http://chmuseums.org for more information. Late February.

MARCH

Festival of Houses and Gardens, Charleston. For nearly 50 years, people have been enjoying some of Charleston's most historic neighborhoods and private gardens on this tour. Contact the Historic Charleston Foundation, 40 E. Bay St. ($\textcircled{C}$ **843/723-1623;** www.historiccharleston.org), for details. Mid-March to mid-April.

Charleston Food + Wine Festival, Charleston. Four days of parties, events, and seminars mark this world-class culinary festival that draws the likes of Bobby Flay. Call $\textcircled{C}$ **843/727-9998** or visit www.charleston foodandwine.com for details. Late February to early March.

APRIL

Cooper River Bridge Run, Charleston. Sponsored by the Medical University of South Carolina, this 10K run and walk starts in Mount Pleasant, goes over the Cooper River Bridge, and ends in the center of Charleston. For information, call $\textcircled{C}$ **843/856-1949** or visit www.bridgerun.com. Early April.

Carolina Cup, Camden. The elaborate picnics with silver candelabras and crystal champagne flutes make this annual steeplechase race an event to remember. Contact the Springdale Race Course ($\textcircled{C}$ **803/432-6513;** www.carolina-cup.org) for more information. Early April.

World Grits Festival, St. George. This unique festival is a celebration of that famous Southern staple, grits! For years, contestants have competed in grits grinding, corn shelling, grits eating, and best recipes, as well as traditional festivities. Call $\textcircled{C}$ **843/563-7943** to find out more. Early April.

Flowertown Festival, Summerville. More than 180 booths of arts and crafts, a road race, a "Youth Fest," and lots of entertainment are set in this historic city surrounded by brilliant azalea and dogwood blossoms. Contact the YMCA ($\textcircled{C}$ **843/871-9622;** www.summervilleymca.org/flowertown) to learn more. First weekend in April.

Family Circle Cup, Charleston. Moved from Hilton Head to a tennis center in Charleston, the Family Circle Cup WTA tournament is one of the oldest on the women's pro tour. For information, call $\textcircled{C}$ **843/856-7900** or go to www.familycirclecup.com. Mid-April.

Verizon Heritage, Hilton Head. This $5.3-million tournament boasts an outstanding field of PGA tour professionals each year. The weeklong tournament is held at Harbour Town Golf Links in Sea Pines Plantation. Contact Classic Sports, Inc., 71 Lighthouse Rd., Ste. 414 ($\textcircled{C}$ **800/234-1107** or 843/671-2448; www.verizon heritage.com), for more information. Mid-April.

MAY

Spring Fling, Spartanburg. Live entertainment mixed with arts, crafts, and games make this a popular annual event. Contact Spartanburg Community Events ($\textcircled{C}$ **864/594-3105;** www.spartanburgspringfling. com) for details. Early May.

Iris Festival, Sumter. The world-famous Swan Lake Iris Gardens is the setting for this elaborate festival of arts and crafts, food, concerts, garden tours, and a parade. Call $\textcircled{C}$ **803/436-2500** or visit www.sumtersc. gov/VisitingUs/Festivals_Iris.aspx for more information. Late May.

Carolina Dodge Challenger 500 and **Diamond Hill Plywood 200,** Darlington. This is stock car racing's original superspeedway. The NASCAR NEXTEL Cup Series now features a full weekend of night racing, called "under the lights." For tickets, contact

© **843/459-7223** or 395-8877 or visit www.darlingtonraceway.com. Mother's Day weekend.

Coastal Uncorked, Myrtle Beach. This food, wine, and spirits festival features tastings, events, tours, golf tournaments, cooking competitions, and restaurant-week discounts. Celebrity guests such as Paula Deen (2011) host events ranging from cooking demos to book signings. For more info, call © **843/839-8818** or log on to coastal uncorked.com. Mid-May.

Pontiac GMC Freedom Weekend Aloft, Anderson. This 4-day extravaganza features big-name entertainment, amusement rides, 100 hot-air balloons, fireworks, and more at the city's Sports & Entertainment Center. Contact Freedom Weekend Aloft (© **864/ 399-9481;** www.freedomweekend.org) for more information. Memorial Day weekend.

Spoleto Festival USA, Charleston. This is the premier cultural event in the tri-state area. This famous international festival—the American counterpart of the equally celebrated one in Spoleto, Italy—showcases world-renowned performers in drama, dance, music, and art in various venues throughout the city. For details and this year's schedule, contact Spoleto Festival USA (© **843/579-3100;** www.spoletousa. org). Late May through early June.

JUNE

Edisto Riverfest, Walterboro. The main attractions at this festival are guided trips down the "black-water" (water darkened from tree tannins) Edisto River. Call © **803/734-0156** or visit www.edistoriver. org for details. Mid-June.

JULY

Lake Murray's July 4th Celebration, Columbia. Lake Murray plays host to some 100 boats decorated in red, white, and blue. A fireworks display is held at night. Contact the Lake Murray Tourism and Recreation Association (© **866/SC-JEWEL;** www. lakemurraycountry.com) for more information. First Saturday in July.

Two Days, Round the Fourth, Conway. Gather along the Waccamaw River for 2 days of arts and crafts, live entertainment, food, Jell-O jumps, raft races, boat rides, and fireworks. Contact the Conway Area Chamber of Commerce (© **843/248-2273;** http://conwayscchamber.com/chamber-currents/plans-well-underway-for-round-the-4th) for more information. Early July.

AUGUST

Shawfest, Shaw Air Force Base, near Sumter and Cherryvale. Onlookers are treated to an air show featuring some of the air force's top pilots and jets. Call © **800/511- SHAW** (7429) or visit www.shaw.af.mil for additional information. Early August in odd years.

Summerfest, York. Loads of live entertainment is presented here with four stages, crafts, country food, and a classic car show. Contact the York County Chamber of Commerce and Visitors Bureau (© **803/684- 2590;** www.greateryorkchamber.com) for more information. Fourth Saturday in August.

SEPTEMBER

South Carolina's Largest Garage Sale, Myrtle Beach. One person's trash is another person's treasure. Vendors set up shop in a large parking garage to sell clothing, furniture, household goods, and hundreds of other bargains. Contact the Myrtle Beach Area Visitor Information (© **800/36-3016** or 843/626-7444; www.cityofmyrtlebeach. com) for more information. Mid-September.

Scottish Games and Highland Gathering, Charleston. This gathering of Scottish clans features medieval games, bagpipe performances, Scottish dancing, and other traditional activities. Call the Scottish Society of Charleston (© **843/224-7867;** http:// charlestonscots.org) for more information. Third Saturday in September.

Candlelight Tour of Homes & Gardens, Charleston. Sponsored by the Preservation Society of Charleston, this annual event provides an intimate look at many of the area's historic homes, gardens, and churches. For more information, call © **843/722-4630** or visit www.preservationsociety.org. Mid-September to late October.

MOJA Festival, Charleston. Celebrating the rich African-American heritage in the Charleston area, this festival features lectures, art exhibits, stage performances, historical tours, concerts, and much more. Contact the Charleston Office of Cultural Affairs (℗ **843/724-7305;** www.charleston arts.sc/about-cultural-affairs-charleston/festivals-and-special-events/moja-arts-festival) for more information. Late September to early October.

OCTOBER

A Taste of Charleston, Charleston. Traditionally held at Boone Hall Plantation, this annual event offers an afternoon of food, fun, entertainment, and more. A selection of Charleston-area restaurants offers their specialties in bite-size portions so you can sample them all. For more information, call ℗ **843/452-6088** or visit www.charleston restaurantassociation.com. Early October.

Fall for Greenville, Greenville. This annual 3-day event features more than 40 restaurants and food vendors from around the city presenting a wide variety of their tasty wares. Events include a chili cook-off, cooking classes, ice carving demonstrations, a bartender's mix-off, a waiter's race, and a bike race, along with free entertainment. For more information, call **864/467-5741** or visit www.greenvillesc.gov/PublicInfo_Events/SpecialEvents.aspx. Mid-October.

Governor's Cup, Columbia. This event, more than half a century old, is comprised of a half-marathon, an 8km run, a 4-mile EdVenture Walk, and a Kids Fun Run beginning at 8:30am on the State Capitol grounds. Conducted by the Carolina Marathon Association. Call ℗ **803/731-2100** or visit www.carolinamarathon.org for more information. Mid-October.

Fall Festival of Houses, Beaufort. Frank Lloyd Wright's Auldbrass Plantation is only one of the beautiful homes on this tour. The public is invited to get a rare look at this coastal city's most stately residences during a 3-day tour. Call ℗ **843/379-3331** or go to www.historicbeaufort.org for more information. Late October.

NOVEMBER–DECEMBER

Merrily Myrtle: A Holiday Celebration, Myrtle Beach. The Grand Strand is decorated in a profusion of lights. This months-long celebration has a lineup that includes concerts, parades, and festivals. Contact the Myrtle Beach Area Chamber of Commerce (℗ **800/356-3016;** www.mbchamber.com) for more information. November to January 15.

Christmas in Charleston, Charleston. This month-long celebration features home and church tours, Christmas-tree lightings, craft shows, artistry, and a peek at how Old Charleston celebrated the holiday season. For more information on how to participate or to visit, call ℗ **800/774-0006** or visit www.charlestoncvb.com/xmas. Early November to late December.

Colonial Cup, Camden. Every year, this prestigious steeplechase race determines the champion and winner of the NSA's Eclipse award. Tailgating in style is a trademark of this event, with tables covered in linen and patrons dressed in hats and sport coats. Contact the Springdale Race Course (℗ **800/780-8117** or 803/432-6513; www.carolina-cup.org) for more information. Mid-November.

Lights Before Christmas, Columbia. The Riverbanks Zoo becomes a holiday wonderland when thousands of lights are strung around the park. Contact the Riverbanks Zoo (℗ **803/779-8717;** www.riverbanks.org) for more information. Late November to late December.

St. Francis Festival of Trees, Greenville. Professionally decorated trees are displayed in the Hyatt Regency, Westin Poinsett, and Hampton Inn & Suites–Riverplace. A teddy bear tea, Gingerbread Land, and family brunch are special attractions. Call ℗ **800/717-0023** or 864/233-0461 or visit www.greenvillecvb.com/visit/event-info.aspx?coe_id=13906&date_id=593995 for more information. Late November to late December.

Georgia

CLIMATE

The average high and low temperatures at coastal Savannah and central Atlanta show Low Country coastal areas to be warmer year-round than those farther inland. Winter temperatures seldom drop below freezing anywhere in the state. Spring and fall are the longest seasons, and the wettest months are December to April. Spring is a spectacular time to visit, as the azaleas, dogwoods, and camellias burst into bloom.

Savannah Average Temperatures & Rainfall

	JAN	FEB	MAR	APR	MAY	JUNE	JULY	AUG	SEPT	OCT	NOV	DEC
HIGH (°F)	60	62	70	78	84	89	91	90	85	78	70	62
HIGH (°C)	16	17	21	26	29	32	33	32	29	26	21	17
LOW (°F)	38	41	48	55	63	69	72	72	68	57	57	41
LOW (°C)	3	5	9	13	17	21	22	22	20	14	14	5
RAIN (IN.)	3.6	3.2	3.8	3.0	4.1	5.7	6.4	7.5	4.5	2.4	2.2	3.0

Atlanta Average Temperatures & Rainfall

	JAN	FEB	MAR	APR	MAY	JUNE	JULY	AUG	SEPT	OCT	NOV	DEC
HIGH (°F)	51	55	61	71	79	85	87	86	81	73	62	53
HIGH (°C)	11	13	16	22	26	29	31	30	27	23	17	12
LOW (°F)	33	36	41	51	59	67	69	69	63	52	41	34
LOW (°C)	12	5	11	15	19	21	21	17	11	5	1	
RAIN (IN.)	4.8	4.8	5.8	4.3	4.3	3.6	5.0	3.7	3.4	3.1	3.9	4.3

Georgia Calendar of Events

JANUARY

Martin Luther King Celebration, Atlanta. This event, occurring over the King holiday weekend, honors one of Atlanta's native sons in a celebration of the life and accomplishments of the civil rights leader. The program includes a "Salute to Greatness" dinner on Saturday and a commemorative at Ebenezer Baptist Church on the Monday holiday, with speeches by notables from the Reverend King's former pulpit. Contact the King Center (© **404/526-8900;** www.thekingcenter.org) for more information. Second week in January.

Augusta Cutting Horse Futurity, Augusta. This prestigious annual event attracts cowboys and cowgirls from all over the country and the world. Held in the Augusta-Richmond County Civic Center, this event marks the first big date on any equestrian lover's calendar. Call © **706/823-3417** or go to www.augustafuturity.com for more information. Mid-January.

Rattlesnake Roundup, Whigham. This event, held at 84 E. Whigham Rattlesnake Grounds, features arts, crafts, food, entertainment, and snake handling that includes a milking demonstration. Call © **229/762-3774** or visit www.caironet.com/RATTLE.HTM for more information. Last Saturday in January.

FEBRUARY

Georgia Days Colonial Faire and Muster, Savannah. Georgians turn out to celebrate the founding of their colony in Savannah on February 12, 1733, by James Oglethorpe. Various events are staged, including costumed demonstrators depicting skills used by the early settlers. Admission is free. Call © **912/651-2125** or go to www.georgiahistory.com for more information. Early February.

Savannah Irish Festival, Savannah. This Irish heritage celebration promises fun for the entire family, with music, dancing, and food. There's both a children's stage and a main stage. Contact the Irish Committee of Savannah (© **912/604-8298;** www.savannahirish.org) for more information. Mid-February.

MARCH

Golden Corral 500, Hampton. This suburb outside Atlanta is the site of the Atlanta International Raceway and home to this first of two annual NASCAR NEXTEL Cup events. Tickets to the races range from $75 to $165. For information and tickets, call ☏ **877/926-7849** or 770/946-4211 or visit www.atlanta motorspeedway.com. Mid-March.

The Savannah Tour of Homes & Gardens, Savannah. Each spring many residents open the doors to their historic homes for 4-day walking tours in which you are allowed to visit six to eight private homes and gardens every day. Luncheons and afternoon teas are also staged. Contact Tour Headquarters at 18 Abercorn St. (☏ **912/234-8054;** www.savannahtourof homes.org) for more information. Mid-March.

Cherry Blossom Festival, Macon. You'll find everything from hot-air ballooning to a giant parade with 100 bands. The entire city is ablaze with thousands of blooming cherry trees. For more information, contact the Macon Cherry Blossom Festival (☏ **478/751-7429;** www.cherryblossom. com). Mid- to late March.

St. Patrick's Day Celebration on the River, Savannah. The river flows green and so does the beer in one of the largest celebrations held on River Street each year. Enjoy live entertainment, lots of food, and tons of fun. Contact the Savannah Waterfront Association (☏ **912/234-0295;** www.river streetsavannah.com) for more information. St. Patrick's Day weekend.

APRIL

Masters Golf Tournament, Augusta. The first of professional golf's four "major" tournaments, this event was conceived by golf legend Bobby Jones, an Atlantan, who mastered the links as an amateur in the 1920s. Tickets ("badges," as the Augusta National "patrons" call them) are sold out years in advance. However, those who plan well in advance are able to enter a lottery to obtain tickets to practice rounds, which allows you to walk the grounds. The deadline for lottery registration is usually the middle of July for the following year's event. Call ☏ **706/667-6700** or go to www.masters.com/index.html for additional information. First weekend in April.

Georgia Renaissance Festival, Fairburn. Of the more than 100 shows every day, see the King's Joust and the Birds of Prey Show. There are games, rides, and crafts items, not to mention stilt walkers, minstrels, jousters, and magicians in the re-creation of a 16th-century English county fair. Admission is $20 for adults, $18 for seniors, $8.50 for children, and free for children 5 and under. Contact the Georgia Renaissance Festival (☏ **770/964-8575;** www. garenfest.com) for more information. Weekends April to June.

Atlanta Dogwood Festival, Atlanta. Georgia celebrates the coming of spring with garden and house tours, bicycle tours of exclusive Buckhead, concerts, and tons of azaleas and dogwoods in full bloom. On the final weekend, food booths, kids' activities, and concerts are among the events. Piedmont Park events are free, but admission fees apply to many other activities. Call ☏ **404/817-6642** or go to www.dogwood. org for more information. Early April.

The Atlanta Film Festival, Atlanta. This 7- to 10-day festival celebrates the rising independent movie scene in Atlanta. More than 80 films, videos, shorts, and documentaries are screened to the public throughout the city. Steven Spielberg credits this festival with giving his work its first big boost. Call ☏ **404/352-4225** or go to http://atlantafilmfestival.com/index.php for more information. Mid-April.

Riverfest Weekend, Columbus. This family-oriented festival offers an art show and sale, a custom and classic automobile show, a 5km road race, an orchid show and sale, parades, river events, and lots of food and music. Contact Riverfest (☏ **706/322-0756;** www.historiccolumbus.com) for more information. Late April.

MAY

The Cotton Pickin' Fair, Gay. Active for more than half a century, this award-winning festival is a family affair, filled with antiques, arts and crafts, food, and entertainment. You can make a day of it. Admission is $5 for adults and $3 for children 4 to 12. For information, call ✆ 706/538-6814 or go to www.cpfair.org. First weekend in May and in October semiannually.

Aiken-Augusta Spring Regatta, Augusta. The Augusta Rowing Club is perched over the waters of the Savannah River. From the boathouse, the water continues for 11 miles downstream, one of the longest stretches of rowable water in the world. This well-attended event attracts enthusiasts from all over America. For details, call ✆ 706/821-2875 or go to www.augustarowingclub.org. Early May.

Atlanta Downtown Festival & Tour, Atlanta. In the historic Fairlie-Poplar district, this festival features live entertainment, an artists' market, kiddie activities, and a wide range of food and beverages for sale at stalls. The festival's aim is to showcase the fine living in the downtown district. For more information, call ✆ 404/227-0061 or go to www.atlantadna.org/festival/festival.htm.

Memorial Day at Old Fort Jackson, Savannah. The day includes a flag-raising ceremony and a memorial service featuring "Taps." Contact the Coastal Heritage Society (✆ 912/651-6840; www.chsgeorgia.org) for more information. Late May.

JUNE

Juneteenth, Savannah. This event highlights the contributions of more than 200,000 African Americans who fought for their freedom and that of future generations. This event is a celebration of the Emancipation Proclamation. Although this promise of freedom was announced in January, it was not until the middle of June (actual date unknown) that the news reached Savannah, thus prompting the remembrance of "Juneteenth." For more information, contact the Savannah Convention & Visitors Bureau (✆ 877/SAVANNAH [728-2662] or 912/644-6401; http://savannahvisit.com). Mid-June.

JULY

Fourth of July Fireworks and Laser Show, Stone Mountain. Stone Mountain makes a picturesque canvas for the artistry of the popular laser show. You need not enter the park to enjoy the show—you can join the thousands who simply pull off to the shoulder of the road to witness the spectacle. Call ✆ 770/498-5690 or go to www.stonemountainpark.com for more information. July 4th weekend.

Augusta Southern Nationals Dragboat Races, Augusta. The stretch of the Savannah River that runs along the Augusta Riverwalk makes for an ideal setting for this annual thunderous event. High speeds and danger fuel these races as boats "fly" by with engines larger than what is found in most cars. Call ✆ 706/823-0440 or go to www.augustasouthernnationals.org for more information. Mid- to late July.

Georgia Mountain Fair, Hiawassee. Enjoy fun-filled days and nights of activities on the shores of Lake Chatuge. There is country, bluegrass, or gospel music along with clogging, a parade, a midway, and arts and crafts shows. Call ✆ 706/896-4191 or visit www.georgiamountainfairgrounds.com for more information. Mid- to late July.

AUGUST

Music & More at the Orchard at Altapass, Spruce Pine. Live music and traditional mountain dancing are the highlights of this weekly event that also includes nature exhibits, crafts, and activities. Call ✆ 888/765-9531 or visit www.altapassorchard.com for more information. Wednesday to Sunday in August.

SEPTEMBER

Yellow Daisy Festival, Stone Mountain. Every year Georgians gather at Stone Mountain Park to celebrate the blooming of the yellow daisy. Enjoy the arts and crafts, but please don't eat the daisies—they're rare. Call ✆ **800/401-2407** or 770/498-5690 or visit www.stonemountainpark.com for more information. Early September.

Savannah Jazz Festival, Savannah. This festival features national and local jazz-and-blues legends. A jazz brunch and music at different venues throughout the city are among the highlights. Call ✆ **912/525-5050** or go to www.savannahjazzfestival.org for more information. Late September.

Helen's Oktoberfest, Helen. Alpine Helen celebrates the South's longest Oktoberfest (starting in Sept) with live Bavarian music, German food and beverages, and dancing. Contact the Helen Welcome Center (✆ **800/858-8027**; www.helenga.org) for more information. September to late October.

Georgia State Fair, Macon. The state's most joyous occasion takes place at this fair, which has everything from rides to competitions, regional specialties to live music. It's strictly family fun. Usually you pay one price ($15) and get unlimited rides. Contact the Georgia State Fair Office (✆ **478/746-7184;** www.georgiastatefair.org) for more information. Late September.

OCTOBER

Andersonville October Fair, Andersonville. History comes alive in Andersonville, near the site of the Andersonville Prison, of Civil War infamy. Reenactments and demonstrations take you back to the time of the war. Contact ✆ **229/924-2558** or go to www.andersonvillegeorgia.com for more information. First full weekend in October.

The Cotton Pickin' Fair, Gay. Active for more than half a century, this award-winning festival is a family affair, filled with antiques, arts and crafts, food, and entertainment. Admission is $5 for adults or $3 for children. For more information, call ✆ **706/538-6814** or go to www.cpfair.org. First weekend in October and in May semiannually.

Big Pig Jig, Vienna. Hailed by *Travel Agent* magazine as one of the "Top 20 Events in the Southeast," the state's barbecue-cooking championship was born in 1982 when a group of people competed to see who could cook the most succulent pig. The festival has expanded to include a parade, sidewalk art contest, "Hog Jog" race, and carnival rides. For more information, call ✆ **229/268-8275** or go to www.bigpigjig.com. Early October.

NOVEMBER

Cane Grinding and Harvest Festival, Savannah. More than 75 crafts artists from four states sell and demonstrate their art. Music is provided by the Savannah Folk Music Society. Contact Oatland Island (✆ **912/305-15-4;** www.oatlandisland.org) for more information. Mid-November.

Fantasy in Lights, Pine Mountain. Wind your way through 5 miles of holiday lights at Callaway Gardens' magical annual display. The adjacent Christmas Village, with crafts, sights, and edibles, completes the package. Contact the gardens (✆ **800/CALLAWAY** [225-5292]; www.callawaygardens.com) for more information. Mid-November through end of December.

Candlelight Tours, Atlanta. These evening tours of historic homes and gardens offer music and storytelling in the spirit of the holidays. Contact the Atlanta History Center (✆ **404/814-4000;** www.atlantahistorycenter.com) for more information. Late November.

DECEMBER

Candles and Carols of Christmases Past, Mount Berry. This is a Victorian Christmas in the best tradition of the Old South, with candlelight tours and seasonal music and drama. Contact Oak Hill and the Martha Berry Museum (✆ **800/220-5504;** www.berry.edu/oakhill) for more information. First Friday and Saturday in December.

Christmas 1864, Savannah. Fort Jackson hosts the dramatic re-creation of its evacuation on December 20, 1864. More than 60 Civil War reenactors play the part of Fort Jackson's Confederate defenders, who were preparing to evacuate ahead of Union general William Tecumseh Sherman. Contact Old Fort Jackson (✆ **912/232-3945**) for more information. Early December.

Holiday Tour of Homes, Savannah. The doors of Savannah's historic homes are opened to the public during the holiday season. Each home is decorated, and a different group of homes is shown every day. Contact the Downtown Neighborhood Association (© **912/236-8362;** www.dna holidaytour.net) for more information. Early to mid-December.

ENTRY REQUIREMENTS

Passports

As of January 23, 2007, all persons, including U.S. citizens, traveling by air between the United States and Canada, Mexico, Central and South America, the Caribbean, and Bermuda are required to present a valid passport. For information on how to obtain a passport, see **"Passports"** in chapter 22.

Visas

The U.S. State Department has a **Visa Waiver Program (VWP)** allowing citizens of the following countries to enter the United States without a visa for stays of up to 90 days: Andorra, Australia, Austria, Belgium, Brunei, Czech Republic, Denmark, Estonia, Finland, France, Germany, Greece, Hungary, Iceland, Ireland, Italy, Japan, Latvia, Liechtenstein, Lithuania, Luxembourg, Malta, Monaco, the Netherlands, New Zealand, Norway, Portugal, San Marino, Singapore, Slovak Republic, Slovenia, South Korea, Spain, Sweden, Switzerland, and the United Kingdom. (**Note:** This list was accurate at press time; for the most up-to-date list of countries in the VWP, consult www.travel.state.gov/visa.) Canadian citizens may enter the United States without visas; they will need to show passports (if traveling by air) and proof of residence, however. **Note:** Any passport issued on or after October 26, 2006, by a VWP country must be an **e-Passport** for VWP travelers to be eligible to enter the U.S. without a visa. (You can identify an e-Passport by the symbol on the bottom center cover of your passport.) If your passport doesn't have this feature, you can still travel without a visa if it is a valid passport issued before October 26, 2005, and includes a machine-readable zone, or between October 26, 2005, and October 25, 2006, and includes a digital photograph. For more information, go to **www.travel.state.gov/ visa**.

Citizens of all other countries must have (1) a valid passport that expires at least 6 months later than the scheduled end of their visit to the U.S., and (2) a tourist visa, which may be obtained without charge from any U.S. consulate.

As of January 2004, many international visitors traveling on visas to the United States will be photographed and fingerprinted on arrival at Customs in airports and on cruise ships in a program created by the Department of Homeland Security called **US-VISIT.** Exempt from the extra scrutiny are visitors entering by land or those (mostly from Europe; see above) who don't require a visa for short-term visits. For more information, go to the Homeland Security website at **www.dhs.gov/dhspublic**.

For specifics on how to get a visa, see **"Visas"** on p. 520.

Medical Requirements

Unless you're arriving from an area known to be suffering from an epidemic, inoculations or vaccinations are not required for entry into the United States. If you have a medical condition that requires **syringe-administered medications** or treatment with **narcotics,** you should carry documented proof with you.

Customs

WHAT YOU CAN BRING INTO THE U.S.

Every visitor more than 21 years of age may bring in, free of duty, the following: (1) 1 liter of wine or hard liquor; (2) 200 cigarettes, 100 cigars (but not from Cuba), or 3 pounds of smoking tobacco; and (3) $100 worth of gifts. These exemptions are offered to travelers who spend at least 72 hours in the United States and who have not claimed them within the preceding 6 months. It is forbidden to bring almost any meat products (including canned, fresh, and dried meat products such as bouillon, soup mixes, and so on). Generally, condiments including vinegars, oils, spices, coffee, tea, and some cheeses and baked goods are permitted. Avoid rice products, as rice can often harbor insects. Bringing fruits and vegetables is not advised, though not prohibited. Customs will allow produce depending on where you got it and where you're going after you arrive in the U.S. Foreign tourists may carry in or out up to $10,000 in U.S. or foreign currency with no formalities; larger sums must be declared to U.S. Customs on entering or leaving, which includes filing form CM 4790. For details regarding U.S. Customs and Border Protection, consult your nearest U.S. embassy or consulate, or **U.S. Customs** (www.cbp.gov).

WHAT YOU CAN TAKE HOME FROM THE U.S.

Canadian Citizens: For a clear summary of Canadian rules, write for the booklet *I Declare,* issued by the Canada Border Services Agency (✆ **800/622-6232** in Canada or 204/983-3500; www.cbsa-asfc.gc.ca).

U.K. Citizens: Contact **HM Revenue & Customs** at ✆ **0845/010-9000** or 02920/501-261 from outside the U.K., or visit **www.hmrc.gov.uk**.

Australian Citizens: A helpful brochure available from Australian consulates or Customs offices is *Know Before You Go.* For more information, call the **Australian Customs Service** at ✆ **1300/363-263** or visit **www.customs.gov.au**.

New Zealand Citizens: Most questions are answered in a free pamphlet available at New Zealand consulates and Customs offices: *New Zealand Customs Guide for Travellers.* For more information, contact New Zealand Customs, the Customhouse, 17–21 Whitmore St., Box 2218, Wellington, 6140 (✆ **04/473-6099** or 0800/428-786; www.customs.govt.nz).

GETTING THERE & AROUND

North Carolina

BY PLANE

Delta (✆ **800/221-1212**; www.delta.com) and **US Airways** (✆ **800/428-4322**; www.usairways.com) serve the largest number of North Carolina destinations from out of state, although not all flights are direct. **American Airlines** (✆ **800/433-7300**; www.aa.com), **Continental Airlines** (✆ **800/523-3273**; www.continental.com), **JetBlue Airlines** (✆ **800/JET-BLUE** [538-2583]; www.jetblue.com), and **United Airlines** (✆ **800/241-6522**; www.united.com) also have direct flights to many North Carolina cities. **Raleigh-Durham International Airport** (www.rdu.com) and **Charlotte-Douglas International Airport,** in Charlotte (www.charmeck.org) are the major hubs, offering connecting flights to most major U.S. destinations.

US Airways (✆ **800/428-4322**; www.usairways.com) and **Delta** (✆ **800/221-1212**; www.delta.com) have several in-state connecting flights between cities such as Raleigh, Charlotte, Asheville, Wilmington, New Bern, Greensboro, Winston-Salem, Jacksonville, and Fayetteville.

Overseas visitors can take advantage of the **APEX** (Advance Purchase Excursion) reductions offered by all major U.S. and European carriers. In addition, some large airlines offer transatlantic or transpacific passengers special discount tickets under the name **Visit USA,** which allows mostly one-way travel from one U.S. destination to another at very low prices. These discount tickets must be purchased abroad in conjunction with your international fare.

IMMIGRATION & CUSTOMS CLEARANCE   International visitors arriving by air, no matter what the port of entry, should cultivate patience and resignation before setting foot on U.S. soil. U.S. airports have considerably beefed up security clearances in the years since the terrorist attacks of September 11, 2001, and clearing Customs and Immigration can take as long as 2 hours.

BY CAR

From Virginia and South Carolina, you can enter North Carolina on either I-95 or I-85. I-27 and I-77 also lead in from South Carolina. The main Tennessee entry is I-40. All major border points have helpful welcome centers, some with cookout facilities and playground equipment in a parklike setting.

Unless you plan to spend the bulk of your vacation in a city where walking is the best way to get around, the most cost-effective way to travel in North Carolina is by car.

Foreign driver's licenses are usually recognized in the U.S., but you should get an international one if your home license is not in English.

North Carolina has a law that requires all front-seat passengers to wear seat belts. The state also has a child-restraint law that requires children 3 years old and younger to be secured in a child safety seat. Children 3 to 16 years old must ride in a safety seat or use a car seat belt.

North Carolina's 76,000 miles of toll-free, well-maintained highways and some state roads have rest areas with picnic tables and outdoor cooking facilities. Write to **Travel and Tourism NC** (© **919/733-4151;** www.nccommerce.com), Department of Commerce, 301 N. Willmington St., Raleigh, NC 27601, for the *Official North Carolina Highway Map and Guide to Points of Interest,* which is also filled with tourist information.

Leading car-rental firms are at North Carolina's major cities and airports. They are: **Avis** (© **800/331-1212;** www.avis.com), **Budget** (© **800/472-3325;** www.budget.com), **Hertz** (© **800/654-3131;** www.hertz.com), and **Thrifty Car Rental** (© **800/367-2277;** www.thrifty.com).

BY TRAIN

North Carolina is on **Amtrak**'s New York–Miami, New York–Tampa, and New York–Washington–New Orleans runs. Be sure to check for excursion fares or seasonal specials. For reservations and fare information, call © **800/USA-RAIL** (872-7245) or go to www.amtrak.com.

International visitors can buy a **USA Rail Pass,** good for 5, 15, or 30 days of unlimited travel on **Amtrak** (© **800/USA-RAIL** [872-7245]). The pass is available online or through many overseas travel agents.

BY BUS

Bus travel is often the most economical form of public transit for short hops between U.S. cities, but it's certainly not an option for everyone (particularly when Amtrak, which is far more luxurious, offers similar rates). **Greyhound** (© **800/231-2222;** www.greyhound.com) is the sole nationwide bus line. International visitors can obtain information about the **Greyhound North American Discovery Pass.** The pass can be obtained from foreign travel agents or through www.discoverypass.com for unlimited travel and stopovers in the U.S. and Canada.

Southeastern Stages (© **404/591-2750;** www.southeasternstages.com) offers limited bus service linking cities in the Carolinas and Georgia, such as Fayetteville, North Carolina; Atlanta, Georgia; Augusta, Georgia; Columbia, South Carolina; and Charleston, South Carolina.

BY FERRY

North Carolina has a system of car ferries that ply the coastal sounds and rivers; most are toll-free, but there is a fee for longer trips. Crossings can be made between Currituck and Knotts Island, Currituck and Corolla, Hatteras and Ocracoke, Ocracoke and Swan Quarter, Cedar Island and Ocracoke, Bayview and Aurora, Cherry Branch and Minnesott, and Southport and Fort Fisher. To obtain a ferry schedule, contact the **North Carolina Department of Transportation Ferry Division** at © **800/ BY-FERRY** (293-3779) or www.ncdot.org/ferry.

South Carolina
BY PLANE

American Airlines and **American Eagle** (© 800/433-7300; www.aa.com), **Continental Airlines** (© 800/523-3273; www.continental.com), **Delta** and **Delta Connection** (© 800/221-1212; www.delta.com), **United Airlines** and **United Express** (© 800/241-6522; www.united.com), and **US Airways** (© 800/428-4322; www.usairways.com) are the major airlines serving South Carolina. Myrtle Beach has scheduled air service via Continental, Delta, and US Airways. You can fly into Charleston on Continental, Delta, United and United Express, and US Airways. Columbia is served by American and American Eagle, Delta and Delta Connection, and US Airways. Greenville/Spartanburg is served by Continental, Delta, and US Airways. If you're traveling to Hilton Head, you have the option of flying US Airways directly to the island or flying into the Savannah (Georgia) International Airport via Continental or Delta and then driving to Hilton Head, which is 1 hour away.

Delta and **US Airways** (see above) both have flights within South Carolina, although connections are sometimes awkward.

BY CAR

I-95 enters South Carolina from the north near Dillon and runs straight through the state to Hardeeville on the Georgia border. The major east-west artery is I-26, running from Charleston northwest through Columbia and on up to Hendersonville, North Carolina. U.S. 17 runs along the coast, and I-85 crosses the northwestern region.

South Carolina has a network of exceptionally good roads. Even when you leave the major highways for the state-maintained roadways, driving is easy on well-maintained roads. AAA services are available through the **Carolina Motor Club** in Charleston (© **843/744-1043**) and Greenville (© **864/421-9510**). For more information, check out www.AAA.com.

In South Carolina, vehicles must use headlights when windshield wipers are in use as a result of inclement weather. Remember that drivers and front-seat passengers must wear seat belts.

For driving times and distances in South Carolina, see the map on p. 241.

South Carolina furnishes excellent travel information to motorists and has well-equipped, efficiently staffed visitor centers at the state border on most major highways. If you have a cellphone and need help, dial © ***HP** (47) for Highway Patrol Assistance.

BY TRAIN

South Carolina is on the **Amtrak** (© **800/USA-RAIL** [872-7245]; www.amtrak.com) New York–Miami and New York–Tampa runs. Its tour packages include hotel, breakfast, and historic-site tours in Charleston at bargain rates. Be sure to ask about the money-saving "All Aboard America" regional fares or any other current fare specials. Amtrak also offers attractively priced rail/drive packages in the Carolinas and Georgia.

BY BUS

Greyhound (© **800/231-2222**; www.greyhound.com) has good direct service to major cities in South Carolina from out of state, with connections to almost any destination.

See "By Bus" under "North Carolina," above.

Georgia
BY PLANE

Virtually every major national airline flies through Atlanta's **Hartsfield International Airport,** 13 miles south of downtown off I-85 and I-285. From Atlanta, there are connecting flights to points around the state, including Augusta, Columbus, and Savannah. **Delta** (© **800/221-1212**; www.delta.com), based at Hartsfield, is the major carrier to Atlanta, connecting it to pretty much the entire country as well as 32 countries internationally. Other major carriers are **America West** (© **800/235-9292**; www.americawest.com), **American** (© **800/433-7300**; www.aa.com), **British Airways** (© **800/AIRWAYS** [247-9297]; www.britishairways.com), **Continental** (© **800/523-3273**; www.continental.com), **Lufthansa** (© **800/645-3880**; www.lufthansa-usa.com), **Northwest** (© **800/225-2525**; www.nwa.com), **United** (© **800/241-6522**; www.united.com), and **US Airways** (© **800/428-4322**; www.usairways.com).

American, Delta, United, and US Airways all serve Savannah's airport.

From Atlanta, there are connecting flights into Albany, Augusta, Brunswick (for the Golden Isles), Savannah, and (by commuter line) several smaller cities. Check with your travel agent.

BY CAR

Georgia is crisscrossed by major interstate highways: I-75 bisects the state from Dalton in the north to Valdosta in the south; I-95 runs north-south along the Eastern Seaboard. The major east-west routes are I-16, running between Macon and Savannah, and I-20, running from Augusta through Atlanta and into Alabama. I-85 runs northeast-southwest in the northern half of the state. The state-run welcome centers at all major points of entry are staffed with knowledgeable, helpful Georgians. The highway speed limit of 65 mph and the seat-belt law are strictly enforced.

In addition to the interstates, U.S. 84 cuts across the southern part of the state from the Alabama state line through Valdosta and Waycross, and eventually connects to I-95 south of Savannah. U.S. 441 runs from the North Carolina border south to Athens, Dublin, and the Florida state line. For 24-hour road conditions, call © **404/656-5267. AAA** services are available in Atlanta, Augusta, Columbus, Macon, Savannah, Smyrna, and Tucker.

BY TRAIN

Amtrak (*©* **800/USA-RAIL** [872-7245]; www.amtrak.com) has stops in Atlanta, Savannah, Jesup, Gainesville, and Toccoa. Bargain fares are in effect for limited periods. See "By Train" in the "South Carolina" section above.

Amtrak runs from Toccoa to Gainesville and Atlanta, as well as from Savannah to Jesup. The **Georgia Railroad** operates between Atlanta and Augusta.

BY BUS

Greyhound (*©* **800/231-2222;** www.greyhound.com) has good direct service to major cities in Georgia from out of state, with connections to almost any destination you want.

See "By Bus" under "North Carolina," above.

MONEY & COSTS

ATMs

Nationwide, the easiest and best way to get cash away from home is from an ATM (automated teller machine), sometimes referred to as a "cash machine" or "cash-point." The **Cirrus** (*©* **800/424-7787;** www.mastercard.com) and **PLUS** (*©* www.visa.com) networks span the country; you can find them even in remote regions. Look

WHAT THINGS COST IN ASHEVILLE	US$
Taxi from the airport to downtown	45.00
Double room at Grove Park Resort (expensive)	300.00
Double room at Beaufort House Victorian Inn (moderate)	199.00
Double room at Cumberland Falls B&B (inexpensive)	125.00
Lunch for one at Bouchon (moderate)	22.00
Lunch for one at Doc Chey's (inexpensive)	14.00
Dinner for one, without wine, at Horizons (expensive)	40.00
Dinner for one, without wine, at the Corner Kitchen (moderate)	36.00
Dinner for one, without wine, at Zambra (inexpensive)	18.00
Bottle of beer	4.00
Coca-Cola	2.30
Cup of coffee	2.50
Movie ticket	9.00
Ticket to the Asheville Symphony	55.00–155.00
Adult admission to the Biltmore Estate	55.00–60.00
Cup of coffee	1.24
Roll of ASA 100 color film, 36 exposures	4.99
Admission to Palace of Holyroodhouse	5.48
Theater ticket at King's Theatre	4.99–25.42

at the back of your bank card to see which network you're on, then call or check online for ATM locations at your destination. Be sure you know your personal identification number (PIN) and daily withdrawal limit before you depart.

Credit Cards & Debit Cards

Credit cards are the most widely used form of payment in the United States: **Visa** (Barclaycard in Britain), **MasterCard** (Eurocard in Europe, Access in Britain, Chargex in Canada), **American Express, Diners Club,** and **Discover.** You can withdraw cash advances from your credit cards at banks or ATMs, provided you know your PIN.

Visitors from outside the U.S. should inquire whether their bank assesses a 1% to 3% fee on charges incurred abroad.

It's highly recommended that you travel with at least one major credit card. You must have one to rent a car, and hotels and airlines usually require a credit card imprint as a deposit against expenses.

ATM cards with major credit card backing, known as **debit cards,** are now a commonly acceptable form of payment in most stores and restaurants.

Traveler's Checks

Traveler's checks are widely accepted in the U.S., including the Carolinas and Georgia, but foreign visitors should make sure that they're denominated in U.S. dollars; foreign-currency checks are often difficult to exchange.

WHAT THINGS COST IN CHARLESTON	US$
Taxi from Charleston airport to city center	25.00
Bus fare (exact change)	1.50
Double room at the Francis Marion (expensive)	189.00
Double room at Cannonboro Inn (moderate)	119.00
Double room at Red Roof Inn (inexpensive)	55.00
Lunch for one at Magnolias (moderate)	18.00
Lunch for one at Jestine's (inexpensive)	14.00
Dinner for one, without wine, at Fig (expensive)	52.00
Dinner for one, without wine, at 39 Rue de Jean (moderate)	36.00
Dinner for one, without wine, at Hominy Grill (inexpensive)	14.00
Bottle of beer	4.00
Coca-Cola	2.30
Cup of coffee	2.50
Admission to the Gibbes Museum of Art	9.00
Movie ticket	9.00
Ticket to a Charleston Symphony concert	35.00

WHAT THINGS COST IN ATLANTA	US$
Taxi from Atlanta airport to downtown (for one passenger)	30.00
Fare between any two MARTA stops	2.00
Double room at Four Seasons Hotel Atlanta (very expensive)	300.00
Double room at the Ellis Hotel (expensive)	179.00
Double room at Indigo (moderate)	169.00
Double room at Sugar Magnolia (inexpensive)	120.00
Lunch for one at the Atlanta Fish Market (moderate)	26.00
Lunch for one at Mary Mac's Tea Room (inexpensive)	16.00
Dinner for one, without wine, in Dining Room of Bone's (expensive)	55.00
Dinner for one, without wine, at the Buckhead Diner (moderate)	30.00
Dinner for one, without wine, at Varsity (inexpensive)	10.00
Bottle of beer	4.00
Coca-Cola	2.30
Cup of coffee in a cafe	2.50
Admission to Fernbank Museum of Natural History	15.00
Movie ticket	9.00
Theater ticket to the Alliance	20.00–60.00

The most popular traveler's checks are offered by **American Express** (✆ **800/492-3344** or 800/221-7282 for cardholders—this number accepts collect calls, offers service in several foreign languages, and exempts Amex gold and platinum cardholders from the 1% fee); **MasterCard** (✆ **800/223-9920**); and **Visa** (✆ **800/732-1322**)—AAA members can obtain Visa checks for free at most AAA offices or by calling ✆ **866/339-3378**). Non-AAA members are assessed a fee of $4.95.

STAYING HEALTHY

For up-to-date health-related travel advice in the U.S., go to the **Centers for Disease Control and Prevention** website at **wwwnc.cdc.gov/travel**.

You'll have little trouble finding hospitals and doctors in the Carolinas and Georgia—in fact, the region has some of the most highly regarded medical centers and teaching facilities in the country. For the names and contact information of **major hospitals and medical centers** in the region, see "Hospitals & Medical Centers" under "Fast Facts: The Carolinas & Georgia" in chapter 22.

If you suffer from a chronic illness, consult your doctor before your departure. Pack **prescription medications** in your carry-on luggage, and carry them in their original containers, with pharmacy labels—otherwise, they won't make it through airport security. Visitors from outside the U.S. should carry generic names of prescription drugs. For U.S. travelers, most reliable healthcare plans provide coverage if you get

3

PLANNING YOUR TRIP TO THE CAROLINAS & GEORGIA

Staying Healthy

sick away from home. Foreign visitors may have to pay all medical costs upfront and be reimbursed later. See "Insurance" under "Fast Facts: The Carolinas & Georgia" at the end of this guide.

Crime & Safety

Although tourist areas are generally safe in the South, crime can occur anywhere, and U.S. urban areas tend to be less safe than those in western Europe or Japan. Visitors should always stay alert. This is particularly true of large U.S. cities, especially Atlanta. Parts of Savannah, Charleston, and Charlotte can be unsafe at night. Avoid deserted areas at night. Don't go into any city park at night unless there's an event that attracts crowds. Generally speaking, you can feel safe in areas where there are many people and open establishments.

Remember also that hotels are open to the public, and security may not be able to screen everyone who enters. Always lock your room door.

Georgia and the Carolinas are among the safest places in the Southeast, especially in the small towns and villages. Resort areas such as Myrtle Beach attract more crime, of course. But on a per-capita basis, Georgia and the Carolinas have far less crime than does Florida, to the south.

SPECIALIZED TRAVEL RESOURCES

Gay & Lesbian Travelers

NORTH CAROLINA

In **Charlotte,** you can get information on gay issues at **White Rabbit Books & Things,** 1401 Central Ave. (© **704/377-4067;** www.whiterabbitbooks.com). In **Raleigh,** there is a branch of **White Rabbit Books & Things** at 309 W. Martin St. (© **919/856-1429;** www.whiterabbitbooks.com).

The **International Gay and Lesbian Travel Association** (**IGLTA;** © **954/630-1637;** www.iglta.org) is the trade association for the gay and lesbian travel industry, and offers an online directory of gay- and lesbian-friendly travel businesses.

SOUTH CAROLINA

Homophobia is rampant. The most gay hip destinations in the tri-state area are Savannah and Atlanta. But even in those cities, discretion is still advised.

The major information center in the state is the **South Carolina Pride Center,** 1108 Woodrow St., Columbia (© **803/771-7713;** www.scpride.org). On the premises are a library, archives, a "gay pride" shop, an inventory of films, and a meeting space.

GEORGIA

Atlanta is famous for its thriving gay community. You can access its gay offerings through the listings and articles in the *Southern Voice.* Call © **404/418-8901** or go to www.sovo.com for information about distribution points throughout the South and gay resources and activities in Atlanta.

Travelers with Disabilities

Thanks to provisions in the Americans with Disabilities Act, most public places in the U.S. are required to comply with disability-friendly regulations. Almost all public establishments (including hotels, restaurants, museums, and so on, but not certain

National Historic Landmarks), and at least some modes of public transportation provide accessible entrances and other facilities for those with mobility challenges.

The **America the Beautiful—National Parks and Federal Recreational Lands Pass—Access Pass** (formerly the **Golden Access Passport**) gives visually impaired or permanently disabled persons free lifetime entrance to federal recreation sites administered by the National Park Service (NPS).

The America the Beautiful pass can only be obtained in person at any NPS facility that charges an entrance fee. The pass also offers a 50% discount on some federal-use fees for facilities such as camping, swimming, parking, boat launching, and tours. For answers to common questions, visit www.nps.gov/fees_passes.htm or call the United States Geological Survey (USGS; © 888/275-8747), which issues the pass.

NORTH CAROLINA

Though hundreds of hotels and restaurants in North Carolina now provide easy access for those with disabilities, it's always a good idea to call before you book to find out just what the situation is.

Many travel agencies offer customized tours and itineraries for travelers with disabilities. Among them are **Flying Wheels Travel** (© 877/451-5006 or 507/451-5005; www.flyingwheelstravel.com), **Access-Able Travel Source** (© 303/232-2979; www.access-able.com), and **Accessible Journeys** (© 800/846-4537 or 610/521-0339; www.disabilitytravel.com).

Organizations that offer assistance to travelers with disabilities include **MossRehab** (© 800/CALL-MOSS [225-5667]; www.mossresourcenet.org), the **American Foundation for the Blind** (**AFB**; © 800/232-5463; www.afb.org), and **SATH** (Society for Accessible Travel & Hospitality; © 212/447-7284; www.sath.org). **AirAmbulanceCard.com** is now partnered with SATH and allows you to preselect top-notch hospitals in case of an emergency.

Also check out the quarterly magazine *Emerging Horizons* (www.emerging horizons.com).

A helpful website for assistance while traveling in the U.S. is **www.disability resources.org**, a nonprofit group that supplies information about available resources. Just click on the state you are traveling to.

Amtrak (© 800/USA-RAIL [872-7245]; www.amtrak.com), with 24 hours' notice, will provide porter service, special seating, and a discount.

SOUTH CAROLINA

South Carolina has numerous agencies that assist people with disabilities. For specific information, call the **South Carolina Disability Resources** (© 843/795-3951; www.sciway.net). Two other agencies are the **South Carolina Protection & Advocacy System for the Handicapped** (© 803/782-0639) and the **Commission for the Blind** (© 800/922-2222 or 803/898-8731; www.sccb.state.sc.us). For transportation within South Carolina, individuals with disabilities can contact **Wheelchair Getaways, Inc.** (© 800/642-2042 or 425/353-8213; www.wheelchair getaways.com).

The Columbia telephone directory contains a special section of "Community Service Numbers." It's quite comprehensive and includes services for travelers who are mobility challenged.

GEORGIA

Many hotels and restaurants in Georgia provide easy access for persons with disabilities. However, it's always a good idea to call ahead to make sure.

The **Georgia Governor's Developmental Disabilities Council** (℡ **888/275-4233;** http://web.me.com/gcdd/GCDD) may also be of help. The Georgia Department of Industry, Trade & Tourism publishes a guide, *Georgia on My Mind,* that lists attractions and accommodations with access for persons with disabilities. To receive a copy, contact **Tour Georgia,** 75 5th St., Technology Sq., Atlanta, GA 30308 (℡ **800/VISIT-GA** [847-4842], ext. 1903; www.exploregeorgia.org).

For transportation within Georgia, individuals with disabilities can contact **Handicapped Driver Services** (℡ **877/437-8267** or 457-9851; www.hdsvans.com) or **Wheelchair Getaways, Inc.** (℡ **800/642-2042;** www.wheelchairgetaways.com).

Senior Travelers

The National Park Service (NPS) offers an **America the Beautiful—National Parks and Federal Recreational Lands Pass—Senior Pass** (formerly the **Golden Age Passport**), which gives seniors 62 years or older lifetime entrance to all properties administered by the NPS—national parks, monuments, historic sites, recreation areas, and national wildlife refuges—for a one-time processing fee of $10. The pass must be purchased in person at any NPS facility that charges an entrance fee. Besides free entry, the America the Beautiful pass also offers a 50% discount on some federal-use fees. For more information, go to www.nps.gov/fees_passes.htm or call the United States Geological Survey (USGS), which issues the passes, at ℡ **888/275-8747.**

Nearly all major U.S. hotel and motel chains now offer seniors a discount, so ask for the reduction *when you make the reservation;* there may be restrictions during peak days. Then be sure to carry proof of your age (driver's license, passport, and so on) when you check in. Among the chains that offer the best discounts are **Marriott Hotels** (℡ **800/228-9290**) for those 62 and older, and **La Quinta Inns** (℡ **800/531-5900**) for ages 55 and older.

Members of **AARP,** 601 E St. NW, Washington, DC 20049 (℡ **888/687-2277;** www.aarp.org), get discounts on hotels, airfares, and car rentals. AARP offers members a wide range of benefits, including *AARP The Magazine* and a monthly newsletter. Anyone older than 50 can join.

Many reliable agencies and organizations target the 50-plus market. **Exploritas** (℡ **800/454-5768;** www.exploritas.org) arranges study programs for those 55 and over.

Recommended publications offering travel resources and discounts for seniors include the quarterly magazine *Travel 50 & Beyond* (www.travel50andbeyond.com) and *Unbelievably Good Deals and Great Adventures That You Absolutely Can't Get Unless You're Over 50* (2009), by Joann Rattner Heilman.

RESPONSIBLE TOURISM

Sustainable tourism is conscientious travel. It means being careful with the environments you explore, and respecting the communities you visit. Two overlapping components of sustainable travel are **eco-tourism** and **ethical tourism.** The **International Ecotourism Society** (TIES) defines eco-tourism as responsible travel to natural areas that conserves the environment and improves the well-being of local people.

You can find some eco-friendly travel tips and statistics, as well as touring companies and associations—listed by destination under "Travel Choice"—at the **TIES** website, www.ecotourism.org. Also check out **Ecotravel.com,** which lets you search for sustainable touring companies in several categories (such as water or land based, or spiritually oriented).

While much of the focus of eco-tourism is about reducing impacts on the natural environment, ethical tourism concentrates on ways to preserve and enhance local economies and communities, regardless of location. You can embrace ethical tourism by staying at a locally owned hotel or shopping at a store that employs local workers and sells locally produced goods.

Responsible Travel (www.responsibletravel.com) is a great source of sustainable travel ideas; the site is run by a spokesperson for ethical tourism in the travel industry. **Sustainable Travel International** (www.sustainabletravelinternational.org) promotes ethical tourism practices, and manages an extensive directory of sustainable properties and tour operators around the world.

In the U.K., **Tourism Concern** (www.tourismconcern.org.uk) works to reduce social and environmental problems connected to tourism. The **Association of Independent Tour Operators** (AITO; www.aito.co.uk) is a group of specialist operators leading the field in making holidays sustainable.

Volunteer travel has become increasingly popular among those who want to venture beyond the standard group-tour experience. Some programs provide free housing and food, but many require volunteers to pay for travel expenses, which can add up quickly. For general info on volunteer travel, visit **www.volunteerabroad.org** and **www.idealist.org**. **Volunteer International** (www.volunteerinternational.org) has a helpful list of questions to ask to determine the intentions and the nature of a volunteer program before you commit.

Plants, animals, birds, and fish live in harmony at **Lake Mattamuskeet Wildlife Refuge ★**, the largest natural lake in North Carolina. Since 1934, the U.S. government has owned the lake, which has an abundance of wildlife spread across 50,000 acres of marshes, woods, and water. A swan's neck deep, the lake is 18 miles long, 7 miles wide. More than 800 species of wildlife and birds are found on the refuge during part or all of each year. In the winter, thousands of Tundra swans, snow geese, pintails, and mallards are seen here. To visit the lake, check with the **Mattamuskeet National Wildlife Refuge,** 32 Mattamuskeet Rd., Swan Quarter, NC 27885 (℃ 252/926-4021; www.mattamuskeet.org).

Visitors to the **Blue Ridge Mountains** can escape back to nature by renting a mountain cottage with scenic views. In some of these areas, Appalachian traditions seem frozen in time. In addition, Big Horse Creek and Helton Creek offer some of the best fly fishing in North Carolina. Marked hiking trails are cut through the area, as you pass massive rock formations, paths along streams once trod by the Cherokee, and wetland trails by ponds. Although the settings of these cottages are rustic, modern conveniences have been installed. For more data on these rentals, check with **Windfall Mountain Vacation Cottage Rentals** at ℃ 704/975-3058 or www.onthewindfall.com.

For eco-tourism, head for **Tyrrell County,** North Carolina, not far from the Outer Banks. Eighty-five percent of the county's land is wetland, providing a habitat for more than 20 rare, threatened, or endangered species, along with waterfowl and neotropical migratory birds.

Among the major sites here is the **Buckridge Coastal Reserve** (℃ 252/796-3709), a 27,000-acre site lying between Alligator River and Pocosin Lakes National Wildlife Refuges.

Protected species found on this site include the red wolf, bald eagle, the American alligator, and the red-cockaded woodpecker. You can hike along existing roads or boat along the shoreline. Walking paths, boardwalks, paddle trails, and water-based camp sites are also found here.

For more information contact **Tyrrell County Ecotourism Committee,** 203 S. Ludington Dr., Columbia, NC 27925 (© **252/796-0723**).

The site is accessed by U.S. 64, which connects with N.C. 94 in Columbia, North Carolina.

Also in Tyrrell County, you can visit **Pettigrew State Park,** 2252 Lake Shore Rd., Cresswell (© **252/979-4475;** www.ils.unc.edu/parkproject/visit/pett/home.html). The park encompasses 1,300 acres around Lake Phelps and more than 3,000 acres along Scuppernong River with 16,000 acres of water. Canoe and kayak trails abound, and row boats and power boats can be rented. There is also a family campsite, plus picnic tables and toilets and showers.

A final attraction in Tyrrell County is the **Pocosin Lakes National Wildlife Refuge** (www.pocosinlakes.fws.gov), covering 111,000 acres, containing a variety of wildlife, including endangered species such as the bald eagle and the red wolf.

Visitors to Hilton Head in South Carolina who want to experience the rich nature of the area can hook up with **Outside Hilton Head** (© **800/686-6996** or 843/686-6996; www.outsidehiltonhead.com). The outfitter's 2-hour guided kayak nature tours are the best in the area. Guided by naturalists, you can see the rich wildlife, including the Atlantic bottle-nosed dolphin. Other adventures include a 2-hour dolphin eco-tour and a 3-hour beachcombing cruise.

Fishing charters and eco-boat tours in the Myrtle Beach area are available at **Coastal Eco-Charters Myrtle Beach Fishing Charters and Eco Boat Tours,** Cricket Cove Marina, Little River (© **843/685-2737;** www.coastalecocharters. com). On the tours you can discover amazing creatures in their natural habitat, including rare birds, dolphins, sea turtles, and stingrays. Tours are conducted by a licensed biology teacher, and focus on ways to preserve the vital salt marshes of the area for future generations.

Many eco-conscious visitors like to stay at "green hotels," that is, accommodations that create less impact on the environment than other lodgings. For this type of lodging, check with local tourist offices or visit www.beinggreen.com. Space does not allow us to recommend all these establishments, but one eco-friendly B&B will give you a good idea. It's the **Cedar House Inn & Yurts,** 6463 Hwy. 19 N., Dahlonega, Georgia (www.georgiamountaininn.com), located near the beginning of the Appalachians in the heart of the North Georgia wine country. You can rent a cozy room with knotty pine walls or else a unique yurt with canopied queen-size beds. The location is convenient to all mountain attractions in this part of Georgia. You can go horseback riding, kayaking, canoeing, or tubing down the nearby rivers.

For tours of the Georgia coast, Roy and Peach Hubbard are the people to contact for trips aboard their *SaltDawg* sailing vessel. They are located near Savannah at Fort McAllister Marina, next to Fort McAllister State Park & Battlefield. Both are naturalists and will take you on an unstructured itinerary to see the wonders of the coast, including its amazing wildlife that includes alligators, wild boar, deer, and stingrays. Dolphins are a special attraction. You can enjoy a picnic lunch and spend time on an undeveloped private beach accessible only by boat. For more information, contact them at © **912/657-3927** or http://saltydawgadventures.com.

Also in the Savannah area, **Bull River Cruises,** 8005 Hwy. 80 E. at the Bull River Marina (© **800/311-4779** or 912/898-1800; www.bullriver.com), is hailed as the premier eco-tourism provider. Its **Island Explorer** tour takes you through the Barrier Islands to the black-water inland rivers. You get to explore the marshland ecology, as Georgia has one-third of the marshes on the Eastern Seaboard. Sightings of birds and bottle-nosed dolphins are just two of the many experiences of touring the waterways of the Low Country.

For details on how to visit the **Okefenokee Swamp,** call © **866/THE-SWAMP** (843-7926) or visit www.okefenokeeadventures.com. Refer also to chapter 21. The swamp is the nation's largest wildlife refuge east of the Mississippi River.

SPECIAL INTEREST & ESCORTED TRIPS

Package Tours

Tour companies offer package tours that include the Carolinas and Georgia. Most tours include airport transfers, admission to attractions, meals, and accommodations. Be sure to ask whether your tour is included under the USOTA consumer-protection guarantee (in case of bankruptcy or insolvency).

Barrier Island Kayaks (© **252/393-6457;** www.barrierislandkayaks.com) offers instruction and guided day trips to the barrier islands of the Outer Banks of North Carolina. Day-trip prices range from $40 to $80. Daily equipment rental for outdoors enthusiasts is an additional charge.

Nearly Perfect Tours (© **704/481-9415**) is a western North Carolina mountain-tour company specializing in custom tours of the Blue Ridge Mountains. The company will design a tour to fit your interest—whether it's history, music, mountain culture, architecture, or old general stores. It also offers a North Carolina wineries tour in the Charlotte area. Full-day tours are $125 per person, and tours have five or fewer participants.

The region's leading tour operator, **Mid Atlantic Tour & Receptive Services** (© **800/769-5912;** www.midatlantictours.com), features all-inclusive customized individual group tours. Tours usually begin at 3 days and 2 nights. Destinations include the Outer Banks, Old Salem, and the western mountains.

Active Vacations

NORTH CAROLINA

North Carolina presents an incredible array of landscapes and recreational offerings. The beaches are outstanding, and they're never as crowded as those on South Carolina's Grand Strand. Broad stretches of white sand offer waves to challenge the most skillful surfer, and quiet, family-oriented seaside resorts can be found on both the Outer Banks and along the southern Bogue Banks, also known as Crystal Coast. Fishing, boating, water-skiing, and even hang gliding from gigantic dunes are all part of the fun up and down the coast.

The opposite end of the state holds the Great Smoky Mountains, with some of the most spectacular scenery in the Southeast—not to mention ample opportunities for hiking, fly-fishing, white-water rafting, and camping.

BICYCLING   Miles of back roads and lots of flat terrain (except in the mountains) make North Carolina an ideal venue for bikers.

Those who like biking by the beach can head for the Outer Banks. Starting in Corolla, a separate bike path parallels N.C. 12 for many miles south.

The gently sloping Piedmont, with its hard-packed surfaces, is also good road-biking country. The tourist office in Winston-Salem can provide maps of the Piedmont's most scenic bike tours through the historic Bethabara and Tanglewood parks. Outside Charlotte, McAlpine Creek Park has a 2-mile trail for bikers. The nearly deserted lanes and sleepy hamlets of Pinehurst and Southern Pines are our favorite spots.

For mountain bikers, the Asheville Convention and Visitors Bureau offers a list of outfitters that also provide trail maps. Regrettably, the scenic Blue Ridge Parkway has no lanes for bikers, who are forced to ride single file along the side of the two-lane highway. Helmets and kneepads are required, and white lights and reflectors are necessary to go through some two dozen dark-as-night tunnels. Fog is also a frequent occurrence. Weekends, any holiday, and the traffic-clogged months of May and October are the worst times to bike the Blue Ridge.

For bicycle route maps, contact the **North Carolina Department of Transportation's Bicycle Program,** 250 Oberlin Rd., Ste. 150, Raleigh, NC 27605 (© **877/368-4968;** www.ncdot.org). Bikers can also get a free catalog from **VBT** (© **800/245-3868;** www.vbt.com), which offers deluxe bicycle vacations, such as a tour of the North Carolina coast.

BIRDING   The Outer Banks traditionally draws birders, especially those who are interested in seasonal migrations. Pea Island National Wildlife Refuge on Hatteras Island hosts hundreds of species of birds. Cape Lookout National Seashore is the most remote state beach and a nesting area for piping plover. On Cape Fear, birders head for Sunset Beach. Here, on the west end, they can wade across Mad Inlet at low tide to reach Bird Island, where herons, egrets, osprey, and an array of other beautiful birds come to feed and nest.

CAMPING   Campers can find very good facilities throughout North Carolina, with fees ranging from $18 to $29 per night. RV hookups, however, are available only at selected sites. For details, contact the **Division of Parks and Recreation,** Department of the Environment and Natural Resources, 1615 MSC, Raleigh, NC 27699 (☎ **919/733-4181;** www.ncparks.gov/Visit/main.php). The excellent *Official North Carolina Highway Map and Guide to Points of Interest* also has extensive information about national and state parks and forests.

The **Great Smoky Mountains,** named for the smoky blue haze that crowns their tops, run for more than 70 miles, picking up where the Blue Ridge Parkway ends. The 520,000-acre park lies half in North Carolina and half in Tennessee. It shelters bears, deer, wild turkeys, and grouse, among other forms of wildlife. Summer brings an ever-changing kaleidoscope of color from flowering plants. Within the park boundaries are no fewer than 130 native species of trees in 180,000 acres of virgin forest.

Camping is best along the 70 miles of the Appalachian Trail, which follows the ridge that forms the North Carolina–Tennessee border. *Note:* Reservations are required between mid-May and October. Contact **National Park Reservation Service,** PO Box 1600, Cumberland, MD 21501 (☎ **877/444-6777;** http://recreation.gov).

FISHING   From fly-fishing to deep-sea or light-tackle fishing, the **Outer Banks** provide some of the best opportunities for anglers in the United States. You can catch channel bass in the spring; whiting, flounder, and Spanish mackerel during the summer; and small bluefish in autumn. Pompano run from spring until the beginning of winter, and big bluefish are hunted almost year-round. Unless you want to go deep-sea fishing, you won't need a boat along the 300 miles of coastline, studded with jetties and piers; some 25% of all Atlantic piers are in North Carolina. Some piers are better known than others: Nags Head for flounder, bluefish, mullet, and striped bass; and Ocracoke Island for sea mullet, bluefish, and pompano. Pursuers of big amber-jack and tarpon head for the piers along the Bogue Banks in the Neuse River region.

The lakes, rivers, and streams of the mountains are the second major venue for fishers, especially for those who seek trout, muskies, catfish, and small- and large-mouth bass. The best places for fishing include the Linville River, the Toe River and its tributaries, the Globe section of the Johns River Gorge, and Howard's Creek (north of Boone). Local tourist offices can supply complete details. For trout fanciers, the lakes and streams of the Blue Ridge are ideal. Trout fishers are also drawn to the Great Smoky Mountains, with hundreds of miles of streams and creeks that are home to smallmouth bass, rock bass, and brown and rainbow trout. (It's illegal to catch brook trout.) Rangers at the visitor centers provide guidelines, and serious anglers can buy Don Kirk's *Smoky Mountains Trout Fishing Guide.*

Most hardware and general stores supply fishing licenses, which are required for all freshwater fishers 16 or older ($15 in state, $30 out of state). With the license comes a list of rules and state laws, especially regarding fish size.

You may also buy a fishing or hunting license online at **www.ncwildlife.org** or by calling ☎ **1-888/2HUNTFISH** (248-6834) Monday to Friday 9am to 5pm. The *North Carolina Inland Fishing, Hunting and Trapping Regulations Digest* booklet is free to the public and may be obtained by writing to North Carolina Wildlife Resources Commission, 1707 Mail Service Center, Raleigh, NC 27699-1722.

GOLF   North Carolina is one of the best states for golf in the nation. Southern Pines and the Pinehurst Sandhills (see chapter 8) are called the Golf Capital of the World—with good reason. Some 35 golf courses fill these sandhills, which have attracted most of the greatest names in the sport. The Pinehurst Resort—the only resort with eight signature courses—is legendary. Equally good are the Pine Needles Lodge and the Club at Longleaf.

Charlotte is mad for the highly publicized Scottish-style Charlotte Golf Links. The Raleigh-Durham area is filled with master courses, including the one at Duke University designed by Robert Trent Jones.

The best course in the mountains is at Asheville's Grove Park Inn. Yet another high-elevation golfing destination is the town of Blowing Rock, a summer haven for golf-loving coastal dwellers who prefer golfing in the much cooler environs of the mountains. Good golfing is also possible on the coast. Cape Fear, near Wilmington, has the most courses, including a George Cobb masterpiece with ocean views at Bald Head Island. Consult the regional chapters that follow or go to **http://golf.visitnc. com** for further details.

HIKING & BACKPACKING   The best place for hiking and backpacking in the entire state is Great Smoky Mountains National Park, where you'll find approximately 800 miles of trails. The guide *Walks and Hikes* lists more than 60 of these trails (the best ones) and is available at the visitor centers. Another good source for hiking and backpacking information is the **Great Smoky Mountains Natural History Association,** 115 Park Headquarters Rd., Gatlinburg, TN 37738 (© **865/436-7318;** www.smokiesstore.org). For the best hiking in North Carolina, contact the **Sierra Club,** 85 Second St., San Francisco, CA 94105 (© **415/977-5500;** www.sierra club.org), and the **Appalachian Mountain Club,** 5 Joy St., Boston, MA 02108 (© **800/372-1758** or 617/523-0636; www.outdoors.org).

HORSEBACK RIDING   North Carolina's southern mountains, linked by U.S. 64 south of Asheville, were once the home of the Cherokees, who didn't have horses. But the residents nowadays surely do. Dozens upon dozens of trails offer some of the best riding in the state. Trails are cut through both Nantahala National Forest and Pisgah National Forest. If you'd like to drive down from Asheville for an equestrian day, call the best of the stables: either **Pisgah Forest Stables,** 476 Pisgah Dr., Brevard (© **828/883-8258;** www.pisgahstables.com), or **Earthshine Mountain Lodge,** 1600 Golden Rd., Lake Toxaway (© **828/862-4207;** www.earthshinemtn lodge.com).

HUNTING   Deer hunting is a passionate pastime for many Southerners. The mating habits and short gestation season of deer count for an overwhelming annual explosion of the population. If you're a hunting enthusiast, you already understand the conservation and preservation tenets of the sport. For information on obtaining a hunting license, see "Fishing," above.

RAFTING   The best white-water rafting in the state—perhaps in the entire country—is in the Great Smoky Mountains along the Nantahala River. Beginners can take a rafting course at the **Nantahala Outdoor Center,** U.S. 19/74 (© **888/905-7238;** www.noc.com), 13 miles west of Bryson City. It offers 1- to 7-day courses. The best outfit to call if you already know how to raft is **Rafting in the Smokies** (© **800/776-7238;** www.raftinginthesmokies.com), which rafts both the Pigeon and Nantahala rivers.

SKIING   For the best skiing in the tri-state area, head for the High Country, where the mountains range from 4,000 to 5,500 feet. Appalachian Ski Mountain, Ski Beech, Hawksnest Golf and Ski Resort, and Sugar Mountain Resort offer snow-laden slopes for both beginners and advanced skiers. The major resorts are close together, and you can easily resort-hop until you find the winter conditions that are suitable for you. Beginners should try the easier slopes of Sugar Mountain. Ski Beech is the highest ski area in eastern North America; the vertical drop is only 830 feet, but it's straight down—so it's only for daredevils. Hawksnest has two short beginner runs, and Appalachian Ski Mountain attracts families and beginners. All ski areas are open for night runs. For more information about skiing the North Carolina mountains, get in touch with **High Country Host,** 1700 Blowing Rock Rd., Boone, NC 28607 (✆ **800/438-7500;** www.highcountryhost.com).

TENNIS   The Piedmont has the greatest number of public courts, including some 20 in the Winston-Salem area alone. All the cities, big and small, in North Carolina have courts, as do all the major resorts. Most courts in the High Country are outdoors, so you'll want to restrict your playing to spring through autumn.

SOUTH CAROLINA

BEACHES   The South Carolina coast is the true gem of the state. Along more than 280 miles of seashore are white-sand beaches shaded by palms, stretching from the Grand Strand to the mouth of the Savannah River. Myrtle Beach offers a carnival atmosphere and emphasizes family entertainment. Edisto Beach is a secluded spot. Fripp Island and Hilton Head are luxury resorts.

BIKING   South Carolina's basically flat terrain offers some of the country's best biking. The hard-packed sand of the beaches is particularly good for riding. Resorts such as Hilton Head have extensive paved bike trails, and many rental outfits operate just off the beaches.

CAMPING   Many of South Carolina's lakes have lakefront campsites. Reservations are not necessary, but you are strongly advised to book ahead for big weekends such as Memorial Day or Labor Day. Campsites are also available in 34 of South Carolina's state parks. For more information, contact **South Carolina Department of Parks, Recreation, and Tourism,** 1205 Pendleton St., Columbia, SC 29201 (✆ **866/224-9339** or 803/734-0156; www.southcarolinaparks.com).

CANOEING   The Broad and Saluda rivers, which flow near Columbia in the center of the state, provide excellent canoeing. Contact the parks department, above, for more information.

FISHING & HUNTING   On the coast, fish for amberjack, barracuda, shark, king mackerel, and other species. In South Carolina's many lakes and streams, fish for trout, bass, and blue and channel catfish. No license is required for saltwater fishing, but a freshwater license is needed. The Upstate is a mecca for waterfowl and wild turkey. The season stretches over fall and winter and sometimes into spring. Hunting on public lands is illegal, but many hunting clubs will allow you to join temporarily if you provide references. For information, write the **South Carolina Department of Natural Resources,** 1000 Assembly St., Columbia, SC 29201 (✆ **803/734-3833;** www.dnr.sc.gov).

GOLF   Some of the best golf in the country is available in South Carolina, at courses such as the fabled Harbour Town at Hilton Head. For information, contact the **South Carolina Department of Parks, Recreation, and Tourism,** 1205 Pendleton St., Columbia, SC 29201 (✆ **866/224-9339** or 803/734-0156; www.southcarolinaparks.com). Ask for the *South Carolina Golf Guide.*

HORSEBACK RIDING   Without question, Aiken County is king of the equine industry in the area. The Carolina Cup and the Colonial Cup steeplechase races are held in Camden each year. For information, contact **Thoroughbred Country** (📞 **888/834-1654** or 803/649-7981; www.tbredcountry.org), or the **Aiken Chamber of Commerce,** 121 Richland Ave. E., Aiken, SC 29802 (📞 **803/642-1100;** www.aikenchamber.net).

THE LAKES   South Carolina's rivers feed lakes all over the state, offering boating, fishing, and camping. With 450 miles of shoreline, the lakes are a magnet for commercial development. While lakeside resort communities are booming, 70% of the lakeshore is slated to remain in a natural state. Many operators and marinas rent boats and watercraft. For information about staying lakeside, contact the **South Carolina Department of Parks, Recreation, and Tourism,** 1205 Pendleton St., Columbia, SC 29201; or call 📞 **866/224-9339.**

STATE PARKS   Camping, fishing, boating, and extensive hiking are available in South Carolina's many state parks. Cabin accommodations are rented year-round in 14 of the parks. All cabins are heated, air-conditioned, and fully equipped with cooking utensils, tableware, and linens. Rates range from $48 to $172 per night. Cabins can accommodate from 4 to 12 people. Advance reservations are necessary for summer. For full details, get in touch with the **South Carolina State Parks,** 1205 Pendleton St., Columbia, SC 29201 (📞 **866/224-9339** or 803/734-0156; www.southcarolinaparks.com).

WHITE-WATER RAFTING   The Chattooga River forms part of the lower northeast border with Georgia and offers some of the best white-water rafting and canoeing in the country. **Wildwater Ltd.,** PO Box 309, Long Creek, SC 29658 (📞 **866/319-8870;** www.wildwaterrafting.com), schedules white-water trips on the Chattooga. Packages including instruction, meals, and lodging are available.

GEORGIA

From the Golden Isles to the North Georgia uplands, the Peach State offers fishing, golf, sailing, and everything in between. If you're a biking enthusiast, you can order a catalog from **Backroads** (📞 **800/462-2848;** www.backroads.com), a reliable firm based in Berkeley, California. It offers organized bike tours to the Georgia islands, among others.

BEACHES   Georgia's beaches don't enjoy the fame of those in the Carolinas. But at one time, the Georgia coast was frequented by the likes of the Rockefellers and Vanderbilts. Even though this grand life has faded, the coast remains a quiet retreat for those seeking a true getaway. The Georgia coast is dotted with what are known as the Golden Isles: Historic Jekyll Island, luxurious Sea Island, and secluded Cumberland Island are the Eastern Seaboard's best-kept secrets. For information, call 📞 **800/VISIT-GA** (847-4842), visit www.exploregeorgia.org, or write to the **Division of Tourism,** Georgia Department of Industry, Trade & Tourism, PO Box 1776, Atlanta, GA 30301.

CAMPING   For information on Georgia's state parks and their camping facilities, contact the **Georgia Department of Natural Resources,** Office of Information, 2 Martin Luther King Jr. Dr., SE, Ste. 1215, Atlanta, GA 30334 (📞 **404/656-9448;** www.gadnr.org). Forty of the state parks in Georgia welcome campers to sites that rent for $10 to $30 per night. Some 30 parks have vacation cottages that rent for $50 to $140 nightly. These rates are for the summer and are reduced during other months. Reservations may be made by calling 📞 **800/864-PARK** (7275) or visiting www.gastateparks.org. Be aware that some of the Georgia state parks have become privatized. Site and cabin rentals could be higher at these parks.

FISHING & HUNTING No license is needed for saltwater fishing, but fishing in Georgia's lakes, streams, and ponds does require a license. Hunting is a sport used to curtail the annual exponential growth of the white-tailed deer population. Wild turkey and quail also abound. For information on hunting and fishing regulations, contact the **Georgia Wildlife Resources Division** (www.georgiawildlife.com) or the **Georgia Department of Natural Resources,** 2 Martin Luther King Jr. Dr., SE, Atlanta, GA 30334 (© **404/656-3500;** www.gadnr.org). Many hunting clubs will allow you to join provided you have references or can be sponsored by a local friend or family member.

GOLF Golf is big in Georgia. Augusta is home to the venerable Augusta National Golf Club, where the Masters Golf Tournament is played (the club's course is not open to the public). Lake Oconee is the golf capital of Georgia, boasting more than seven championship courses by designers like Jack Nicklaus and Ben Crenshaw. Mickey Mantle loved it so much that he spent most of his last days at the Harbor Club golf resort. Its neighbor, Reynolds Plantation, is host to the American qualifications for the World Championship. For information on private and public golf courses across the state of Georgia, the Georgia State Golf Association (© **800/949-4742;** www.gsga.org) offers the free guide *Georgia Golf on My Mind.*

HIKING The Appalachian Trail begins in North Georgia. For those who want easier hikes, some 40 state parks in Georgia offer trails of varying difficulty. Call © **800/864-PARKS** (864-7275) for more information.

LAKES Georgia is a virtual land of lakes, providing water, electricity, and recreation. East Georgia's Clarks Hill Lake (the Georgia side of South Carolina's Thurmond Lake), northeast Georgia's Lake Hartwell, and middle Georgia's lakes Oconee, Sinclair, and Lanier are the premier spots for boating and fishing. Contact the **Georgia Department of Natural Resources,** Office of Information, 2 Martin Luther King Jr. Dr., SE, Atlanta, GA 30334 (© **404/656-3500;** www.gadnr.org).

PANNING FOR GOLD Believe it or not, the San Francisco gold rush fever actually started in Dahlonega, Georgia. Contact the **Dahlonega Georgia Visitor Center** (© **800/231-5543;** www.dahlonega.org) for information on vacations and day trips to the gold mines, 250 feet below the surface. You get to keep the gold you find, but don't expect a king's ransom.

WHITE-WATER CANOEING & RAFTING The Amicalola River (pronounced Am-e-co-*lo*-la) is one of the state's more stunning sites, with the towering Amicalola Falls. **Appalachian Outfitters** (© **800/426-7117;** www.canoegeorgia.com) is the leading operation, offering trips for beginners with experienced guides.

STAYING CONNECTED

Internet Access Without Your Own Computer

To find cybercafes in your destination check **www.cybercaptive.com** and **www. cybercafe.com**.

Aside from formal cybercafes, most **youth hostels** and **public libraries** offer Internet access.

Most major airports now have **Internet kiosks** scattered throughout their gates. These give you basic Web access for a per-minute fee that's usually higher than cybercafe prices.

Internet Access with Your Own Computer

More and more hotels, resorts, airports, cafes, retailers, campgrounds, RV parks, and even entire towns are becoming *hot spots* for high-speed Wi-Fi (wireless fidelity or wireless Internet) access. Hotspot Finder at **www.jiwire.com** holds the world's largest directory of public wireless hot spots.

For dial-up access, most business-class hotels in the U.S. offer dataports for laptop modems, and a few thousand hotels in the U.S. and Europe now offer free high-speed Internet access.

For information on electrical conversions, see "Electricity," in "Fast Facts The Carolinas & Georgia" in chapter 22.

Cellphone Use in the U.S.

Just because your cellphone works at home doesn't mean it'll work everywhere in the U.S. (thanks to our nation's fragmented cellphone system). It's a good bet that your phone will work in major cities, but take a look at your wireless company's coverage map on its website before heading out. If you need to stay in touch at a destination where you know your phone won't work, **rent** a phone that does from **InTouch USA** (**℃ 800/872-7626;** www.intouchglobal.com) or a rental car location.

If you're not from the U.S., you'll be appalled at the poor reach of our **GSM (Global System for Mobiles) wireless network,** which is used by much of the rest of the world. Your phone will probably work in most major U.S. cities; it definitely won't work in many rural areas. (To see where GSM phones work in the U.S., check out www.t-mobile.com/coverage/national_popup.asp.) And you may or may not be able to send SMS (text messages) home.

SUGGESTED ITINERARIES IN THE CAROLINAS & GEORGIA

4

The itineraries that follow take you to many major attractions and some of the most scenic Southern villages. The pace may be a bit breathtaking for some visitors, so skip a town or sight occasionally to have some chill-out time. If your time is limited, you may want to concentrate on just one scenic adventure at a time, such as "The Outer Banks in 1 Week" tour. If you've been to the South before, especially to Savannah, Charleston, or Atlanta, you may want to spend a week in the western mountains of North Carolina, taking "The Western Mountains of North Carolina" tour. Families might want to consider "The South Carolina Coast with Kids" tour.

THE REGIONS IN BRIEF
North Carolina

THE HIGH COUNTRY The **Blue Ridge Parkway** seems to touch the sky as it traces the jutting peaks and rising plateaus of the North Carolina mountains. Set in the splendor of these hills are the mountain folk, who strive to retain their lifestyle despite the headaches and traffic caused by tourists taking in the sights along the parkway.

The peak time for entering the parkway is May through October, when hotel accommodations are plentiful and visitor facilities are open. Fall is when the landscape is at its best. The natural foliage of the mountain evergreens is magically enhanced by a brisk palette of reds, yellows, oranges, and golds. Although winter rates are appealing, cold-weather conditions may make roads inaccessible. As though the mountains were not inspiring enough, North Carolina also offers other sites filled with natural splendor.

You can create your own script for this 470-mile drive—called the "Most Scenic Highway in America"—by entering at the southern end of Shenandoah National Park near the Virginia border. The slow drive that follows the road's sharp curves and narrow straightaways is full of serendipitous discoveries, from fresh-grown apples sold at stands along the roadside to rustic "junk" stores.

The rolling pasturelands of the Blue Ridge's northern access lie in Allegheny and Ashe counties, picture-perfect with grazing cows and lichen-covered split-rail fences. As you approach Watauga, Avery, and Mitchell counties, the mountains seem to rise like images in a fast-paced video game. **Grandfather Mountain** is the site of a staggering engineering feat: a roadway that swings treacherously 1,243 feet around the curve of the craggy mountain. With down-home eateries, inns, panoramic views of misty blue mountains, and hiking trails spread along the length of the parkway, plus the highest peak in the eastern United States at **Mount Mitchell State Park** (6,684 ft.), you'll be amazed by the sights you'll see along the road, in spite of the traffic.

There are ways to avoid crowds and traffic even during the peak season. Park rangers suggest that you drive the parkway Monday through Friday, when the roads are less congested. Avoid Sunday afternoon altogether, and be adventurous: Go off the beaten track. Numerous side roads run parallel to the parkway or branch off from it. Visitor centers furnish detailed maps, but rangers recommend that you get specific instructions before venturing out onto one of these roads.

Plan on spending at least 2 days in the **Cherokee** area. Although the town is a little touristy, a smattering of intimate hideaways is concealed along the back roads of Great Smoky Mountains National Park near Cherokee.

Set just off the Blue Ridge Parkway, about 40 miles east of Cherokee, is **Asheville,** a stunning small city worthy of a 3-day stay, with attractions such as the Biltmore Estate, the Thomas Wolfe Memorial, and the Folk Art Center.

THE PIEDMONT   After you visit the mountains, head east to **Winston-Salem,** our favorite Piedmont City. The former seat of the powerful Reynolds tobacco fortune, Winston-Salem is also home to Old Salem, a restored 18th- and 19th-century village settled by German-speaking Moravians, and Wake Forest University.

Another component of the Piedmont is the **Raleigh-Durham–Chapel Hill area,** often referred to as the Research Triangle. This area has attracted all sorts of high-tech industry to the state—no wonder, because three of the premier universities in the South (Duke, the University of North Carolina [UNC], and North Carolina State) are located here, within a stone's throw of one another. The proximity of Duke to UNC has given rise to perhaps the greatest rivalry in college-basketball history—although State's consistently competitive hoops program can never be counted out of the equation. Chapel Hill is the charming college town, Durham the up-and-coming hot spot, and Raleigh the bustling state capital.

The largest city in the Piedmont is **Charlotte.** Surprisingly cosmopolitan and set amid rolling hills, this fast-paced city rivals Orlando or Birmingham and dismisses the down-home label. It's a major banking center and transportation hub, and its diversified manufacturing capabilities include machinery, textiles, metals, and food products. Charlotte has also been transformed into a big-time sports town: The state's first pro-football team, the Carolina Panthers, continues to draw fans to its state-of-the-art open-air "retro" stadium.

THE COAST   A trip through North Carolina wouldn't be complete without sticking your toes in the brisk Atlantic. The largest city on the coast is **Wilmington,** although much of North Carolina's shoreline remains much less developed than the frenetic scene along South Carolina's beaches. In spite of the slowpoke summer traffic, **Nags Head** especially has a little something for every family member, from a rustic fishing pier to nearby video arcades. It also offers some of the finest seafood restaurants on the East Coast, many in modest settings. Local specialties include Hatteras-style clam chowder, crab cakes, and deep-fried hush puppies. Surprisingly, Nags Head lacks one thing that most of its rival resorts do have: high-rise condos. Instead, towering overhead is Jockey's Ridge, a giant sand dune that forms the tallest *médano* (large, isolated hill of sand) in the East. Climb to the top of the mile-long dune for outstanding views of the ocean and sound.

Another wonderful spot is **Ocracoke Island,** a 45-minute ride across the waters of Pamlico Sound. A free ferry departs Hatteras village every 30 minutes, beginning daily at 5am. Disembark at the north-end ferry visitor station, and head for the village of Ocracoke while enjoying the expanses of wild dunes and forests of cedar and pine. The beaches leading into Ocracoke Village are some of the best on the East Coast.

Much of the island is a National Seashore area where large development is prohibited. While this is a place where you still can go into the post office barefoot to check your mail, it's not the sleepy little backwater it was even 10 years ago. The town of Ocracoke has ceded to the demands of tourism, building several multistory hotels around Silver Lake; restaurants; and shops selling the requisite beach hammocks, taffy, T-shirts, and souvenirs. In the summer, the tourist crush can be overwhelming; visit in the fall, when you'll see the island at its best, a real North Carolina charmer.

South Carolina

THE HEARTLAND The attraction of these backwater stops is the interaction with the people who live here. A Southern drawl as long as Rhett Butler's coattails prevails here, as do "Yes, ma'am," "No, ma'am," and afternoon naps. You're likely to come upon an old gas station complete with working Pure pumps and ice-cold Coca-Cola in bottles, and you're even more likely to pass a flock of camouflage-clad deer hunters lining a country road with trucks and guns.

A rail-and-highway hub, **Florence** is simply a convenience off the interstate, with fast-food joints; clean, inexpensive motels; and a midsize mall with a cafeteria and restrooms.

A more charming town for a half-day visit is **Darlington,** home of the famed raceway. The small, old-time downtown area features attractive Victorian-style homes and several good restaurants serving home-cooked meals. The Mountain Dew Southern 500, held each Labor Day, and the Stock Car Hall of Fame are ideal for a taste of NASCAR-style racing.

With that small-town feel, South Carolina is a film producer's dream location and a delight for Northerners seeking a taste of the traditional South. There are courthouses that rival the national Capitol building (on a smaller scale) sitting smack in the middle of Main Street. There are white-picket-fenced homes sporting Victorian woodwork lining two-lane, moss-hung streets. There's a general hardware store that doubles as a Greyhound bus station. There are a couple of churches where the membership has stayed pretty much the same (with the annual number of births equaling the number of deaths) for who knows how long. There are places such as **Camden** (the former home of the late William F. Buckley, Sr.), which hosts two nationally known horse races: the Camden Classic and the Carolina Classic. **Kingstree** is the home of Nobel Peace Prize–winner Dr. Joseph Goldstein.

COLUMBIA The state capital, located in the heart of South Carolina, is the home of "the Worst Boiled Peanuts in the World," at Cromer's, a state institution for munchies.

Columbia also happens to be the state's largest city, hosting more than 300 factories. In addition, the city is the marketing and distribution center for a large farming area, and it's crawling with college students who attend the University of South Carolina.

A day's worth of exploring will take you to Ainsley Hall Mansion, President Woodrow Wilson's boyhood home; the State House and Governor's Mansion; the Columbia Museum of Art; and the Town Theatre (1919), one of the oldest theaters in the country. The Riverbanks Park Zoo is an outstanding modern zoo that celebrates Christmas by draping thousands of twinkling lights throughout the park.

THE UPSTATE The northwestern region of South Carolina lies in the foothills of the Blue Ridge Mountains. Originally, it was the place where residents of Charleston fled to escape the summer heat and the mosquitoes. What they discovered was a land of scenic wonders, with mountain peaks, unspoiled forests, waterfalls, and country hamlets. The chief city is **Greenville.**

But cities are not the major reason to visit the Upstate. Escape instead to **Pendleton,** an entire town listed on the National Register of Historic Places. Here you can visit Ashtabula Plantation, dating from the 1820s and once the most beautiful farm in the Upstate. Parks and battlefields abound, including Cowpens National Battlefield at Chesnee, famous for Daniel Morgan's 1781 defeat of the British. Finally, the Cherokee Foothills Scenic Highway curves for 130 miles through the heart of South Carolina's Blue Ridge foothills.

MYRTLE BEACH & THE GRAND STRAND Like Las Vegas in the desert, Myrtle Beach rises above the Southern coastline in a blaze of neon so bright that you might want to keep your shades handy, even after sunset. This city, a far cry from the historic South, has been transformed into a megawatt entertainment mecca. A golfer's paradise, the area now boasts more than 120 championship golf courses. There are water slides, arcades, giant shopping malls, and a host of kids' attractions. Numerous country-music shows are available and, as in Branson, Missouri, renowned musicians appear here year-round.

If you're hungry for seafood, dining is best at nearby **Murrells Inlet,** a strip along the marsh that's packed with seafood places. The late mystery novelist Mickey Spillane made his home here.

CHARLESTON What can we possibly say about a city so charming that nearly every celebrity who visits ends up driving around town with a real-estate agent? Located on the peninsula between the Cooper and Ashley rivers in southeastern South Carolina, Charleston is the oldest and second-largest city in the state, full of antebellum homes and carefully preserved buildings. Each spring, Charleston hosts Spoleto Festival USA, one of the most prestigious performing-arts events in the South.

One of the finest examples of colonial architecture in the country is Drayton Hall, a mansion set amid huge oaks draped with Spanish moss. This National Historic Landmark is the only Ashley River plantation house to survive the Civil War intact.

Every day of the week, Charleston's City Market bustles with craftspeople jammed under the covered breezeways. Sweet-grass basket-weavers hum old spirituals, horse-drawn carriages clop down the street, and thousands of tourists eat, drink, and shop their way along.

A minimum 3-day stay is required if you are to discover Charleston by day and night. Try to include a trip over the Cooper River Bridge to the string of islands that have rebounded from the massive destruction of Hurricane Hugo. Take time to stop in **Beaufort,** the inspiration for Pat Conroy's novel *The Prince of Tides* (among other bestsellers). The town is full of old-fashioned inns, rustic pubs, and tiny stores along a tailored waterfront park.

HILTON HEAD   Much more commercial than Charleston is Hilton Head Island, home of wealthy Northerners (mostly retired) and vacationers from all parts of the country. With myriad contemporary beachfront restaurants and rows of hotels, time-share villas, and cottages, the island has recently sprouted boutiques and upscale shopping areas. Although the traffic is horrendous (there is only one main thorough-fare both on and off the island), development hasn't obliterated nature on Hilton Head, and you can find solitude at the north end of the beach.

On the positive side, the island has become socially and culturally oriented, playing host to presidents and world leaders, and also supporting its own symphony orchestra and ballet company. Sea Pines on Hilton Head is one of the country's premier golf resorts, located on a 605-acre Wildlife Foundation Preserve that's home to birds, squirrels, dolphins, and alligators. Hilton Head has 15 miles of bike paths and 5 miles of pristine beaches.

Georgia

THE ATLANTA AREA   Gateway to the Deep South, Atlanta is one of the most progressive cities in America. The hometown of Martin Luther King, Jr., bears no relationship to the city from which Scarlett O'Hara and Aunt Pittypat fled during Sherman's march. It's a fast-paced capital city that, while still sporting a few magnolia blossoms and mint juleps, is marching forward in commerce and culture. *Fortune* magazine has called Atlanta "America's Best City for Business," and the title still holds into the 21st century.

NORTHERN GEORGIA   This area, within 70 to 120 miles of Atlanta, may be the best-kept travel secret in the South. Northern Georgia is a virtual national or state park, a rugged outback that stands in sharp contrast to the Blue Ridge Mountains in the northeastern part of the state. The northwest has many Native American sites, as well as the Chickamauga and Chattanooga National Military Park, where critical Civil War battles were staged. Lookout Mountain rises like a 100-mile linear barrier from the valleys below.

The southern Appalachians contain a mountain culture that hasn't been com-pletely wiped out, and many of the old ways prevail. **Dahlonega** makes a great base for exploring Georgia's Blue Ridge Mountains, much of which lies within 727,000-acre **Chattahoochee National Forest.**

SAVANNAH   The very name evokes a romantic antebellum aura. Savannah is the city that General Sherman gave President Lincoln as a Christmas present.

Founded in 1733 by James Oglethorpe as Georgia's first settlement, the city is located 18 miles inland on the Savannah River at the South Carolina border. A deep channel connects Savannah to the ocean, attracting massive freighters to the termi-nals at the Georgia Ports Authority. Visitors can almost touch the ships as they slowly make their way up the river. Lined with classy nightspots and upscale restaurants, as well as a few rough pubs and artsy boutiques, cobblestone River Street has become a hub for tourists.

MACON & THE SOUTHWEST   Macon is best seen in March during the Cherry Blossom Festival, but this historic town has year-round attractions, too. It once grew fat on the cotton trade and still boasts some nice antebellum homes that Sherman's armies didn't completely destroy. Today it's one of the most rewarding destinations in Georgia. The two other major attractions in the state's southwest are **Callaway Gardens** and **Warm Springs** (where Franklin Delano Roosevelt died). You can visit both towns on a day trip from Atlanta, or you can find plenty of old inns in the area if you want to spend the night.

THE GOLDEN ISLES Don't leave Georgia without exploring the Golden Isles. Start at U.S. 17 about 17 miles south of Darien (or exit off I-95 South at the Golden Isles Pkwy.), head toward Brunswick, and then travel to St. Simons and Sea islands. The drive culminates in **Jekyll Island,** once the private enclave of wintering wealthy families like the Rockefellers and the Vanderbilts, but now open to all.

If you can afford it, plan to spend at least 1 night at the **Cloister** on Sea Island, the grandest resort in the tri-state area. For escapists, there are also Little St. Simons Island and Cumberland Island, the idyllic wilderness where John Kennedy, Jr., married Carolyn Bessette 3 years before their tragic plane crash.

Based at a hotel on the Golden Isles, you can make a day trip to one of the greatest attractions in Georgia: the **Okefenokee Swamp,** the largest freshwater swamp still preserved in the United States.

THE OUTER BANKS IN 1 WEEK

The 175-mile ribbon of sandy islands that forms the Outer Banks and Cape Hatteras National Seashore runs roughly parallel to the North Carolina coast. It is a seaside wilderness, an extremely vulnerable ecosystem of barrier islands jutting out into the Atlantic Ocean. More than 500 ships, including the Union ironclad *Monitor,* have gone down on the shifting shoals of the Outer Banks coastline, an area grimly called "the Graveyard of the Atlantic." Blackbeard once holed up along these shores, and you can follow in the pirate's footsteps, perhaps discovering a few remaining fishing villages on your own. An overly developed section, a motel row, stretches from Kitty Hawk to Nags Head, but much of the rest of the Outer Banks is still unspoiled, especially its offbeat islands reached by ferry. The good news is that in just a week, you can tour the highlights of this region.

Day 1: Elizabeth City to Kill Devil Hills ★★★

Many visitors use Elizabeth City as their gateway to the northern Outer Banks. From here you can head east along Route 158, which will take you through the town of Grandy to Point Harbor. Cross the bridge at Point Harbor near the end of Route 158 and arrive at Kitty Hawk, a distance of 49 miles east of Elizabeth City. Before lunch you can drive north to the little beach community of **Corolla,** passing through **Duck,** 7 miles north of Kitty Hawk. The final lap from Duck to Corolla is 10 miles to the north. The **Currituck Beach Lighthouse** in Corolla (p. 94) is the northernmost lighthouse on the Outer Banks. Count yourself lucky if you see some of the wild horses that still live in the area.

At this point, you'll need to double back, heading south along Route 12 to Kitty Hawk again. There are many eateries along the way, mostly serving seafood specials.

At Kitty Hawk, continue south, following the signs into Kill Devil Hills, where you can overnight. If you're flush with money, you can live more elegantly at the **Sanderling** (p. 98), back in Duck.

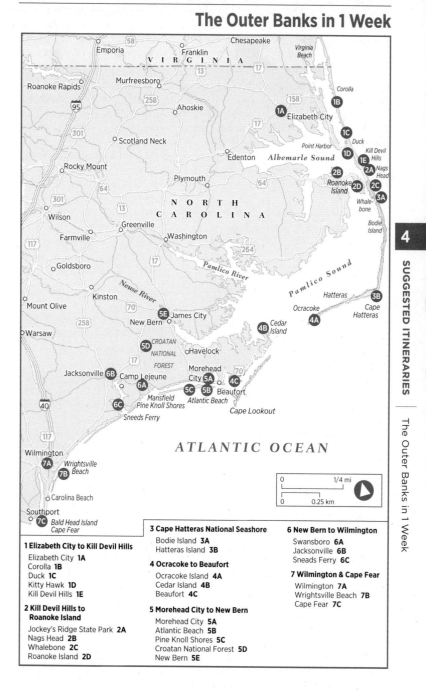

1 Elizabeth City to Kill Devil Hills

Elizabeth City **1A**
Corolla **1B**
Duck **1C**
Kitty Hawk **1D**
Kill Devil Hills **1E**

2 Kill Devil Hills to Roanoke Island

Jockey's Ridge State Park **2A**
Nags Head **2B**
Whalebone **2C**
Roanoke Island **2D**

3 Cape Hatteras National Seashore

Bodie Island **3A**
Hatteras Island **3B**

4 Ocracoke to Beaufort

Ocracoke Island **4A**
Cedar Island **4B**
Beaufort **4C**

5 Morehead City to New Bern

Morehead City **5A**
Atlantic Beach **5B**
Pine Knoll Shores **5C**
Croatan National Forest **5D**
New Bern **5E**

6 New Bern to Wilmington

Swansboro **6A**
Jacksonville **6B**
Sneads Ferry **6C**

7 Wilmington & Cape Fear

Wilmington **7A**
Wrightsville Beach **7B**
Cape Fear **7C**

The major attraction in Kill Devil Hills is the **Wright Brothers National Memorial** (p. 94). The bicycle-making brothers launched the aviation age along this coast in 1903. Both the hangar and Orville and Wilbur's living quarters have been restored, and replicas of the 1902 glider and 1903 flying machine are on display.

Day 2: Kill Devil Hills to Roanoke Island ★

Fortified with a Carolina country breakfast, set out the next morning from Kill Devil Hills, continuing south along Route 12 until you come to **Jockey's Ridge State Park** (p. 92). Known for its hang gliding, the park offers you a breezy walk along a 360-foot boardwalk, ideal for a morning break. For a beach break, you face 5 miles of sand, with more than two dozen public access areas off Route 12.

Nags Head is the last town before the Cape Hatteras National Seashore, with its beautiful landscapes. Before you head to Hatteras, a detour is suggested. From Nags Head, drive the short distance south to Whalebone Junction, then cut west along the causeway leading to **Roanoke Island,** a distance of 10 miles to the southwest. Follow U.S. 64/264 from the 158 bypass to **Manteo,** capital of Roanoke Island and the best place for overnighting.

Before the day fades, take in the **Fort Raleigh National Historic Site** in a landscaped park (p. 94). At the north end of Roanoke Island, follow the signs to the **North Carolina Aquarium** (p. 95), home to the state's largest ocean tank. If time remains, visit the **Elizabethan Gardens** (p. 94).

The real reason to anchor into Manteo for the night is to see *The Lost Colony*, the country's first and longest-running outdoor drama, telling the story of the first colonists who landed here in 1587 but mysteriously disappeared (p. 92).

Day 3: Cape Hatteras National Seashore ★★

After overnighting on Roanoke Island, head east again, returning to Whalebone Junction and then going south along Hwy. 12 for the most dramatic seashore drive along the East Coast until you reach the Florida Keys.

The first island you traverse is **Bodie Island,** with its black-and-white lighthouse (ca. 1872) at the southern end. You'll see an observation platform nearby for viewing local bird life. A visitor center here lies 6½ miles south of Whalebone.

From Bodie Island, continue south, passing through **Pea Island National Wildlife Refuge** (p. 105), only 10 miles to the south of Nags Head. This is one of the East Coast's most populated avian roosting places, with aquatic and migratory birds appearing year-round.

A high point is crossing over the Herbert C. Bonner Bridge, arching for 3 miles over Oregon Inlet as it arrives at **Hatteras Island,** known to all blue marlin fishermen. At any point along the way, break your day by hitting one of the 70 miles of beaches that stretch along the Cape Hatteras National Seashore to Ocracoke Island (see below). The best fishing pier is at Rodanthe.

Thirty miles to the south of Rodanthe is the **Cape Hatteras Lighthouse,** at 208 feet, the tallest along the East Coast. The little town of Hatteras is the embarkation point for the free ferry to **Ocracoke Island,** where you can overnight after a 40-minute sea trip.

Day 4: Ocracoke to Beaufort ★★

After breakfast on Ocracoke Island, photograph its lighthouse and wander about the village with its many shops centered around Silver Lake Harbor; here Blackbeard was killed back in 1718. Later you can take a car ferry from Ocracoke to **Cedar Island,** a 2¼-hour trip over Pamlico Sound. Many visitors secure the makings of a picnic lunch on Ocracoke, enjoying their food as they sail along.

Once you land, you can explore the **Cedar Island National Wildlife Refuge** (p. 111), a feeding ground for migratory waterfowl. Cedar Island is linked to the mainland by Route 12. After seeing the refuge, continue southwest along 12, which becomes Route 70, taking you into **Beaufort,** North Carolina's third-oldest town (not to be confused with Beaufort, South Carolina).

Beaufort has a number of attractions, plus some good accommodations, so consider an overnight here. Chief among the attractions is the **Beaufort Historic Site** (p. 123), with an old burial ground, an 1829 restored jail, a courthouse (ca. 1796), an apothecary shop, and restored homes from 1767 to 1825. As the afternoon fades, make your way to the **North Carolina Maritime Museum** (p. 123), one of the best in the Carolinas.

Day 5: Morehead City to New Bern ★

Leave Beaufort in the morning and drive 3 miles west to **Morehead City,** a year-round resort town founded in 1857. Fishermen come here in pursuit of king mackerel and blue marlin.

Morehead City is the best base for exploring the **Bogue Banks,** a 28-mile barrier island lying off its coast. You can drive across a bridge spanning Bogue Sound to the little town of Atlantic Beach, where there is a boardwalk and swimming.

Go east on 58 a couple of miles until you reach the tip of Bogue Island and **Fort Macon** (p. 128), a restored Civil War landmark. Then head west along Route 58 (the island's only road), stopping in at Pine Knoll Shores to see the vastly expanded **North Carolina Aquarium** (p. 128).

At this point, you can make a decision. If time is running short, you can leave Bogue Island and follow the signs along the coast southwest to Wilmington. Otherwise, you can spend an extra day exploring the **Croatan National Forest.** This refuge covers 161,000 acres and is riddled with waterways and estuaries, the alligator's northernmost habitat. If you have that extra day, follow Route 58 back to the mainland but cut east on Route 24 heading back to Morehead City. This is a scenic drive along the southern tier of the park. At the junction with Route 70, head north through the eastern part of the park until you reach **New Bern,** where you can overnight. New Bern lies 50 miles inland from the coast we've just visited, but it's only 87 miles northeast of Wilmington.

Day 6: New Bern ★ to Wilmington ★

You can spend most of the morning exploring **Tryon Palace Historic Sites & Gardens** (p. 130). Tryon Palace itself was once called "the most beautiful building in colonial America." You can also visit the **John Wright Stanly House** and the **Dixon-Stevenson House.** Take a final look at the **Birthplace of Pepsi-Cola Store** (p. 130), unless you're a fan of Coca-Cola.

Leave New Bern on Route 17, which takes you along the western border of **Croatan National Forest.** At the junction with Route 58, continue south to the coast once again, cutting right on Route 24, which will take you into the historic waterfront town of **Swansboro** (p. 129). We always like to spend an hour or two checking out its antiques shops and wandering the harborfront where shrimp boats pull in.

After a visit, continue due west to the town of **Jacksonville,** where you can visit the areas of the **Camp Lejeune marine base** that are not closed to the public.

For a seafood lunch in the area, leave Jacksonville and head south along Route 17 to the junction with Route 210, taking you to the old fishing village of **Sneads Ferry,** where you can find some of the best fish lunches along the coast. After a good "tuck-in," you can head north again to the junction with Route 17, following it southwest for 52 miles into **Wilmington,** the biggest city along the coast.

Day 7: Wilmington & Cape Fear ★

The best way to spend the morning in Wilmington is to sail the *Henrietta III* (p. 114) on a 45-minute narrated cruise that takes in the waterfront and traverses a 5-mile loop of the **Cape Fear River.** Back in town, you can visit the big attractions such as **Airlie Gardens** (p. 115), the **USS *North Carolina* Battleship Memorial** (p. 116), and the **Fort Fisher State Historic Site** (p. 116). Any time left over can be devoted to fun in the sands along **Wrightsville Beach** (p. 117), 6 miles east of Wilmington.

At this point, you can end your tour or head down the coast to some of the major tourist meccas in the Southeast: **Myrtle Beach, Charleston, Hilton Head,** and **Savannah.**

THE SOUTH CAROLINA COAST WITH KIDS

Coastal South Carolina is infamously known as the "Redneck Riviera," especially the area around **Myrtle Beach.** But it also boasts the South's grandest antebellum city, **Charleston,** and one of the great playgrounds along the East Coast at **Hilton Head.** Along the way are towns of charm and grace, especially **Georgetown,** as well as a favorite with kids, **Tybee Island** (although this is just across the South Carolina state line in Georgia).

Days 1 & 2: Myrtle Beach & the Grand Strand ★★

If you went along with us on the first week's tour of the Outer Banks (see above), you can pick up where we left off in the city of Wilmington and continue south for 75 miles into Myrtle Beach, where we recommend a 2-night stopover.

At times the entire 60-mile string of beaches, aptly called the Grand Strand, seems to have been designed expressly for children, with kid-friendly facilities and amusements as well as dozens of resorts serving kids' menus. Family rates at many of the hotels are yet another enticement.

The Strand stretches from the border with North Carolina in the north all the way south to Georgetown (see "Day 3," below). At the hub is Myrtle Beach itself. Most families like to organize their time between the beach and man-made amusements. Parents may want to sneak away for some serious golfing (see "Golf," in chapter 13).

The SC Coast with Kids in 1 Week

1 & 2 Myrtle Beach & the Grand Strand
3 Georgetown
4 & 5 Charleston
6 Hilton Head
7 Savannah

On the first day, allowing time for the beach, families can visit the **Myrtle Waves Water Park** (p. 306) and **Ripley's Aquarium** (p. 307), the most visited attraction in South Carolina.

While still based at a hotel along the Grand Strand, you can spend the morning of Day 2 exploring **Myrtle Beach State Park** (p. 307), with its sandy beach and pavilions, picnic tables, and a swimming pool. It's riddled with nature trails. In the afternoon, drive down to **Murrells Inlet** (p. 322), 11 miles south. It's called the Seafood Capital of South Carolina. While in the area, you can pay a call on the beautiful **Brookgreen Gardens** (p. 323). Back in Myrtle Beach, attend one of the many variety shows in the area, including the **Alabama Theatre** (p. 320) for family fun.

Day 3: Georgetown ★★

On the morning of Day 3, head down the coast along Route 17 until you see the turnoff for **Huntington Beach State Park,** 3 miles south of Murrells Inlet and across from Brookgreen Gardens, which we've already visited. The 2,500-acre park offers a completely different experience from the gardens, and it opens onto one of the best sandy beaches along the Grand Strand. We suggest you spend the morning here and also enjoy a picnic under one of the shelters and a stroll along the boardwalk.

After lunch, continue the rest of the way to Georgetown, a distance of only 28 miles south of Myrtle Beach. After checking in to a hotel, we suggest one of the river cruises aboard the **Carolina Rover** or the **Jolly Rover** that set sail from Georgetown Harbor. For more details, see "River Cruises" on p. 327. Georgetown has more than 50 historic buildings that date back as far as 1737. For information on tours of Georgetown, see p. 327.

Days 4 & 5: Charleston ★★★

From Georgetown on the morning of Day 4, drive southwest along Route 17 for 62 miles into the historic seaport of Charleston, the highlight of most visits to South Carolina and a very kid-friendly town. Check into a hotel for 2 nights and begin your adventure.

For a lesson in history outside the classroom, kids can see where the Civil War began at the **Fort Sumter National Monument** (p. 261). Later the whole family will be fascinated by the **H. L. Hunley Confederate submarine** (p. 261), which sank one fateful day in 1864 but was later raised. A good 2 or 3 hours can be spent at **Charles Towne Landing** (p. 265) enjoying its 663 acres; for kids, this is one of the highlights of a visit to Charleston. Wind down the afternoon with a visit to the **South Carolina Aquarium** (p. 266).

For Day 5, you should try to hit one or more of the following four major attractions in the Charleston environs. The most Mercury-footed families manage to see all of them in 1 day. If that's too fast a pace for you, skip one or two. In order of importance, they are **Magnolia Plantation** (p. 263), **Middleton Place** (p. 264), **Cypress Gardens** (p. 264), and **Drayton Hall** (p. 263).

Day 6: Hilton Head ★★★

It's a 100-mile drive to our next overnight stopover at Hilton Head, so you should leave as early as you can in the morning. Follow the signs out of Charleston to Route 17, heading southwest until it reaches Route 21 going west to I-95. Follow this until you come to the junction with Route 278, which will take you east into Hilton Head.

The most fun place to stay for families is **Disney's Hilton Head Island Resort** (p. 290). Devote the day to romps along the beaches and taking one of the boat cruises (see "Cruises & Tours" in chapter 12). In the afternoon, you can take your kids to the nature preserve of **Sea Pines Forest Preserve** (p. 286) for walks among the wildlife, including white-tailed deer. There are several picnic areas here for lunch. Overnight in Hilton Head.

Day 7: Savannah ★★★

You have a choice. You can stay yet another day on Hilton Head, enjoying its beaches and outdoor activities, or you can drive across the Georgia state line for a visit to Savannah, 120 miles south of Charleston. Should you choose the latter, drive west once again to I-95, which you follow south until you see the exits for Savannah. I-95 lies 10 miles west of Savannah. Just follow the signs leading to the Historic District, where you can overnight.

Savannah is packed with attractions the entire family can enjoy, including the **Ships of the Sea Maritime Museum** (p. 481); the **Massie Heritage Interpretation Center** (p. 478), geared to children; a tour of the **Civil War forts** (see "Forts" in chapter 20); and **Savannah riverboat cruises** (p. 482).

The South Carolina Coast with Kids | SUGGESTED ITINERARIES

THE WESTERN MOUNTAINS OF NORTH CAROLINA

The most spectacular drives in the tri-state area take in the western mountains of North Carolina. The city of **Asheville,** the most cultural and beautiful of North Carolina, can be your gateway. The major attraction is the **Great Smoky Mountains National Park,** but you can also take some of the grand scenic tours of the South, especially a trek along the **Blue Ridge Parkway** and a ride on the **Great Smoky Mountains Railroad.**

Day 1: Asheville ★★★

Noted for its eclectic architecture, Asheville lies 115 miles west of Charlotte. Many visitors prefer to make it their vacation center for touring the Blue Ridge Mountains; it is also the city closest to the Great Smoky Mountains National Park. Asheville's major attraction is the **Biltmore Estate** (p. 196), the former country mansion of the Vanderbilts (allow at least 2 hr.). You can also spend an hour or so shopping in **Biltmore Village** (p. 204). You can visit the memorials to Asheville's famous literary star, novelist Thomas Wolfe of *Look Homeward, Angel* fame. Overnight here at the best accommodations in the mountains.

Day 2: Cherokee

On the morning of Day 2, it's only a 48-mile drive southwest to Cherokee, which can be your actual entrance into the Great Smoky Mountains National Park. Follow I-40 west out of Asheville, detouring onto Route 19 for the final run west into Cherokee. Here you can visit the **Museum of the Cherokee Indian** (p. 223) and the **Oconaluftee Indian Village** (p. 223). That night, attend the most popular outdoor drama in America, *Unto These Hills* (p. 224). Overnight in Cherokee.

Day 3: The Great Smoky Mountains Railroad ★★★

While still based in Cherokee, you can head west on Day 3 along Route 19 to Bryson City to board the **Great Smoky Mountains Railroad** (p. 235). (Cherokee to Bryson City is only 11 miles.) It's the greatest train ride in all the South, crossing 53 miles of track and going across 25 bridges. Most tours take 4½ hours. Considering driving time from Cherokee and lunch breaks, allow the better part of a day for this fascinating journey into nostalgia. Return to Cherokee for the night.

Days 4 & 5: Great Smoky Mountains National Park ★★★

For more extensive touring notes, see "The Park's Highlights," in chapter 10. On the morning of Day 4, head northwest along Route 441 in the heart of the park, detouring to **Clingmans Dome** (p. 228), the highest peak in the park, at 6,642 feet. It's signposted. A secondary road leads to a parking lot, a distance of 7 miles. From here, you can climb the half-mile to the greatest viewing platform in the park.

Return to the main road (441) and continue northwest to **Newfound Gap,** the center of the park. After stopping to take in the views, continue up the road

4

SUGGESTED ITINERARIES

The Western Mountains of North Carolina

83

for another stop at the twin peaks of **Chimney Tops** (p. 228). Route 441 continues to the northwest for a final stopover at the **Sugarlands Visitor Center** (p. 228). For accommodations for the night, consider driving the short distance into Gatlinburg across the border in Tennessee, which has the area's widest range of accommodations, especially in the budget category.

On Day 5, leave Gatlinburg in the morning, continuing west on Route 321 until you see the turnoff for **Cades Cove,** which is reached by following Little River Road into the cove. For more details, see p. 228. After touring the 11-mile Cades Cove loop, you can see more of the park by following a series of winding roads that cut south through the western scenery of the park, leading you past Fontana Dam into **Fontana Village,** found along Route 28 on the southern rim of the park.

After stopping for refueling and a snack, head east to the town of Dillsboro, which has some of the best accommodations in the area (our hotel recommendations begin on p. 234). From Fontana Village to Dillsboro, a distance of 46 miles, go east on Route 28 but turn left onto U.S. 74 at the junction. Continue along until you reach U.S. 23 and U.S. 441, which will take you into Dillsboro (just follow the signs).

Day 6: The Blue Ridge Parkway ★★★

Part of the National Park Service, the Blue Ridge Parkway, traversing five counties of the High Country, is the greatest scenic ride in the entire South. It actually begins at Rockfish Gap between Charlottesville and Waynesboro in Virginia, stretching for some 469 miles. Many visitors travel the entire length. If you don't have a generous amount of time, you can join the parkway after a night in Dillsboro. You can spend a day if you travel leisurely with stopovers along the parkway, reaching the Boone/Blowing Rock area in the late afternoon. From Dillsboro, head east along Route 23 until you reach the entrance to the parkway. Get on this scenic route and travel it all the way to Blowing Rock, a distance of 142 miles to the northeast. It's one of the drives of a lifetime.

Overnight in Blowing Rock (p. 214), Boone (p. 207), or Banner Elk.

Day 7: Blowing Rock, Boone ★ & Banner Elk ★

These scenic towns lie close to one another, so you can easily explore them all in 1 day. If you began the morning at Blowing Rock, you can see the fabled rock itself, enjoying panoramic views from its observation tower. Take Route 321 north to Boone, which lies in the heart of the Blue Ridge Mountains. If you're traveling with kids, stop at the **Tweetsie Railroad Theme Park** (p. 208) along the way.

The distance between Boone and Blowing Rock is 8 miles. At Boone, explore the **Daniel Boone Native Gardens** (p. 208) and the **Hickory Ridge Homestead Museum.**

After Boone, drive along N.C. 194 to Banner Elk, a distance of 17 miles from Boone. Here you'll find one of the highlights of the trip, a visit to **Grandfather Mountain,** the highest peak in the Blue Ridge.

And that's it. For those with more time, the highlights of Georgia loom on our fourth and final drive through the Old South.

The Western Mountains of North Carolina

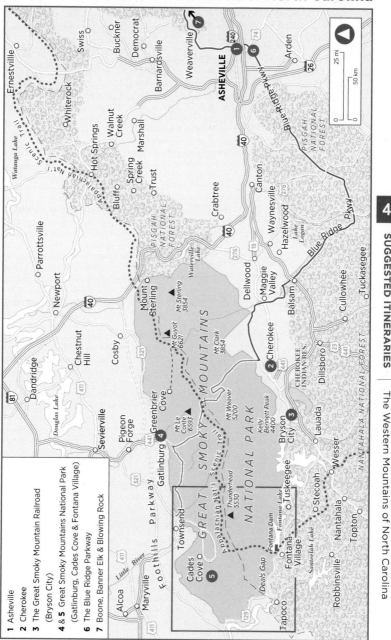

1 Asheville
2 Cherokee
3 The Great Smoky Mountain Railroad (Bryson City)
4 & 5 Great Smoky Mountains National Park (Gatlinburg, Cades Cove & Fontana Village)
6 The Blue Ridge Parkway
7 Boone, Banner Elk & Blowing Rock

HIGHLIGHTS OF GEORGIA IN 1 WEEK

Having tackled the best of the Carolinas, we're ready to take on a really big state, Georgia, from its capital of **Atlanta** to its shoreline, highlighted by **Savannah** and the **Golden Isles.** One could spend a month just touring the state, but good road links let you tackle its highlights in just 7 days, including visits to the famous **Callaway Gardens** and to **Warm Springs,** where FDR went for R & R.

Days 1 & 2: Atlanta ★★★

Use Atlanta as your gateway to Georgia. (It's the transportation hub of the Deep South.) Once here, plan to stay for at least 2 nights. You'll need a car to see Atlanta: The city is spread out, with many sights located outside the city center and inconvenient to reach by public transportation.

Plenty of places in Atlanta offer family fun. The two must-visits for families are the theme park **Six Flags Over Georgia** (p. 397) and **Zoo Atlanta** (p. 397). It's recommended that you also work in an organized tour for a quick overview of the city—you simply won't be able to see it all in 2 days. If you didn't have time for the tour on the first day, take it on the second day and also consider separate visits to **Underground Atlanta** (p. 402), the **World of Coca-Cola** (p. 392), and, most definitely, the new **Georgia Aquarium** (p. 389).

Day 3: Callaway Gardens ★★★ & Warm Springs ★★

In your rented car on Day 3, get an early morning start and drive south of Atlanta for 70 miles. For directions to the **Callaway Gardens** from Atlanta, see "Getting There" on p. 447. The gardens and the hiking trails will take up most of your day, and you can enjoy a picnic lunch on the grounds. Before the afternoon fades, drive 17 miles east of Callaway Gardens to Warm Springs and FDR's **Little White House.** For directions from Callaway Gardens, see "Getting There" on p. 451. You can tour the Little House, where the wartime president, a polio victim, went for the healing waters, and you can also visit the **FDR Memorial Museum.** Accommodations are limited in Warm Springs. You might opt to stay overnight in Callaway Gardens and just drive over and back on an excursion to Warm Springs.

Day 4: Macon, Milledgeville & Augusta ★★

If you move fast enough, you can do a three-city tour in 1 day. Leave Warm Springs in the morning, and take Route 41 south to 80 East, a driving distance of 91 miles, to the city of **Macon,** which is 84 miles southeast of Atlanta. Here allow at least enough time to see the **Georgia Music Hall of Fame** (p. 444) and the elegant **Hay House** (p. 445), in the Italian Renaissance Revival style. After lunch in Macon, head northeast along Route 49 to the town of **Milledgeville,** a distance of 30 miles from Macon.

In **Milledgeville,** pay a call on **Andalusia—Flannery O'Connor's Farm** (p. 417)—where the famous novelist lived until her death in 1964.

Continue east along Route 24 to 88. Then head northeast on Route 1 to the city of **Augusta,** home to the famous Masters golf tournament. The driving

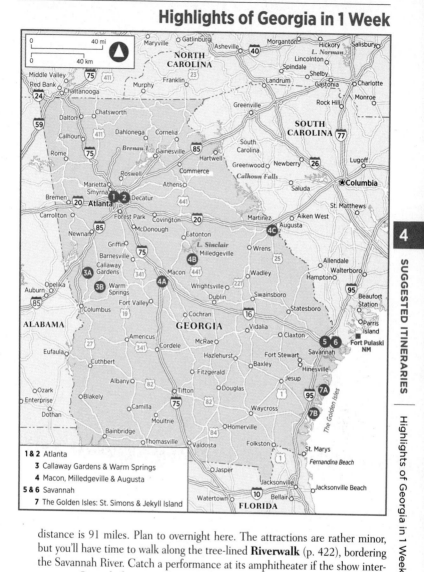

Highlights of Georgia in 1 Week

1 & 2 Atlanta
3 Callaway Gardens & Warm Springs
4 Macon, Milledgeville & Augusta
5 & 6 Savannah
7 The Golden Isles: St. Simons & Jekyll Island

distance is 91 miles. Plan to overnight here. The attractions are rather minor, but you'll have time to walk along the tree-lined **Riverwalk** (p. 422), bordering the Savannah River. Catch a performance at its amphitheater if the show interests you. Or settle for a moonlit stroll.

Days 5 & 6: Savannah ★★★

On the morning of Day 5, leave Augusta, taking Route 25 south to I-16 East, which brings you right into Savannah, a distance of 141 miles.

You'll be based in Savannah for 2 nights. Set out as soon as you check into a hotel to explore the Historic District. The best way to get acquainted is to take one of the **Old Town Trolley Tours** (p. 481) for orientation purposes, if nothing else. In the afternoon, visit the **Mercer Williams House Museum** (p. 479) and the **Telfair Mansion and Art Museum** (p. 478). Select one of the restaurants along the Savannah riverfront for dinner. On the morning of Day 6, take in the **Owen-Thomas House and Museum** (p. 478) and the **Davenport House Museum** (p. 477). In the afternoon, go on one of the Savannah riverboat cruises operated by the **River Street Riverboat Co.** (p. 482). If you finish in time, browse some of the **shops** of Savannah (our coverage of the possibilities begins on p. 484).

Day 7: The Golden Isles: St. Simons ★★ & Jekyll ★★★

Leave Savannah on the morning of Day 7, heading for the town of **Brunswick,** 75 miles to the south. From Savannah, follow the signs to I-95 to the Brunswick turnoff.

Once at Brunswick, follow the signs to the E. J. Torras Causeway, which leads to **St. Simons Island.** Pick up the makings of a picnic in the village along Mallory Street and enjoy it at the south end of the island at **Neptune Park,** where there's a freshwater swimming pool, a play park for the kiddies, and picnic tables. Instead of driving around, we recommend you take the informative **St. Simons Trolley Island Tour** (p. 496).

Back in your car, cross the causeway leading to Brunswick, where you follow Route 17 south for 9 miles to **Jekyll Island;** here you can overnight. Like St. Simons Island, this is mostly an island for play, with its fine beaches and other outdoor pursuits. Drive south on North Beachview Drive to some of the island's 10 miles of public beaches with picnic areas. Try to time your visit to take one of the guided tours of the **Historic District** (p. 504) to see the fabled "cottages" of America's Gilded Age millionaires.

THE OUTER BANKS

They're maddeningly overcrowded in the summer, and development has been rampant over the last 20 years, but North Carolina's Outer Banks (OBX) are unlike anything else along the East Coast. The infamous pirate Blackbeard met his end here, and this is the place where the Lost Colony mysteriously disappeared. On these shores, Virginia Dare was born, and centuries later, Wilbur and Orville Wright learned to fly. The Outer Banks once enjoyed a dubious reputation as "the graveyard of the Atlantic," and to this day, you'll see the many lighthouses that stood vigil over centuries of shipwrecks. You can even see the actual shipwrecks—at several places along the shore, the rusted bones of schooners and cargo ships are mired in the breakers. The East Coast's tallest lighthouse is at Cape Hatteras, and the oldest is at Ocracoke Island. Sand dunes tower over long stretches of undeveloped national seashore, and you can hop a ferry to explore islands where the residents (descended from the Elizabethans) say "hoigh toids" instead of "high tides" and call tourists "comers 'n' goers."

Both the size of fish and the diversity of species have put the Outer Banks on the map as one of the hottest fishing spots in the world. The 80-mile-long Pamlico Sound is a vast estuarine breeding ground for most of the fish caught off the coast, and the Gulf Stream lies just 12 miles offshore—the closest that this fish-laden current comes to land this side of Florida. The water teems with tuna and such trophy fish as blue marlin, white marlin, and sailfish.

Constant winds—the same ones that brought the Wright brothers here in the early 1900s—blow across the Outer Banks, bringing with them invigorating sea air. The area is a recreational playground, with 800 square miles of accessible water. Wind, water, and temperature conditions are right for ideal sailing from early spring until late autumn. And, as any windsurfer can tell you, the best conditions for sailboarding on the East Coast are along the Banks—in particular, at a place called Canadian Hole, on Hatteras Island.

COROLLA TO OREGON INLET

Nags Head: 234 miles N of Wilmington

The Outer Banks—the bony finger of land that separates the Atlantic Ocean from the sounds and estuaries of North Carolina's coast—actually begins near the Virginia border. But much of the northern Banks is accessible only by four-wheel-drive, and residents need a permit to access the area from Virginia. Highway 12, which runs the length of the Outer Banks to Ocracoke, begins near the town of Corolla, not so long ago a sleepy little coastal village with little more than a lighthouse and wild horses. Today it's the Corolla of supersize beach "cottages," shops, and roads. And the number of wild horses, alas, is so greatly diminished that they have become an endangered species.

To the south of Corolla are the largely residential towns of Sanderling, Duck, and Southern Shores, oceanside communities that, like Corolla, have been utterly transformed by development in the last 20 years. Duck, in particular, has gone from a tiny one-stoplight town with a quaint outhouselike post office to a manicured community with multimillion-dollar homes in developments tucked discreetly into dense thickets of island shrub.

Indeed, building has been brisk in the other barrier-island communities south of Duck but north of Oregon Inlet—Kitty Hawk, Kill Devil Hills, Nags Head, Manteo, and Wanchese. But blessedly, there remain miles and miles of fine, clean beaches; good eats; plenty of family entertainment; and wonderful opportunities for water-based recreation.

Essentials

GETTING THERE The 16-mile, four-lane Chesapeake Expressway linking Virginia and North Carolina makes it easier to reach the Outer Banks. The highway links I-64 in Chesapeake, Virginia, to North Carolina and the Outer Banks. The 5¼-mile-long **Virginia Dare Memorial Bridge,** the longest bridge in the state, opened in August 2002, providing a much-needed alternative transportation link between the mainland and the barrier islands. The other routes are from Raleigh, via U.S. 64, and from Wilmington, via the Cedar Island ferry (see "Cedar Island," later in this chapter). N.C. 12 (also called Virginia Dare Trail, or the Beach Rd. from Kitty Hawk to Whalebone Junction) runs the length of the Outer Banks, from Ocracoke to Corolla. The four-lane U.S. 158 Bypass runs from Kitty Hawk to Whalebone Junction.

The nearest airport is 80 miles northwest in Norfolk, Virginia. **Norfolk International Airport** (© 757/857-3351; www.norfolkairport.com) is served by **American Airlines** (© 800/433-7300; www.aa.com), **Continental Airlines** (© 800/525-0280; www.continental.com), **Delta** (© 800/221-1212; www.delta.com), **US Airways** (© 800/428-4322; www.usairways.com), **United Airlines** (© 800/864-8331; www.united.com), and **Southwest Airlines** (© 800/435-9792; www.southwest.com).

You can **rent a car** at Norfolk International Airport from national chains such as **Alamo** (© 800/462-5266; www.alamo.com), **Avis** (© 800/831-2847; www.avis.com), **Budget** (© 800/527-0700; www.budget.com), **Dollar** (© 800/800-3665; www.dollar.com), **Enterprise** (© 800/736-8222; www.enterprise.com), **Hertz** (© 800/654-3131; www.hertz.com), **National** (© 800/227-7368; www.national car.com), and **Thrifty** (© 800/367-2277; www.thrifty.com).

If you're not planning on renting a car for some reason, taking a shuttle or limo is a viable, though expensive, option. For example, the **Connection** (© 252/449-2777; www.calltheconnection.com) offers direct van service from the airport to the Outer Banks. Rates are $135 to $345 for one person, one way, and additional passengers are charged $50 each. **Beach Limousine** (© 252/255-5466; www.obx beachlimo.com) offers private limo service for $95 per hour, and the ride to Nags Head is approximately 2 hours.

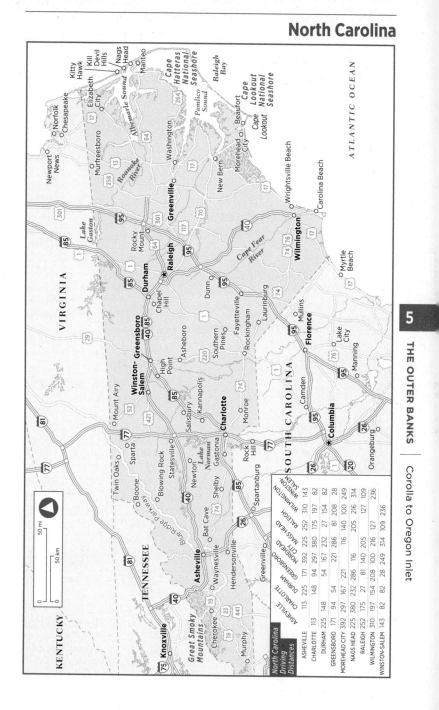

VISITOR INFORMATION Contact the **Outer Banks Visitors Bureau,** 704 S. Hwy. 64/264, Manteo, NC 27954 (© **877/OBX-4FUN** [629-4386]; www.outerbanks. org), for information about accommodations and outdoor activities. The bureau is open Monday to Friday 9am to 5:30pm, and Saturday and Sunday 10am to 4pm.

SPECIAL EVENTS On Roanoke Island, where it all happened, Paul Green's moving drama *The Lost Colony* ★★ is presented in the Waterside Theatre from June to late August, Monday to Saturday at 8:30pm. It's no West End show, but it is the country's oldest outdoor drama, running since 1937. Contact the **Waterside Theatre,** 1409 National Park Dr., Manteo, NC 27954 (© **866/468-7630** or 252/473-3414; www.thelostcolony.org), for Visa or MasterCard bookings. Tickets to the play cost from $10 to $24.

Exploring the Area

Nags Head ★ is the largest resort in the Outer Banks area. Its odd name, according to local legend, comes from the practice of wily old land pirates who used to hang lanterns from the necks of ponies and parade them along the dunes at night to lure unsuspecting ships onto shoals. When the ships ran aground, the waiting robbers promptly stripped their cargoes. Another theory holds that the town was named for the highest point of the Isles of Scilly, which was the last sight English colonists had of their homeland. However it got its name, Nags Head has been one of North Carolina's most popular beach resorts for more than a century. The town is crowded in the summer; roadsides are chockablock with modern motels, restaurants, and watersports stores; and erosion has taken its toll on the once-grand beaches in recent years. Still, it has a barefoot charm, and the many handsome old wooden homes from the late 19th century—known as the "Unpainted Aristocracy"—hearken back to the time when the town was an idyllic seaside retreat.

The highest sand dune on the East Coast—and a hugely popular destination for watching the sunset—Jockey's Ridge, is the focal point of **Jockey's Ridge State Park** (entrance on Carolista Dr., at milepost 12 off U.S. 158 Bypass; © **252/441-7132;** www.jockeysridgestatepark.com). A self-guided trail, stretching for 1.5 miles, begins at the parking lot and goes over the dunes and back. If you don't want to get sand in your shoes, you can take a shorter walk along a 360-foot boardwalk. With its smooth, sandy, 138-foot-high slopes and reliable winds, this is also one of the best hang-gliding destinations in the United States. You can get in a high-flying spirit perhaps in memory of the Wright Brothers by taking a hang-gliding lesson from **Kitty Hawk Kites,** near the park visitor center. This is the world's largest hang-gliding school. For reservations, call © **877/359-8447** or 252/441-4127, or go to www. kittyhawk.com. Beginning, intermediate, and advanced instruction are provided.

Just north of Nags Head is **Kill Devil Hills** (named for a particularly potent rum once shipped from here), where the Wright brothers made their historic first air flight back in 1903 (see "Wright Brothers National Memorial," below).

In Kill Devil Hills, December 12 to December 17, 2003, the **First Flight Centennial** (© **252/491-5165;** www.firstflightcentennial.org) held a celebration of the Wright brothers' 1903 aeronautical feat, featuring a re-creation of the original flight in what is being touted as the only accurate reproduction of the *Wright Flyer.* If you didn't make the celebration, you can browse the First Flight Centennial Photo Album or order the Official First Flight Centennial Video (check the website).

The Outer Banks

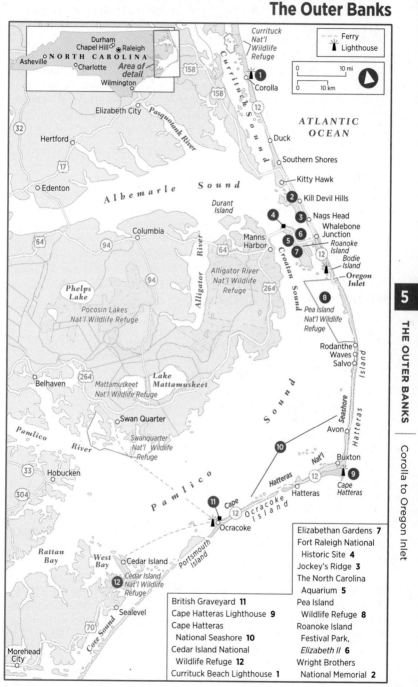

Elizabethan Gardens **7**
Fort Raleigh National
  Historic Site **4**
Jockey's Ridge **3**
The North Carolina
  Aquarium **5**
Pea Island
  Wildlife Refuge **8**
Roanoke Island
  Festival Park,
  Elizabeth II **6**
Wright Brothers
  National Memorial **2**

British Graveyard **11**
Cape Hatteras Lighthouse **9**
Cape Hatteras
  National Seashore **10**
Cedar Island National
  Wildlife Refuge **12**
Currituck Beach Lighthouse **1**

Sights & Attractions

CURRITUCK BEACH LIGHTHOUSE

At Corolla, one of the three working lighthouses on the Outer Banks stands 158 feet above the dunes. It flashed its first beacon on December 1, 1875, filling in that dark spot on the coast between Bodie Island in the south and Cape Henry, Virginia, in the north. Before construction of this lighthouse, whose beam can be seen for 18 miles, many ships foundered in the 80-mile "Sea of Darkness." Weather permitting, the lighthouse can be climbed daily Easter to Thanksgiving 10am to 6pm for $6 ($3 per person for group tours with advance reservations). For more information, call ⓒ 252/453-8152 or go to http://currituckbeachlight.com.

WRIGHT BROTHERS NATIONAL MEMORIAL

The **Wright Brothers National Memorial** (milepost 8, U.S. 158 Bypass, Kill Devil Hills; ⓒ 252/441-7430; www.nps.gov/wrbr) is open to the public. Admission is $4 for adults, free for seniors 62 and older with a valid America the Beautiful Senior Pass, and free for children 16 and under. Both the hangar and Orville and Wilbur's living quarters have been restored, and the visitor center has replicas of the 1902 glider and the 1903 flying machine. Exhibits tell the story of the brothers who came here from their Dayton, Ohio, bicycle business to turn their dream into reality. The memorial is open daily 9am to 6pm (9am–5pm in winter). It is closed Christmas Day. A park ranger gives two tours at 11am and 3pm year-round.

MANTEO & ROANOKE ISLAND

From Whalebone Junction, U.S. 64/264 leads to Roanoke Island and the pastoral village of Manteo, with docks, restaurants, and shops along Shallowbag Bay. Four miles west, you'll reach **Fort Raleigh National Historic Site,** where the fort from 1585 is but a mound of dirt. But the beauty of the landscaped park is reason enough to visit. The **visitor center** (ⓒ 252/473-5772; www.nps.gov/fora) is a first stop; a museum and an audiovisual program acquaint visitors with the park's story. The site is open daily 9am to 5pm (until 6pm in summer). There is no admission charge.

Many people visit Roanoke Island to see a performance of *The Lost Colony* at the Waterside Theatre (see "Special Events," in the "Essentials" section, above, and "The Lost Colony," below). The nearby 11-acre **Elizabethan Gardens,** 1411 National Park Dr., Manteo (ⓒ 252/473-3234; www.elizabethangardens.org), as well as the Tudor-style auxiliary buildings, remind us that this area was the first connection between Elizabethan England and what was to become the United States of America. Admission is $8 for adults, $7 for seniors, $5 for children 6 to 17, and free for children 5 and under. It's open December through February daily 10am to 4pm (closed Christmas Eve, Christmas Day, and New Year's Day), March daily 9am to 5pm, April and May daily 9am to 6pm, June to August daily 9am to 7pm, September daily 9am to 6pm, and October and November daily 9am to 5pm (closed Thanksgiving Day).

Escaping the Hordes

The traffic along the Outer Banks can be maddening in summer. Avoid gridlock by arriving or leaving on days other than Saturday and Sunday, when the weekly rentals begin and end, or by traveling at unusual hours. Most checkouts are at 11am, so the roads get packed around then.

THE LOST COLONY

Roanoke Island, between the Outer Banks and the mainland, is where Sir Walter Raleigh's colony of more than 100 men, women, and children settled in 1585 in what was to be England's first permanent New World foothold. Virginia Dare—granddaughter of the little band's governor, John White—was born that year, the first child of English parents to be born in America. When White sailed back to England on the ships that brought the settlers, it was his intention to return within the year. Instead, because of political events in England, White wasn't able to get back to Roanoke until 1590. What he found on his return was a mystery. The rudimentary houses that he had helped build were all dismantled, and the entire area was enclosed by a high palisade that he later described as "very fortlike." At the entrance, crude letters on a post from which the bark had been peeled spelled out the word CROATOAN.

Because White didn't find the prearranged distress signal—a cross—and no evidence suggested violence, his conclusion was that those he'd left on Roanoke Island had joined the friendly Croatoan tribe. An unhappy chain of circumstances, however, forced him to set sail for England before a search could be made. Despite all sorts of theories about the colony's fate, no link was ever established between the "lost" colonists and the Native Americans. Recent analysis of tree rings has indicated that the colonists may have suffered horrific drought conditions, but no clue has been unearthed revealing exactly what happened.

The **Fort Raleigh National Historic Site** (www.nps.gov/fora) at Roanoke was named in 1941, and its visitor center tells the colony's story in exhibits and film. Paul Green's symphonic drama *The Lost Colony* brings the events to life in the amphitheater at the edge of Roanoke Sound.

The **North Carolina Aquarium** ★, off Hwy. 64/264, Airport Road, north end of Roanoke Island (© **866/332-3475;** www.ncaquariums.com), has expanded to twice its former size. Home to the state's largest ocean tank, the aquarium features hundreds of animals found in North Carolina waters, including rivers, marshes, and sounds. A wooden path takes visitors through a sky-lit atrium complete with towering trees, creeks, and streams. In the natural habitat are creatures of the marsh, including alligators, frogs, turtles, and otters. Bluefish, drum, pinfish, eels, and other sea creatures are exhibited in the Saltwater Gallery. In the Discovery Gallery, a favorite with children, skates, rays, crabs, sea stars, urchins, and other invertebrates can be handled. The centerpiece is the 285,000-gallon ocean tank housing the skeletal remains of the USS *Monitor* shipwreck. Large sharks and sea turtles combine to make this exhibit realistic and spectacular. Hours are daily from 9am to 5pm. Admission is $8 for adults 13 to 61, $7 for seniors and active military, $6 for children 3 to 12, and free for children 2 and under. It is closed Thanksgiving Day, Christmas Day, and New Year's Day.

Visitors journey to Manteo to see the 27-acre **Roanoke Island Festival Park,** which features the *Elizabeth II* (© **252/475-1500;** http://roanokeisland.com), moored across from the renovated waterfront. This 69-foot-long three-masted bark, a composite design of 16th-century ships, was built in 1984 with private funds for the 400th anniversary of the 1584 and 1587 Roanoke voyages. From mid-June to late August, Tuesday to Saturday, living-history interpreters portray colonists and mariners. The site is open February 18 to March 31 daily 9am to 6pm, April to November 1 daily 9am to 6pm, and November 9 to December 31 daily 9am to 5pm (closed Dec 24–26). Admission is $8 for adults and seniors, $5 for students 6 to 17, and free for children 5 and under.

SIDE TRIP: EDENTON, COLONIAL WATERFRONT TOWN

About 1½ hours away from Nags Head, a later phase of U.S. history is preserved at **Edenton ★**, an atmospheric old town whose streets are lined with homes built by the planters and merchants who settled along the Albemarle Sound. The women of Edenton held their own "tea party" in 1774—one of the first recorded instances of American women taking political action. Take U.S. 64, turn right at N.C. 37, and then turn left when you reach N.C. 32.

Visit the **Historic Edenton Visitor Center** at 108 N. Broad St. (signs are posted throughout the town; ☏ 252/482-2637; www.nchistoricsites.org/iredell) to view a free 14-minute slide show and purchase a Historic District map. The center is open Monday to Saturday 9am to 5pm and on Sunday 1 to 4pm. Guided tours of five historic buildings—the 1767 Chowan County Courthouse, the 1758 Cupola House, the 1780s Barker House, the 1800/1827 James Iredell House State Historic Site, and the restored St. Paul's Episcopal Church—can be booked here for $10 for adults, $2 for students under 18, and $20 per family (free for preschool children). From April to October, tours are Monday to Saturday 9am to 5pm and Sunday 1 to 5pm, off season Monday to Saturday 10am to 4pm and Sunday 1 to 4pm.

Beaches & Outdoor Pursuits

BEACHES The coterie of northern-bank beaches include those at Kitty Hawk, Kill Devil Hills, and Nags Head, all of which lie along the Beach Road (N.C. 12). Ferocious tides, strong currents, and fickle, constantly changing winds alter the beach scene from day to day on the Outer Banks, and that wide beach you see today may be narrower tomorrow. Water temperatures in summer average in the 70s (20s Celsius), sometimes at the low point. On a glorious July day, the cool, clean seawater and fresh salt air riding the constant winds make beach-going a fine, invigorating experience.

Signs direct you to the various small (and too-often-inadequate) parking lots in the vicinity of the dunes. Toilets, showers, bathhouses, and picnic shelters line some 70 miles of beaches here, many at public beach-access parking lots.

FISHING **Nags Head Fishing Pier,** milepost 12, Beach Road, Nags Head (☏ **252/441-5141;** www.nagsheadpier.com), has its devotees, who rent rod and reel for $6 per day. The pier itself is open to fishermen. The fee is $10 for adults, $5 for

---

📎 Beach Safety

The very conditions that make beach-going so pleasant here can make ocean swimming hazardous at times, with strong riptides and undertows. All beach areas theoretically have roving lifeguards and supervisors, but hours and locations are subject to change without notice. Caution flags are flown if swimming is not advised. A red warning flag means that swimming is prohibited; take heed of these warnings even if the water doesn't look particularly rough. Nonswimmers are advised to wear some sort of flotation device and should not go out past the breakers alone. Finally, if you see lightning or hear thunder, leave the beach for safe shelter immediately.

children, and $1.50 for sightseers. From Memorial Day to Labor Day, the pier is open daily 24 hours; off season it is open daily 6am to midnight.

GOLF A popular course is **Nags Head Golf Links,** 5615 S. Seachase Dr., Nags Head (© **252/441-8073;** www.clubcorp.com), with an 18-hole, 6,126-yard, par-71 course that's open daily 7am to 6pm. Greens fees, including the use of a mandatory cart, range from $40 to $135. Reservations are required. At the clubhouse, you'll find a restaurant and a pro shop.

NATURE WALKS **Nags Head Woods Preserve,** 701 W. Ocean Acres Dr., off U.S. 158, milepost 9.5 (© **252/441-2525;** www.nature.org), is a fine example of a mid-Atlantic maritime forest. The seashore includes 640 acres of protected wetlands, dunes, and hardwood forest, and is a National Natural Landmark.

At **Jockey's Ridge State Park,** milepost 12 on U.S. 158 (© **252/441-7132;** www.jockeysridgestatepark.com), you'll find the East Coast's highest sand-dune formation. This 400-acre park makes you feel that you're traversing the Sahara, with its self-guided nature trail through sifting sands and blowing winds. Park at the northern rim of the park.

WATERSPORTS **Kitty Hawk Watersports Sailing Site,** Bypass Highway, milepost 16, Nags Head (© **800/948-0759** or 252/441-6800; www.kittyhawk sports.com), offers watersports equipment. Windsurfers, in particular, flock here, renting equipment for $25 per hour, $55 per 3 hours, or $69 for a full day. WaveRunners cost $90 to $95 for a full hour. You can rent kayaks, for $29 to $45 per half-day, for a trip along the waterways. Toilets and picnic facilities are on-site, and the center is open daily from 9am to 6pm.

Windsurfing Hatteras, N.C. 12, Avon (© **866/995-6644** or 252/995-5000), rents a wide range of watersports equipment. Two-hour kayak rentals range from $25 to $35; surfboards rent for $25 a day, $40 a week; windsurfing gear is available for 24-hour rental at $40 for the board alone or $65 for a full rig. In addition, a 2-hour introductory windsurfing class is offered for $59.

Where to Stay

Although the beaches are lined with cottage rentals, many of them are spoken for on a year-to-year basis, so it's essential to make reservations well in advance. If you'd like to settle down for a week or more, your best bet is to contact the **Outer Banks Visitors Bureau** (see "Essentials," earlier in this section). It is also worth noting that a good number of national motel chains, along with numerous independently owned lodges, are dotted along the coastline and can provide adequate accommodations if you're traveling without reservations.

Nags Head, Kill Devil Hills, and Kitty Hawk are so close together that you can choose your accommodations according to style and facilities rather than by location. Duck, about 18 miles north of Nags Head, is the site of an exceptional seaside hotel that's well worth the short drive.

Another option is **camping.** For information on private campgrounds, contact the Outer Banks Visitors Bureau (see "Essentials," earlier in this section).

IN DUCK

Advice 5¢ ★ 🏨 As an alternative to the more expensive Sanderling, this B&B lies in the heart of Duck, close to shops and restaurants. It's a small, casual place but a choice one. It's located in the tranquil neighborhood of Sea Pines between the ocean and Currituck Sound. Dating from 1995, Advice 5¢ is thoroughly modernized, with spacious and well-furnished guest rooms, most with private bathrooms with tub and shower plus sun decks. One room has a shower (no tub), and the one suite features a Jacuzzi-style bathtub. There's a pool at Sea Pines and a tennis court, plus a private walkway from Sea Pines to a good beach. The breakfast goodies are baked from scratch.

111 Scarborough Lane, Duck, NC 27949. © **800/238-4235** or 252/255-1050. www.advice5.com/ Advice5/Welcome_to_Advice_5_in_Duck_NC.html. 5 units. $155–$265 double. MC, V. No children 16 and under. **Amenities:** Breakfast room. *In room:* TV (in some), Internet (free).

The Sanderling Resort & Spa ★★★   Composed of a complex of three large, beach-house-style buildings, with a separate annex containing two restaurants and bar (and another restaurant across the street), this resort and spa was established in 1985. It is one of the most affluent and eco-sensitive pockets of posh in the Outer Banks, and one of the three great resorts in the entire state. At the narrowest point of the archipelago, on a manicured set of lawns close to the 3,400-acre Pine Island National Audubon Sanctuary, it features a postmodern design that emulates an 18th-century plantation house, complete with weathered shingle siding and wraparound verandas. The allure is calm, sedate, and soothing, all within a sand-and-sea-colored enclave that contains more Carolina pinewood trim than virtually any other recently built hotel in the country. Guest rooms are filled with deep carpets, deep upholsteries, and an almost overwhelming sense of serenity. In addition to suites, four ocean-front villas have three to four bedrooms each, with such luxurious features as a covered garage and outdoor showers. Public areas contain majestic spiraling staircases, blazing fireplaces, and what's reputed to be $2 million worth of bird and animal sculptures by a locally famous artist named Grainger McKoy. The **Lifesaving Station** restaurant is recommended separately in "Where to Dine," below.

1461 Duck Rd., Duck, NC 27949. © **877/650-4812** or 252/261-4111. Fax 252/261-1638. www.sanderling inn.com. 88 units. June 25–Sept $250–$500 double, $500–$550 suite, from $950 villa; off season $110–$375 double, $250–$400 suite, from $600 villa. Additional person $50. Rates include continental breakfast. AE, DC, DISC, MC, V. Take N.C. 12 about 5 miles north of Duck. **Amenities:** 2 restaurants, including Lifesaving Station (see review, p. 101); 2 bars; exercise room; room service; spa. *In room:* A/C, TV, hair dryer, kitchenette, minibar, Wi-Fi (free).

IN EDENTON

The Captain's Quarters Inn   Only 3 blocks from Albemarle Sound, the lovely Captain's Quarters Inn offers nautical-themed guest rooms decorated with antiques. Built in 1907, its rooms have four-poster, canopy, brass, or wicker beds; two are decorated with beautiful handmade quilts. The Captain of Her Heart room has a two-person Jacuzzi tub with a full shower. Award-winning chef and owner Diane Pariseau and her husband, Don, present gourmet meals. Relax in the swing on the 65-foot wraparound porch while enjoying your afternoon tea and homemade treats. Ask about the Sail and Dine, Golf and Dine, Mystery Weekends, and Golf and Sail packages. While Visa and MasterCard are accepted, cash or personal checks are preferred at checkout. Holiday weekends require a 2-night minimum stay. Children 8 and older are welcome.

202 W. Queen St., Edenton, NC 27932. © **800/482-8945** or 252/482-8945. Fax 252/482-5314. www. captainsquartersinn.com. 8 units. $125 double; $135 Captain of Her Heart room. Rates include breakfast. MC, V. No children 7 and under. **Amenities:** Dining room. *In room:* A/C, TV, Wi-Fi (free).

Trestle House Inn ★ 🏠   Overlooking a pond and lake fed by the Albemarle Sound, the Trestle House Inn was built in 1972 as a 7-acre retreat, surrounded on three sides by water and on the fourth side by an 88-acre wildlife refuge that's ideal for bikers, birders, canoeists, and fishermen. Host Peter L. Bogus has maintained the true tradition of the retreat since he became the innkeeper in 1996. The interior is highlighted by massive beams of California redwood and cedar. Before they became part of the Trestle House Inn, the beams were actual train trestles for the Southern Railway Company. The rooms—Osprey, Cormorant, Mallard, Heron, and Egret—are named for the grand birds that can be viewed from the windows of the respective units. Spacious and furnished with antiques, the rooms contain twin beds or two double beds, or a queen- or king-size bed. The management can arrange day trips and tours in either Edenton or the Outer Banks.

632 Soundside Rd., Edenton, NC 27932. ✆ **800/645-8466** or 252/482-2282. Fax 252/482-7003. www.trestlehouseinn.com. 5 units. $99–$134 double. Additional person $20 per day. Rates include full gourmet breakfast. AE, DISC, MC, V. **Amenities:** Breakfast room; lounge. *In room:* A/C, no phone, Wi-Fi (free).

IN KILL DEVIL HILLS

Cypress House Inn ★   This historic B&B dates from the 1940s, when it was first constructed as a hunting and fishing lodge. An aura of the Outer Banks "as it used to be" is still preserved here, as evoked by its soft cypress tongue-and-groove paneled walls and ceilings. The midsize guest rooms have an old-fashioned feel with white ruffled curtains, ceiling fans, and cheery but comfortable furnishings. Guests gather around the fireplace in the public lounge, and a large wraparound porch is just right for absorbing the seascapes. A hearty home-baked breakfast and afternoon tea are served in the dining room.

500 N. Virginia Dare Trail, Kill Devil Hills, NC 27948. ✆ **800/554-2764** or 252/441-6127. Fax 252/441-2009. www.cypresshouseinn.com. 7 units. $99–$199 double. Rates include breakfast. AE, DISC, MC, V. No children 13 and under. **Amenities:** Dining room; lounge. *In room:* A/C, TV, fridge, hair dryer, no phone, Wi-Fi (free).

Ramada Plaza Nags Head Beach ★ ☺   Directly on the beach, this is one of the largest and most substantial oceanfront hotels. It is convenient to many of the area attractions, including the Lost Colony and Kitty Hawk. The midsize bedrooms are immaculately kept and well furnished, each with a private balcony overlooking the water. There is also an on-site full-service restaurant with oceanview seating, and a lounge that features weekend entertainment. Some rooms contain a Jacuzzi, and units offer two double beds, making the hotel one of the most family friendly in the Outer Banks—although there are no specific programs for children.

1701 S. Virginia Dare Trail, Kill Devil Hills, NC 27948. ✆ **800/272-6232** or 252/441-2151. Fax 252/441-1830. www.ramada.com. 171 units. $95–$168 double. AE, DC, DISC, MC, V. **Amenities:** Restaurant; bar; free health club nearby; room service. *In room:* A/C, TV, hair dryer, minibar, Wi-Fi (free).

IN MANTEO

Roanoke Island Inn   Nestled in one of the most spectacular gardens in town, this white-sided clapboard house dates to the 1860s. Each of several subsequent generations has added on to the core to create the rambling, graciously appointed Colonial Revival home it is today. In 1992, a hip and urbanized new generation of family members, headed by John Wilson, added big-city gloss to the place with a sophisticated array of *trompe l'oeil* murals in an Italian Renaissance theme, adding greatly to the establishment's sense of cutting-edge allure. Guest rooms are stately, even imperial, in their appointments, with glowing hardwoods, louvered or Venetian blinds, and many concessions to the 18th-century aesthetic of the Outer Banks.

305 Fernando St., PO Box 970, Manteo, NC 27954. ✆ **877/473-5511** or 252/473-5511. Fax 252/473-1019. www.roanokeislandinn.com. 8 units. $138–$198 double; $178–$238 suite. Rates include breakfast. AE, MC, V. **Amenities:** Breakfast room; Wi-Fi (free). *In room:* A/C, TV.

Scarborough House Inn   This charming inn does much to recapture the feel of old-time Roanoke Island. Each unit is filled with antiques, including netting draped over four-poster beds, and a beautifully maintained private bathroom. Each is also stocked for a continental breakfast. For many, the most desirable rental is the cottage loft with a whirlpool. The owners, Phil and Sally Scarborough, are islanders whose roots in the Outer Banks go back centuries, with ancestors who were boat builders, fishermen, and craftsmen. Practically the whole Scarborough family at one time or another has appeared in the long-running stage drama *The Lost Colony.* Living here is comfortable and laid-back, with rocking chairs on the porch. Gleaming pine floors and local artifacts add to the allure. *Note:* Children are permitted only in the guesthouse.

323 Fernando St., PO Box 1310, Manteo, NC 27954. © **252/473-3849.** www.scarboroughhouseinn.com. 5 units. High season $100–$105 double, $115 cottage, $125 guesthouse; low season $60–$85 double, $70–$85 cottage, $100 guesthouse. Rates include continental breakfast. MC, V. No children except in the guesthouse. *In room:* A/C, TV, fridge, hair dryer.

The Tranquil House Inn ★★   Though we prefer the Sanderling in Duck (see the Sanderling Resort & Spa, above), the Tranquil House Inn, sheathed in weather-beaten cedar shingles, is our second choice on the Outer Banks. A weather-beaten three-story structure, this waterfront resort resembles those old seaboard inns that were part of 19th-century Manteo; yet it dates from 1988. Rear porches face the water, boats bob at anchor in the marina, and an entranceway opens onto the charming historic core of Manteo. Guest rooms are spacious and furnished with reproductions of antiques. Bikes are available for guests during daylight hours, and wine and cheese are served each evening from 5 to 6pm.

The hotel's **1587 Restaurant** offers not only excellent Continental and *cuisine moderne* dishes, but also a water view. See "Where to Dine," below.

405 Queen Elizabeth St. (PO Box 2045), Manteo, NC 27954. © **800/458-7069** or 252/473-1404. Fax 252/473-1526. www.1587.com. 25 units. May 14–Sept 6 $199–$239 double; off season $109–$189 double. Rates include continental breakfast. AE, DISC, MC, V. Take U.S. 158 south to Whalebone Junction in South Nags Head, then U.S. 64/264 6 miles west to Manteo. The inn is on the harborfront. (Turn right at the 1st traffic light onto Sir Walter Raleigh St.) **Amenities:** Restaurant (see review, p. 103); bar; room service. *In room:* A/C, TV, hair dryer.

The White Doe Inn ★★   Built in 1898 as the Meekins' family home, this old-fashioned inn is now on the National Register of Historic Places. The wraparound porch, where you are likely to meet fellow guests absorbing the breezes, sets the tone of the place. Its Queen Anne architecture is so appreciated that many nonguests pause to photograph it. The innkeepers welcome you with down-home friendliness into one of their "bedchambers," which are furnished with antiques or reproductions and often have century-old architectural features. Gas fireplaces evoke a return to yesterday, but modern amenities include whirlpools and private bathrooms with claw-foot tubs. A satisfying three-course Southern-style breakfast is the highlight of the day. *Note:* Children 11 and under are not welcome.

319 Sir Walter Raleigh St., Manteo, NC 27954. © **800/473-6091** or 252/473-9851. Fax 252/473-4708. www.whitedoeinn.com. 8 units. Summer $232–$335 double; off season $175–$290 double. MC, V. Children 12 and older are welcome. **Amenities:** Breakfast room; bike rentals; spa. *In room:* A/C, TV, hair dryer, Wi-Fi (in some free).

IN NAGS HEAD

Cahoons Cottages   Low slung, weather beaten, and separated from the surf by a sand dune anchored tenuously with fragile scrub grasses, this cluster of simple cottages was built in stages between 1948 and 1968, in a postwar unpretentiousness many jaded travelers find endearing. Modern building codes prevent equivalent structures from being constructed directly on the dunes, so a stay here is a retro-charming kind of holiday: Expect not a smidgeon of grandeur in these bungalows awash with sun-bleached wooden porches, faux-wood paneling, and battered but comfy furniture. Of the 11 cottages, two are efficiencies and one is a bungalow. Each unit has its own kitchen and two, three, or four bedrooms.

7213 S. Virginia Dare Trail, milepost 16.5, Nags Head, NC 27959. ✆ **252/441-5358.** Fax 252/441-1734. www.cahoonscottages.com. 11 cottages. Summer $575–$1,400 per week; off season $350–$750 per week. DISC, MC, V. *In room:* A/C, TV, kitchen or kitchenette.

The First Colony Inn ★★   This impressive three-story inn near the ocean was constructed in 1932 and has a wraparound veranda with rocking chairs. It was built without the help of an architect, which might explain why the veranda is almost as big as the interior space. The finest inn in the area, it is owned by Alan Lawrence and his family. It has received AAA's rating of four diamonds and is listed on the National Register of Historic Places. The interior is furnished with reproductions of turn-of-the-20th-century items. Units with sitting areas are also available. Grills and picnic tables are on hand for guests' use on the 4½-acre grounds, and a private access leads across the highway to the beach, known for its sea breezes and seemingly endless gentle dunes.

6720 S. Virginia Dare Trail, Nags Head, NC 27959. ✆ **800/368-9390** or 252/441-2343. Fax 252/441-9234. www.firstcolonyinn.com. 26 units. Summer $229–$329 double; off season $79–$249 double. Rates include breakfast and afternoon tea. AE, DC, DISC, MC, V. **Amenities:** Breakfast room; bar; outdoor pool; room service. *In room:* A/C, TV, hair dryer, kitchenette, Wi-Fi (free).

The Nags Head Inn ★   Don't let the word *inn* mislead you. This is a thoroughly modern and well-kept hotel, one of the best in the area. Right on the oceanfront, it offers fairly luxurious and spacious rooms, with private balconies opening onto the view. In a sea of chain hotels, the inn is independently owned and nestled on 450 feet of sand dunes, beach, and well-kept lawns and gardens. One of its finest amenities is a heated oceanfront indoor pool along with a large spa and sun deck. The staff is among the most helpful in the area.

4701 S. Virginia Dare Trail, Nags Head, NC 27959. ✆ **800/327-8881** or 252/441-0454. Fax 252/441-0454. www.nagsheadinn.com. 100 units. Late May to Labor Day $154–$260 double. Children 12 and over $10 extra; children 11 and under stay free in parent's room. Off-season discounts available. AE, DISC, MC, V. **Amenities:** Indoor pool; spa. *In room:* A/C, TV, fridge, hair dryer, Wi-Fi (free).

Where to Dine
IN DUCK
The Lifesaving Station ★ COASTAL/SEAFOOD   Although it's one of two premier dining enclaves in the most upscale and exclusive resort in the Outer Banks, something is refreshingly simple—even spartan—about this place. Much of it derives from its origins in 1879 as a government-funded rescue station, when lifeguards and mariners set out from here to rescue crew and passengers from ships foundering on the region's notoriously treacherous shoals. Look for memorabilia associated with the 1899 heroic rescue of the barkentine *Priscilla* that earned the site national attention. A brass bell from the original rescue station is prominently displayed. Top-quality ingredients go into the masterful dishes where sauces or other adornments never overpower the natural flavors. The chef likes to cook in the New South style, suggesting a lighter cuisine. A signature chowder is made with corn, scallions, and shrimp. You might also enjoy crispy tempura-battered fish and oysters with a tangy rémoulade, or one of the daily

seafood and pasta specials. The chocolate raspberry crème brûlée is divine. On the second floor, the **Swan** bar's severe dignity evokes an antique schoolhouse.

In the Sanderling Inn Resort and Spa, 1461 Duck Rd. ✆ **800/701-4111** or 252/261-4111. www.sanderling inn.com. Reservations recommended. Main courses $3.95–$14 lunch, $14–$25 dinner. AE, DC, DISC, MC, V. Sun–Thurs 7:30am–2:20pm and 5–9pm; Fri–Sat 7:30am–2:20pm and 5–9:30pm.

IN KILL DEVIL HILLS

Flying Fish Café SEAFOOD/CONTINENTAL   Open only for dinner, the Flying Fish Café is a cut above many other North Carolina coastal restaurants for featuring not only delicious seafood, but steak, chicken, and succulent veal chops as well. We started our evening with Thai coconut shrimp bisque, followed by golden-fried calamari tossed in lemon-garlic sauce, served with marinara. For our main course, we opted for the pan-fried Carolina crab cakes with homemade corn pudding and black-bean salsa. Guests who don't like seafood might try the seared filet mignon with Gorgonzola crust, or the free-range chicken breast stuffed with Gruyère and fresh asparagus. The restaurant is open year-round.

2003 S. Croatan Hwy. (milepost 10). ✆ **252/441-6894.** www.flyingfishcafeobx.com. Main courses $24–$31. AE, DC, MC, V. Daily 5–10pm.

Outer Banks Brewing Station AMERICAN/FUSION   Every item from sushi to vegetarian fare appears on the menu at this modern eatery. Along with the fresh catch of the day, there's always a freshly made soup (perhaps she-crab) as well as an appetizer special of the day. Although the menu is varied—including steaks cooked as you like them, succulent pastas, and chicken and steak dishes—fried, steamed, or broiled seafood is the way to go. Home-brewed beer is the drink of choice here, of course, and the friendly waitstaff will gladly help you pair beer with your meal. Save room for one of the luscious homemade desserts, especially the cheesecake or peach cobbler. If live entertainment, especially C & W music, isn't featured, a DJ rules the tunes heard throughout the largest bar on the Outer Banks.

600 S. Croatan Hwy. (milepost 8.5 on the Bypass). ✆ **252/449-2739.** www.obbrewing.com. Main courses $6–$12 lunch, $14–$30 dinner. AE, DISC, MC, V. Daily 11:30am–10pm.

IN KITTY HAWK

Rundown Cafe & Tsunami Surf Bar CARIBBEAN/PACIFIC RIM/AMERICAN Tired of all those fried fish? Then give this place a chance to enliven your taste buds with something different. Its freshly made salads are the best in the area, and you can order them house style, or else with meat toppings (chicken, steak), and also seafood toppings (calamari, shrimp, or tuna). The lunch crowd often fills up on these salads along with juicy burgers or seafood. Chef's specials appear on the dinner menu, as do vegetarian selections. The raw bar and the steamer bar are superb, and Caribbean and Pacific Rim dishes dominate the dinner selections. Microbrews are served along with a martini menu, and drink specials rule the night, including the Shark Attack with grenadine that is served in a plastic shark. This Caribbean-style joint opens onto the beach road, and is found when you come over the bridge from the mainland.

5218 N. Virginia Dare Trail (milepost 1; Beach Rd., across from Kitty Hawk Pier). ✆ **252/255-0026.** Main courses $10–$16. AE, DISC, MC, V. Mon–Sat 11am–10pm; Sun 11:30am–10pm.

IN MANTEO

Darrell's ☺ SEAFOOD   Since 1960, Darrell's has been the family favorite for fresh seafood. The day begins early as both locals and tourists show up for delights such as pecan hot cakes and crabmeat omelets. Locals cite the fried oysters as their favorite dish, and it comes with all the fixin's, including creamy coleslaw and golden hush puppies. Clam chowder or oyster stew is always on the menu at lunch along with a barbecue plate or broiled scallops. Some of the best sandwiches along the coast are dished out here, and children's plates are also available. At night, the most popular choices are seafood dinners, ranging from the broiled catch of the day to farm-raised catfish. Typical Southern proteins such as pork chops and fried chicken are also served, as well as family-style takeout dinners.

523 S. U.S. Hwy. 64/264. © **252/473-5366.** Main courses $2.95–$11 breakfast, $3.95–$13 lunch, $12–$21 dinner. AE, DISC, MC, V. Mon–Sat 11am–8:30pm.

1587 Restaurant ★★ AMERICAN   This restaurant offers the best creative cuisine along the Outer Banks. Expect a sense of relaxed chic and elegant food in a subtly lit, nautically inspired setting, with expensive boats bobbing at anchor in the nearby marina. Preface your meal with a drink at the convivial bar, where a bar top sheathed in polished copper reflects the faces and voices of many of the town's amicable locals. Good food and service await you here, and the menu is more sophisticated than most in the area. The best examples include sesame-seared sea scallops with a soy-and-wasabi-flavored cream sauce and sautéed tiger shrimp in a charred tomato butter sauce with artichoke hearts, kalamata olives, prosciutto, and Fontina cheese, atop a crisp puff pastry. Main courses might include grilled tuna steak over Asian shrimp fried rice, surrounded by wasabi vinaigrette and topped with marinated hearts of palm and matchstick vegetables. A vegetarian menu is also available.

In the Tranquil House Inn, 405 Queen Elizabeth St. © **800/458-7069** or 252/473-1587. www.1587.com. Reservations recommended. Main courses $17–$31. AE, MC, V. Daily 5–9pm.

IN NAGS HEAD

Fat Boyz ★ BURGERS/AMERICAN   This takeout joint is aptly named, but Fat Boyz arguably serves the best burgers along the Outer Banks, most of which say to hell with cholesterol, especially such specialties as the bacon cheeseburger with lots of mayo. You might also choose a crab-cake sandwich, chili cheese dog, or a Carolina barbecue pork sandwich with creamy coleslaw. The eatery takes the prize for such retro desserts as butterscotch sundaes and banana splits—and Elvis would love the banana and peanut butter milkshakes. The "flurries" are sin itself, especially the chocolate slammer (a vanilla shake with chocolate syrup and Oreos cookies). Grab your food to go, or eat outside at one of the handful of picnic tables on the covered porch.

Milepost 16.5, Beach Rd. © **252/441-6514.** Sandwiches $4.30–$8; burgers $3.50–$6.50. MC, V. Daily 11am–11pm.

Fishermen's Wharf ★ SEAFOOD   At the south end of Roanoke Island, overlooking the harbor, this restaurant serves the freshest seafood around. It also has a connected retail seafood market. Founded in 1974, it started out serving about 50 diners per day; today that number has grown to about 500. Lunch sandwiches range from fresh local fish filet to a crab-cake delight, everything served with coleslaw and hush puppies. Dinners are more elaborate, including a gargantuan seafood platter with just about everything. Other menu items might include (depending on what's in the larder on the day of your arrival) Miss Maude's crab cakes, a "big" seafood platter, fresh-caught tuna, local flounder, sea scallops, and various preparations of shrimp. Virtually anything you order here can be fried, broiled, or blackened to your taste.

Roanoke Island, N.C. 345, Wanchese. © **252/473-6004.** www.fishermanswharfobx.com. Main courses $7–$15 lunch, $12–$26 dinner. DC, DISC, MC, V. Mon–Sat 11:30am–3pm and 4–9pm.

Sam & Omie's SEAFOOD   A father-son partnership established this eatery in the 1930s as a spot where fishermen could get a rib-sticking breakfast before heading out onto the high seas. Today it's a deliberately downscale, endlessly raffish place that has attracted most of North Carolina's leading, and most notorious, politicians—as well as locals who like the quintessentially funky Outer Banks vibe. There's a convivial bar area where old salts and young beauties alike mingle, and a series of pinewood banquettes where copious portions of well-prepared seafood are always in demand. Though a little played-out and overcrowded these days, it still offers hefty doses of local color, a sense of folksy authenticity, and food items that include marinated tuna steaks served either as a platter or as a sandwich, she-crab soup, fried locally caught oysters, crab cakes, and burgers. This is a popular breakfast spot (expect a wait). It's also an early-to-bed kind of place; the last food order is accepted at 10pm, and the bar closes shortly thereafter.

7228 S. Virginia Dare Trail, milepost 16.5. ℂ **252/441-7366.** www.samandomies.net. Reservations not accepted. Breakfast $3.95–$13; main courses $4.95–$10 lunch, $11–$21 dinner. DISC, MC, V. Mon–Sat 7am–10pm; Sun 7am–9pm. Closed Thanksgiving–Mar 1.

CAPE HATTERAS NATIONAL SEASHORE ★★

From Whalebone Junction in South Nags Head, Cape Hatteras National Seashore stretches 70 miles south down the Outer Banks barrier islands. The drive along N.C. 12 (about 4½ hr.) takes you through a wildlife refuge and pleasant villages, past miles of sandy beaches untainted by commercial development, and on to Buxton and the Cape Hatteras Lighthouse, the tallest on the coast. Since 1870, the light has been a beacon for ships passing through these treacherous waters, which have claimed more than 1,500 victims by means of foul weather, strong rip currents, and shifting shoals. This is where the ironclad Union gunboat *Monitor* went down during a storm in December 1862.

From the little village of Hatteras, a car ferry crosses to **Ocracoke Island,** where more than 5,000 acres, including 16 miles of beach, are preserved by the National Park Service for recreation. From the southern end of the island, you can take a ferry across the vast, shallow Pamlico Sound to **Cedar Island.**

The seashore is best explored on an all-day trip, or on several half-day trips from a Nags Head base. Give yourself plenty of time for swimming, fishing, or just walking along the sand and for visiting the newly moved Cape Hatteras Lighthouse. It's an informal, barefoot kind of place—you can easily beach hop from one shimmering beach to another; just pull into any of the many beach-access parking lots, cross a small boardwalk over dunes of sea oats, and plop yourself in the tawny sand or race to the surf. Then have lunch (a crab-cake sandwich, perhaps, and a bowl of Hatteras-style clam chowder) and get to know the local people who call this patch of sand home. The hardy "Bankers" can recount tales of heroism at sea and tell you about the ghostly light that bobs over Teach's (Blackbeard's) Hole, as well as the wild ponies that have roamed Ocracoke Island for more than 400 years—all in a lilting accent that some people say harks back to Devon, England, home base of a band of shipwrecked sailors who came ashore here and stayed.

Visitor Information

You can get more information at one of the following national park facilities: the **Bodie Island Visitor Center,** Bodie Island Lighthouse, 6½ miles south of Whalebone Junction (© **252/441-8144;** www.outerbankschamber.com; daily 9am–6pm in summer, 9am–5pm all other times), or the **Hatteras Island Visitor Center,** Cape Hatteras Lighthouse, Buxton (© **252/995-4474;** www.hatterasguide.com; daily 9am–6pm in summer, 9am–5pm all other times). Contact the **Superintendent, Cape Hatteras National Seashore,** Route 1, Box 675, Manteo, NC 27954, for information about accommodations and outdoor activities.

Exploring the Area

Turn left off N.C. 12 about 8 miles south of U.S. 158 to reach **Coquina Beach,** which offers bath shelters, lifeguards (mid-June to Labor Day), picnic shelters, and beach walks guided by National Park Service naturalists. Back on N.C. 12, to the southwest you will soon see the 156-foot-tall black-and-white-striped **Bodie Island Lighthouse,** in operation since 1872.

Two miles south, the **Herbert C. Bonner Bridge** cuts an elegant swath over the waters of Oregon Inlet; look down to see anglers wrestling with puppy drum on the spits of sand beneath the bridge. Across Oregon Inlet, the 5,834 acres of **Pea Island National Wildlife Refuge** (© **252/473-1131;** www.fws.gov/peaisland), on Hatteras Island (the northern part, south of Bonner Bridge), attract birders from all over the country to see snow geese in winter and wading shore and upland birds in summer. Some 265 species of birds winter here. There's a parking area and raised platforms. The wildlife refuge, 10 miles south of Nags Head, is open daily 9am to 4pm; admission is free.

All along N.C. 12, you'll see places to pull off and park to reach the beaches, which are hidden from view by huge protective sand dunes. *Note:* Don't try to park anywhere else; the sands are very soft, and it's easy to get stuck.

Warning: Whether you're camping or just stopping at beaches where there are no lifeguards, you should always keep in mind that tides and currents along the Outer Banks are *very* strong, and ocean swimming can be dangerous at times.

When you get to Buxton, turn left off N.C. 12 to see the famed **Cape Hatteras Lighthouse** (© **252/473-2111;** www.nps.gov/caha). The iconic lighthouse was reopened to the public in 2000 following a massive relocation effort, which moved the lighthouse back 2,900 feet to save it from toppling into the encroaching sea. Its rotating duplex beacon has a 1,000-watt, 250,000-candlepower lamp on each side and is visible for 20 miles. The lighthouse is open May 1 until October 19, 9am to 5pm. Climbing passes for the lighthouse are $7 for adults, $3.50 for seniors and children 12 and under. Tickets can be purchased in person, on-site, the day of the climb.

The little town of **Avon** makes the best stopover for dining (see below). Historically named Kinnakeet, the town was renamed Avon when a post office was established here in 1883. Today, Avon, with its two traffic lights, is home to lots of rental properties on the oceanfront, with easy beach access.

The village of **Hatteras** ★ exists now, as it has from the 1700s, as a fishing center, with large commercial and sport fleets operating from its docks and marinas. In the spring and fall, boats bring in catches of sea trout, king and Spanish mackerel, red drum, and striped bass. In summer, most of the action is offshore, where blue marlin and other billfish are in plentiful supply. If you're interested in doing some fishing yourself, the Outer Banks Chamber of Commerce can supply a list of charter boats and fishing information. Even if you don't fish, it's fun to watch the boats come in between 4 and 6pm.

Outdoor Pursuits

Hatteras Island Fishing Pier, 24251 Atlantic Ave., Rodanthe (© **800/331-6541** or 252/987-2323; www.hatterasislandresort.com), stretches 653 feet into the Atlantic. The fee for fishing is $10 for adults and $5.75 for children; the fee for sightseeing is $1 per person. Fishers can rent rod and reel from the bait shop for $7.50 per day, plus a refundable $30 deposit. Live and artificial bait are available, along with the necessary tackle. At the beach end of the pier is a restaurant, plus toilets, a motel, and cottages for rent. The pier is open April 1 to December 31, from 7am to 11pm.

Windsurfers flock to the area—and especially to **Canadian Hole,** between Avon and Buxton, so named for its popularity among Canadian windsurfers. The best place to get hooked up with gear is the **Hatteras Island Surf Shop,** N.C. 12, Waves (© **866/HIB-WAVE** [442-9283]; www.hiboardsports.com), open Monday to Saturday 9am to noon and 3 to 6pm, and on Sunday 10am to 6pm. Windsurfing equipment is available for rent for $20 per hour, surfboards for $15 per day, and boogie boards for $8 per day.

Where to Stay

Cape Hatteras Bed & Breakfast ★ 🏠   In the town of Buxton, directly north of Hatteras, this relatively unknown inn is down a quiet lane just a stone's throw from the beach. Two miles south of the East Coast windsurfing site of Canadian Hole, this welcoming and thoroughly modernized house has an array of amenities. Each guest room is handsomely maintained, containing a private bathroom with shower and a private entrance. Oddly, the rooms are named after famous hurricanes that have brought destruction to the Outer Banks—talk about paying homage to the enemy. It's a casual place, with guests meeting and exchanging tips on the sun deck or from the beach chairs. There are also outdoor showers for your return from the beach. The owners are proud of their Hatteras-style breakfast—fit fortification for the day.

46223 Old Lighthouse Rd., PO Box 490, Buxton, NC 27920. ©/fax **800/252-3316** or 252/995-6004. 10 units. $105–$139 double. Rates include full breakfast. MC, V. **Amenities:** Dining room; lounge. *In room:* A/C, TV, no phone, Wi-Fi (free).

Where to Dine

Mack Daddy's Restaurant ★ SEAFOOD   If you linger for a few days along the Outer Banks, this casual eatery is likely to be your preferred choice for dining. The food is market fresh, especially the catch of the day. Sit next to locals as you dig into the crab cakes (jumbo lump crab) with a Cajun jambalaya, or the best shrimp and grits we've had along the coast. The seafood lasagna is a delectable choice for pasta lovers. A limited number of poultry and meat dishes are offered, such as the organic chicken breast coated in a black pepper crust and served with buttermilk mash potatoes. Chef Seth Foutz comes from a long line of family cooks, and he's a master at deftly handling the bounty from land or sea. There's also a raw bar.

Hwy. 12, Avon. © **252/995-5060.** www.mackdaddysobx.com. Reservations not accepted. Main courses $12–$22. MC, V. Daily 5–10pm.

OCRACOKE ISLAND ★★

From Hatteras, a free car ferry crosses the inlet to **Ocracoke Island** in 40 minutes; during the peak summer tourist season, the line may be long, so you'll need to get there early to get a place.

Ocracoke has shown up on maps as far back as the late 1500s, when Sir Walter Raleigh's Roanoke Island party landed here. It's rumored to have been the last headquarters of Blackbeard, who died here. The wily pirate, after years of terrorizing merchant ships along the Atlantic coast, made his peace with the British crown in 1712 and received a full pardon from the king. Soon thereafter, however, he came out of retirement and resumed preying on ships from the Caribbean to the Virginia capes, working hand in glove with the colonial governor, Charles Eden, and colonial secretary Tobias Knight.

When Ocracoke Island was isolated from the mainland and few visitors came by boat, as many as 1,000 wild ponies roamed its dunes. Where they came from—shipwrecks, early Spanish explorers, or English settlers—is uncertain. Eventually, as more and more people traveled to and from the island, many ponies were rounded up and shipped to the mainland. The remnants of the herd (about two dozen) now live at the **Ocracoke Pony Pens,** a range 7 miles north of Ocracoke village, where the National Park Service looks after them.

In a quiet little corner of Ocracoke Island, you'll find a bit of England: the **British Graveyard,** where four British seamen are buried. Their bodies washed ashore after the HMS *Bedfordshire* was torpedoed by a German submarine in 1942. The graveyard is leased by the British government but is lovingly tended by townspeople.

Ocracoke village has seen some changes since World War II, when the U.S. Navy dredged out Silver Lake Harbor (still called "Cockle Creek" by many natives) and built a base here. They also brought the first public telephones and paved roads. In spite of the invasion of 20th-century improvements and the influx of tourist-oriented businesses, Ocracoke is essentially what it has always been: a fishing village whose manners and speech reflect its 17th-century ancestry.

Where to Stay

The Anchorage Inn & Marina   This four-story hotel, completely modern and up-to-date, lies near the entrance to Silver Lake Harbor. It's an island favorite, mainly because of its good-size, comfortably furnished rooms, which open onto some of Ocracoke's best views. The sunsets over Pamlico Sound, of course, are better the higher up your room: We prefer the fourth-floor rooms with balconies. An elevator services all floors. Boaters and fishermen are fond of this place because of its easy access to the harbor. The hotel also operates a dockside cafe adjacent to its swimming pool at the marina, and grills and picnic tables are outside for do-it-yourself cooks. Even nonguests can enjoy the Anchorage's raw bar, which offers fresh local clams, oysters, shrimp, and the catch of the day.

Hwy. 12 at Anchorage Marina, Ocracoke, NC 27960. © **252/928-1101.** Fax 252/928-6322. www.the anchorageinn.com. 35 units. Summer $139 double, $250 suite; low season $89 double, $189–$219 suite. Rates include continental breakfast. AE, DISC, MC, V. **Amenities:** Restaurant; bike and scooter rentals; outdoor pool. *In room:* A/C, TV, hair dryer, kitchenette or full kitchen (in suite).

TWO CUTS TO BLACKBEARD'S NECK

The British expected their American colonies to produce *profits*—as in having the colonists grow the raw materials that factories in Great Britain would use to produce the goods, which the colonists, in turn, would buy at inflated prices. To make sure that this happened, Parliament enacted a series of import duties designed to keep cheaper goods made elsewhere out of its colonies. The tax levies, which later fomented revolutionary sentiment, helped bring about the so-called golden age of piracy between 1689 and 1718. What better way to get duty-free goods than through smuggling? And who better to do it than the pirates who stole the loot in the first place?

Edward "Blackbeard" Teach and others began by roaming the Caribbean, legally plundering French and Spanish ships during Queen Anne's War from 1701 to 1713. But they kept at their trade after the war, so, in 1718, the British navy chased them out of the area. Blackbeard relocated to the tangled web of islands and shifting shoals along the North Carolina coast. Teach's cheap smuggled goods were welcomed, and some colonial officials—including Gov. Charles Eden, for whom Edenton is named—were suspected of helping him make a little money.

But the folks down in South Carolina felt differently because they were now the pirates' prime targets. When Blackbeard struck Charleston in June 1718, looting merchant ships at anchor and taking hostages for ransom, the South Carolinians had had enough. Over the next 2 months, South Carolinians caught and hanged 20 pirates. Two Royal Navy sloops from Virginia under Lt. Robert Maynard eventually found Blackbeard—off Ocracoke Island at dawn on November 22, 1718. Blackbeard and half his crew of 18 were killed during fierce hand-to-hand combat. The survivors were taken to Virginia and executed.

The incident was reported in the *Boston News-Letter:* "One of Maynard's men, being a Highlander, ingaged [sic] Teach with his broadsword, who gave Teach a cut of the Neck, Teach saying well done, Lad, the Highlander reply'd, if it be not well done, I'll do it better, and with that he gave him a second stroke, which cut off his head, laying it flat on his shoulder."

Maynard sailed back to Virginia with Blackbeard's head hanging from his ship's rigging to warn pirates that their golden age was over. Still, tales persist of treasure stashed away along the North Carolina coast, but none has ever been found; Blackbeard likely sold his spoils quickly and squandered the proceeds.

Cove Bed & Breakfast   Staying here is like being in a private home. Each of the tastefully decorated guest rooms or suites has an immaculate private bathroom. With such names as Dolphin or Sandpiper, the midsize to spacious rooms are comfortably furnished, often with four-poster beds. Suites have whirlpool tub/showers. Guests can enjoy their own private balcony, or meet fellow guests while sitting on the screened-in porch. The day begins with one of the most scrumptious breakfasts on the island. Jim and Mary Ellen Piland welcome guests from all over America and treat them to true Outer Banks hospitality.

21 Loop Rd., Ocracoke, NC 27960. ☏ **252/928-4192.** Fax 252/928-4092. www.thecovebb.com. 6 units. High season $175 double, $225 suite; low season $125 double, $175 suite. Rates include continental breakfast and wine reception. MC, V. Children 14 and under not welcome. **Amenities:** Bike and kayak rentals. *In room:* TV, hair dryer, no phone.

The Ocracoke Harbor Inn   Built in 1998, this three-story hotel is one of the most up-to-date, comfortable, and inviting inns on the island. Its front guest rooms open onto Silver Lake Harbor, and guests often sit out on the porches to take in the views. Private decks allow you to take in the sunset as well, perhaps with a cocktail. The waterfront deck is where continental breakfast can be enjoyed as the Ocracoke fishermen depart in their boats for the day. Guest rooms, small to midsize, are attractively furnished in a vaguely Caribbean style, and the seven suites offer a separate bedroom and a queen-size sleeper in the living room. Special features of the suites are kitchenettes and Jacuzzis. The hosts also offer boat docking and a patio deck with charcoal and gas grills, should you want to try your hand at a North Carolina barbecue.

144 Silver Lake Rd., Ocracoke, NC 27960. **888/456-1998** or 252/928-5731. Fax 252/928-6260. www. ocracokeharborinn.com. 23 units. Summer $105–$160 double, $175–$235 suite; spring–fall $99–$139 double, $155–$210 suite; winter $80–$120 double, $130–$180 suite. Additional person $10. Rates include continental breakfast. AE, DISC, MC, V. **Amenities:** Restaurant; bike and boat rentals; fitness center. *In room:* A/C, TV, fridge, hair dryer, Wi-Fi (free).

The Thurston House Inn ★ 🍴   For some 75 years, this cedar-shake cottage (ca. 1920s) was the home of native guide Capt. Thurston Gaskill, who took visitors into the wilds of Ocracoke on fishing and hunting expeditions. Today the sun-filled B&B is a modern addition next to the original cottage. At this inn, you don't have to rough it to enjoy Ocracoke; the rooms are state-of-the-art, with queen- or king-size beds, feather comforters, spacious private bathrooms with showers, and an elegant, understated feel. The inn is just off the town's main road in a grove of oak trees and flowering shrubs; you can breakfast in the shade on one of the cottage porches.

Hwy. 12, Ocracoke Island, NC 27960. **252/928-6037.** www.thurstonhouseinn.com. 6 units. $95–$155 double. Rates include continental breakfast. AE, DISC, MC, V. No children 11 and under. **Amenities:** Airport pickup (free). *In room:* A/C, TV, Wi-Fi (free).

Where to Dine

Back Porch ★★ SEAFOOD/AMERICAN   Offering something more ambitious than other restaurants in Ocracoke, Back Porch emphasizes fresh local seafood and is a great favorite among islanders. Tables are set on an elegant screened-in porch and in the air-conditioned dining room. All the dishes have a down-home flavor. Fish is prepared plain or else "tarted up" with interesting combos like Vietnamese lime sauce, pineapple salsa, or balsamic brown butter. We love the crab cakes in pepper sauce and smoked bluefish appetizers. The sumptuous Back Porch seafood platter is justifiably a favorite and includes baked fish, sautéed shrimp, and a deep-fried crab beignet. The scrumptious desserts—a calories-be-damned selection—and the fresh breads are baked daily in the kitchen.

110 Back Rd. **252/928-6401.** www.backporchrestaurant.com. Main courses $16–$31. MC, V. Daily 5–9:30pm.

Howard's Pub and Raw Bar Restaurant SEAFOOD/AMERICAN   There's more lore associated with this place, and a greater sense of community among its devoted fans, than any other restaurant on Ocracoke Island. Set inside an imposing but weather-beaten building that's the first major business you'll see after heading south from the Hatteras Ferry landing, it occupies the site of what flourished briefly in the 1850s as a pub (Howard's) before it sank into the sands of this reputedly haunted island. Inside the mostly wooden interior, you'll find a cheerful staff that's

Before the Civil War, **Portsmouth** ★ was a thriving little community of some 700 souls. It proudly boasted the first maritime hospital and the first lifesaving station. But when Jefferson Davis ordered that Confederate troops be stationed here during the Civil War, Portsmouth's fate was sealed. Union forces bombarded the island, and most residents fled elsewhere. After the war, the shoaling in of Portsmouth inlet and the coming of the steamboat drove away its final business—the island's harbor was too small for steamboats.

Today the National Park Service maintains the quaint buildings still standing, including a church, a general store, and a lifesaving station, but it's a ghost town. From Ocracoke village you can take two daily guided tours on all-terrain vehicles (ATVs) offered by **Portsmouth Island ATV Excursions** (✆ 252/928-4484; www.portsmouth islandatvs.com), costing $85 per person, six-person maximum per trip (reservations are recommended). Service is from April 1 until the end of November. Do-it-yourselfers can go less expensively by taking one of the **Portsmouth Island boat tours** (✆ 252/928-4361; www.portsmouthnc.com), costing $25 for a half-day for adults and $13 for children 6 to 12. Reservations must be made 1 day in advance. Once at Portsmouth, swimming, fishing, shelling, and bird-watching are diversions.

proud of the establishment's self-sufficiency—thanks to their own generators, they've provided sustenance to famished locals even in the aftermath of hurricanes. Menu items include burgers, steaks, fresh oysters and shellfish, barbecued ribs, grilled fish, Maine lobster, and massive amounts of shrimp.

Local ordinances restrict the serving of hard liquor by the glass, so as a means of compensating, Howard's stocks the largest selection of beer—more than 200 kinds—on the Outer Banks. The bar is the single most popular rendezvous point on the island, serving drinks and good cheer every night.

Hwy. 12. ✆ **252/928-4441.** www.howardspub.com. Salads and sandwiches $5–$11; main courses $14–$25. DC, DISC, MC, V. Daily 11am–2am.

CEDAR ISLAND

You can get to more southerly beaches in leisurely fashion by taking the car ferry from Ocracoke to Cedar Island. You'll need to make a reservation for the 2¼-hour trip over the calm, sparkling waters of the Pamlico Sound. Take along a picnic lunch, and don't be surprised to see dolphins cavorting alongside the boat. Call to reserve space on one of the scheduled sailings. To sail from Cedar Island or Ocracoke, call ✆ **800/293-3779** or visit www.ncdot.org. *Note: Reservations are not honored if your car is not in the loading zone at least 30 minutes before departure time.* The fare is $15 to $30 per car and occupants, $3 per bicycle and rider, and $1 for pedestrians. For a complete list of ferries, schedules, and fares, contact the **Ferry Division,** Department of Transportation, 113 Arendell St., Morehead City, NC 28557 (✆ **252/726-6446;** www.ncdot.org).

On the island, you can explore the **Cedar Island National Wildlife Refuge** (© **252/926-4021;** www.fws.gov), a feeding ground for migratory waterfowl. Since 1964, this refuge has taken in 11,000 acres of irregularly flooded and brackish marsh, with such plants as saltmeadow hay, needlerush, and salt-marsh cordgrass. The land is a winter habitat for thousands of ducks and a nesting habitat for colonial water birds. Endangered species such as the American alligator and the brown pelican find a safe haven here.

Where to Stay & Dine

Driftwood Motel & Restaurant 🗡 Simple yet cozy, this budget-minded motel is a 3-minute walk from the beach. The lobby is on the second floor, above the first-floor gift shop, which has items in the expected nautical theme. Rooms are traditional motel, and the biggest amenity is the low price. The motel also maintains a restaurant, serving lunch from 11am to 2:30pm and dinner nightly from 5 to 9pm. The fare is adequate, with enough seafood and Continental dishes to satisfy everyone in your party. Try the cream of crab soup, the fried oysters, or homemade desserts, such as lemon meringue pie. Barbecue is also popular here.

3575 N. Cedar Island, NC 28520. © **252/225-4861.** Fax 252/225-1113. www.clis.com/deg. 37 units. $85 double. Rate includes continental breakfast. Children $10 extra. AE, DISC, MC, V. **Amenities:** Restaurant; bar. *In room:* A/C, TV.

WILMINGTON & THE SOUTHERN BANKS

The Southern Banks are dominated by the town of Wilmington, which boasts some 200 restored city blocks, forming one of the largest such districts in the National Register of Historic Places. Wilmington is the gateway to the Cape Fear coast, which, in spite of its ominous-sounding name, is filled with azalea gardens and sun-dappled plantation houses.

Base yourself along the Southern Banks (also known as the Crystal Coast), in historic old Beaufort, in Morehead City, or in a cottage along the string of beaches from Atlantic Beach to Emerald Isle, to sun and swim in the ocean or visit area attractions. Or stay in Wilmington, to see plantations and gardens, Fort Fisher, and fine beaches.

If you're thinking about camping, you will find campgrounds throughout the region. But you should know in advance that they're flat and sandy, with no shade, and that you'll need tent stakes longer than you'd normally use. Also, no hookups are provided. Sites are available on a first-come, first-served basis, and the maximum stay is 14 days from mid-April to September 10. For private campgrounds in the area, which do have hookups, call the tourist offices listed.

WILMINGTON ★ & CAPE FEAR ★

123 miles SE of Raleigh

As the chief port of North Carolina, Wilmington is a major retail, trade, and manufacturing center, but tourism is looming larger than ever in its economy. Known first as New Carthage and then as New Liverpool, New Town, and Newton, this city was given its present name in 1739 in honor of the earl of Wilmington. Technically, it's inland a bit, at the junction of the Cape Fear River's northeast and northwest branches. Despite the treacherous shoals that guarded the mouth of Cape Fear when explorers first arrived in 1524, upriver Wilmington developed into an important port for goods shipped to and from Europe during colonial days.

The city's history is evident in the old residential section of town, on the grounds of Orton Plantation, in the excavated foundations of Brunswick town houses, and in the blockade-runner relics at Fort Fisher.

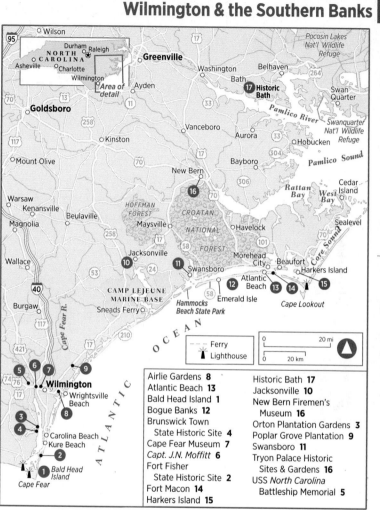

Airlie Gardens **8**
Atlantic Beach **13**
Bald Head Island **1**
Bogue Banks **12**
Brunswick Town
    State Historic Site **4**
Cape Fear Museum **7**
Capt. J.N. Moffitt **6**
Fort Fisher
    State Historic Site **2**
Fort Macon **14**
Harkers Island **15**

Historic Bath **17**
Jacksonville **10**
New Bern Firemen's
    Museum **16**
Orton Plantation Gardens **3**
Poplar Grove Plantation **9**
Swansboro **11**
Tryon Palace Historic
    Sites & Gardens **16**
USS *North Carolina*
    Battleship Memorial **5**

Boasting one of the largest districts listed in the National Register of Historic Places, Wilmington is known for its preservation efforts, which are reflected in the grandeur of its restored antebellum, Victorian, Georgian, and Italianate homes.

During both world wars, Wilmington was a major port for naval supplies. Today the river is busier than ever with industrial shipping. In recent years, a thriving new industry has developed: filmmaking. Ever since 1983, when Dino De Laurentiis came here to film *Firestarter,* Wilmington has been a major site for the movie industry, hosting the production of more than 400 movie features, miniseries, and TV movies. In fact, according to a survey by the International Association of Film Commissioners, Wilmington generated more film revenue than any U.S. city except Los Angeles and New York—giving rise to its nickname "Hollywood East." Among the films made in Wilmington are *Divine Secrets of the Ya-Ya Sisterhood, Forrest Gump, I Know What You Did Last Summer, Sleeping with the Enemy, Before Night Falls,* and *Bread and Tulips;* the TV series *One Tree Hill* is filmed on location here.

Essentials

GETTING THERE   You can reach Wilmington via I-40, U.S. 117, and U.S. 421 from the northwest; U.S. 74/76 from the west; and U.S. 17 from the northeast and south.

Wilmington International Airport, 1740 Airport Blvd. (© **910/341-4125;** www.flyilm.com), lies half a mile from the center of town. Taxis meet arriving planes. The airport is host to the following major and commuter airlines: **US Airways** (© **800/ 428-4322;** www.usairways.com) and **A.S.A. Delta Connection to Atlanta** (© **800/ 282-3424;** www.delta.com).

Greyhound (© **800/231-2222;** www.greyhound.com) offers regular service to Wilmington. The **bus station** is at 201 Harnett St. (© 910/762-6073).

VISITOR INFORMATION   The **Cape Fear Coast Convention and Visitors Bureau,** 24 N. 3rd St., Wilmington, NC 28401 (© **877/406-2356** or 910/341-4030; www.cape-fear.nc.us), offers free brochures on the many attractions and accommodations of the Cape Fear Coast. The efficient staff can provide a self-guided walking-tour map of historic Wilmington and background details on other area attractions. The center is open Monday to Friday from 8:30am to 5pm, on Saturday from 9am to 4pm, and on Sunday from 1 to 4pm.

SPECIAL EVENTS   The **North Carolina Azalea Festival** (© **910/794-4650;** www.ncazaleafestival.org), held in early April, is the city's most-frequented event. City gardens burst into bloom, and the festivities include garden tours, beauty pageants, and a parade. The dogwoods get almost as much attention as the azaleas. Call or visit the website for more details.

Seeing the Sights

IN TOWN

To get an overview of the historic Wilmington waterfront, hop aboard the *Henrietta III* ★ (© **800/676-0162** or 910/343-1611; www.cfrboats.com), which departs from Dock and South Water streets for a 5-mile loop of the Cape Fear River. The 45-minute narrated cruise skirts the busy harbor, passes the Cotton Exchange and the Riverfront Park, and stops at the dock for passengers who want to disembark to tour the battleship USS *North Carolina* (see "Sights Nearby," below). The season runs from April to October; tours depart daily at 11am and 2pm. Call for availability of Monday cruises. The fare is $10 for adults and $5 for children 2 to 12. It also offers murder-mystery cruises, evening party cruises, and nature cruises, among others.

The **Cotton Exchange** (© **910/343-9896;** www.shopcottonexchange.com), an in-town shopping center, is in the old exchange building, with 2-foot-thick brick walls and hurricane rods. The small shops and restaurants are a delight, and the wrought-iron lanterns and benches add to the setting's charm. It's right on the riverfront, and an ample parking deck is just next door. Shops are open Monday to Saturday 10am to 5:30pm. Some shops are also open on Sunday noon to 4pm.

In Historic Wilmington—the old residential area bounded roughly by Nun, Princess, Front, and 4th streets—the **Burgwin-Wright House,** 224 Market St. (© **910/ 762-0570;** www.burgwinwrighthouse.com), was constructed in 1771 and used by

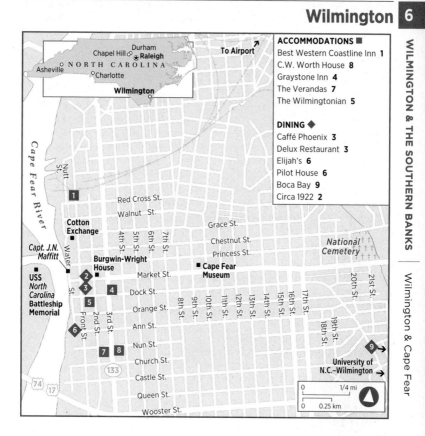

ACCOMMODATIONS ■
Best Western Coastline Inn **1**
C.W. Worth House **8**
Graystone Inn **4**
The Verandas **7**
The Wilmingtonian **5**

DINING ◆
Caffé Phoenix **3**
Delux Restaurant **3**
Elijah's **6**
Pilot House **6**
Boca Bay **9**
Circa 1922 **2**

Cornwallis as his headquarters in 1781. The colonial town house was built over an abandoned city jail. You can tour the interior Tuesday to Saturday 10am to 4pm. Admission is $10 for adults, $4 for children 5 to 12, and free for children 4 and under.

Airlie Gardens   Once the plantation home of a wealthy rice planter, these 67-acre Gilded Age gardens are surrounded by huge lawns, serene lakes, and wooded gardens that hold just about every kind of azalea in existence. The blooms are at their height in the early spring, but even when they're faded, this is a lovely spot. Unveiled in 2007, an open-air greenhouse is home to some 20 native species of butterflies, and visitors can watch them as they take flight. Guides are on hand to give you tips on re-creating a small-scale butterfly garden in your own backyard.

300 Arlie Rd., U.S. 76. 𝄢 **910/798-7700.** www.airliegardens.org. Admission $5 adults, $3 children 6–12, free for children 5 and under. Apr–Oct daily 9am–5pm; off season Mon–Sat 9am–5pm. Take U.S. 76 toward the beach and look for the signpost.

Cape Fear Museum   This museum showcases the history, science, and culture of the lower Cape Fear region from prehistoric times to the present. Noteworthy are Civil War artifacts and dioramas of the Battle of Fort Fisher and the Wilmington

115

The longer the movie industry continues to operate in the city, the more the business of making movies draws tourists itching to pay a few bucks to see where films are made. **EUE/Screen Gems Studios,** headed by Frank Capra, Jr., offers tours of its studio, the largest full-service film lot outside California (1223 N. 23rd St.). If you're coming from U.S. 17/74, go straight on Dawson Street and take a left onto 17th Street; follow the airport signs to the corner of 23rd Street and Martin Luther King Jr. Parkway. For more information, directions, and group reservations, call ℂ **910/343-3500** or check the website at www.euescreengems.com. Because this is a *working* studio, and not set up as a tourist attraction, tours may be canceled because of production schedules. The hour-long tours are at noon on Saturday from September to May, and on Saturday and Sunday at noon and 2pm from Memorial Day to Labor Day. Tickets cost $12 for adults and $5 for children 11 and under.

waterfront from around 1863. Children will be interested in the discovery gallery and various hands-on activities.

814 Market St. ℂ **910/341-4350.** www.capefearmuseum.com. Admission $6 adults, $5 seniors and college students, $3 children 3-17. Memorial Day to Labor Day Mon-Sat 9am-5pm, Sun 1-5pm; off season Tues-Sat 9am-5pm, Sun 1-5pm.

SIGHTS NEARBY

Fort Fisher State Historic Site ★ One of the Confederacy's largest and most technically advanced forts, Fort Fisher was the last stronghold of the Confederate army. Following the defeats at Savannah and Mobile, Confederate general Robert E. Lee depended solely on Fort Fisher for supplies. President Lincoln recognized that to end the war, Fort Fisher would have to be taken. After withstanding two of the heaviest naval bombardments of the Civil War, the fort finally fell to Union forces in what was the largest land-sea battle in U.S. history until World War II. The unconditional Confederate surrender came only 3 months after the fall of Fort Fisher. The visitor center exhibits artifacts of that era, and there's an audiovisual program as well. Costumed tour guides welcome visitors, and living-history events are depicted during the summer.

Kure Beach. ℂ **910/458-5538.** www.nchistoricsites.org. Free admission. Apr-Sept Mon-Sat 9am-5pm, Sun 1-5pm; Oct-Mar Tues-Sat 9am-5pm. Follow U.S. 421 south to Kure Beach.

Poplar Grove Plantation This restored Greek Revival manor house and estate dates from 1850. The outbuildings include a smokehouse, tenant house, and old kitchen. Attractions include demonstrations by a basket weaver, a fabric weaver, and a blacksmith.

10200 U.S. 17. ℂ **910/686-9518.** www.poplargrove.com. Admission $10 adults, $9 seniors, $5 children 6-15. Mon-Sat 9am-5pm; Sun noon-5pm. Take U.S. 17 9 miles northeast of Wilmington.

USS North Carolina Battleship Memorial The USS *North Carolina* was commissioned in 1941 and is permanently berthed here as a memorial to the state's World War II dead. The ship and brave crew fought in every major naval offensive in the Pacific during World War II, making the vessel the most decorated U.S. battleship of WWII and winning it 15 battle stars. You can tour most of the ship, and the Exhibit Hall houses a "through their eyes" exhibit focusing on recollections of the battleship's former crew. The ship is still painted in its 1944-to-1945 camouflage. A visitor center offers a large gift shop and snack bar.

Eagle Island. © **910/251-5797.** www.battleshipnc.com. Admission $12 adults, $10 seniors 65 and over, $6 children 6–11, free for children 5 and under. June–Aug daily 8am–8pm; off season daily 8am–5pm. On Cape Fear River across from the Historic District at junction of Hwy. 17/74/76/421. Easily accessible from I-95 or I-40.

Beaches & Outdoor Pursuits

BEACHES   The main summer target is **Wrightsville Beach ★** (© **800/650-9106** or 910/256-8116; www.visitwrightsville.com), 6 miles east of Wilmington on U.S. 74/76—and don't expect to have the beach to yourself during the high season. The island is separated from the mainland by a small drawbridge. A year-round residence for some 3,200 dwellers, Wrightsville Beach, once known only as "the Banks," is the widest beach on the Cape Fear coast, stretching for a mile along the oceanfront, its beige sands set against a backdrop of hearty vegetation such as sea oats. The south end isn't ideal for swimming; you'll find better conditions between the rebuilt Johnnie Mercer Pier and Crystal Pier (patrolled by lifeguards in summer).

Another good spot is **Carolina Beach State Park** (© **910/458-8206**; www.ncparks.gov/Visit/parks/cabe/main.php), sprawling across 1,770 acres 10 miles north of Wilmington off U.S. 421. This beach, flanked on one bank by the Cape Fear River and on the other by the Intracoastal Waterway, lies at the northern edge of aptly named Pleasure Island. The significance of the park lies not in the beach—in fact, swimming is not allowed—but in the natural flora, including the rare Venus' flytrap and other insect-eating plants, which abound in the swamp forest. The park has 5 miles of hiking trails. Facilities include toilets, a marina, a picnic area, and a family campground.

At the southern tip of Pleasure Island is the small, family-friendly community of **Kure Beach** (www.visitkure.com). From here, you can see Cape Fear River and the Atlantic Ocean. The white-sand beaches are generally uncrowded, restaurants are informal, and the Kure Beach fishing pier is a magnet for anglers. You can wander through the remains of Fort Fisher (see "Sights Nearby," above).

FISHING   **Batson's Charter Boats,** Carolina Beach (© **910/367-2317;** www.carolinabeachcharterfishing.com), departs from the Carolina Beach Municipal Marina, offering trolling and bottom-fishing charters. The charter boat can accommodate up to six fishers besides the crew. Prices are $400 for 5 hours, $790 for 8 hours, and $1,050 for 10 hours; rates include rod, reel, and bait.

GOLF   The **Belvedere Country Club,** 2368 Country Club Dr., Hampstead (© **910/270-2703**), has one of the best and most popular courses in the Wilmington area, offering a par-72, 6,315-yard, 18-hole course open daily from 7am to 7pm. From Monday to Thursday, greens fees are $36 before 11am, $31 from 11am to 2pm, and $26 after 2pm. Friday to Sunday, greens fees are $40 before 11am, $36 from 11am to 2pm, and $32 after 2pm. Clubs can be rented from $10 to $20 for 18 holes. Tee-time reservations are requested. Facilities include a clubhouse, a restaurant, and a pro shop. Professional instruction is available at $50 per hour. The club lies 15 miles outside Wilmington. Take U.S. 17 north to Hampstead (about 10 miles), and continue on the same route the final 4½ miles.

SCUBA/SNORKELING   The best outfitter is **Aquatic Safaris & Divers Emporium,** 6800-1A Wrightsville Ave. (© **910/392-4-FUN** [4386]; www.aquaticsafaris.com). Hours are Monday to Saturday 10am to 5pm, Sunday noon to 4pm.

6 Where to Stay

The **Cape Fear Coast Convention and Visitors Bureau** (see "Essentials," above) will do more than just send you its *Accommodations Guide*. If you're in the market for an apartment or cottage for a week or more (a dollar-saving approach that's hard to beat), write well in advance, describing just what you have in mind. The bureau will circulate your requirements in a bulletin that goes to area owners and managers, who will then contact you directly.

Campers can check out the **Camelot Campground,** 7415 Market St., Wilmington, NC 28411 (℃ **888/562-5699** or 800/454-7705; www.koacampingnc.com/wilmington), which sits on 43 wooded acres on U.S. 17. Facilities include a pool, recreation room, playground, laundry, and grocery store, and propane gas is available for stoves. Rates range from $35 for tent sites to $55 for full hookups.

Best Western Coastline Inn Next door to the Coastline Conference & Event Center, this inn was designed to complement the restored historic rail depot that it's named for. The adjacent full-service restaurant actually occupies one of the original railroad buildings and has a popular bar and periodic live entertainment. The inn's rooms all have good views of the Cape Fear River. Some units, such as the Overlook Suite, afford two river views.

503 Nutt St., Wilmington, NC 28401. ℃ **800/617-7732** or 910/763-2800. Fax 910/763-2785. www.coastlineinn.com. 53 units. $119–$169 double; $179–$249 suite. Rates include continental breakfast. AE, DC, DISC, MC, V. **Amenities:** Restaurant; exercise center; room service. *In room:* A/C, TV, hair dryer, Wi-Fi (free)

C.W. Worth House This 1893 Victorian three-story B&B is a real escape from the modern world. The decorative motif matches the Victorian design of the structure, with rooms furnished in 19th-century antiques. One unit, dubbed the Louisiana Room, breaks the mold with an all-French design. Children 10 and under are not admitted. A TV is provided in the sitting room.

412 S. 3rd St., Wilmington, NC 28401. ℃ **800/340-8559** or 910/762-8562. Fax 910/763-2173. www.worthhouse.com. 7 units. $144–$184 double. Each additional person $25. Rates include full breakfast. AE, DISC, MC, V. Free parking. No children 10 and under. **Amenities:** Breakfast room; lounge. *In room:* A/C, hair dryer, Wi-Fi (free).

Graystone Inn ★★ This is the grandest of Wilmington's B&B inns. A neoclassical stone mansion from 1905, it offers 12- to 14-foot ceilings and Victorian-period furnishings. It has a large three-story portico and a grand staircase made of hand-carved red oak. A formal dining room, where breakfast is served; the original drawing room and music room; and a library lined with old volumes take you back in time. All the handsomely furnished guest rooms are on the third floor.

100 S. 3rd St., Wilmington, NC 28401. ℃ **888/763-4773** or 910/763-2000. Fax 910/763-5555. www.graystoneinn.com. 7 units. $169–$279 double; $229–$379 suite. Rates include full breakfast. AE, DC, DISC, MC, V. Free parking. No children 11 and under. **Amenities:** Dining room; exercise room. *In room:* A/C, TV, hair dryer, Wi-Fi (free).

The Verandas ★ One of the most appealing and fairly priced B&Bs in Wilmington is a stately, white-sided mansion that, with eight units, is one of the largest owner-occupied guesthouses in town. It was built in 1853 by a local merchant and then transformed into a convent in the 1860s. A century later, the then-dilapidated building was the site of Wilmington's most popular whorehouse before a devastating fire in 1992 reduced its back side to a smoldering ruin. Three years later, after a radical restoration rebuilt it from its studs, adding modern infrastructures and lots of antiques, it blossomed into an utterly charming inn. Each unit is a corner room flooded with sunlight. The second-floor rooms are grander than those on the third floor, which are deliberately cozier and less formal. Children 11 and under are not encouraged.

202 Nun St., Wilmington, NC 28401. © **910/251-2212.** www.verandas.com. 8 units. $169–$269 double. AE, DC, DISC, MC, V. **Amenities:** Breakfast room; Wi-Fi (free). *In room:* A/C, TV, hair dryer.

The Wilmingtonian ★★   This renovated 1906 commercial building is rightly regarded as the premier inn of Wilmington, although sparse on public amenities. Actually, it's a glorified B&B in which all the rooms are suites. The suites on the second and third floors have balconies, and all suites contain kitchenettes. The two-bedroom suites sleep four guests comfortably, and the special-occasion suite (ideal for a honeymoon) has a fireplace and a whirlpool tub. All rooms have either queen- or king-size beds and well-kept bathrooms. A small library is near the front desk, and an intimate on-site pub offers beer and wine Wednesday to Saturday from 5:30pm to 1am. About a dozen restaurants lie within safe walking distance. The owners also operate an antebellum (ca. 1840s) home with an additional six luxury suites, each with a whirlpool, a wet bar, antique reproduction furniture, and fireplaces.

101 S. 2nd St., Wilmington, NC 28401. © **800/525-0909** or 910/343-1800. Fax 910/251-1149. www. thewilmingtonian.com. 32 units. $89–$305 1-bedroom suite; $185–$325 special-occasion suite. Rates include continental breakfast. AE, DC, DISC, MC, V. Free parking. **Amenities:** Pub. *In room:* A/C, TV, hair dryer, kitchenette, Wi-Fi (free).

STAYING ON THE BEACH NEARBY
Blockade Runner Beach Resort Hotel & Conference Center   In the middle of Wrightsville Beach, opening onto views of the ocean, this seven-story hotel is far superior to the lackluster string of motels along Lumina Avenue, north and south. Guest rooms are comfortably and attractively furnished and often have private patios. Many of its rooms, especially the oceanfront balcony units, have been fashionably refurbished and greatly improved, with bathrooms redone in marble with rain shower heads. Its modern and airy **East Restaurant** is better than ever. The **SeaEscape** beach bar offers drinks in a poolside setting, complete with beach volleyball and a beachfront dining patio.

275 Waynick Blvd. (PO Box 555), Wrightsville Beach, NC 28480. © **800/541-1161** or 910/256-2251. Fax 910/256-2251. www.blockade-runner.com. 150 units. Mid-June to mid-Sept $169–$379 double; off season $89–$215 double. Children 11 and under stay free in parent's room. AE, DC, DISC, MC, V. **Amenities:** Restaurant; 2 bars; babysitting; exercise center; Jacuzzi; room service; sauna. *In room:* A/C, TV, fridge, hair dryer, Wi-Fi (free).

Where to Dine

As is true of so many coastal towns, Wilmington's best dining spots are at the beaches or on their fringes, and many of them specialize in seafood.

Sooner or later, you're bound to hear the name **Calabash** ★, especially if you love seafood. This tiny town of 150 residents, 35 miles south of Wilmington on U.S. 17, is renowned for its bounty of seafood restaurants—about 30 of them within 1 square mile, vying with one another to serve the biggest and best platter of seafood at the lowest price. Calabash restaurants use family recipes handed down from generation to generation.

We head to a tiny little place called **Calabash Seafood Hut,** 1125 River Rd. (© **910/579-6723**). The line of customers waiting for a table often stretches around the corner. The fried shrimp, fresh fish, and hush puppies are the best in the area.

Portions are really big, and, in the words of one patron, "the sweet tea is to die for." Platters range from $12 to $14. The bigger restaurants along the waterfront are also good, but avoid the all-you-can-eat buffets and order fresh from the a la carte menu instead.

MODERATE

Caffè Phoenix ★ MEDITERRANEAN   This cafe, a block from the water in the center of town, is easily the best bistro in Wilmington. In a renovated and transformed former dry-goods store, it has a light, open, airy decor, with lots of plants. Luncheon choices include homemade soups, freshly prepared salads, pasta, and sandwiches. Dinner becomes more elaborate, featuring delicacies like paella. Specials change weekly. Many Wilmington artists dine here, and the place has a gay following.

9 S. Front St. ⓒ **910/343-1395.** Main courses $9–$12 lunch, $17–$27 dinner. AE, DC, DISC, MC, V. Mon-Sat 11:30am–10pm (light fare served 3–5pm); Sun 10am–3pm.

Deluxe Restaurant NOUVELLE AMERICAN   Don't underestimate the value of this restaurant's bar as a meeting point for the artistic and the articulate. Lots of musicians and artists are drawn here because of the ambience and the eclectic, vaguely Southwestern decor, which might have been designed by Frank Lloyd Wright on psychedelics. It was established as a coffeehouse in 1995 and expanded into this full-fledged restaurant in 1998. Menu items are imaginative—a welcome change from the catfish and collards that are staples at some of the local competitors. Reflecting a solid technique and a flair for flavor, the chef delights with such dishes as white soy–molasses grilled sirloin, or panko-dusted North Carolina soft-shell crabs. Brunch is always a treat here, with cinnamon-pecan-swirl French toast and hickory-smoked salmon. Wines are appropriately eclectic, with origins from around the world.

114 Market St. ⓒ **910/251-0333.** www.deluxenc.com. Reservations recommended. Main courses $13–$34; Sun brunch $6–$14. AE, DISC, MC, V. Mon-Sat 5:30pm–2am; Sun 10:30am–2pm (brunch) and 5:30pm–2am.

Elijah's ★ AMERICAN/SEAFOOD   This is one of the largest and best-established restaurants along Wilmington's historic riverfront. Elijah's occupies a low-slung, wood-sided building that was originally conceived as a maritime museum. It still contains some of its seafaring memorabilia, which looks striking against the rich paneling that sheathes most of the interior. In the evenings, a wraparound bar with views of the river becomes a convivial nightlife venue. On warm nights, head for the huge waterfront terrace, where a bar is rolled on or off the deck, depending on the weather. Lunches here tend to emphasize sandwiches and simple platters that always include a fine version of crab cakes. Dinners are more elaborate, with classic and well-prepared dishes that include deep-fried calamari, soft-shell crabs, shrimp in a Dijon mustard and garlic sauce, and tender, juicy steaks.

2 Ann St., Chandler's Wharf. ⓒ **910/343-1448.** www.elijahs.com. Reservations recommended for 8 or more. Main courses $7–$13 lunch, $10–$28 dinner. AE, DC, DISC, MC, V. Outdoors Sun–Thurs 11:30am–10pm, Fri-Sat 11:30am–11pm; indoors Sun–Thurs 11:30am–3pm and 5–10pm, Fri-Sat 11:30am–3pm and 5–11pm.

Freddie's Restaurante ★ ITALIAN/AMERICAN   Open since 1995, the popular Freddie's at the beach serves savory Italian specialties in the atmosphere of an Irish pub. The bartender is said to make the best martinis in town. The chef—known as King of the Pork Chop—creates masterful versions of this dish, including chops made with special rum molasses sauce, or flame-grilled and topped with sliced peaches, pecans, and peach liquor. Italian dishes include the seafood ravioli with shrimp, clams, and scallops, or veal parmigiana. The melt-in-your-mouth lasagna is enveloped in a tomato Bolognese sauce (simmered for 8 hr.) and ricotta cheese and topped with a blanket of melted mozzarella.

111 K Ave., Kure Beach. ✆ **910/458-5979.** www.freddieskurebeach.com. Reservations recommended. Main courses $11–$35. AE, MC, V. Tues–Wed 5–9:30pm; Thurs–Sat 5–10pm; Sun 5–9pm.

Hieronymus Seafood Restaurant & Oyster Bar ★ ☺ SEAFOOD The motto of this well-established restaurant is "Fresh is best," and the chefs live up to that promise. They buy seafood directly from the local fishermen and turn it into tempting dishes—and have done so for 3 decades. The coziest place on a cool day is by the fireplace in the Oyster Bar: Diners drive from many miles away to sample the fresh oysters and clams. She-crab soup is another special appetizer with Cape Fear, hand-picked crabmeat. For a main course, the filet of flounder can be fried, grilled, or blackened. Fresh-shucked oysters lightly fried can also be prepared as a main dish. The Captain's Platter is the most popular dish for the seafood connoisseur. The chefs also make a tempting jambalaya inspired by the kitchens of New Orleans. *Tip:* The kids' menu makes this place a family favorite.

5035 Market St. ✆ **910/392-6313.** www.hieronymusseafood.com. Reservations recommended. Main courses $15–$29. AE, MC, V. Mon–Fri 11am–4pm; daily 4–10pm.

Pilot House ★ LOW COUNTRY/SEAFOOD On the Cape Fear River in the historic restored Craig House, the Pilot House serves some of the best seafood dishes in the Wilmington area. Set within a yellow-painted clapboard house (ca. 1870) immediately adjacent to the Cape Fear River, it was moved to this site in 1978. This is the Wilmington restaurant that's more attuned to the gourmet allure of Low Country cuisine than any other, offering both classic and nouvelle twists on traditional dishes. More upscale than its neighbor, Elijah's (with which it shares the same owner), the Pilot House seats most of its diners on a sprawling riverfront terrace, with an additional 10 tables in an isolated upstairs garret room. Preface your meal with a drink at the cozy nautical-style bar before diving into the specialties, such as shrimp and grits or crunchy catfish, a true Southern delicacy. The seafood platter is the most-ordered dish. A choice selection of meats is offered, especially prime cuts of beef, and it wouldn't be a Carolina restaurant if it didn't serve pork chops.

2 Ann St., Chandler's Wharf. ✆ **910/343-0200.** www.pilothouserest.com. Reservations recommended. Main courses $9–$12 lunch, $18–$27 dinner. AE, DC, DISC, MC, V. Daily 10am–10pm.

INEXPENSIVE

Boca Bay SOUTHERN/INTERNATIONAL The special feature here is a fountainside outdoor covered patio for dining. That and the good food at reasonable prices have put this place on the culinary map of Wilmington. The menu is unusual, in that it is so wide ranging and includes an array of tapas, sushi, and sashimi, plus a bevy of delightful main courses. Many guests make their entire order from the tapas selections, including stuffed grape leaves, vodka-cured salmon, Mediterranean hummus, and marinated mushrooms. From the main menu, you may be intrigued by the main course of lobster cheesecake with rock shrimp served with a champagne-and-pink-peppercorn sauce. Desserts are appropriately nicknamed "Colossal Confections" and are best exemplified by the hazel truffle cake with hazelnut cream.

2025 Eastwood Rd. ✆ **910/256-1887.** www.bocabayrestaurant.com. Reservations recommended. Main courses $8–$14. AE, DISC, MC, V. Mon–Wed 5–10pm; Thurs–Sat 5–11pm; Sun 9am–2pm and 5–10pm.

Circa 1922 ★ 🍴 SOUTHERN/INTERNATIONAL One of Wilmington's most affordable restaurants opened in 2000 in a 1920s bank building. Inside you'll find a stately, high-ceilinged interior filled with hardwoods and mirrors, and a menu that features tapas, the small-portioned and savory bar food of Spain. The best way to navigate your way through a meal here is to order a medley of the savory dishes to share among your fellow diners. The culinary inspirations range from Asian to Mediterranean. For starters, Prince Edward Sound mussels are delectable in green curry and coconut milk. The lobster ravioli is sublime and prepared with a lobster bisque. Sushi and sashimi also adorn the menu, and you can order such main courses as pan-seared scallops served with a smoked oyster fondue. We'd walk a mile for the B-52 cheesecake.

8 N. Front St. ✆ **910/762-1922.** www.circa1922.com. Reservations recommended. Main courses $11–$25; tapas $4–$5; Sun–Thurs 3-course menu $19. AE, DC, DISC, MC, V. Sun–Thurs 5–10pm; Fri–Sat 5–11pm. Bar daily 5pm–midnight (until 1–2am Fri–Sat).

Wilmington After Dark

Hell's Kitchen This is the hot spot in town. The bar itself was created from the set used for the now-defunct TV show *Dawson's Creek.* It's a full liquor bar with a wide selection of microbrew suds and draft beer. If you're hungry, you can devour a

---

SIDE TRIP: BALD HEAD ISLAND

A 45-minute drive southeast from Wilmington on U.S. 17 South, with a left turn onto N.C. 87, takes you to the little town of Southport, the jumping-off point for the passenger ferry to **Bald Head Island ★**. (The terminal is at Indigo Plantation.) You must call ahead to book the ferry (✆ **910/457-5003;** www.baldheadisland.com). The day trip costs $11 for adults and $9 for children 3 to 12; children 2 and under ride free.

Bald Head Island invites nature lovers to visit for much longer than 1 day. There are some 3,000 pristine acres, with 14 miles of sandy beachfront and miles and miles of salt marshes, tidal creeks, and maritime forests. An 18-hole championship golf course and the Village of Bald Head Island—with shops, restaurants, private homes, and condominiums—offer other diversions. Activities on the island include swimming (the island has a pool as well as all those miles of beaches), biking, tennis, golf, canoeing, fishing, birding, and just plain beachcombing.

Still, human intrusion is kept to a minimum. No cars are permitted on the island; transportation is provided by golf carts and jitneys. Sea oats, yucca, beach grasses, live oak, red cedar, palmetto,

sabal palms, loblolly pines, and a yellow wildflower called gaillardia thrive here. White ibises, great blue herons, snowy egrets, black ducks, mallards, and pintails frequent the island, and a protected population of loggerhead sea turtles nests here.

If you'd like to stay over, private homes, as well as condominiums, are available as rentals. You can also rent either of two historic cottages that were the homes of lighthouse keepers and their families from 1903 to 1958. All units are tastefully furnished, with full kitchens, TVs, and other modern conveniences, and most rates include the use of one of the electric passenger carts. There is a 3-night minimum stay at the condos and a weekly only rental for houses. In summer, daily rates range from $260 to $550, with weekly rates going from $1,700 to $13,000. Off season, the daily rate is from $200 to $550, with weekly rentals costing $1,500 to $13,000. All kinds of package deals are available. For full details and bookings, contact **Bald Head Island,** PO Box 3069, Bald Head Island, NC 28461 (✆ **800/515-1038** or 910/457-5000; www.bald headisland.com).

pub selection of burgers, nachos, wings, and other such fare, with most plates costing less than $7. It's open Monday to Friday 11:30am to 2am and Saturday and Sunday 5pm to 2am. 118 Princess St. © **910/763-4133.** www.hellskitchenbar.com.

The Thalian Hall Theater   If there's a big event being staged in Wilmington, this is likely to be the venue. This restored 1858 theater hosts about 250 events annually. Local theater groups and the symphony also use the theater as their home base for productions. Performances range from live dance to children's dramas performed by local companies. Contact the box office to learn what's happening at the time of your visit. Ticket prices depend on the event. Center box-office hours are noon to 6pm Tuesday to Friday, 2 to 6pm Saturday, and 2 hours before curtain time on Sunday. 310 Chestnut St. © **800/523-2820,** 910/343-3660, or the box office 632-2285. www.thalianhall.com.

BEAUFORT ★

35 miles E of New Bern

North Carolina's third-oldest town, **Beaufort ★** (pronounced *Bo*-fort) dates back to 1713 and still reflects its early history. Along its narrow streets are two 200-year-old houses, and more than a hundred houses are over a century old. On the last weekend in June, residents open their homes for the annual Old Homes Tour. Beaufort lies on the Taylor Creek waterfront, where a boardwalk with restaurants, shops, and piers offers pleasant strolling.

Essentials

GETTING THERE   Access is on U.S. 70 just over the Grayden Paul Bridge from Morehead City. From New Bern, take U.S. 70 East.

VISITOR INFORMATION   For sightseeing and accommodations information, contact the **Crystal Coast Tourism Authority** (© **877/206-0929** or 252/726-8148; www.crystalcoastnc.org).

The **Beaufort Historical Association,** 130 Turner St. (PO Box 1709), Beaufort, NC 28516 (© **252/728-5225;** www.beauforthistoricsite.org), is open March to November Monday to Saturday 9:30am to 5pm and in the off season Monday to Saturday 10am to 4pm.

Exploring the Area

Beaufort Historic Site ★, in the 100 block of Turner Street, includes the 1767 Joseph Bell House, the 1825 Josiah Bell House, the 1796 Carteret County Court-house, the 1829 county jail, the 1859 apothecary shop and doctor's office, and the 1778 Samuel Leffers House, home of the town's first schoolmaster. Tours are given Monday to Saturday at 10am, 11:30am, 1pm, and 3pm. A tour costs $8 for adults and $4 for children 6 and older. Not included on the tour is the 1732 Rustell House, an art gallery; entry is free of charge.

A block away is the **Old Burying Ground,** dating from 1709 and listed on the National Register of Historic Places. Both self-guided and narrated tours are available. Narrated tours aboard a British double-decker bus are offered on Tuesday, Wednesday, and Thursday at 2:30pm year-round for $8 per person. You can also purchase a self-guided tour brochure for $1. Call © **252/728-5225** for more information.

From modest beginnings, the **North Carolina Maritime Museum,** 315 Front St. (© **252/728-7317;** www.ncmaritime.org), grew into a $2.2-million complex. It has natural- and maritime-history exhibits, ship models, and shell collections, and it offers intriguing field trips and programs for all ages. The Wooden Boat Show is held here the first weekend in May. Admission is free. The museum is open Monday to Friday from 9am to 5pm, Saturday from 10am to 5pm, and Sunday from 1 to 5pm; it's closed on major holidays.

Divers are attracted to this area because of the many wrecks off the coast. If you want to get into this action, contact **Discovery Diving Co.,** 414 Orange St. (© **252/ 728-2265;** www.discoverydiving.com), where the staff knows the local waters best. The company offers charter diving tours for prices ranging from $65 to $115 per person, plus use of the company's equipment. Tanks rent for $12 to $18, with regulators going for $6 to $9 and weights for $2. Masks and fins are priced at $3 each, and extra amenities (such as cameras and computers) cost $10 to $20 (film is extra). Call ahead for equipment reservations. Tours include one dive at a shipwreck site offshore, one farther offshore, and two dives on the reefs closer to shore.

Where to Stay

Beaufort Inn ★   Katie and Bruce Ethridge have managed to give their Historic District inn a historical feel, even though it's of recent vintage. Rooms are tastefully decorated, with lots of homey touches. Some 15 boat slips are provided for guests who arrive by water, and bicycles are available for rent. A scrumptious hot breakfast is served in the dining area (don't miss Katie's breakfast pie, made of sausages, eggs, and cheese), and good restaurants are within walking distance.

101 Ann St., Beaufort, NC 28516. © **800/726-0321** or 252/728-2600. www.beaufort-inn.com. 44 units. June–Sept $119–$159 double; off season $79–$139 double; year-round $218–$338 suite. Additional person $20. Rates include breakfast. AE, DC, DISC, MC, V. **Amenities:** Breakfast room; exercise room; outdoor Jacuzzi. In room: A/C, TV, hair dryer, Wi-Fi (free).

Old Seaport ★ 🐾   In 1866, immediately following the Civil War, Jacob Gibbie built this home for his expanding family. This enlarged saltbox-style cottage is fringed with perennial borders and rosebushes. The homelike and cozy B&B is one of the finest and best run in Beaufort. Each guest room has a king-size Jenny Lind bed. Only four antiques-furnished guest rooms (each with private bathroom) are offered, so reservations are important in summer. Mary and F. J. Hurst are the courteous and helpful hosts. They can also make reservations for ferry connections, advise you about nearby golf, or help you board a charter fishing boat. You can even borrow their bicycles, beach chairs, umbrellas, coolers, and beach towels.

217 Turner St., Beaufort, NC 28516. © **800/349-5823** or 252/728-4300. www.oldseaportinn.com. 3 units. $99–$140 double. Rates include continental breakfast. MC, V. No children 18 and under. **Amenities:** Breakfast room; lounge; Wi-Fi (free). In room: A/C, no phone.

Pecan Tree Inn ★   Named for the 2-century-old pecan trees that grace the property, the Pecan Tree Inn is housed in a building that was constructed during the mid-1800s. The Victorian porches, turrets, and gingerbread trim that make the house unique were added in 1890. Recent renovations have improved the inn while maintaining its original architectural essence. The rooms and parlor are furnished with a collection of antiques, designed to highlight the use of pine in the construction. Guest rooms feature king-size, queen-size, or twin beds; specify which you want when you make reservations. Each suite contains a Jacuzzi, and the king-size canopied bed evokes the Southern-plantation ambience. A 5,500-square-foot English garden in the back features more than 1,000 plants, each labeled to aid the budding botanist.

SIDE TRIP: HARKERS ISLAND

If you're a boat owner, you can tie up across the sound from Beaufort at **Calico Jack's Marina** (✆ 252/728-3575) on Harkers Island. If you don't have a boat, a **ferry** (✆ 800/BY-FERRY [293-3779]; www.ncdot.org) leaves from Calico Jack's for the 35-minute trip to Cape Lookout. The ferry runs between April and December, and the fare is $10 for adults and $6 for children 6 and under.

A jitney service between Cape Point and the lighthouse moves visitors from one spot to another. Bring a picnic, insect repellent, and your own water supply. The island's atmosphere is ideal for those who like sailboats, lots of sun, and miles of sandy beaches. It's also a good venue for fishing and beachcombing. The unique diamond-patterned lighthouse has stood here since 1859.

116 Queen St., Beaufort, NC 28516. ✆ **800/728-7871** or 252/728-6733. www.pecantree.com. 9 units. $100–$150 double; $125–$180 suite. Rates include continental breakfast. AE, DISC, MC, V. No children 9 and under. **Amenities:** Breakfast room; lounge; bikes. *In room:* A/C, TV, hair dryer, Wi-Fi (free).

Where to Dine

Clawson's 1905 Restaurant AMERICAN   One of downtown Beaufort's most consistently popular restaurants was built in 1905 by a Swedish immigrant who needed a warehouse. The rough-hewed plank, timber, and brick building has been pierced with skylights and gentrified, with every cranny of its labyrinthine interior jampacked with nostalgia, diners, and drinkers. If you have to wait at the bar for a table, you'll rub elbows with boat owners, local hell-raisers, and golf-playing retirees. Lunches are a lot simpler than dinners, consisting of fried oysters, shrimp or scallops, salads, and overstuffed sandwiches. Dinners feature larger portions and lots of combination platters piled high with ribs and shrimp, steak, pork, and chicken. A specialty is a very large potato stuffed with broccoli, red pepper, onions, and mushrooms, then topped with cheese and sour cream.

425 Front St. ✆ **252/728-2133.** Reservations recommended. Main courses $5.95–$24. DISC, MC, V. Mon–Sat 11:30am–9:30pm; Sun 4–9pm.

The Spouter Inn SEAFOOD   Waterfront dining and fresh seafood keep this place humming. The atmosphere is casual, even though the tables are lighted by candles in the evening. Popular with both locals and visitors, the restaurant offers lunches with pastas, salads, chowders, and sandwiches. In the evening, more elaborate meals are served, depending largely on the availability of fresh seafood. Continental dishes—rare in this region—are also featured. For dessert, chocolate silk pie, cream cheese lemon pie, or rum cake may appear on the menu.

218 Front St. ✆ **252/728-5190.** www.spouterinn.net. Reservations recommended for dinner. Main courses $8–$24 lunch, $19–$32 dinner. AE, MC, V. Daily 11:30am–2:30pm and 5–9pm.

MOREHEAD CITY

147 miles SE of Raleigh; 3 miles W of Beaufort; 45 miles SE of New Bern; 87 miles NE of Wilmington

This has been an important port for oceangoing vessels since 1857 and is the world's largest tobacco-export terminal. Across the Intracoastal Waterway from Beaufort, and the gateway to the Atlantic Beach–Emerald Isle area (see "The Bogue Banks," below), it attracts many fishermen. Both onshore and offshore fishing trips are offered here, and tournaments are held throughout the year. The biggest event is the **Big Rock Blue Marlin Tournament** (© 252/247-3575; www.thebigrock.com), staged over 6 days, beginning the second Monday in June. Stroll the little waterfront boardwalk, where boats hired for deep-sea fishing trips clean the day's catch. Or stop in for a platter of fresh shrimp and hush puppies in "old-timey" seafood restaurants like Captain Bill's and the Sanitary Fish Market (see "Where to Dine," below), both with waterfront dining.

Essentials

GETTING THERE   Morehead City is about a 45-minute drive on U.S. 70 East from New Bern.

The closest commuter-flight connection is the airport at New Bern. (See "New Bern," below.)

The nearest **Amtrak** stop is at Raleigh on the New York–Miami or New York–Tampa run. Call © 800/USA-RAIL (872-7245) or go to www.amtrak.com for schedules and fares.

VISITOR INFORMATION   For sightseeing and accommodations information, contact the **Crystal Coast Tourism Authority,** 3409 Arendell St., Morehead City, NC 28557 (© 877/206-0929 or 252/726-8148; www.crystalcoastnc.org). The office is open Monday to Friday 8am to 5pm and Sunday 9am to 5pm.

Outdoor Pursuits

Fishing is especially good here—in fact, it's the reason most visitors come to Morehead City. The Gulf Stream brings in blue marlin, tarpon, amberjack, and other prizes, in addition to inshore fish. Gulf Stream fishing is possible April through November. The area has about 80 miles of surf and 400 miles of protected waterways.

A near-perfect day or evening on the water can be enjoyed on the ***Carolina Princess,*** 604 Evans St. (© 800/682-3456 or 252/726-5479; www.carolinaprincess.com). The *Princess* is a trim vessel that accommodates up to 95 passengers and has a snack bar and sun deck. Full-day bottom fishing trips cost $100 for adults, $70 for children 12 and under, and $40 for a passenger who goes along just for the ride and doesn't fish. The boat supplies the rod, reel, and bait. Ice can be purchased to take with you.

Where to Stay

The Buccaneer Inn ☺   If you're looking for a family-friendly place, head for this motel. It's not the largest in the area, but it's one of the best. Housekeeping is good. The hotel's standard rooms are comfortable and rather tasteful; some have Jacuzzi tubs. Amenities include free coffee, free local phone calls (with a $10 deposit), and a pool.

2806 Arendell St. (Hwy. 70), Morehead City, NC 28557. © 800/682-4982 or 252/726-3115. Fax 252/726-3864. 91 units. $60–$130 double. Children 16 and under stay free in parent's room. Rates include continental breakfast. AE, DC, DISC, MC, V. **Amenities:** Restaurant; bar; outdoor pool. *In room:* A/C, TV, fridge, hair dryer, Wi-Fi (free).

The Harborlight Guest House ★★ 🛏   We much prefer a B&B with some charm and character to any big chain motel when we visit the Carolina coast. Graced with shady palms along the waterfront, this guesthouse is something of a secret, and no signs from the road give it away. The Harborlight is encircled on three sides by water, giving guests good views of the Intracoastal Waterway and Bogue Sound from every guest room; sometimes you can see porpoises feeding in the waters. Each guest room is a suite with attractive furnishings, expansive windows, and excellent bathrooms. The best units contain two-person whirlpool tubs and/or fireplaces. The most coveted suites are the Beaufort and Emerald rooms. With filet mignon, rum-laced French toast with honeybee ambrosia, and blueberry crepes, breakfast is one more good reason to stay here.

332 Live Oak Dr., Cape Carteret, NC 28584. ✆ **800/624-VIEW** (8439) or 252/393-6868. Fax 252/393-6868. www.harborlightnc.com. 7 units. $165–$315 suite. No children 16 and under. AE, MC, V. **Amenities:** Golf privileges; health club privileges. *In room:* A/C, TV, fridge, hair dryer, Wi-Fi.

Where to Dine

Bistro by the Sea ★ ATLANTIC COASTAL   The town's best restaurant (and its stylish bar) occupies a contemporary, stone-sided building set beside Highway 70, near the Hampton Inn, in a commercial neighborhood west of the waterfront. Within the dignified dining rooms, you'll be offered savory dishes that include peppercorn-encrusted seared tuna; sautéed bistro-style crab cakes, shrimp, and a julienne of vegetables; prime rib of beef; pastas that include capellini in pesto sauce with fresh-roasted vegetables; and an assortment of burgers. Your hosts are Tim Coyne and his wife, Libby Eaton, who began their restaurant careers in a beachfront shack in the 1980s, and who eventually expanded into the substantial building that stands today.

4031 Arendell St. ✆ **253/247-2777.** www.bistro-by-the-sea.com. Reservations recommended for 6 or more. Main courses $14–$25. AE, DC, MC, V. Tues–Thurs 5–9:30pm; Fri–Sat 5–10pm. Closed Jan.

Captain Bill's Waterfront Restaurant SEAFOOD   A tradition since the 1940s, this local favorite overlooks the colorful fishing boats on Bogue Sound. With a name like Captain Bill's, the restaurant obviously specializes in seafood, which is very fresh. Locals look forward to the conch stew on Wednesday and Saturday, as well as all-you-can-eat seafood specials on Friday. Prices are a bargain. There's also a good selection of nonfinny dishes. The Down East lemon pie is justly celebrated. A children's menu is available.

701 Evans St. ✆ **252/726-2166.** www.captbills.com. Reservations recommended. Main courses $6.95–$11 lunch, $12–$30 dinner. MC, V. Sun–Thurs 11:30am–9pm; Fri–Sat 11:30am–10pm.

Sanitary Fish Market & Restaurant SEAFOOD   This 600-seat restaurant started out as 12 stools, a counter, and a kerosene stove in 1938. It became a regional favorite for families over the years as much for its sunny waterside ambience (vintage wood paneling, windows overlooking the sound, faded photos of politicians and beauty queens of old) as for its reliable seafood platters. And lo and behold, after years of abstinence, the place today serves beer and wine. The shrimp salad is a winner, and the hush puppies here are the best around—hot, crisp, and never cloyingly sweet.

501 Evans St. ✆ **252/247-3111.** www.sanitaryfishmarket.com. Main courses $7.50–$11 lunch, $12–$26 dinner. DISC, MC, V. Daily 11am–9pm. Closed Dec 1–Feb 1.

The Bogue Banks ★

Atlantic Beach is the oldest of the resorts on the 28-mile stretch of barrier island known as the Bogue Banks, which includes the vacation centers directly south, **Pine Knoll Shores, Salter Path, Indian Beach,** and **Emerald Isle.** The area is also being positioned by tourism officials as "the Crystal Coast" (encompassing Beaufort and Morehead City to the north; see earlier in this chapter). Whatever its moniker, the long, thin island was relatively undeveloped until 1927, when the first bridge was built across Bogue Sound to Morehead City. It's now one of the state's most popular coastal areas, with fishing festivals and tournaments held in early spring and late fall. A south-facing exposure makes the island's weather less volatile and temperatures milder than those found on the northern Outer Banks, and it's virtually a year-round resort. When you begin to feel waterlogged, plenty of sightseeing is within easy reach.

For sightseeing and accommodations information, contact the **Crystal Coast Tourism Authority** (✆ 877/206-0929 or 252/726-8148; www.crystalcoastnc.org).

At the tip of Bogue Island sits **Fort Macon** (✆ 252/726-3775; www.ncparks. gov/Visit/parks/foma/main.php), a restored Civil War landmark that's open to the public at no charge. The jetties (designed by Gen. Robert E. Lee), moats, gun emplacements, and dungeons make it worth the trip. The museum displays weapons, tools, and artifacts. The public beach has bathhouses, a snack bar, and lifeguards. Fort Macon lies 2 miles east of Atlantic Beach off N.C. 58 and is open daily from 9am to 5:30pm. Free guided tours of the fort are offered only in summer at 11am, 1pm, and 3pm. The museum is open in summer from 9am to 5:30pm.

The **North Carolina Aquarium** at Pine Knoll Shores has undergone a $24-million expansion (✆ 866/294-3477 or 252/247-4003; www.ncaquariums.com). It is three times larger, with a 300,000-gallon Living Shipwreck Ocean Tank featuring the wreckage of a German sub U-352 and a big collection of marine life. Open daily 9am to 5pm, it charges $8 admission, $6 for children 12 and under.

WHERE TO STAY

The Oceanana Family Resort ☺   This motel at Atlantic Beach proper, directly beside the ocean, offers a free fishing pier for guests. If you want to turn the day's catch into the evening meal, you'll find grills and a supply of charcoal, starter fluid, and even ketchup and mustard out by the pool, as well as picnic tables nearby. For the small fry, there's a playground, and for vacationers of all ages, the biweekly watermelon party out by the pool is a festive occasion. A tropical breakfast, spread under an open poolside pavilion, features more than 15 fresh fruits. A fast-food grill is out by the fishing pier. Every room has a well-maintained bathroom, and suites have

---

🄾 A Real-Life Deserted Island

For those who really want to get away from it all, head to **Bear Island** ★ by taking Hammocks Beach Road (State Rd. 1511) off Hwy. 24 in Swansboro to a passenger ferry. You can reach this uninhabited barrier island, where the pristine beaches are strewn with little more than snow-white sand dollars and the delicate tracings of bird feet, only by private boat or by seasonal ferry—and visitation is limited to how many people can cross on the ferry, so you really do feel as if the island is your own. Bear Island is the island portion of **Hammocks Beach State Park,** 1572 Hammocks Beach Rd. (park office ✆ 910/326-4881; www.ncparks.gov),

a 3-mile-long barrier island dominated by high sand dunes, a maritime forest, and unspoiled beach. Primitive camping is allowed here year-round—except for 3 nights each month during the summer nesting season of endangered loggerhead sea turtles, which come here under the full moon to lay their eggs. The ferry leaves from the Hammocks Beach Road park entrance on the hour on Monday and Tuesday Memorial Day to Labor Day, and on the half-hour Wednesday to Sunday. The fare is $5 for adults, $3 for seniors and children 6 to 12, and free for children 5 and under. Call to confirm ferry hours.

stoves. You can take portable grills to the lawn area in front of your room (but not on upper-floor decks) and cook dinner right at your door.

700 E. Fort Macon Rd. (PO Box 250), Atlantic Beach, NC 28512. © **252/726-4111.** Fax 252/726-4113. www.oceanana.com. 110 units. May 26 to Labor Day $138 double, $200–$334 suite; off season $80–$100 double, $120–$200 suite. Rates include tropical breakfast. MC, V. Closed Nov–Mar. **Amenities:** Restaurant; outdoor pool. *In room:* A/C, TV.

WHERE TO DINE

The Crab Shack SEAFOOD   While much was written about the devastating 2005 hurricanes Katrina and Rita, Hurricane Ophelia took a bite out of the Salter Path sound front that same deadly season, essentially blowing this restaurant to the ground. It's since been rebuilt and remains everything a Down East seafood "shack" should be: It's a local favorite with an expansive backside view of Bogue Sound and consistently reliable seafood standards. If it's steamed spiced crabs you crave, here's the spot to order up a dozen or two in season. You won't find fancy sauces here: The Crab Shack offers fresh, unadulterated seafood, fried, grilled, or broiled; a solid Hatteras-style clam chowder (broth based); and state-of-the-art hush puppies. Families love the friendly, casual ambience. The decor is nothing to write home about, and in the summer, you may have to wait in line for a table, but for good and simple, you can't beat it. Beer and wine are available.

144 Shore Dr., off Hwy. 58 (behind the Methodist Church), Salter Path. © **252/247-3444.** Main courses $7.95 lunch, $14–$34 dinner. MC, V. Daily 11am–9pm. Hours change seasonally so call ahead.

Swansboro

Along the coast southwest of Morehead City, the historic waterfront town of **Swansboro** (www.tourswansboro.com), bordering the White Oak River across from Cape Carteret, is a diminutive charmer, with shops in renovated centuries-old structures and shrimp boats along the harbor. The **Mullet Festival,** held here every fall, draws huge crowds from around the Southeast.

NEW BERN ★

87 miles NE of Wilmington

Less than 50 miles inland, on U.S. 70 and U.S. 17, New Bern is the state's second-oldest town (after Bath, see below), lying between the Neuse and Trent rivers, where swimming, boating, and both fresh- and saltwater fishing are favorite pastimes. Its Historic District merits a visit—it's filled with Georgian, Victorian, and classical-Revival architecture.

Essentials

GETTING THERE   From Beaufort, take U.S. 70 West to Morehead City, and continue along the same western route straight into New Bern. From Wilmington, head north on U.S. 17 through Jacksonville and directly into New Bern. From Raleigh, go east along U.S. 70 to New Bern.

The recently expanded **Craven Regional Airport,** 1501 Airport Rd., 2 miles outside New Bern (© 252/638-8591; www.newbernairport.com), is served by **US Airways** (© 800/428-4322), with connections from major cities in North Carolina. A taxi from the **Cherry Cab Co.** (© 252/447-3101) will take passengers into the city. A taxi to the center of New Bern from the airport costs approximately $11.

VISITOR INFORMATION The **Craven County Convention and Visitors Bureau,** 203 S. Front St. (© **800/437-5767;** www.visitnewbern.com), is open Monday to Friday from 8am to 5pm, and Saturday 10am to 2pm. The **New Bern Historical Society,** at 512 Pollack St. (© **252/638-8558;** www.newbernhistorical.org), is located in the historic 1790 Attmore-Oliver House, which exhibits 18th- and 19th-century furniture and artifacts. Hours are 1 to 4pm Thursday to Saturday (May–Oct).

SPECIAL EVENTS In the last week of March or first week of April, when the azaleas and dogwoods burst into bloom, New Bern sponsors the **Spring Historic Homes & Gardens Tour.** About 10 historic homes in town are open to the public, and tours also feature churches. Tickets cost $15 to $20 per person. For information, call the New Bern Historical Society (© **252/638-8558**).

Exploring the Area

In town, more than 180 18th- and 19th-century structures are listed in the National Register of Historic Places. Among the highlights are the following:

New Bern Firemen's Museum The original firefighting equipment of New Bern, dating back to the early 19th century, is on display, including an 1884 horse-drawn steamer and leather fire helmets. There's also a Civil War display case.

408 Hancock St. © **252/636-4087.** www.newbernmuseums.com. Admission $5 adults, $2.50 children. Mon–Sat 10am–4pm.

Tryon Palace Historic Sites & Gardens ★ This 19-room museum, built from 1767 to 1770 as both the state capitol and the residence of the royal governor, has been authentically restored. Walking through the elegant rooms, it's easy to see why this mansion was once called the most beautiful in America. The main building burned in 1798 and lay in ruins until the restoration from 1952 to 1959. The handsome grounds and gardens surrounding Tryon Palace are designed in 18th-century style.

Two other landmarks in the 13-acre Tryon Palace complex are the **John Wright Stanly House** (1780), a late-Georgian-style mansion with town-house gardens, and the **Dixon-Stevenson House** (1805), noted for its rare Federal antiques. Crafts shows and historical dramas are presented, and seasonal guided tours are available.

610 Pollock St. © **800/767-1560** or 252/514-4900. www.tryonpalace.org. Admission $15 adults, $6 children, free for children with an adult. Palace viewable by guided tour only Mon–Sat 9am–5pm; Sun 1–5pm. Closed New Year's Day, Thanksgiving, and Dec 24–26.

Shopping

The Birthplace of Pepsi-Cola Store The antique storefront that contains this place once functioned as Caleb Bradham's Pharmacy, the site where the entrepreneur invented the formula for Pepsi-Cola in 1898, 13 years after the development of the original formula for Coca-Cola. Today the site functions as a hybrid store-museum, dispensing nostalgia along with 8-ounce glasses of Pepsi from a replica of an old-time soda fountain for 64¢ each. Also on display are Frisbees and commemorative T-shirts, each lauding Pepsi and/or its claim on the American soul, in one way or another. Subsidized by the Pepsi-Cola Bottling Company of New Bern, serving several counties of eastern North Carolina, the site is open Monday to Saturday 10am to 6pm. 256 Middle St. (corner of Pollack St.). © **252/636-5898**. www.pepsistore.com.

Where to Stay

Aerie Inn Bed & Breakfast ★ A block east of Tryon Palace, within walking distance of several restaurants, this gracious inn is among the top two or three in town. It was fully restored and redecorated in 1985. Built in 1882, it has only two floors. Inside, the rooms are furnished with antiques or reproductions from the 1880s and 1890s. Breakfasts are country style, and afternoon refreshments, served in the tearoom, have become a local tradition.

509 Pollock St., New Bern, NC 28562. © **800/849-5553** or 252/636-5553. Fax 252/514-2157. www. aeriebedandbreakfast.com. 7 units. $119–$169 double. Rates include full breakfast and evening wine and hors d'oeuvres. Additional person $20 extra. AE, DISC, MC, V. **Amenities:** Breakfast room; lounge. *In room:* A/C, TV, hair dryer, Wi-Fi (free).

Harmony House Inn ★ Close to the Aerie—and a worthy competitor in every way—this Greek Revival house from 1850 receives guests on two floors in the Historic District. The furnishings are contemporary, however, not antiques, and the attractive, well-maintained rooms have king-size, queen-size, or twin beds. The owner displays her own needlepoint and artwork throughout the house. Guests quickly gravitate to their favorite rockers on the front porch. In the evening, wine is served. The house maintains a two-room suite, consisting of two bedrooms and a living room with a sleeper sofa, which is ideal for families and small traveling groups. In addition, the inn has two other Jacuzzi suites, ideal for honeymoons, anniversaries, or any other romantic getaway.

215 Pollock St., New Bern, NC 28560. © **800/636-3113** or 252/636-3810. www.harmonyhouseinn.com. 10 units. $109–$139 double; $175 suite. Rates include full breakfast. Additional person $20 extra. DISC, MC, V. **Amenities:** Breakfast room; lounge. *In room:* A/C, TV, Wi-Fi (free).

Meadows Inn B&B On the same street as the Aerie and Harmony House, the 1848 Meadows Inn is almost comparable in rating and ambience. This Greek Revival–style home is furnished with antiques and period reproductions. Several restaurants are within walking distance.

212 Pollock St., New Bern, NC 28560. © **877/551-1776** or 252/634-1776. Fax 252/634-1776. www. meadowsinn-nc.com. 10 units. $119–$139 double; $169 suite. Additional person $20 extra. Rates include full breakfast. Children 6 and under stay free in parent's room at discretion of management. AE, MC, V. **Amenities:** Breakfast room; lounge. *In room:* A/C, TV, hair dryer, Wi-Fi (free).

Where to Dine

Captain Ratty's AMERICAN/LOW COUNTRY One of New Bern's most popular restaurants occupies a brick structure (ca. 1897) that functioned throughout most local residents' memory as a pharmacy. Its owners, who know virtually everyone in town, define the place as a tavern in the Carolinas style and print a calendar of events advertising the evenings when oysters, for example, will sell for only 50¢ each. Live music is presented every Thursday, Friday, and Saturday from 7 to 10pm. The menu includes such dishes as platters of king crab legs, New York strip steak (served with or without shrimp), mussels in a white-wine sauce, any of several other kinds of shellfish and fresh fish, and daily specials. It's hardly haute cuisine, but the food is fresh and crowd pleasing.

202–206 Middle St. © **800/633-5292** or 252/633-2088. www.captainrattys.com. Reservations recommended. Sandwiches and salads $3.50–$16; main courses $16–$20. AE, MC, V. Daily 11:30am–9:30pm.

Chelsea ★ ECLECTIC AMERICAN   With its ambitious and innovative menu, this restaurant is in a historic building first used by local pharmacist Caleb Bradham, who invented Pepsi-Cola. Take the elevator to the main dining room with its original transom windows and old-fashioned high ceilings, or hang out on the ground floor for casual dining in the bar. At lunch, get started with a lump crab cake and creamy grits and follow with bacon-wrapped scallops tossed in garlic butter. At night, many traditional Southern specialties are featured, including brown butter barbecued chicken or shrimp and fried green-tomato rémoulade. Some of the best and freshest seafood in the area is served here as well, including shrimp, scallops, tomatoes, and mushrooms over a chorizo angel-hair "cheesecake."

335 Middle St. (℅ **252/637-5469.** http://thechelsea.com. Reservations recommended in main dining room. Main courses $6–$20 lunch, $14–$32 dinner. AE, DISC, MC, V. Mon–Thurs 11am–9pm; Fri–Sat 11am–10pm.

HISTORIC BATH: THE STATE'S OLDEST TOWN ★★

10 miles E of Washington

This tiny historic hamlet on the Pamlico River is the oldest incorporated town in North Carolina. A well-known explorer and surveyor, John Lawson, laid out the original town back in 1706, with Bath's dozen or so settlers allocating a site for a marketplace, a courthouse, and a church, of course. Its most famous citizen was Blackbeard, who married and settled here for a "gentlemanly life," which he found so boring he abandoned it all, including his woman, to return to his life of piracy.

From 2005 to 2006, the town celebrated its **Tricentennial** (1705–2005) with outdoor dramas, military reenactments, a gala ball, and a visit by the archbishop of Canterbury.

Essentials

GETTING THERE   Bath is reached by heading north of New Bern (see above) on Route 17, until you come to the intersection with Route 264 going east. At the intersection with Route 92, continue east into Bath.

If you have the time, you can also get to Bath by taking the toll-free **Aurora/Bayview auto ferry** (www.ncferry.org) north on Route 306 over the Pamlico Sound leaving from the sleepy little town of Aurora, home to the gigantic PCS Phosphate Mine. Over the years, the phosphate mines have produced a rich trove of ancient marine fossils (such as giant prehistoric sharks' teeth) from the time when this area was underwater. You can see the collection at the **Aurora Fossil Museum,** 400 Main St., Aurora (℅ **252/322-4238;** www.aurorafossilmuseum.com; open Mon–Sat 9am–4:30pm, Sun 12:30–4:30pm; free admission, donations accepted).

Sailors can easily make a stopover in Bath; it's just 12 miles from the Intracoastal Waterway.

VISITOR INFORMATION   For more information, stop at the **Historic Bath Visitor Center,** on 207 Carteret St. (℅ **252/923-3971;** www.nchistoricsites.org; open Tues–Sat 9am–5pm). You can view an orientation film, get a street map, or sign up for a guided walking tour. Self-guided tours are also available.

Exploring the Area

Armed with a map, set out on a self-guided tour to take in the major houses of historical interest. These include a town museum in the 1790 **Van Der Veer House,** right out the back door of the visitor center; the 1751 **Palmer-Marsh House,** reached along an oyster-shell walkway; and **Harding's Landing,** accessed by going across Main Street.

From Harding's Landing, head south on Main Street to the corner of Craven Street, where you come to **Glebe House.** Several notable citizens of Bath have occupied this building (ca. 1835), which can be viewed only from the outside.

Beside the Glebe House on Craven Street is Bath's grandest landmark, **St. Thomas Church,** built between 1734 and 1762. It's the oldest church in the state.

One more block along Main Street leads to the 1830 **Bonner House,** the best example of North Carolina coastal architecture in Bath. It's characterized by spacious porches in front and back. An early-20th-century general store, **Swindell's Store,** on Main Street, is still in operation.

There is a $2 admission to either the Palmer-Marsh House or the Bonner House (sold at the visitor center).

Where to Stay & Dine

If you fall in love with the picturesque nostalgia of Bath, as many visitors do, you can stay overnight. The town now has a B&B. The **Inn on Bath Creek,** 116 S. Main St. (© **252/923-9571;** www.innonbathcreek.com), looks as if it's been around a long time. But innkeepers Mark and Kae Penner-Howell, tired of finding an old house to restore, built a new one, albeit in the style of the older historic homes in town. Each guest room is tastefully and comfortably decorated, with its own private bathroom (with shower). All prices are based on double occupancy and include a full breakfast featuring fresh fruit. Rates are $130 to $225 a night. MasterCard, Visa, and Discover cards are accepted. You can putter around town on one of the B&B's bikes or take a sailboat onto the river from the town dock.

The accurately named **Old Town Country Kitchen,** 436 Carteret St. (© **252/923-1840**), serves up the best grub in town against a backdrop of seascapes, anchors on the wall, and handcrafted models of pirate ships. During the week, locals file in here for such Southern fare as fried pork chops and fresh collard greens. Fried shrimp is also a house specialty. On the weekend, seafood dominates the menu, including the house special: fresh fried oysters served with hush puppies. Main courses range from $6.50 to $18 (open Wed–Sat 7am–8pm, Sun–Tues 7am–2pm; cash only).

THE PIEDMONT

Nowhere in the South do old and new come together quite so dramatically as in North Carolina's Piedmont, between the coastal plains and the mountains. The contrast is especially marked in cities such as Winston-Salem, where the mammoth tobacco industry is represented by R.J. Reynolds, and the Stroh Brewery produces millions of barrels of beer each year. Across town, the streets and buildings of Old Salem have been restored to reflect the life of the Moravians who planned the community in 1753. The landscape here—red-clay hills, tobacco fields, and peach orchards—is as varied as the region's industry and agriculture.

The Piedmont is the home of the vaunted Research Triangle, a multidisciplinary scientific institute founded in 1958 by Duke University in Durham, the University of North Carolina in Chapel Hill, and North Carolina State University in Raleigh. The region boasts a wealth of other educational institutions, including Wake Forest University in Winston-Salem, and Shaw University in Raleigh, founded in 1865 and the oldest historically black university in the South.

The Piedmont is very much the New South, and its residents won't hesitate to brag a bit about the economic miracle that's transformed the area in the past 3 decades. They're especially proud of their big-time sports scene. (College basketball is practically a religion in these parts.) But the cities of the Piedmont haven't lost their manners, and a leisurely pace of life persists in the midst of all the growth and change. Travelers will see that streets lined with gorgeous homes and blooming dogwoods haven't been lost in the name of progress. And outside the cities, there's a lot waiting to be discovered, including some of the nation's greatest championship golf courses.

RALEIGH ★

143 miles NE of Charlotte

State government has been Raleigh's principal business since 1792, when it became North Carolina's capital. Just before the Civil War, the city was the setting of the fiery legislative debate that led to North Carolina's secession from the Union in 1861. Raleigh endured Union occupation by General Sherman in 1865, and during Reconstruction saw the west wing of its imposing Grecian Doric capitol building turned into a rowdy barroom by "carpetbagger" and "scalawag" legislators, its steps permanently nicked from whiskey barrels rolling in and out of the building.

Today the 5-acre square fronting the capitol is the focal point for a cluster of state office buildings in the heart of the city. From it radiate wide boulevards and tree-shaded residential streets. Downtown Raleigh

The Research Triangle: Raleigh, Durham & Chapel Hill

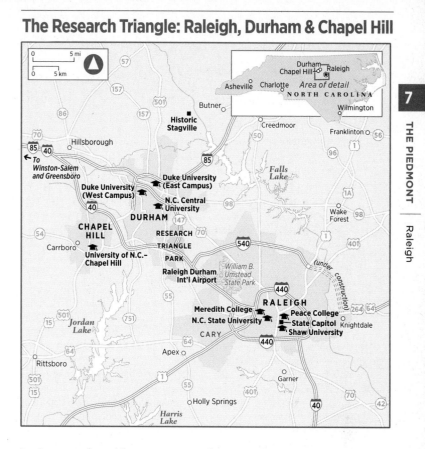

has been transformed by an attractive pedestrian mall where trees, fountains, and statuary create a shopping oasis. No fewer than six college campuses dot the city's streets, with wide lawns and impressive brick buildings. The oldest, St. Mary's College, was founded in 1842. The big name in town, though, is North Carolina State University, and cheering for the Wolfpack in basketball or football is more than just an idle pastime. New suburbs and gigantic shopping centers dominate the outskirts of Raleigh, characterized by nicely designed homes blending into a landscape that retains much of its original wooded character.

All this, plus the abundance of good accommodations, makes Raleigh a fine base from which to explore the Research Triangle area. Both Chapel Hill and Durham are within easy reach for day trips, and after a day of sightseeing, the capital city offers a good variety of entertainment options, from college bars to supper-club shows.

Essentials

GETTING THERE   U.S. 64 and U.S. 70 run east and west from Raleigh; U.S. 1 runs north and south, joining I-85, which runs northeast and is joined by I-40 to the west and I-95 to the east. U.S. 401 also runs northeast and southwest. The AAA is represented by the **Carolina Motor Club,** 2301 Blue Ridge Rd. (© **919/ 832-0543;** ww.aaany.com).

135

The Raleigh-Durham International Airport (RDU) is about 15 miles west of Raleigh, just off I-40. Major airlines serving the airport from out-of-state destinations include **Air Tran** (✆ 800/247-8726; www.airtran.com), **American Airlines** (✆ **800/433-7300;** www.aa.com), **Continental Airlines** (✆ **800/525-0280;** www.continental.com), **Delta** (✆ **800/221-1212;** www.delta.com), **United Airlines** (✆ **800/241-6522;** www.united.com), **US Airways** (✆ **800/428-4322;** www.usairways.com), **Southwest Airlines** (✆ 800/435-9792; www.southwest.com), **Air Canada** (✆ **888/247-2262;** www.aircanada.com), and **JetBlue** (✆ **800/JETBLUE** [538-2583]; www.jetblue.com).

Amtrak (✆ **800/USA-RAIL** [872-7245]; www.amtrak.com) provides rail service to and from New York and Washington, D.C., to the north, and to and from Florida to the south, with one train daily from each direction.

Greyhound (✆ **800/231-2222;** www.greyhound.com) offers regular service to both Raleigh and Durham. The **Raleigh bus station** is at 314 W. Jones St. (✆ **919/834-8275**) and the **Durham bus station** is at 515 W. Pettigrew St. (✆ **919/687-4800**).

VISITOR INFORMATION   Contact the **Greater Raleigh Convention and Visitors Bureau,** 421 Fayetteville St. Mall, Ste. 1505, Raleigh, NC 27601-1755 (✆ **800/849-8499** or 919/834-5900; www.visitraleigh.com). Hours are Monday to Saturday 8:30am to 5pm. **Capital Area Visitor Services,** in the lobby of the North Carolina Museum of History, 5 E. Edenton St. (✆ **919/807-7950;** www.ncmuseum ofhistory.org/vs/index.html), provides information about the state-government complex, local attractions, and historic sites; bus-route brochures are available. The center is open Monday to Friday 9am to 5pm, Saturday 10am to 4pm, and Sunday 1 to 3pm.

SPECIAL EVENTS   In mid-February, the **Southern Ideal Home Shows** draws thousands of visitors from all over the South; call ✆ **800/849-0248** or 704/376-6594 or visit www.southernshows.com for more information. In mid-October, the **North Carolina State Fair** (www.ncstatefair.org) also draws crowds from all over with its livestock competitions, culinary bake-offs, and corn pone charm. The fairgrounds are located 5 miles west of town on I-440 and then 1 mile west on N.C. 54. For exact dates, call ✆ **919/821-7400.** In early December, the city hosts an old-fashioned **Holiday Festival** at the North Carolina Museum of Art (✆ **919/839-6262;** http://ncartmuseum.org).

Exploring the Capitol & Environs

For the best possible tour of the capital city, make the **Capital Area Visitor Services** your first stop (see "Visitor Information," above). The staff starts you off with an orientation film, arms you with brochures, and coordinates walking or driving tours. Most of the attractions listed in this section are within easy walking distance of the state capitol.

The Hobbit Garden ★ 📷   Willie Pilkington and John Edward Dilley created a "secret garden" on a small plot of land in 1978. Their garden is dedicated to growing unusual plants—from carnivorous pitcher plants to evergreen dogwoods—many of which were thought impossible to cultivate in North Carolina. Speaking of which, have you ever come face to face with a Cornus Kousa Wolf Eye?

9400 Sauls Rd. ✆ **919/772-6761.** Reservations required. Admission $10. 2-hr. guided tours by appointment.

North Carolina Museum of Art ★   This museum houses a major collection of European paintings, plus American, 20th-century, ancient, African, Oceanic, and

Judaic exhibits. The permanent collection—with works by Raphael, Rubens, Van Dyck, Monet, Homer, and Wyeth—is complemented by a program of 12 to 15 special exhibitions annually. A special feature of the museum is the Virginia Camp Smith 17th-century Flemish *Kunstkamer,* a re-creation of a Flemish style "art room" with exhibits illustrating both decorative and fine arts. A 2009 $138-million extension added to the permanent collections with pieces such as casts of 22 bronze sculptures by Auguste Rodin, including *The Thinker* and *The Kiss.*

2110 Blue Ridge Rd. *©* **919/839-6262.** www.ncartmuseum.org. Free admission (there may be an admission fee for special exhibits). Tues–Thurs and Sat 10am–5pm; Fri 10am–9pm; Sun 10am–5pm.

North Carolina Museum of History The state's long and colorful history comes alive through innovative exhibits and programs in this state-of-the-art facility. It's all here, beginning with the Roanoke Island colonists to the present, including the contributions to the state by women and African Americans. The state, which was initially reluctant to enter what it called "a rich man's war and a poor man's fight," lost more native sons in battle than any other state in the Confederacy. The folk-life gallery showcases the state's cultural and crafts heritage, exhibiting music, pottery, baskets, and textiles.

5 E. Edenton St. *©* **919/807-7900.** www.ncmuseumofhistory.org. Free admission. Mon–Sat 9am–5pm; Sun noon–5pm.

North Carolina Museum of Natural Sciences ★ ☺ The state's oldest museum has found a bigger and better home, situated between the capitol and the legislature building. The museum's Exhibit Hall presents a variety of programs daily to the public, often featuring live animals. Exhibits focus on North Carolina's geology and geography, notably its plant and animal life. One of the biggest draws is "Willo," the world's only dinosaur with a fossilized heart. Among the big bones is *Acrocanthosaurus,* a spiny-lizard-type dinosaur, the only skeleton of its type in the world. The museum has one of America's greatest displays of whale skeletons as well. The Naturalist Center has a collection of specimens ranging from mammals to reptiles, fossils to minerals, and more.

11 W. Jones St. *©* **919/733-7450.** www.naturalsciences.org. Free admission, donations accepted; admission fees for special exhibits. Mon–Sat 9am–5pm; Sun noon–5pm. Open until 9pm the 1st Fri of every month. Closed Thanksgiving, 2 days at Christmas, and New Year's Day.

The State Capitol ★ This stately Greek Revival structure (constructed 1833–40) is a National Historic Landmark. All state business was conducted here until 1888. The building now contains the offices of the governor and lieutenant governor, as well as restored legislative chambers. Beneath the awe-inspiring 97-foot copper dome is a duplicate of Antonio Canova's marble statue of George Washington dressed as a Roman general. The capitol takes about 30 to 45 minutes to tour. Reservations are necessary for guided tours. Call the capitol for additional information and times.

Capitol Sq. *©* **919/733-4994.** www.nchistoricsites.org/capitol/default.htm. Free admission. Mon–Sat 9am–5pm; Sun 1–4pm.

State Legislative Building Allow about 30 minutes to go through this striking contemporary building, designed by Edward Durrell Stone. But take longer if you happen to be here when the legislature is in session. You'll be able to watch the proceedings and perhaps even spot a young, postmillennial Jesse Helms in the making.

16 W. Jones St. *©* **919/733-7928.** www.ncga.state.nc.us. Free admission. Mon–Fri 8am–5pm; Sat 9am–5pm; Sun 1–5pm.

Outdoor Pursuits

Raleigh's **parks** and recreational facilities have won awards. In all, there are 3,904 acres of parkland and 1,332 acres of water. A greenway system covers 1,297 acres, offering hiking and jogging trails that link many of Raleigh's 141 parks.

One of the major recreational centers is **Lake Wheeler,** 6404 Lake Wheeler Rd. (© 919/662-5704; www.raleighnc.gov), comprising 60 acres of parkland and 600 acres of lake, 5 miles southwest of Raleigh. Activities include sailing, rowing, kayaking, canoeing, and fishing. Hours are sunrise to sunset daily.

Dead Broke Farm, 6921 Wildlife Trail (© **919/596-8975** www.deadbroke horsefarm.com), offers horseback riding and summer camping trips on 60 wooded acres of hills, creeks, lush vegetation, and wildlife that includes deer, cranes, and turkeys. Open daily year-round, the farm charges $50 per person for each hour of trail riding, or $75 for 2 hours. The cost is $175 per person daily for a camping trip.

William B. Umstead State Park, 8801 Glenwood Ave. (© **919/571-4170;** www.ncparks.gov/Visit/parks/wium/main.php), is actually two parks, including Crabtree and Reedy Creek, comprising a total acreage of 5,439. We prefer Crabtree; it has better facilities and a big lake where you can rent boats for $5 and go fishing ($20 deposit). It also has a visitor center and picnic tables. Biking trails riddle the park, as do hiking trails.

The best golf is at the **Tobacco Road Course,** 442 Tobacco Rd. in Sanford (© **877/ 284-3762** or 919/775-1940; www.tobaccoroadgolf.com), an 18-hole, 6,500-yard, most challenging course. Greens fees range from $49 to $134 (depending on the season), and the course is open Monday to Friday 8am to dusk, on Saturday 7am to dusk, and on Sunday 8am to dusk. Greens fees include cart rentals.

Raleigh also has about 24 miles of greenway for **bikers.** For trail maps, contact the **Raleigh Parks and Recreation Center,** 2401 Wade Ave. (© **919/831-6640;** www.raleigh-nc.org).

The best **camping** is at **Raven Rock State Park,** 3009 Raven Rock Rd. at Lillington (© **910/893-4888;** www.ncparks.gov/Visit/parks/raro/main.php), and at **Falls Lake State Recreational Area,** 3304 Creedmoor Rd., 12 miles via N.C. 50 (© **919/ 676-1027;** www.ncparks.gov/Visit/parks/fala/main.php). Call for information, which varies seasonally.

Raleigh has at least 112 **tennis** courts in its city parks.

Where to Stay

EXPENSIVE

Raleigh Marriott Crabtree Valley ★   Located 10 minutes northwest of the city center and 7 miles from the airport, this is Raleigh's leading hotel. It lacks some of the charm of the Oakwood Inn (see below) but is professional in every way and caters to a large business clientele. The city's largest hotel,offers well-furnished guest rooms and large bathrooms spread over its six floors. The most luxurious and expensive rooms are on the concierge level.

4500 Marriott Dr. (U.S. 70 W. opposite the Crabtree Valley Mall), Raleigh, NC 27612. © **800/909-8289** or 919/781-7000. Fax 919/781-3059. www.marriott.com. 375 units. $99–$189 double; $289–$489 suite. Children 17 and under stay free in parent's room. AE, DC, DISC, MC, V. Free parking. **Amenities:** 2 restaurants; bar; exercise center; Jacuzzi; 2 pools (1 indoor, 1 outdoor). *In room:* A/C, TV, hair dryer, Wi-Fi ($13 per day).

Sheraton Capital Center Hotel Raleigh ★   A 17-story redbrick skyscraper that factored prominently into an urban renewal of downtown Raleigh when it was built in 1982, this is the tallest, most visible, most consistently occupied, and most appealing large hotel in the city center. The uniformed staff here is polite and well versed in the layout of Raleigh. The hotel has a coffee-shop-inspired restaurant within the glass-roofed atrium, a lobby level covered with either travertine marble or flagstones, soaring redbrick arches, and comfortable, conservatively contemporary midsize guest rooms. The hotel is directly connected, through a covered passageway, to the city's convention facilities.

421 S. Salisbury St., Raleigh, NC·27601. ✆ **800/325-3535** or 919/834-9900. Fax 919/833-1217. www. starwoodhotels.com. 355 units. $99–$179 double; $129–$289 club room; $250–$550 suite. AE, DC, DISC, MC, V. Parking $10. **Amenities:** Restaurant; bar; 2 cafes; babysitting; concierge; health club; room service. *In room:* A/C, TV, hair dryer, minibar, Wi-Fi ($10 per day).

Umstead Hotel & Spa ★★★   Only minutes from the center of Raleigh is this oasis of tranquillity and luxury set on 12 wooded acres. Its public spaces are filled with art, and there are notes of charm and grace throughout, as evoked by the carefully furnished bedrooms. You can wander the sculpted gardens and later dine on first-class, locally sourced cuisine. The beautifully appointed bedrooms with balconies opening onto panoramic views are the most luxurious and spacious in the area. Organic materials like limestone and granite bring a touch of the outdoors in.

Woodland Pond Dr., Cary, NC 27513. ✆ **866/877-4141** or 919/447-4000. www.theumstead.com. 150 units. $219–$289 double; from $309 suite. AE, DC, DISC, MC, V. **Amenities:** Restaurant; bar; concierge; exercise room; room service; spa. *In room:* A/C, TV/DVD, CD player, MP3 docking station, Wi-Fi (free).

MODERATE

The Oakwood Inn ★★ 🛍   Raleigh has no shortage of hotels, motor hotels, and motels, but it has almost no inns. The Oakwood fills the vacuum; it's an inn of charm and character. Built in 1871, the Victorian building lies in the Historic District, and guests can stroll to attractions downtown. A wraparound porch evokes the best of Southern architecture in the 19th century. Leaded glass and mahogany and walnut furniture re-create a long-gone era, as do the well-kept bathrooms with showers and claw-foot tubs. The inn, listed on the National Register of Historic Places, serves the best breakfast in the area.

411 N. Bloodworth St., Raleigh, NC 27604. ✆ **800/267-9712** or 919/832-9712. Fax 919/836-9263. www. oakwoodinnbb.com. 6 units. $119–$159 double. Rates include full breakfast. AE, DC, DISC, MC, V. Free parking. **Amenities:** Breakfast room; lounge. *In room:* A/C, TV, hair dryer, Wi-Fi (free).

Where to Dine

EXPENSIVE

Bloomsbury Bistro ★ FRENCH/INTERNATIONAL   At Five Points, in the center of the city, chef John Toler offers a delightful cuisine that features a seasonal menu adjusted every 6 weeks to take advantage of what's fresh in the local markets. For some, the decor evokes a country club, and the waitstaff is among the most helpful, polished, and, yes, friendliest in the Triangle. The selections include both old favorites and innovative new ones. An appetizer with a touch of exoticism is the Chinese-style gingered pork "dim dum" dumplings wrapped in napa cabbage leaves with shiitake mushrooms and Lap Chong sausage. For a main course, try the sautéed boneless Carolina mountain trout wrapped in pancetta.

509 W. Whitaker Mill Rd. © **919/834-9011.** www.bloomsburybistro.com. Reservations recommended. Main courses $18–$32. AE, DC, MC, V. Mon–Sat 5:30–10pm.

Margaux's ★ INTERNATIONAL   Its strip-mall setting belies the serene and elegant enclave within. Seafood and steak are the specialties, but the chefs are also particularly strong in Pacific Rim cuisine. Plow through the menu in a quest for such delights as Parmesan-dusted oysters, rillettes of rabbit, and fried calamari. For a main course, try the panko-crumbed grouper with ginger-lime hollandaise sauce. There's live music on Friday, and, on the upper level, a bartender who makes the best martinis in the capital.

8111 Creedmoor Rd. in Brennan Station. © **919/846-9846.** www.margauxsrestaurant.com. Main courses $20–$90; 3-course dinner $28. AE, DC, DISC, MC, V. Mon–Thurs 5:30–9pm; Thurs–Fri 11:30am–1:30pm; Sat 5:30–10pm.

Second Empire Restaurant and Tavern ★ INTERNATIONAL   The historically important landmark that contains these two restaurants is one of the most visible antique houses in downtown Raleigh. Originally built in 1879 in the French-inspired Second Empire style, it devotes most of its architectural glamour to the restaurant, and a somewhat folksier and less-formal venue to its (less-expensive) tavern. Frankly, we feel a bit more comfortable in the tavern (the restaurant, at its worst, can be a wee bit pompous). Among the restaurant's well-prepared menu items are buttermilk-fried quail and arugula salad, steamed local clams with penne pasta, pan-roasted halibut, and grilled Angus beef rib-eye. The food in the tavern is less expensive and less fussed over, and includes fried calamari, "pulled chicken" pasta, Kobe beef hamburger, and seafood paella.

330 Hillsborough St. © **919/829-3663.** www.second-empire.com. Reservations recommended. Main courses $24–$36 restaurant, $17–$30 tavern. AE, DC, MC, V. Restaurant Mon–Thurs 5:30–10pm; Fri–Sat 4:30–11pm. Tavern Mon–Sat 4:30–10pm.

Sullivan's Steakhouse ★ STEAKS   This is the best, most posh, and most upscale steakhouse in Raleigh—the kind of classy, hard-drinking, and indulgent grill room where Sinatra and his Rat Pack might have felt very much at home. Opulent and full of machismo, with an open-to-view kitchen and lots of exposed brick, it emulates a Chicago-style steakhouse with a speak-easy aura. A resident butcher trims the steaks artfully, and a bar area (which some guests enjoy even more than the restaurant) near the entrance is for whiling away time before your table is ready. Here live jazz begins every evening at 5:30pm. Past guests have included former senator John Edwards, as well as local sports coaches and players. Steaks come in two-fisted portions of rib-eye, filet, porterhouse, and New York strip. Lamb, veal, chicken, and a selection of fish (ahi tuna steak and tequila-and-lime-flavored shrimp) are also available.

414 Glenwood Ave. © **919/833-2888.** www.sullivanssteakhouse.com. Reservations recommended. Main courses $25–$36. AE, DC, MC, V. Mon–Fri 11:30am–2pm and 5:30–11pm; Sat–Sun 5–10pm.

MODERATE

BuKu ★★ INTERNATIONAL   Attracting a young crowd, this exotic restaurant (and venue for live entertainment) is presided over by William D'Auvray, who grew up in the Philippines and practices "borderless" cooking. He is a true global chef, taking what he wants from menus and recipes around the world, but adding his own distinctive style. As a starter you might go for the shrimp puffs with cashew nuts, *sambal*, and a tamarind broth or else lamb *kefta* meatballs with lentils and Moroccan *harissa*. Market-fresh seafood is a fixture, as are sashimi selections and both fast- and

Where Highbrow Meets Biscuits & Grits

Raleigh has its share of posh cosmopolitan dining spots, but a defiantly down-home restaurant in the City Market is still packing 'em in. **Big Ed's City Market Restaurant,** 229 Wolfe St. (© 919/836-9909), remains stubbornly old-fashioned despite the encroaching gentrification that surrounds it. Its allegiance to old-time country tradition has endeared it to hundreds of local residents, who crowd in every day for much more than just breakfast and lunch: Some social commentators have likened this place to a deep cultural immersion into Hillbilly Chic. Breakfast platters cost $4 to $9 each and come with grits and red-eyed peas flavored with ham hocks. Main courses at lunch cost $8.20 to $12. Don't even think of showing up here on a Sunday or after 2pm. The folksy-looking dining room evokes a cross between a church bazaar and a grange, all of it layered with nostalgic mementos from the rural South of old. It's open Monday to Friday 7am to 2pm and Saturday 7am until noon. No credit cards are accepted.

slow-cooked meats, everything from beef *tataki* with wasabi greens to sake-braised short ribs with Japanese rice. He uses only wild-caught, sustainable fish, shellfish, and mollusks obtained from fisheries using artesian methods.

110 E. Davie St. © **919/834-6963.** http://bukuraleigh.com/buku. Reservations recommended. Main courses $9–$24. AE, DISC, MC, V. Mon–Sat 11am–2am.

The Duck & Dumpling ASIAN   Our favorite Asian restaurant in Raleigh has the kind of glossy, minimalist decor that evokes an upscale neighborhood in Hong Kong—a cocoon of burnished teak and cherrywood. Reasonably priced and charmingly unpretentious, it has a large and accommodating bar near its entrance and a sophisticated array of martinis, some made with sake. The chef is likely to pay a personal visit to your table during the course of your meal, asking how, for example, you like the deep-fried pork-and-shrimp dumplings, the spring rolls, the steamed filet of sea bass with ginger, the lamb chops cooked with curried coconut milk, or the "lion's head" meatball stuffed with scallops and served in a clay pot with baby bok choy.

Moore Sq., 222 Blount St. © **919/838-0085.** www.theduckanddumpling.com. Reservations recommended. Main courses $7.95–$9.45 lunch, $9.45–$19 dinner. AE, DC, MC, V. Mon–Fri 11:30am–2:30pm; Mon–Thurs 5–10pm; Fri–Sat 5–11pm.

42nd St. Oyster Bar & Seafood Grill ★ SEAFOOD   In a restored 1931 warehouse, this lively restaurant is your best bet for raw oysters, clams, and mussels, plus an array of other seafood ranging from mesquite-grilled catfish to soft-shell crabs. The oyster stew and the clam chowder are the best in the area, and the catch of the day (check the blackboard) is served broiled, blackened, or grilled. Although this is primarily a seafood restaurant, the chefs also serve pastas and some of the most tender steaks in Raleigh, especially the 10-ounce Angus sirloin. The hush puppies are almost a meal unto themselves.

508 W. Jones St. © **919/831-2811.** www.42ndstoysterbar.com. Reservations recommended. Main courses $16–$40; lunch specials $7.95–$16. AE, DC, MC, V. Mon–Fri 11:30am–3pm; Mon–Wed 4–10pm; Thurs–Fri 4–11pm; Sat 5–11pm; Sun 5–10pm.

Michael Dean's ★ AMERICAN/SEAFOOD This seafood grill and oyster bar is the creation of Dean Ogan, who wanted an alternative to the chain restaurants sweeping across the Raleigh-Durham area. Against the backdrop of a sedate, modern decor, informality reigns, especially Thursday to Saturday nights in the Oyster Bar where a DJ spins. Known to be the best in the area, the fish and chips feature Guinness-battered tilapia. You can also order such dishes as North Carolina flounder stuffed with Tasso ham and shrimp or pistachio-encrusted salmon with papaya. "Food Without Fins" offers dishes such as wood-grilled marinated chicken or grilled Black Angus rib-eye with a blue cheese potato cake. The Sunday buffet brunch is the best in Raleigh.

6004 Falls of Neuse Rd. ✆ **919/790-9992.** www.michaeldeans.com. Reservations recommended. Main courses $9–$24; Sun brunch $15 adults, $6 children 9 and under. AE, DISC, MC, V. Restaurant Mon–Thurs 11am–2pm and 5–10pm; Fri–Sat 11am–2pm and 5–11pm; Sun 10am–2pm and 5–10pm. Oyster Bar Sun–Thurs 11am–midnight; Fri–Sat 11am–1am.

Mo's Diner SOUTHERN The owners of this popular restaurant are known for their sense of humor and good food. Despite a location on an uninspired street corner in downtown Raleigh, in a blue-sided cottage adjacent to a homeless shelter, it's one of the most sought-after dining spots in town. You'll eat behind lace curtains in an appealingly cluttered warren of small, parlorlike rooms that evoke the home of someone's genteel Southern grandmother. Menu items change with the inspiration of the chef but might include baked oysters with fresh spinach and bacon-flavored hollandaise, sautéed chicken livers with Madeira sauce, grilled pork tenderloin with caramelized onions and balsamic vinegar, and seared tenderloin of beef with mashed potatoes and port-wine sauce.

306 E. Hargett St. ✆ **919/856-9938.** www.mosdiner.net. Reservations recommended. Main courses $14–$29. AE, DISC, MC, V. Tues–Sat 5:30–9pm.

INEXPENSIVE

Carolina Ale House AMERICAN This is both a munch-down eatery and a place to occupy your late nights. The design of this good-time bar is a sort of hybrid, the marriage of an Alaskan timber baron's mansion and a Victorian sawmill—sprawling, high-ceilinged, beer-stained, and woodsy. Expect a state of creative cacophony that gets louder as the evening progresses, thanks to about 25 TV screens (some of them jumbo-size). Monday features enormous platters of shrimp for around $10 per platter, and the rest of the week the culinary norm involves quesadillas, sandwiches, burgers, pastas, salads, grilled steaks, and seafood.

4512 Falls of Neuse Rd. ✆ **919/431-0001.** www.carolinaalehouse.com. Reservations not necessary. Main courses $9–$17. AE, DC, MC, V. Daily 11am–2am.

Clyde Cooper's Barbecue ★ BARBECUE Since 1938, this old-timer has been *the* place in Raleigh for barbecue. Even if you think you prefer the Texas stuff, Cooper's will convert you. Prices are reasonable, and portions are generous. The chef slow cooks only top-grade pork shoulders until they're so tender they practically melt. They're then mixed with a zesty barbecue sauce good enough to be bottled. For dessert, try the super-moist carrot cake.

109 E. Davie St. (1 block east of the mall). ✆ **919/832-7614.** www.clydecooperbbq.com. Reservations not accepted. Main courses $6–$7.50. No credit cards. Mon–Sat 10am–6pm.

NoFo INTERNATIONAL When this likable restaurant and its crowded-with-novelties gift emporium opened here, in what was originally conceived in the 1950s as a member of the Piggly Wiggly grocery store chain, a team of designers added

The Most Historic Hot Dog in North Carolina

The most famous hot dogs in North Carolina are dispensed from one of the state's most unassuming storefronts. The **Roast Grill** was established in 1940 by members of the Salikis family, who had just arrived as new immigrants from Greece. During its tenure at this address, the Roast Grill's hot dogs have been sampled by every politician in North Carolina, including formidable right-winger Jesse Helms, whose picture and written thank-you letter join several such pieces of nostalgia decorating the grill walls. Today the likable owner is George Poniros, grandson of the founders, who, like his forebears, imports his hot dogs from Michigan, serves them on thin sheets of waxed paper, and outlaws ketchup as antithetical to the proper flavor of the hot dog. (Chili, mustard, and cheese sauce are still well-accepted garnishes, however.) Hot dogs cost $2 each. No other food items are served, with the exception of desserts, priced at $1.35 to $2.50 each. The joint has only two or three tiny tables, plus a half-dozen seats at the luncheonette-style countertop. The Roast Grill is at 7 S. West St., Raleigh (© 919/832-8292; www.roastgrill. com). It's open Monday to Saturday 11am to 4pm and accepts cash only.

decorative touches such as a spectacular Murano glass chandelier. Menu items are savory, flavorful, and popular, including shrimp and grits; Thai-style chicken wraps; shrimp-studded BLTs; grilled chicken salads; and a blue-plate special that, on the night of our visit, included stuffed chicken breasts with mozzarella, basil, and tomato. Come here for a sense of fun and whimsy and artfully offhanded cuisine. Brunch is a popular tradition here.

2014 Fairview Rd., Five Points. © **919/821-1240.** www.nofo.com. Reservations recommended for dinner Fri-Sat. Breakfast and brunch platters and lunch sandwiches and salads $7.25–$9.50; dinner main courses $15–$18; brunch main courses $8.25–$13. AE, DC, MC, V. Mon–Thurs 11am–3pm and 5:30–9pm; Fri 11am–3pm and 5–10pm; Sat 10am–3pm and 5–10pm; Sun 10am–3pm.

Shopping

Raleigh, with its population of up-and-coming financiers, computer experts, and yuppies, is known for an elegant array of home decorating stores, many of them specializing in antiques. A dense cluster of antiques stores lies along Fairview Road in the suburban neighborhood known as Five Points because of its intersection of five different streets. One of the most appealing is **Antiques at Five Points,** 2005 Fairview Rd. (© 919/834-4900), which focuses on mid-19th- to mid-20th-century American, English, and European antiques and paintings. A nearby competitor loaded with French and English antiques, many of a higher quality than those available from less upscale competitors, is **Acquisitions, Ltd.,** 2003 Fairview Rd. (© 919/755-1110; www.acquisitionslimited.com).

Peché du Chocolat, 14 Glenwood Ave. (© 919/264-1674), is the finest chocolate shop in Raleigh, a tastefully upscale, European-style venue for confections that derive from Belgium, Italy, France, Turkey, and Lebanon.

Raleigh After Dark

The elegantly renovated **Progress Energy Center for the Performing Arts,** 1 E. South St. (© 919/831-6011; www.progressenergycenter.com), is the home of the

North Carolina Symphony Orchestra and the North Carolina Theatre. The orchestra gives around 50 performances annually in Raleigh; Gerhardt Zimmermann is its conductor laureate. Critics have hailed the North Carolina Theatre as "the best it gets this side of Broadway." It specializes in large-scale Broadway musicals such as *Hello, Dolly*. This is the state's only resident professional musical theater. The box office is open Monday to Friday 10am to 5pm.

The hottest sports tickets in a sports-crazy town are for seats to a **Carolina Hurricanes game** (http://hurricanes.nhl.com). The Raleigh hockey franchise catapulted to greatness when it won its first Stanley Cup in 2006, defeating the Edmonton Oilers. The Canes play in the **RBC Center,** 1400 Edwards Mill Rd. (✆ **919/861-2300;** www.rbccenter.com). For tickets, call ✆ **866/645-2263.**

Berkeley Cafe   This is a blues bar with a back deck. In addition to blues, you're likely to hear everything from folk rock to R&B. Open Wednesday to Saturday from 8pm to 2am, and for lunch Monday to Friday from 11am to 2:30pm. 217 W. Martin St. ✆ **919/821-0777.** www.berkeleycafe.net. Cover varies, depending on the band.

Flex   Set within a dank and somewhat claustrophobic cellar, and painted mostly black, this is the most visible and popular gay bar in Raleigh. Many of its patrons drive for miles from the rural hamlets throughout the Piedmont for access, especially on Friday and Saturday nights. Beginning at midnight every Thursday, there's a "Trailer Park Prize Night" when all of the *artistes* are in drag, and where many members of the crowd are nubile young women, who scream and giggle appropriately. Thursday to Sunday, the club charges a cover of between $2 and $4 per person. Open Monday to Saturday 5pm to 2:30am and Sunday 2pm to 2am. 2 S. West St. ✆ **919/832-8855.** www.flex-club.com. Cover $2–$4.

Napper Tandy's Irish Pub   Formerly the Rí Rá Irish Pub, Napper Tandy's (named after an Irish politician) has infused new life into this favorite local hangout and claims to be the "pub that parties like a club." Featuring specials every night, the pub also has widescreen TVs for sporting events and live Irish music on Friday. Don't miss the $6 20-ounce Guinness pints all day, every day. Pub fare includes everything from fish and chips to bangers and mash. It's open daily from 11am to 2am. 126 N. West St. ✆ **919/833-5535.** www.nappertandysirishpub.com.

The Pour House   This is perhaps the most popular bar in the Triangle area. Set on two different levels, it offers live music and pool games. Entertainment might be a jam band, a group of local musicians, or a popular touring act. Bartenders offer 30 quality draft beers, with pints ranging in price from $3.50 to $6.50. Each band decides what to charge at the door. The house doesn't add to the cover, and the musicians get all the money. When there is a cover, it's $5 to $12. *Tip:* The bouncer doesn't get here until around 10pm, so go early and get in free. Open Thursday to Saturday 5pm to 2am and Sunday to Wednesday 8pm to 2am. 224 S. Blount St. ✆ **919/821-1120.** www.the-pour-house.com. Cover $5–$12.

DURHAM ★

23 miles W of Raleigh

In the late 1860s, Washington Duke left the Confederate army and walked 137 miles back to his farm in Durham, where he took up life again as a tobacco farmer. That first year, he started grinding and packaging the crop to sell in small packets. In 1880, he decided that there was a future in cigarettes—then a new idea—and, along with his three sons, set to work to manufacture them on a small scale. By 1890, the family had formed the American Tobacco Company, and a legendary American manufacturing empire was underway.

Durham, a small village when Duke returned, blossomed into an industrial city, taking its commercial life from the "golden weed." And it still does. From September until the end of December, tobacco warehouses ring with the chants of auctioneers moving from one batch of the cured tobacco to the next, followed by buyers who indicate their bids with nods or hand signals.

Even Duke University, the cultural heart of Durham, is linked to tobacco. The university was quiet little Trinity College until national and international prominence came with a Duke family endowment of $40 million in 1924. Its medical center is one of the most highly respected in the world.

Essentials

GETTING THERE   Durham is reached from the east via U.S. 70 and I-40 to N.C. 147, from the north via I-85, from the west via I-40/85 to I-85, and from the south via U.S. 15/501 joining I-40 to N.C. 147. The AAA office in Durham is the **Carolina Motor Club,** 3909 University Dr. (© **919/489-3306**).

For service to Raleigh-Durham International Airport (RDU), see "Essentials," under "Raleigh," earlier in this chapter. **Amtrak** (© **800/USA-RAIL** [872-7245]; www.amtrak.com) has a station on Pettegrew Street (© **919/956-7932**).

VISITOR INFORMATION   Contact the **Durham Convention & Visitors Bureau,** 101 E. Morgan St., Durham, NC 27701 (© **800/446-8604** or 919/687-0288; www.durham-nc.com), which can supply local bus-route information.

SPECIAL EVENTS   Beginning in mid-June and lasting for the first 3 weeks in July, the **American Dance Festival** showcases modern dance on the campus of Duke University. Sometimes as many as 17 dance companies participate, and both national and international works have premiered. For information and tickets, call © **919/684-6402** or go to **www.americandancefestival.org**.

Exploring the Town & University

Duke Homestead State Historic Site ★★   The Duke homestead, where Washington Duke opened his first tobacco factory in a rickety one-room barn, is today a National Historic Landmark. As a Confederate soldier, Duke learned about the Union soldiers' love of bright-leaf tobacco, and he returned home to begin the humble enterprise that would one day establish North Carolina as the heart of a worldwide tobacco empire. The homestead has been called a "living museum of tobacco history," and the early farming techniques and manufacturing processes used in the production of tobacco are demonstrated. (Don't mention cancer around here.)

2828 Duke Homestead Rd. © **919/477-5498.** www.ibiblio.org/dukehome. Free admission. Tues–Sat 9am–5pm. Hours may vary. Take the Guess Rd. exit 175 from I-85 and drive ½ mile north.

Museum of Life and Science ☺   This museum is especially designed for children, but no matter what your age, you'll love the interactive, high-tech exhibits on the human body, weather, geology, and aerospace. One exhibit displays the *Apollo 15* lunar landing module, complete with a sample moon rock. Hands-on exhibits are in the Science Arcade and the Scientific Discovery Room. The 70-acre site also holds a farmyard, Loblolly Park, and a mile-long narrow-gauge railroad charging $2 for a ride.

433 Murray Ave. ℂ **919/220-5429.** www.ncmls.org. Admission $13 adults, $11 seniors, $9.50 children 3–12, free for children 2 and under. Labor Day to Memorial Day Mon–Sat 10am–5pm; Sun noon–5pm. Head north of I-85 off Duke St.

DUKE UNIVERSITY

The campuses of Duke University (ℂ **919/684-8111;** www.duke.edu) cover more than 1,000 acres on the west side of the city. The **East Campus,** which was the old Trinity College, features Georgian architecture, and its redbrick and limestone buildings border a half-mile-long grassy mall. The East Campus has a certain charm, but it's the **West Campus** (a short drive away on winding, wooded Campus Dr.) that really steals the show. Its Gothic-style buildings and beautifully landscaped grounds are nothing short of breathtaking.

The highlight of this showplace is the **Duke Chapel ★** (ℂ **919/684-2572**), reminiscent of England's Canterbury Cathedral. The bell tower of the majestic cruciform chapel rises 210 feet and houses a 50-bell carillon that rings out at the end of each workday and on Sunday. A half-million-dollar Flentrop organ with more than 5,000 pipes (said to be one of the finest in the Western Hemisphere) is in a special oak gallery, its case 40 feet high. Renowned organists perform public recitals on the first Sunday of each month. The long nave, with its ornate screen and carved-oak choir stalls, is lighted in soft shades of red, blue, green, and yellow from 77 stained-glass windows. Chapel hours are 8am to 10pm Monday to Friday during school terms, and there are interdenominational services every Sunday at 11am. Summer hours are Monday to Friday 8am to 8pm.

A visit to the West Campus would not be complete without a peek at **Cameron Indoor Stadium,** since 1935 the home of the Duke Blue Devils basketball team. Also on the West Campus is the **Duke University Medical Center,** which has gained worldwide fame for its extensive treatment facilities and varied research programs.

To arrange special **guided tours** of the campus and find out more about Duke, call the Admissions Office (ℂ **919/684-3214**) Monday to Friday 9am to 5pm and Saturday 9am to 1pm. We recommend a visit to the **Sarah P. Duke Gardens,** 55 lovely acres on the West Campus that draw more than 200,000 visitors each year. In a valley bordered by a pine forest, the gardens feature a lily pond, stone terraces, a rose garden, a native-plant garden, an Asiatic arboretum, a wisteria-draped pergola, and colorful seasonal plantings. The gardens are open daily from 8am until dark, and admission is free. Free tours of the gardens are available daily from 8am to dusk, and special private tours can be arranged through the Duke Gardens office (ℂ **919/684-3698;** www.hr.duke.edu/dukegardens). Private tours last 1½ hours, and the group rate for 1 to 15 people is $50, plus $5 per additional person. These tours must be booked 2 weeks in advance.

Where to Stay

Keep in mind that hotel rates go up during Duke University's graduation ceremonies and for major sporting events.

Arrowhead Inn ★★ This inn (ca. 1775) is one of the most highly honored inns in the area, acknowledged by such publications as USA *Today, Southern Living,* and *Food & Wine.* Your hosts, Gloria and Phil Teber, strive to continue the excellence that they have established at this inn. There's a choice of beautifully furnished rooms, each with king-, queen-, or twin-size beds. Seven of the rooms have a fireplace. The inn is complete with a sleeping loft, sitting room with fireplace, and front porch with rocking

FIELD OF DREAMS

It's true that the real name of the game in these parts is basketball—people take their hoops mighty seriously around here. But thousands of locals and tourists continue to fill the stands each summer as the **Durham Bulls** play a full season in the Class A Carolina League as an affiliate of the Atlanta Braves. The Bulls shot to fame on the shoulders of Kevin Costner catching for hotshot rookie pitcher Tim Robbins in the 1988 flick *Bull Durham*. But if you're in town for a game, don't expect to see the wonderful old-time ballpark where the film was actually shot. In 1995, the Bulls abandoned the old ballpark for snazzy new digs on Magnum Street, designed by the same architects who conceived Camden Yards in Baltimore. By the way, the famous snorting bull in the movie was a mere prop that proved such a hit that it's now a Bulls fixture. And there really *was* a Crash Davis on the team in the 1940s. Other famous alums of the Bulls include Joe Morgan, Mark Lemke, Steve Avery, Ryan Klesko, David Justice, and Rusty Staub. The season runs early April through early September. Unfortunately, tickets are very hard to get. As far in advance as possible, contact the Durham Bulls, 409 Blackwell St., PO Box 507, Durham, NC 27702 (© **919/956-2855;** www.dbulls.com).

---

chairs. A full breakfast is served from 8 to 9am in the dining room, in the "keeping room," or on the patio; a continental breakfast, left out for the earliest and latest risers, is available from 7:30 to 9:30am. There are hammocks outside for your leisure.

106 Mason Rd., Durham, NC 27712. © **800/528-2207** or 919/477-8430. Fax 919/471-9538. www.arrowheadinn.com. 9 units. $135–$265 double; $180–$250 suite; $295–$325 2-room log cabin; $265–$295 cottage. Rates include full or continental breakfast. AE, DC, DISC, MC, V. **Amenities:** Restaurant; babysitting; room service. *In room:* A/C, TV/DVD, hair dryer, MP3 docking station, Wi-Fi (free).

Holiday Inn Express at Research Triangle Park   Built in 2002, this is the best and most comfortable of the many modern hotels that have been built in the past dozen or so years on the rural outskirts of Durham. Expect a modern, well-maintained building painted a shade of pale coral, rising from a rural, rather isolated spot that's convenient (if you have a car) to the businesses of the Research Triangle Park. Rooms are comfortable, and although the neighborhood has few, if any, real diversions, the many business travelers who check in find it restful and easy to get to.

4912 S. Miami Blvd., Durham, NC 27703. © **888/465-4329** or 919/474-9800. Fax 919/474-9803. www.hiexpress.com. 81 units. $75 double; $85 suite. Rates include breakfast. AE, DC, MC, V. From downtown Durham, drive south along the Durham Fwy. (or 147 South) to I-40 East, get off at exit 281 (S. Miami Blvd.), and turn left after the exit ramp. **Amenities:** Restaurant; bar; airport shuttle (free); exercise room. *In room:* A/C, TV, fridge, hair dryer, Wi-Fi (free).

Washington Duke Inn & Golf Club ★★   On the Duke University campus, about a mile from U.S. 15/501, this is the premier inn of Durham, with an 18-hole golf course designed by Robert Trent Jones. Named for the original tobacco tycoon, it's filled with Duke memorabilia, including Washington Duke's own antique desk. The property is like a castle, with an L-shaped lower wing. Many of the helpful staff members are university students. Although the impressive redbrick mansion is traditional in style, the bedrooms are modern, with big mullioned windows, upholstered chairs, quilted spreads, and either one or two double beds.

Naturally, someone had to name the bar **Bull Durham.** The full-service restaurant, **Fairview,** the most comfortable in town, serves an excellent contemporary cuisine and features piano music.

3001 Cameron Blvd., Durham, NC 27705. ℂ **800/443-3853** or 919/490-0999. Fax 919/688-0105. www. washingtondukeinn.com. 271 units. $199–$229 double; from $259 suite. AE, DC, DISC, MC, V. Free parking. **Amenities:** Restaurant; bar; babysitting; 18-hole golf course; exercise room; indoor pool; room service; spa. *In room:* A/C, TV, hair dryer, minibar, Wi-Fi (free).

Where to Dine

Brightleaf Square, a complex of former warehouses built between 1900 and 1904, has a host of restaurants as well as shopping. You can enjoy a stroll and an ice cream in the courtyards.

EXPENSIVE

Four Square ★★ AMERICAN/INTERNATIONAL   Owners Elizabeth Woodhouse and Shane Ingram, a husband-and-wife team, have taken a Greek Revival mansion and put in place an exceptional restaurant. Constructed in 1908, this Edwardian manse is imbued with such architectural delights as leaded-glass windows. Expect some of the best service in town from the experienced and gracious waitstaff. Everything we've ordered here has been enjoyable, full of flavor, and made with very fresh-tasting ingredients. Try the grouper bouillabaisse with clams, mussels, fennel, tomatoes, and lobster ravioli. Loin of rabbit is served on pine-nut, currant, and olive polenta with rapini and braised rabbit jus. Many in-the-know guests, if the weather agrees, select a table on the wraparound veranda.

2701 Chapel Hill Rd. ℂ **919/401-9877.** www.foursquarerestaurant.com. Reservations required. Main courses $22–$33. AE, DC, MC, V. Mon–Sat 5:30–9:30pm.

Magnolia Grill ★★★ SOUTHERN/INTERNATIONAL/REGIONAL AMERICAN The grandest dining experience in Durham and one of North Carolina's treasures, the Magnolia Grill, with its peach and dark-green interior, delivers old Southern charm with a degree of urban sophistication inspired not just by the region, but by such faraway places as Thailand, Mexico, and the Mediterranean. This restaurant, better described as a bistro, evokes an unexpected coastal feel. Start with the wine list, which features more than 130 bottled varieties, 10 to 12 of which are sold by the glass. The menu changes frequently. During a recent visit, we started with the green-tomato soup with crab and country ham, followed by the grilled pork porterhouse with Low Country risotto and crawfish ale. The restaurant bar opens at 5pm for predinner drinks.

1002 9th St. ℂ **919/286-3609.** www.magnoliagrill.net. Reservations recommended. Main courses $25–$29. AE, MC, V. Restaurant Tues–Thurs 6–9:30pm; Fri–Sat 5:30–10pm. Bar 5–9:30pm. Closed major holidays.

Nana's ★ NEW AMERICAN   Chef-owner Scott Howell has presided over this local favorite since 1992, after having worked with David Bouley at his renowned New York restaurant Bouley. He has also cooked in Imola, Italy, at San Domenico's, and sous-chefed at Magnolia Grill (see above). An Asheville native, Howell combined his culinary experience with a love for Tarheel regional cooking, and the result is fresh and delicious. The menu changes daily; on one evening, the risotto special contained local sweet corn and coastal white shrimp and was topped off with spinach, Smithfield country ham, and scallions. The prosciutto-wrapped duck breast is served over roasted butternut squash and fennel. Nana's is known for its special wine dinners and has won *Wine Spectator* magazine's Award of Excellence every year since 1993.

2514 University Dr. ℂ **919/493-8545.** www.nanasdurham.com. Reservations recommended. Main courses $17–$30. AE, DC, DISC, MC, V. Mon–Sat 5:30–10pm.

MODERATE

Parizäde ★ INTERNATIONAL   Set on the ground floor of Durham's most visible skyscraper (the Wachovia Building), this is the most sophisticated, flashy, and gastronomically eclectic restaurant in town. The place is airy, high-ceilinged, and stylish. Lots of "suits and ties" dine here at lunchtime; a somewhat more-relaxed and less-work-driven crowd shows up at dinner. The menu features a sophisticated array of pastas, including a fine version of linguine with clams. Roasted pork loin comes with a fennel rosemary crust; roast chicken is accompanied by a rice pilaf of currant, grape leaves, pine nuts, and cinnamon served with a roasted garlic rosemary jus; and a local version of bouillabaisse is replete with fresh fish, shrimp, mussels, and a saffron-orange and tomato-fennel-flavored broth.

In the Wachovia Building, Irwin Sq., 2200 Main St. ℂ **919/286-9712.** www.ghgrestaurants.com. Reservations recommended. Main courses $7–$16 lunch, $14–$26 dinner. AE, DC, MC, V. Mon–Fri 11:30am–2pm and 5:30–10pm; Fri–Sat 5:30–11pm; Sun 5:30–9pm.

Pop's ITALIAN   Owners John Vandergrift and Chris Stinnett fill their menu with locally grown ingredients that they turn into an array of hearty Italian fare. We'd go here just for the warmed olives and the large bowl of savory mussels in a delectable broth, ideal for dipping the homemade bread into. The calamari and the field greens salad are also alluring, and you can sample other dishes such as linguine with local lump crabmeat, basil, bacon, and a creamed corn sauce. Another favorite dish that never leaves the menu is Pop's chicken filet "cooked under a brick," a technique that flattens the filet and seals in the juices. Patrons claim their pizzas are the best in town—try the pie topped with salted eggs, prosciutto, roasted garlic, and olives. You can opt for a romantic table for two in the corner or a high-top table in the center of all the action.

605 W. Main St. ℂ **919/956-7677.** www.pops-durham.com. Reservations recommended. Main courses $9–$22. AE, MC, V. Mon–Fri 11am–2pm; daily 5:30–9pm.

Watts Grocery ★ 🛍 SOUTHERN   In the Ninth Street shopping area, this down-home eatery run by Durham native Amy Tornquist serves the best farm-fresh fare in the area. The chef-owner believes in serving the best of Piedmont produce, and every rib-sticking dish is homemade. You can get fried chicken gizzards here just like grandma used to make when she wasn't baking those red velvet cupcakes. Sandwiches, burgers, and salads dominate the luncheon menu, featuring a fried green tomato BLT, even (our favorite) hand-cut buttermilk onion rings with a chipotle–blue cheese dipping sauce. At night it gets fancier with entrees ranging from braised rabbit in red wine to yellowtail snapper filets stuffed with crabmeat. Buttermilk pancakes and shrimp and grits highlight the breakfast menu.

1116 Broad St. at Club Blvd. ℂ **919/416-5040.** Reservations not necessary. Breakfast dishes $4–$9.50; lunch sandwiches $7–$11; dinner main courses $15–$20. MC, V. Tues–Sun 11am–2:30pm and 5:30–10pm.

INEXPENSIVE

Elmo's Diner AMERICAN   This is the busiest, most popular, and most nostalgia-laden diner in Durham, the ultimate burger joint where endless amounts of coffee are dispensed during exam week, and where a Southern-American menu has many locals recalling their childhoods. Set in what was originally designed as a bakery, and housing a staff that's clad in T-shirts, Elmo's has Naugahyde-covered banquettes and counter stools, spinning ceiling fans, and areas of exposed brick. Expect a simple, all-American menu that incorporates burgers, meatloaf, chicken burritos, salmon cakes, and omelets, as well as "full square meals" that stick to the ribs at affordable prices. Biscuits and gravy accompany virtually any main course you select.

776 Ninth St. ℂ **919/416-3823.** www.elmosdiner.com. Reservations not accepted. Main courses $5.50–$11. MC, V. Daily 6:30am–10pm.

International Delights ☺ MIDDLE EASTERN   For a change of pace you can come here and fill up on your choice of gyros, falafel, *kafta*, kabobs, freshly made salads, pizzas piping hot from the oven, and baklava. The hummus is the best in town, and the chefs are marvelous at cooking *foul* (fava beans), perfectly seasoned with tangy lemon. The baba ghanouj had some kick to it and comes in generous helpings. A lunchtime favorite is the chicken *shawarma* sandwich, with meaty chicken and flavorings of fresh cilantro and mint. Just don't ask for ketchup.

740 Ninth St. ℂ **919/286-2884.** Reservations not needed. Main courses $7–$12. MC, V. Mon–Sat 11am–9pm.

Vita MEDITERRANEAN   Few restaurants in Durham celebrate with as much zest the original, natural flavors of the Mediterranean. The lunch menu features an array of mixed salads, pizzas, and sandwiches. Pastas such as a traditional lasagna are always served. At night the menu broadens with a selection of some of the most delectable antipasti in town, including roasted eggplant and Parma prosciutto. Pizza is another popular dinner choice: Try the lamb sausage with feta cheese. Main dish specialties include chicken *osso buco* as well as scampi with angel-hair pasta laced with garlic and herbs.

2200 W. Main St. ℂ **919/286-9755.** www.ghgrestaurants.com. Reservations not required. Pizzas $7–$12; main courses $8–$14. AE, DC, MC, V. Mon–Thurs 11am–10pm; Fri–Sat 11am–11pm.

Durham After Dark

You can spend an entire evening at the **American Tobacco Company** (ℂ **919/433-1566;** www.americantobaccohistoricdistrict.com), a complex of bars and restaurants on the site of a 19th-century tobacco company. The facility is bordered by I-40, beside the Durham Bulls Triple A Baseball park, adjacent to the 2,800-seat **Durham Performing Arts Center** (ℂ **919/688-3722;** www.dpacnc.com), opened in November 2008. Among the choices for eating and drinking are **Café Zen** (sushi and Asian specialties), **Mellow Mushroom** (the best pizzas), **Symposium** (the best martinis), and **Tyler's** (best American comfort food and most varied import beers on tap).

The Down Under Pub   Wooden doors open into a chummy pub with a neighborhood feel, where an interesting cross section of Durhamites meet. Located in the historic downtown area, the Down Under Pub offers a good selection of beers, from European ales and lagers to American microbrews, and more than decent pub food. Play pool, throw darts, or, if you're really parched, belly up to the bar for a beer in yard- or half-yard-size glasses. Hours are Monday to Saturday 11:30am to 2am and Sunday from noon to 2am. 802 W. Main St. ℂ **919/682-0039.**

Satisfaction   This is one of Durham's most enduringly raucous and sometimes frenetic sports bars. It occupies part of what was built in 1904 as a tobacco warehouse, a structure that was renovated in the mid-1980s into a rustic, heavily timbered shopping-and-restaurant complex. The woodsy-looking decor is such that you can easily imagine endless pitchers of beer spilled on it. Virtually everybody here makes a fuss over the homemade potato chips, served with ranch dressing. It also serves steak, chicken, or submarine sandwiches, as well as burgers, pastas, and platters. The bar is open Monday to Saturday from 11am to 2am, and Sunday from noon until 10pm. In Bright Leaf Sq., 905 W. Main St. ℂ **919/682-7397.** www.historicbrightleaf.com.

CHAPEL HILL ★

28 miles W of Raleigh; 12 miles SW of Durham

The third point of the Research Triangle area is Chapel Hill, a small city that has managed to hold on to its village atmosphere in spite of the presence of a university that annually enrolls more than 25,000 students. Chapel Hill *is* the University of North Carolina (UNC) and has been in existence since 1795, when it was the first state university in the country. The 2,000-acre campus holds 125 buildings, ranging from Old East, the oldest state university building in the country (its cornerstone was laid in 1793), to the Morehead Planetarium, which was an astronaut-training center in the early days of the U.S. space program.

Just before the Civil War erupted, the student body was the second largest in the country, after Yale's. Then the fighting started, and most of UNC's undergraduates and faculty left for the battlefield. The school closed down from 1868 to 1875.

The university has consistently been a leader in American education—Chapel Hill has the highest concentrations of Ph.D.s in the United States—and a center of liberal intellectualism in a generally conservative state.

Schedule your visit ideally in spring to see the dogwoods and crape myrtle burst into bloom. At any time, you can wander past the stately pillared houses of Franklin Street and—surprise—find an espresso outlet on virtually every street corner, just as you can in Seattle.

Essentials

GETTING THERE   Chapel Hill is reached from the east by I-40 and I-85, from the west by I-85, from the north by N.C. 57, and from the south by N.C. 54.

The nearest airport is in Raleigh.

VISITOR INFORMATION   Information is provided by the **Chapel Hill/Orange County Visitors Bureau,** 501 W. Franklin St., Suite 600 (ℂ **888/968-2060** or 919/968-2060; www.visitchapelhill.org), open Monday to Friday 8:30am to 5pm and Saturday 10am to 2pm.

Exploring On & Off Campus

Your best introduction to the university is a free 1-hour **campus tour ★** that leaves from the Morehead Planetarium (the west entrance) at 250 E. Franklin St. For details, contact the UNC Visitors Center located within the Morehead Planetarium (ℂ **919/962-1630;** www.unc.edu/visitors). Hours are 9am to 5pm Monday to Friday.

With the tour or on your own, look for the **Old Well,** once the only source of drinking water for Chapel Hill. It stands in the center of the campus on Cameron Avenue, in a small, templelike enclosure with a dome supported by classic columns. Just east of it is **Old East,** begun in 1793 and the country's oldest state-university building. Across the way stands the "newcomer," **Old West,** built in 1824. **South Main Building** was begun nearby in 1798 and wasn't finished until 1814; in the interim, students lived inside the empty shell in rude huts. At the **Coker Arboretum,** at Cameron Avenue and Raleigh Street, 5 acres are planted with a wide variety of plants. As you walk around the campus, you'll hear popular tunes coming from the 167-foot **Morehead-Patterson Bell Tower,** an Italian Renaissance–style campanile.

Morehead Planetarium, on East Franklin Street (© **919/549-6863;** www.moreheadplanetarium.org), was the first planetarium owned by a university, and it was once used as a NASA training center. The star of the permanent scientific exhibits here is a large orrery, showing the simultaneous action of planets revolving around the sun, moons revolving around planets, and planets rotating on their axes. The stargazing theater has a 68-foot dome. Admission to the planetarium is free; admission to the show is $7.25 for adults and $6 for seniors, students, and children. Hours are Monday to Saturday 10am to 3:30pm (plus Fri–Sat 6:30–9pm) and Sunday 1 to 4:30pm.

UNC has one of the largest athletic programs in the South. The Tarheels field 26 varsity teams and maintain a 24-hour Carolina hot line number, providing recorded information about all upcoming sporting events on campus. Information is also available from the **Smith Center Ticket Office** (© **800/722-4335** or 919/962-2296; Mon–Fri 8am–5pm). Carolina has a long history of recruiting top players; its famous alums include Michael Jordan and James Worthy.

Off campus, one of the most appealing botanical gardens in the Southeast comprises nearly 600 acres of mostly donated land. Accessible via laboriously laid-out paths and walking trails, the **North Carolina Botanical Garden ★★**, Totten Center (© **919/962-0522;** www.ncbg.unc.edu), includes about 2,500 of the 4,700 plant species that are known to be native or naturalized in North and South Carolina, as well as herbs and plants from around the world. Allow at least 45 minutes for the simplest overview of this amazingly complex compound of gardens and natural habitats. It's open Monday to Friday year-round 8am to 5pm; Saturday hours are 9am to 6pm; Sunday hours are 1 to 6pm. Admission is free.

Outdoor Pursuits

You'll find several fine golf courses around Chapel Hill. Public ones include the 18-hole **Cedar Grove Golf Course,** 700 McDade Store Rd., Hillsborough (© **866/211-2051** or 919/732-8397; www.cedargrovegolfcourse.com), with greens fees ranging from $9 to $25. Another good course, also an 18-holer, is **Finley Golf Course,** Finley Golf Course Road, Chapel Hill (© **919/962-2349**), with greens fees ranging from $23 to $82.

Orange County has an abundance of parks, gardens, and recreational facilities for visitors, including such activities as boating, fishing, camping, biking, and picnicking. For more information, call the following numbers and tell the staff which activities you'd like to pursue: **Chapel Hill Parks and Recreation** (© **919/968-2743;** www.ci.chapel-hill.nc.us) and **Orange County Recreation and Parks** (© **919/245-2660;** www.co.orange.nc.us/recparks/contactus.asp).

Where to Stay

The Carolina Inn ★★   Owned (but not operated) by the University of North Carolina, this hotel occupies sprawling redbrick premises that date from 1924 and have been artfully upgraded many times since. Part of its appeal derives from its public areas (an interconnected series of graciously appointed living rooms), which emit a genteel Southern dignity. Guest rooms are tastefully and conservatively outfitted in 18th- and 19th-century themes, with flower-patterned upholsteries and a restrained and relatively formal dignity that evokes the decor of an upscale private home.

211 Pittsboro St., Chapel Hill, NC 27516. ℂ **800/962-8519** or 919/933-2001. Fax 919/962-3400. www. carolinainn.com. 184 units. $239–$309 double; $269–$329 suite. AE, DC, DISC, MC, V. Valet parking $10. **Amenities:** Restaurant; bar; exercise room; room service. *In room:* A/C, TV, hair dryer, Wi-Fi (free).

The Franklin Hotel ★★★ This is a pocket of posh, somehow combining the intimacy and charm of an upmarket B&B with the luxuries and amenities of a swank hotel. A stay here in one of the penthouse suites is the ultimate in luxury for Chapel Hill. Bedrooms are deluxe, with custom-designed furniture, elegant fabrics, and colors in a palette of celadon, champagne, and chocolate. Black-and-white photographs of historic Franklin Street adorn the walls. In some units, glass doors open onto patio balconies. From a personalized phone number to luxurious bath amenities, everything is designed for the VIP, which is how every guest is treated.

311 W. Franklin St., Chapel Hill, NC 27516. ℂ **866/831-5999** or 919/442-9000. www.franklinhotelnc. com. 67 units. $169–$199 double; from $209 suite. AE, DC, DISC, MC, V. Free parking. **Amenities:** Restaurant; bar; concierge; exercise room; room service; spa. *In room:* A/C, TV/DVD, fridge, hair dryer, MP3 docking station, Wi-Fi (free).

Sheraton Chapel Hill Hotel ★ This is Chapel Hill's leading hotel, although the Fearrington House, on the outskirts (see "Staying Nearby," below), has more character. Parents of university students often stay here. The hotel offers ground-floor rooms with private patios and upper-floor rooms with balconies. All units contain well-kept bathrooms. The decor is tasteful and the place is well furnished, but it's somewhat unimaginative. Nevertheless, it's the most reliable choice for good, solid comfort. It offers a central location and nearby golf privileges. The hotel restaurant serves ordinary fare.

1 Europa Dr., Chapel Hill, NC 27517. ℂ **800/325-3535** or 919/968-4900. Fax 919/968-3520. www.star woodhotels.com. 168 units. $134–$229 double; $239–$310 suite. Children 15 and under stay free in parent's room. AE, DC, DISC, MC, V. Free parking. **Amenities:** Restaurant; bar; fitness center; outdoor pool. *In room:* A/C, TV, hair dryer, Wi-Fi (free).

Siena Hotel ★★ 🛎 Much of the charm of this well-groomed and well-managed hotel derives from its refusal to copy the Southern theme that's the norm at many of its competitors. Built in the mid-1980s in a distinguished-looking U-shaped design that evokes a villa in Tuscany, it's the closest thing in North Carolina to the kind of hotel you might have selected for a romantic second honeymoon in the Italian countryside. Inside, a lavish use of russet-colored marble, copies of 19th-century antiques, and reproductions of Italian Renaissance paintings (which line the upstairs hallways) create an ambience that's distinct. Rooms are large and accented with plush, elegant furnishings that include writing desks and comfortably upholstered armchairs for reading, rich (Italian) brocades, and marble-trimmed bathrooms.

1505 E. Franklin St., Chapel Hill, NC 27514. ℂ **800/223-7393** or 919/929-4000. Fax 919/968-8527. www.sienahotel.com. 80 units. $169 double; $199–$209 suite. AE, DC, MC, V. Free parking. **Amenities:** Restaurant; bar; complimentary membership at nearby health club; room service. *In room:* A/C, TV, hair dryer, Wi-Fi (free).

STAYING NEARBY

Fearrington House Country Inn ★★★ Created in 1974 in a planned community of gracious town houses surrounding a village center, the 60-acre grounds are meticulously kept, with the rose gardens adding a special burst of color. The guest rooms are just as inviting, with lots of little details: silk or dried flowers, antiques mixed with high-quality reproductions, double ottomans, cathedral ceilings, some seating areas, marble tables, various bed arrangements, and luxuriously appointed bathrooms. Some extras at the inn include screened porches, vintage Schwinns ready for your ride around the village, and even fresh flowers in the bathroom.

2000 Fearrington Village Center (15 min. south of Chapel Hill on U.S. 15/501), Pittsboro, NC 27312. ✆ **919/542-2121.** Fax 919/542-4202. www.fearrington.com. 33 units. $275–$350 double; $450–$575 suite. Rates include breakfast and afternoon tea. AE, MC, V. **Amenities:** 2 restaurants; bar; babysitting; exercise room; outdoor pool; room service ($20 per-person fee). *In room:* A/C, TV, hair dryer, Wi-Fi (free).

Where to Dine

A delightful spot for desserts, ice cream, and home-baked cakes is aptly named **Sugarland,** 140 E. Franklin St. (✆ **919/929-2100**), open daily from 10am to 10pm (until midnight on Sat–Sun). Every dessert is made from scratch, using local ingredients such as flour from Alamance County, eggs from Roxboro, and fresh dairy from Carolina cows.

EXPENSIVE

The Carolina Crossroads ★★ MODERN SOUTHERN/INTERNATIONAL

This charming, sophisticated restaurant has unofficially evolved into the local university's parlor and living room: a place where trustees and benefactors can be wined and dined, where collegiate sports heroes are celebrated, where the intricacies of academic politics are sometimes hammered into policy, and where the world at large can get a fast, favorable, and extremely hospitable overview of North Carolina's most distinguished academic institution. It's set inside a trio of dining rooms in the also-recommended Carolina Inn, amid Chippendale furniture and colonial tones of yellow and blue. It's supervised by executive chef Brian Stapleton (formerly associated with the Ritz-Carlton Hotel chain), whose craftsmanship is artfully tied to the seasons and infused with the best tenets of modern Southern cuisine. Especially tasty starters include prosciutto-wrapped arctic char on fall ratatouille or Southern barbecued quail. Main courses include oven-roasted snapper with shrimp jambalaya, grilled wild Irish salmon, roasted free-range chicken, or braised lamb shank.

In the Carolina Inn, 211 Pittsboro St. ✆ **919/933-2001.** Reservations recommended. Main courses $23–$32; afternoon tea $18–$28 per person (Thurs–Sun 2:30–4:30pm). AE, DC, MC, V. Daily 6:30–11am, 11:30am–2pm, and 5:30–9pm (until 10pm Fri–Sat).

Elaine's on Franklin ★★ 🍴 REGIONAL AMERICAN Virginia native Bret Jennings grew up eating "angel biscuits" (buttermilk biscuits), country ham with red-eye gravy, and fresh tomato sandwiches. Formerly a busboy, waiter, and caterer, Jennings worked himself up to the top. After training with two of America's top chefs, he decided to branch out on his own and create his own culinary style. On a recent visit to Elaine's, we delighted in such appetizers as spicy green-tomato and avocado gazpacho with North Carolina shrimp, and Vietnamese barbecued quail. For your main course, try the delicious grilled Colorado bison New York strip with honey lavender butter, or grilled wild salmon on barbecued lima beans.

454 W. Franklin St. ✆ **919/960-2770.** www.elainesonfranklin.com. Reservations required. Main courses $28–$36. AE, DISC, MC, V. Tues–Thurs 5:30–9:30pm; Fri–Sat 5:30–10pm.

Il Palio ★★ ITALIAN This culinary landmark is the best, most appealing, and most formal Italian restaurant in North Carolina. Set on the lobby level of the Siena Hotel (see "Where to Stay," above), a 5-minute drive north of the center of Chapel Hill, it's a showcase for the cuisine of chef Jim Anile, one of the most celebrated

culinary stars in the region. Expect a meal based on Tuscan priorities, but with a sophisticated use of ultrafresh local ingredients. Begin with a medley of marinated octopus and roasted peppers, or succulent smoked ahi tuna with endive, pear, and sweet mustard. Pasta might be garnished with cockles, rapini, and pancetta ham, or perhaps studded with lobster and laced with saffron sauce. The double-braised veal *osso buco* is absolutely splendid. About 95% of the wines offered here are Italian, reasonably priced, and presented with finesse.

In the Siena Hotel, 1505 E. Franklin St. © **919/929-4000.** Reservations recommended. Main courses $11–$19 lunch, $23–$36 dinner; 3-course set menu $39. AE, DC, MC, V. Mon–Wed 11:30am–2pm and 5:30–9pm; Thurs–Fri 11:30am–2pm and 5:30–10pm; Sat 5:30–10pm; Sun 11:30am–2pm.

Lantern Restaurant ★ PAN-ASIAN Named one of the top 50 restaurants in America in 2006 by *Gourmet* magazine, the Lantern is like no other in Chapel Hill. It's set against a cool decor of walls the color of green tea and tables like black coral. A brother-and-sister act, Brendan and Andrea Reusing, are the guiding lights. Our party got so intrigued with sharing appetizers that we almost didn't make it to the main courses. The cuisine is lively, original, and tasteful: The crackling calamari salad with seasonal greens and a lime miso vinaigrette or the Bang Bang chicken with Szechuan peppers did much to establish this place's well-deserved reputation for fiery flavors. We were enchanted by the steamed grouper with seared ginger, scallions, and black beans, and also found the "tea and spice" smoked chicken with yang chow pork and shrimp fried rice delightful.

423 W. Franklin St. © **919/969-8846.** www.lanternrestaurant.com. Reservations not accepted. Main courses $16–$30; 3-course tasting menu with wine $60–$75 per person. MC, V. Mon–Sat 5:30–10pm.

MODERATE

Crook's Corner ★ SOUTHERN Behind the rather quirky facade of Crook's Corner lurks one of Chapel Hill's superb restaurants. The seasonal menu may include such delights as shrimp and grits with mushrooms, bacon, and scallions; green Tabasco chicken; or barbecued St. Louis ribs. Among the side dishes are such down-home delicacies as fresh collard greens and hoppin' John (black-eyed peas and rice with scallions, tomato, and cheddar cheese). Waiters review the "War of Northern Aggression" as they haul out those jalapeño hush puppies along with the oyster and filet mignon scalawags. The wine-by-the-glass list is excellent. You may have to wait for a table, but it's worth it.

610 W. Franklin St. © **919/929-7643.** www.crookscorner.com. Reservations recommended. Main courses $16–$25. AE, DC, DISC, MC, V. Tues–Sat 5:30–10:30pm; Sun 10:30am–2pm and 5:30–10:30pm.

Pazzo! ★ ♟ ITALIAN/PIZZA/AMERICAN Local chef Seth Kingsbury has cooked at some of the great restaurants of North Carolina, including Magnolia Grill, but is now forging ahead in his own spot in the heart of Southern Village. Kingsbury uses fresh ingredients to concoct a finely toned cuisine that delights local foodies. Sample a range of delightful appetizers, such as a *fritto misto* of fried local green tomatoes, okra spears, and Vidalia onions in a pesto-tomato sauce, and BLT soup: tomato soup with lettuce and crispy pancetta. For a main, dig into the meticulously prepared wild king salmon over wilted greens and grilled veal scaloppine with herb-roasted potatoes. The pizza counter is open daily 11:30am to 10pm. You can eat in the small dining room or alfresco on the patio overlooking Market Street.

700 Market St., Southern Village. © **919/929-9984.** Reservations recommended. Main courses $13–$25. AE, MC, V. Daily 5–10pm.

Spice Street ★ INTERNATIONAL   Evoking a massive Asian spice market, this biggest, most daring, and most experimental theme restaurant in Chapel Hill is in the sprawling premises of what used to be a local department store on the town's eastern outskirts. There's a lot of showmanship, with a specific area designated as a delicatessen-style marketplace (with an impressive collection of olives, cheeses, and spices), a separate area devoted to sushi, a large sunny bar, a dining area that might remind you of a high-ceilinged Zen temple, and a separate area devoted to cooking classes and presentations by local celebrity chefs. Menu items derive from Asia (steamed pork dumplings with *ponzu* sauce; salmon roll tempura), Greece (beef *kefta* with cucumber and yogurt; "mezzo" platters of olives, hummus, *tzadziki*, and flatbread), the Middle East (grilled lamb chops with Egyptian-style lentils and yogurt sauce), and the Mediterranean (grilled calves' liver with pancetta ham and caramelized onions).

In the University Mall, 201 S. Estes Dr. ✆ **919/928-8200.** www.ghgrestaurants.com. Reservations not necessary. Main courses $7-$11 lunch, $13-$24 dinner. AE, DC, MC, V. Mon–Thurs 11:30am-2:30pm and 5-10pm; Fri-Sat 11:30am-2:30pm and 5:30-10:30pm; Sun 5-10pm.

Top of the Hill ★ INTERNATIONAL   This is not only the place to be seen in town, it also serves some of the best food. The home-brewed beer is among the finest in North Carolina. First-rate ingredients go into the wide array of dishes, including the best appetizers in town, ranging from plum barbecue seared tuna with wasabi cream to pan-seared mussels in a spicy white-wine marinara. The main dishes are delectable, including down-home favorites such as buttermilk fried chicken and Cajun grilled salmon with roasted tomato jam.

100 E. Franklin. ✆ **919/929-8676.** www.topofthehillrestaurant.com. Reservations required. Main courses $7.99-$9.99 lunch, $11-$30 dinner. AE, MC, V. Mon–Sat 11am-2am; Sun 11:30am-2am.

INEXPENSIVE

Allen & Son ★ BARBECUE/SOUTHERN   This joint is regionally known for its ribs. The patrons, even those who just got out of church, called the barbecue here "kickass." It's very tender—pulled pork, really, which is torn from the shoulder of the meat by hand. It also has a slightly smoky flavor. As for the Brunswick stew offered nightly, we've had better. The peach cobbler is one of the most luscious desserts served here. The good ol' boy favorite, however, is peanut butter pie. A love of plastic flowers, checked oilcloth, and "pig art" helps you enjoy the place more. Just follow the smell of billowing hickory smoke.

The Barbecue: A Pig-Pickin' Good Time

Collegiate sports and barbecue are things that elicit huge emotion within North Carolina, and when it comes to barbecue, everyone in the state seems to have a strong opinion. Dyed-in-the-wool Tarheels claim they can, blindfolded, tell where they are within their state based on the degree of spiciness of their respective barbecues. Here's a brief primer on what local residents expect when it comes to their favorite football food. Eastern North Carolina, site of the first settlers' landing, and presumably where food-preparation techniques are the most closely tied to Elizabethan England, seasons its barbecue only with salt, pepper, and vinegar. The farther west you head within the state, the darker, redder, and smokier the barbecue becomes.

6203 Millhouse Rd. ✆ **919/942-7576.** Main courses $6–$15. MC, V. Tues–Wed 10am–5pm; Thurs–Sat 10am–8pm.

The Barbecue Joint ☺ BARBECUE/SOUTHERN With its "pig-kitsch" decor, this eatery serves up some of the best barbecue in Chapel Hill. Two Carolina boys (even adult men are called "boys" in the South), Jonathan Childres and Damon Lapas, have teamed up to create this family favorite where mama, papa, and all the kids show up for a good tuck-in. First, the barbecue itself: It has a mellow, smoky taste; it's moist and served in "fist-size" knots of unadulterated pulled pork, with Asian chili sauce resting on the table for extra flavor. Barbecue isn't all you get here. The appetizers are the most imaginative of any so-called barbecue joint in town, including smoked duck quesadillas with roasted chipotle sauce, or the hummus, black bean, and pumpkin-seed dip with homemade tortilla chips. Other main-course delights include grilled wahoo with mango chutney, and a classic Cajun jambalaya, a meal in itself. Few can resist such desserts as the bourbon chocolate pecan pie or the caramelized pecan banana cake.

630 Weaver Dairy Rd. ✆ **919/932-7504.** Reservations recommended. Main courses $6–$15. AE, MC, V. Mon–Sat 11am–9pm.

Mama Dip's Kitchen ★ 🍴 TRADITIONAL COUNTRY COOKING This simple, first-come, first-served place is a great example of how the South likes to live: at the dinner table. The menu serves up succulent fried chicken, zesty beef or pork barbecue, and lip-smacking fried catfish as its tried-and-true specialties, along with a menu so vast it'll make you wish you had room to eat everything. The main courses are old-fashioned meat dishes, served with 2 of the 18 vegetable sides offered each day. Naturally, you get biscuits with everything. The drink of choice, of course, is sweet iced tea. All the vegetables are fresh, and the meat is purchased from the butcher shop down the street. Other good-tasting options include spaghetti, homemade soups, and savory gumbos, along with fresh homemade desserts.

408 W. Rosemary St. ✆ **919/942-5837.** www.mamadips.com. Reservations not accepted. Main courses $7–$18. DISC, MC, V. Mon–Sat 8am–9:30pm; Sun 8am–9pm.

Shopping

Many college towns in the South are noted for their quirky character and artistic penchant, however folksy. Chapel Hill is not without its eclectic beat, and you'll discover shops and boutiques that you would expect to find only in big cities.

A Southern Season, in the Eastgate Shopping Center, 1800 E. Franklin St. (✆ **919/929-7133;** www.southernseason.com), is one of the largest, most up-to-date, sprawling, and comprehensive large-scale shopping emporiums in North Carolina. It offers a fabulous array of delicatessen-style gourmet foods to go, wines and liqueurs, porcelain and crystal, and gift items, many with a distinctive Southern flair. Particularly appealing are gift baskets that, depending on what you specify, might contain kudzu jelly, Moravian spice cookies, chocolate-covered Carolina pecans, Carolina butter-crunch toffee, Blue Ridge bonbons, all manner of North Carolina honey-cured hams, plus about a thousand different gourmet items imported from Europe. You can even order vacuum-packed North Carolina barbecue here, available in either the western (with a touch of tomato sauce) or eastern North Carolina (with salt, pepper, and vinegar) style. The center is open Monday to Saturday 10am to 9pm, Sunday noon to 6pm.

Growing Your Own Endangered Plants

The **North Carolina Botanical Garden** (📞 919/962-0522; www.ncbg.unc.edu), which is maintained by the Horticultural Department of the University of North Carolina, is described in "Exploring On & Off Campus," earlier in this chapter. But what many visitors don't realize is that the staff that maintains the gardens also devotes enormous time and effort to its "conservation through propagation program," wherein rare (and sometimes imperiled) Carolina plants are propagated through seeds and cuttings, and then sold at rock-bottom prices to visitors in the hopes that they'll cultivate them in their own private gardens. A staff member or volunteer is usually on hand to explain the origin of the plants and their preferred growing conditions. Potted plants, depending on their rarity and how hard they were to propagate, cost from $3.50 to $15 each and tend to include species that are more rare and unusual than what you'd find, say, in a Home Depot garden center. If you love plants and want a living souvenir of your visit to North Carolina, a selection of plants culled from these gardens would be a brilliant idea. The center is open year-round Monday to Friday 8am to 5pm, Saturday 9am to 6pm, and Sunday 1 to 6pm.

The **Weathervane** (📞 919/929-9466), a restaurant associated with A Southern Season shopping emporium, takes the best of its affiliate's produce and turns it into a sophisticated array of salads and sandwiches priced from $5 to $12 and main courses priced from $13 to $25. Set in a woodsy family-friendly format immediately adjacent to the store, it's open Monday to Thursday from 7am to 9pm, Friday to Saturday from 7am to 10pm, and Sunday 10:30am to 6pm (see A Southern Season, above for address and phone). American Express, Diners Club, MasterCard, and Visa are accepted.

Well-read Chapel Hill has a large book-buying public, and Franklin Street is the site of most bookstores. The **Bookshop, Inc.,** 400 W. Franklin St. (📞 919/942-5178; www.bookshopinc.com; Mon–Fri 11am–9pm, Sat 11am–6pm, and Sun 1–5pm), has been a civic monument in Chapel Hill since 1981. This bookshop sells only used books and (in the words of its owner, Bill Loeser) "everything except textbooks and romance novels." It doesn't seem very large, but its cramped, crowded, and somewhat dingy premises contain some 150,000 books, ranging in price from 50¢ to a rare 1770 edition of Catesby's *History of the Carolinas,* selling here for around $40,000.

Immediately across the street, and selling a radically different style and type of book, is Chapel Hill's most visible counterculture bookstore. The **Internationalist Book & Magazine Cooperative,** 405 W. Franklin St. (📞 919/942-1740; www.internationalistbooks.org; Mon–Sat 11am–8pm and Sun noon–6pm), is funky, artsy, and the darling of Chapel Hill residents with a slightly leftist bent; it focuses on feminist, gay, lesbian, graphic arts, and poetry tomes.

Some 3 miles east of the center of Chapel Hill stands **Meadowmont Village,** adjacent to Route 54 (eastbound). This upscale multipurpose shopping, residential, office, and dining complex is evocative of the way visitors and locals dine and shop in the New South.

A unique food market is the **Weaver Street Market,** 101 E. Weaver St. (📞 919/929-0010; www.weaverstreetmarket.coop), 1 mile west of Chapel Hill. It is a rambling but modern warehouselike structure near the center of Carrboro that's piled almost to the rafters with all-organic foodstuffs. You can buy things that are fresh,

Carolinian, and healthful here, and you can also purchase the fixings for a picnic lunch. Many locals visit its self-service, buffet-style restaurant, the **Weaver Street Market Café** (same address and phone), where a $6 buffet (especially pleasing to vegetarians) is served on picnic tables under soaring oak trees, and where Thursday nights include performances from live jazz bands. Both the market and its restaurant are open Monday to Friday 7:30am to 9pm and Saturday and Sunday 8am to 9pm.

Chapel Hill After Dark

Arts Center   The Arts Center presents events Thursday to Sunday for about 50 weeks annually, including regional, national, and international concert tours, plays, and children's programs. Call for information. The box office is open Monday to Friday 10am to 6pm and on Saturday 10am to 4pm. Ticket price depends on the event. 300-G E. Main St., in Carrboro. ✆ **919/929-2787.** www.artscenterlive.org.

Cat's Cradle   This casual, intimate space is still going strong as *the* venue to see the latest bands—rock 'n' roll, alternative, bluegrass, you name it. The talent is often native bred, and the scheduling is made with an eye to quality musicianship. Chapel Hill is the hometown of big-time picker James Taylor, after all. 300 E. Main St., in Carrboro. ✆ **919/967-9053.** www.catscradle.com. Cover varies.

WINSTON-SALEM ★

104 miles W of Raleigh

In 1913, the twin communities of Winston and Salem were incorporated into a single city. Winston, founded in 1849, contributed an industry-based economy, whereas Salem added an emphasis on education and crafts, and the sense of order that its Moravian settlers brought from Pennsylvania in 1766. The union has proved to be happy and productive.

Salem (the name comes from the Hebrew word *shalom,* meaning "peace") was the last of three settlements established in the Piedmont by Moravian clergymen and laymen in the early 1750s; the little towns of Bethabara and Bethania came first. The hardworking newcomers were devout people who had fled persecution in Europe and brought to the New World their artisans' skills, a deep love of music and education, and an absolute rejection of violence in any form.

In the 20th century, "progress" encroached on the boundaries of the beautiful old congregational town. But in 1949, an organized restoration effort was begun, and today, more than 30 buildings have been restored with meticulous attention to authenticity; renovation is still underway on others. Devout the Moravians were, but glum they were not: The bright, cheerful reds and blues and soft greens and yellows in the restored interiors and exteriors replicate the colors they used in those early days.

Essentials

GETTING THERE   I-40 (the East-West Expwy.) is the main approach to Winston-Salem from both east and west; from the north, it's U.S. 311, U.S. 52, and U.S. 158; and from the south, it's U.S. 52.

Winston-Salem's **Smith Reynolds International Airport** (✆ **336/767-6361**) is served by **US Airways Express** (✆ **800/428-4322;** www.usairways.com). Charlotte is the nearest airport served by all major carriers.

Greyhound (✆ **800/231-2222;** www.greyhound.com) offers regular service to town. The **bus station** is at 100 W. 5th St. (✆ **336/724-1429**).

The **Convention and Visitors Bureau,** 200 Brookstown Ave., Winston-Salem, NC 27101 (© 866/728-4200 or 336/728-4200; www.visitwinstonsalem.com), can tell you about attractions, accommodations, dining, and local bus transportation. Hours are Monday to Friday 8:30am to 5pm, but from May to August it is also open on Saturday 9am to 5pm and on Sunday noon to 4pm.

SPECIAL EVENTS For a relatively small city, Winston-Salem has quite a calendar of events. The Convention and Visitors Bureau (see above) can provide complete details. In mid-April, the city's 18th-century gardens in Old Salem are open for the **Spring Garden Tour** (call © 888/653-7253 or 919/962-0522; www.chapelhill gardentour.net). Every year, there's a traditional Moravian **Easter Sunrise Service.** An old-fashioned **Independence Day Celebration** is held each year at historic Bethabara. Starting in July is the **National Black Theatre Festival.** Early September brings the **Chili Championship** to Tanglewood Park. Mid-October also brings **Folk Festival IV,** a competition complete with country cooking and entertainment. Beginning in November and running to January 1 is the **Festival of Lights** in Tanglewood Park (© 336/778-6300; www.tanglewoodpark.org). And the holiday season wouldn't be complete without the **Old Salem Christmas and Candle Teas ★** (© 888/653-7253; www.oldsalem.org), a re-creation of yuletide as it was celebrated 200 years ago in Old Salem. (You've got to sample that Moravian sugar cake!)

Exploring the Area

Historic Old Salem ★★ One of the leading attractions of North Carolina, this restoration of a Moravian community demonstrates old-world skills. The **visitor center** has exhibits that trace the Moravians' journey from Europe to America and finally to North Carolina. Costumed hosts and hostesses will show you around, and you'll see craftspeople in Moravian dress practicing the trades of the original settlement. The center is open Monday to Saturday 9am to 5pm and Sunday noon to 4pm.

When boys reached the age of 14, they moved into the **Single Brothers House**— the half-timbered section was built in 1769, the brick wing in 1786—where they began a 7-year apprenticeship to a master artisan. Academic studies continued as they learned to be gunsmiths, tailors, potters, and shoemakers. Adolescent girls lived in the **Single Sisters House,** diagonally across the town square, where they learned the domestic arts that they would need when marrying time arrived. Young single women still live in this building, which is a private dormitory for Salem College.

Be sure to go into the **Tavern,** built in 1784 to replace an earlier one that burned. George Washington spent 2 nights here in 1791, and the dining room, sleeping rooms, barns, and grounds are not much different now from how they were when he stopped by; the cooking utensils in the stone-floored kitchen, with its twin fireplaces, are genuine period artifacts.

You can also visit the **Market-Firehouse** and the **Winkler Bakery,** where breads and cookies are still baked in big wood-burning ovens. Many homes have distinctive signs hanging outside to identify the shops inside. A yellow, weather-boarded log cottage houses one of our favorites: the **tobacco shop** of Matthew Miksch.

Like the Historic District of Williamsburg, Virginia, Old Salem still functions as a living community. Many of the restored homes are private residences, and the young people walking the old streets with such familiarity are no doubt students at Salem College, living a 21st-century campus life in an 18th-century setting.

On the square, the **Home Moravian Church,** which dates from 1800, is the center of the denomination in the South. Visitors are welcome at services; hundreds show up for the Easter Sunrise service, the Christmas Lovefeast (Dec 24), and the New Year's Eve Watch Night service. One block north, the graveyard named God's Acre contains more than 4,000 graves, all marked with nearly identical stones. Princes and paupers are shown the same respect. Opening times are at the discretion of the church.

MESDA (Museum of Early Southern Decorative Arts) ★   One of the most interesting museums in the state, MESDA was conceived as a showcase of furniture design and decorative arts in the American Southeast during the 18th and early 19th centuries. It originated as the result of the outrage generated at a lecture by the then-president of the Winterthur Museum (Delaware) in 1949, when he implied that nothing of artistic importance was produced south of Baltimore during America's colonial era. MESDA's collection of Southeastern American art and antiques grew up in reaction to his words, and today the organization functions as a research and documentation center, producing large, four-color volumes on esoteric subjects associated with the decorative arts in the American South.

The best way to enter this museum is by navigating your way through the visitor center for Old Salem, passing over a replica of a mortise-and-tenon-covered bridge leading toward Old Salem, and entering the neo-Palladian entryway (inspired by Thomas Jefferson's Monticello) of MESDA. Its collections are set inside replicas of 32 historically important period rooms, many dismantled from places throughout the South, then reassembled, side by side, in a warehouselike structure originally conceived as a Kroger grocery store in the 1950s. Each of the rooms represents a different region of the South and is appointed with furniture from its era. Hours are the same as those for the Old Salem visitor center, and a ticket to Old Salem includes access to this museum.

MESDA allows you to tour period rooms and galleries, showcasing the furniture, paintings, textiles, ceramics, silver, and other metalwares made and used in the South through 1820. The museum stands at the southern edge of Old Salem.

Old Salem Rd. © **888/653-7253** or 336/721-7300. www.oldsalem.org. Admission $17 adults, $10 children 6–16. Tues–Sat 10am–5pm; Sun 1–5pm.

Reynolda House Museum of American Art ★   This museum was a sprawling and richly impractical 64-room bungalow built between 1912 and 1917, during the height of the Jazz Age, as a showcase homestead by tobacco tycoon R. J. Reynolds and his beautiful and charismatic young wife, Katharine. The museum's permanent collection includes American art from the colonial era to the present. Charmingly, about 90% of Katharine Reynolds's original furnishings from 1917 (many of them purchased from Wanamaker's department store in Philadelphia) have been restored and/or replaced, and these, in contrast with the modern and contemporary art, make for some very interesting museum-watching. Katharine's formal gardens, to the left of the main house as you face it, are spectacular.

2250 Reynolda Rd. © **888/663-1149** or 336/758-5150. www.reynoldahouse.org. Admission $10 adults, $9 seniors, free for students 18 and under and college students with ID. Tues–Sat 9:30am–4:30pm; Sun 1:30–4:30pm.

SECCA (Southeastern Center for Contemporary Art) ★ 🎁   One of the most radical, creative, and innovative museums in North Carolina, the SECCA was established in 1956 within the solid stone walls of the estate that was originally built in 1929 by the James G. Hanes family. Hanes was an energetic textile mogul and founder of the company best known today for the manufacture of underwear. The

THE SEARCH FOR mayberry

Mayberry, the hometown of Sheriff Andy Taylor on *The Andy Griffith Show*, never existed, of course. But its inspiration is said to have been **Mount Airy**, lying off U.S. 52 in the Upper Piedmont, to the south of the Virginia–North Carolina border. Andy Griffith was born and raised in this sleepy little town.

The town is an example of television's power to affect tourism. Thousands visit Mount Airy yearly, and the town they see looks very much like the fictional Mayberry of the long-running TV series. Southern oaks border the streets, and "just plain folks" sit out on the verandas, swinging and rocking as though it were still 1902. You expect to see Barney Fife appear at any minute.

Mayberry Days, held the last Thursday, Friday, and Saturday of September, draw visitors from all over the country for traditional "pig-pickin's" cooking and pie-eating contests. Call the **Mount Airy Arts Council** (✆ **336/786-7998;** www.surryarts.org) for information. If you'd like a **walking-tour map** of the town, go to the **Mount Airy Chamber of Commerce** at 200 N. Main St. (✆ **800/948-0949** or 336/786-6116), open Monday to Friday from 8:30am to 5pm.

Mount Airy Visitors Center, 200 N. Main St. (✆ **800/948-0949** or 336/786-6116; www.visitmayberry.com), is open Monday to Saturday 8:30am to 5pm and on Sunday 1 to 4pm. It guides visitors through the town, pointing out the still-standing birthplace of Andy Griffith and local businesses that were the inspiration for places seen in the TV series, including the replica of the old jail (Mon–Thurs 8am–4:30pm). Call ✆ **336/786-6116** for more information.

You can even get arrested in Andy Taylor's old squad car, or at least a restored 1962 Ford Galaxie that looks like the Mayberry patrol car. A former Chamber of Commerce president, Jim Grimes, in his Barney Fife outfit, runs 25-minute tours in the car, charging $30 for up to five people. To book a tour, call ✆ **336/789-6743** or visit www.tourmayberry.com.

If you'd like to follow in the footsteps of Sheriff Andy, head for the **Snappy Lunch** at 125 N. Main St. (✆ **336/786-4931**) for a pork-chop sandwich. The old-time lunch counter is a virtual showcase for *The Andy Griffith Show*. Andy himself frequented the place as a boy. The proprietor, Charles Dowell, claims to sell about 1,000 pork-chop sandwiches every week. The sandwiches, costing $1.55–$3.65, are consumed at old school desks. The sandwich is a boneless pork chop between steamy bun halves, covered with mustard. It's served Monday to Saturday from 5:45am to 1:45pm (the lunch counter closes at 1:15pm Thurs and Sat).

original structure, bequeathed by Hanes to SECCA "for the enjoyment of art in a home-like setting," was designed to resemble a much-enlarged version of a stone manor house in the Cotswold district of England. Two massive greenhouse-style enlargements were added in the mid-1970s. This is a showplace for the exposition of avant-garde and cutting-edge contemporary art. One of the strengths (and weaknesses) of this place is its lack of a permanent collection. Everything you'll see here is conceived and constructed only for exhibitions that last up to a maximum of about 3 months.

In the Historic Hanes Estate, 750 Marguerite Dr. ✆ **336/725-1904.** www.secca.org. Free admission. Wed–Sat 10am–5pm (1st Thurs of every month 10am–8pm); Sun 2–5pm.

Outdoor Pursuits

We believe that the best way to get a sense of the early origins of Winston-Salem involves a detour to the 175-acre tract known as **Historic Bethabara Park ★**, 2147 Bethabara Rd. (© **336/924-8191**; www.cityofws.com). Positioned 7½ miles north of Old Salem, and the beneficiary of intensive excavation since the mid-1970s, at which time much of it lay in ruins, it was established in 1753 as the site of the first Moravian settlement in North Carolina. Later it played an important role in the local politics surrounding the French and Indian War. Fifteen Moravian men came to this part of North Carolina from Bethlehem, Pennsylvania, the site of an even earlier Moravian settlement, and quickly built a small agrarian community of log houses, a crudely fortified palisade, a meetinghouse and church (the stone-sided Gemeinhaus), and a medicinal garden (the first well-documented garden of its kind in what later became the United States) whose restored version is one of the highlights of the modern-day park. By 1766, the newer town of Salem was established, and Bethabara (which had originally been envisioned only as a temporary community) gradually sank into obscurity. Today, however, in its restored form, Bethabara illuminates much of the early history of this part of North Carolina. Additionally, the mass of written records, journals, inventories, and maps generated by the early Moravian settlers at Bethabara forms one of the most important bodies of research materials for the study of U.S. colonial history.

Highlights of the much-restored settlement include a 15-minute video presentation in the visitor center, a guided walking tour of the compound conducted by well-informed volunteers, and access to walking trails that fan out over the surrounding acreage.

Historic Bethabara's buildings, gardens, and visitor center are open Tuesday to Friday 10:30am to 4:30pm and Saturday and Sunday 1:30 to 4:30pm. Admission is $2 for adults and $1 for children.

Tanglewood Park, U.S. 158 West in Clemmons (© **336/778-6370**), is a year-round recreational facility set on some 1,100 acres. You can enjoy golf on two of *Golf Digest*'s top-rated courses, or tennis on one of nine tennis courts, both hard and clay. Stop by the horse stables to ask about trail rides and riding lessons or to arrange a leisurely carriage drive around the park. A nature trail also meanders through the acreage. The park has two modern, fully equipped children's playgrounds, plus an Olympic-size pool. It's open daily from 7am to dusk. Admission is $2 per car.

Where to Stay

Augustus T. Zevely Inn ★★   This 1844 home of Old Salem physician A. T. Zevely was saved from decay in the 1950s by Old Salem, Inc. This group of citizens who preserve historic Moravian structures restored the home into the grandest B&B in Old Salem. A first glimpse of the classic 19th-century brick facade evokes the Old Moravian style. Beautifully furnished in Old South style, it's well maintained, snug, and cozy. The inn is centrally located in the Historic District, near many sights, shops, and activities, including golfing, tennis, and boating. Rooms are done in 1800s period style, complete with antique furnishings. All units have well-kept bathrooms. Some rooms feature fireplaces, refrigerators, and balconies. When you are making reservations, be sure to be specific about which extras you prefer.

803 S. Main St., Winston-Salem, NC 27101. ℂ **800/928-9299** or 336/748-9299. Fax 336/721-2211. www. winston-salem-inn.com. 12 units. $95–$145 double; $240 suite. Rates include continental breakfast Mon–Fri and full breakfast Sat–Sun. AE, MC, V. Free parking. **Amenities:** Breakfast room; lounge. *In room:* A/C, TV, hair dryer, Wi-Fi (free).

The Brookstown Inn ★★★

The premier inn of Winston-Salem, the Brookstown is housed in an 1837 cotton mill that supplied material for Confederate uniforms. This jewel of a building offers spacious rooms with two double beds, a chest of drawers, an armoire, a love seat, a desk, chairs, and tables. Most suites have a separate sitting room and garden tub. Silk flowers, quilts, baskets, and wooden decoys adorn the parlor areas, decorated in Wedgwood blue, burgundy, gold, and olive. The inn, listed on the National Register of Historic Places, is conveniently near the Old Salem restoration. Another area of the mill, where its boiler was once located, is the site of a visitor center.

200 Brookstown Ave., Winston-Salem, NC 27101. ℂ **800/845-4262** or 336/725-1120. Fax 336/773-0147. www.brookstowninn.com. 70 units. $94–$120 double; $136–$186 suite. Rates include continental breakfast. Children 12 and under stay free in parent's room. AE, DC, DISC, MC, V. Free parking. Take the Cherry St. exit from I-40. **Amenities:** Breakfast room; lounge; exercise room. *In room:* A/C, TV, hair dryer, Wi-Fi (free).

Embassy Suites ★★

In the heart of the business district, the landmark Adam's Mark was the leading hotel of Winston-Salem—but no more. After a $45-million investment into the property, the twin towers have been converted into this upscale hotel, plus a Marriott (see below). Local residents have named the two hotels and the adjoining Benton Convention Center "the Twin City Quarter." Of the two, we prefer the smaller Embassy Suites, with its elegantly furnished suites, each with two spacious rooms and a complimentary cooked-to-order breakfast.

460 N. Cherry St., Winston-Salem, NC 27101. ℂ **336/724-2300.** Fax 336/721-2240. http://embassy suites1.hilton.com. 146 units. $179–$189 double; $209–$239 suite. AE, DC, MC, V. Parking $6–$12. **Amenities:** Restaurant; exercise room; indoor pool; room service. *In room:* A/C, TV, fridge, hair dryer, Wi-Fi (free).

The Manor House Bed & Breakfast ★ 👔

In Tanglewood Park, part of the former 1,100-acre estate of William Reynolds (the brother of R. J.), this stately former house lies southwest of Winston-Salem in a landscape of Carolina pines and dogwoods. The 1859 home has been restored and adapted for the use of guests. All the rooms are spacious and handsomely furnished, like the rooms in an English country house. The tasteful decor is in cranberry and hunter green, with louvered wooden blinds and Austrian swag-style draperies. The cost of swimming and fishing nearby is included.

4061 Clemmons Rd., Tanglewood Park (PO Box 1040), Clemmons, NC 27012. ℂ **336/778-6370.** Fax 336/778-6379. http://manorhouse.tanglewoodpark.org. 10 units. $80–$125 double. Rates include continental breakfast (manor house only). AE, DC, MC, V. Free parking. **Amenities:** Breakfast room; 2 18-hole golf courses; outdoor pool. *In room:* A/C, TV, fridge.

Marriott Winston Plaza ★★

The leading hotel of Winston-Salem and one of the state's best, the Marriott Winston Plaza (formerly Adam's Mark) is located in the heart of the business district and is connected underground to the Benton Convention Center. Consisting of a 17-story and a nine-story building, the complex is like a grand hotel in a major world city. The most expensive rooms are at the luxury-club level on three floors, with a private lounge, complimentary continental breakfast, and concierge. All the guest rooms are tasteful and spacious, and many have panoramic views. Some rooms open onto balconies that overlook the atrium.

425 N. Cherry St., Winston-Salem, NC 27101. © **888/236-2427** or 336/725-3500. Fax 336/728-4025. www.marriott.com. 315 units. $109–$179 double; $199–$229 suite. Children 17 and under stay free in parent's room. AE, DC, DISC, MC, V. Parking $6–$12. **Amenities:** Restaurant; 2 bars; exercise room; indoor pool; room service; sauna. *In room:* A/C, TV, hair dryer, Wi-Fi (free).

The Summit Street Bed & Breakfast Inns ★★ 👔 This is the most sophisticated, elegant, and adult-oriented B&B in Winston-Salem, the kind that appeals to worldly business travelers and romantic couples. It occupies a pair of elaborately decorated and lavishly restored side-by-side West End Victorian houses, one built in 1895, the other 2 years later. We've rarely seen a bed-and-breakfast that's better accessorized than this one, or one with management as discreet and cooperative. Each house has stylish public rooms that look like pages from *Architectural Digest,* and each has lavish and whimsical furnishings that evoke the most charming aspects of the late Victorian Age. All but one of the rooms has a Jacuzzi for two, and each has a state-of-the-art stereo system and access to a collection of movies. One of the houses has the largest and most up-to-date exercise room we've ever seen in a comparably small hotel. Local entrepreneur Ken Land, a man well versed in the dining options of Winston-Salem, is your host.

420 and 434 Summit St. at the corner of W. 5th St., Winston-Salem, NC 27101. © **336/777-1887.** www. bbinn.com. 9 units. Sun–Thurs $129–$179 double; Fri–Sat $149–$189 double. AE, DC, MC, V. Free parking. **Amenities:** Exercise room; room service. *In room:* A/C, TV, Wi-Fi (free).

Where to Dine

IN OLD SALEM

Old Salem Tavern Dining Room ★ AMERICAN/CONTINENTAL Here, as everywhere else in the restored village, authenticity is the keynote. The three ground-floor dining rooms were built in 1816 as an annex to the 1784 Tavern next door. Upstairs is a trio of three additional dining rooms; dining is also available on the rear veranda. In summer only, you can eat under a wisteria arbor in the rear garden. The simple furnishings and colonial-costumed staff provide an appropriate 18th-century ambience. The manager, Doris Hamilton, works hard to keep original Moravian culinary tenets alive, basing at least some of her recipes (meatloaf fortified with rolled oats, Moravian chicken pie, Moravian gingerbread for dessert, and ample use of apples, fresh lemons, and sauerkraut) on authentic 19th-century recipes. The pumpkin-and-raisin muffins are a specialty.

736 S. Main St. © **336/748-8585.** www.oldsalemtavern.com. Reservations recommended for dinner and for lunch for parties of 6 or more. Main courses $7.50–$8.75 lunch, $12–$24 dinner. AE, MC, V. Mon–Thurs 11:30am–2pm and 5–9pm; Fri 11:30am–2pm and 5–9:30pm; Sat 11:30am–2:30pm and 5–9:30pm; Sun 11:30am–2pm.

Ollie's Bakery SANDWICHES/PASTRIES This is Winston-Salem's most popular and sophisticated bakery, chugging out a staggering variety (at least two dozen types) of breads every day, as well as an assortment of pastries, some of which are influenced by the traditions of the Moravians. Although we respect this place for its role as a bakery, we especially value its sandwiches, which, when consumed with a steaming cup of coffee, make for a satisfying light lunch. The place originated in the 19th century as a grocery store, and much of that antique sense of fresh-baked wholesomeness remains. You'll find it in the center of historic Salem, opening onto the back side of the city's tourist information office.

300 S. Marshall St. © **336/727-0404.** www.olliesbakeryws.com. Sandwiches $7.95 each; loaves of bread and individual portions of pastries $2–$6. DISC, MC, V. Tues–Fri 7am–5:30pm; Sat 8am–5pm; Sun 8am–4pm.

IN WINSTON-SALEM
Expensive

Ryan's ★ CONTINENTAL   This restaurant is every bit the equal of Zevely House (recommended below), with which it's often compared. In a wooded setting overlooking a stream, Ryan's is rustic in decor but has a truly sophisticated Continental menu. Dishes are executed with polished technique. Beef dishes are specialties, as are some excellent seafood creations. The homemade soups are exceptional, and there's a good wine list. It's estimated that you could eat here all the time and always find something new to surprise and delight you.

719 Coliseum Dr. ✆ **336/724-6132.** www.ryansrestaurant.com. Reservations recommended. Main courses $22–$45. AE, DC, MC, V. Mon–Thurs 5–10pm; Fri–Sat 5–10:30pm. Closed major holidays. Take the Cherry St. exit from I-40 Business.

Zevely House ★ CONTINENTAL   Antiques and a fireplace decorate this house, which dates back to 1815. It was constructed by Van Neuman Zevely, a Moravian cabinetmaker, and became the center of his plantation. In 1974, the building was hauled to its present site and authentically restored. This restaurant has steadily improved and truly justifies its star rating. The cuisine is creative and accomplished, the sauces are in harmony, and the wine list is well chosen and reasonable in price. Try the potato cakes with sour cream and caviar, or maybe something simple and grandmotherly—chicken potpie, for example. A pork tenderloin is perfectly prepared. Venison and beef filet are often featured, but pan-fried trout is the signature dish. The brown sugar pound cake is always a good choice. A fireplace keeps the place snug in winter, although you'll want to retreat to the patio when the weather's fair.

901 W. Fourth St. ✆ **336/725-6666.** www.zevelyhouse.com. Reservations recommended. Main courses $13–$32; Sun brunch $6.25–$18. AE, DC, DISC, MC, V. Tues–Sat 5–9pm; Sun 11am–2pm (brunch).

Moderate
The Old Fourth Street Filling Station CONTEMPORARY AMERICAN   Whenever a Carolina TV station wants to include a local restaurant in one of its reality-TV programs, they tend to schedule it here at this hip and trendy spot. Don't expect anything even vaguely related to a gas station, since most of its architectural remnants were ripped out long ago. There's a walled-in and partially covered dining terrace, plus an interior that's partially devoted to an animated bar where you're likely to find a high percentage of the city's available and nubile young women. Menu items are well prepared and based on a creative interpretation of modern American cuisine. Examples include deep-fried wontons stuffed with crabmeat, cream cheese, and scallions; a portobello mushroom sandwich; pizzas (the favorite comes with spicy Thai-style chicken); a succulent brie-and-spinach-stuffed chicken; filet steak with bacon and Gorgonzola sauce; and Carolina shrimp and grits served with Cajun-style andouille sausage and hominy cakes.

871 W. Fourth St. ✆ **336/724-7600.** www.theoldfourthstreetfillingstation.com. Reservations recommended for tables inside, not accepted for the patio. Pizzas, salads, and sandwiches $3–$9; pastas and main courses $15–$24. AE, DC, MC, V. Mon–Tues 11am–9pm; Wed–Thurs 11am–10pm; Fri–Sat 11am–11pm; Sun 10am–3pm and 5–9pm.

Inexpensive
Rana Loca LATIN   This is the leading South-of-the-border restaurant in Winston-Salem, serving a variety of dishes based on various Latin cultures. Expect all the familiar dishes, but a few surprises from the chef's daily specials. On Tuesday there's a special pork plate along with tacos, and on Wednesday an affordable prime rib is

offered. On Saturday nights a bucket of Bud or Miller is $9. In fair weather, dining can be enjoyed on the outdoor patio.

411 W. Fourth St. (℃ **336/722-9911.** www.ranaloca.com. Reservations not accepted. Salads, sandwiches, and platters $4–$9; main courses $8–$18. MC, V. Daily 11am–10pm; Thurs–Sat until 2am.

Shopping

Winston-Salem offers all types of shopping options, thanks to its dual Southern and Moravian heritage. **Stratford Place,** Stratford Road at I-40 Business (℃ **336/723-2221;** http://stratfordvillageonline.com), offers a collection of specialty shops and restaurants in one locale.

Winston-Salem has a selection of antiques stores, as do the neighboring cities. One worth a look is the **Reynolda Antique Gallery,** 114-C Reynolda Village (℃ **336/728-2500**). These shops are open Monday to Saturday 10am to 6pm.

If rare and old used books are your passion, we recommend a stop at **Larry Laster Old and Rare Books,** 2416 Maplewood Ave. (℃ **336/724-7544**), a great place to make that rare find. Visits are by appointment only and must be made 1 day in advance.

Everything you might ever have associated with the Moravians is available in the cozily claustrophobic premises of the **Moravian Gift Shop,** 614 S. Main St. (℃ **336/723-6262**), where the folkloric and Christmas traditions of the town's earliest settlers remain alive. Expect an inventory of arts and crafts, beeswax candles, Moravian stars in all shapes and sizes, upscale gift items, and a stodgy collection of conservative reading material. A nearby competitor with roughly equivalent merchandise is **T. Bagge,** 626 S. Main St. (℃ **336/721-7387**).

Winkler Bakery, 529 Main St. in Old Salem (℃ **336/721-7302**), is known for its domed and wood-fired brick oven dating back to the turn of the 19th century. Drop in for a bevy of goodies, including old-fashioned and paper-thin Old Salem Moravian ginger, lemon, sugar, and black walnut cookies.

The funky and appealing **Earthbound Arts (Gifts from Nature),** 610 N. Trade St. (℃ **336/773-1043**), is what you get when you mix a psychedelic-era "head shop" with New Age philosophy, an art gallery, and a dose of hillbilly charm. The result is an emporium of scented soaps that seem to pull you into the nearest bathtub or shower. Also for sale are handcrafted jewelry and scented herbs. Everything on display here shows a great sense of fun and whimsy—always with a North Carolina accent and a strong sense of the state's mountains and hideaway hollers.

Piedmont Craftsmen ★, 601 N. Trade St. (℃ **336/725-1516;** www.piedmont craftsmen.org), is richly inventoried with products from more than 350 craftspersons based throughout central North Carolina, each of whom is required by company charter to pass minimum standards of quality, creativity, and originality. As such, its merchandise is more appealing and, in many cases, much more humorous than that found in competing shops. Much of its creative force derives from its founder and executive director, Tomi Melson. Come here expecting to be charmed.

Just a 7-mile drive north of Winston-Salem is the town of Germanton, settled in 1790 by German immigrants. It's the home of the **Germanton Art Gallery and Winery,** Highway 8, Germanton (℃ **336/969-6121;** www.germantongallery.com), where you can find originals and prints by many internationally known artists. The gallery is an authorized dealer for art dealers all over the world. The wines are well worth tasting; the climate of the foothills of the Blue Ridge Mountains provides an ideal setting for the French-American hybrid grape to flourish. Allow time for shopping, and bring a credit card. Open Tuesday to Friday 10am to 6pm and Saturday 9am to 5pm.

Winston-Salem After Dark

Club Odyssey This is the most visible gay bar in the region. Located 6 miles from Old Salem, in a small-scale shopping center beside a busy traffic artery, it includes two bar areas (only one of which is open whenever the place isn't busy), a pool table (where older patrons sporting just a whiff of leather tend to congregate), and a dance floor. It's open Tuesday to Sunday 9pm to 2:30am, but the place is never really crowded except on Friday and Saturday nights after around 10pm. Be prepared to show your ID at the door. 4019A Country Club Rd. ✆ **336/774-7071.** www.clubodyssey.info/main.html. Cover $5–$10.

The Garage Both country music and rock fans head for this decade-old joint that offers some of the best live entertainment in the city, including the occasional open-mic night. The cover, ranging from $3 to $20, depends on what's happening. Open Tuesday to Saturday 6pm to 2am. 1110 West 7th St. ✆ **336/777-1127.**

The Hideout Live blues, jazz, and alternative rock artists perform here Thursday to Saturday evenings. It has an outdoor area where national bands are the attraction spring through fall. The place is usually packed, often with male customers drawn to sports broadcasts on the large flatscreen TVs. There is also free Wi-Fi, and beers start at $2. Open Tuesday to Saturday 8pm to 2am. 864 W. Northwest Blvd. ✆ **336/722-0888.**

GREENSBORO

78 miles W of Raleigh; 54 miles W of Durham; 48 miles W of Chapel Hill; 27 miles E of Winston-Salem; and 91 miles NE of Charlotte

Greensboro was settled by freedom-loving Scots-Irish, Germans, and Quakers. The Scots-Irish and Germans fought valiantly in the American Revolution and the War of 1812, but when North Carolina seceded from the Union in 1861, Greensboro became an important Confederate supply depot. Jefferson Davis met here with Union General Johnston to arrange surrender terms after the Southern cause was lost. Today, the thriving city is a leader in higher education and the manufacture of textiles, cigarettes, and electronic equipment, as well as the home of a large insurance industry.

Greensboro, although considered to be one of the most desirable places to live in America for families, is not the first place in the Piedmont that you'd think of visiting. Winston-Salem is far more interesting; but if you're in the area, Greensboro has several attractions that are worthy of attention.

Essentials

GETTING THERE   By Plane Planes arrive at Piedmont Triad International Airport, Airport Parkway, off Highway 68 N (✆ **336/665-5666;** www.flyfrompti.com). Greensboro is served by **American Airlines** (✆ 800/433-7300; www.aa.com), **Continental Airlines** (✆ 800/433-7300; www.flycontinental.com), **Delta Air Lines** (✆ 800/221-1212; www.delta.com), **United Airlines** (✆ 800/241-6522; www.united.com), and **US Airways** (✆ 800/428-4322; www.usairways.com).

By Train   Amtrak has one northbound and one southbound train through Greensboro daily (✆ **800/USA-RAIL**).

By Bus The **Greyhound/Trailways** depot is at 501 W. Lee St. (✆ **336/272-8950**).

By Car Reach Greensboro from the east and southwest via I-85, from the west via U.S. 40, and from the south via U.S. 220. For AAA services, contact the **Carolina**

Motor Club, 14-A Oak Branch Dr., Greensboro, NC 27407 (✆ **336/852-0506; www.aaany.com**).

VISITOR INFORMATION For tourist information on Greensboro and the vicinity, contact the **Greensboro Convention and Visitors Bureau,** 2200 Pinecroft Rd. Suite 200, Greensboro, NC 27407 (✆ **800/344-2282** or 336/274-2282; www.greensboronc.org). Also ask for information on city bus routes and schedules. Hours are Monday to Friday 8:30am to 5:30pm, Saturday 9am to 4pm, and Sunday 1 to 4pm.

Exploring the Area

Bargain hunters will want to visit two nearby towns, both of which are overflowing with factory outlet shops. **High Point,** 17 miles south of Greensboro (so named because it was the highest point along the 1853 North Carolina and Midland Railroad from Salem to Fayetteville), is notable for its furniture and hosiery shops. **Burlington,** 21 miles east of Greensboro, is a major textile center, with scores of factory outlets for clothing, fabrics, sheets, towels, blankets, and the like.

IN TOWN

Greensboro Historical Museum Greensboro was the hometown of O. Henry, the short-story writer known in these parts as William Sidney Porter. Here, you'll find an exhibit illustrating his life and work, plus a fine collection from Dolley Madison's life. Born in Greensboro, Madison was the only native-born North Carolinian to be First Lady. Other exhibits include early modes of transportation, furnishings, pottery, and textiles. An exhibit of note remembers the civil-rights lunch-counter sit-ins at F.W. Woolworth, when, in 1960, four African Americans launched the nation's first major protest against segregation.

130 Summit Ave. ✆ **336/373-2043.** www.greensborohistory.org. Free admission. Tues–Sat 10am–5pm, Sun 2–5pm.

SIGHTS NEARBY

Guilford Courthouse National Military Park This 220-acre park marks one of the closing battles of the Revolution—the Battle of Guilford Courthouse on March 15, 1781. Gen. Nathanael Greene (Greensboro was named for him) led a group of

---

 Furniture in North Carolina

The town of Hickory is the undisputed king of furniture in North Carolina. Sixty percent of the state's furniture manufacturing industry is located in this town, and people come here from far and wide—because if you want the best deals, of course, you must go directly to the source. Hickory has obliged by offering two furniture malls and what is known as the "20-mile stretch"—20 miles of stores and outlets standing end-to-end, stretching from Hickory to Lenoir. The best outlet is the **Hickory Furniture Mart,** 2220 Hwy. 70 SE (✆ **800/462-MART [6278]; www.hickoryfurniture.com**), which describes itself as "20 acres of furniture." It has the look of a typical mall, except there are no Neiman Marcuses here—rather, 85 stores of furniture and more furniture, representing more than 800 manufacturers of high-end merchandise.

Both of these latter outlets are open Monday to Saturday 9am to 6pm.

inexperienced troops against British general Lord Cornwallis. Although he was defeated, Greene inflicted severe losses on the British. Cornwallis hotfooted it out of this part of the country and headed for Yorktown, where he surrendered his depleted forces just 7 months later, on October 19. The visitor center has films, brochures, and displays about the historic battle. There are also wayside exhibits along the 2-mile road that connects some of the many monuments.

2332 New Garden Rd. ✆ **336/288-1776.** www.nps.gov/guco. Free admission. Visitors' center daily 8:30am–5pm. Closed Thanksgiving Day, Christmas Day and New Year's Day. 6 miles northwest of downtown Greensboro on U.S. 220.

Alamance Battleground State Historic Site   This is where those upstart farmers marched against Royal Governor Tryon in 1771 to protest corrupt government practices. Ill-trained and poorly equipped, they were soundly defeated—the battle lasted only 2 hours—but the stout-hearted Regulators were among the first Southern colonists to demonstrate their objection to royal rule. The visitor center has an audio-visual presentation detailing the rebellion. Built by John Allen for his family around 1780, the John Allen House is a restored log dwelling typical of North Carolina backwoods homes at the time of the battle.

N.C. 62, Burlington. ✆ **336/227-4785.** www.nchistoricsites.org. Free admission. Visitors center, Mon-Sat 9am–5pm, Take I-85/40 Exit 143 to N.C. 62; then go 6 miles to site.

North Carolina Transportation Museum   About halfway between Greensboro and Charlotte (near historic Salisbury), this museum in the little town of Spencer is a mecca for dyed-in-the-wool railway buffs. The shops were established in 1896 as a major repair facility for the Southern Railway. Opened as a museum in 1983, the Master Mechanics Building is the focal point of the 57-acre site. Visitors are free to wander and inspect the growing collection of transportation memorabilia. Once, during the 1930s, this facility built a locomotive in one day. Staff members are likely to add anecdotes about the shops' history at your first show of enthusiasm. Rail rides are sometimes available, and a large museum shop offers unusual railroad items, ranging from maps to *Orient Express* crystal.

411 S. Salisbury Ave., Spencer. ✆ **704/636-2889.** www.nctrans.org. Free admission, but donations accepted. Train rides $6 adults, $5 children (3-12), free for children 2 and under who don't need a seat. May–Oct, Mon-Sat 9am–5pm, Sun 1–5pm. Nov–Apr, Tues–Sat 9am–5pm, Sun 1–5pm. Take Exit 79 off I-85.

Outdoor Pursuits

Greensboro lives up to the *green* in its name with 110 parks, sprawling over 3,000 acres. On the northwest edge of the city, **Jaycee Park,** off Pisgah Church Road on Forest Lawn Drive adjacent to Country Park (✆ **336/545-5343**), is the site of the North Carolina Tennis Hall of Fame, offering facilities for baseball, softball, soccer, football, and tennis, plus a playground beside a lake. The North Carolina Closed Tennis Championship is played here annually on the best of the city's 156 courts.

The previously mentioned **Country Park** (✆ **336/545-5343; www.carolina country.com**), adjacent to the Natural Science Center off Lawndale Drive, offers two stocked fishing lakes, pedal boats, three playgrounds, picnic shelters, a softball field, and trails for jogging, hiking, and bicycling.

The **Bryan Park Complex and Lake Townsend,** 27 north on Bryan Park Rd., Browns Summit (✆ **336/375-2222;** www.bryanpark.com), boasts two 18-hole championship golf courses, tennis courts, picnic areas, and soccer fields, along with sailing, fishing, and boating at adjacent Lake Townsend. The site is open Monday to Friday 8am to 5pm.

Golfing is a major pastime in Greensboro, especially during the **Wyndham Championship** held at the Sedgefield Country Club, which hosts one of the PGA Tour's longest running events, dating from 1938. Prior golfing champs have included every golfer from Sam Sneed to Ben Hogan. Some 300,000 fans show up in August for the event. Tickets are available online at www.wyndhamchampionship.com or through the tournament office at 336/379-1570. The event takes place at the Sedgefield Country Club at 3201 Forsyth Dr. (© 336/299-5324).

Most of the major sporting events in town—everything from hockey to college basketball—take place at the **Greensboro Coliseum Complex,** 1921 W. Lee St. Call © **336/373-7474,** or visit www.greensborocoliseum.com for a complete list of events. This is the largest and most diversified entertainment, civic, and sports facility in the Southeast, and it's the home of the Carolina Hurricanes of the National Hockey League.

The best golf is at **Bel Aire Golf Club,** 1518 Pleasant Ridge Rd. at Highway 68, 1½ miles north of Piedmont Triad International Airport (© **336/668-2413;** http://greensboro.golfnation.org/course153/bel-aire-golf-and-country-club). Eighteen holes of golf are set in a scenic, hilly terrain featuring four challenging and heavily wooded lakeside par-3 holes. Other good golf is available at **Bryan Park Complex** (recommended previously in this section). Two 18-hole courses here were designed by George Cobb and Rees Jones. The Players course is a championship layout with 84 bunkers and 8 ponds or lakes, and the Champions course opened 1990 to critical acclaim and continues to get national rankings each year It has 100 sand and grass bunkers, and its six holes border scenic Lake Townsend. Greens fees at most of these courses range from $29 to $31.

Where to Stay

Biltmore Greensboro Hotel ★   Built in 1895, this three-story brick hotel in the center of town is listed on the National Register of Historic Places. One of Greensboro's leading hotels, it's smaller and more intimate than the typical Marriotts and Sheratons that dominate the hotel scene for the business-client dollar. It has been heavily renovated and boasts excellent rooms with hardwood floors, canopied four-poster beds, armoires, 18th-century reproduction furniture, and either king-size beds or two doubles or two queen-size beds. All units also come equipped with a well-kept bathroom containing mostly shower-tub combinations. A continental breakfast is served in a paneled lobby with a fireplace. Other extras include a small business center.

111 W. Washington St., Greensboro, NC 27401. © **800/332-0303** or 336/272-3474. Fax 336/275-2523. 28 units. $129 double, $149 junior suite. Rates include continental breakfast. AE, CB, DC, DISC, MC, V. Free parking. Amenities: Breakfast room, babysitting. In room: A/C, TV, minibar, hairdryer, Wi-Fi (free).

Marriott Greensboro   Although not as good as it once was, this is the only member of a major chain in the downtown area. The lobby, rising three floors, is impressive, and the health club joined to the hotel is the best in the city. Bedrooms are spacious, with big windows—the best feature, because the decor is lackluster. The rooms offer double or king-size beds and well-kept bathrooms with shower-tub combinations. Parking is not a problem, because a seven-story garage is available. The hotel shares a building with the Greensboro Athletic Club; it has two bars and a reasonably priced restaurant.

304 North Greene Street, Greensboro, NC 27401. © **336/379-8000**. Fax 336/275-2810. www.marriott. com. 281 units. Sun–Thurs from $99.95, Fri–Sat from $119.95 double. Children under 17 stay free in parents' room. Each additional person $10. Weekend discounts. AE, CB, DC, DISC, MC, V. Parking $11. **Amenities:** Restaurant, bar; baby-sitting; café; fitness center; Jacuzzi; pool; room service. *In room:* A/C, TV, hair dryer, Wi-Fi ($9.95–$12.95 per day).

Park Lane Hotel-Four Seasons ★   This motor hotel on the road to High Point is well run and offers comfort and security. Its major competitors are the mammoth Holiday Inn-Four Seasons, rising 17 floors with 524 rooms, and the less glamorous 175-room Howard Johnson Coliseum. All these hotels are crawling with business clients during the week, but the pace slows on weekends. We give the nod to Park Lane because it's got better and more personal service than the other giants. Its rooms are comfortably and attractively furnished; some have whirlpools and all have well-kept bathrooms. Suites have wet bars. Some units are especially designed for people with disabilities. An onsite restaurant serves soups and sandwiches, and the bar is open Monday to Friday from 4:30 to 10pm.

3005 High Point Rd., Greensboro, NC 27403. © **336/294-4565.** Fax 336/294-0572. 161 units. $79–$99 double, $100–$150 suite. Rates include continental breakfast. AE, CB, DC, DISC, MC, V. Free parking. **Amenities:** Restaurant, bar; outdoor pool; fitness center; sauna; room service. *In room:* A/C, TV, hair dryer, Wi-Fi (in some free).

Where to Dine

Cellar Anton's INTERNATIONAL   The loyal local clientele keeps returning—for the food, not the decor. Wholesome cookery at moderate tabs is the deal here. The no-nonsense menu of steak, pasta, and seafood succeeds because the ingredients are fresh and deftly handled. Lunch can be simple fare, such as salad and sandwiches, but at night, the chef reveals more talent, turning out such dishes as beef Leonardo, a creamy lasagna, or spaghetti, which is especially delectable. The cooking and home-spun charm of the staff will leave you well fed and smiling.

1628 Battleground Ave. © **336/273-1386.** Salads and sandwiches $4–$9; dinner main courses $10.95–$24.95. AE, MC, V. Mon–Thurs 11am–9:30pm, Fri 11am–10pm, Sat 4–10pm. Closed major holidays.

1618 West Seafood Grille ★ SEAFOOD   Management claims, rightly so, that everyone from the "hipster to the homebody" is attracted to the well-crafted food served here in this busy restaurant that was created from an old farmhouse. The carnivore isn't overlooked, as the chef turns out filet mignon, ribeye steaks, or grilled thick-cut pork chops. But most diners prefer the fresh seafood, such as black grouper with a sweet chili and peanut sauce or the sesame-seed crusted tuna with wasabi mashed potatoes. Pan-seared mountain trout is another favorite, as are the grilled sea scallops served with a cheesy cake made of grits.

1618 W. Friendly Ave. © **336/235-0898.** http://1618west.com. Reservations recommended. Main courses $19–$29. AE, MC, V. Sun–Mon 5:30–9pm, Tues–Sat 5:30–10pm.

Southern LightsBistro AMERICAN   This is the best of the city's bistros, a bright and airy place offering freshly prepared food made with choice ingredients. As a budget eatery, it draws a fair share of young people. Enough variety is on the menu to make it appealing for lunch or dinner. Locals seem to agree that the cooks turn out the best sandwiches and burgers in town, each coming with a cup of soup, pesto pasta, or a tossed salad. "The Sonoma" sandwich consists of roast turkey, applewood smoked bacon, pepper jack cheese, and condiments served on a baguette. Main dishes include either the classic Bistro steak or else grilled salmon in a cucumber dill sauce. Desserts are delectable, especially the chocolate walnut pie. Fresh daily seafood is also offered, and you can look for the daily changing chalkboard specialties. 10 or more wines are availbale to order by the glass—a nice touch, as Hemingway would say.

105 N. Smyres Place. © **336/379-9414.** http://southernlightsbistro.com. Reservations not accepted. Main courses $8–$12. Tues-Thurs 11am-9pm, Fri-Sat 11am-10pm. AE, MC, V.

Greensboro After Dark

Music, drama, art, and dance flourish in Greensboro, which is no longer the country town that it once was. At the **Eastern Music Festival,** held over 6 weeks every summer, 300 professional musicians and students from the United States and abroad perform about 40 classical concerts. The visitors' bureau (p. 174) will have complete details.

The **Community Theater of Greensboro,** 200 N. Davie St. (© **336/333-7470;** http://ctgso.org), has been presenting Broadway shows and musicals for nearly half a century. It also offers classical and contemporary drama.

The **Carolina Theatre,** 310 S. Greene St. (© **336/333-2600;** http://www.carolina theatre.com), opened in 1927 as a venue for vaudeville. Listed on the National Register of Historic Places, it is now a showcase for theater, dance, concerts, and films.

One of the oldest dinner theaters in the country, the **Barn Dinner Theatre,** 120 Stage Coach Trail (© **800/668-1764 or 336/292-2211;** www.barndinner.com), presents Broadway-type plays after a hearty buffet, complete with such dishes as roast top sirloin and baked Alaskan halibut. Dinner and performances take place Wednesday to Sunday from January to November, and 7 days a week in December, from 6 to 10:30pm. Admission costs $40 to $45 for adults, or $20 to $22.50 for children 12 and under.

The **Comedy Zone,** Holden and Patterson St. (© **336/333-1034;** www.the comedyzone.com), features some of the country's funniest comedians on Friday and Saturday nights. It was recently voted Greensboro's best place to go on a date. Admission charges are $8.50 to $9.50 per person. One show Friday is at 9pm, with two shows Saturday at 8 and at 10pm.

CHARLOTTE

143 miles SW of Raleigh; 91 miles S of Winston-Salem

In the past decade or so, Charlotte has been sprouting skyscrapers, including the 40-story, trapezoidal steel-and-glass tower of the Bank of America Plaza and the stunning 46-story Hearst Tower, which was completed in 2002. The city has attracted and taken to heart a professional football team—the Carolina Panthers—that was good enough to get to the Super Bowl in 2004 and nearly pull off an upset against the favorite, the New England Patriots. Suburban districts have mushroomed, with landscaped housing developments and enormous shopping malls springing up in every direction.

The city is booming, and business is just fine, thank you very much. The banking, insurance, and transportation industries keep feeding the economy. With all this growth, a new generation of Charlotteans is champing at the bit for recognition that their city has hit the big time.

Essentials

GETTING THERE   North-south routes through Charlotte are I-85 and I-77; I-40, a major east-west highway, crosses I-77 some 40 miles to the north. Contact the AAA through the **Carolina Motor Club,** 9433 Pineville-Matthews Rd., Ste. A, Pineville, NC 28134 (✆ **704/541-7409**).

Charlotte-Douglas International Airport (✆ **704/359-4027,** http://airport-charlotte.com) is served by **American Airlines** (✆ 800/433-7300; www.aa.com); **Air Canada** (✆ 888/247-2262; www.aircanada.com); **Continental Airlines** (✆ 800/525-0280; www.continental.com); **Delta, Delta ASA,** and **Delta Comair** (✆ 800/221-1212; www.delta.com); **United Airlines** (✆ 800/241-6522; www.united.com); **US Airways** and **US Airways Express** (✆ 800/428-4322; www.usairways.com); and **Lufthansa** (✆ 800/399-5838; www.lufthansa.com), among others.

The daily **Amtrak** (✆ **800/USA-RAIL** [872-7245]; www.amtrak.com) service to Washington, D.C., and Atlanta through Charlotte both depart in the early-morning hours.

Greyhound (✆ **800/231-2222;** www.greyhound.com) offers regular service to Charlotte. The **bus station** is at 601 W. Trade St. (✆ **704/375-3332**).

VISITOR INFORMATION   Contact the **Charlotte Convention & Visitors Bureau,** Visitor Information Center, 330 S. Tryon St., Charlotte, NC 28202 (✆ **800/231-4636** or 704/331-2753; www.charlottesgotalot.com), open Monday to Friday from 8:30am to 5pm and Saturday from 9am to 3pm. **Charlotte Transit** (✆ **704/336-7433;** www.charmeck.org) can furnish local bus-route and schedule information.

SPECIAL EVENTS   In late April, **Springfest** is a 3-day festival held in uptown Charlotte. The streets come alive with music and other entertainment, and street vendors dispense a wide variety of foods. For 6 full days in mid-September, the **Festival in the Park** in Freedom Park celebrates regional arts and crafts.

Seeing the Sights

If you're in Charlotte during April and May, drive north on N.C. 49 to the **University of North Carolina at Charlotte** campus to see the **botanical gardens ★** (✆ **704/547-2364;** www.uncc.edu) in full bloom. The gardens are a wonderland of rhododendrons, azaleas, and native Carolina trees, shrubs, wildflowers, and ferns. A tropical-rainforest conservatory in the gardens' McMillan Greenhouse is open Monday to Saturday 10am to 3pm; admission is free. The outdoor garden is open daily during daylight hours.

Discovery Place & the Nature Museum   Discovery Place is one of the top hands-on science and technology museums in the region. This uptown center features such permanent exhibits as a tropical rainforest and an aquarium. There's also an OMNIMAX theater. The static-electricity demonstration, which literally makes your hair stand on end, is a perennial favorite. Temporary exhibits on loan from other science centers keep the place forever changing.

301 N. Tryon St. ✆ **800/935-0553** or 704/372-6261. www.discoveryplace.org. Admission $10 adults, $8 children 2–13, free for children 1 and under. Mon–Fri 9am–5pm; Sat 9am–6pm; Sun noon–6pm.

Mint Museum of Art   With the recently added Dalton Wing, this stately museum displays a fine survey of European and American art, as well as the internationally recognized Delhom Collection of porcelain and pottery. Also featured are pre-Columbian art, contemporary American prints, African objects, vast collections of costumes and antique maps, and gold coins originally minted at the facility. New galleries

Charlotte

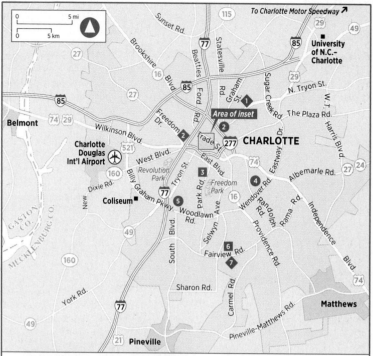

ACCOMMODATIONS ■
Charlotte Marriott SouthPark **6**
Dunhill **9**
The Morehead Inn **3**

DINING ◆
Blue B **10**
LaVecchia's Seafood Grille **11**
Rock Bottom **1**
Upstream **7**

ATTRACTIONS ●
Bank of America Stadium **8**
Discovery Place & the Nature
  Museum *2*
Mint Museum of Art **4**
Wing Haven Gardens
  & Bird Sanctuary **5**

exhibit studio glass and pottery from North Carolina studios. An admission ticket also gains you admittance to the Mint Museum of Craft & Design (220 N. Tryon St.).

2730 Randolph Rd. ℂ **704/337-2000.** www.mintmuseum.org. Admission $10 adults, $8 students and seniors, $5 children 5–17, free for children 4 and under, free for everyone Tues 5–10pm. Tues 10am–10pm; Wed–Sat 10am–5pm; Sun noon–5pm. Closed holidays.

Wing Haven Gardens & Bird Sanctuary ★ ⚏   Since 1927, one of Charlotte's special attractions, created by Elizabeth and Edwin Clarkson, has been a 3-acre enclosed area in the heart of a residential neighborhood. Mrs. Clarkson was known as the city's "bird lady." Some 142 winged species have been sighted in the walled garden, which was once a bare clay field. Birders and garden lovers will have a field day as they browse through the Upper, Lower, Main, Wild, Herb, and Rose gardens. The gardens are at their most splendid in the spring, when birds are returning from their winter migration.

248 Ridgewood Ave. ℂ **704/331-0664.** www.winghavengardens.com. Free admission. Tues 3–5pm; Wed 10am–noon; Sun 2–5pm.

Outdoor Pursuits

Charlotte is ringed by nature preserves and parks, including the nearly 1,000-acre **McDowell Park and Nature Preserve,** about 12 miles south of the city center on N.C. 49 (ℂ **704/588-5224;** http://charmeck.org/mecklenburg/county/ParkandRec/ InsideTheDepartment/Divisions/StewardshipServices/NaturePreserves/Pages/ McDowell.aspx). Its heart is Lake Wylie. The preserve has many hiking trails, and paddleboats can be rented on the lake. Swimming isn't allowed, but fishing is. Call for more information.

The **U.S. National Whitewater Center,** 820 Hawfield Rd. (ℂ **704/391-3900,** www.usnwc.org), on the banks of the Catawba River, is the world's largest artificial white-water river. At a cost of $38 million, the center is part of a 307-acre public adventure sports facility that includes not only white-water rafting but kayaking, mountain biking, and hiking trails. An all-sports daily pass costs $49 for adults, $29 for ages 4 to 10.

Even bigger is **Latta Plantation Park,** the largest in the county, at 5225 Sample Rd. in Huntersville (ℂ **704/875-2312;** www.lattaplantation.org), 12 miles northeast of the city center. It's a favorite resting place for waterfowl and has some 2,500 acres devoted to nature. It also has stables where you can rent horses and ride along 7 miles of trail. A nature center and picnic tables are available. Fishing is permitted; swimming is not.

For **bikers,** the best route is between SouthPark and uptown Charlotte. If you'd like a route map, write to the North Carolina Department of Transportation, PO Box 25201, Raleigh, NC 27611.

Because there are so many **fishing** possibilities in the Greater Charlotte area, you may want to obtain a state license from the North Carolina Wildlife Commission; call ℂ **919/707-0050** or visit www.ncwildlife.org for more information. License prices vary.

Tennis courts are available at many places in the area, including several city parks. Among the best are Hornet's Nest, Park Road, and Freedom. The **Mecklenburg County Park and Recreation Department** (ℂ **704/336-3854;** www. charmeck.org) can advise you on which ones are closest to your hotel or motel, assuming that there isn't a court where you're staying. The people of Charlotte, like those in all Piedmont cities, are devoted to **golf.** For a preview of what's available, visit www.golfholes.com. The **Visitor Information Center** (ℂ **704/331-2753;** www.charlottesgotalot.com) has a complete list of courses that are open to the public.

Where to Stay

The massive 700-room **Westin Charlotte,** 601 S. College St. (© **704/375-2600;** www.starwoodhotels.com), lies in a prime location uptown in the financial district near the Convention Center and the Bank of America Stadium (home of the Carolina Panthers); look for weekend bargains.

The Ballantyne Resort ★★★   Within the city limits, this is one of the most elegant resorts in the western part of the state and a haven for golfers who come to play one of North Carolina's best 18-hole courses. The setting is a beautiful 2,000-acre site south of the center of Charlotte. The par-71, five-star golf course is masterfully designed and a challenge to golfers of all levels. The on-site spa is also one of the best in the west, with head-to-toe body-care services. Guest rooms are spacious and classically decorated, with many lavish touches, including marble bathrooms. A creative cuisine—contemporary yet classic—is served in the refined Gallery Restaurant.

10000 Ballantyne Commons Pkwy., Charlotte, NC 82877. © **866/248-4824** or 704/248-4000. Fax 704/248-4005. www.theballantynehotel.com. 251 units. $189–$539 double. AE, DC, MC, V. **Amenities:** Restaurant; 2 bars; 18-hole golf course; indoor grotto pool; outdoor pool; room service; spa; 4 tennis courts (2 lit). *In room:* A/C, TV, hair dryer, minibar, Wi-Fi ($13 per day).

Charlotte Marriott SouthPark ★★   Formerly the Park Hotel, this is Charlotte's government-rated four-star hotel. If money is no object, stay here and enjoy the classic styling, with fluted columns and tasteful, luxurious appointments. In SouthPark's commercial center, this six-story hostelry attracts those discriminating travelers who want the ultimate in city comfort. The green marble floors are matched by upholstery in Caribbean sea-green colors—an effect that is tasteful and stylish. The guest rooms, some of the best in town, often have a set of double beds or sometimes a four-poster king-size bed. Some rooms contain refrigerators. The restaurant is elegant, the service attentive and unobtrusive. A refined and quite sophisticated cuisine is served. In summer, guests can enjoy piano music Thursday to Saturday.

2200 Rexford Rd., Charlotte, NC 28211. © **800/228-9290** or 704/364-8220. Fax 704/365-4712. www.marriott.com. 192 units. $109–$184 double; $229–$589 suite. Children 17 and under stay free in parent's room. AE, DC, DISC, MC, V. Free parking. **Amenities:** Restaurant; bar; health club; outdoor pool; room service; spa. *In room:* A/C, TV, hair dryer, Wi-Fi ($13 per day).

Dunhill ★   Constructed in 1929, this is one of Charlotte's oldest and most historic hotels. These days, the big names often go elsewhere, but old-timers still prefer the Dunhill's European-style comfort and charm. (The doorman out front often greets returning guests by name.) In the old days, it was called the Mayfair Manor, and some of its most loyal clients still refer to it that way. The artwork in the public areas is by North Carolinian Philip Moose, and a piano player entertains in the stylish lobby. The restored guest rooms have a warm, cozy feeling; they're furnished with handsome reproductions and often with four-poster beds. **Monticello's** is the hotel restaurant, offering excellent cuisine throughout the day. Health-club privileges can be arranged.

237 N. Tryon St., Charlotte, NC 28202. © **800/354-4141** or 704/332-4141. Fax 704/376-4117. 60 units. $159–$239 double; $179–$259 suite. Children 15 and under stay free in parent's room. AE, DC, DISC, MC, V. **Amenities:** Restaurant; bar; babysitting; room service. *In room:* A/C, TV, hair dryer, Wi-Fi (free).

The Morehead Inn ★★ 🛏   This Southern estate lies in one of Charlotte's oldest neighborhoods, just minutes from uptown. With its tranquil elegance and fine antiques, it is easily one of the finer inns in western North Carolina. Installed in the historic Dilworth home, the inn is a popular center for local weddings. Its public areas are spacious but offer many cozy nooks, often with intimate fireplaces. Eight private suites are in the main house, and a secluded carriage house across the courtyard offers an additional quartet of suites. The furnishings are tasteful and comfortable. One favorite is "the Romany," a corner room with a queen-size four-poster bed and a separate office den. "The Mount Vernon" has a king-size sleigh bed facing an original fireplace, along with a large sunroom.

Breakfast is the only meal served, but the staff will direct you to many good restaurants nearby for lunch and dinner.

1122 E. Morehead St., Charlotte, NC 28204. © **888/667-3432** or 704/376-3357. Fax 704/335-1110. www. moreheadinn.com. 12 units. $129–$269 double. Rates include breakfast. AE, DC, DISC, MC, V. **Amenities:** Breakfast room. *In room:* A/C, TV, hair dryer, Wi-Fi (free).

Where to Dine

Blue B ★ MEDITERRANEAN This sophisticated uptown restaurant serves a market-fresh, multicultural menu with an emphasis on Spanish, French, Italian, and Moroccan cuisine. Live jazz is a feature Wednesday to Saturday. Begin with such appetizers as Provence style lobster and crab cakes in a beurre blanc or else crispy calamari fried North African style in a chickpea flour. Main courses range from grilled lamb loin in a pomegranate glaze to roast pork tenderloin with orange blossom honey. Or try the whole roasted Mediterranean sea bass, perhaps a Moroccan tagine, a duo of wild boar, or beef tenderloin à la blue. The cheese selection is the best in town.

Hearst Tower, corner of 5th and College St. © **704/927-2583.** Reservations required. Main courses $17–$33. AE, DC, MC, V. Mon–Thurs 5–10pm; Fri–Sat 5–11pm.

LaVecchia's Seafood Grille ★★ SEAFOOD This family-owned-and-operated business is celebrated locally as the best all-around restaurant and the best seafood dining room in greater Charlotte. It's an elegant setting with many works of art and sculpture by the Columbia, South Carolina–born artist Mike Williams. Dig into such delights as Maine lobster, aged beef, and both fresh- and saltwater fish, along with the finest assortment of shellfish in the area. In warm weather, tables on the patio fill up quickly, with diners sampling such dishes as she-crab soup (exceptional) and stuffed shrimp with crabmeat. The calamari with creamy herb garlic aioli is a delight, as is a platter of rope-cultured mussels steamed with white wine, garlic, and shallots with a touch of Pernod. Our favorite is the crispy seared salmon with Thai white rice, roasted wild mushrooms, julienne vegetables, and Asian hoisin honey glaze.

225-E 6th St. © **704/370-6776.** www.lavecchias.com. Reservations required. Main courses $18–$37. AE, DC, MC, V. Mon–Thurs 5:30–10pm; Fri–Sat 5:30–11pm.

Rock Bottom ☺ AMERICAN/PIZZA In the Transamerican Building in the heart of downtown, this is a good stopover spot for wood-fired pizzas, ales and lagers, and a large menu of family favorites including homemade soups, salads, the best burgers in town, and a selection of main dishes ranging from brown ale chicken to pork ribs in a sweet magnolia sauce. The outdoor patio is one of Charlotte's favorite gathering spots. Salads range from a salmon Caesar to hummus and goat cheese, and there's always a freshly made soup of the day. Pizzas come with a wide selection of toppings. Main dish specialties range from pasta jambalaya to cod filets in a beer batter. The bartenders make the longest list of specialty cocktails and martinis in town, including both a limoncello lemon drop martini and a pomegranate one.

401 N. Tryon St., Ste. 100. © **704/334-2739.** Main courses $9.50–$16. AE, DC, MC, V. Sun 11am–11pm; Mon–Sat 11am–2am.

Upstream ★★ SEAFOOD Near South Park Mall, this is the place for seafood in Charlotte, especially on "lobster Mondays." A local favorite, Upstream offers a sushi and oyster bar, an extensive wine list, and a market-fresh menu of delights from the sea. Dinner is its finest hour, although lunch here is a temptation with such starters as lobster bisque with crème fraîche and caviar, followed by large salads, perhaps chilled seafood, or else Japanese bento boxes. There is also a wide selection of sandwiches and main courses, including pecan-crusted Snake River trout. At dinner you can sample fresh oysters or wild mushroom–stuffed quail. Fish choices range from diver sea scallops to grilled mahimahi. The raw bar features the town's best seviche, especially jumbo shrimp and mango.

6902 Phillips Place. ✆ **704/556-7730.** Reservations recommended. Lunch sandwiches and main courses $9–$14; dinner main courses $23–$38. AE, DC, MC, V. Mon–Thurs 11:30am–10pm; Fri–Sat 11:30am–11pm; Sun 10:30am–10pm.

Charlotte After Dark

The **Charlotte Symphony Orchestra** (✆ **704/972-2003;** www.charlottesymphony. org) season runs from September to May; check local newspapers or call for performance dates. **Opera Carolina** (✆ **704/332-7177;** www.operacarolina.org) presents performances from October to April. Classic plays are often performed by **Theatre Charlotte,** 501 Queens Rd. (✆ **704/376-3777;** www.theatrecharlotte. org), usually Thursday to Sunday. The **Blumenthal Performing Arts Center,** 130 N. Tryon St. (✆ **704/372-1000;** www.blumenthalcenter.org), is the newest facility to join the performance venues; it features three theaters for productions ranging from rock concerts to intimate stage events.

If you want to catch a pro football game, a limited number of single-game tickets are available. For tickets to see the **Carolina Panthers** (www.panthers.com), visit the Bank of America Stadium Ticket Office at 800 S. Mint St., southeast side of the stadium, Monday to Friday 8:30am to 5:30pm (✆ **704/358-7800**), or order through Ticketmaster (✆ **704/522-6500;** www.ticketmaster.com). The city also has a pro basketball team, the **Charlotte Bobcats** (✆ **704/262-2287;** www.nba.com/bobcats). The majority holder is Robert Johnson, the Black Entertainment Channel (BET) multimillionaire and the first prominent African-American owner in U.S. sports. The Bobcats' new $265-million uptown arena opened in 2005.

Double Door Inn Some of the blues musicians who appeared here went on to become famous, such as Willie Dixon, Buddy Guy, and Stevie Ray Vaughn. The setting is a renovated 1920s house on the border of downtown Charlotte and the Elizabeth district, with a likable, battered, absolutely unpretentious ambience. You might catch a zydeco band if you're lucky. Hours are Monday to Friday from 11am to 2am and Saturday and Sunday from 8:30pm to 2am, but live music is featured only between 10pm and 2am nightly. 218 E. Independence Blvd. ✆ **704/376-1446.** www.doubledoor inn.com. Cover $6–$15 when music is offered.

Scorpio This popular lesbian and gay nightclub has been going strong for years. Many gays drive for miles—even from across the border in Tennessee—to have a lively night on the town at this bustling joint. Actually, it's several clubs within a club. There's a large dance bar that attracts "same-sexualists" (to use Gore Vidal's term). There's also a country bar called the Queen City Saloon. On certain Friday and Saturday nights, the crowd is so vast here that you'll think everybody in Charlotte has gone gay—at least for the night. The club is open nightly from 9pm to 2am. 2301 Freedom Dr. ✆ **704/373-9124.** www.scorpios.com. Cover $5–$10.

SOUTHERN PINES & THE PINEHURST SANDHILLS

8

The Sandhills' porous, sandy soil is a reminder that in prehistoric times, this land was under the turbulent waters of the Atlantic. This soil provides the ideal drainage that's crucial to the Golf Capital of the World, for no matter what the rainfall, no puddles accumulate on its rolling golf courses. And with mean temperatures ranging between 44° and 78°F (7°–26°C), the game is played here year-round.

In 1895, when Boston philanthropist James Walker Tufts bought 5,000 acres of land for $1 per acre, his plan was to build the little resort village of Pinehurst as a retreat for wealthy Northerners. Tufts's attention turned to golf, which had only recently arrived from Great Britain, when one of his dairy employees complained that guests were "hitting the cows with a little white ball." By 1900, Tufts had enlisted Donald Ross (who had honed his skills at Scotland's St. Andrews) to design courses that eventually drew the world's most distinguished golfers.

In 1973, the first World Open Championship was played in Pinehurst; the event was replaced in 1977 by the Colgate Hall of Fame Classic. In September 1974, President Gerald Ford presided at the opening of the World Golf Hall of Fame, overlooking Ross's famous No. 2 Course (one of the country's top 10).

Midland Road (N.C. 2) is a highway divided by a stately 6-mile row of pine trees, sedate homes, and lavish gardens. From the second green of the Pinehurst No. 2 Golf Course (site of the 1999 U.S. Open) at one end to the little village of Southern Pines at the other, about a third of the area's more than 35 courses are accessible via this road.

In addition to golf, competitive **tennis** made its mark when the first major tournament, the United North and South Tennis Tournament, hit the courts of the Pinehurst Tennis Club in 1918. That amateur event ran until 1942 and was the proving ground for many nationally ranked players, including the Davis Cup Team of the 1930s. Today this area enjoys a reputation for having some of America's best tennis facilities and programs.

The Sandhills region is also known for its **equestrian competitions.** Most of these events are free to spectators. *Horse Days,* a monthly publication about events that features calendar listings, is available locally at information offices. From late October to May, there are horse trials, shows, and even fox hunts.

PINEHURST ★

71 miles SW of Raleigh

Pinehurst, built by Frederick Law Olmsted (the architect-landscaper who planned New York's Central Park), has retained its New England village air, with green and shaded residential streets. Year-round greenery is provided by pines (some with needles 15 in. long), stately magnolias, and hollies. Moderate temperatures mean color through all seasons with camellias, azaleas, wisteria, dogwoods, and summer-blooming flowers. Shops, restaurants, hotels, and other business enterprises make this community self-sufficient. Pinehurst offers plenty of recreational facilities for those who aren't interested in chasing after that little white ball: a tennis club with excellent courts; more than 200 miles of riding trails, as well as stables with good mounts for hire; boating on a 200-acre lake; trap and skeet ranges; archery; 9,000 acres of woods to explore via meandering pathways; and, of course, shopping in the boutiques.

But golf is definitely king. If there's a hotel or motel in the area that doesn't arrange play for its guests, we couldn't find it. For a complete list of golf courses, ask the visitors bureau (see "Essentials," below) for its *Accommodations/Golfing* brochure.

Essentials

GETTING THERE U.S. 1 runs north and south through Southern Pines, N.C. 211 runs east and west, U.S. 15/501 reaches Pinehurst from the north, and there's direct area access to I-95, I-85, and I-40. You really need a car to get around this entire area.

Raleigh-Durham is the nearest commercial airport (see "Raleigh," in chapter 7). Moore County has a small private airport with a 5,500-foot runway. If you are flying in yourself, call for ramp-space reservations (© **910/692-3212**). A Hertz car-rental desk is at the terminal (© **910/692-5858**). Call ahead for reservations. **Amtrak** (© **800/USA-RAIL** [872-7245]; www.amtrak.com) has one northbound and one southbound train daily through Southern Pines.

VISITOR INFORMATION We strongly recommend that you write or phone ahead for details on golfing and other sports, sightseeing, accommodations, and dining. Contact the **Pinehurst Area Convention and Visitors Bureau,** 10677 Hwy. 15-501, Southern Pines, NC 28388 (© **800/346-5362;** www.homeofgolf.com).

Hitting the Links

Pinehurst is like a quaint village with the kind of total-golf atmosphere you find in St. Andrews in Scotland. With its more than 35 superb championship golf courses, some of which are among the highest rated in the world, the town represents golf's grandest era. Legends were born here—names such as Nelson, Zaharias, Jones, Hogan, Snead, and Palmer. Some of the finest golf architects of the 20th century designed courses in the area—Donald Ross, Ellis Maples, and Robert Trent Jones among them. The courses here are too numerous to list. Following are our favorites.

THE LINKS OF pinehurst

Nowhere in America do golf past and golf present walk hand in hand as they do in Pinehurst/Southern Pines. The area is a museum of golf architecture and a living laboratory of golf design. The first 18-hole course was laid out by Dr. D. LeRoy Culver of New York. It opened in 1899. Since then, the array of architects has included Ellis and Dan Maples, Tom Fazio, Robert Trent Jones, Peter Tufts, and (one of the latest) Arnold Palmer. When the greens of Pinehurst No. 2 were dug up and resurfaced with bent grass in 1987, workers found an old horseshoe buried under the 18th green—a souvenir left by one of the animals that used to drag and shape the putting surface some 80 years ago. When Rees Jones, the famous golf architect, was laying out holes for Pinehurst No. 7 in 1984, he came across several ancient bunkers of a long-abandoned golf course. He ordered the bunkers restored, and they sit today in front of the tee to the 4th hole.

Some holes are nearly a century old, and others have small greens rounded off on the corners—the "upside-down-saucer" effect that Scotsman Donald Ross used so frequently. Some courses have huge greens that require a 7-iron approach if the pin's at the front and a 4-iron if it's in the rear. Still other holes require heroic shots over water or pits of sand, and some have open green entrances that invite the old bump-and-run shot.

North Carolina's Pinehurst/Southern Pines was the site of the U.S. Open Championship, which marked the second time that the U.S. Open has been played in the Southeast (the first time was in 1976).

The **Club at Longleaf,** Pinehurst (© **800/542-0450** or 910/692-6100; www.longleafgolf.com), was called by *Golf Digest* "the most playable course in Pinehurst." It was designed by Dan Maples, architect of the nationally acclaimed Pit Golf Links. The front 9 at Longleaf was designed in the Scottish open style, with rolling fairways. Greens fees cost $29 to $89 with cart rental.

Legacy Golf Links, U.S. 15/501 South, Aberdeen (© **800/314-7560** or 910/944-8825; www.legacygolfnc.com), is the only links in the area to blend the accessibility of a public course with the amenities of a private club. It's also the only public course to receive *Golf Digest*'s four-star rating. Greens fees are $39 to $79 per person, including cart rental.

Pine Needles Lodge & Golf Club ★★, Southern Pines (© **800/747-7272** or 910/692-7111; www.pineneedles-midpines.com), is a Donald Ross masterpiece built in 1927, a challenging par-71 course for golfers of all skill levels. The course, playing to 6,708 yards from the championship tees, has been immaculately groomed and restored to its original splendor. Its Bermuda fairways and bent-grass greens are available only to guests staying at the Pine Needles and Mid Pines (for details, see the reviews for Pine Needles Lodge & Golf Club and Mid Pines Inn & Golf Club, later in this chapter). Greens fees are $125 to $195. Package rates are also available in combination with hotel tariffs.

The **Pinehurst Resort Golf Courses ★★★**, 1 Carolina Vista at Pinehurst (© **800/ITS-GOLF** [487-4653] or 910/295-6811; www.pinehurst.com), is the only resort with eight signature courses, and you must be a guest of the resort to play. Many guests book golf packages. The original architect was Donald Ross. This is golf in the grandest tradition, and shots played by Hogan, Nelson, and Jones still echo down the fairways. For these 126 holes of golf, the classic designs are by Donald Ross and Ellis Maples; the modern concepts are by Tom Fazio and Rees Jones.

Other Outdoor Pursuits

Tennis buffs will find nearly 100 public courts in the area; call ✆ **910/692-3330** for locations, hours, and fees. Most of the resorts have their own court facilities. The Pine Needles Lodge & Golf Club has the only local grass courts, and lighted courts are available in both Southern Pines and Aberdeen.

Bicycling is another major sport. The Pinehurst area has long been regarded as a top-flight training area and proving ground for the U.S., Canadian, and other international cycling teams. Riders of all skill levels can enjoy a variety of mapped courses along peaceful lanes and through country villages. Annual cycling events include the **Tour de Moore,** a grueling 100-mile road race held the last Saturday in April around the perimeter of Moore County. This race draws cyclists from all over the world, who compete for the coveted Pinehurst Cup.

Because of the lack of bicycle-rental shops in the area, hotels keep their own stock to rent to guests who'd like to cycle along the relatively easy terrain. Traffic is generally light, and conditions for cycling are good.

Where to Stay

Although the **Carolina Hotel** is still *the* place to stay in Pinehurst, several other hotels in the village offer luxury on a smaller scale and graciousness at the same level, at somewhat more moderate prices.

The Carolina Hotel ★★★ Established in 1901, the Carolina Hotel is one of America's premier golf and tennis resorts. It is now better than ever following a multimillion-dollar renovation. Set on 10,000 acres of landscaped grounds, this white, four-story clapboard landmark, with porches lined with comfortable rocking chairs, encourages the art of gracious living. Bright, cheerful colors predominate in the spacious guest rooms, which have an air of subdued elegance. In addition, the resort offers villas, which are ideal for foursomes or eightsomes, and there's always the cozy Manor Inn for quiet getaways. Some guests prefer a condo by one of the golf courses or facing Lake Pinehurst. The resort also owns the hotel's divinely comfortable neighbor, the Holly Inn, a charming turn-of-the-20th-century structure that offers deluxe accommodations and an imported Scottish bar.

For information about the **Carolina Dining Room,** see "Where to Dine," below.

Carolina Vista (PO Box 4000), Pinehurst, NC 28374. ✆ **800/ITS-GOLF** (487-4653) or 910/235-8507. Fax 910/235-8507. www.pinehurst.com. 220 units, 170 condos. 3-day, 3-night golf package $795 per person double. Rates include breakfast and dinner. AE, DC, DISC, MC, V. **Amenities:** 9 restaurants, including Carolina Dining Room (see review, p. 184); 3 bars; babysitting; kids club; 8 18-hole golf courses; exercise room; Jacuzzi; 3 pools; room service; sauna; spa; 24 tennis courts (5 lit). *In room:* A/C, TV, hair dryer, minibar, Wi-Fi (free).

Magnolia Inn This three-story, white clapboard building, dating from 1895, is set in the midst of well-landscaped gardens. *Casablanca*-style fans rotate overhead on the front porch, and out back is a little pool. The rooms are sunny and flowery, with double, queen-size, or twin beds. Some of the bathrooms, with their claw-foot tubs, are a little too old-fashioned for comfort; the others have tub/shower combinations. The Olmsted and Page rooms, each of which has a fireplace, are our favorites. A tavern offers your basic pub menu. Breakfast and dinner are served in the dining room. The fare's seasonings (or lack of them) won't frighten away this inn's mostly older patrons.

65 Magnolia Rd. (at Chinquapin Rd.; PO Box 818), Pinehurst, NC 28370. ⓒ **800/526-5562** or 910/295-6900. Fax 910/215-0858. www.themagnoliainn.com. 11 units. $95–$160 per person. Rates include breakfast Thurs–Sun. AE, MC, V. **Amenities:** Restaurant; pub; outdoor pool. *In room:* A/C, TV, Wi-Fi (free).

The Pine Crest Inn Right in the heart of the village, the Pine Crest Inn has all the flavor and courtesies of an English countryside inn. Bob Barrett (proprietor since 1961) tells us that approximately 80% of his guests are returnees—and small wonder, for the three-story, white-columned building radiates warmth from the moment you enter the lobby, with its comfortable armchairs, fireplace, and bar. Our favorite place to stay is the Telephone Cottage, named after its former function as a telephone switching station. Roomy and comfortable, it's a separate cottage nestled under the trees. Meals in the three dining rooms (with fireplaces and tasteful wallpaper) are so popular that they draw people from as far away as Raleigh and Charlotte.

50 Dogwood Rd. (PO Box 879), Pinehurst, NC 28370. ⓒ **800/371-2545** or 910/295-6121. Fax 910/295-4880. www.pinecrestinnpinehurst.com. 40 units. $72–$122 double. Rates include breakfast and dinner. Golf and sports packages available. AE, DC, DISC, MC, V. **Amenities:** Restaurant; bar. *In room:* A/C, TV, Wi-Fi (free).

Where to Dine

Carolina Dining Room ★★ AMERICAN The food here is the finest in the area. Only fresh, first-rate ingredients are used, and the dining room itself is worthy of the cuisine, with its series of Murano (Venetian) chandeliers. Breakfast, which is more expensive than the luncheon buffet, is the best in the area and recommended even if you're not a guest. Chefs prepare made-to-order omelets and waffles. The dinner menu is extensive, and the service is impeccable. Seafood fresh from Carolina coastal waters is presented in classic style. Beef so tender you can cut it with your fork, veal, and succulently flavored chicken (depending on the whim of the chef) also appear on the menu. In summer, there's top-flight entertainment, as well as dinner dancing.

In the Carolina Hotel, 80 Carolina Vista. ⓒ **910/295-6811.** Reservations required. Jacket preferred for men at dinner. Breakfast buffet $25; main courses $10–$15 lunch, $26–$34 dinner; fixed-price 3-course dinner $70–$75. AE, DC, DISC, MC, V. Daily 6–10am and 6:30–9pm. Tavern daily 11:30am–5pm.

Dugan's Pub CONTINENTAL/IRISH Across from the Holly Inn, this is the town's leading independent restaurant. Featuring a nautical decor, with natural woods, it also has a pub. Sandwiches and salads are lunch favorites. At night, a selection of seafood, mainly from the Carolina coast, is available. Pasta dishes are often overcooked, but the veal is great. Live music is offered here on Friday and Saturday nights.

2 Market Sq. ⓒ **910/295-3400.** www.duganspub.net. Main courses $8–$15 lunch, $10–$22 dinner. AE, DISC, MC, V. Restaurant Mon–Sat 11:30am–10pm; Sun noon–9pm. Bar Mon–Sat 11:30am–1am.

Elliotts on Linden ★★ FUSION Its loyal devotees claim Elliotts is the best restaurant in North Carolina. While we wouldn't go quite that far, English-born Mark Elliott has turned this address into not only a fine restaurant, but also a retail wine shop, kitchenware store, cooking school, and deli with artisan cheeses and prepared dishes. The inventive cuisine is made from high-quality fresh ingredients, and seasonal specialties are often featured. Appetizers include chicken livers sautéed with bacon and shallots and flambéed in brandy, and seared scallops in a ginger and citrus garlic sauce. The main dishes are classically grounded yet imaginative, as evoked by grilled elk rack with a pomegranate glaze or stuffed quail and duck with sweet corn fritters and a ginger-spiked catsup. Roast bison filet—wrapped with prosciutto and wild mushrooms—is served with a red-wine sauce.

905 Linden Rd. ℃ **910/215-0775.** www.elliottsonlinden.com. Reservations required. Main courses $17–$39. AE, DC, MC, V. Mon–Sat 11:30am–2:30pm and 6–9:30pm; Sun 6–9:30pm.

Pinehurst After Dark

Entertainment is mostly available at the golf resorts. Check, though, to see what's going on at **Sandhills Community College,** 3395 Airport Rd. (℃ **800/338-3944** or 910/692-6185; www.sandhills.edu), which often stages jazz and other variety shows, with tickets costing from $5 to $20. There are also free outdoor summer concerts.

Side Trips in the Area

ASHEBORO: NORTH CAROLINA ZOOLOGICAL PARK

A few miles north of Seagrove on U.S. 220 is the town of Asheboro, and 6 miles southeast of Asheboro off U.S. 64 and U.S. 220 is the **North Carolina Zoological Park ★**, 4401 Zoo Pkwy. (℃ **800/488-0444;** www.nczoo.org). The 300-acre Africa region and the 200-acre North America region are the first of seven continental regions planned for the 1,448-acre park, featuring more than 1,000 animals in natural habitats. In this still-developing world-class zoo, gorillas and 200 rare animals such as meerkats inhabit the African Pavilion. Lions, elephants, bears, bison, elk, alligators, chimpanzees, and many other animals dwell in spacious outdoor habitats. A 37-acre African Plains exhibit is the home of a dozen species of antelope, gazelle, and oryx. The R. J. Reynolds Forest Aviary displays 150 exotic birds flying free amid lush tropical trees and plants. There are picnic areas, restaurants, gift shops, and a tram ride. The zoo is open daily 9am to 5pm from April to October and 9am to 4pm November to March. The park is closed Christmas Day. Admission is $10 for adults, $8 for seniors and students, $6 for children 2 to 12, and free for children 1 and under.

SEAGROVE: THE POTTERIES

About an hour's drive to the northwest on U.S. 220 is the little town of Seagrove, which has been turning out quality pottery for more than 200 years. This region's red and gray clays were first used by settlers from Staffordshire, England; the first items produced were jugs for transporting whiskey. The same art is practiced today just as it was then. Clays are ground and mixed by machines turned by mules, simple designs are fashioned on kick wheels, and glazing is done in wood-burning kilns. Many of the potters work in or behind their homes, with only a small sign outside to identify their trade. If you have difficulty finding them, stop and ask; everybody does, so don't be shy. There are some sales rooms in town, but the real fun is seeing the pottery actually being made.

While you're here, visit **Jugtown Pottery,** a group of rustic, log-hewn buildings in a grove of pines, at 330 Jugtown Rd. (℃ **910/464-3266;** www.jugtownware.com). The main potters here are owner Vernon Owens and his wife, Pam, both award-winning craftspeople. You'll find traditional jugs and candlesticks in wood-fired salt glaze and frog skin, among many other items. **Friends of the North Carolina Pottery Center** (℃ **336/873-8430** or 873-7887; www.ncpotterycenter.com) is located at 233 East Ave. and offers 30-minute demonstrations between 11:30am and 2:30pm Tuesday to Saturday. This center displays examples of most of the potters' wares in the area and also serves as an information source, with guide maps available upon request. It's open Tuesday to Saturday 10am to 4pm. Admission is $2 for adults, $1 for children, and free for children 11 and under. Guided tours are $3 per person, regardless of age.

Of some 40 potters operating in the Seagrove area, one especially has caught our fancy. At the **Fish House and Blue Moon Gallery,** 1387 Hwy. 705 S., Seagrove (⌀ **336/879-3270;** www.blue-moon-gallery.com), Brian and Georgia Knight's potter's wheel turns out delicate cutout candleholders, as well as a full line of more traditional bowls, vases, teapots, and casserole dishes. The shop is open January to March Tuesday to Saturday 10am to 5pm and April to December Monday to Saturday 10am to 5pm. The gallery features the work of artists from all over the country.

SOUTHERN PINES

5 miles E of Pinehurst

The pleasant village of Southern Pines has its own attractions lying among longleaf and loblolly pines in what is known as "sand country." A resort since the 1880s, it became a golfing mecca in 1920. It's rare for a building here to be more than two stories tall. Locals readily admit that the main reason to come here is to follow that little white ball, but they are quick to point out that the town has some interesting sights as well.

Essentials

SPECIAL EVENTS   Expect a full calendar of equestrian events throughout the year, including the **Southern Pines Horse Trials** at Carolina Horse Park at Five Points, annually in mid-March (⌀ **910/875-2074;** www.carolinahorsepark.com). During the first week of April, the **Pinehurst Harness Track Matinee Races** are held at the Pinehurst Harness Mile Track, 200 Beulah Hill Rd. S. (⌀ **910/295-4446**). The **Carolina Carriage Classic in the Pines** is presented at the end of April and in early May at the Pinehurst Harness Mile Track, Route 5, Pinehurst (⌀ **910/295-4446**). This is one of the major driving events in the Southeast, with three rings of competition—dressage, pleasure classes, and obstacles. The **Pinehurst Area Convention and Visitors Bureau,** PO Box 2270, Southern Pines, NC 28388 (⌀ **800/346-5362;** www.homeofgolf.com), can furnish exact dates and full details on all these events, as well as others throughout the year.

Seeing the Sights

The **Campbell House,** a handsome Georgian former family residence on East Connecticut Avenue, now houses the Arts Council of Moore County, and its galleries display the work of local artists.

Shaw House, at Southwest Broad Street and Morganton Road (⌀ **910/692-2051** or 692-4885; www.moorehistory.com), is a stylish antebellum house with unusual carved-cypress mantels. It's the oldest structure in town, dating from the 1770s, and serves as headquarters of the Moore County Historical Association. It's open Wednesday to Sunday from 1 to 4pm, and admission is free. It's closed during the summer, but tours are available. For information on tour times and operators, call the Shaw House.

On the Fort Bragg–Aberdeen road, 1 mile southeast of Southern Pines, you'll come to **Weymouth Woods–Sandhills Nature Preserve** (⌀ **910/692-2167;** www.

ncparks.gov/Visit/parks/wewo/main.php), a nature spot with foot and bridle paths and about 600 acres of pine-covered "sand ridges." The natural history museum is open daily 9am to 6pm (until 7pm Apr–Oct); admission is free. It's closed on Christmas Day.

You'll find a lot of fine horse farms in the Sandhills. Steeplechasers trained here show up regularly at tracks around the country, and trotters and pacers are also trained in the area. The late Del Cameron, renowned three-time winner of the Hambletonian, kept a winter training stable here for more than 30 years.

Seek out **Downtown Southern Pines,** U.S. 1 in the Broad Street area, for a collection of shops and restaurants in the Historic District.

Where to Stay

Days Inn   This is the best motel in the area, attracting a lot of golfers. Although lacking personality, it compensates with good-size rooms, a high level of housekeeping, and personal service. The staff is helpful, providing such extras as free cribs for families who need them. Room service is also available. The fare in the **Hennings Restaurant** is only ordinary, but the restaurant is conveniently open throughout the day. Charbroiled steaks are a specialty.

805 Southwest Service Rd., Southern Pines, NC 28387. (Ⓒ) **800/329-7466** or 910/692-8585. Fax 910/692-5213. www.daysinn.com. 162 units. $69–$99 double. Children 17 and under stay free in parent's room. AE, DC, DISC, MC, V. **Amenities:** Restaurant; bar; exercise room; outdoor pool; room service. *In room:* A/C, TV, hair dryer, Internet (free).

Hampton Inn Southern Pines   Hampton Inn is one of the leading motels in the area. Although decorated in standard chain format, it is one of the better-run inns, with styling in the Early American mode. Guest rooms are comfortably furnished, making for an inviting family atmosphere. Rates rise during special events, such as NASCAR races, the PGA tournament, and the Stoneybrook Steeplechase races. Tennis and golf can be arranged, as can entrance to a nearby health club. There is also a restaurant nearby.

1675 U.S. 1 S., Southern Pines, NC 28387. (Ⓒ) **800/HAMPTON** (426-7866) or 910/693-4330. Fax 910/693-4329. www.hamptoninn.com. 103 units. $109 double; $119–$159 suite. Children 17 and under stay free in parent's room. Golf packages available. Rates include continental breakfast. AE, DC, DISC, MC, V. **Amenities:** Breakfast room; lounge; outdoor pool. *In room:* A/C, TV, Wi-Fi (free).

Hyland Hills Resort   In an attractive wooded setting, this small resort is nowhere near the match of such better-known places as Mid Pines, but what it has going for it is economy. The efficiencies and rather spacious guest rooms, often with patios, aren't luxurious in any way, but they're comfortable and well maintained, and you can prepare light meals here.

U.S. 1 N., Southern Pines, NC 28387. (Ⓒ) **800/841-0638** or 910/692-7615. www.hylandhillsresort.net. 41 units. $59–$69 double; $75 efficiency. Golf packages available. DISC, MC, V. **Amenities:** Restaurant; bar; pool. *In room:* A/C, TV.

Mid Pines Inn & Golf Club ★   Five miles east of Pinehurst, this 1921 inn retains its old-fashioned comfort and a certain flair. It is owned and run by Pine Needles Lodge & Golf Club (see below). Every hole on the golf course remains as it was in 1921 when Donald Ross first conceived this challenging course. A devoted clientele returns every year, but newcomers are also given a hearty welcome. The inn consists of a graceful three-story, colonial-style main building with wings flanking the entrance. The lobby rotunda is gracious, with twin white staircases. The rooms are decorated with style and taste, although you may prefer one of the golf cottages or villas on the grounds—some have their own fireplaces. The villas are the most spacious choices. Generous meals are prepared in the formal dining room. In summer, lunch is served on an informal terrace overlooking the fairways of the championship golf course.

1010 Midland Rd., Southern Pines, NC 28387. ✆ **800/747-7272** or 910/692-2114. Fax 910/692-4615. www.pineneedles-midpines.com. 108 units, 7 cottages, 10 lakeside villas. $108–$156 double; $168–$288 cottage or villa. Children 11 and under stay free in parent's room. AE, DC, DISC, MC, V. **Amenities:** Restaurant; bar; babysitting; 18-hole golf course; health club privileges; outdoor pool; room service; tennis court (lit). *In room:* A/C, TV, hair dryer, Wi-Fi (free).

Pine Needles Lodge & Golf Club ★★   With all the pine trees in the area, someone had to name a hotel "Pine Needles," and someone did. The resort—home to the U.S. Women's Open Championships—is the creation of local legend Peggy Kirk Bell, a champion golfer and golf instructor, who opened it with her late husband. It has won many a devoted fan over the years. The golf course here was designed in 1927 by Donald Ross, the famous golf architect. The handsome rooms are spread across 10 rustic two- and four-story lodges that can hold groups of 10 to 20 people each; returnees often select their favorite. Decidedly informal, the guest rooms have rustic styling, often with exposed beams. The Bell family purchased the Mid Pines Inn & Golf Club in 1994 (see above).

1005 Midland Rd., Southern Pines, NC 28387. ✆ **800/747-7272** or 910/692-7111. Fax 910/692-5349. www.pineneedles-midpines.com. 78 units. $140–$450 double. Golf packages available. Children 4 and under stay free in parent's room. AE, MC, V. **Amenities:** 2 restaurants; 3 bars; babysitting; bike rentals; 2 18-hole golf courses; exercise room; outdoor pool; room service. *In room:* A/C, TV, hair dryer, Wi-Fi (free).

Where to Dine

The Lob Steer Inn ☺ STEAK/SEAFOOD   This family favorite is a sure bet for fine dining at a reasonable cost. Tasty preparations of the kind of fare locals like are served, including broiled seafood and prime rib. Guests help themselves at the freshly prepared salad bar and somehow always find room to go to the dessert bar to finish their meal. This is a rather upscale dining choice, despite the casual dress. As a waiter confided, "We're no redneck joint." It's deservedly one of the best and most popular places in the area. Children's plates are offered in a wider variety than usual.

U.S. 1 N. ✆ **910/692-3503.** www.thelobsteerinn.com. Reservations recommended Fri–Sat. Main courses $12–$43. AE, DC, DISC, MC, V. Sun–Thurs 5–10pm; Fri–Sat 5–10:30pm.

195 American Fusion Cuisine ★ AMERICAN   Organic ingredients, fresh produce, and dishes that taste homemade are the hallmarks of this fine restaurant just off Old U.S. 1 South. The owners operated a natural foods store for many years, and a casual, contemporary comfort prevails. Freshly made soups come either by the cup or bowl, and the appetizers are tempting, perhaps blackened scallops with an avocado corn relish over crispy flour tortillas or else calamari over a baby spinach salad with shiitake mushrooms, leeks, and a warm bacon vinaigrette. At night you can enjoy freshly made breads, artful salads, and some of the best seafood in the area. Desserts are always a temptation.

195 Bell Ave. ✆ **910/692-7110.** www.195pinehurstdining.com. Reservations recommended. Main courses $15–$32. DISC, MC, V. Tues 11am–3pm; Wed–Sat 11am–3pm and 5:30–9:30pm.

Southern Pines After Dark

Most area golf resorts offer dancing and occasional evening entertainment. The **Arts Council of Moore County,** PO Box 405, Southern Pines, NC 28388 (*℃* **910/692-2787;** www.artscouncil-moore.org), maintains a cultural calendar and sponsors local concert and entertainment groups and periodic arts-council shows.

A Side Trip to Cameron

The entire little town of **Cameron,** 10 miles north of Southern Pines (off U.S. 1/15/501), has been designated a historic district, with some 19 vintage sites and buildings. More than 60 antiques dealers have shops here, and an annual antiques street fair is held the first Saturday in May and again in October. Most shops are open Wednesday to Saturday from 10am to 5pm. After a morning of sightseeing and shopping, have lunch at the **Dewberry Deli,** 485 Carthage St. (*℃* **910/245-3697**). Call ahead for opening hours, which are subject to change. In an old hardware store, this eatery is ideal for a salad or a sandwich.

ASHEVILLE & THE HIGH COUNTRY

Men and women have made their homes in North Carolina's Blue Ridge Mountains since the first push westward, but nature endures. In late spring, green creeps up the peaks as trees leaf out. In summer, wildflowers make a carpet of colorful blooms. Fall brings vivid reds, yellows, and oranges to give every mountainside a flamelike hue. Wildlife still flourishes, streams are clear, and forests of birch, poplar, beech, hickory, and oak are undisturbed. This is one of those rare places where civilization has been smart enough to protect the natural environment as well as enjoy it.

The largest city in the High Country is handsome Asheville, home of author Thomas Wolfe (*Look Homeward, Angel*) and long a residence of the wealthy and famous. In recent years, neighboring Boone, Banner Elk, and Blowing Rock have become important ski centers in the South, especially since the introduction of snowmaking equipment. The best skiing in the area includes Ski Beech, Appalachian Ski Mountain, Hawksnest Golf & Ski Resort, and Sugar Mountain.

THE GREAT OUTDOORS IN THE HIGH COUNTRY

Sparkling white winters, fragrant springs, cool summers, and brisk, burnished autumns characterize North Carolina's High Country. Skiing in winter gives way in milder weather to swimming, golfing, fishing, tennis, rafting, horseback riding, backpacking, rock climbing, and rappelling.

The **Blue Ridge Parkway,** a unit of the National Park Service, passes through all five counties of the High Country, offering a vista of natural beauty and rural landscapes (see "The Blue Ridge Parkway," later in this chapter).

Moses Cone Memorial Park, near Blowing Rock on the parkway, has 25 miles of easily graded **hiking** trails. It's also popular for cross-country skiing. The Linville Falls–Linville Gorge area on the parkway has several trails leading to the head of the falls, with views of the cataract and the Linville Gorge Wilderness Area. Moderate trails lead to Grandfather Mountain, and challenging hikes take in part of the fabled Appalachian Trail, stretching from Georgia to Maine. In North Carolina, the trail

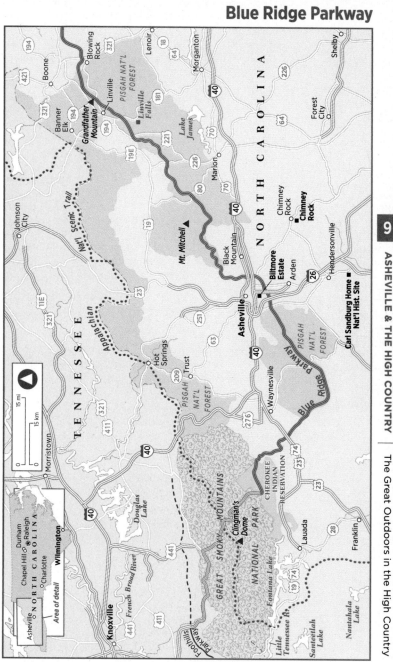

crosses Roan Mountain, Hump Mountain, and Yellow Mountain, all of which are known for their large expanses of meadows with panoramic views. Trail heads are in Elk Park and at Carver's Gap on Roan.

The High Country is also filled with **state and federal parks,** including Moses Cone Memorial Park, north of Blowing Rock. This 3,600-acre park offers bridle paths, hiking trails, trout streams, and two lakes. The other major park is the Linville Gorge Wilderness Area, a 7,600-acre tract set aside to provide a natural environment. The steep walls of the gorge enclose the Linville River, which descends 2,000 feet in only 12 miles. Access is by foot trails via the Forest Service Road off U.S. 221 at the Linville Falls exit.

Cross-country **skiing** is the finest in the South. Excellent trails are at Moses Cone Memorial Park, Beech Mountain, and several other locations along the Blue Ridge Parkway.

For **fishing,** area streams and lakes abound in trout, bass, catfish, blue gill, and other varieties. The game fish waters of the Blue Ridge Parkway (Price, Cone, and Doughton parks) are under federal regulation and require a license or permit. The fishing season begins the first Saturday in April and runs through the last day of February.

ASHEVILLE ★★★

241 miles W of Raleigh

Asheville, once just a tiny mountain trading village at the confluence of the French Broad and Swannanoa rivers, has grown up and turned into a year-round resort, complete with architectural gems from several eras and a lively cultural scene.

People who could have lived almost anywhere in the world, including Thomas Edison, settled in Asheville. Those Jazz Age kids F. Scott and Zelda Fitzgerald were among the most famous visitors. Fitzgerald arrived in the summer of 1935, recuperating from a mild case of tuberculosis, and his wife, Zelda, who had suffered a series of nervous breakdowns, was incarcerated at Highland Hospital, a private sanitarium charging $240 a month—an exorbitant fee in those days.

The most famous person associated with Asheville is Thomas Wolfe, whose mother ran a boardinghouse here called the Old Kentucky Home. It was disguised as "Dixie-land" in Wolfe's autobiographical novel, *Look Homeward, Angel*. Fitzgerald and Wolfe had some things in common: TB, an eye for the women, and alcohol. They even shared an editor: the famous Maxwell Perkins. Wolfe's novel (still called "that book" by old-timers in Asheville) was blacklisted here as late as 1949. Although he claimed that "you can't go home again," he eventually did, in 1938. Thousands assembled outside his mother's old boardinghouse to bid him farewell upon his premature death.

Essentials

GETTING THERE I-40 passes through Asheville from the east and west, I-26 runs southeast (as far as Charleston), U.S. 23/19A runs north and west, and I-240 is a perimeter highway circling the city. For AAA services, contact the **Carolina Motor Club,** 1000 Merrimon Ave., Ste. B, Asheville (⌀ **800/274-2621** or 828/253-5376).

Asheville Regional Airport (⌀ **828/684-2226;** www.flyavl.com) is just off I-26. Major airlines serving this airport are **Delta ASA** and **Comair** (⌀ **800/221-1212;** www.delta.com), **Continental Express** (⌀ **800/525-0280;** www.continental.com), and **US Airways** (⌀ **800/428-4322;** www.usairways.com).

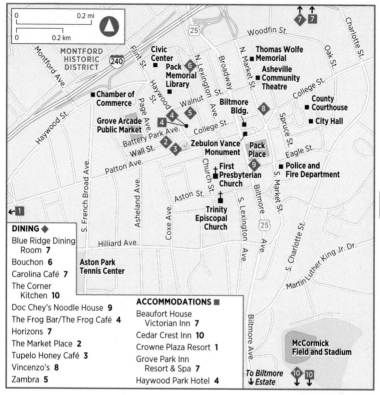

Downtown Asheville

DINING ◆

Blue Ridge Dining Room **7**
Bouchon **6**
Carolina Café **7**
The Corner Kitchen **10**
Doc Chey's Noodle House **9**
The Frog Bar/The Frog Café **4**
Horizons **7**
The Market Place **2**
Tupelo Honey Café **3**
Vincenzo's **8**
Zambra **5**

ACCOMMODATIONS ■

Beaufort House Victorian Inn **7**
Cedar Crest Inn **10**
Crowne Plaza Resort **1**
Grove Park Inn Resort & Spa **7**
Haywood Park Hotel **4**

9 ASHEVILLE & THE HIGH COUNTRY | Asheville

Greyhound (📞 **800/231-2222;** www.greyhound.com) offers bus service to Asheville. The **bus station** is at 2 Tunnel Rd. (📞 **828/253-8451**).

VISITOR INFORMATION The **Asheville Convention and Visitors Bureau,** 36 Montford Ave. (PO Box 1010), Asheville, NC 28802 (📞 **888/247-9811** or 828/258-6101; www.exploreasheville.com), is open daily 9am to 5pm. You can also request the *Asheville Visitor Guide* from the **Asheville Chamber of Commerce** (📞 **888/247-9811** or 828/258-6101; www.ashevillechamber.org).

SPECIAL EVENTS Special happenings at the **Biltmore Estate** (see "Seeing the Sights," below) include a spring Festival of Flowers, a September International Exposition, and Christmas at Biltmore—call ahead for specific dates.

Special events at the **Folk Art Center** (www.southernhighlandguild.org; see "Side Trips from Asheville," later in this chapter) include Fiber Day in May, the World Gee Haw Whimmy Diddle Competition in August, Celebrate Folk Art in September, and Christmas with the Guild in December.

If you're here the first weekend of August, you can attend the **Annual Mountain Dance and Folk Festival** (📞 **828/258-6101;** www.folkheritage.org), held at the Civic Center on Haywood Street. The fiddlers, banjo pickers, ballad singers, dulcimer players, and clog dancers don't call it quits until nobody is interested in one more dance. This is the oldest such festival in the country, and you're encouraged to join in even if you don't know a "do-si-do" from a "swing your partner." Every Saturday night from early July to August (except for the first Sat in Aug), there's a **Shindig-on-the-Green** (www.folkheritage.org), where you'll find many of the same mountain musicians and dancers having an old-fashioned wingding. It's free and lots of fun. Take along a blanket or chair.

Brevard, 27 miles southwest of Asheville, hosts a music festival from late June through mid-August at the **Brevard Music Center** (www.brevardmusic.org). Nationally and internationally famous artists perform daily in symphony, chamber-music, band, and choral concerts, as well as musical comedy and opera. Write to PO Box 312, Brevard, NC 28712; or call © 888/384-8682 or 888/862-2105 for schedules and reservations. Some events are free; others cost from $12 to $70.

The **North Carolina International Folk Festival (Folkmoot),** Waynesville, is an annual cultural heritage of folk music and dances held the second and third weeks in July. Participants travel from around the world to join in the event. For information, get in touch with Folkmoot USA, 112 Virginia Ave. in Waynesville (© **877/FOLK-USA** [365-5872] or 828/452-2997; www.folkmootusa.org).

Billed as "the largest free outdoor street festival in the Southeast," **Bele Chere** is a great summer festival of food and entertainment in Arts Park in Asheville and is held in July. Feast on such delights as hickory smoked pork, peach and blueberry pie, and corn dogs. "A Taste of Asheville" food booths feature local cuisine along with specialties ranging from Mexican to Chinese. In addition, top regional artisans and craftspeople showcase handmade clothing, pottery, and jewelry. Such big-name artists as Blues Traveler, Shooter Jennings, and John Anderson have played the festival. Contact the Department of Parks and Recreation (© **828/259-5800;** www.belecherefestival.com) for more information.

Seeing the Sights

In recent years, a vigorous local effort has been made to preserve and restore remnants of the city's colorful past. The *Asheville Urban Trail* brochure, available free from the Asheville Chamber of Commerce or at the Asheville Visitor Center, is a self-guided tour through the historic downtown district.

Biltmore Village (www.biltmorevillage.com) is a cluster of 24 cottages housing boutiques, crafts shops, and restaurants. The best of these shops is the **New Morning Gallery,** 7 Boston Way (© **828/274-2831;** www.newmorninggallerync.com); it started in 1972 and today is a 6,000-square-foot showcase of "art for living." The New Morning Gallery is one of the South's largest galleries of arts and crafts. It offers a fresh mix of functional and sculptural pottery, fine-art glass, furniture, jewelry, and other handmade objects. It's open Monday to Saturday from 10am to 7pm and on Sunday from noon to 5pm.

Another attraction, the **Montford Historic District,** has more than 200 turn-of-the-20th-century residences. In the downtown area, amid Art Deco buildings, you'll see the **Lexington Park** area, a center for artists and artisans whose workshops are tucked down a little alleyway, and **Pack Place,** a developing center for a wide variety of cultural activities.

THE GREATEST mansion IN THE MOUNTAINS

George Washington Vanderbilt, a young man of 25 in the late 1880s, came upon the perfect spot in the Blue Ridge for his French Renaissance–style château, which was to be built by his friend, architect Richard Morris Hunt.

The great château would be called Biltmore. Vanderbilt's initial purchase of 125,000 acres outside Asheville has diminished to 8,000. It includes formal and informal gardens designed by the father of landscape architecture in America, Frederick Law Olmsted.

Biltmore remains the largest private residence in the United States, a National Historic Landmark now owned by Vanderbilt's grandson. Begun in 1890, the house is constructed of tons of Indiana limestone, transported by a special railway spur built specifically to bring the massive amounts of material and supplies to the site. It took hundreds of workers 5 years to complete the house. On Christmas Eve 1895, George Vanderbilt formally opened the doors for the first time to friends and family members.

Like William Randolph Hearst, Vanderbilt journeyed through Europe and Asia buying paintings, porcelains, bronzes, carpets, and antiques, all of which would become part of the collection of 50,000 objects that are still in Biltmore today. Artwork is by Renoir, Sargent, Whistler, Pellegrini, and Boldini, and furniture includes designs by Chippendale and Sheraton.

Fully electric and centrally heated, Biltmore was one of the most technologically advanced structures ever built at the time of its completion. It used some of Thomas Edison's first light bulbs and boasted a fire-alarm system, an electrical call-box system for servants, two elevators, elaborate indoor plumbing for all 34 bedrooms—and a relatively newfangled invention called the telephone.

Thomas Wolfe, a native of Asheville, immortalized the town and its citizens in his first novel, *Look Homeward, Angel.* His mother's **boardinghouse,** at 48 Spruce St., is maintained as a literary shrine. The house was severely damaged by a fire set by an arsonist in 1998, but the building was restored and it reopened in 2004. The author lived here from 1906 to 1916. ("I was a child here, here the stairs, and here was darkness; this was I, and this was Time.") Called Old Kentucky Home, the 30-room house with a wooden porch was referred to as "Dixieland" in his novels. Tours of the house are offered Tuesday to Sunday every hour on the half-hour, costing $1 and lasting 45 minutes. Before the fire, the city of Asheville opened the **Thomas Wolfe Memorial;** because many of his personal belongings, such as his typewriter and writing table, were on display in the site's visitor center, they were not destroyed. The exhibit was expanded just after the fire to include a 22-minute video biography and a slide show that depicts the Wolfe house as it was before the devastation. The biography is shown at the beginning of every half-hour from 9am to 4pm, and the slide show runs from 9:30am to 4:30pm. For information, call or visit the **Visitors Center,** 52 N. Market St., Asheville (© **828/253-8304;** www.wolfememorial.com). Hours are Tuesday to Saturday 9am to 5pm and Sunday 1 to 5pm (winter hours Tues–Sat 10am–4pm and Sun 1–4pm). Admission is $1 for adults or 50¢ for ages 17 and under.

Both Wolfe and short-story writer **O. Henry** (William Sydney Porter) are buried in **Riverside Cemetery** (entrance on Birch St. off Pearson Dr.).

Asheville's **Grovewood Gallery** (© **877/622-7238** or 828/253-7651; www. grovewood.com) features the work of some of the Southeast's finest craftspeople, including the artists of **Grovewood Studios,** whose workshops are in the adjoining buildings. The gallery is located in what was for 70 years the home of the Biltmore Homespun Shops, adjacent to the Grove Park Inn Resort (see "Where to Stay," later in this chapter). Grovewood Studios continues the tradition of craftsmanship begun by Edith Vanderbilt in 1901 as Biltmore Estate Industries. Established as an industrial school to teach boys and girls the traditional skills of woodcarving and hand weaving, the Industries became a thriving business, producing homespun cloth, woodcarvings, and furniture. Industries was sold in 1917 to Fred Seely, manager of the Grove Park Inn, who built the charming cluster of English-style workshops known as the Biltmore Homespun Shops and further developed the woolen cloth into a product known around the world. Cloth production finally ceased in 1980, but the history of Biltmore Estate Industries and the Biltmore Homespun Shops is told here at the **North Carolina Homespun Museum.** Also on the grounds are the **Estes-Winn Memorial Automobile Museum** and the **Grovewood Cafe.** The gallery is open year-round Monday to Saturday 10am to 6pm and Sunday 11am to 5pm. The museums are open April to December Monday to Saturday 10am to 5pm and Sunday 11am to 5pm. Admission to the two museums is free. You can reach the gallery and the Grove Park Inn via Charlotte Street and Macon Avenue. Once you are on the grounds of the inn, follow the signs.

As intriguing as all the preceding attractions may be, they're dwarfed by the premier attraction in Asheville: the magnificent Biltmore Estate.

Biltmore Estate ★★★ The French Renaissance château, built by George W. Vanderbilt, has 250 rooms. This is one of the largest and most impressive privately owned historic estates in the world, still under the control of the rich Vanderbilt clan. The estate is divided into four different attractions, including the mansion itself (four floors of the building and the basement), part of a 2- to 2½-hour self-directed tour. Immediately adjacent to the mansion are the greenhouses and conservatories. Three miles from the main house is the Winery and Biltmore Farm Village, the most visited winery in the U.S., featuring tours and wine tastings. Finally, there's the Explore Biltmore Center, devoted to outdoor sports and family activities, including horseback riding, cycling, trips on the French Broad River, and other events. There isn't an ordinary spot in the place—not even the kitchen. Vanderbilt gathered furnishings and art treasures from all over the world for this palace (Napoleon's chess set and table from St. Helena are here, for example) and then went further, creating one of the most lavish formal gardens you'll ever see.

The Behind the Scenes Tour provides further access to the house, and the Rooftop Tour provides panoramic views. Visitors should allow a minimum of 5 hours. If you get your pass stamped when you leave the estate at the end of your first day, you can return anytime the following day for a flat fee of $10.

1 N. Pack Sq. (on U.S. 25, 2 blocks north of I-40). © **800/411-3812** or 828/225-1333. www.biltmore.com. Admission house and gardens $55–$60 adults, $28–$30 children 10–16, free for children 9 and under when accompanied by paying adult. Behind the Scenes Tour and Rooftop Tour are each an additional $15 to $25 per person. Daily 9am–6pm.

Outdoor Pursuits

BICYCLING The Asheville area is terrific for mountain biking. Bicycle shops and outfitters can provide trail maps and bike rentals. Call the chamber of commerce at © **828/258-6101** or visit www.ashevillecycling.com for a complete list.

FISHING Best for lake fishing is **Lake Julian,** south of Asheville, which is well stocked with bass and bream. Canoes and picnic facilities are available. **Lake Powhatan,** on N.C. 191 in the Pisgah National Forest, has a sand beach, swimming, camping, and picnicking in addition to fishing. No boats are available, however. **Lake Lure,** on U.S. 74 about 30 minutes southeast of Asheville, has trout, bass, bream, and watersports; motorboats are available. An abundance of well-stocked rivers and highland streams are also within easy reach of Asheville. For more information about fishing in the area, contact the **Hunter Banks Store** (© **800/227-6732** or 828/ 252-3005; www.hunterbanks.com).

GOLF The rolling terrain of the mountains around Asheville presents golfers with hundreds of uncrowded fairways. There are more than 50 golf courses in the state's western region. Our favorite is the course at the **Grove Park Inn Resort,** 290 Macon Ave. (© **800/438-5800** or 828/252-2711; www.groveparkinn.com). Open daily throughout the year, the par-71 course is steeped in tradition, having first opened in 1899. It was redesigned in 1924 by master golf architect Donald Ross. The oldest operating course in North Carolina, it evokes memories of Harry Vardon, Bobby Jones, and Ben Hogan. Arnold Palmer and Jack Nicklaus are only two of the great golfers who have played here. Greens fees are $50 to $85 for 9 holes and $85 to $149 for 18 holes.

HIKING The famous **Appalachian Trail** (www.appalachiantrail.org) passes through a large section of Pisgah National Forest and Great Smoky Mountains National Park. The Greater Asheville area is a hiker's paradise, with trails in almost every direction and in every major park. You can purchase the booklet *100 Favorite Trails* at the visitors bureau (© **828/258-6101**). You can also contact the North Carolina division of the U.S. Forest Service (© **828/257-4200;** www.cs.unca.edu/ nfsnc) for trail maps and more information.

ROCK CLIMBING Based in Brevard, near Asheville, **Fox Mountain Guides,** 3228 Asheville Hwy., Pisgah Forest (© **888/284-8433;** www.foxmountainguides. com), is the only outfitter in the Southeast accredited by the American Mountain Guide Association. Experienced guides take families climbing in the Pisgah National Forest. The outfit offers everything from international mountaineering expeditions to teen rock-climbing summer camps. Kids 6 years old and up can participate in a 2-hour Intro to Climbing Class for $40. Groups of seven can go on climbing expeditions at a cost of $70 per person for a full day, and a family of four can experience "top roping"—requiring no previous experience—for $320 per day, including all equipment. Camping and individual instruction in rock climbing are also available.

TENNIS The **Grove Park Inn Resort,** 190 Macon Ave. (© **800/438-5800;** www. groveparkinn.com), leads not only in golf, but also in tennis. The resort has been ranked as one of the 50 greatest tennis resorts in the U.S. by *Tennis* magazine. It offers three outdoor courts and three indoor courts. Rates per hour range from $20 outdoors to $25 indoors.

WHITE-WATER RAFTING You can choose a raft, kayak, or canoe to ride the white-water rapids. The rivers of western North Carolina and the Tennessee border offer rapids of Class I to V difficulty. Outfitters offer trips ranging from a half-day to a full weekend. Try the Nolichucky and French Broad rivers to the north or the Nantahala, Ocoee, Chattooga, and Green rivers to the west and south. Call the chamber of commerce (see above) for more information.

Where to Stay

Beaufort House Victorian Inn ★★   Designed in 1894 by A. L. Melton, a well-known local architect, this landmark Queen Anne confection is among the top two or three B&Bs in Asheville. It lies half a mile from the center of town, in the Grove Park district. The house is operated by Jacqueline and Robert Glasgow and is listed on the National Register of Historic Places. The individually decorated guest rooms are full of antiques. One room occupies the top floor, and another is in a carriage house with a loft bedroom, kitchenette, private deck, and living room. Three of the four rooms in the main house have whirlpools. The country breakfast with freshly squeezed juice is a serious reason to stay here.

61 N. Liberty St., Asheville, NC 28801. ✆ **800/261-2221** or 828/254-8334. Fax 828/254-9935. www.beauforthouse.com. 11 units. $199–$350 double. Rates include full breakfast and afternoon tea. AE, DISC, MC, V. **Amenities:** Breakfast room; lounge. *In room:* A/C, TV, hair dryer, Wi-Fi (free).

Cedar Crest Inn ★   This Queen Anne mansion is one of the largest and most opulent residences surviving from Asheville's 1890s boom. The mansion has a captain's walk, projecting turrets, and expansive verandas, and the inside is a fantasy of leaded glass, ornately carved fireplaces, and antique furnishings, with a massive oak staircase. Owners Rita and Bruce Wightman have indulged their romantic and whimsical imaginations in furnishing the guest rooms: All have period antiques and individual decor—a canopied ceiling in the Romeo and Juliet room, a carved walnut bed in another room, and brass bedsteads in a third. Several units contain working fireplaces. A cottage with two suites is adjacent to the main house.

674 Biltmore Ave., Asheville, NC 28803. ✆ **877/251-1389** or 828/252-1389. Fax 828/253-7667. www.cedarcrestvictorianinn.com. 11 units. $145–$255 double; $230–$300 suite. Rates include breakfast and afternoon refreshments. AE, DC, DISC, MC, V. Free parking. No children 11 and under. **Amenities:** Breakfast room; lounge. *In room:* A/C, TV, hair dryer, kitchenette (in some), Wi-Fi (free).

Crowne Plaza Resort   This is Asheville's leading motor hotel, lying directly off I-240, 3 miles from the center of town. The Crowne Plaza chain took over this former Holiday Inn resort and completed a $4-million renovation. Standard double rooms have comfortable beds and such extras as refrigerators. There are tennis courts and an 18-hole golf course nearby. The restaurant, popular with families, serves typically American fare.

1 Resort Dr., Asheville, NC 28806. ✆ **800/733-3211** or 828/254-3211. Fax 828/285-2688. www.ashevillecp.com. 274 units. $144–$194 double; $164–$299 suite. AE, DC, DISC, MC, V. **Amenities:** Restaurant; bar; babysitting; 18-hole golf course; exercise room; outdoor pool; room service; sauna; 20 tennis courts (4 indoor, 2 lit outside). *In room:* A/C, TV, fridge, hair dryer, minibar, Wi-Fi (free).

Cumberland Falls B&B ★★   The sound of a waterfall greets you as you mount the steps to this cute B&B only 3 miles from the Biltmore Estate or about a 15-minute drive to the Blue Ridge Parkway. You can walk to the historic center of Asheville. The house itself is from the turn of the 20th century, and each bedroom is luxuriously and beautifully furnished and named after its theme, such as "Victorian Parlor." The most romantic couples retreat to the under-the-eaves "Daydream Room." Expect dozens of thoughtful extras, including a gourmet breakfast served by candlelight and home-baked afternoon treats with a hot beverage bar.

254 Cumberland Ave., Asheville, NC 28801. ✆ **888/743-2557** or 828/253-4085. Fax 828/253-5566. www.cumberlandfalls.com. 6 units. $125–$260 double. Rates include breakfast. MC, V. **Amenities:** Breakfast room. *In room:* Ceiling fan, TV/DVD/VCR, hair dryer, Wi-Fi (free).

Grove Park Inn Resort & Spa ★★★   This resort, built in 1913 on the side of Sunset Mountain at an elevation of 3,100 feet, is one of the oldest and most famous in the South. Listed on the National Register of Historic Places, it's a favorite year-round destination, providing old-world charm and panoramic views of the city's skyline and the Blue Ridge Mountains. Its great-hall lobby is flanked by 14-foot fireplaces; comfortably padded chairs and sofas create a feeling of coziness despite the size of the 120-foot-long room. Twenty-eight of the guest rooms are oversize and contain extras such as whirlpools. The resort has hosted some famous names, including Thomas Edison, Henry Ford, Harvey Firestone, and presidents Franklin Delano Roosevelt and Woodrow Wilson. Novelist F. Scott Fitzgerald stayed at the hotel while his wife, Zelda, spent her nights in a sanitarium nearby, hence the hotel's "romantic" getaway package called the Great Gatsby.

290 Macon Ave., Asheville, NC 28804. ✆ **800/438-5800** or 828/252-2711. Fax 828/253-7053. www.groveparkinn.com. 510 units. Summer $300–$800 double, $1,075–$1,300 suite; off season $305–$815 double, $875–$1,100 suite. AE, DC, DISC, MC, V. **Amenities:** 3 restaurants; 3 bars; babysitting; 18-hole golf course; exercise room; 2 pools (1 indoor); room service; sauna; spa; 6 tennis courts (3 outdoor, 3 indoor). *In room:* A/C, TV, hair dryer, kitchenette, Wi-Fi (free).

Haywood Park Hotel ★   In the heart of downtown Asheville, this rather elegant all-suite place is the leading hotel in the city center. The suites are crisp and airy, a blend of luxury—some have Iberian marble bathrooms, recessed closets, showers with oversize tubs, and whirlpools—and practical details such as computer hookups. All beds are either queen- or king-size. The hotel's deluxe restaurant has a Continental menu specializing in French, German, and Indian cuisine, as well as an extensive wine list. It also has a beer garden.

1 Battery Park Ave., Asheville, NC 28801. ✆ **800/228-2522** or 828/252-2522. Fax 828/253-0481. www.haywoodpark.com. 33 units. $170–$370 suite. Rates include continental breakfast. Children 17 and under stay free in parent's room. AE, DC, DISC, MC, V. Free parking. **Amenities:** Restaurant; bar; exercise room; room service; sauna. *In room:* A/C, TV, hair dryer, minibar, Wi-Fi (free).

STAYING NEARBY

The Greystone Inn ★   Henry Ford and John D. Rockefeller once whiled away their summers on the 14 miles of leafy shoreline around Lake Toxaway. Set on a wooded peninsula along the lake, this imposing Swiss Revival mansion, listed on the National Register of Historic Places, was created for Savannah heiress Lucy Armstrong Moltz as a seasonal "cottage." Refurbished in 1985, it welcomes guests with an engaging mix of antique furnishings and modern comforts. Each guest room has its own character, and many have working fireplaces. The stone fireplace is a focal point in the oak-paneled living room, the library is a tastefully appointed oasis, and the terrace is the ideal setting for before-dinner drinks. For dedicated do-nothings, there are wicker rocking chairs on the glassed-in sun porch overlooking the lake.

Meals in the **Lakeside** dining room (for guests only) feature such gourmet selections as seared Texas antelope and Georgian pecan chicken. Dinner is a six-course affair.

Greystone Lane, Lake Toxaway, NC 28747. ✆ **800/824-5766** or 828/966-4700. Fax 828/862-5689. www.greystoneinn.com. 33 units. Sun–Thurs $370–$450 double, $490–$600 suite; Fri–Sat $430–$510 double, $550–$660 suite. Rates include breakfast, champagne, afternoon tea, dinner, and sports activities except golf. MC, V. **Amenities:** Restaurant; bar; babysitting; health club; outdoor pool; room service; sauna; spa; 4 tennis courts. *In room:* A/C, TV, hair dryer (in some).

Inn on Biltmore Estate ★★★   A. V. Cecil, Jr., great-grandson of George W. Vanderbilt, poured $31 million into the creation of this elegant inn, 2 miles from the

French Renaissance country estate originally built by the tycoon himself, deep within the grounds of the Biltmore Estate. No one can drive up to it without proof of a reservation or a general pass to tour the compound. Most rooms are booked as part of packages that include admission to the grounds and mansion.

Each season brings new pleasures—cozy fireside evenings in the library, tranquil Indian summer afternoons rocking on the big veranda, or spring brunches on the dining terrace as daffodils burst into bloom. The inn faces Mount Pisgah, with 270 degrees of uninterrupted wilderness on view from the windows.

Guest rooms are spacious, comfortable, and elegantly furnished, with state-of-the-art bathrooms. Suites are sometimes named for friends of Vanderbilt, including the one honoring novelist Edith Wharton. The cuisine—one of the reasons to stay here—is among the finest in western North Carolina.

1 Antler Hill Rd., Asheville, NC 28803. ℂ **800/411-3812** or 828/225-1600. Fax 828/225-1629. www.biltmore.com. 249 units. $189–$379 double; from $499 suite. AE, DC, MC, V. **Amenities:** 2 restaurants; bar; babysitting; exercise room; Jacuzzi; outdoor pool; room service. *In room:* A/C, TV, hair dryer, Wi-Fi (free).

The Lion and the Rose ★ This antiques-filled inn opened in 1987 in a Georgian–Queen Anne–style home in the historic Montford district. The house was built in 1898, during the heyday of Asheville's summer resort boom. Restored to its original grandeur, the inn is run by Jim and Linda Palmer. Sherry (served on the porch) and discreetly placed fresh flowers add grace notes that make this a tranquil retreat—one of the best-run B&Bs in Greater Asheville. Guests dine around the fireplace in cold weather or on the porch in summer. The traditionally styled guest rooms have queen-size beds, and some have a sitting area with a couch. The two-bedroom suite is decorated with white wicker and lace; one bedroom has a queen-size bed, and the other has twin beds. The well-kept bathrooms have either walk-in showers or tub/shower combinations, and a private balcony. Children 13 and over are welcome on weekends only.

276 Montford Ave., Asheville, NC 28801. ℂ **800/546-6988** or 828/255-7673. Fax 828/285-9810. www.lion-rose.com. 5 units. $130–$190 double; $190–$215 suite. Rates include full breakfast and afternoon tea. AE, DISC, MC, V. Free parking. No children 12 and under allowed; children 13 and over allowed on weekends only. **Amenities:** Breakfast room; lounge; room service. *In room:* A/C, TV/DVD, hair dryer, Wi-Fi (free).

Richmond Hill Inn ★★ Listed on the National Register of Historic Places, this inn was named one of the "Ten Outstanding New Inns in America" by *Inn Review Newsletter*. Constructed in 1889 of granite, slate, and local woods, the house was designed by James Hill, the supervising architect of the U.S. Treasury buildings, and is Asheville's remaining example of Queen Anne–style architecture. The main building is a spacious two-story mansion, painted yellow, with a wraparound porch. The interior is graced by family-heirloom portraits and the house's original oak paneling. Guest rooms are charming, featuring bathrooms with showers and claw-foot tubs, balconies overlooking a small stream, canopied beds, and fireplaces. The seven rooms on the second floor are preferable to the smaller rooms on the third. Nine cottages containing rooms and suites, all with small porches and rockers, are across the way. Other than the much-larger Grove Park, this is our favorite address in Asheville.

87 Richmond Hill Dr., Asheville, NC 28806. ℂ **800/545-9238** or 828/239-1074. Fax 828/252-8726. www.richmondhillinn.net. 36 units. $270–$445 double; $435–$615 suite. Rates include full breakfast. Children 16 and under stay free in parent's room. AE, MC, V. Free parking. **Amenities:** Restaurant; babysitting; exercise room. *In room:* A/C, TV, hair dryer, Wi-Fi (free).

Where to Dine

EXPENSIVE

Blue Ridge Dining Room AMERICAN   This is the moderately priced choice at Asheville's premier resort. The food is not as good as at Horizons (see below), but the prices are more affordable, and you get excellent quality and generous helpings. The view of the Blue Ridge Mountains alone is worth the trip here. This longtime family favorite is an Asheville tradition, known for its sumptuous international buffet tables laden with many "plantation extras." Omelets and waffles are on the buffet at breakfast. The Friday-night seafood buffet and Saturday prime-rib buffet are so popular with locals that early reservations are recommended. Sunday brunch is Asheville's best, and it's usually packed.

In the Grove Park Inn Resort, 290 Macon Ave. ⓒ **800/438-5800.** www.groveparkinn.com. Reservations recommended. Jacket and collared shirt required for men. Main courses $16–$33; Fri seafood buffet $33; Sat prime-rib buffet $33; Sun brunch $30. AE, DC, DISC, MC, V. Mon–Sat 6:30–11am and 5:30–9:30pm; Sun 6:30–10:30am, 11am–2:30pm, and 5:30–9:30pm.

The Frog Bar Deli/The Flying Frog Café CONTINENTAL/INDIAN   This is the most culturally diverse and, in some ways, the most intriguing cafe and restaurant in Asheville, with enough different themes to keep prospective diners moving through its premises until they settle on the venue they like best. The street level (the Frog Bar Deli) offers a disjointed and relatively informal warren of outdoor and indoor tables in at least four different seating areas, each accented with copper trim, beige tiles, and a new-wave sense of "live and let live." Downstairs, in the cellar, is a more formal dining area (the Flying Frog Café), one that celebrates the enigmatic fusion of French, German, and Indian cuisine. Here, at banquettes that romantically engulf their occupants in yard upon yard of milk-colored mosquito netting, you can order from a menu that's 50% devoted to the spicy cuisine of India (the lamb *vindaloo* is delicious) and 50% devoted to French and German items that include sauerbraten, Wiener schnitzel, and bouillabaisse.

At the corner of Haywood St. and Battery Park. ⓒ **828/254-9411.** www.flyingfrogcafe.com. Reservations not necessary for the deli, recommended for the cafe. Deli sandwiches and platters $7.50–$11; cafe main courses $16–$33. AE, DC, MC, V. Deli daily 11:30am–2am. Cafe Wed–Thurs 5:30–9:30pm; Fri–Sat 5:30–11pm.

Horizons ★★ CONTINENTAL   This most formal, and also the best, restaurant in Greater Asheville occupies a prominent position in the city's grandest resort. It's consistently rated among the finest in the nation and has earned AAA's rating of four diamonds for 8 consecutive years. Patrons are rewarded with exceptional service and gratifying cuisine such as brook trout, bouillabaisse, and medallions of venison. In its ground-level setting in the Grove Park Inn's Sammons Wing, Horizons serves innovative yet classic, market-fresh cuisine. Dinner includes soup or salad, a main course, dessert, and a nonalcoholic beverage. The wine list is very extensive.

In the Grove Park Inn Resort, 290 Macon Ave. ⓒ **800/438-5800** or 828/252-2711. www.groveparkinn.com. Reservations required. Jacket and collared shirt required for men. 3-course fixed-price menu $75–$125; main courses $18–$39. AE, DC, DISC, MC, V. Mon–Thurs 6–9pm; Fri–Sat 6–9:30pm.

The Market Place CONTINENTAL   An upscale casual restaurant with candlelit tables, this establishment has impeccable service. The chef uses extra-fresh ingredients, and all herbs and vegetables are grown locally. For all its attributes, the restaurant—although popular with savvy locals—seems to be undervalued and underappreciated, and rarely appears in a guidebook. Yet some of its dishes rival those at the Grove Park Inn. Try, for example, the fresh grilled salmon, the fresh tenderloin, or the duo—a platter of lamb and marinated grilled venison. Many dishes are nouvelle in style and preparation, and the professional staff is knowledgeable about the extensive wine list.

20 Wall St. © **828/252-4162.** www.marketplace-restaurant.com. Reservations recommended. Main courses $16–$28. AE, DC, MC, V. Mon–Sat 5:30–9pm.

MODERATE

Bouchon CONTINENTAL   If Gaudí, the brilliant architect of late-19th-century Barcelona, could have designed a modern-day cafe, it might look a lot like this earth-toned hideaway in downtown Asheville, all curved walls and sinuous lines. Established by a team of French and Argentine expatriates, Bouchon (formerly Café Soleil) has positioned itself as *the* gathering place for members of Asheville's foreign (mostly European) community, as such evoking some aspects of a busy, arts-conscious cafe in, say, Paris or Madrid. The cafe has a list of good wines, many sold by the glass; an impressive roster of both salted and sweet crepes made with buckwheat flour in the French tradition and stuffed with your choice of dozens of different fillings; and quiches and salads. Main courses include French mussels steamed in white wine, shallots, garlic, tomato, and thyme, served with delicious *pommes frites.*

62 N. Lexington Ave. © **828/350-1140.** www.ashevillebouchon.com. Reservations not accepted. Main courses $11–$18. MC, V. Mon–Sat 5pm–1:30am.

The Corner Kitchen ★ PAN-AMERICAN   Owners Kevin Westmoreland and Chef Joe Scully spent 2 months renovating this historic turn-of-the-20th-century Victorian home and turned it into one of Asheville's favorite dining locations. Originally designed by Richard Sharpe Smith, the on-site architect for the Biltmore Estate, the home was rented at one time by the Waddell family (whose son was one of the estate's engineers). Chef Scully calls his cuisine "Pan-American," and main courses feature such delights as sweet-potato salad, homemade chowchow, and a Napoleon of fried green tomatoes layered with herb cheese, or barbecue-glazed salmon, grilled and served on feta potato salad and spinach greens tossed in an apple vinaigrette. The Corner Kitchen serves a very affordable breakfast and dinner, and also delivers a delicious a la carte Sunday brunch. The restaurant is in historic Biltmore Village.

3 Boston Way. © **828/274-2439.** www.thecornerkitchen.com. Reservations not required. Main courses $5–$10 breakfast, $5–$11 lunch, $18–$25 dinner. AE, MC, V. Mon–Sat 7:30–11am, 11:30am–3pm, and 5–11pm; Sun 9am–3pm (brunch) and 5–11pm.

Tupelo Honey Café SOUTHERN   No other restaurant in Asheville so effectively captures the imagination of both the down-home breakfast crowd and, on Friday and Saturday nights, the very-late-night supper crowd. Behind a storefront in downtown Asheville, it's a place where Sunday-morning breakfast crowds line up and wait (in some cases, for up to an hour) for an available table. Students at the nearby university also drag their parents here for a sense of how much Asheville really does respect old-fashioned Southern virtues and cooking. Breakfast is served throughout the day, with such dishes as grit cakes stuffed with cheddar cheese and served with green tomato salsa; sweet-potato pancakes; many kinds of omelets; and crab cakes topped with poached eggs and hollandaise sauce. Lunches and dinners focus on updated Southern favorites such as shrimp and goat cheese grits, Cajun-seared catfish, and Tupelo burgers. In honor of Elvis, you can order a grilled peanut butter and banana sandwich, prepared with either honey or (if you're a hard-core Southerner) mayonnaise.

12 College St. © **828/255-4863.** www.tupelohoneycafe.com. Main courses $6–$12 breakfast, $4–$13 lunch, $7–$18 dinner. AE, MC, V. Tues–Thurs 9am–3pm and 5:30–10pm; Fri–Sat 9am–3pm and 5:30pm–midnight; Sun 9am–3pm.

Vincenzo's NORTHERN ITALIAN   The premier Italian restaurant in Asheville is in the central part of the Historic District. A bustling trattoria with a piano bar, it has an eclectic decor with Art Deco overtones. True, chances are that you will have had finer Italian dinners than this in your life, but what you get isn't bad. Try veal chop Milanese with pasta, or filet medallions in a brandied mushroom, scallion, and Dijon cream sauce. *Cioppino* is filled with goodies, including fresh whitefish, scallops, and shrimp over linguine flavored with a spicy red sauce. The penne pasta with char-broiled chicken, peppers, pepperoni, and spinach is excellent, as are the veal dishes.

10 N. Market St. (✆ **828/254-4698.** www.vincenzos.com. Reservations suggested but not required. Main courses $12–$30. AE, DC, DISC, MC, V. Mon–Thurs 5:30–10pm; Fri–Sat 5:30–11pm; Sun 5:30–9pm.

INEXPENSIVE

Doc Chey's Noodle House ★ 🍴 ASIAN FUSION   Perhaps the slogan on the T-shirts the waitstaff wears sets the mood for this popular downtown Asheville restaurant: PEACE, LOVE AND NOODLES. Voted the number-one Asian restaurant in western North Carolina and set in the oldest building in downtown Asheville, Doc Chey's blends Chinese, Japanese, Thai, Vietnamese, and vegetarian influences to create freshly prepared noodle bowls, rice bowls, and stir-fries. Everything is prepared fresh to order, including all of the sauces. Start your meal with Thai shrimp rolls—shrimp, garlic, ginger, and scallions in a crispy spring-roll wrapper. You could also select the Chinese lo mein, a traditional stir-fry of cabbage, carrots, onions, and egg noodles. Your fellow restaurant patrons will be a representative blend of urban hippies, out-door-loving granola crunchers, retired wealthy couples, students, and the conservative church folk who stop by after Sunday services.

37 Biltmore Ave. (✆ **828/252-8220.** www.doccheys.com. Reservations not required. Main courses $7–$9. AE, DISC, MC, V. Sun–Tues and Thurs 11:30am–10pm; Fri–Sat 11:30am–11pm.

Zambra MEDITERRANEAN   In a unique location under Asheville's most famous bookstore, Malaprop's, Zambra serves an equally unique blend of Spanish, Portu-guese, and Moroccan tapas. The enticing list of tapas and an extensive Iberian wine list make this one of Asheville's favorite dining spots. With rustic Spanish decor and dark paneled wood, the restaurant has the ambience of a quaint spot on the Iberian coast. Zambra has a lounge that opens at 4:30pm. Music groups often perform here, lending an extra romantic touch to a fine-dining evening. We recommend the lamb, as well as the steak tapas. Vegetarian selections are also available.

85 Walnut St. (✆ **828/232-1060.** www.zambratapas.com. Reservations recommended. Tapas $3–$20; paella $10–$17. AE, DISC, MC, V. Mon–Sat 5:30pm–midnight; Sun 5:30–11pm.

Shopping

The historic **Grove Arcade Public Market** at 1 Page Ave. (✆ **828/252-7799;** www.grovearcade.com) showcases some 50 shops and restaurants. The arcade is the largest commercial building in the city, and the market itself has been restored to its previous prominence. This 269,000-square-foot structure (ca. 1929), closed since World War II, was in its heyday a bustling part of the city landscape and one of the country's first indoor public markets. It is much in the style of Seattle's Pike Place Market, with food stalls, restaurants, crafts stalls, and more. One of the more popular shops in the Grove Arcade is **Morning Star Galleries** (✆ **828/350-8585**). It stocks heirloom-quality replicas of armoires from the Victorian Age, Art Deco litho-graphs and prints, stained-glass lamps inspired by Louis Comfort Tiffany, lots of estate jewelry, and, perhaps best of all, a staggering number of handmade quilts imported from at least 20 different quilting co-ops in Kentucky and Missouri. A few even come from India and Eastern Europe.

One of the foremost arts-and-crafts shops is the **Grovewood Gallery** at the **Homespun Shops,** which also enjoys the distinction of being a historical landmark (see "Seeing the Sights," earlier in this chapter).

Asheville is the home of more than 50 galleries exhibiting works by local and national artists, including folk art, Native American art, and antiques. A gallery worth noting is the **Appalachian Craft Center,** 10 N. Spruce St. (© **828/253-8499;** www.appalachiancraftcenter.com). Hours are Monday to Saturday from 10am to 5pm.

A popular counterculture bookstore and gathering place is **Malaprop's Bookstore/Cafe,** 55 Haywood St. (© **800/441-9829** or 828/254-6734; www.malaprops. com). This is the most interesting and most deeply entrenched independently owned bookstore in western North Carolina, a cultural beacon by anyone's standards and the subject of devoted loyalty from thousands of readers in the surrounding towns and counties. It's divided into more than 300 different subject categories, with specific emphasis on regional studies, Asheville lore, films and movies, women's studies, astrology, New Age philosophy, and more, with a distinctive interest in the liberal, countercultural venues with which Asheville has long been associated. The bookstore is open most nights until 9 or 10pm.

Asheville Wine Market ★ 🏛 You hardly think of North Carolina as a wine-producing state. Once associated exclusively with moonshine, it today produces the likes of cabernet francs, viogniers, and chardonnays. In America, North Carolina now ranks 10th in grape production. You can see what the excitement is all about Monday to Friday 10am to 7pm and Saturday 10am to 6pm. 65 Biltmore Ave. © **828/253-0060.** www.ashevillewine.com.

Biltmore Village This shopping village is reminiscent of a time capsule. As you walk the cobblestone sidewalk, you feel that you might catch a glimpse of old George Vanderbilt himself. Shops, restaurants, and galleries abound, so allow yourself plenty of time to see everything. One store, the Biltmore Village Co., is quite charming and affordable; it bills itself as a gift shop containing everything—at half price. Hours are Monday to Saturday 9:30am to 6pm, and Sunday 1 to 5pm. Across from main entrance gate of the Biltmore Estate, Swan St. off Biltmore Ave. © **828/225-1333.** www.biltmorevillage.com.

Blue Spiral 1 This is one of the hottest galleries in Asheville, representing some 100 Southeastern artists in a three-story space. Hours are Monday to Saturday 10am to 6pm; from May through October it is also open Sunday noon to 5pm. 38 Biltmore Ave. © **800/291-2513** or 828/251-0202. www.bluespiral1.com.

The Chocolate Fetish This is the home of the most delicious, elegant, and sophisticated chocolates in the entire region. Bill and Sue Foley have been the owners of this place since the mid-1980s, supervising the manufacture, on-site, of small-scale batches of more than 21 kinds of chocolate that are made according to the highest standards of chocolate manufacturing in Belgium. Some of the bestsellers include truffles, sold by the piece; Ecstasy Blossom, which is flavored with lemon zest, saffron, and ginger, and embellished with a crystallized violet; and a divine Dragon's Kiss that's artfully flavored with Japanese wasabi. Open Monday to Thursday 11:30am to 6pm, Friday and Saturday 11am to 9pm, and Sunday noon to 5pm. 36 Haywood St. © **828/258-2353.** www.chocolatefetish.com.

The Kress Emporium ★ 🏛 This store serves as a showcase for more than 80 artists and craftspeople in the area. Stained-glass mosaics, lace handwork, fine miniature-furnishing collectibles, silk paintings, frames, and prints are just a few of the things that you will find here. The 1928 building that houses the emporium is a reason to visit in its own right; it is an architectural landmark designed in neoclassical style. Hours are Monday to Thursday 11am to 6pm and Friday and Saturday 11am to 7pm. Between summer and Christmas, it is also open on Sunday from noon to 5pm. 19 Patton Ave., Asheville. ☎ **828/281-2252.** www.thekressemporium.com.

The Mast General Store   In terms of down-home Blue Ridge shopping options, the Mast has it all. It's situated on the sprawling premises of a general department store from the 1940s. The merchandise here is more rustic, more rural, and more folksy than you'll find in more modern department stores. You can buy the accessories you'd need (from lingerie to camping supplies) for a season in the "hillbilly hollers" of the region. Don't overlook the furniture stocked in the balcony. Hours are Monday to Thursday 10am to 6pm, Friday and Saturday 10am to 8pm, and Sunday noon to 5pm. 15 Biltmore Ave. ☎ **828/232-1883.** www.mastgeneralstore.com.

Woolworth Walk   The best crafts emporium in town lies on the main street in the sprawling premises of what was originally built as—you guessed it—a Woolworth's department store from the 1930s. Inside, clustered into a series of side-by-side self-contained boutiques, and scattered over two separate floors, are the carefully displayed works of 175 local artists, each of whose work had to be approved by a local jury. Representative art forms include silversmithing, pottery, leatherware, stained glass, metalwork, bookbindery, and cabinetmaking. Adding to the ambience might be live music from a flute player or guitarist. Open Monday to Thursday and Sunday 11am to 6pm and Friday and Saturday 11am to 8pm. 25 Haywood St. ☎ **828/254-9234.** www.woolworthwalk.com.

Asheville After Dark

Barley's   This pub has a vast array of imported beer. There's never a cover charge, although the club is a venue for live entertainment, including jazz, blues, rock, and alternative rock. Pizza, nachos, salads, and soups are offered. Hours are Monday to Saturday from 11:30am to 2am and Sunday from noon to midnight. 42 Biltmore Ave. ☎ **828/255-0504.** www.barleystaproom.com.

Club Hairspray   Named after the John Waters camp classic starring the late drag queen, Divine, this club attracts mainly a gay and lesbian crowd but welcomes "open-minded straights" as well. There's a funky bar here along with several pool tables, and downstairs is a cabaret and dance club. Call to inquire about their special events for the week. Dancing is usually on the weekends. Technically, this is a private club, but you can gain membership at the door for $5. Open daily at 8pm until as late as business warrants. 38N French Broad Ave. ☎ **828/258-2027.** www.clubhairspray.com.

Fine Arts Theatre   See first-run, art, and independent films at this elegant Art Deco–modern theater. Call for movie titles, times, and ticket prices. No credit cards. 36 Biltmore Ave. ☎ **828/232-1536.** www.fineartstheater.com.

Hannah Flanagan's Irish Pub   Asheville's most authentically Irish pub draws after-hours workers who congregate either on an outdoor terrace, surrounded by masonry walls draped with ivy, or inside a woodsy-looking interior that evokes the early 20th century. The pub was named after the owner's grandmother, Hannah Flanagan, whose sepia-tone portrait hangs above the bar. Menu items derive from Irish traditions (corned beef and cabbage, Irish stew laced with Guinness, chargrilled salmon with mashed potatoes and a "wee" dinner salad). Open Monday to Saturday

11:30am to 2am and Sunday noon to 2am. 27 Biltmore Ave. ℂ **828/252-1922.** http://the
originalhannahflanagans.com.

Orange Peel Club ★   This is the focal point of the music scene in Asheville,
booking everybody from Bob Dylan to Merle Haggard. Even though the city has a
convention center for big acts, a lot of name performers prefer the more relaxed ambience of the Orange Peel. Popular local bands also get exposure here. The building
itself was young in 1950, and much of the original architecture remains, including a
barrel-vaulted truss ceiling. At the stainless-steel bar, an array of 40 brews is on tap.
The dance floor was voted best place in western North Carolina for dancing by the
readers of *Mountain Xpress.* Call for performance times. 101 Biltmore Ave. ℂ **828/225-
5851.** www.theorangepeel.net. The box office does not take phone orders; call ℂ 866/468-7630 instead.

Smokey Tavern   This is Asheville's favorite gay and lesbian tavern. Established in
the 1960s, it's the oldest continuously operating bar of any persuasion in Asheville
and contains a collection of barroom kitsch that would gladden the heart of any
antiques dealer. An amiable crowd of multigenerational drinkers begins tippling every
afternoon a few minutes after the place opens. You'll find a pair of pool tables, plenty
of local homeowners to ask for advice, and, as the night progresses, enough good-
looking local gays to make any visiting queer feel interested. Open daily 4pm until last
call at 2am. 18 Broadway. ℂ **828/253-2155.**

Tressa's Downtown Jazz & Blues ★★   Over the years, this multicultural bar
has been considered by some as the best bar in western North Carolina. It's in the
restored 1913 Richard Sharpe Smith building and is the town's best place to dance
and listen to jazz and blues. The martinis are absolutely fab, and a light European-
inspired menu is also served. Open Friday 4pm to 2am, Monday to Thursday and
Saturday 7pm to 2am. 28 Broadway. ℂ **828/254-7072.** www.tressas.com.

Side Trips from Asheville

About 5 miles east of downtown Asheville, at milepost 382 on the Blue Ridge Parkway,
the **Folk Art Center ★** (ℂ **828/298-7928;** www.southernhighlandguild.org) is operated by the Southern Highland Handicraft Guild, a not-for-profit organization of craftspeople in the nine-state southern Appalachian region. The contemporary wood-and-stone
structure houses the finest of both traditional and contemporary handicrafts of the
region. In the Folk Art Center, the **Allanstand Craft Shop,** established in 1895, is one
of the oldest crafts shops in the country, featuring exhibitions and museum areas. Pottery,
ceramics, weavings, jewelry, and handmade quilts, among other merchandise, are for
sale. The center does not charge for admission but does accept donations. It's open daily
from 9am to 6pm. The crafts shop maintains the same hours.

   Chimney Rock Park is 25 miles southeast of Asheville on U.S. 64/74A. The
park's focal point is a granite monolith that rises to a height of 360 feet; you can reach
its top by a stairway, a trail, or an elevator. An observation lounge is open daily
(weather permitting), and the charge is $14 for adults, $6 for children 6 to 15, and
free for children 5 and under. Trails lead to Needle's Eye, Moonshiner's Cave, and
Devil's Head (on the way to Hickory Nut Falls, which is twice the height of Niagara).
The Last of the Mohicans was filmed here, and costumes and other artifacts from the
movie are on display in the observation lounge. Food is available for $8 or less, and
there are picnic facilities. For full details, a free color brochure, and a trail map,
contact Chimney Rock Park, PO Box 39, Chimney Rock, NC 28720 (ℂ **800/277-
9611** or 828/625-9611; www.chimneyrockpark.com).

Stately **Mount Mitchell,** highest point in the eastern U.S., is in Mount Mitchell State Park, 2388 State Hwy. 128, Burnsville (✆ **828/675-4611;** www.northcarolina outdoors.com), some 33 miles northeast on the parkway and then 5 miles north on N.C. 128. Mount Mitchell has a museum, a tower, and an observation lodge; camping and picnicking facilities are available in the park.

About 30 miles southeast of Asheville on I-26 is the pastoral little town of Flat Rock, most famous as the former home of Carl Sandburg. The two-time Pulitzer Prize–winning writer-poet-historian known for his biography of Abraham Lincoln lived at **Connemara Farms ★**, 81 Carl Sandburg Lane, just west of I-26 (✆ **828/ 693-4178;** www.nps.gov/carl). It's open daily from 9am to 5pm; admission is $5 for adults and free for children 15 and under. Now a National Historic Site, the big white farmhouse is administered by the National Park Service, which offers guided formal tours. Sandburg purchased the 240-acre farm in 1945 for $40,000. He called it Connemara after the mountains of Ireland. The walls of Sandburg's modest abode are filled with approximately 10,000 volumes of books, bookmarked and dog-eared; in the living room is his collection of walking sticks. The grounds include a goat house occupied by the charming descendants of a prize herd of goats raised by Sandburg's wife.

Flat Rock is also the home of the North Carolina State Theater's **Flat Rock Playhouse** (✆ **828/693-0731;** www.flatrockplayhouse.org), which opened in 1952. It hosts the popular Vagabond Players, a troupe launched on Broadway in 1937. The group presents *The World of Carl Sandburg* and *The Rootabaga Stories* annually, not at the actual playhouse, but across the street at Sandburg's Connemara Farms.

Five minutes from the Flat Rock Playhouse is **Highland Lake Inn** (✆ **800/635- 5101;** www.hlinn.com) and its award-winning restaurant, **Season's** (✆ **828/696- 9094**). On 26 gently wooded acres, Highland Lake Inn offers a variety of lodging choices, including everything from cabins to an elegant bed-and-breakfast inn. Rates are $89 to $299 for a double, depending on the season and type of lodging you choose. With a 40-acre lake, swimming pool, tennis courts, and walking trails, Highland Lake Inn is a perfect relaxing escape. **Season's Restaurant** delivers delightful dining in a casual country setting, based on garden-inspired cuisine. When in season, the restaurant uses fresh ingredients from the on-site 2-acre organic garden to prepare three meals a day. Don't miss the Southern Country Breakfast buffet (included in your room rate) or the extraordinary Sunday brunches, renowned throughout the western North Carolina mountains.

BOONE ★

95 miles NE of Asheville

In the heart of the Blue Ridge Mountains, Boone has long been a favorite vacation destination. During the 1880s, Southerners came here to escape the summer heat. In recent years, Boone has also become a winter ski destination. Daniel Boone traveled through this area on his way to Kentucky in the late 1700s—hence, the town's name.

Boone has been called "the coolest spot in the South," with an average temperature of 68°F (20°C) in summer. Golf, tennis, swimming, fishing, skiing, and sightseeing are part of the local attractions. The region's rugged terrain lends itself to a variety of high-adventure outdoor sports, from mountain biking and canoeing to white-water rafting and rock climbing. For summer visitors, there's also Kermit Hunter's play *Horn in the West,* as well as an Appalachian Summer Festival of concerts, drama, and art exhibits.

Essentials

GETTING THERE   Boone lies 1 hour from I-77, I-81, and I-40, and is accessible from a trio of major highways, including U.S. 321, U.S. 421, and U.S. 221. N.C. 105 provides access from U.S. 221.

The nearest **airport** is at Asheville (☏ **828/684-2226;** www.flyavl.com).

VISITOR INFORMATION   The **Boone Convention and Visitors Bureau,** 208 Howard St., Boone, NC 28607 (☏ **800/852-9506** or 828/262-3516; www.visit boonenc.com), is open Monday to Friday 9am to 5pm. Information is also available at the **High Country Host,** 1700 Blowing Rock Rd. (☏ **800/438-7500;** www. mountainsofnc.com), which is open Monday to Saturday 9am to 5pm and Sunday 9am to 3pm.

Seeing the Sights

Daniel Boone Native Gardens, 651 Horn in the West Dr., 1 mile east of U.S. 421 (☏ **828/264-6390;** www.danielboonegardens.org), next door to the Daniel Boone Theatre, offers a collection of native North Carolina plants in an informal landscaped design set amid 6 acres. Weather permitting, the gardens are open daily from May 1 to October 15 and on weekends in October from 10am to 6pm. June 15 to August 15, they remain open until 8pm. Admission is $2 for visitors 16 and older.

Also adjacent to the theater is the **Hickory Ridge Homestead Museum** (☏ **828/ 264-2120;** www.horninthewest.com/museum.htm), an 18th-century living-history museum in a re-created log cabin. Traditional craftspeople demonstrate their skills, and there's a homestead store. An apple festival is held on the grounds in late October, and Christmas events are on tap in mid-December. Hours are Tuesday to Sunday 1 to 5pm from May to October, and Saturday 10am to 4pm and Sunday 1 to 4pm from November to April. Admission is free, but they like donations.

Tweetsie Railroad Theme Park, Blowing Rock Road, halfway between Boone and Banner Elk (☏ **800/526-5740** or 828/264-9061; www.tweetsie.com), is fun for the whole family. An old narrow-gauge train winds along a 3-mile route, enduring mock attacks by Indians and outlaws. There's mountain music and other entertainment, along with restaurants, Western shops, country-fair rides, a petting zoo, and a crafts area. The park is open April 30 to May 23 Friday to Sunday from 9am to 6pm, May 28 to August 22 daily from 9am to 6pm, and August 27 to October 31 Friday to Sunday from 9am to 6pm. The park is also open on Labor Day. Admission is $32 for adults and $22 for children 3 to 12; children 2 and under are admitted free. Get your tickets early for the popular Ghost Train night rides ($27 adults and children 3–12; free for children 2 and under), part of Tweetsie's Halloween Festival, held on October weekends. An assortment of entertainment and games is available for very young children, for whom the Ghost Train ride is not recommended. Admission to the festival is $26 per person, and gates open at 7:30pm.

Outdoor Pursuits

GOLF   The **Boone Golf Club,** U.S. 321/221, Blowing Rock Road (☏ **866/532- 4653** or 828/264-8760; www.boonegolfclub.com), an 18-hole, par-70 course designed by Ellis Maples, is 6,400 yards long from its longest tees. It's the standard against which all High Country public courses are measured. Opened in 1958, with its natural routing and electrifying greens, it remains a perennial favorite. Greens fees from May 25 to October are $32 to $39 Monday to Thursday, rising to $37 to $44 Friday to Sunday. Professional instruction costs $40 for 40 minutes, and clubs are available for rent at $20 for 18 holes. A pro shop is on-site, and there's a restaurant at the clubhouse.

RAFTING & OTHER SPORTS **Wahoos,** on U.S. 321 between Boone and the Tweetsie Railroad Theme Park (© **800/444-RAFT** [444-7238] or 828/262-5774; www.wahoosadventures.com), is the best all-around center to connect you with outdoor adventures, ranging from white-water rafting to tubing. Tours are available for all ages. The office is open daily 8am to 8pm in summer.

Nolichucky River rafting is for those 6 years old or older, costs $80 to $105 per person, and lasts 4 to 5 hours, including transportation and lunch. Watauga River rafting, for those 3 and older, lasts 2 hours and costs $55 to $75 per person, including lunch and transportation. Tubing ($20), canoeing ($40), and kayaking ($45) are all possible in the New River, with three 1- to 3½-hour excursions. Wahoos can also make reservations at local campsites.

Where to Stay

Holiday Inn Express Within 20 minutes of the downhill ski runs, this is one of the best motels in the Boone area. The rooms are well maintained and exactly what you'd expect from this dependable chain. The hotel has no on-site restaurant, although several restaurants and diners are within walking distance.

1943 Blowing Rock Rd., Boone, NC 28607. © **888/465-4329** or 828/264-2451. Fax 828/265-3861. www.holidayinn.com. 129 units. $80–$199 double; $119–$249 suite. Rates include continental breakfast. AE, DC, DISC, MC, V. **Amenities:** Breakfast room; exercise room; outdoor pool. *In room:* A/C, TV, hair dryer, kitchenette (in some), Wi-Fi (free).

Lovill House Inn ★ Dating from 1875, this inn was originally a private home. The house stands on 11 wooded acres. Scott and Anne Peecook welcome you to one of the finest places to stay in the area. Floors and walls are double insulated, and the guest rooms are tastefully furnished. Quality linens and comforters are just two of the thoughtful touches. Three of the original brick fireplaces remain. Breakfast is served in a dining room with picture-view windows. In summer, guests gather on a spacious veranda before dinner to meet one another.

404 Old Bristol Rd., Boone, NC 28607. © **800/849-9466** or 828/264-4204. www.lovillhouseinn.com. 6 units. $119–$219 double. Rates include full breakfast. MC, V. No children 11 and under. **Amenities:** Breakfast room; lounge; Jacuzzi. *In room:* TV, hair dryer, Wi-Fi (free).

Where to Dine

Dan'l Boone Inn ★ SOUTHERN Such a local legend is this place that many motorists drive the 5 miles from the parkway to dine here. The inn is one of the oldest buildings in town, with a rustic atmosphere. But what really brings 'em in is the down-home Southern cooking, served family style in huge portions for a set price. That means Southern fried chicken, country-fried steak, and a choice of five vegetables. Lunch or dinner comes with soup or salad, vegetables, a choice of three meats, homemade biscuits, a homemade dessert (usually rich and creamy), and a beverage. Breakfast includes such Southern savories as country ham, grits, and stewed apples. If you come here on New Year's Day, you can participate in the Southern tradition of eating black-eyed peas and collard greens, for good luck in the coming year.

130 Hardin St. (© **828/264-8657.** www.danlbooneinn.com. Reservations accepted for parties of 15 or more. $8.95 breakfast, children (4-11) $3.95-$5.95; $16 lunch and dinner, children $4.95-$8.95; children 3 and under eat free. No credit cards. June-Oct Mon-Fri 11:30am-9pm, Sat-Sun 8am-9pm; off season Mon-Thurs 5-8pm, Fri 5-9pm, Sat 8am-9pm, Sun 8am-8pm.

Shopping

In the tiny town of Valle Crucis, 10 miles west of Boone, **Mast General Store ★**, 3565 Hwy. 194 S. (© **866/367-6278** or 828/963-6511; www.mastgeneralstore. com), is arguably the most famous store in Appalachia. Dating from 1883, it is listed on the National Register of Historic Places. Its plank floors are worn to a smooth sheen, and on cold mountain mornings, a potbellied stove is still fired up. From overalls to brogans, red ribbons to calico patterns, the store has a wide assortment of sturdy clothing, shoes, and boots—all the outdoor gear you'll need to become a mountain man or mountain mama. You'll also find old-time salves, wind-up toys, regional music, rock candy, and peanut brittle on sale. Hours are Monday to Saturday 7am to 6:30pm and Sunday 11am to 6pm. If you don't want to drive out to the hamlet of Valle Crucis, you'll find similar merchandise at the outlet in Boone, **Mast General West,** 630 West King St. (© **828/262-0000**), in business since 1883. Hours are Monday to Saturday 10am to 6pm and Sunday 11am to 6pm.

Boone After Dark

Kermit Hunter's ***Horn in the West*** ★ is presented in the Daniel Boone Theatre, 591 Horn in the West Dr., Boone, NC 28607 (© **828/264-2120;** www.horninthewest. com), every night except Monday from late June through mid-August. The play tells a vivid story of the pioneers' efforts to win freedom during the American Revolution. Performances begin at 8pm, and admission is $15 (tickets are half price for children 12 and under). Tickets can be ordered in advance by mail and will be held at the box office for pickup.

BANNER ELK ★

136 miles NW of Charlotte

The village of Banner Elk used to be about the sleepiest place in the High Country until it was discovered by scenery hounds in summer and skiers in winter. Banner Elk is on N.C. 194, enclosed by mountains. In winter, skiers can head for Sugar Mountain or Ski Beech. The town also makes a good center for exploring Grandfather Mountain, just north of Linville, a wealthy enclave where many folks have summer homes.

Essentials

GETTING THERE   To reach Banner Elk from Asheville, take I-40 East to U.S. 221 North, passing through Marion to Linville. Exit onto N.C. 105 North at Linville and travel until you reach the intersection of N.C. 194 East. Turn left onto N.C. 194 East and proceed for roughly 4 miles into Banner Elk.

VISITOR INFORMATION   The **Avery/Banner Elk Chamber of Commerce,** N.C. 184, no. 2 Shoppes at Tynecastle (PO Box 335), Banner Elk, NC 28604 (© **800/972-2183** or 828/898-5605; http://averycounty.com), will mail you information on activities in the area. It's open Monday to Saturday 10am to 4pm and Sunday 10am to 3pm.

SPECIAL EVENTS Kilt-clad Scots from Scotland (as well as from all parts of North America) gather here early in July for the annual **Grandfather Mountain Highland Games and Gathering o' Scottish Clans** (© 828/733-1333; www. gmhg.org). Bagpipe music, dancing, wrestling, and tossing the caber (a shaft that resembles a telephone pole), as well as the colorful mix of people bent on 4 days of fun, make this a spectacle not to be missed.

Grandfather Mountain

Grandfather Mountain ★★, on U.S. 221 near Linville (© **800/468-7325** or 828/733-4337; www.grandfather.com), a mile off the Blue Ridge Parkway, is the highest peak in the Blue Ridge. You can see as far as 100 miles from the **Mile High Swinging Bridge;** the **Environmental Habitat** is the home of Mildred the Bear and her black-bear friends. In a spacious separate section, you can view native deer, cougars, and bald and golden eagles (which have been injured and cannot live in the wild on their own). Grandfather Mountain is open daily except Thanksgiving and Christmas from 8am to 5pm in winter, to 6pm in spring and fall, and to 7pm in summer. Admission is $15 for adults, $13 for seniors, $7 for children 4 to 12, and free for children 3 and under.

Outdoor Pursuits

GOLF **Village of Sugar Mountain Golf Course,** N.C. 184 (© **800/SUGAR-MT** [784-2768] or 828/898-6464; www.seesugar.com), outside Banner Elk, is an 18-hole, par-64 course at the foot of the Sugar Mountain Ski Resort. This executive course offers variety and a par-5 hole designed by Arnold Palmer. Greens fees are $15 to $40.

SKIING The **Hawksnest Ski Resort,** 2058 Skyland Dr., Seven Devils, NC 28604 (© **800/822-HAWK** [4295] or 828/963-6561; www.hawksnest-resort.com), is northeast of Banner Elk and 10 miles south off N.C. 105. It offers 12 slopes—one expert, three advanced, five intermediate, and three beginner—with a peak elevation of 4,819 feet and a 669-foot vertical drop. Lift tickets cost $15 to $70, depending on the time of season and the length of time for which you plan to ski. Ski rentals start from $20. The resort also offers a children's camp for $85 for a full day. During the December-to-March season, the resort is open Sunday to Thursday from 9am to 10pm, Friday from 9am to 2am, and Saturday from 9am to midnight. Ski instruction is available for $42 to $82.

Sugar Mountain Resort, N.C. 194, a mile from N.C. 105 (PO Box 369), Banner Elk, NC 28604 (© **800/SUGAR-MT** [784-2768] or 828/898-4521; www.skisugar. com), has 20 slopes—20% expert, 40% intermediate, and 40% beginner—with an elevation of 5,300 feet and a vertical drop of 1,200 feet. The resort is open from mid-November to mid-March. Lifts operate daily from 9am to 4:30pm and 6 to 10pm, with tickets ranging from $18 to $64. Ski rentals range from $8 to $25, depending on the time of day and the type of skis, and professional lessons are also available, at $20 per member of a group or $48 per person hourly. Children ages 5 to 10 can participate in a Sugarbear Ski School from 10am to 3pm daily, including lunch, for $75 per child. The resort also offers snowboarding, with lift tickets costing from $22 to $33.

Where to Stay

Archers Mountain Inn ★ On Beech Mountain between the towns of Banner Elk and Beech Mountain, this resort is a good choice if you want to sample all the skiing in the area. The inn features 15 rooms in two buildings plus five separate log cabins. Laurel Lodge and the Hawk's View both have views of Sugar Mountain and the Grandfather Mountains just outside your window. The rooms in Laurel Lodge are essentially designed for couples; all have fireplaces. Some of the more expensive rooms and suites feature whirlpools. Hawk's View offers more spacious rooms, with efficiency kitchens and fireplaces. These rooms are better equipped for large parties. The building has large porches with rockers where guests can take in views of the mountain range. The inn's restaurant, **Jackalope's View,** serves international fare prepared by the restaurant's two chefs.

2489 Beech Mountain Pkwy., Banner Elk, NC 28604. ℂ **888/827-6155** or 828/898-9004. www. archersinn.com. 15 units. $80–$130 double; $90–$205 suite. Top rates include full breakfast. Each additional person $10. DISC, MC, V. **Amenities:** Restaurant, Jackalope's View (see review, below); bar; babysitting; Wi-Fi. *In room:* TV, hair dryer, no phone.

The Mast Farm Inn ★★   This member of the National Register of Historic Places provides historic lodging and gourmet dining in a traditional, North Carolina–style mountain inn. All the attractive, comfortable guest rooms have old-fashioned charm, including fireplaces and four-poster beds. Each unit is decorated differently, and rustic cottages and cabins are also available. Seven unique rooms are found in the main 1880s farmhouse itself. Some of the cabins are ideal for a family, others for only a couple.

2543 Broadstone Rd., Banner Elk, NC 28604. ℂ **888/963-5857** or 828/963-5857. http://mastfarminn. com. 14 units. $99–$269 double; $149–$459 cottages and cabins. Rates include a 2-course gourmet breakfast. AE, MC, V. **Amenities:** Restaurant, Simplicity (see review, below). *In room:* A/C.

Where to Dine

Jackalope's View Restaurant AMERICAN   In the cozy Archers Mountain Inn (see "Where to Stay," above), Jackalope's is nestled on the side of Beech Mountain. Even if you're not a guest at the inn, you'll want to dine here—the cuisine is among the finest in the area. After dinner in winter, guests relax in front of fireplaces; in summer they sit in rockers on the porch. The personal service in the dining room makes you feel pampered. The menu changes from time to time. If it's available, you might begin with the sweet Vidalia onion stuffed with sautéed mushrooms, roasted garlic, and Gorgonzola cheese, or else Tuscan shrimp bruschetta. The main courses are always tantalizing, especially the delectable sautéed North Carolina trout nut rusted with raspberries, or the tiger shrimp flavored with bacon and tomatoes and tossed in an Alfredo sauce with ziti. Homemade desserts are featured nightly.

2489 Beech Mountain Pkwy. ℂ **828/898-9004.** Reservations recommended. Main courses $15–$32; fixed-price menu $18–$35. AE, DISC, MC, V. Daily 5–9pm.

Simplicity ★★ AMERICAN   In an old-fashioned former mountain farmhouse, a mother-and-daughter team turn out some of the finest dishes in the area. Dining here is a slow and well-thought-out affair, with a meticulous cuisine noted for its freshness and the skill of its preparations. All the natural ingredients used for your fare are of high quality, and the personal service is another allure. Much of the produce comes from the farm's own organic gardens, along with pasture-raised meats and free-range dairy and eggs. Start perhaps with cream of three mushrooms flavored with fresh herbs and white wine and go onto the "Love Me Tender" beef tenderloin stuffed with smoked ham and cheese and cooled with a cranberry, pear, and raspberry chutney. Finish with a delightful brown sugar cheesecake.

In the Mast Farm Inn, 2543 Broadstone Rd. © **828/963-5857.** www.mastfarm.net/mfi-simplicity. Reservations required. Fixed-price menu $38 per person. AE, MC, V. July and Oct Thurs–Sun seatings at 6, 7, and 8pm; Nov–Feb, Apr–June, Aug–Sept Thurs–Sat seatings at 6, 7, and 8pm. Closed March.

BEECH MOUNTAIN

141 miles NW of Charlotte; 5 miles NW of Banner Elk

Beech Mountain boasts the highest elevated ski area in the east, with a peak of 5,506 feet. It was voted the number-one ski area by readers of *Blue Ridge Country,* competing with the slopes in Tennessee, West Virginia, Virginia, and other areas of North Carolina. The Ski Beech mountain area lies on N.C. 184 along the Beech Mountain Parkway.

Beech Mountain is a resort of all seasons. You can enjoy golf, tennis, hiking, and biking in summer, or else skiing, tubing, and snowboarding—among the best in the Southeast—in winter.

A former hunting ground for the Cherokees, Beech Mountain was once called *Klonteska,* or "pheasant." The Great Trading Path that ran from Virginia to Georgia is said to have passed through Beech Mountain, and the 1864 Battle of Beech Mountain was fought here during the Civil War.

Essentials

GETTING THERE   After you reach Banner Elk (see "Getting There," in section above), you'll see Beech Mountain signposted. It's a 5-mile drive along the Beech Mountain Parkway to the top of the mountain.

VISITOR INFORMATION   Dispensing information is the very helpful staff at the **Beech Mountain Chamber of Commerce,** 403A Beech Mountain Pkwy. (© 800/468-5506 or 828/387-9283; www.beechmtn.com). It's open Monday to Saturday 9am to 5pm.

Fun in the Outdoors

SUMMER   The private Beech **Mountain Club** (© 828/387-4208; www.beech mtnclub.org) has a magnificent Willard Byrd–designed 18-hole championship golf course. Access to the course is available to guests renting qualified lodging; ask your rental office for more details.

This same private club has both hard-surface and clay tennis courts. Access to tennis is available to guests renting qualified lodging; ask your rental office for details. The **Pinnacle Inn** (© 800/405-7888; www.pinnacleinn.com) offers two asphalt courts for registered guests.

The swimming pool at the Beech Mountain Club is available to guests renting qualified lodging. There are indoor pools at the Pinnacle Inn and at **Cedar Village Condos** (© 828/387-4748; www.cedarvillagebeechmountain.com) for registered guests.

Beech Mountain Sports offers rentals of mountain bikes for the eight marked trails on Beech Mountain. For more information, call © **828/387-9283.**

Fishers will find the 7-acre Buckeye Lake stocked throughout the year with trout. Facilities here include a boat ramp, picnic pavilion, and toilet facilities. The fishing season runs from the first Saturday in April until the end of February. Lake Coffey, another lake on Beech Mountain, is also stocked with trout. Persons over the age of

Beech Mountain

16 need a license costing $20 to $40; you can get one at **Fred's General Mercantile** (© 828/387-4838).

If you like hiking, the best trail is **Pond Creek Trail,** stretching for 2 miles beginning at Tarnarack Road, following the creek past Lake Coffey, and continuing to Locust Ridge Road. The lower end of the trail has a few small waterfalls.

WINTER The **Ski Beech Express** (© 800/438-2093 or 828/387-2011; www.skibeech.com), a high-speed quad chairlift, is one of 10 lifts that service 15 slopes in the area: three beginner, eight intermediate, and four advanced. There is an 830-foot vertical drop from the summit to the base.

The ski season lasts from mid-November until mid-March. Daily lift rates are $32 Monday to Friday and $52 on Saturday and Sunday. Lifts operate daily from 8:30am to 4:30pm and from 6 to 10pm. Ski rental is $19 Monday to Friday and $23 on weekends. Professional lessons are available at $20 per hour for group lessons or $55 for private lessons. Snow tubing and ice-skating are also available for $15 each for a 2-hour period.

The town has created a free sledding hill next to the town hall. This is eastern America's highest sled run, and it's open daily from 8am to 10pm.

Where to Stay

The Banner Elk Inn ★★   This 1912 inn is one of our favorite getaways in the Appalachian Mountains. Innkeeper and owner Beverly Lait is one of the more gracious hosts in western Carolina. Only 2 miles from Sugar Mountain ski resort and a few more miles from Ski Beech ski resort, the inn is in the village across the street from the Banner Elk Town Park, with its walking path and meandering stream. You can sit out on the side porch enjoying the mountain breezes or else admire the prizewinning gardens. The comfy-cozy guest rooms in the main building (adults only) have an old-fashioned charm, and bathrooms have both tub and shower. In addition to three cottages, family-friendly cabins are also available. Hearty and memorable breakfasts are served on fine china.

407 Main St. E., Banner Elk, NC 28604. © 888/487-8263 or 828/898-6223. Fax 828/898-6224. www. bannerelkinn.com. 9 units. $85–$125 double; $90–$180 suite; $150–$175 cottage. MC, V. **Amenities:** Breakfast room. *In room:* TV, kitchenette (in some), Wi-Fi (free).

The Pinnacle Inn ★ ☺   Among the vast array of guest rooms at this modern resort are the one- and two-bedroom Ski Suites. The one-bedroom suite can sleep two to four guests comfortably, and the two-bedroom suite can accommodate up to six. Each suite is well maintained and comfortably furnished, and comes with a fully equipped kitchen, a fireplace, and a private balcony for taking in those mountain views. All the rooms have been painted and decorated with bright colors and furnished in a cozy style. There is no restaurant on-site, but nine different dining choices are within a 3-mile driving radius, and twice as many are only minutes away in Banner Elk.

301 Pinnacle Inn Rd., Banner Elk, NC 28604. © 800/405-7888 or 828/387-2231. Fax 828/387-3745. www.pinnacleinn.com. 242 units. Winter $85–$140 1-bedroom suite; $135–$195 2-bedroom suite; summer $65–$100 1-bedroom suite; $100–$125 2-bedroom suite. AE, MC, V. **Amenities:** Children's playground and activities (mid-June to mid-Sept); exercise room; Jacuzzi; indoor pool; sauna; steam room; 2 tennis courts (lit). *In room:* TV, hair dryer, kitchen, Wi-Fi (free; in some).

BLOWING ROCK

90 miles NE of Asheville

One of the oldest resorts in North Carolina, Blowing Rock dates back to the 1800s. Sitting on the Continental Divide at an elevation of 4,000 feet, Blowing Rock is filled with little B&Bs, inns, and galleries. It makes a good base for exploring and offers some of the state's best snow skiing (at Appalachian Mountain).

Essentials

GETTING THERE   To reach Blowing Rock from Asheville, head north on the Blue Ridge Parkway or take I-40 East out of Asheville to U.S. 321 North and follow the signs into Blowing Rock. From Boone, take U.S. 321 South directly into Blowing Rock.

VISITOR INFORMATION   The **Blowing Rock Chamber of Commerce,** 132 Park Ave., Blowing Rock, NC 28605 (© **800/295-7851** or 828/295-7851; www. blowingrock.com), is open Monday to Saturday 9am to 5pm, dispensing information about the area.

Exploring the Area

The area's biggest attraction, from which the town takes its name, is the **Blowing Rock ★** (© **828/295-7111;** www.theblowingrock.com), on U.S. 321, 2 miles south of town. Rising 4,000 feet above John's River Gorge, the mountain has a strong updraft that returns any light object (such as a handkerchief) that's thrown into the void. The observation tower, gazebos, and gardens offer panoramic views of John's River Gorge and nearby Blue Ridge peaks. You can visit the mountain January to February Saturday and Sunday 9am to 5pm, March to May daily 9am to 5pm, June to Labor Day daily 8:30am to 7pm, September and October daily 9am to 6pm, and November and December daily 9am to 5pm. Admission is $6 for adults and $1 for children 4 to 11.

Another natural phenomenon at Blowing Rock is **Mystery Hill** (© **828/264-2792;** www.mysteryhill-nc.com), where balls and water run uphill.

Outdoor Pursuits

SKIING   The **Appalachian Ski Mountain,** PO Box 106, Blowing Rock, NC 28605 (© **800/322-2373** or 828/295-7828; www.appskimtn.com), lies 2 miles off U.S. 221/321 between Boone and Blowing Rock near the Blue Ridge Parkway intersection. It offers nine slopes: two beginner, four intermediate, and three advanced. It stands at an elevation of 4,000 feet, with a 365-foot vertical drop. The season runs from the weekend before Thanksgiving to the third weekend in March, when it's open daily from 9am to 4pm and 6 to 10pm. Lift tickets cost $25 to $61 for adults Monday to Friday and $41 to $52 on weekends and holidays. Tickets for children 12 and under cost $16 and $44, respectively. Ski lessons are available for $40 per hour for private instruction, but cost only $17 per person in a group. Skis can be rented for $10 to $26. Children 5 and under get a free ticket with a paying adult.

Shopping

The **Main Street Gallery,** Main Street (© **828/295-7839;** www.blowingrockfine crafts.com), is a cooperative gallery featuring handmade contemporary art and crafts from the North Carolina mountains. The location is in the center of Blowing Rock across from the post office. Hours are daily 10am to 6pm.

Orchard at Altapass, milepost 328.4 on the Blue Ridge Parkway, at Spruce Pine on Orchard Road (© **888/765-9531** or 828/765-9531; www.altapassorchard.com), sells apples from July to November; you pick, or they pick. The orchard has an array of fresh baked goods, free tours, and even music and tall tales. The proprietors will arrange hayrides for you on Saturday and Sunday. From May to October, hours for Monday to Saturday are 10am to 6pm; on Sunday they're 11am to 6pm. The rest of the year, the store is open only on Saturday 10am to 6pm and Sunday noon to 6pm. Finally, **Parkway Craft Center** (© **828/295-7938;** www.southernhighlandguild. org) is at milepost 294 on the Blue Ridge Parkway in the Moses Cone Manor just off Route 321. Here, you'll find the finest-quality Appalachian Mountain crafts, hand-made by members of the Southern Highland Craft Guild. Craft demonstrations are presented on the porch. Open daily 9am to 5pm.

Where to Stay

Crippen's Country Inn & Restaurant (see "Where to Dine," below) also rents guest rooms.

Chetola Resort at Blowing Rock ★★ ☺ *Chetola,* Cherokee for "rest haven," is the right name for this idyllic spot. This is the grandest resort in the area, set on 87 acres within walking distance of the center of the village, with the 3,600-acre Moses H. Cone National Park and the Blue Ridge Mountains enveloping it. Guests can select a first-class room in the lodge or choose one of the luxury condos. Much of the property is new, but remnants of yesterday remain, including the fireplace (from the mid-1800s) in the manor house. Many private homes are also part of the complex. In 1988, the Chetola Lodge & Conference Center opened on-site. We prefer staying in the lodge, where the spacious rooms and suites are comfortably and attractively fur-nished. (The condos' decor depends on the taste of the individual owners.)

500 N. Main St., Blowing Rock, NC 28605. © **800/243-8652** or 828/295-5500. Fax 828/295-5529. www.chetola.com. 104 units. $142–$315 double; $159–$660 condo. AE, DISC, MC, V. **Amenities:** Restau-rant; bar; soda shop; babysitting; children's activities; golf privileges; exercise room; indoor pool; room service; sauna; 3 tennis courts (lit); Wi-Fi (free in lobby). *In room:* A/C, TV, hair dryer, kitchenette (in some), minibar.

Cliff Dwellers Inn This aptly named motel-like structure is just 1 mile south of the Blue Ridge Parkway on the side of a mountain, offering panoramic views. It is across from a shopping center where you can stock up on supplies. Guests often branch off from this location for a day of fly fishing, water rafting, or golf (discounts granted for guests). Bedrooms are spacious and furnished in a homey way, often with sunken living rooms and private terraces.

116 Lakeview Terrace, Blowing Rock, NC 28605. © **800/322-7380** or 828/295-3122. Fax 828/295-3121. http://cliffdwellers.com. 22 units. $74–$161 double; $174–$286 suite. AE, DISC, MC, V. **Amenities:** Con-cierge. *In room:* A/C, TV, fridge, hair dryer.

Hound Ears Lodge ★★ If you want high style, this exclusive resort should be your mountain retreat. Its unusual name derives from a nearby rock formation. The setting is panoramic, on 700 acres with an 18-hole golf course. Guest rooms, except for seven in the main clubhouse, are in chalets complete with pitched roofs and balconies with fantastic views. Guest rooms are spacious and have well-kept bath-rooms. Fishing is a major pastime. So is golf.

Off N.C. 105 S. near Boone, PO Box 188, Blowing Rock, NC 28605. © **828/963-4321.** Fax 828/963-8030. www.houndears.com. 28 units. $235 double; $325 suite. Rates include breakfast and dinner. AE, MC, V. **Amenities:** Restaurant; bar; 18-hole golf course; outdoor pool; room service; sauna; 6 tennis courts (3 lit); Wi-Fi (free in lobby). *In room:* A/C, TV.

Where to Dine

Best Cellar Incorporated ★ CONTINENTAL This restaurant is housed inside an authentic log cabin dating from 1938. Set on a hillside off the bypass in Blowing Rock, it's run by Rob Dyer and Lisa Stripling, who welcome visitors from all over the world. They've turned their kitchen over to chef Richard Jones (everybody calls him "Dickie"), a master at his craft. He admits that he didn't learn to cook from his mama, whose specialty was TV dinners. Dickie is a heavy-cream-and-butter type of chef—South Beach dieters might prefer to book a table elsewhere. Fresh seafood and aged beef are the chef's delightful specialties, and he also does wonders with rack of lamb and duck. We've enjoyed the smoky mountain trout with smoked bacon and onions, and grilled blackened rib-eye rubbed with Cajun spices. The homemade desserts are worth making room for; the chef's favorite is a rich brownie with vanilla ice cream and hot fudge.

203 Sunset Dr. (off 321 Bypass). © **828/295-3466.** www.ragged-gardens.com. Reservations required. Main courses $22–$42. AE, MC, V. Mon–Thurs 5:30–9pm; Fri–Sat 5:30–9:30pm.

Crippen's Country Inn & Restaurant ★ AMERICAN   The restaurant's sophisticated cuisine is one of the reasons people stay at Crippen's Country Inn. The spacious dining area with circular tables offers a surprising amount of intimacy despite the crowds. The menu changes daily, offering many creative delights. Ever had Coca-Cola–marinated kangaroo or chocolate steak with Bailey's sauce? You may begin with a shrimp brûlée, pan roasted with blue-spot prawns, or a crispy duck confit with spring rolls and peanut-ginger dressing. Chef's specialties include chili-rubbed grilled rib-eye steak, and sesame-seared yellowfin tuna. Reservations are essential. The inn also rents nine guest rooms, each of which is comfortable and well furnished; prices range from $99 to $159 (double occupancy).

239 Sunset Dr., Blowing Rock. © **828/295-3487.** www.crippens.com. Reservations required. Main courses $22–$42. AE, DISC, MC, V. Daily 6–9pm.

THE BLUE RIDGE PARKWAY ★★★

The **Blue Ridge Parkway** takes up where Virginia's Skyline Drive leaves off at Rockfish Gap, between Charlottesville and Waynesboro. It then continues winding and twisting along the mountain crests for 469 miles, passing through most of western North Carolina before it reaches Great Smoky Mountains National Park near the Tennessee border.

The parkway links the southern end of Shenandoah National Park in Virginia with the eastern entrance of Great Smoky Mountains National Park in North Carolina. When it was begun 60 years ago, the parkway was a great engineering challenge. During the Roosevelt era, it was designed as a federal public-works project to relieve massive unemployment in the region. Its final segment, the Linn Cove Viaduct, was constructed in the 1980s.

The northern section of the parkway skims the crest of the towering Blue Ridge Mountains, with panoramic views of grand valleys on both sides of the road. But when the parkway twists and curls in the more rugged Pisgah and Black mountains to the south, the panoramas become even more dramatic.

October is the peak visiting month, and thousands of people come to see the incredible scarlet of sourwoods, orange sassafras, and golden poplars, to name only a few. Traffic moves at a snail's pace in October, and Saturday and Sunday are especially crowded on the parkway. Reservations for lodging and certain attractions in summer and especially in October are essential.

You can detour to Waynesville around the third week of October for the best apple festival in the region. On sale are crafts, cider, apple butter, and fresh and dried apples. Square dancers perform, and bluegrass bands entertain the crowds. Waynesville

The Blue Ridge Parkway

lies 7 miles from the parkway at milepost 443.1. For more information, contact the **Haywood County Apple Harvest Festival,** PO Box 600, Waynesville, NC 28786 (✆ **828/456-3021;** www.haywood-nc.com).

Elevations range from 649 to 6,053 feet. The parkway has frequent exits to nearby towns but no tolls. There are 11 visitor stations; nine campgrounds (May–Oct only; some need reservations) with drinking water and comfort stations but no shower or utility hookups; restaurants and gas stations; and three lodges, plus one site featuring rustic cabins for overnight stays (reservations recommended). Opening and closing dates for campgrounds and cabins are flexible, so be sure to check in advance. Before you set out, write ahead for maps and detailed information. Contact Superintendent, **Blue Ridge Parkway,** 199 Hemphill Knob Rd., 1 Pack Sq., Asheville, NC 28803 (✆ **828/298-0398;** www.nps.gov/blri).

At many overlooks, a sign is posted showing the symbol of a man with a hiking stick and the word TRAIL, which means that there are marked walking trails through the woods. Some trails take only 10 or 20 minutes and provide a leg-stretching break from the confines of the car; others are longer and steeper and may take an hour or more if you go the entire way.

A few simple rules have been laid down by the National Park Service: no commercial vehicles, no swimming in lakes and ponds, no hunting, no pets without a leash, and, above all, no fires except in campground or picnic-area fireplaces. Another good rule is to keep your gas tank half full at all times; this is no place to be stranded. The speed limit is strictly 45 miles an hour.

Don't plan to hurry down the Blue Ridge: Take time to amble and drink in the beauty. If you want to drive the entire length of the parkway, allow at least 2 or 3 days. On the first day, drive the Virginia half; then stop for the night at Boone, North Carolina, not far from the state border. The final two legs of the trip—from Boone to Asheville and from there to Fontana Village—can easily be accomplished in another day's drive.

SIGHTS NEAR THE PARKWAY   You can veer off the parkway to see several attractions, including **Linville Falls Visitor Center** (✆ **828/765-1045;** www.virtual blueridge.com/parkway_tour/VisitorCenters/316_0/index.asp), between Linville and Marion. Parking is available at milepost 316 on the parkway. This is a series of two falls, with an upper level of 12 feet and a lower level of 90 feet. The falls plunge into the 2,000-foot-deep Linville Gorge. A 1-mile round-trip hike takes you to the upper falls; other trails lead to more views. Some of the trails are quite challenging. Open April to November, the falls are free.

The 7,600-acre **Linville Gorge Wilderness Area** (www.northcarolinaoutdoors. com/places/mountains/linvillegorge.html) is a primitive natural environment, accessed by foot trails off N.C. 183. You need a permit to enter the area and can obtain one at the district ranger's office (signposted) in Marion.

Another major attraction, **Linville Caverns,** lies about 65 miles north of the Folk Art Center (milepost 382 on the Blue Ridge Pkwy.), just off U.S. 221 between Linville and Marion (✆ **828/756-4171;** www.linvillecaverns.com). The only caverns in North Carolina, these tunnels go 2,000 feet underground. The year-round temperature is 51°F (11°C). Admission is $7 for adults, $5.50 for seniors, and $5 for children 5 to 12. The caverns are open June 1 to Labor Day daily 9am to 6pm; April, May, September, October daily 9am to 5pm; November and March daily 9am to 4:30pm; and December, January, February weekends 9am to 4:30pm.

North Carolina is not necessarily a state you associate with wine production, yet it is home to more than 90 wineries and ranks seventh in wine production in the United States.

More than 400 individually owned vineyards are spread across the state, covering 1,800 acres. From the mountains to the Outer Banks, to the vast Yadkin Valley, you can taste everything from merlot to muscadine, perhaps enjoy a picnic as well, even some live country music in some of the vineyards.

The best of the lot is the **Biltmore Estate Winery** on the Biltmore Estate (p. 196). It is in Antler Hill Village, 1 Antler Hill Rd. (✆ **800/411-3812** or 828/225-1333; www.biltmore.com/visit/antler_hill_village/winery/default.asp). Open daily 11am to 8pm, it charges $60 for adults, $30 for ages 16 and under. You can visit the historic cellars finishing in the tasting room for a complimentary sampling of the crisp whites, refreshing rosés, and robust reds. A self-guided tour of the winery and complimentary wine tasting is included in the estate admission, or else you can visit the winery separately.

Dublin Winery, 505 N. Sycamore St., Rose Hill (✆ **800/774-9634**), offers free tours of its production facilities Monday to Friday 9am to 11am and 1 to 4pm, and 9am to 4pm on Saturday. You can also visit a museum of wine artifacts. Established in 1975, Dublin produces about 303,000 cases of wine per year, especially muscadine.

In the Haw River Valley, **Benjamin Vineyards,** 6516 Whitney Rd., Graham (Saxapahaw; ✆ **336/376-1080;** www.hawrivervalleyava.com; Thurs–Sun noon–5pm), is known for its muscadine grapes, but also for a number of French-American hybrid grapes. Tasting fees range from $3 to $5 per person. You can even pick some of the grapes for sampling and enjoy lunch at a picnic table.

Laurel Gray Vineyards is at 5726 Old Hwy. 421, Hamptonville, in the Swan Creek area (✆ **336/468-9463;** www.laurelgrayvineyards.com). It is open Wednesday to Saturday 10am to 5pm and Sunday 1 to 5pm annually except in January. Entrance is free but a wine tasting costs $5. This family owned and operated winery produces estate-grown French wines in the Yadkin Valley. Sip wine on the vineyard's spacious front porch old-timey style in gliders and rockers.

Also in the Yadkin Valley, **Elkin Creek Winery,** 318 Elkin Creek Mill Rd. (✆ **336/526-5119;** www.elkincreekvineyard.com), is the domain of the Greene family, who will let you sample their wines for $5 Thursday to Sunday 11am to 5pm. You can also order a meal in the Kitchen at Elkin Creek, with its wood-burning brick oven.

9

ASHEVILLE & THE HIGH COUNTRY

The Blue Ridge Parkway

SHOPPING   The best shopping for handmade mountain crafts is at **Allanstand Craft Shop,** Folk Art Center, Blue Ridge Parkway, milepost 382 (✆ **828/298-7928;** www.southernhighlandguild.org/pages/guild-shops/allanstand-craft-shop.php). Here you'll find beautifully made quilts, Granny style, along with pottery, wooden bowls, and even musical instruments. Works displayed were made by members of the Southern Highland Craft Guild.

GREAT SMOKY MOUNTAINS NATIONAL PARK

C loaked in mystery, the **Great Smoky Mountains ★★★** were once known by the Cherokees as *sha-cona-ge,* "land of the blue mist" (or smoke). According to Cherokee legend, people and animals originally lived in the sky above the ocean. When the sky became overcrowded, a water beetle was sent to find land but could not, so it dove to the bottom of the ocean and brought up mud to form the earth. The Smokies were then formed by a great buzzard whose wings touched the mud, hardening it into a mountain range. Geologists have a counter theory that says this range was actually formed by many upheavals and erosions of the land.

10

The Great Smoky Mountains, formed hundreds of millions of years ago, are the oldest mountains in the world. They're comprised of peaks that range in elevation from 840 to 6,642 feet. The mountainsides are covered with a wide variety of flora and fauna that have few equals throughout the Temperate Zone.

To preserve the pristine beauty of this environment, Great Smoky Mountains National Park was officially established in June 1934. The area had been threatened with destruction by the logging industry. A librarian from St. Louis, Horace Kephart, spearheaded the effort to save the area. He was joined by several prominent citizens from Knoxville. The National Park Service, John D. Rockefeller, and eventually the federal government backed their efforts. The people gave the government the land, making it the first national park to be created in this fashion. In September 1940, Great Smoky Mountains National Park was dedicated by President Franklin D. Roosevelt at the Rockefeller monument at Newfound Gap. The park has become one of the most-frequented national parks in the United States, hosting more than nine million visitors annually.

The oval park, bisected by the North Carolina–Tennessee border, encompasses more than 520,000 acres of forests, streams, rivers, waterfalls, and hiking trails. These trails pass through valleys, peaks, forests, and overlooks that provide scenic views. The park also contains balds—patches of clear land in the midst of the wooded slopes. It's still a mystery why these spots do not support tree growth.

The United Nations has designated the park an International Biosphere Reserve because of its multitude of plants, trees, mammals, birds, and fish. More than 100 species of trees thrive in the park. Growing on some of the relatively drier slopes in the lower to middle elevations (up to 4,500 ft.) are pines, oaks, hickories, yellow poplars, and dogwood trees. Hike the trails at Cades Cove and Laurel Falls to see the species that are typical of this elevation. In several areas, you can find gigantic ancient hemlocks that escaped the loggers' destruction; these hemlocks are located along trails leading from the Roaring Fork Motor Nature Trail to Grotto Falls or from the Newfound Gap Road to Alum Cave Bluffs. At slightly higher elevations are hardwoods typical of those that grow in northern states: beeches and yellow birches. Look for these species at Newfound Gap and along Clingmans Dome Road. The higher elevations (above 4,500 ft.) support evergreens such as the Fraser fir and red spruce, which you can find along the Appalachian Trail through most of the eastern half of the park, as well as along Clingmans Dome Road.

Abundant wildflowers offer a kaleidoscope of colors in spring and early summer and a blanket of lush greenery in later summer. Often non-native flowers—trilliums, violets, lady's slippers, and jack-in-the-pulpits—have taken over entire areas. Blooming shrubs, numbering more than 1,500 species, are scattered throughout the park. The height of the blooming season is in mid-June, when you'll find rhododendrons, mountain laurels, and azaleas in full glory. The best places to look for these blooms are among the various balds (such as Gregory, Andrews, and Silers) and along the Cove Hardwoods Nature, the Chimney Tops, and the Noah Bud Ogle Farm trails.

As you ascend the peaks, you'll travel through the blue mists that once were wholly the work of Mother Nature. Unfortunately, they are now composed of almost 70% pollution from factories and cities, and are causing damage to the delicate balance of this area's ecosystem. Pollution has also reduced visibility by 30% over the past several decades. Yet, as you traverse the park, the mists still surround you with a centuries-old aura of mystery.

The park is the home of more than 200 species of birds. The junco, a small gray bird with white outer tail feathers, patrols the parking lots of Newfound Gap and Clingmans Dome. Although wild turkeys appear throughout the park, you'll most likely view them in the early-morning and evening hours around Cades Cove. More than 70 types of fish and 30 varieties of amphibians can be found in the streams, including the red-cheeked salamander, which lives only in the park.

More than 70 species of mammals live in the park, known especially for its black bears that weigh an average of 200 to 300 pounds. Other mammals are white-tailed deer, groundhogs, raccoons, skunks, and bobcats. Park rangers stress that no visitor should try to approach or feed these creatures—for the safety of both humans and animals.

CHEROKEE: GATEWAY TO THE SMOKIES ★

48 miles SW of Asheville

The Cherokee Nation once claimed around 135,000 square miles of land encompassing sections of South Carolina, North Carolina, Tennessee, Virginia, West Virginia, and Kentucky. When Hernando de Soto, the Spanish explorer, moved into the southern mountains of the Appalachian range in 1540, the Cherokees numbered only about 25,000—a very small number compared with the millions who now occupy former Cherokee land.

When Soto arrived, he forever changed the way the Cherokees lived. With him on his quest for gold in the name of Spain came misery, disease, and death. Some of Soto's men killed or enslaved many of the Native Americans, believing that they were holding back information about the location of treasure. It's estimated that during the first 200 years of European occupation, 95% of the Cherokees died of diseases that the foreigners brought with them. The treatment of the Cherokees did not improve in later centuries. When the Cherokees adapted well to the white man's ways and set up a flourishing society, greed and envy eventually culminated, in 1838, in the Trail of Tears. Most of the Cherokees were driven out of the area by military force, and their ancestral lands were taken away.

Today the Smoky Mountain home of the Cherokees has dwindled to 56,000 acres that make up the Qualla Boundary, also known as the Cherokee Indian Reservation. This land was purchased by a white man, Will Thomas, who gave it to the Cherokee people in the late 1800s. When you visit the reservation, you're entering a sovereign land held in trust specifically for the tribe by the United States government. Known as the Eastern Band of the Cherokee Nation, the Cherokees who still reside here are descendants of the approximately 1,000 Cherokees who hid in these mountains to avoid forced removal to Oklahoma. These people can rightfully claim to be the original inhabitants of the vast Smoky Mountains.

Only a generation ago, the Cherokee language—both the spoken form and the written form—was in danger of becoming extinct. But since the late 1940s, annual increases in tourist-related business and the resultant growth of tribal resources have helped keep it alive. Today visitors can hear the language spoken at attractions such as the Oconaluftee Indian Village and during the outdoor drama *Unto These Hills*. In Cherokee schools, it's a required subject, and it has also become part of the curriculum such as Western Carolina University in Cullowhee, North Carolina. Tourism is the mainstay of the economy; about 75% of the tribe's revenue is derived from this industry. All business locations within the Qualla Boundary are Native American–owned, but by the authority of the tribal council, Native Americans can lease their buildings or businesses to other people. Nearly 30 businesses hold trader's licenses and collect a 6% tribal levy on sales. No other sales tax applies within the boundary, including North Carolina sales tax.

On your visit here, you'll notice several "chiefs" dressed in Western attire. You can have your picture taken with them for a small fee or tip. Many of these "chiefs" have been around for quite a while, priding themselves on having their picture taken with two or three generations of the same family.

Foodies flock here at the end of March for the **Rainbows & Ramps Festival,** celebrating mountain trout along with ramps (the pungent, wild-onion-and-garlic-like root vegetable). The festival includes music, horseshoe competitions, and a barbecue cook-off along with bushels of trout and ramps. For more information, call the **Cherokee Welcome Center** at ℂ **800/438-1601.**

Essentials

GETTING THERE From the southern end of the Blue Ridge Parkway and points south, U.S. 441 leads to Cherokee; U.S. 19 runs east and west through the town.

The nearest airport is at Asheville (see "Essentials," in the "Asheville" section of chapter 9).

VISITOR INFORMATION For more information, contact the **Cherokee Visitor Center,** 498 Psali Blvd., off 441 North, Cherokee, NC 28719 (© **800/438-1601** or 828/497-9195; www.cherokee-nc.com), open daily 8:15am to 5pm.

Discovering Cherokee Culture

The Museum of the Cherokee Indian ★

The objective of this museum is to "authentically present and preserve thousands of years of Cherokee history and culture." This it does, displaying one of the finest exhibits of Native American artifacts in the United States. One exhibit includes a digital movie of the creation of the Cherokee Nation. When you enter the building, you begin walking along a timeline, beginning with the Paleolithic era some 10,000 years ago and continuing chronologically to modern times. Artifacts that you'll find here include farming utensils, weapons for hunting and war, clothing, copies of the first photographs taken of the Cherokee people, pottery, baskets, and an art gallery displaying native art and photography. Also included are lighting special effects, the most impressive of which is a holographic exhibit of the Cherokees. A gift shop is also open in the museum. On the grounds is a 20-foot-tall, hand-carved statue of Sequoyah, the inventor of the Cherokee alphabet.

U.S. 441 at Drama Rd. © **828/497-3481.** www.cherokeemuseum.org. Admission $10 adults, $6 children, free for children 5 and under. Daily 9am–5pm. Closed major holidays.

Oconaluftee Indian Village

Operated by the Cherokee Historical Association, this living museum offers a step back in time to the mid-1750s Cherokee way of life. On your tour of the village, you'll see women shaping clay into pottery, arrowheads being chipped, naturally dyed river cane being woven into baskets, and blowguns being demonstrated. Lectures are held at the Ceremonial Grounds, where you'll hear about dances, masks, rattles, feathers, and other facets of Cherokee life, and at the Council House, where presentations are given about Cherokee government, Council House designs, territories, language, and other nonceremonial topics. There's also a mile-long nature trail adjacent to the village. The seven-sided Council House conjures up images of the leaders of seven tribes gathered to thrash out problems or to worship their gods together.

U.S. 441. © **828/497-2315.** www.cherokee-nc.com. Admission $20–$22 adults, $12–$14 children 6–12. Mid-May to Oct daily 9am–5:30pm.

Trout Fishing

The major outdoor pursuit on the reservation is **fishing.** Thirty miles of streams are stocked with 400,000 trout annually. Supplemental fish stocks include rainbow, brook, and brown trout, ranging up to trophy size. Those 12 or older need a tribal permit to fish the Cherokee streams and ponds, and these are available at most convenience stores. The annual season begins the last Saturday of March and ends the last day of February in the following year. Fishing is allowed beginning a half-hour before sunrise and ending a half-hour after sunset. The creel limit is 10 trout per day per permit holder. Certain enterprise waters are open only to tribal members.

For complete fishing information, contact **Cherokee Fish and Game Management,** PO Box 302, Cherokee, NC 28719 (© **828/497-5201**), or the visitor center (see "Essentials," above).

UNTO THESE hills

Unto These Hills ★★★ has been presented each summer at Cherokee since 1950. It relates the story of the Cherokees from 1540 until the Trail of Tears exodus to Oklahoma in 1838, during which thousands died.

The 2-hour show, recently rewritten by Hanay Geiogamah, involves 130 performers, including actual Cherokee Indians, and technicians. All performances are at the 2,800-seat **Mountainside Theater,** off U.S. 441 (© **800/438-1601;** www.cherokee-nc.com). Opening night is around June 10, and the curtain closes on August 19. Tickets cost $22 for reserved seating, $18 for general admission, and $10 for children 6 to 12 years old. Free for children 5 and under in the general-admission seating area. No shows are presented on Sunday.

Where to Stay

Cherokee has an abundance of motel and hotel rooms offering basic accommodations. In addition to the following listings is the **Holiday Inn-Cherokee,** U.S. 19 South (© **888/HOLIDAY** [465-4329] or 828/497-9181; www.holidayinn.com).

Baymont Inn   Built in 1995, this economy choice offers comfortable but decidedly straightforward accommodations. Guest rooms are basic, with neatly kept bathrooms. Suites offer such amenities as small refrigerators, microwaves, and sleeper sofas. The rates include in-room coffee and continental breakfast delivered to your door. Stay here only for the value.

1455 Acquoni Rd. (PO Box 1865), Cherokee, NC 28719. © **877/229-6668** or 828/497-2102. Fax 828/497-5242. www.baymontinns.com. 67 units. $109–$149 double; $126–$159 suite. Rates include continental breakfast. AE, DC, DISC, MC, V. **Amenities:** Breakfast room; lounge; outdoor pool. *In room:* A/C, TV, hair dryer, Wi-Fi (free).

Harrah's Cherokee Casino & Hotel ★   Directly connected to the casino, this first-class hotel rises 15 floors, each level decorated with local Indian crafts and artwork. An elevated mountain walkway over a fast-flowing stream takes patrons from the casino into the hotel precincts, where the spacious lobby is adorned with Native American artifacts. Guest rooms are big and attractively furnished.

777 Casino Dr., Cherokee, NC 28719. © **800/HARRAHS** (427-7247) or 828/497-7777. Fax 828/497-5076. www.harrahscherokee.com/casinos/harrahs-cherokee/hotel-casino/property-home.shtml. 576 units. $109–$229 double. AE, DC, DISC, MC, V. **Amenities:** 2 restaurants; cafe; babysitting; exercise center; indoor pool; room service; sauna. *In room:* A/C, TV, fridge, hair dryer, Internet ($12 per day).

Newfound Lodge   On the Oconaluftee River, this centrally located motel is divided into two sections. One section is set on the mountainside, the other is located across the street and contains balconied rooms overlooking the river. The rooms are spacious; some are decorated in a standard floral motif, whereas others display a more modern geometric design. The grounds include picnic areas with grills and a deck that leads down to the rocks below.

1192 Tsali Blvd., N. Cherokee, NC 28719. © **828/497-2746.** Fax 828/497-7136. 72 units. Late Mar to mid-June $69 double; mid-June to Oct $95 double. AE, DISC, MC, V. Closed Nov to late Mar. **Amenities:** Outdoor pool. *In room:* A/C, TV, fridge.

Riverside Motel and Campground   Set off the road, this motel offers comfortable, standard rooms overlooking the river. Each well-kept unit has a bathroom containing a tub/shower combination. The stone structure fits in well with the environment, not distracting from the beauty of the mountains. The grounds hold a sheltered picnic area plus a campground with 30 rental sites. Overnighters bring their own camper, RV, or tent.

U.S. 441 S. at Old Rte. 441 (PO Box 58), Cherokee, NC 28719. ℭ **877/643-1439** or 828/497-9311. www. riversidemotelnc.com. 34 units. $75–$79 double. DISC, MC, V. Closed Nov–Mar. **Amenities:** Outdoor pool. *In room:* A/C, TV.

Where to Dine

Most restaurants here serve your basic chicken, steak, seafood, and (of course) freshwater fish from local waters. Also, the familiar national chains have long since arrived.

New Happy Garden Restaurant CHINESE   This red-and-gold restaurant offers hearty helpings served by an attentive staff. The specialties include battered shrimp lightly fried with a five-spice and salt blend, green peppers, and green onions, and Seven Star around the Moon, which is scallops, chicken, and barbecued pork with broccoli, carrots, snow peas, bamboo shoots, and rice in a brown sauce, with seven fried shrimp surrounding the entire concoction. Although it's not the most original Chinese restaurant, it is consistent and a welcome relief from all the Big Macs.

Acquoni Rd., Saunooke Village. ℭ **828/497-4310.** Main courses $5.60–$12; buffet $6.50 lunch, $8.95 dinner. AE, MC, V. Tues–Sun 11am–9pm.

Peter's Pancakes & Waffles AMERICAN   This pancake house offers hearty breakfasts and light lunches featuring sandwiches, soups, and salads. The birdhouse-adorned dining room has tables as well as counter service. Lunch options include Reubens, hot ham and cheese, chili dogs, and even PB&J, but the meal to eat here is breakfast. As you walk in the door, the aroma of fresh-cooked waffles and pancakes greets you. Waffles come topped with fresh fruit, and pancakes can be made with pecans. Hearty breakfast platters include the Ranch Hand: country ham, two eggs, two pancakes or biscuits, and grits.

34 Hwy. 441. ℭ **828/497-5116.** Breakfast items $3.25–$6.95; lunch main courses $4.25–$5.50. DISC, MC, V. Apr–Oct daily 7am–2pm.

Shopping

You'll find many opportunities to take some Cherokee culture home with you. A wide selection of handmade Cherokee products is available, as well as authentic Native American items from other areas. About 16 stores on the Cherokee reservation specialize in crafts, clothing, paintings, or jewelry made by local craftspeople or craftspeople from other tribes. The largest is **Qualla Arts and Crafts Mutual** (ℭ **828/497-3103**), on U.S. 441 at Drama Road, at the entrance to the *Unto These Hills* arena. Formed in the mid-1940s as a cooperative, Qualla has a current membership of 300 Cherokees, whose items are sold exclusively at the store. It ships products worldwide and is frequently visited by other tribal representatives who are interested in establishing a similar facility on their lands. Whether the craftsperson is a woodcarver, pottery maker, finger-weaver, artist, or basket maker, the products show individual artistry and convey a personal link to the makers' ancestors. Hours are Monday to Saturday 8am to 7pm and Sunday 9am to 5pm.

Cherokee After Dark

Drawing people from across the state is **Harrah's Cherokee Casino,** 777 Casino Dr. (ℭ **828/497-7777**), open 24 hours daily. All your favorite games of chance are here, plus a 1,500-seat Cherokee Pavilion Theater and five major restaurants. You must be 21 years of age or older to enter. This complex is part of a vast project that has transformed the Cherokee tribe's chronically depressed reservation into the only place in North Carolina where people can legally gamble. Rows of slots, video poker, and blackjack machines, along with other games, provide the tribe with an annual payout from Harrah's of $175 million—each member gets a $7,000 check every year. About once a month, the theater presents a headliner, and tickets range from $15 to $90.

THE SMOKIES: JUST THE FACTS

GETTING THERE Take I-40 from Asheville to U.S. 19, then take U.S. 441 to the park's southern entrance near Cherokee, a distance of 50 miles west.

ACCESS POINTS & ORIENTATION Although there are several side roads into the park, the best routes are through one of the three main entrances, two of which are located on Newfound Gap Road, U.S. 441, a 33-mile road that stretches north-south through the park. The southern entrance is near Cherokee, North Carolina, whereas the northern entrance is located 33 miles away near Gatlinburg, Tennessee. The third main entrance is on the western side of the park at Townsend, Tennessee. Other access points are from the campgrounds at the edge of the park. The park is open year-round, and admission is free.

VISITOR CENTERS At each of the three main entrances is a visitor center for the park. Each center offers information on roads, weather, camping, and backcountry conditions. You'll also find books, maps, and first-aid information.

Sugarlands Visitor Center and Park Headquarters (for park headquarters and all three visitor centers: © **865/436-1200;** www.nps.gov/grsm) is at the northern entrance, near Gatlinburg, Tennessee. This center is the largest and offers a 20-minute movie. A natural-history exhibit features stuffed animals such as a wild boar and other wildlife of the region.

The smaller **Oconaluftee Visitor Center** is at the southern entrance and offers a few exhibits on what to see and do in the park.

Cades Cove Visitor Center, at the western end of the park on Parson Branch Road about 12 miles southwest of Townsend, Tennessee, is set among a cluster of historic 19th-century farms and buildings.

The visitor centers are open daily from April to October: in April, May, and August 31 to October from 8am to 6pm (9am at the Cades Cove center) and June to August 30 from 8am to 7pm (9am at the Cades Cove center).

FEES, REGULATIONS & PERMITS Entrance to the park, backcountry permits, and parking permits for people with disabilities (which can be obtained from the visitor centers and ranger stations) are all free.

Park visitors must adhere to quite a few regulations, which help preserve the surroundings and keep visitors, as well as wildlife, safe:

- Alcohol is allowed only in designated picnic and campsite areas and at LeConte Lodge. Open containers in automobiles are illegal.
- No hunting, weapons, or fireworks are allowed, including bows, arrows, and slingshots.
- Fires are allowed only in designated areas, such as established fire rings and fireplaces. No trees can be cut down for firewood, although dead and downed trees

may be used. Firewood is sold by concessionaires at the Cades Cove, Elkmont, and Smokemont campgrounds.

- You may camp in designated areas only. To camp overnight in the backcountry, you must obtain a permit from a ranger station, one of the campgrounds, or one of the visitor centers (but not at Cades Cove).
- Motorcycles, bicycles, and mountain bikes are allowed on paved roads and in campgrounds. They are not permitted on trails and administrative roads. Helmets are required for motorcyclists. Skateboarding is prohibited in the park.
- Pets are allowed in parking lots, in campgrounds that are accessible by motor vehicle, and along paved roads. They are not allowed on the trails, in public buildings, or in the backcountry—with the exception of Seeing Eye and hearing guide dogs, which are permitted to travel throughout the park.
- It is illegal to pick, damage, destroy, and/or disturb any natural feature of the park. Federal law protects the forests and wildflowers of the Great Smokies.
- Food should never be left out. You'll find bear-proof trash cans and dumpsters throughout the park for depositing any food, wrappings, and containers.

SEASONS   From late March to June, spring brings great bursts of color from the wildflowers. Flowering shrubs spread across the countryside. At the higher elevations, mild daytime temperatures around the mid-70s (mid-20s Celsius) are recorded, although evenings are much cooler, dipping into the mid-40s (single digits Celsius).

As the season changes to summer, which lasts from June to August, the lush greenery comes into its full splendor and the weather gets warm and humid. Although the higher elevations offer milder temperatures, ranging from the low 50s to the mid-60s (teens Celsius), the lower ones can bring on days that are in the 90s (30s Celsius). Autumn colors first appear at higher elevations when the leaves on the fire cherry tree change to brilliant shades of crimson. Around the beginning of October, elevations above a mile have seen the end of fall, but lower elevations are just coming into their own. The best time to experience this change is from mid- to late October. Winter in the park can be very scenic, with snowfalls blanketing the countryside. At higher elevations, the temperature can drop below 0°F (–18°C). Throughout the year, weather can change often and rapidly, often within the same day. The wettest months are generally March and July.

RANGER PROGRAMS   Park rangers provide assistance to visitors at the ranger stations scattered throughout the park, as well as at the visitor centers. Rangers also offer films, short talks, guided nature and history walks, and evening campfire programs, along with slide presentations covering geology, bears, plant life, and early settler life. These programs are posted daily at the visitor centers.

THE PARK'S HIGHLIGHTS

Start early in the morning to avoid the crowds that increase during the day. When crossing the park on the Newfound Gap Road (U.S. 441), you should allow, at the very least, 1 hour. The speed limit does not rise above 45 mph anywhere in the park. When ascending the mountain slopes, you can rarely go over 30 mph because of the winding roads. Pack a lunch since the park has no restaurants.

DAY 1   Your best strategy is to visit the sights along the Newfound Gap Road. Begin at the **Oconaluftee Visitor Center,** where you can pick up park information and get details about the weather. Oconaluftee (which means "by the river") was owned by the Cherokees until settlers acquired the land through treaties. Today the **Oconaluftee Mountain Farm Museum,** a replica of a pioneer farmstead, operates here in a collection of original log buildings. Park staff members, dressed in period costumes, make this a living-history farm from April to October.

Travel about half a mile north on the Newfound Gap Road to the **Mingus Mill,** constructed in 1886 by Dr. John Jacob Mingus, son of this area's first permanent settler. It closed in 1940 and was reopened in 1968 by the park service. This water-powered mill is still in operation, grinding wheat and corn for flour and cornmeal from mid-April to October.

As you travel north, you'll come to a turnoff for **Clingmans Dome,** the highest peak in the park, soaring 6,642 feet and named for Thomas Lanier Clingman, a 19th-century North Carolina senator. After you turn onto this road, you travel 7 miles southwest to a parking lot, where you can walk a steep half-mile to a viewing platform that features one of the park's best views. The platform is generally closed from December to April.

Next comes **Newfound Gap,** which, at 5,048 feet, is the center of the park. A path that the Cherokees traveled was 2 miles west of the present-day gap. Later the path was widened and renamed Indian Gap Road. If the sky is clear, you can see for miles around. It's best to call ✆ **865/436-1200,** the park's main number, for weather conditions before you set out.

The next point of interest is the **Chimney Tops,** twin peaks that rise close to 2,000 feet. The Cherokees named these peaks Duniskwalguni (which means "forked antlers"), whereas the settlers named them for the 30-foot-deep fluelike cavity in one of them. If you'd like a closer look, you can hike a 4-mile trail round-trip.

The drive across the park takes you to the **Sugarlands Visitor Center,** where you can stroll through the nature exhibit, view a slide show, or browse through the gift shop. At this point, you can either head into Gatlinburg for the night or go west about 5 miles on Little River Road to **Elkmont Campground.** It's best to make reservations (accepted only from mid-May to Oct).

DAY 2 Continue your journey west on Little River Road to **Cades Cove,** where you'll find more pioneer structures than at any other location in the park. The best time to go is early in the morning, when you have a better chance of spotting deer grazing in the fields. Plan to spend half a day exploring the many attractions along the 11-mile Cades Cove Loop. Stop at the visitor center for a pamphlet that contains a key to the numbered sights.

Originally called Kate's Cove, after the wife of John Oliver, the cove's first settler, the name evolved over the years into Cades Cove. Founded in 1818, the cove was a thriving, self-supporting community for more than 100 years. Original log homes still stand today. Other buildings include smokehouses, cantilevered barns, a blacksmith shop, and corncribs. You'll also find cemeteries with such epitaphs as one from the Civil War that reads BAS SHAW—KILLED BY REBELS. The three historic churches are **Methodist Church, Missionary Baptist Church,** and the oldest, **Primitive Baptist Church,** built in 1827. Included on the loop is the John P. Cable farm, where you'll find the **1868 Cable Mill** still in operation. Cades Cove offers several nature trails; the shortest in the Cable Mill area consists of a half-mile round-trip.

After you complete the Cades Cove loop, head toward the **Sugarlands Visitor Center** to the Newfound Gap Road to recross the park, this time taking advantage of the numerous pulloff areas dotting the roadside. At most of them, you'll find Quiet Walkways—short paths created for moments of solitude in which visitors can experience nature. Don't be discouraged if a pulloff is full, because another one will appear within a mile.

SPORTS & OUTDOOR PURSUITS

BACKPACKING   Backpacking enthusiasts are required to obtain permits from one of the ranger stations, the Oconaluftee and Sugarlands visitor centers, or the Cades Cove Campground Kiosk, before setting out. These permits are used to keep track of visitors for safety reasons, as well as to prevent popular campsites from becoming overcrowded. Campers are allowed to use only designated campsites and shelters. You will be fined if you're caught camping outside one of these sites. A rationing program limits the number of campers at 13 of the 80 campsites and at all 18 of the shelters. Plan your route in advance to determine whether you'll need any of these designated areas. The maximum number of people allowed in a hiking group is eight.

You must obtain shelter and ration campsite (aka, those with electrical and water hookups) permits in person before departing on any given trail, calling for permits between 8am and 6pm only. Stays are limited to 1 night at shelters and 3 nights at campsites. Tents are not allowed in the shelter areas or along the Appalachian Trail. Shelters are located on the Appalachian Trail and at Laurel Gap, Kephart Prong, Mount LeConte, Rich Mountain, and Scott Gap. Permits for nonration (those without electrical and water hookups) sites can be obtained upon arrival. For more information, call ✆ 865/436-1200 from 9am to 1pm daily, visit www.nps.gov/grsm, or write to **Great Smoky Mountains National Park,** Attn.: Backcountry Office, 107 Park Headquarters Rd., Gatlinburg, TN 37738.

BIKING   Bicycles are not allowed on the trails, so areas for cyclists are limited. You can ride on roads, but traffic can be very heavy and the inclines quite steep. Try the 11-mile **Cades Cove Loop** from May to mid-October on Saturday mornings before 10am, when it's closed to all automobile traffic. Another possibility is the **Cataloochee Valley.** From April to October, you can rent a bicycle from the **Cades Cove Campground Store** (✆ 865/448-9034) for $4 to $6 daily 9am to 7pm.

BIRDING   With more than 200 species of birds in the park, you should be able to spot a few on your ramblings. The higher elevations support bird life that's typical of parts of northern New England. Also to be seen in the high country along mountain crags are falcons, hawks, and ravens. Throughout the park, you may spot grouse and wild turkey, although the latter are quite shy of people.

FISHING   The park contains more than 700 miles of streams suitable for fishing. Fishers must have a valid North Carolina or Tennessee state fishing license, which can be purchased in the gateway towns at sporting-goods stores. In North Carolina, anyone 16 or older must have a license. Trout stamps are not required. Fishing is permitted from sunrise to sunset year-round, although the optimum seasons are spring and fall. Popular fishing areas include **Abrams Creek, Big Creek, Fontana Lake,** and **Little River.** The limit is five fish, with the exception of brook trout, which are illegal to possess.

GOLF   Named as one of *Southern Living*'s Top 50 Golf Courses, the **Maggie Valley Golf Course** is located on U.S. 19, 35 miles east of Asheville (✆ 828/926-6013; www.maggievalleyclub.com). A par-72, 6,377-yard course, it offers 18 holes. Greens fees range from $45 to $80, including cart.

HIKING With over 800 miles of **hiking trails** (www.allthesmokies.com/hiking_trails.html), the park offers visitors of all fitness levels a chance to experience the great outdoors firsthand (see "Nature Trails," below). Before setting out, make sure to check the weather forecast for the duration of your trip, be it a few hours or a few days. If you find yourself caught in a thunderstorm, make sure to avoid all open areas to lessen your chance of being struck by lightning. Carry rain gear because sudden storms are normal for this area, and leave a copy of your itinerary at one of the ranger stations or visitor centers in case you become lost or injured.

Following are a few of the most popular trails that the park offers:

Indian Creek Falls Trail has an elevation gain of 100 feet and begins at Deep Creek Road near the Deep Creek Campground. The 1.5-mile flat trail leads to the 60-foot-high Indian Creek Falls. Physical level: moderate.

Laurel Falls Trail ★ is the most popular waterfall trail in the park, with an elevation gain of 200 feet. You travel 1.25 miles to the falls from the Laurel Falls parking area, a few miles from the Sugarlands Visitor Center. It's paved and relatively flat. Physical level: easy.

Abrams Falls Trail has an elevation gain of 340 feet. You travel 2.5 miles from the Abrams Falls parking lot at the west end of Cades Cove Loop Road to a 20-foot-high waterfall. The trail follows a clear stream and is relatively flat. Physical level: moderate.

Alum Cave Bluffs Trail is deceiving because it starts off easy and grows more difficult. The elevation gain is 2,800 feet, and the distance is 10 miles round-trip. The first 1.5 miles take you to Arch Rock, which contains a tunnel created by erosion. Then the trail becomes steeper and takes you to the 100-foot-high Alum Cave Bluffs. The last leg of the trail is quite steep, and many hikers find it necessary to use trailside cables to maneuver the cliffs. The journey ends at Mount LeConte, which offers one of the park's best views. Begin at Newfound Gap Road at the Alum Cave Bluffs parking lot, 9 miles south of the Sugarlands Visitor Center. Physical level: moderate.

Charlies Bunion Trail is a 4-mile trek to a 1,000-foot-high cliff where the forest was destroyed by fire in 1925. Part of the Appalachian Trail, it offers an elevation gain of 980 feet and begins at the Newfound Gap Overlook parking lot. Physical level: strenuous.

Although the **Boulevard Trail** is the easiest and most popular trail to Mount LeConte, the 16-mile round-trip categorizes it as strenuous for a lot of people. The elevation gain is 1,545 feet. You must travel the Appalachian Trail from Newfound Gap to reach this trail. Physical level: strenuous.

Ramsay Cascades Trail has a total elevation gain of 2,375 feet and is 8 miles long round-trip. This trail also leads to Ramsay Cascades, a 100-foot-high waterfall, the park's highest. From Greenbrier Cove, follow the signs to the trail head. Physical level: strenuous.

The **Appalachian Trail** ★★★ is the most famous trail, stretching from Maine to Georgia, and has 68 of its 2,100 miles situated in the park, following the Smokies ridgeline from east to west almost the entire length of the park. Access points are Newfound Gap, Clingmans Dome, the end of Tenn. 32 just north of the Big Creek Campground, and the Fontana Dam. The most popular section is from Newfound Gap to Charlies Bunion (see Charlies Bunion Trail, above). Elevation gain is 980 feet. Physical level: strenuous.

HORSEBACK RIDING The park offers some of the state's most panoramic scenery for equestrians. All off-trail and cross-country riding, as well as use of trails

Sports & Outdoor Pursuits

GREAT SMOKY MOUNTAINS

designated as foot trails, is prohibited in the park. Horses are restricted from developed campgrounds and picnic areas and on maintained portions of park roadways. Any overnight riders must obtain backcountry permits (see "Backpacking," above). The following five drive-in horse camps offer easy access to designated trails: Anthony Creek, Big Creek, Cataloochee, Round Bottom, and Towstring. You can make reservations 30 days in advance with the **Backcountry Reservations Office** by calling *©* **865/436-1231.**

If you have your own horse, write for an information packet that describes the park's trails, campsites, and regulations. Contact the Superintendent at Great Smoky Mountains National Park, 107 Park Headquarters Rd., Gatlinburg, TN 37738 (*©* **865/436-1200**).

Horses can be rented for $20 an hour April to October. Ask for details at the individual concessions within the park at **Cades Cove** (*©* **865/448-6286**), **Smokemont Riding Stable** (*©* **828/497-2373;** www.smokemontridingstable.com), **Smoky Mountain Riding Stables** (*©* **865/436-3535**), and **Smoky Mountains Riding Stables,** U.S. 321 (*©* **865/436-5634;** www.smokymountainridingstables. com). The park service requires that a guide accompany all rental treks.

NATURE TRAILS   Self-guided nature trails offer even couch potatoes an opportunity to commune with nature. These trails are staked and keyed to pamphlets with descriptions of points of interest along the way. You can obtain a keyed pamphlet from one of the visitor centers or stands at the trail heads. There are about a dozen such trails, ranging in length from a third of a mile to 6 miles. All offer easy walks through peaceful surroundings.

WHITE-WATER RAFTING ★★   Starting at the Waterville Power Plant, a 5-mile stretch of the Pigeon River has 10 rapids and offers some of the most challenging white-water rafting in the South. Water for rafting is released by the Carolina Power & Light Company. **Rafting in the Smokies** rafts both the Pigeon and the Nantahala rivers. A trip on the Pigeon costs $39 per person, but only $18 per person on the Nantahala. For reservations and details, contact the company's central office in Gatlinburg, Tennessee (*©* **800/776-7238** or 865/436-5008; www.raftinginthe smokies.com).

WILDLIFE-WATCHING   Your chances for seeing wildlife are best in the spring, summer, and fall. Mammals are the main interest for many park visitors. As in all national parks, native wildlife is protected by federal law. Printed material, available at the visitor centers, can provide additional information. For your safety as well as the protection of the wildlife, do *not* tease, harass, feed, or approach any wild animal, and be especially cautious when encountering mothers with their young.

The best-known park mammal is the black bear, which has been known to stop traffic—a situation that park officials try to keep from happening because bears can become too used to humans. If this happens, bears are relocated to other, less-traveled areas of the park. When bears lose their innate fear of humans, they become more susceptible to poachers. Visitors should heed the rules about bears and the warnings given out by park authorities.

Frequently sighted smaller mammals include cottontail rabbits, squirrels, and woodchucks (groundhogs). Mammals that are seldom seen are raccoons, skunks, opossums, weasels, bobcats, red and gray foxes, mink, and beavers.

The park is home to at least 23 varieties of snakes. The poisonous ones are timber rattlesnakes and copperheads. If you stay on the trails and away from warm rocky slopes, abandoned buildings, and stone fences, you should have no close encounters. These snakes are not aggressive and generally stay away from areas used by people. Among the nonpoisonous snakes, the most common are the Eastern garter and Northern water snakes. Other varieties include the Northern ringneck, the Eastern king snake, and the Northern black racer.

CAMPING

The park contains 10 campgrounds with picnic tables, fire grills, cold running water, and flush toilets, but they don't have showers or water and electrical hookups (see "Backpacking," above). There are three major campgrounds. **Cades Cove** (151 sites) features a camp store, bike rentals, a disposal station, wood for sale, and naturalist programs held in the small amphitheater. **Elkmont** (220 sites) offers a disposal station, firewood for sale, vending machines, and a telephone. **Smokemont** (142 sites) has a disposal station and firewood for sale.

Reservations (© **800/365-CAMP** [2267]; www.recreation.gov) can be made up to 5 months in advance online or daily from 10am to 10pm. The campgrounds are full on weekends beginning in April and daily from July to October. The busiest months are July and October, and you should make reservations at least 4 weeks in advance. Mid-May to October, there's a 7-day maximum stay, and the charge is $29 per day for two. November to mid-May, with limited sites available, the maximum stay is 14 days, and the charge is $14 to $25 per day. The seven smaller campgrounds, open mid-May to October, are along the boundaries of the park and are $14 per day.

WHERE TO STAY

In the Park

The park's only lodging, **LeConte Lodge** ★ (© **865/429-5704** for reservations; www.lecontelodge.com), is on the top of Mount LeConte. The lodge is very back to basics: It has no electricity, TV, phone, or indoor plumbing, although there are four flush toilets in outhouses. The only means of access to the lodge is by hiking. The shortest and steepest route is the Alum Cave Bluffs Trail (see "Hiking," above), a 5.5-mile one-way trip. The lodge offers private bedrooms in cabins with a shared living room, as well as private cabins. Prices range from $60 to $79 per person daily. Adults pay another $37 per person for breakfast and dinner, and children ages 4 to 12 are charged $25. Reservations are difficult to come by if you don't make them in October for the following year. The lodge is open from the last week in March to late November. No credit cards are accepted.

Bryson City

The Chalet Inn On 22 acres of forested mountainsides and ridges with trails, this inn offers the blend of rusticity and traditional comforts of an alpine *gasthaus*. George and Hanneke Ware own this inn, which offers uniquely decorated rooms with balconies or porches. Although the rooms have no phones, you have access to cordless phones that you're welcome to use in your room. You can view Doubletop Mountain from the Chalet's Great Room, and if the window is open, you can hear the sounds of the babbling brook that winds its way around the inn. On wintry evenings, you can enjoy one of the books from the inn's library while sitting in front of the fire in the stone fireplace. The grounds include lawn games and a picnic area, as well as hiking trails. From mid-June to mid-August, only children 8 and older are accepted. During the rest of the year, children 12 and older are accepted. A whirlpool is available in the Romantic suite.

285 Lone Oak Dr., Dillsboro, NC 28725 (U.S. 74/441 btw. Bryson City and Dillsboro). © **800/789-8024** or 828/586-0251. www.chaletinn.com. 6 units. $96–$145 double; $160–$188 suite. Rates include full breakfast. AE, DISC, MC, V. Closed Jan 2–Mar. No children 7 and under from Labor Day to Jan 1; no children 11 and under in winter. **Amenities:** Breakfast room; lounge; privileges at nearby country club. *In room:* A/C, no phone, Wi-Fi (free).

The Folkestone Inn ★   Originally a 1920s farmhouse, the Folkestone Inn, which bills itself as a place to escape and explore, has the benefit of location. The structure is framed by a grove of Norway spruce trees, with a mountain stream serving as a boundary with the wilderness. Guests can explore the park and play golf at a nearby course. Asheville and other towns are just an hour's drive away. Rustic is the most apt term to describe the rooms, which are furnished with antiques, including the beds (some have queen-size beds). Each unit has its own bathroom with a shower and an old-fashioned claw-foot tub. The upstairs rooms have balconies with mountain views; the downstairs rooms have flagstone floors and pressed-tin ceilings. Breakfast is the only meal served, and what you get is a little less common than your standard eggs and bacon; you might see eggs Benedict when you sit down at the table. Dinner is now available for groups of eight or more for $30 per person. Dinner reservations must be made in advance.

101 Folkestone Rd., Bryson City, NC 28713. © **888/812-3385** or 828/488-2730. Fax 828/488-0722. www.folkestone.com. 10 units. $99–$163 double. Additional person $20 per night. Rates include full breakfast. AE, DISC, MC, V. No children 10 and under. **Amenities:** Breakfast room; lounge. *In room:* A/C, hair dryer, no phone.

Fryemont Inn ★★   Listed on the National Register of Historic Places, this inn has been in operation since 1923. Amos Frye, head of a timber empire in the late 1800s, built it of the best chestnut, oak, and maple in the region. The exterior is covered with the bark of huge poplar trees, as sturdy today as when the strips were first cut. Sue and George Brown are the owners of the inn, which the *Atlanta Journal-Constitution* cited as being "a rustic, bark-covered architectural masterpiece." Each of the chestnut-paneled rooms is individually decorated, and some bathrooms contain old-fashioned pedestal tubs; all have showers. The large rooms have country touches such as homespun curtains. The cottage suites, open year-round, are housed in a stone structure. Each suite has a loft bedroom overlooking a living area with a fireplace, TV, and wet bar. There is also a secluded and well-furnished cabin near the pool. Meals are served in the dining room in the main lodge, open April 14 through October 29. The lobby has a TV, two game tables, and a fireplace that can burn 8-foot logs, and the porch has rocking chairs. Closely supervised children are allowed in the main lodge, but the cottage suites are for adults only.

Fryemont St. (PO Box 459), Bryson City, NC 28713. © **800/845-4879** or 828/488-2159. www.fryemont inn.com. 41 units. $95–$180 double; $175–$260 suite; $75–$245 cottage; $130–$270 cabin. Additional person $20–$40. Rates include breakfast and dinner. DISC, MC, V. Main lodge closed Dec to mid-Mar. **Amenities:** Restaurant; bar; outdoor pool. *In room:* A/C, no phone.

Lloyd's on the River   This inn offers clean, decent rooms in a relaxed atmosphere, with comfortable furnishings and wood paneling or tasteful wallpaper. No meals are served, although the grounds contain picnic tables along the river and outdoor grills. With its columned porches accented by hanging plants and rocking chairs, the look is that of an oversize country home—or, as one guest stated, "It's like staying at a B&B without the breakfast." The owner, Bob Starks, offers warm hospitality and can create a personalized trail guide for you.

U.S. 19 (PO Box 429), Bryson City, NC 28713. © **888/611-6872** or 828/488-3767. Fax 828/488-9020. www.lloydsontheriver.com. 21 units. Winter $49–$69 double; summer $79–$109 double. DISC, MC, V. **Amenities:** Lounge; outdoor pool. *In room:* A/C, TV, Wi-Fi (free).

Dillsboro & Balsam

Balsam Mountain Inn ★★   Only a 5- to 7-minute drive from Dillsboro, this long-established inn is on the National Register of Historic Places. It's set in a drop-dead-gorgeous part of the mountains, overlooking the little town of Balsam. For those who want to escape the curse of cheapskate roadside motels, this is the place. Lying just a quarter of a mile from the Blue Ridge Parkway, the inn was constructed in a neo-classical style, with a mansard roof and wraparound porches; it welcomed its first guests in 1908. Completely restored, it offers comfortably furnished and well-maintained rooms, with either a claw-foot tub or a shower. The more expensive and much better "bedsitting" rooms—minisuites—are more spacious, each opening onto mountain views. Suites range from cozy, romantic havens for couples to units suitable for families. Grace notes include a piano in the dining room, a library, a lobby with fireplaces, and 24 acres of trails.

68 Seven Springs Dr., Balsam, NC 28707. © **800/224-9498** or 828/456-9498. www.balsaminn.com. 50 units. $145 double; $165–$229 suite. Rates include breakfast. AE, DISC, MC, V. **Amenities:** Restaurant. *In room:* No phone, Wi-Fi (free).

Jarrett House ★★ ♥   One of the oldest inns in western North Carolina, this 1884 hostelry goes back to the days of the horse and buggy. It is on the National Register of Historic Places. Expect home-style food such as hot biscuits served with honey, affordable prices, and an old-time ambience (rockers on the front porch) where guests can practice the lost art of loafing. Rooms are handsomely furnished and come with neat, well-maintained bathrooms. The on-site restaurant is open to the public daily April to December.

100 Haywood St., Dillsboro, NC 28725. © **800/972-5623** or 828/586-0265. www.jarretthouse.com. 22 units. $80–$90 per person. MC, V. **Amenities:** Restaurant. *In room:* A/C, no phone.

Olde Towne Inn   This inn is a restored 1878 home in the heart of Dillsboro. The rooms have a country flair and are tastefully appointed with antiques and ceiling fans. The inn has been referred to as "a comfortable old home place"—ideally located near shops, restaurants, and the train station. You'll find many guests enjoying the breezes that roll off the mountainside as they rock on the front porch. In the morning, you're greeted by the aroma of a freshly prepared breakfast that's sure to fill you up. Children 10 and older are welcome.

364 Haywood Rd. (PO Box 485), Dillsboro, NC 28725. © **888/528-8840** or 828/586-3461. www.dillsboro-oldetowne.com. 4 units. $95–$135 double; $120–$155 suite. Rates include full breakfast. AE, DC, MC, V. No children 9 and under. **Amenities:** Breakfast room; lounge. *In room:* A/C, TV, hair dryer.

Squire Watkins Inn   A casual lodging set in peaceful surroundings on 3 acres of gardens, this 1880s inn touts itself as "a place to enjoy the sunrise and fireflies, peaches from the garden and eggs from the farm." That's right. Tom and Emma Wertenberger, who bought and restored this old home in 1983, make their guests feel right at home, providing helpful advice on places to go and activities not to miss. Each morning, you're greeted with freshly baked breads, homemade casseroles, eggs from

The Great Smoky Mountains Railroad

Among the most popular attractions in the mountains are year-round scenic railroad excursions. For schedules and reservations, call ℭ **800/872-4681** or 828/586-8811 or visit www.gsmr.com. This **scenic train journey ★★★**, an exercise in nostalgia, takes you across valleys and river gorges and through tunnels. In all, there are 53 miles of track, two tunnels, and 25 bridges. A variety of round-trip excursions are offered, departing from depots in both Dillsboro and Bryson City. The trip takes from 4 to 4½ hours. Prices are $49 to $61 for adults, $31 to $35 for children 3 to 12, and free for children 2 and under. There is also a Gourmet Dinner Train ride for $89 to $115 per person.

a farm just down the road, and fresh fruits and juices, all served on sparkling china and silver. Rooms are furnished with period antiques and have well-maintained bathrooms.

U.S. 441 and Haywood Rd. (PO Box 430), Dillsboro, NC 28725. ℭ **800/586-2429** or 828/586-5244. 5 units. $115–$125 double; $135 suite; $150 cottage. Double and suite rates include full breakfast. No credit cards. No children 11 and under. **Amenities:** Breakfast room; lounge. *In room:* A/C, no phone.

Fontana Dam

Fontana Village Resort On January 1, 1942, 24 days after the attack on Pearl Harbor, the Tennessee Valley Authority (TVA) got permission to build a dam 480 feet high to produce critically needed hydroelectric energy. This led to the birth of a village to support the dam workers and their families, including a school, a 50-bed hospital, churches, and space to play. This village has become the largest and most complete resort in the Great Smoky Mountains. Choose a room at the inn, a cabin with a kitchenette, or a campsite. (There are 20 campsites, 10 with hookups; the cost is $25 a night without hookup and $35 with hookup.)

Activities abound for every taste: biking (30 trails), horseback riding, cookouts, square dancing, crafts classes, mountain-bike races, and boating.

N.C. 28 (PO Box 68), Fontana Dam, NC 28733. ℭ **800/849-2258** or 828/498-2211. Fax 828/498-2345. www.fontanavillage.com. 64 units, 135 cabins. $59–$199 double; $99–$249 cabin. AE, DISC, MC, V. **Amenities:** Restaurant; exercise room; 3 outdoor pools; sauna; 4 tennis courts (lit); Wi-Fi (free). *In room:* A/C, TV, hair dryer, kitchenette (in cabins).

Maggie Valley

The Abbey Inn On the northern slope of Setzer Mountain, this hostelry has a 1950s feel and offers views up to 5 miles away. Owners Mike and Natalie Nelson deliver friendly hospitality and advice on what to see in the area. The rooms are small yet reasonably comfortable and contain refinished furniture specifically made for the inn. Some rooms have kitchenettes with small refrigerators, stoves, and microwaves. Rooms have front porches with great views where you can while away the hours. The 2-acre grounds boast patio swings, a picnic area, and grills.

6375 Soco Rd. (U.S. 19), Maggie Valley, NC 28751. ℭ **800/545-5853** or 828/926-1188. Fax 828/926-2389. www.abbeyinn.com. 20 units. Apr–Oct $49–$99 double. DISC, MC, V. Closed Nov–Mar. **Amenities:** Lounge. *In room:* TV, kitchenette (in some), Wi-Fi (free).

Cataloochee Ranch ★★ On the border of Great Smoky Mountains National Park, this 1,000-acre ranch offers a wide range of activities. The property includes a main lodge with six double rooms; the Silver Belle, containing the remaining rooms; and six cabins, each of which is rustic and individual. All units contain well-kept bathrooms with tub/shower combinations. One small house is suitable for four. Meals are served family style, and very few people ever leave hungry. The property includes a trout pond for fishing and trails for hiking.

119 Ranch Dr., Maggie Valley, NC 28751. © **800/868-1401** or 828/926-1401. Fax 828/926-9249. www.cataloocheeranch.com. 25 units. Apr–Nov $205–$247 double; $247–$320 cabin. Rates include breakfast and dinner. AE, MC, V. Closed Dec–Mar. **Amenities:** Dining room; lounge; outdoor pool; tennis court (lit). *In room:* TV (in some), kitchenette (in some), no phone.

Maggie Valley Resort and Country Club Opening onto panoramic vistas, this resort offers a wide variety of activities to accommodate the whole family. The spacious rooms come with a rather standard decor. The premium ones overlook the front 9 holes of the golf course; the villas open onto the back 9. Greens fees for the golf course range from $53 to $58. A dining room serves steak, seafood, and an array of international dishes. Live entertainment is featured Wednesday to Saturday evenings.

1819 Country Club Rd. (near the intersection of U.S. 19 and U.S. 276), Maggie Valley, NC 28751. © **800/438-3861** or 828/926-1616. Fax 828/926-2906. www.maggievalleyclub.com. 75 units. Apr–Oct $249–$299 double, $329 villa; Nov–Mar $249 double, $269 villa. Golf packages available. AE, DISC, MC, V. **Amenities:** Restaurant; bar; 18-hole golf course; exercise room; outdoor pool. *In room:* A/C, TV, hair dryer, kitchenette (in some), Wi-Fi (free).

The Swag ★★ Just a 30-mile drive west of Asheville puts you into Appalachian High Country, the setting for one of North Carolina's finest inns. With direct park access from the inn, the Swag is our best recommendation as a base for touring the Great Smoky Mountains. Hand-hewn logs and local fieldstone went into the construction, which led to luxurious rooms (some in log cabins), with rustic beamed vaulted ceilings and balconies in most cases opening onto panoramic mountain views from a 5,000-foot ridge. Barn-siding lines one room, a copper soaking tub is installed in another, and, in most rooms, a blazing stone fireplace keeps the chill at bay on cool mountain nights. Even though they are part-time Manhattanites, hosts Dan and Deener Matthews put a capital "S" in "Southern hospitality." Their hideaway lies on 250 acres of scenic property, with trails in all directions. Gourmet-oriented, four-course meals are served during social group dinners that focus on seasonal ingredients, including some from the inn's own gardens.

2300 Swag Rd., Waynesville, NC 28785. © **800/789-7672** or 828/926-0430. Fax 828/926-2036. www.theswag.com. 15 units. $400–$630 double; $625–$750 suite. Additional person $100 extra; children 7 and under $60 extra. 10% tax and 15% service fee extra. Rates include all meals. Guests bring their own alcohol. AE, DISC, MC, V. Closed mid-Nov to Apr. **Amenities:** Restaurant. *In room:* Fridge, hair dryer, Wi-Fi (free).

Timberwolf Creek Bed & Breakfast ★★ 🎁 This is a well-run, welcoming place set in one of the most scenic spots in the area. A stream runs through the middle of the property between the two buildings, tumbling down the mountainside in a series of little waterfalls. The setting amid old trees lends a kind of rainforest-like atmosphere. Bedrooms are good size and stylishly decorated, with many homelike touches. Sounds of the nearby creek set the stage for romance or relaxation. Each accommodation has a private deck by the stream. Units vary, from a fireplace suite, or else a skylight suite, to a four-poster room. A well-furnished and most comfortable vacation cabin is also rented, as is a three-bedroom house. The breakfast is one of the best in the area, from the homemade buttermilk biscuits with honey butter to the *chapelure* filled with berries, nuts, granola, and spices, and served with whipped cream and maple syrup.

391 Johnson Branch, Maggie Valley, NC 28751. ℂ **888/525-4218** or 828/926-2608. www.timberwolf creek.com. 4 units. $195–$225 double; $275–$325 suite; 2-bedroom cottage $350 for 4; 3-bedroom house $450 for 8. Rates include breakfast. AE, DISC, MC, V. **Amenities:** Breakfast room. *In room:* TV/ DVD/VCR, CD player.

Walland (Tennessee)

Blackberry Farm ★★★   The best way to take in the mist-shrouded panorama might be from a rocking chair on the terrace of this hotel on a 4,200-acre estate in the Great Smoky Mountains. Rated by Zagat in 2004 as the best small hotel in America, the luxury property evokes an English manor house, with guest rooms divided among two stone-built structures and a colony of cottages in the woods. Luxuries abound in the elegant antiques-filled bedrooms, with feather beds and wood-burning fireplaces. Modernity is not ignored either, as evoked by the whirlpool soaking tubs. The cuisine is renowned, much of the produce coming from the hotel's own farm.

1471 W. Millers Cove Rd., Walland, TN 37886. (The estate lies at the northwestern top of the park, reached along the Foothills Pkwy. over the state line in Tenn.) ℂ **800/648-4252** or 865/984-8166. Fax 865/681-7753. http://blackberryfarm.com. 44 units. $995–$1,995 double. Rates include all meals. AE, MC, V. **Amenities:** Restaurant; outdoor pool; room service; spa; 4 tennis courts (lit). *In room:* A/C, TV, hair dryer.

WHERE TO DINE

Forget the tourist brochures. Some of the worst restaurants in the South are in the towns that cater to the millions of visitors to the Smokies. Fast-food joints are everywhere, and many a cook's idea of a good dinner is a frozen hamburger slapped on a grill. Some good places with country cooking do exist, but they can be hard to find. Here's a representative sampling to get you going.

Bryson City

Nantahala Village Restaurant SOUTHERN   The food at this family-style haven ranges from down-home favorites like mountain trout, fried chicken, and country ham to more eclectic and lighter varieties that reflect an up-to-date approach to dining. Of the latter, dig into wild forest pasta, sautéed shrimp, and nightly vegetarian specialties. Many guests arrive early to enjoy the sunsets over the Smoky Mountains through the large windows. In cool weather, a fireplace burns brightly. Homemade soups (such as corn chowder or lentil) and homemade pies and cakes round out the wide variety of meats, poultry, and fish offered as main courses. As one local habitué informed us, "This place serves portions big enough to satisfy the biggest, hungriest bear."

9400 Hwy. 19. ℂ **828/488-2826.** Breakfast $6–$12; main courses $6–$12 lunch, $16–$26 dinner. DC, MC, V. Daily 7:30–9:30am, 11am–2pm (May 24–Sept 1), and 5:30–9pm. Closed Dec 1–Mar 8.

Relia's Garden ☺ AMERICAN/SOUTHERN   Part of the Nantahala Outdoor Center, this lodgelike place is worth the trip out of town. Hearty food and a helpful staff make it a family favorite, with a kids' menu and a policy of doggie bagging. The menu is a bit overfamiliar, but time-tested favorites include rainbow trout and beef kabobs. Everybody likes the baked Cajun catfish. Vegetarian meals are also available. In fair weather, try for a table on the porch. You can "brown bag" your own alcohol if you choose to do so.

U.S. 19 S. (13 miles southwest of the Nantahala Outdoor Center). © **828/488-2175.** Main courses $8–$18. MC, V. Sun–Thurs 5–9pm; Fri–Sat 5–10pm.

Dillsboro

Dillsboro Smokehouse BARBECUE   One of your best bets in town is hickory-flavored mountain barbecue at this smokehouse, 2 blocks down the street from the post office. It's known mainly for its fall-off-the-bones baby back ribs in a peach-flavored sauce. The pork barbecue, served chopped or sliced, has the best flavor, and the smoked brisket of beef is excellent. The chicken, either dark or white meat, can dry out fast when barbecued. Dinners are served with coleslaw, barbecue beans, yams, french fries, and hush puppies (what else?). The restaurant also sells barbecue by the pound to go, in case you've rented a cabin nearby.

403 Haywood St. © **828/586-9556.** Main courses $3.95–$16. AE, DISC, MC, V. May–Oct Mon–Thurs 11am–9pm, Fri–Sat 11am–10pm, Sun 11am–8pm; Nov–Apr Mon–Thurs 11am–8pm, Fri–Sat 11am–9pm, Sun 11am–3pm.

Maggie Valley

Meals can also be booked at the **Swag country inn,** listed above.

J. Arthur's Restaurant ☺ AMERICAN/BEEF   In a classic mountain building, J. Arthur's (which is affiliated with Manero's Restaurant in Palm City, Florida) is an odd name for a Smoky Mountain restaurant. It's a winning choice, however; in fact, it's the best in town. Offering a loft dining area, the restaurant is a family favorite and tailors its menus to diners 12 and under. The kitchen is known for its Gorgonzola cheese salad, which is backed by a choice of prime rib, New York sirloin, broiled filet mignon, and grilled rib-eye. The meat is succulent and very tender (in other words, not the kind that you can purchase in a supermarket). Southerners really know how to cook pork chops, and this joint doesn't diminish that culinary reputation. The menu is limited but quite choice. The fresh North Carolina rainbow trout is delicious.

2843 Soco Rd. (U.S. 19). © **828/926-1817.** Main courses $16–$27. MC, V. Daily 4:30–9pm.

Joey's Pancake House ☺ PANCAKES/SOUTHERN   A popular family dining room for Ma and Pa Kettle and all the kids, this eatery is featured in the book *100 Secrets of the Smokies.* It has been pleasing hungry diners for some 40 years. Pancakes are made according to the chefs' secret formula, featuring such delights as Smoky Mountain blueberry, peanut butter, chocolate chip, pecan, and whole wheat smothered in cinnamon apples. A wide variety of specialty items are offered, including a hash brown casserole, French toast, and savory eggs Benedict. Biscuits are made from scratch and served along with country-sausage gravy, Southern grits, and creamed chipped beef.

4309 Soco Rd. © **828/926-0212.** Reservations not required. Main courses $5–$12; children's menu $2–$2.75. MC, V. Sun–Wed and Fri–Sat 7am–noon.

CHARLESTON

I
f the Old South lives on in South Carolina's Low Country, it positively thrives in Charleston. All our romantic notions of antebellum days—stately homes, courtly manners, gracious hospitality, and, above all, gentle dignity—are facts of every-day life in this old city, in spite of a few scoundrels here and there, from pirates to politicians.

Notwithstanding a history dotted with earthquakes, hurricanes, fires, and Yankee bombardments, Charleston remains one of the best-preserved cities in America's Old South. It boasts 73 pre–Revolutionary War buildings, 136 from the late 18th century and more than 600 built before the 1840s. With its cobblestone streets and horse-drawn carriages, Charleston is a place of visual images and sensory pleasures. Jasmine and wisteria fragrances fill the air, the aroma of she-crab soup (a local favorite) wafts from sidewalk cafes, and antebellum architecture graces the historic cityscape. "No wonder they are so full of themselves," said an envious visitor from Columbia, which may be the state capital but has little of Charleston's style and grace.

In its 2008 reader survey, *Condé Nast Traveler* named Charleston the number-two city to visit in America, which places it ahead of such perennial favorites as New York, Chicago, and Sedona. Visitors are drawn here from all over the world, and it is now quite common to hear German and French spoken.

Does this city have a modern side? Yes, but it's well hidden. Chic shops abound, as do a few supermodern hotels, but Charleston has no skyscrapers. You don't come to Charleston for anything cutting-edge, though. You come to glimpse an earlier, almost-forgotten era.

Many local families still own and live in the homes that their planter ancestors built. Charlestonians manage to maintain a way of life that in many respects has little to do with wealth. The simplest encounter with Charleston natives seems to be invested with a social air, as though the visitor were a valued guest. Yet there are those who detect a certain snobbishness in Charleston—and truth be told, you'd have to stay a few hundred years to be considered an insider here.

ORIENTATION
Getting There

BY PLANE   See "Getting There & Around," in chapter 3. **Charleston International Airport** is in North Charleston on I-26, about 12 miles west of the city. The fixed rate for a taxi from the airport into the city is

$9 per passenger, not to exceed $27 per trip. The airport **shuttle service** (© 843/767-1100; www.chs-airport.com) has a $12 fare. All major car-rental facilities, including Hertz and Avis, are available at the airport. If you're driving, follow the airport-access road to I-26 into the heart of Charleston.

BY CAR The main north-south coastal route, U.S. 17, passes through Charleston; I-26 runs northwest to southeast, ending in Charleston. Charleston is 120 miles southeast of Columbia via I-26 and 98 miles south of Myrtle Beach via U.S. 17.

BY TRAIN Amtrak (© 800/USA-RAIL [872-7245]; www.amtrak.com) trains arrive at 4565 Gaynor Ave., North Charleston.

BY BUS Greyhound (© 800/231-2222; www.greyhound.com) offers regular service to North Charleston, as does **Southeastern Stages** (© 404/591-2750; www.southeasternstages.com). The **bus station** is at 3610 Dorchester Rd. (© 843/744-4247).

Visitor Information

The visitor center for the **Charleston Area Convention and Visitors Bureau (CACVB),** 375 Meeting St., Charleston, SC 29402 (© 800/774-0006 or 843/853-8000; www.charlestoncvb.com), just across from the Charleston Museum, provides maps and brochures, and the helpful staff can also assist you in finding accommodations. Numerous tours depart hourly from the visitors bureau, and restroom facilities, as well as parking, are available. Be sure to allow time to view the 24-minute multi-image presentation *Forever Charleston* (admission $2) and pick up a copy of the visitor's guide. The center is open daily from 8:30am to 5:30pm (closing at 5pm Nov–Feb; closed Christmas Day, New Year's Day, and Thanksgiving Day).

City Layout

Charleston's streets are laid out in an easy-to-follow grid pattern. The main north-south thoroughfares are King, Meeting, and East Bay streets. Tradd, Broad, Queen, and Calhoun streets cross the city from east to west. South of Broad Street, East Bay becomes East Battery.

The CACVB offers wonderful maps that are downloadable from its website (www.charlestoncvb.com), including an activities map showing the streets of the Historic District as well as surrounding areas. You can also pick up free maps at the **Charleston Visitor Center,** 375 Meeting St., at John Street (© 843/853-8000).

Neighborhoods in Brief

The Historic District In 1860, according to one Charlestonian, "South Carolina seceded from the Union, Charleston seceded from South Carolina, and south of Broad Street seceded from Charleston." The city preserves its early years at its southernmost point: the conjunction of the Cooper and Ashley rivers. White Point Gardens, right in the elbow of the two rivers, provide a sort of gateway into this area, where virtually every home is of historic or architectural interest. Between Broad Street and Murray Boulevard (which runs along the south waterfront), you'll find such sightseeing highlights as St. Michael's Episcopal Church, the Edmondston-Alston House, the Heyward-Washington House, Catfish Row, and the Nathaniel Russell House.

Downtown Extending north from Broad Street to Marion Square at the intersection of Calhoun and Meeting streets, this area encloses noteworthy points of interest, good shopping, and a gaggle of historic churches. Just a few of its highlights are the Old City Market, the Dock Street Theatre, Market Hall, the Old Powder Magazine, the

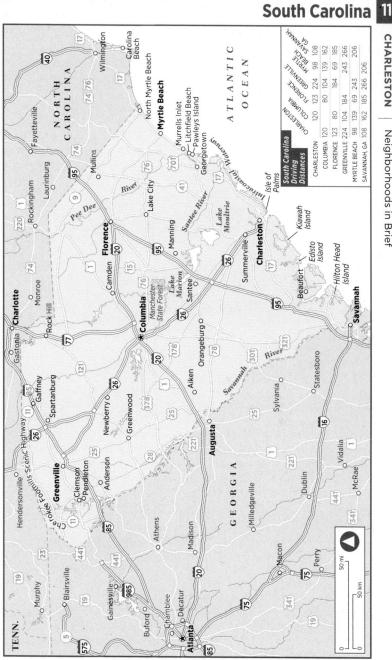

South Carolina Driving Distances	CHARLESTON	COLUMBIA	FLORENCE	GREENVILLE	MYRTLE BEACH	SAVANNAH, GA
CHARLESTON	120	123	224	98	108	
COLUMBIA	120		80	104	139	162
FLORENCE	123	80		184	69	185
GREENVILLE	224	104	184		243	266
MYRTLE BEACH	98	139	69	243		206
SAVANNAH, GA	108	162	185	266	206	

Thomas Elfe Workshop, Congregation Beth Elohim, the French Huguenot Church, and St. John's Church.

Above Marion Square The visitor center is located on Meeting Street north of Calhoun. The Charleston Museum is just across the street, and the Aiken-Rhett Mansion, Joseph Manigault Mansion, and Old Citadel are within easy walking distance in the area bounded by Calhoun Street to the south and Mary Street to the north.

North Charleston Charleston International Airport is at the point at which I-26 and I-526 intersect. This makes North Charleston a Low Country transportation hub. Primarily a residential and industrial community, it lacks the charm of the Historic District. It's the home of the North Charleston Coliseum, the largest indoor entertainment venue in the state.

Mount Pleasant East of the Cooper River, just minutes from the Historic District, this community is worth a detour. Filled with lodgings, restaurants, and some attractions, it encloses a historic district along the riverfront known as the Old Village, which is on the National Register of Historic Places. Its major attraction is Patriots Point, the world's largest naval and maritime museum; it's also the home of the aircraft carrier *Yorktown*.

Outlying Areas Within easy reach of the city are Boone Hall Plantation and the public beaches at Sullivan's Island and Isle of Palms. Head west across the Ashley River Bridge to pay tribute to Charleston's birth at Charles Towne Landing and visit such highlights as Drayton Hall, Magnolia Gardens, and Middleton Place.

GETTING AROUND

BY BUS City bus fare is $1.50, and service is available from 5:35am to 10pm (until 1am to North Charleston). Between 9am and 3:30pm and after 6pm, seniors pay 60¢. The fare for persons with disabilities (all day) is 40¢. Exact change is required. For route and schedule information, call © **843/724-7420** or visit www.ridecarta.com.

BY TROLLEY The **Downtown Area Shuttle (DASH)** is the quickest way to get around the main downtown area daily. The fare is $1.50, and you'll need exact change. A day pass costs $5. For hours and routes, call © **843/724-7420.**

BY TAXI Leading taxi companies are **Yellow Cab** (© **843/577-6565**) and **Safety Cab** (© **843/722-4066**). Each company has its own fare structure. Within the city, however, fares seldom exceed $6 or $12. You must call for a taxi; there are no pickups on the street.

BY CAR If you're staying in the city proper, park your car and save it for day trips to outlying areas. You'll find **parking facilities** scattered about the city, with some of the most convenient at Hutson Street and Calhoun Street, both of which are near Marion Square; on King Street between Queen and Broad; and on George Street between King and Meeting. If you can't find space on the street to park, the two most centrally located **garages** are on Wentworth Street (© **843/724-7383**) and at Concord and Cumberland (© **843/724-7387**). The fee is $16 all day.

Leading car-rental companies are **Avis Rent A Car** (© **800/331-1212** or 843/767-7030; www.avis.com), **Budget Car and Truck Rentals** (© **800/527-0700,** 843/767-7051 at the airport, 760-1410 in North Charleston, or 577-5195 downtown; www.budget.com), and **Hertz** (© **800/654-3131** or 843/767-4554; www.hertz.com).

American Express The local American Express office is at 10 Carriage Lane (© **843/556-9051;** www. abbottandhilltravel.com), open Monday to Friday 9am to 5pm.

Car Rentals See "Getting Around," above.

Climate See "When to Go," in chapter 3.

Dentist Consult **Atlantic Dental Association,** 61 West Building, Ste. 105 (© **800/310-1292,** ext. 2, or 843/356-3838; www. charlestonsfinest.com).

Doctor For a physician referral or 24-hour emergency-room treatment, contact **Roper Hospital,** 316 Calhoun St. (© **843/724-2000;** www.ropersaint francis.com), or **Doctor's Care** (© **843/556-5585;** www.doctorscare.com) for the names of walk-in clinics.

Emergencies In an emergency, dial © **911.** If the situation isn't life threatening, call © **843/577-7070** for the fire department and © **843/577-7077** for the police.

Eyeglass Repair Try **Jackson Davenport Vision,** 379 King St. (© **866/228-8430** or 843/722-4416; www.jacksondavenport vision.com), open Monday to Friday 9am to 5:30pm and Saturday 9am to 5pm.

Hospitals Local hospitals operating 24-hour emergency rooms include **AMI East Cooper Community Hospital,** 2000 Hospital Dr., Mount Pleasant (© **843/881-0100;** www. eastcoopermedctr.com), and **Medical University of South Carolina,** 171 Ashley Ave. (© **843/792-2300;** www.musc.edu). For medical emergencies, call © **911.**

Newspapers & Magazines The *Post and Courier* is the local daily.

Pharmacies Try **CVS Drugs,** 1603 Hwy. 17 N. (© **843/971-0764**), open Monday to Saturday from 8am to 10pm and on Sunday from 10am to 8pm.

Post Office The main post office is at 83 Broad St. (© **843/577-0688**), open Monday to Friday from 9am to 5pm.

Safety Downtown Charleston is well lighted and patrolled throughout the night to ensure public safety. People can generally walk about downtown at night without fear of violence.

Taxes South Carolina has a 6% sales tax. Charleston tacks a 6% accommodations tax (room or occupancy) onto your hotel bill and 7% on food.

Toilets These are available throughout the downtown area, including at Broad and Meeting streets, at Queen and Church streets, on Market Street between Meeting and Church streets, and at other clearly marked strategic points in the historic and downtown districts.

Transit Information Contact the **Charleston Area Convention Visitor Reception & Transportation Center,** 375 Meeting St. (© **843/853-8000;** www.charlestoncvb. com).

Weather Call © **843/744-3207** for an update.

WHERE TO STAY

Charleston has many of the best historic inns in America, surpassing even those of Savannah. Hotels and motels are priced in direct ratio to their proximity to the 789-acre Historic District; if prices in the center are too high for your budget, find a place west of the Ashley River, and drive into town for sightseeing. In the last decade, the restoration of inns and hotels in Charleston has been phenomenal, although it's slowing somewhat. Charleston ranks among the top cities of America for hotels of charm and character.

Bed-and-breakfast accommodations range from historic homes to carriage houses to simple cottages, and they're located in virtually every section of the city. For details and reservations, contact **Historic Charleston Bed and Breakfast,** 57 Broad St., Charleston, SC 29401 (℃ **800/743-3583** or 843/722-6606; www.historiccharleston bedandbreakfast.com; Mon–Fri 9am–5pm).

During the Spring Festival of Houses and the Spoleto Festival, rates go up, and owners charge pretty much what the market will bear. Advance reservations are essential at those times.

In a city that has rooms of so many shapes and sizes in the same historic building, classifying hotels by price is difficult. Price often depends on the room itself. Some expensive hotels may, in fact, have many moderately priced rooms. Moderately priced hotels, on the other hand, may have special rooms that are quite expensive. When booking a hotel, ask about package plans—deals are most often granted to those who are staying 3 days or more.

The downside regarding all these inns of charm and grace is that they are among the most expensive in this tri-state guide. Staying at an inn or B&B in the Historic District is one of the reasons to go to Charleston and can do more to evoke the elegance of the city than almost anything else. Innkeepers and B&B owners know this all too well and charge accordingly, especially in the summer season.

If you simply can't afford a stay at one of these historic inns, you can confine your consumption of Charleston to dining in the old city and sightseeing and, at night, retire to one of the many clean, comfortable—and, yes, utterly dull—chain motels on the outskirts. See the most representative samples under our "Inexpensive" category, later in this chapter.

By and large, the double rooms in the recommended hotels and inns below have private bathrooms with tub/shower combinations, unless otherwise noted.

Very Expensive

Charleston Place Hotel ★★★ Charleston's premier hostelry, an Orient Express Property, is an eight-story landmark in the Historic District that looks like a postmodern French château. It's big-time, uptown, glossy, and urban—at least, one former visitor, Prince Charles, thought so. Governors and prime ministers from around the world, as well as members of Fortune 500 companies, even visiting celebs such as Mel Gibson, prefer to stay here instead of at one of the more intimate B&Bs. Guest rooms are among the most spacious and handsomely furnished in town—stately, modern, and maintained in state-of-the-art condition. This hotel represents the New South at its most confident, a stylish giant in a district of B&Bs and small converted inns. Acres of Italian marble grace the place, leading to plush guest rooms with decor inspired by colonial Carolina. The deluxe restaurant, **Charleston Grill,** is recommended in the "Where to Dine" section, later in this chapter. A cafe provides a more casual option.

205 Meeting St., Charleston, SC 29401. ℃ **888/635-2350** or 843/722-4900. Fax 843/722-0728. www. charlestonplacehotel.com. 440 units. $235–$590 double; $285–$880 suite. Seasonal packages available. AE, DC, DISC, MC, V. Parking $14. **Amenities:** 2 restaurants, including Charleston Grill (see review, p. 252); bar; exercise room; indoor/outdoor pool; room service; sauna; spa. *In room:* A/C, TV, hair dryer, kitchenette (in some), minibar, Wi-Fi (free).

Market Pavilion Hotel ★ The hotel evokes old-time Charleston so effectively that virtually everyone is amazed that the structure is from 2003. With only 66 rooms, it's defined as a classy boutique hotel with a spectacularly attractive bistro, **Grill**

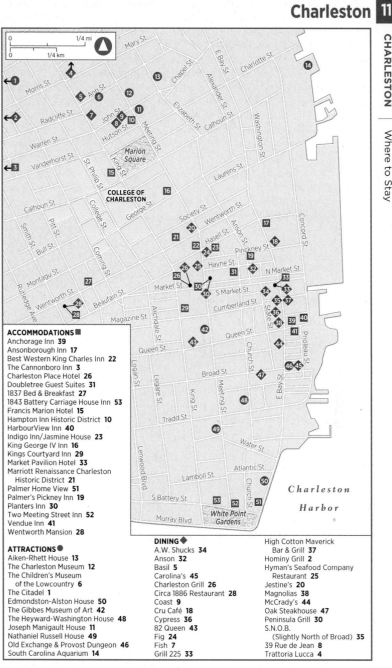

ACCOMMODATIONS ■
Anchorage Inn **39**
Ansonborough Inn **17**
Best Western King Charles Inn **22**
The Cannonboro Inn **3**
Charleston Place Hotel **26**
Doubletree Guest Suites **31**
1837 Bed & Breakfast **27**
1843 Battery Carriage House Inn **53**
Francis Marion Hotel **15**
Hampton Inn Historic District **10**
HarbourView Inn **40**
Indigo Inn/Jasmine House **23**
King George IV Inn **16**
Kings Courtyard Inn **29**
Market Pavilion Hotel **33**
Marriott Renaissance Charleston
   Historic District **21**
Palmer Home View **51**
Palmer's Pickney Inn **19**
Planters Inn **30**
Two Meeting Street Inn **52**
Vendue Inn **41**
Wentworth Mansion **28**

ATTRACTIONS ●
Aiken-Rhett House **13**
The Charleston Museum **12**
The Children's Museum
   of the Lowcountry **6**
The Citadel **1**
Edmondston-Alston House **50**
The Gibbes Museum of Art **42**
The Heyward-Washington House **48**
Joseph Manigault House **11**
Nathaniel Russell House **49**
Old Exchange & Provost Dungeon **46**
South Carolina Aquarium **14**

DINING ◆
A.W. Shucks **34**
Anson **32**
Basil **5**
Carolina's **45**
Charleston Grill **26**
Circa 1886 Restaurant **28**
Coast **9**
Cru Café **18**
Cypress **36**
82 Queen **43**
Fig **24**
Fish **7**
Grill 225 **33**

High Cotton Maverick
   Bar & Grill **37**
Hominy Grill **2**
Hyman's Seafood Company
   Restaurant **25**
Jestine's **20**
Magnolias **38**
McCrady's **44**
Oak Steakhouse **47**
Peninsula Grill **30**
S.N.O.B.
   (Slightly North of Broad) **35**
39 Rue de Jean **8**
Trattoria Lucca **4**

225, which fills up most of its street-level entrance in a style that evokes a grandly imperious turn-of-the-20th-century bank. Accommodations are unashamedly posh, unashamedly conservative, and deeply connected to 18th-century English and colonial American (especially South Carolinian planters-style) furnishings and fabrics. There's a rooftop pool, terrace, and the Pavilion Bar, and a sense that this hotel attracts high-profile guests as diverse as John Kerry and Rush Limbaugh. The hotel's most visible and obvious competitor is the also-recommended and much larger and better-accessorized Charleston Place, which evokes a greater degree of European flair, more elaborate service, and even greater degrees of plush.

255 E. Bay St., Charleston, SC 29401. ✆ **877/440-2250** or 843/723-0500. Fax 843/723-4320. www.marketpavilion.com. 66 units. $209–$329 double; from $550 suite. AE, DC, DISC, MC, V. Valet parking $20. **Amenities:** Restaurant (see review, p. 253); bar; rooftop bar/lounge; exercise room; rooftop pool; room service. *In room:* A/C, TV, hair dryer, Internet (free).

Planters Inn ★★★ This distinguished brick-sided inn stands next to the City Market. Renovations transformed the place into a cozy but tasteful and opulent enclave of colonial charm, turning it into one of the finest small luxury hotels of the South. The inn has a lobby filled with reproductions of 18th-century furniture and engravings, a staff clad in silk vests, and a parking area with exactly the right number of spaces for the number of rooms in the hotel. The spacious guest rooms have hardwood floors, marble bathrooms, and 18th-century decor (the work of award-winning decorators). The suites are appealing, outfitted very much like rooms in an upscale private home. Afternoon tea is served in the lobby, and a well-recommended restaurant, the **Peninsula Grill,** is described in the "Where to Dine" section, later in this chapter.

112 N. Market St., Charleston, SC 29401. ✆ **800/845-7082** or 843/722-2345. Fax 843/577-2125. www.plantersinn.com. 64 units. $285–$365 double; from $550 suite. AE, DC, DISC, MC, V. Parking $18. **Amenities:** Restaurant (see review, p. 253); room service. *In room:* A/C, TV, hair dryer, Wi-Fi (free).

Wentworth Mansion ★★★ A splendid example of America's Gilded Age, this 1886 Second Empire inn touts such amenities as hand-carved marble fireplaces, Tiffany stained-glass windows, and detailed wood and plasterwork. If it is grand accommodations that you seek, you've found them. When a cotton merchant built the property in the 1800s, it cost $200,000, an astronomical sum back then. In the mid-1990s, a team of local entrepreneurs spent millions renovating it into the smooth and seamless inn you see today. The guest rooms and suites are large enough to have sitting areas. All units have a king-size bed and a well-kept bathroom with a shower and whirlpool tub, and most have working gas fireplaces. The mansion rooms and suites come with a sleeper sofa for extra guests, who are charged an additional $50 per night.

149 Wentworth St., Charleston, SC 29401. ✆ **888/466-1886** or 843/853-1886. Fax 843/720-5290. www.wentworthmansion.com. 21 units. $395–$470 double; $450–$750 suite. Additional person $50 extra per night. Rates include breakfast buffet and afternoon tea and cordials. AE, DC, DISC, MC, V. Free parking. **Amenities:** Restaurant, Circa 1886 Restaurant (see review, p. 253); bar; babysitting; room service; spa. *In room:* A/C, TV/DVD, CD player, hair dryer, minibar (soft drinks only), Wi-Fi (free).

Expensive

Ansonborough Inn ★ ☺ This is one of the oddest hotels in the Historic District. Most visitors really like the unusual configuration of rooms, many of which are spacious enough to house families. Set close to the waterfront, the massive building, once a 1900 warehouse, has a lobby that features exposed timbers and a soaring atrium filled with plants. Despite the building's height, it has only three floors, which allows guest rooms to have ceilings of 14 to 16 feet and, in many cases, sleeping lofts. Guest rooms are outfitted with copies of 18th-century furniture and accessories. Breakfast is the only meal served, but many fine restaurants are located nearby.

21 Hasell St., Charleston, SC 29401. ℭ **800/522-2073** or 843/723-1655. Fax 843/577-6888. www. ansonboroughinn.com. 37 units. $159–$239 double. Rates include continental breakfast. Children 11 and under stay free in parent's room. AE, DISC, MC, V. Parking $12. **Amenities:** Breakfast room; babysitting. *In room:* A/C, TV, fridge, hair dryer.

1843 Battery Carriage House Inn ★

In one of the largest antebellum neighborhoods of Charleston, this inn offers guest rooms in a somewhat eccentric carriage house behind the main building. In other words, the owners use the top living accommodations for themselves but have restored the bedrooms out back to a high standard. Recent renovations added four-poster beds and a colonial frill to the not-overly large bedrooms. Don't stay here if you want an inn with lots of public space; that, you don't get. But you can enjoy the location, which is a short walk off the Battery—a seafront peninsula where you can easily imagine a flotilla of Yankee ships enforcing the Civil War blockade.

20 S. Battery, Charleston, SC 29401. ℭ **800/775-5575** or 843/727-3100. Fax 843/727-3130. www.battery carriagehouse.com. 11 units. $159–$249 double. Rates include continental breakfast served in courtyard or room. AE, DISC, MC, V. Free parking. No children 11 and under. **Amenities:** Lounge; Wi-Fi (free). *In room:* A/C, TV.

Francis Marion Hotel ★

A $14-million award-winning restoration has returned this historic hotel to its original elegance. Although the 12-story structure breaks from the standard Charleston decorative motif and has rooms furnished in traditional European style, it is not devoid of Charleston charm. Guest rooms feature a king-size, queen-size, or double bed, and the renovated bathrooms contain tub/shower combinations with brass fixtures. The hotel's restaurant, **Swamp Fox Restaurant & Bar,** serves breakfast, lunch, and dinner, and features classic Southern cuisine.

387 King St., Charleston, SC 29403. ℭ **877/756-2121** or 843/722-0600. Fax 843/853-2186. www. francismarioncharleston.com. 233 units. $189–$279 standard double; $229–$299 deluxe double; $299–$379 suite. Children 11 and under stay free in parent's room. AE, DC, DISC, MC, V. Parking $10–$15. **Amenities:** Restaurant; bar; babysitting; exercise room; room service. *In room:* A/C, TV, hair dryer, Wi-Fi (free).

HarbourView Inn ★

Spruced up and looking better than ever, this four-story inn lies in the heart of Charleston, across from the landmark Waterfront Park. From its windows you can see some of the best seascapes in the city. Known for its Old South hospitality and attentive service, this is one of the best and most comfortable inns in the historic zone. Guest rooms have an understated elegance, with plush four-poster beds, wicker chests, sea-grass rugs, and rattan chairs—decor very much in the style of an old-time Charleston sea captain's town house. Expect pampering here, from morning (when a continental breakfast is delivered to your door) to night (when turndown service comes with candy on your pillow). The beautifully maintained private bathrooms come with both tub and shower. The most elegant unit is the penthouse with its whirlpool bathroom, working fireplace, and private balcony.

2 Venue Range, Charleston, SC 29401. ℭ **888/853-8439** or 843/853-8439. Fax 843/853-4034. www. harbourviewcharleston.com. 52 units. Double $149–$369; penthouse $299–$459, 2-night minimum weekends. Rates include continental breakfast. AE, DC, DISC, MC, V. Parking $16. **Amenities:** Babysitting; room service. *In room:* A/C, TV, hair dryer, Wi-Fi (free).

Indigo Inn/Jasmine House ★ These two hotels are set across the street from each other, with the same owners and the same reception area in the Indigo Inn. Built as an indigo warehouse in the mid–19th century, and gutted and radically reconstructed, the Indigo Inn (the larger of the two) offers rooms with 18th-century decor and comfortable furnishings. Rooms in the Jasmine House, an 1843 Greek Revival mansion whose exterior is painted buttercup yellow, are much more individualized. Each unit in the Jasmine House has a ceiling of about 14 feet, its own color scheme and theme, crown moldings, bathrooms with shower and whirlpool tubs, and floral-patterned upholsteries. Both inns serve breakfast on-site for their respective guests. Children are welcome at the Indigo Inn but not at the Jasmine House.

1 Maiden Lane, Charleston, SC 29401. ℂ **800/845-7639** or 843/577-5900. Fax 843/577-0378. www. indigoinn.com. 40 units Indigo Inn, 10 units Jasmine House. Double $139–$199 Indigo Inn, $179–$289 Jasmine House. Rates include continental breakfast. 10% discounts available in midwinter. AE, DC, DISC, MC, V. Parking $10. No children accepted at Jasmine House. **Amenities:** Breakfast room; babysitting (at Indigo Inn); Jacuzzi. *In room:* A/C, TV, hair dryer, Wi-Fi (in Jasmine; free).

The Inn at Middleton Place ★★ 🏨 It's a long way from Tara and Rhett Butler, but if your lodging preferences south of the Mason-Dixon line run toward strikingly modern luxury hotels, this is the place for you. The inn is a direct counterpoint to the adjoining Middleton Place (p. 264), an 18th-century plantation that's a sightseeing attraction. Charles Duell, a descendant of Middleton's original owners, wanted a departure from ersatz colonial and deliberately commissioned architects to create an inn devoid of "Scarlett and her antebellum charm." That said, the inn, with its live oaks and setting on the bluffs of the Ashley River, still has Southern grace and a warm and inviting interior. The guest rooms are filled with handcrafted furniture, wood-burning fireplaces, and cypress paneling; bathrooms have oversize tubs and private showers. You can patronize the inn's restaurant if you're not a guest, enjoying classic plantation fare ranging from pan-fried quail to crawfish cakes.

4290 Ashley River Rd., Charleston, SC 29414. ℂ **800/543-4774** or 843/556-0500. Fax 843/556-5673. www.theinnatmiddletonplace.com. 53 units. $170–$285 double; $400–$500 suite. Rates include full breakfast. AE, DISC, MC, V. Free parking. **Amenities:** Restaurant; babysitting; bike rentals; outdoor pool. *In room:* A/C, TV, hair dryer, Wi-Fi (free).

Kings Courtyard Inn ★ The tiny entry to this three-story 1854 inn in the Historic District is deceiving because it opens into a brick courtyard with a fountain. A fireplace warms the small lobby, which has a brass chandelier. Besides the main courtyard, two courts offer fine views from the breakfast room. The owners bought the building next door and incorporated 10 more rooms into the existing inn. Your room might be outfitted with a canopy bed, an Oriental rug over a hardwood floor, an armoire, or even a gas fireplace. A whirlpool is on-site. A continental breakfast is included in the rate; a full breakfast is available for an additional charge.

198 King St., Charleston, SC 19401. ℂ **800/845-6119** or 843/723-7000. Fax 843/720-2608. www. charminginns.com. 41 units. $175–$295 double. Rates include continental breakfast. Children 11 and under stay free in parent's room. Off-season 3-day packages available. AE, DC, DISC, MC, V. Parking $12. **Amenities:** Breakfast room; lounge; Jacuzzi; room service. *In room:* A/C, TV, fridge, hair dryer, Wi-Fi (free).

Marriott Renaissance Charleston Historic District Hotel Built in 2001, with a massive renovation completed in 2008, this is the most upscale member of the extended Marriott family of chain hotels in historic Charleston. It's bigger than you might originally have thought given its visage facing Wentworth Street, thanks to a long and sprawling design that extends way, way back from the street. Bedrooms have mahogany paneling, high ceilings, and furnishings that evoke the best aspects of the genteel plantation-based South, but it's not as chic as the more appealing Charleston Place. If you opt for a stay in one of the comfortably appointed rooms at this hotel, expect lots of emphasis on corporate conventions, whose comings and goings are rather visible in the hotel's public areas.

68 Wentworth St., Charleston, SC 29401. (ⓒ) **877/256-9840** or 843/534-0300. Fax 843/534-0700. www.marriott.com. 166 units. $249–$279 double; $269–$309 suite. AE, DC, DISC, MC, V. Parking: $12–$19 per day. **Amenities:** Restaurant; bar; exercise room; rooftop outdoor pool. *In room:* A/C, TV, Wi-Fi ($13 per day).

Palmer Home View ★★★   This media favorite has been consistently voted one of the most outstanding B&Bs in the country by everybody from the Travel Channel to *Travel + Leisure* magazine. Now operated by the third-generation owner, the house was built in 1848 by John Ravenel, whose son designed the *Little David,* the first semisubmersible vessel and the forerunner to the submarine. A B&B since 1977, Palmer Home is beautifully decorated and furnished with antiques. Guest rooms are midsize to spacious and open onto panoramic views of Charleston Harbor and historic Fort Sumter. Many of the bedrooms contain four-poster beds. The most elegant—also the most expensive—way to stay here is to rent the on-site carriage house.

5 East Battery, Charleston, SC 29401. (ⓒ) **843/853-1574.** Fax 843/723-7983. www.bbonline.com. 4 units. $165–$385 double; $420 suite. AE, MC, V. **Amenities:** Breakfast room; outdoor pool. *In room:* A/C, TV.

Two Meeting Street Inn ★   Set in an enviable position near the Battery, this house was built in 1892 as a wedding gift from a prosperous father to his daughter. Inside, the proportions are as lavish and gracious as the Gilded Age could provide. Stained-glass windows, mementos, and paintings were either part of the original decorations or collected by the present owners, the Spell family. Most guest rooms contain bathrooms with tub/shower combinations, four-poster beds, ceiling fans, and (in some cases) access to a network of balconies. A continental breakfast with home-baked breads and pastries is available.

2 Meeting St., Charleston, SC 29401. (ⓒ) **888/723-7322** or 843/723-7322. www.twomeetingstreet.com. 9 units. $199–$479 double. Rates include continental breakfast and afternoon tea. No credit cards. No children 11 and under. **Amenities:** Breakfast room. *In room:* A/C, TV, hair dryer, MP3 docking station, Wi-Fi (free).

Vendue Inn ★   This three-story inn manages to convey some of the personalized touches of a B&B. Its public areas—a series of narrow, labyrinthine spaces—are full of antiques and colonial accessories that evoke a cluttered, and slightly cramped inn in Europe. Guest rooms do not necessarily follow the lobby's European model, however, and appear to be the result of decorative experiments by the owners. Room themes may be based on aspects of Florida, rococo Italy, or 18th-century Charleston. Marble floors and tabletops, wooden sleigh beds, and (in some rooms) wrought-iron canopy beds, while eclectically charming, might be inconsistent with your vision of colonial Charleston. Overflow guests are housed in a historic, brick-fronted annex across the cobblestone-covered street. The inn's restaurant is called the **Kitchen House** (for dinner only). The chef here offers a menu of local favorites with unusual twists. The other restaurant, the **Roof Top Terrace,** offers a complete lunch and dinner menu in a more informal atmosphere with a panoramic view of the harbor and of the Historic District.

19 Vendue Range, Charleston, SC 29401. © **800/845-7900** or 843/577-7970. Fax 843/577-2913. www.vendueinn.com. 66 units. $155–$205 double; $215–$255 suite. Rates include full Southern breakfast. AE, DC, DISC, MC, V. Parking $16. **Amenities:** 2 restaurants; bar; babysitting; room service. *In room:* A/C, TV, hair dryer, kitchenette (in some), Wi-Fi (free).

Moderate

Reliable motel accommodations are also available at the **Hampton Inn Historic District,** 345 Meeting St. (© **800/HAMPTON** [426-7866] or 843/723-4000; www.hamptoninn.com), across from the visitor center.

Anchorage Inn ★★   Other than a heraldic shield out front, few ornaments mark this bulky structure, which was built in the 1840s as a cotton warehouse. The inn boasts the only decorative theme of its type in Charleston: a mock-Tudor interior with lots of dark paneling; references to Olde England; canopied beds with matching tapestries; pastoral or nautical engravings; leaded casement windows; and, in some places, half-timbering. Because bulky buildings are adjacent to the hotel on both sides, the architects designed all but a few rooms with views overlooking the lobby. (Light is indirectly filtered inside through the lobby's overhead skylights—a plus during Charleston's hot summers.) Each room's shape is different from that of its neighbors, and the expensive ones have bona fide windows overlooking the street outside.

26 Vendue Range, Charleston, SC 29401. © **800/421-2952** or 843/723-8300. Fax 843/723-9543. www.anchoragencharleston.com. 19 units. $119–$279 double; $169–$309 suite. Rates include continental breakfast and afternoon tea. AE, MC, V. Parking $12. **Amenities:** Breakfast room; babysitting. *In room:* A/C, TV, hair dryer, Wi-Fi (free).

The Cannonboro Inn   This buff-and-beige 1853 house was once the private home of a rice planter. The decor isn't as carefully coordinated or as relentlessly upscale as those of many of its competitors; throughout, it has a sense of folksy informality. Although there's virtually no land around this building, a wide veranda on the side creates a "sit-and-talk-a-while" mood. Each unit contains a canopy bed and formal, old-fashioned furniture. ·

184 Ashley Ave., Charleston, SC 29403. © **800/235-8039** or 843/723-8572. Fax 843/723-8007. www.charleston-sc-inns.com. 6 units. $119–$239 double; $199–$259 suite. Rates include full breakfast and afternoon tea and sherry. AE, DISC, MC, V. Free parking. No children 9 and under. **Amenities:** Breakfast room; bike rentals. *In room:* A/C, TV, kitchenette, Wi-Fi (free).

Doubletree Guest Suites   A somber five-story 1991 building adjacent to the historic City Market, the Doubletree offers family-friendly suites instead of rooms, each outfitted with a wet bar, refrigerator, and microwave oven. The accommodations tend to receive heavy use, thanks to their appeal to families, tour groups, and business travelers.

181 Church St., Charleston, SC 29401. © **800/222-TREE** (8733) or 843/577-2644. Fax 843/577-2697. http://doubletree1.hilton.com. 212 units. $189–$209 double suite. AE, DC, DISC, MC, V. Parking $19. **Amenities:** 3 restaurants; babysitting; exercise room. *In room:* A/C, TV, hair dryer, Wi-Fi (free).

1837 Bed & Breakfast   Built in 1837 by Nicholas Cobia, a cotton planter, this place is called a "single house" because it's only a single room wide. Our favorite room is no. 2 in the Carriage House, which has authentic designs, exposed-brick walls, warm decor, a beamed ceiling, and three windows. All the rooms have refrigerators and separate entrances because of the layout, and all contain well-kept bathrooms and canopied poster rice beds. On one of the verandas, you can sit under whirling ceiling fans and enjoy your breakfast (sausage pie or eggs Benedict, and homemade breads) or afternoon tea. The parlor room has cypress wainscoting and a black-marble fireplace; the breakfast room is really part of the kitchen.

126 Wentworth St., Charleston, SC 29401. © **877/723-1837** or 843/723-7166. Fax 843/722-7179. www.1837bb.com. 9 units. $99–$209 double. Rates include full breakfast and afternoon tea. AE, DISC, MC, V. Free off-street parking. No children 6 and under. **Amenities:** Breakfast room. *In room:* A/C, TV, fridge, hair dryer.

Palmer's Pinckney Inn ★   This is one of Charleston's most inviting B&B's, in the historic market in the center of town. Charleston native Francess Palmer welcomes you to five well-appointed bedrooms, often with a four-poster bed. Most have king-size beds, and some offer gas fireplaces. Two of the units each come with a Jacuzzi. Stair climbing is required if you choose a room on the second floor. In the Southern style, rocking chairs are placed on the veranda.

19 Pinckney St., Charleston, SC 29401. © **843/722-1733.** www.pinckneyinn.com. 5 units. $150–$300 double. Rates include breakfast. MC, V. **Amenities:** Breakfast room. *In room:* A/C, TV, Wi-Fi (free).

Inexpensive

Those on tight budgets might try one of the chain motels such as **Days Inn,** 2998 W. Montague Ave., Charleston, SC 29418 (© **800/329-7466** or 843/747-4101; fax 843/566-0378; www.daysinn.com), near the international airport. Doubles range from $87 to $179. Children 11 and under stay free in their parent's room, and cribs are also free. **Lands Inn,** 2545 Savannah Hwy., Charleston, SC 29414 (© **843/763-8885;** fax 843/556-9536; www.landsinnsc.com), is another bargain, with doubles costing from $67 to $139, and $10 extra charged for each additional person. Children 15 and under stay free with parent. At **Red Roof Inn,** 7480 Northwoods Blvd., Charleston, SC 29406 (© **800/RED-ROOF** [733-7663] or 843/572-9100; fax 843/572-0061; www.redroof.com), doubles cost $55 to $70, and $6 is charged for each additional person; children 18 and under stay free in parent's room.

Best Western King Charles Inn ☺   One block from the Historic District's market area, this three-story hotel has rooms that are better than you might expect from a motel and are likely to be discounted in the off season. Some rooms have balconies, but the views are limited. Although short on style, the hotel is a good value and convenient to most everything. An all-you-can-eat buffet breakfast is served in a colonial-inspired restaurant, and the hotel has a small pool and a helpful staff.

237 Meeting St. (btw. Wentworth and Hazel sts.), Charleston, SC 29401. © **866/546-4700** or 843/723-7451. Fax 843/723-2041. www.kingcharlesinn.com. 91 units. $139–$299 double. Children 18 and under stay free in parent's room. AE, DC, DISC, MC, V. Free parking. **Amenities:** Restaurant; outdoor pool; room service. *In room:* A/C, TV, hair dryer, MP3 docking station, Wi-Fi (free).

King George IV Inn   This four-story 1790 Federal-style home in the heart of the Historic District serves as an example of the way Charleston used to live..Named the Peter Freneau House, it was formerly the residence of a reporter and co-owner of the *Charleston City Gazette.* All rooms have wide-planked hardwood floors, plaster moldings, fireplaces, and 12-foot ceilings, and are furnished with antiques. Beds are either Victorian or four-poster double or queen-size. All guests are allowed access to the three levels of porches on the house. The location is convenient to many downtown Charleston restaurants; tennis is a 5-minute drive away, the beach is 15 minutes away, and some 35 golf courses are nearby. The continental breakfast consists of cereals, breads, muffins, pastries, and fruit.

32 George St., Charleston, SC 29401. ☎ **888/723-1667** or 843/723-9339. Fax 843/723-7749. www. kinggeorgeiv.com. 10 units, 2 with shared bathrooms. $89–$219 double. Rates include continental breakfast. AE, DISC, MC, V. Free parking. **Amenities:** Breakfast room; Wi-Fi (free). *In room:* A/C, TV.

North Charleston

La Quinta Charleston ☺   This sturdy, well-designed, and childproof member of a nationwide hotel chain has an exterior that's attractively designed like a Spanish hacienda, replete with terra-cotta roof tiles, thick stucco walls, a bell tower, and references to the mission churches of California. It lies near the busy interstate and close to row upon row of shopping malls, chain restaurants, and fast-food joints. Historic Charleston is a 25-minute drive away. Each guest room is midsize and comfortably laid out with a sense of Tex-Mex whimsy.

2499 La Quinta Lane, Charleston, SC 29420. ☎ **800/753-3757** or 843/797-8181. Fax 843/569-1608. www.lq.com. 122 units. $74–$79 double; $89–$99 suite. Rates include continental breakfast. Children 17 and under stay free in parent's room. AE, DC, DISC, MC, V. Free parking. **Amenities:** Outdoor pool. *In room:* A/C, TV, hair dryer, Wi-Fi (free).

Mount Pleasant

Old Village Post House ★ 🏨   This is the best inn in the old town of Mount Pleasant, across the bridge from downtown Charleston. The B&B's rooms have original hardwood floors, 10-foot ceilings, and soothing whirlpool tubs. Many guests prefer to stay here among the moss-draped oaks of the Old Village instead of downtown Charleston. The property dates from the days when wayside inns attracted passersby for overnight stopovers. You can also dine on-site at its **Maverick** restaurant. Traditional charm meets modern amenities at this well-run inn. Each accommodation varies in size and decor. Room 6, known as the Honeymoon Suite, features a four-poster bed, a sitting area, and an extra-large private bath for two.

101 Pitt St., Mount Pleasant, SC 29464. ☎ **843/388-8935.** www.oldvillageposthouse.com. 6 units. $99–$109 double. Rates include breakfast. AE, MC, V. **Amenities:** Restaurant (see review, p. 260); bar. *In room:* A/C, TV, Wi-Fi (free).

WHERE TO DINE

Foodies from all over flock to Charleston for some of the finest dining in the tri-state area. You get not only the refined cookery of the Low Country, but also an array of French and international specialties. Space does not permit us to preview all the outstanding restaurants of Charleston—much less the merely good ones.

Very Expensive

Charleston Grill ★★★ LOW COUNTRY/FRENCH   This is the most prestigious, most formal, and most sophisticated restaurant in Charleston, with superb service, grand food, an impeccably trained staff, and one of the city's best selections of wine. The cuisine of the celebrity chef, Bob Waggoner, draws rave reviews from as far away as Paris. The marble-floored, mahogany-sheathed dining room is one of the city's most luxurious and the one that's the most at ease with haute European sophistication. Menu items change with the seasons, and you will be pleasantly surprised by how well Low Country and French cuisine meld. Appetizers might be something rather simple but delectable—perhaps young lettuce in a champagne vinegar, or something more complicated such as venison carpaccio with arugula, Parmesan, and fried shallots. Main courses burst with freshness and originality, including diver scallops and lobster risotto with white asparagus and a lemon vermouth sauce, or else grilled swordfish with capers, *piccolini* olives, and sun-dried tomatoes. Modern interpretations of Southern dishes also appear on the menu—try the duck confit with "dirty grits," baby turnips, and a bacon sage gravy.

In the Charleston Place Hotel, 224 King St. © **843/577-4522.** www.charlestongrill.com. Reservations recommended. Main courses $25–$48. AE, DC, DISC, MC, V. Sun–Thurs 5:30–10pm; Fri–Sat 5:30–10:30pm.

Circa 1886 Restaurant ★★ AMERICAN/FRENCH   In the carriage house of the Wentworth Mansion (p. 246), this deluxe restaurant offers grand food, a beautiful decor, and formal service. Begin by accepting the invitation of the concierge for a view of Charleston from the cupola, where you can see all the bodies of water surrounding the city. Seating 50, two main rooms are beautifully set in the most idyllic place for a romantic dinner in Charleston. The chef prepares an updated version of Low Country cookery, giving it a light, contemporary touch but retaining the flavors of the Old South. Menus are rotated seasonally to take advantage of the best and freshest produce. For a first course, try the candied carrot soup with roasted garlic, or the spicy grilled shrimp over fried green tomatoes. Here the traditional gazpacho comes with celery instead of tomato and is flavored with carrot-Tabasco oil. Featured main courses are prepared with consummate skill, especially the truffle-oil fried catfish and the vanilla-glazed Berkshire pork chop. We're still smacking our lips over the strawberry shortcake soufflé hazelnut tart.

In the Wentworth Mansion, 149 Wentworth St. © **843/853-7828.** www.circa1886.com. Reservations recommended. Main courses $23–$32. AE, DC, DISC, MC, V. Mon–Sat 5:30–9:30pm.

Grill 225 ★ AMERICAN/INTERNATIONAL   Although this upscale bistro opened in 2003, you'd swear its setting was a converted bank lobby from a century earlier. Paneled and interspersed with soaring columns and elaborate references to early-20th-century models, it occupies most of the lobby level of the also-recommended hotel. A cheerful staff serves food on crisp napery: The best examples include at least eight massive portions of grilled steaks, such as a version of filet mignon layered with foie gras and served with béarnaise sauce. Seafood features "encrusted" halibut with spicy scallops, lump crabmeat, and miso-flavored lemongrass broth. Cuba Gooding, Jr., and the Bush twins have eaten at this place.

In the Market Pavilion Hotel, 225 E. Bay St. © **843/723-0500.** Reservations recommended. Main courses $26–$68. AE, DC, MC, V. Daily 11am–3pm and 5:30–11pm.

Oak Steakhouse ★ STEAK   In 2005, Chef Brett McKee opened this restaurant in a historic building dating back to 1850. Brooklyn-born McKee re-creates an Italian-style steakhouse, with 18-foot ceilings, mahogany paneling, and pine floors. The menu focuses on traditional items, such as New York strip or porterhouse, but infuses dishes with an Italian flavor. Start with such appetizers as tuna tartare or Brett's specialty meatballs with melted mozzarella. Oak specialties include a 12-ounce burger with cottage fries or a lobster and shrimp macaroni. Vegetarians and vegans are also catered to with excellent salads including McKee's chopped mixed green salad that contains everything from radicchio to sweet Vidalia onions.

17 Broad St. © **843/722-4220.** Reservations recommended. Main courses $22–$49. AE, MC, V. Mon–Sat 5–11pm; Sun 5–10pm.

Peninsula Grill ★★ CONTINENTAL/INTERNATIONAL   There's an old Southern saying about "country come to city." This is one case where the city has come to country. The Peninsula Grill, in the also-recommended Planters Inn, manages to be quaint, historic, hip, and just a wee bit pricier than it perhaps should be—all at the same time. There's a cramped but convivial bar near the entrance that has introduced goodly numbers of prowling singles, and a warm, dimly lit interior that's romantic, proudly Southern, and posh. The menu changes frequently. You might start with a platter that's artfully arranged with three different preparations of lobster: as ravioli, tempura, and sautéed. This might be followed with bourbon grilled jumbo shrimp with Low Country hoppin' John and lobster-basil hush puppies. A full array of steaks, chops, and seafood can be prepared any way you like. Even the *New York Times* and *Bon Appétit* magazine have praised "the ultimate coconut cake," based on a recipe from the chef's grandmother.

In the Planters Inn, 112 N. Market St. (𝄞 **843/723-0700.** www.peninsulagrill.com. Reservations required. Main courses $28–$39. AE, DC, DISC, MC, V. Sun–Thurs 5:30–10pm; Fri–Sat 5:30–11pm.

Expensive

Anson ★★★ LOW COUNTRY/MODERN AMERICAN   Charlestonians know that they can spot the local society types in this hip, stylish brick-sided ice warehouse. The present owners have added New Orleans–style iron balconies, Corinthian pilasters salvaged from demolished colonial houses, and enough Victorian rococo for anyone's taste. A well-trained staff in long white aprons describes dishes that are inspired by traditions of the coastal Southeast. But this isn't exactly down-home cookery; France meets the Deep South in one seafood selection: cashew-crusted grouper with hoppin' John, green beans, and a champagne cream sauce. Our favorite is the crispy flounder, which rival chefs have tried to duplicate but haven't equaled. Some of the best meat selections include slow-roasted duck with duck confit potato cake and local peaches, or else a New York strip with Maytag blue cheese and an onion marmalade. A children's menu is available.

12 Anson St. (𝄞 **843/577-0551.** www.ansonrestaurant.com. Reservations recommended. Main courses $18–$39. AE, DC, DISC, MC, V. Sun–Thurs 5–10pm; Fri–Sat 5–11pm.

Cypress ★ LOW COUNTRY   Some of the most imaginative Low Country food is served here, focusing on hearty platters with lots of rice, shrimp, and regional herbs. For starters, treat yourself to crab cakes or almond-fried Brie with a cranberry and walnut chutney. Main course specialties include a crisp wasabi tuna with shiitake mushrooms or a filet of beef in Madeira sauce. Tableside presentations for two include a chateaubriand with Parmesan potato gratin. James River oysters from Virginia are a feature in season, as is grilled pork belly in a butter glaze. The wood-burning grill churns out such main dishes as "Reconstruction lamb T-bone."

167 E. Bay St. (𝄞 **843/727-0111.** www.magnolias-blossom-cypress.com. Reservations recommended. Main courses $20–$49. AE, DC, MC, V. Sun–Thurs 5:30–10pm; Fri–Sat 5:30–11pm.

Fig ★★ SOUTHERN/INTERNATIONAL   Mustardy deviled eggs are served while you peruse the tempting menu that ranges from the best Portuguese fish soup in Charleston (complete with salt cod, squid, and chorizo) to roast suckling pig with a cabbage casserole and roasted beets. We like chef-owner Mike Lata's dedication to locally grown vegetables and his respect for the best produce in any season. We've made an entire meal out of his vegetables alone, including a garlic-studded sautéed rapini or butterbeans with prosciutto and basil butter. His hanger steak with caramelized shallots and an old-fashioned Bordelaise sauce, with a butterball potato purée on the side, is a delight to the senses. The appetizers are also perfectly harmonious, including Swiss chard ravioli with walnuts and a white-corn soup with applewood-smoked bacon and scallions.

232 Meeting St. © 843/805-5900. www.eatatfig.com. Reservations required. Main courses $26–$34. AE, MC, V. Mon–Thurs 5:30–10:30pm; Fri–Sat 5:30–11pm.

High Cotton Maverick Bar & Grill ★★ SOUTHERN/STEAK   This blockbuster of a restaurant caters to a devoted clientele of locals who prefer its two-fisted drinks in an upscale macho decor, and a tasty cuisine that defines the restaurant as a Southern-style steakhouse. It's also a good choice for nightlife because of its casual elegance and its busy and cozy bar where live music, usually jazz, is performed nightly from 6 to 10pm. Cuisine here, under the direction of Anthony Gray, is genuinely wonderful. Dig into the buttermilk-fried oysters with arugula in a green goddess dressing, or a house-made version of the most sophisticated platter of charcuterie in the Carolinas. It's all there—processed terrines and sausages and cold cuts butchered and processed on-site in ways that evoke 19th-century France. Gourmets gravitate to the barbecue-spiced seared flounder, sliced medallions of venison *au poivre,* or succulent Carolina rabbit, wrapped in prosciutto; but most diners go for one of the juicy, tender steaks.

199 E. Bay St. © 843/724-3815. www.mavericksouthernkitchens.com. Reservations recommended. Main courses $21–$36. AE, DC, DISC, MC, V. Mon–Thurs 5:30–10pm; Fri 5:30–11pm; Sat 11am–2:30pm and 5:30–11pm; Sun 10am–2pm (brunch with live music) and 5:30–10pm.

McCrady's ★★ AMERICAN/FRENCH   Charleston's oldest eating establishment, where none other than George Washington dined, is one of the finest kitchens in the Low Country. Praising both its wine list and well-chosen menu, *Esquire* named it one of the best new restaurants in America. Entered down a mysterious-looking "Jack the Ripper" alley, it looks like an elegant wine cellar, with rough brick walls, exposed beams, and wide-plank floors. Cooking times are unerringly accurate, and a certain charm and fragrance is given to every dish. We still remember the peekytoe-crab and lobster salad. Ditto for the tartare of tuna with olives, red pepper, and basil. A perfectly done sautéed halibut appears on your plate with sides of spinach and cauliflower purée. Slow-roasted Moulard duck breast comes with chocolate balsamic *jus,* or else you might happily settle for the herb-marinated rack of lamb.

2 Unity Alley. © 843/577-0025. www.mccradysrestaurant.com. Reservations required. Main courses $25–$32; Sun–Thurs 3-course fixed-price dinner $39; tasting menu (all week) $85. AE, MC, V. Sun–Thurs 5:30–9:30pm; Fri–Sat 5:30–10:30pm.

Moderate

Carolina's ★ 🏛 SOUTHERN   Amid the wharves and turned-posh town houses of Lower East Bay Street, Carolina's is a Charlestonian staple that fell out of fashion and is now fighting its way back into the city's gastronomic good graces. Since opening as "Perdita's" in the early 1950s, it's had a revolving door of chefs and culinary styles. Today, much stabilized under the guidance of chef Jeremiah Bacon, it now exerts a broad-based appeal to locals, with special value at lunch. Platters include shrimp and grits with sweet peppers and andouille gravy or pan-seared salmon with apricots, Swiss chard, and lentils. Dinners are more elaborate, with glazed quail with collard greens, and such artfully exotic fare as shrimp and crabmeat wontons with soy lime ginger aioli. A worthy selection might be crisp-fried flounder with peach jam, but traditionalists appreciate the New York strip steak perched atop mashed potatoes.

10 Exchange St. ⓒ **843/724-3800.** www.carolinasrestaurant.com. Reservations recommended. Main courses $7–$12 lunch, $23–$34 dinner; 4-course tasting menu $42; Sun brunch main courses $9–$14. AE, DC, DISC, MC, V. Mon–Fri 11:30am–2:30pm and 5–10pm; Sat 5–11pm; Sun 11am–2:30pm and 5–10pm.

Coast ★ SEAFOOD   Savvy local foodies fill up the tin-roofed booths in a former indigo warehouse, where this casual and hip restaurant is known for its menu of specialties, from oak wood grilled items to Charleston classics. The chefs prepare Charleston's best seviche, one made with lobster, and you can make selections from the raw bar sampler. Appetizers are worth the trip, and some diners make a meal of them tapas-style. Try the cornmeal-encrusted oysters in a papaya coulis with caviar or the yellowfin tuna pan-seared with tropical salsa. Fish such as mahimahi or grouper sizzles on the grill and is served with a variety of sauces including a pineapple chili salsa. Other seafood specialties include a delectable paella or a Portuguese calamari stew.

39D John St. ⓒ **843/722-8838.** www.coastbarandgrill.com. Reservations recommended. Main courses $15–$32. AE, DC, MC, V. Daily 5:30–10pm.

Cru Café ★ 🍴 AMERICAN/INTERNATIONAL   In a small 18th-century house, this two-room cafe is a local favorite. Diners sit at small banquettes or at a bar-cum–chef's table facing the open kitchen to watch Chef John Zucker prepare his imaginative specialties. Start, perhaps, with his buttermilk fried oyster salad with apple smoked bacon or his duck confit arugula salad with candied pecans in a port wine vinaigrette. Zucker makes some of the best pastas in town, including garlic scallops and angel-hair pasta, and especially his Thai seafood risotto. From the a la carte grille you can try a 12-ounce jerk rib-eye, or else go for the tasty seared maple leaf duck breast in a sherry thyme demi-glace.

18 Pinckney St. ⓒ **843/534-2434.** www.crucafe.com. Reservations recommended. Main courses $14–$24. AE, MC, V. Tues–Sat 11am–3pm; Tues–Thurs 5–10pm; Fri–Sat 5–11pm.

82 Queen ★ LOW COUNTRY   In its way, this is probably the most unusual compendium of real estate in Charleston: three 18th- and 19th-century houses clustered around an ancient magnolia tree, with outdoor tables arranged in its shade. Menu items filled with flavor and flair include an award-winning version of she-crab soup laced with sherry. Some of the best Low Country meals in Charleston are served here, especially the Charleston bouillabaisse made with market-fresh seafood and the seasoned shrimp and crawfish jambalaya with tasso ham and red rice. Grilled dinners are also a specialty of the chef, especially the black-pepper New York strip with mashed red-skin potatoes and balsamic-marinated portobello mushrooms.

82 Queen St. ⓒ **843/723-7591.** www.82queen.com. Reservations recommended for dinner. Main courses $10–$15 lunch, $8–$15 Sun brunch, $19–$30 dinner. AE, DC, DISC, MC, V. Daily 11:30am–3pm and 5:30–10:30pm (Sun brunch 11am–3pm).

Fish ★ SEAFOOD   Restaurant owners Charles and Celeste Patrick spearheaded the revitalization of North King Street when they restored and opened a restaurant in this 1830s former private home. Now visitors are flocking to an area once viewed as unsafe to enjoy some of the freshest and best seafood in the Low Country. The menu is seasonally adjusted. We dined on such starters as scallop seviche and seared foie gras with gherkins and champagne grapes. For a main course, perhaps "naked fish" is best. It's the fresh catch of the day and is prepared simply to bring out its natural flavor. Shrimp and grits prepared with chorizo cream, peppers, and onion is a winning combination—as is the seared halibut in a cucumber yogurt sauce. An array of "sides," or fresh vegetables, is among the city's best and freshest.

442 King St. © **843/722-3474.** www.fishrestaurant.net. Reservations recommended. Main courses $10–$12 lunch, $17–$25 dinner. AE, MC, V. Mon–Fri 11am–2:30pm; Sat 5:30–10pm.

Magnolias 😊 SOUTHERN   Magnolias manages to elevate the regional, vernacular cuisine of the Deep South to a hip, postmodern art form that's suitable for big-city trendies but is more likely to draw visiting families instead. The city's former Customs House has been revised into a sprawling network of interconnected spaces with heart-pine floors, faux-marble columns, and massive beams. Many diners fill up on soups and salads at lunch, ranging from a creamy tomato with lump crabmeat to a salmon BLT salad. But blackened catfish, fried green tomatoes, cheese grits, and buttermilk fried chicken breast—how Southern can you get?

185 E. Bay St. © **843/577-7771.** www.magnolias-blossom-cypress.com. Reservations recommended. Main courses $9–$19 lunch, $19–$32 dinner, $9–$19 Sun brunch. AE, DC, MC, V. Mon–Sat 11:30am–3:30pm; Sun 10am–3:45pm; Sun–Thurs 4–10pm; Fri–Sat 4–11pm.

S.N.O.B. (Slightly North of Broad) ★ ✇ SOUTHERN/INTERNATIONAL
This is an eclectic and energetic bistro with a casual attitude and some potent references to fine dining. You'll find an exposed kitchen, a high ceiling crisscrossed with ventilation ducts, and vague references to the South of long ago in this snazzily rehabbed 18th-century warehouse. Winner of many culinary awards, it justifiably promotes itself as Charleston's culinary maverick, priding itself on having introduced, in the early 1990s, stylishly updated versions of the vittles that kept the South alive for 300 years. Yet S.N.O.B. remains a potent contender on the culinary who's who of Charleston. Main courses can be ordered in medium and large sizes. An array of freshly made salads, soups, sandwiches, and daily specials greet you at lunch. Dinners are more elaborate, including grilled barbecued tuna glazed with mustard sauce and topped with fried oysters, country ham, and green onions; or roasted rack of lamb with green beans, pearl onions, and a rosemary-flavored cabernet sauce.

192 E. Bay St. © **843/723-3424.** www.mavericksouthernkitchens.com. Reservations accepted only for parties of 5 or more for lunch, recommended for all for dinner. Main courses $9–$16 lunch, $10–$29 dinner. AE, DC, DISC, MC, V. Mon–Fri 11:30am–3pm and 5:30–11pm; Sat–Sun 5:30–11pm.

39 Rue de Jean ★ ✇ FRENCH/SUSHI   You'll think you've been transported to the Left Bank at this new bistro, which pays homage (exceedingly well) to the classic brasserie cuisine of Paris. Justifiably popular for its inexpensive French cuisine, the restaurant comes complete with a traditional zinc bar, steak frites, and a great bottle of wine. Patio dining is an added attraction. The only incongruous note is the sudden culinary departure into Japanese sushi. All our favorite French appetizers are on the menu, including onion soup, truffle potato soup, and frisée lettuce with bacon lardoons. Each day a special *plat du jour* is featured, and we always go for that, especially the Sunday rendition of a delectable bouillabaisse. It wouldn't be a Parisian bistro without escargots gratinée, steak frites, and foie gras, and the chefs do these time-honored dishes well. Special features are six preparations of mussels and a whole fish du jour from the marketplace that morning.

39 John St. © **843/722-8881.** www.39ruedejean.com. Reservations required. Main courses $7.50–$15 lunch, $19–$25 dinner, $8–$19 Sun brunch. AE, DC, DISC, MC, V. Mon–Sat 11:30am–1am; Sun 10am–3pm and 5:30–11pm.

Trattoria Lucca ★ ☺ Chef Ken Vedrinkski of Siena brings to Charleston Italian family-style dining inspired by the Tuscan city of Lucca, known for its bevy of olive oils and savory Italian dishes. Unpretentious fare is served trattoria style at communal dining tables, and there are family suppers on Sunday. The homemade pastas are among the best in town, including *bucatini* with goat butter, trumpet mushrooms, and homemade Italian duck sausage. Other specialties include grilled farm chicken with local fresh peas, and beans or pork chop Milanese with Speck ham and arugula. One splendid dish is grilled black Angus flat-iron steak with Vidalia onion *fonduta* and Gorgonzola macaroni.

41A Bogart St. ☎ **843/973-3323.** Reservations recommended. Main courses $19–$24. AE, MC, V. Tues–Thurs 6–10pm; Fri–Sat 6–11pm; Sun 5–8pm.

Inexpensive

A. W. Shucks ★ 🦐 SEAFOOD This hearty oyster bar is a sprawling, salty tribute to the pleasures of shellfish and the fishermen who gather them. A short walk from the Public Market, set in a solid, restored warehouse with rough timbers, the restaurant has a long bar where thousands of crustaceans have been cracked open and consumed, as well as a dining room. The menu highlights oysters and clams on the half-shell, tasty seafood chowders, deviled crab, shrimp Creole, and succulent oysters prepared in at least a half a dozen ways. Chicken and beef dishes are also listed on the menu, but they're nothing special. A wide selection of international beers is sold. Absolutely no one cares how you dress; just dig in.

70 State St. ☎ **843/723-1151.** www.a-w-shucks.com. Main courses $14–$24. AE, DC, DISC, MC, V. Sun–Thurs 11am–10pm; Fri–Sat 11am–11pm.

Basil THAI The busiest restaurant of North King Street, this is one of only two Thai restaurants in Charlestown, and as such, it's something of a gastronomic landmark. Within a somewhat cramped setting of ocher-colored walls and hardwood floors, you can order all the usual Thai curries and lemon-grass specials. Especially popular are Tom Kha Gai (chicken-coconut soup); duck salads with celery, onions, pineapple, carrots, ginger, and cashew nuts; and a wide array of green, red, and yellow curries. Henry Eang is your hardworking host, an entrepreneur from Cambodia who has a tale or two to tell about the Pol Pot regime.

460 King St. ☎ **843/724-3490.** www.eatatbasil.com. Reservations not accepted. Main courses $8.95–$11 lunch, $14–$17 dinner. AE, DC, MC, V. Mon–Thurs 11am–2:30pm and 5–10:30pm; Fri–Sat 11am–2:30pm and 5–11pm; Sun 5–10pm.

Hominy Grill ★ ☺ LOW COUNTRY Owned and operated by chef Robert Stehling, Hominy Grill features simply and beautifully prepared dishes inspired by the kitchens of the Low Country. Since its opening, it has gained a devoted family following, who come here to feast on such specialties as barbecue chicken sandwiches, avocado and wehani rice salad with grilled vegetables, okra and shrimp beignets, and—a brunch favorite—smothered or poached eggs on homemade biscuits with mushroom gravy. At night, opt for one of the down-home specials such as grilled soft-shell crab with baked cheese grits and almond slaw, or else country-style pork ribs with red rice and pinto beans. Stehling claims that he likes to introduce people to new grains in the place of pasta or potatoes; many of his dishes, including salads, are prepared with grains such as barley and cracked wheat. The menu is well balanced between old- and new-cookery styles. Dropping in for breakfast? Go for the buttermilk biscuits, the meaty bacon, and the home-style fried apples.

207 Rutledge Ave. ℭ **843/937-0930.** http://hominygrill.com. Main courses $6.95–$16. AE, MC, V. Mon–Fri 7:30am–9pm; Sat 9am–9pm; Sun 9am–3pm.

Hyman's Seafood Company Restaurant ★ SEAFOOD   Hyman's was established a century ago and honors old-fashioned traditions. The building sprawls over most of a city block in the heart of Charleston's business district. Inside are at least six dining rooms and a take-away deli loaded with salmon, lox, and smoked herring, all displayed in the style of the great kosher delis of New York City. One sit-down section is devoted to deli-style sandwiches, chicken soup, and salads; another to a delectably messy choice of fish, shellfish, lobsters, and oysters.

215 Meeting St. ℭ **843/723-6000.** www.hymanseafood.com. Reservations recommended. Main courses $18–$43. AE, DC, DISC, MC, V. Daily 11am–1pm.

Jestine's SOUTHERN/SOUL FOOD   When the tourist board is asked "for a native place to eat," they most often send visitors here for some real Low Country flavors. This restaurant was named after the cook and housekeeper who reared the founder of the restaurant, Shera Lee Berlin. All of Jestine's recipes have been preserved to delight a new generation of diners who like to feast on such local favorites as country-fried steak, okra gumbo, fried chicken, shrimp Creole, fried oyster po'boys, country cream corn, black-eyed peas, and blueberry cobbler. There is a daily blueplate special, and even a green-plate special for vegetarians. If you ever wondered what "red rice" is, ask for it here. The "table wine" is actually sugary tea in tumblers.

251 Meeting St. ℭ **843/722-7224.** No reservations accepted. Main courses $7.95–$15. AE, DC, DISC, MC, V. Tues–Thurs 11am–9:30pm; Fri–Sat 11am–10pm; Sun 11am–9pm. Closed Dec 25 and Jewish holidays.

Awendaw

See Wee ★ 🛏 LOW COUNTRY   At See Wee, the cooks make an art of Low Country frying, serving the best fried green tomatoes—dusted with corn flour—in the Charleston area. Its perfect accompaniment is a mild horseradish sauce. Cooks also fry okra, oysters, and yellow summer squash. And no one makes better fried pickles than the bubbas in the kitchen. Locals devour the freshest shrimp in the area with collard greens. But you don't have to go fried all the way. Why not try the grilled shrimp with a tomato-basil cream sauce with lump crabmeat over pasta? The cook is rightly proud of his chocolate pie, and the *Post and Courier* claimed that the "incredible cakes and pies will bring you to your knees with thanks and praise."

4808 Hwy. 17 N., Awendaw. ℭ **843/928-3609.** Reservations not needed. Main courses $6.95–$13 lunch, $8.95–$19 dinner. MC, V. Mon–Fri 9am–9pm; Sat 8am–9:30pm; Sun 11am–3pm.

Mount Pleasant

Gullah Cuisine ★ 🛏 SOUTHERN   This unpretentious little dive pays tribute to the cuisine of the Gullahs, among the first African Americans to live in the Low Country sea islands. Gullah cooking is evocative of Creole flavors, and the dirty rice served here delectably comes with fresh shrimp, chicken, and andouille sausage. Here the okra pod is elevated to its rightful place in the pantheon of a great vegetable: We love the crisp, vividly green okra that not only thickens the gumbos, but is also served deep-fried. The okra gumbo is a delight to us, as is the she-crab soup, one of the best served in Charleston. Locals come for miles around to sample Charlotte Jenkins's Southern fried chicken served with extra-cheesy macaroni. The fried oysters are succulent.

1717 U.S. 17, Mount Pleasant. ✆ **843/881-9076.** www.gullahcuisine.com/index.html. Reservations not needed. Main courses $7–$11; daily lunch buffet Mon–Sat $7.25; Sun brunch $14. MC, V. Mon–Sat 11am–9:30pm (buffet 'til 2:30pm); Sun 11am–3:30pm.

Maverick ★ LOW COUNTRY/AMERICAN   At the previously recommended Old Village Post House, you can enjoy the best prepared food in Mount Pleasant, that suburb across the bridge from Charleston. In this classic restaurant, Low Country dining favorites are a nightly feature, including Post House crab cakes with butter beans and okra or the classic shrimp and grits flavored with scallions and garlic. Another specialty is crusted chicken breast filled with Gruyère cheese and spinach and served with a country ham gravy. Pan-seared halibut also appears on the menu, served with a gazpacho salsa, avocado salad, and savory black beans with crispy tortillas.

101 Pitt St., Mount Pleasant. ✆ **843/388-8935.** Main courses $17–$24. AE, MC, V. Sun 10am–2pm; Sun–Thurs 5:30–10pm; Fri–Sat 5–11pm.

The Red Drum ★★★ AMERICAN/SOUTHWESTERN   Calling itself a gastropub, a sort of London version of the French brasserie, this restaurant draws visitors to Mount Pleasant, just over the Cooper River bridge. The chef and owner, Ben Berryhill, claims that food wasn't frozen in 1865 and sees no reason for it to be so in the 21st century. Winner of numerous culinary awards, Berryhill believes in impeccably fresh ingredients: He maintains a constant search for the best produce South Carolina has to offer. The influence of the Southwest is applied to seafood such as wood-grilled salmon with a roasted red-pepper purée and a sweet corn pudding in corn husks. The free-range chicken won us over when it was served with barbecued sweet potatoes and caramelized pumpkin seeds. You might also wisely opt for the roasted rack of lamb with a wild mushroom and potato crepe topped with a red currant pastille chili sauce. All the appetizers we've sampled have been full of flavor, especially the molasses-grilled quail with a cinnamon-roasted corn bread and applewood bacon, and the rare yellowfin tuna in a spicy ginger vinaigrette.

803 Coleman Blvd., Mount Pleasant. ✆ **843/849-0313.** www.reddrumrestaurant.com. Reservations recommended. Main courses $12–$38. AE, MC, V. Tues–Sat 5:30–10pm.

EXPLORING CHARLESTON

We always head for the **Battery** (officially, the White Point Gardens) to get into the feel of this city. It's right on the end of the peninsula, facing the Cooper River and the harbor. It has a landscaped park, shaded by palmettos and live oaks, with walkways lined with old monuments and other war relics. The view toward the harbor goes out to Fort Sumter. We like to walk along the seawall on East Battery and Murray Boulevard and slowly absorb the Charleston ambience.

Before you go, contact the **Charleston Area Convention and Visitors Bureau** (**CACVB;** ✆ **800/774-0006** or 843/853-8000; www.charlestoncvb.com) for information on tours, attractions, and special events.

Note: You can visit nine of the city's most visible historic attractions by buying a 2-day **Heritage Passport ticket** for $45 ($30 for children 6–12, free for children 5 and under). The ticket provides admission to the Charleston Museum, the Heyward-Washington House, the Joseph Manigault House, Middleton Place, Drayton Hall, the Nathaniel Russell House, Gibbes Museum, the Aiken-Rhett House, and the Edmondston-Alston House. The ticket allows one-time admission to each of those monuments, with the understanding that each is visited during the course of 2 consecutive days. Tickets are available only from the main downtown branch of the **CACVB,** 375 Meeting St. (☏ **800/774-0006** or 843/853-8000), which is open daily 8:30am to 5pm.

The Top Attractions
A CONFEDERATE FORT & A SUBMARINE

Fort Sumter National Monument ★★★　It was here on April 12, 1861, that Confederate forces launched a 34-hour bombardment of the fort. Union forces eventually surrendered, and the rebels occupied federal ground that became a symbol of Southern resistance. This action, however, led to a declaration of war in Washington. Amazingly, Confederate troops held onto Sumter for nearly 4 years, although it was almost continually bombarded by the Yankees. When evacuation finally came, the fort was nothing but a heap of rubble.

Today park rangers are on hand to answer your questions, and you can explore gun emplacements and visit a small museum filled with artifacts related to the siege. A complete tour of the fort, conducted daily from 9am to 5pm, takes about 2 hours.

Though you can travel to the fort via your own boat, most people take the tour of the fort and harbor offered by **Fort Sumter Tours,** 360 Concord St., Ste. 201 (☏ **800/789-3678** or 843/881-7337; www.spiritlinecruises.com). You can board at either of two locations: Liberty Square, in downtown Charleston, or Mount Pleasant's Patriots Point, the site of one of the world's largest naval and maritime museums. Sailing times change every month or so, but from March to Labor Day, there generally are three sailings per day from each location, beginning at 9:30 or 10:45am. Winter sailings are more curtailed. Call for details. Each departure point offers ample parking, and the boats that carry you to Fort Sumter are sightseeing yachts built for the purpose; they're clean, safe, and equipped with modern conveniences.

In Charleston Harbor. ☏ **843/881-7337.** www.spiritlinecruises.com. Free admission to fort; boat trip $16 adults, $15 seniors, $10 children 6–11, free for children 5 and under.

H. L. Hunley Confederate Submarine ★★★　One of the greatest and most sought-after artifacts in the history of naval warfare can now be viewed by the public. The Confederate submarine *H. L. Hunley,* a hand-cranked vessel fashioned of locomotive boilers, sank the Union blockade vessel USS *Housatonic* in February 1864. The sinking of the Union ship launched the age of submarine warfare. The submarine and its nine-member crew mysteriously vanished off Sullivan's Island shortly after completing its historic mission. The vessel was finally located in 1995, sparking headlines across the world. The submarine was eventually raised and brought to the old Charleston navy base for preservation. The bones of its crew members were buried in a historic ceremony on April 17, 2004, at Magnolia Cemetery. The sub, which rests in a tank of 50°F (10°C) water, can be visited only weekends on 20-minute tours.

Warren Lasch Conservation Center, 1250 Supply St., Building 255, North Charleston. ☏ **877/448-6539** or 843/744-2186. www.hunley.org. Admission $12, free for children 5 and under. Sat 10am–5pm; Sun noon–5pm.

HISTORIC HOMES

Aiken-Rhett House　Now deep into its decay, the Aiken-Rhett House, a ghost of its former self, was constructed by merchant John Robinson in 1818 and greatly expanded by Governor and Mrs. William Aiken in the 1830s and 1850s. The property must have looked glorious in 1858, before the outbreak of the Civil War. From

Europe the governor and his lady brought back crystal and bronze chandeliers, classical sculpture, and paintings, plus antiques. Original outbuildings include the kitchens, slave quarters, stables, privies, and cattle sheds.

48 Elizabeth St. ☏ **843/723-1159.** www.historiccharleston.org. Admission $10. Mon–Sat 10am–5pm; Sun 2–5pm.

Edmondston-Alston House ★★★ On High Battery, an elegant section of Charleston, this house (built in 1825 by Charles Edmondston, a Charleston merchant and wharf owner) was one of the earliest constructed in the city in the late Federal style. Edmondston sold it to Charles Alston, a Low Country rice planter, who modified it in Greek Revival style. The house has remained in the Alston family, who open the first two floors to visitors (on guided tours only). Inside are heirloom furnishings, silver, and paintings. It was here in 1861 that General Beauregard joined the Alston family to watch the bombardment of Fort Sumter. Gen. Robert E. Lee once found refuge here when his hotel uptown caught fire.

21 E. Battery. ☏ **843/722-7171.** www.middletonplace.org. Admission $10 adults, $8 children 7–15, free for children 6 and under. Guided tours Tues–Sat 10am–4:30pm; Sun–Mon 1:30–4:30pm. Last tour 4:15pm.

The Heyward-Washington House ★★★ In a district of Charleston called Cabbage Row, this 1772 house was built by Daniel Heyward, called "the rice king," and is the setting for DuBose Heyward's *Porgy*. It was also the home of Thomas Heyward, Jr., a signer of the Declaration of Independence. President George Washington bedded down here in 1791. Many of the fine period pieces in the house are the work of Thomas Elfe, one of America's most famous cabinetmakers. The restored 18th-century kitchen is the only historic kitchen in the city that is open to the public. It stands behind the main house, along with the servants' quarters and the garden.

87 Church St. (btw. Tradd and Broad sts.). ☏ **843/722-0354.** www.charlestonmuseum.org. Admission $10 adults, $5 children 3–12. Adult combination ticket for Heyward-Washington House, the Joseph Manigault House, and the Charleston Museum $22. Mon–Sat 10am–5pm; Sun 1–5pm. Tours leave every half-hour until 4:30pm.

Joseph Manigault House ★ This 1803 Adams-style residence, a National Historic Landmark, was a wealthy rice planter's home. The house features a curving central staircase and an outstanding collection of Charlestonian, American, English, and French period furnishings. It's located diagonally across from the visitor center.

350 Meeting St. (at John St.). ☏ **843/722-2996.** www.charlestonmuseum.org. Admission $10 adults, $5 children 3–12. Adult combination ticket for the Joseph Manigault House, the Heyward-Washington House, and the Charleston Museum $22. Mon–Sat 10am–5pm; Sun 1–5pm. Last tour 4:30pm.

Nathaniel Russell House ★★★ One of America's finest examples of Federal architecture, this 1808 house was completed by Nathaniel Russell, one of Charleston's richest merchants. It is celebrated architecturally for its "free-flying" staircase, spiraling unsupported for three floors. The staircase's elliptical shape is repeated throughout the house. The interiors are ornate with period furnishings, especially the elegant music room with its golden harp and neoclassical-style sofa. The house is accessible to visitors only on guided tours.

51 Meeting St. ☏ **843/724-8481.** http://historiccharleston.org. Admission $10 adults, $5 children 6–16, free for children 5 and under. Guided tours Mon–Sat 10am–5pm; Sun and holidays 2–5pm. Last tour 4:30pm.

NEARBY PLANTATIONS

Boone Hall Plantation & Gardens   This unique plantation is approached by a famous **Avenue of Oaks ★★★**, huge old moss-draped trees planted in 1743 by Captain Thomas Boone. The first floor of the plantation house is elegantly furnished and open to the public. Outbuildings include the circular smokehouse and slave cabins constructed of bricks made on the plantation. A large grove of pecan trees lies behind the house. Note that Boone Hall is not an original structure, but a replica; die-hard history purists may be disappointed in the plantation house, but the grounds are stunning and very much worth visiting. **Boone Hall Farms** opened in 2006, selling produce grown on the plantation and offering seasonal pick-your-own crops.

1235 Long Point Rd. (U.S. 17/701), Mt. Pleasant. *©* **843/884-4371.** www.boonehallplantation.com. Admission $18 adults, $15 seniors 65 and over, $7.50 children 6–12, free for children 5 and under. Apr to Labor Day Mon–Sat 8:30am–6:30pm, Sun 1–5pm; after Labor Day to Mar Mon–Sat 9am–5pm, Sun 1–4pm. Take U.S. 17/701 9 miles north of Charleston.

Drayton Hall ★★   This is one of the oldest surviving plantations, built in 1738 and owned by the Drayton family until 1974. Framed by majestic live oaks, the Georgian-Palladian house is a property of the National Trust for Historic Preservation. Its hand-carved woodwork and plasterwork represent New World craftsmanship at its finest. Because such modern elements as electricity, plumbing, and central heating have never put in an appearance, the house is much as it was in its early years; in fact, it is displayed unfurnished. You can visit an African-American cemetery and take self-guided walks along the river.

Old Ashley River Rd. (S.C. 61). *©* **843/769-2600.** www.draytonhall.org. Admission $15 adults, $8 children 12–18, $6 children 6–11, free for children 5 and under. Mar–Oct daily 8:30am–4:30pm; Nov–Feb daily 8:30am–4pm. Tours on the hour. Closed Thanksgiving Day and Dec 25. Take U.S. 17 S. to S.C. 61; it's 9 miles northwest of Charleston.

Magnolia Plantation and Its Gardens ★★★   Ten generations of the Drayton family have lived here continuously since the 1670s. They haven't had much luck keeping a roof over their heads; the first mansion burned just after the Revolution, and the second was set afire by General Sherman. But you can't call the replacement modern. A simple pre-Revolutionary house was barged down from Summerville and set on the basement foundations of its unfortunate predecessors.

The house is filled with museum-quality Early American furniture, appraised to exceed $500,000 in value. An art gallery has been added to the house as well.

The flowery gardens of camellias and azaleas—among the most beautiful in America—reach their peak bloom in March and April but are colorful year-round. You can tour the house, the gardens (including an herb garden, horticultural maze, topiary garden, and biblical garden), a petting zoo, and a waterfowl refuge, or walk or bike through wildlife trails.

Other sights include an antebellum cabin that was restored and furnished, a plantation rice barge on display beside the Ashley River, and a Nature Train that carries guests on a 45-minute ride around the plantation's perimeter.

Low Country wildlife is visible in marsh, woodland, and swamp settings. The **Audubon Swamp Garden,** also on the grounds, is an independently operated 60-acre cypress swamp that offers a close look at other wildlife, such as egrets, alligators, wood ducks, otters, turtles, and herons.

S.C. 61. *©* **800/367-3517** or 843/571-1266. www.magnoliaplantation.com. Admission to garden and grounds $15 adults, $14 seniors, $10 children 6–12, free for children 5 and under. Plantation house tour is $7 extra for ages 6 and up; children 5 and under not allowed to tour the house. Admission to Audubon Swamp Garden $7 adults, $6 seniors, $5 children 6–12, free for children 5 and under. Magnolia Plantation and Audubon Swamp Gardens summer daily 8am–5:30pm; call for winter hours.

Middleton Place ★★★   This was the home of Henry Middleton, president of the First Continental Congress, whose son, Arthur, was a signer of the Declaration of Independence. Today this National Historic Landmark includes America's oldest landscaped gardens, the Middleton Place House, and the Plantation Stableyards.

The gardens, begun in 1741, reflect the elegant symmetry of European gardens of that period. Ornamental lakes, terraces, and plantings of camellias, azaleas, magnolias, and crape myrtle accent the grand design.

The Middleton Place House itself was built in 1755, but in 1865, all but the south flank was ransacked and burned by Union troops. The house was restored in the 1870s as a family residence and today houses collections of fine silver, furniture, rare first editions by Catesby and Audubon, and portraits by Benjamin West and Thomas Sully. In the stable yards, craftspeople demonstrate life on a plantation of yesteryear. There are also horses, mules, hogs, cows, sheep, and goats.

A plantation lunch is served at the **Middleton Place Restaurant,** which is a replica of an original rice mill. *American Way* magazine cited this restaurant as one of the top 10 representing American cuisine at its best. Specialties include she-crab soup, hoppin' John and ham biscuits, okra gumbo, Sea Island shrimp, and corn pudding. Service is daily from 11am to 3pm. Dinner is served daily 5 to 9pm and is likely to include panned (pan-seared) quail with ham (a recipe from the late chef Edna Lewis, who was a consultant-in-residence here for years), sea scallops, or broiled oysters. For dinner reservations, call ℂ **843/556-6020.**

Ashley River Rd. ℂ **800/782-3608** or 843/556-6020. www.middletonplace.org. Admission to gardens and stable yard $25 adults, $5 children 7–15, free for children 6 and under. House tour $10 adults, $6 children 6–12. Gardens and stable yards daily 9am–5pm. House Mon noon–4:30pm; Tues–Sun 10am–4:30pm. Take U.S. 17 W. to S.C. 61 (Ashley River Rd.) 14 miles northwest of Charleston.

SPECTACULAR GARDENS

See also the listing for Magnolia Plantation in "Nearby Plantations," above.

Cypress Gardens ★★   This 163-acre swamp garden was used as a freshwater reserve for Dean Hall, a huge Cooper River rice plantation, and was given to the city in 1963. Today the giant cypress trees draped with Spanish moss provide an unforgettable setting for flat-bottom boats that glide among their knobby roots. Footpaths in the garden wind through a profusion of azaleas, camellias, daffodils, and other colorful blooms. Visitors share the swamp with alligators, pileated woodpeckers, wood ducks, otters, barred owls, and other abundant species. The gardens are worth a visit at any time of year, but they're at their most colorful in March and April. Also on-site are a reptile center, aquarium, and aviary, plus a butterfly house.

U.S. 52, Moncks Corner. ℂ **843/553-0515.** www.cypressgardens.info. Admission $10 adults, $9 seniors, $5 children 6–12, free for children 5 and under. Daily 9am–5pm. Closed major holidays. Take U.S. 52 some 24 miles north of Charleston.

MUSEUMS

The Charleston Museum ★★   The Charleston Museum, founded in 1773, is the first and oldest museum in America. The collections preserve and interpret the social and natural history of Charleston and the South Carolina coastal region. The full-scale replica of the famed Confederate submarine *H. L. Hunley* standing outside the museum is one of the most-photographed subjects in the city. The museum also exhibits the largest silver collection in Charleston, early crafts, historic relics, and the "Discover Me" room, which has hands-on exhibits for children.

360 Meeting St. ⓒ **843/722-2996.** www.charlestonmuseum.org. Admission $10 adults, $5 children 3-12. Adult combination ticket for the Charleston Museum, the Joseph Manigault House, and Heyward-Washington House $22. Mon–Sat 9am–5pm; Sun 1–5pm.

The Gibbes Museum of Art ★   Established in 1905 by the Carolina Art Association, the Gibbes Museum contains an intriguing collection of prints and drawings from the 18th century to the present. On display are landscapes, genre scenes, panoramic views of Charleston Harbor, and portraits of South Carolinians (see *Thomas Middleton* by Benjamin West, *Charles Izard Manigault* by Thomas Sully, and *John C. Calhoun* by Rembrandt Peale). The museum's collection of some 400 miniature portraits ranks as one of the most comprehensive in the country.

135 Meeting St. ⓒ **843/722-2706.** www.gibbesmuseum.org. Admission $9 adults; $7 seniors, students, and military; $5 children 6-18; free for children 5 and under. Tues–Sat 10am–5pm; Sun 1–5pm. Closed holidays.

More Attractions

Charles Towne Landing State Historic Site ★★   This 663-acre park is located on the site where English settlers first landed in 1670, thereby establishing the birthplace of the Carolina colony and the plantation system that eventually spread throughout the American South. The park's infrastructure and pathways were redefined and upgraded, and a visitor center/museum was added with lots of interactive exhibits describing the history of the first permanent English settlement in the Carolinas. A history trail, with the option of listening to a prerecorded audio tour, enables visitors to experience the reality of those first settlers. Interpretive park rangers in 17th-century dress tend heirloom crops such as rice, indigo, and cotton; fire cannons and muskets; and deliver information about the daily life of the era's indentured servants. You can wander through informal English gardens and the Animal Forest, home to species which were native to the area at the time of the original settlement. There's absolutely no flashy theme-park atmosphere here: Just a commitment to archaeology, natural beauty, and the transmission of history.

500 Old Towne Rd. (S.C. 171, btw. U.S. 17 and I-26). ⓒ **843/852-4200.** http://southcarolinaparks.com. Admission $7.50 adults, $3.50 children 6-15, free for those with disabilities. Daily 9am–5pm. Closed Dec 24-25.

The Children's Museum of the Lowcountry ☺   This hands-on learning place for both young'uns and their parents aims to spark a love of learning in children as young as 3 months and up to 12 years through interactive, hands-on experiences in the arts and sciences. Children can, for example, explore the life of a shrimper on the *Anna Marie,* or get lost in medieval life in a castle. Other adventures include racing boats down rapids, boarding a pirate ship, making rain indoors, and growing vegetables in an all-organic kids' garden.

25 Ann St. ⓒ **843/853-8962.** www.explorecml.org. Admission $7 per person but free for kids under 12 months. Tues–Sat 9am–5pm; Sun 1–5pm.

The Citadel ★   The all-male (at that time) Citadel was established in 1842 as an arsenal and a refuge for whites in the event of a slave uprising. In 1922, it moved to its present location. Pat Conroy's novel *The Lords of Discipline* is based on his 4 years at the military college. Since 1995, when the first woman notoriously joined the ranks of cadets, women have joined the ranks with young men. The campus of the school features buildings of Moorish design, with crenelated battlements and sentry towers. It is especially interesting to visit on Friday, when the college is in session and the public is invited to a precision-drill parade on the quadrangle at 3:45pm. For a history of the Citadel, stop at the **Citadel Memorial Archives Museum** (☏ 843/953-6846).

Moultrie St. and Elmwood Ave. ☏ **843/225-3294.** www.citadel.edu. Free admission. Daily 24 hr. for drive-through visits. Museum Sun–Fri 2–5pm; Sat noon–5pm; closed religious, national, and school holidays.

Fort Moultrie   Only a palmetto-log fortification at the time of the American Revolution, the half-completed fort was attacked by a British fleet in 1776. Col. William Moultrie's troops repelled the invasion in one of the first decisive American victories of the Revolution. The fort was subsequently enlarged into a five-sided structure with earth-and-timber walls 17 feet high. The British didn't do it in, but an 1804 hurricane ripped it apart. By the War of 1812, it was back and ready for action. Osceola, the fabled leader of the Seminoles in Florida, was incarcerated at the fort and eventually died here. During the 1830s, Edgar Allen Poe served as a soldier at the fort. He set his famous short story "The Gold Bug" on Sullivan's Island. The fort also played roles in the Civil War, the Mexican War, the Spanish-American War, and even in the two world wars, but by 1947, it had retired from action.

1214 Middle St., on Sullivan's Island. ☏ **843/883-3123.** www.nps.gov/fomo. Admission $3 adults, $1 seniors 62 and over, free for children 15 and under, $5 family. Federal Recreation Passports honored. Daily 9am–5pm. Closed Christmas Day and New Year's Day. Take S.C. 703 from Mt. Pleasant to Sullivan's Island.

International Center for Birds of Prey   This attraction contains more than 80 species of birds of prey, set on a 152-acre site. The location is 12 miles north of Mount Pleasant and 15 miles from the center of Charleston. The collection includes eagles, hawks, owls, falcons, kites, and vultures. Guided walking tours are available, and free-flight demonstrations are staged.

4872 Seewee Rd., Awendaw. ☏ **843/971-7474.** www.thecenterforbirdsofprey.org. Admission $12 adults, $10 ages 6–18, free for ages 5 and under. Thurs–Sat only 10am–5pm. Follow U.S. 17 north through Mount Pleasant to Awendaw and look for the signs.

Old Exchange and Provost Dungeon ★   This is a stop that many visitors overlook, but it's one of the three most important colonial buildings in the United States because of its role as a prison during the American Revolution. In 1873, the building became City Hall. You'll find a large collection of antique chairs, supplied by the local Daughters of the American Revolution, each of whom brought a chair here from home in 1921.

122 E. Bay St. ☏ **843/727-2165.** www.oldexchange.com. Admission $8 adults, $4 children 7–12, free for children 6 and under. Daily 9am–5pm. Closed Thanksgiving Day and Dec 23–25.

South Carolina Aquarium ★   Visitors can explore Southern aquatic life in an attraction filled with thousands of enchanting creatures and plants in amazing habitats, from five major regions of the Appalachian Watershed. Jutting into the Charleston Harbor for 2,000 feet, the focal point is a 93,000-square-foot aquarium featuring a two-story Great Ocean Tank Exhibition. Contained within are more than 800 animals, including deadly sharks but also sea turtles and stingrays. Every afternoon at

4pm, the aquarium offers a dolphin program, where bottle-nosed dolphins can be viewed from an open-air terrace. One of the most offbeat exhibits replicates a black-water swamp, with atmospheric fog, a spongy floor, and twinkling lights. **Secrets of the Amazon** features the diversity of this endangered region in sights, sounds, and adventure. New in 2008 was the inauguration of the Camp Carolina exhibit, a child-friendly, interactive display about how to successfully appreciate the great Carolina outdoors without leaving an ecologically destructive "footprint."

100 Aquarium Wharf. ℂ **843/720-1990.** www.scaquarium.org. Admission $18 adults, $17 seniors 62 and over, $11 children 2-11, free for children 1 and under. Apr 1-Aug 15 Mon-Sat 9am-6pm, Sun noon-6pm; Aug 16-Mar 31 Mon-Sat 9am-5pm, Sun noon-5pm.

Especially for Kids

For more than 300 years, Charleston has been the home of pirates, patriots, and presidents. Your child can see firsthand the **Great Hall at the Old Exchange,** where President Washington danced; view the **Provost Dungeons,** where South Carolina patriots spent their last days; and touch the last remaining structural evidence of the **Charleston Seawall.** Children will take special delight in **Charles Towne Landing** and **Middleton Place.** At **Fort Sumter,** they can see where the Civil War began. Children will also enjoy **Magnolia Plantation,** with its Audubon Swamp Garden.

Kids and navy vets will also love the aircraft carrier **USS *Yorktown*,** at Patriots Point, 2 miles east of the Cooper River Bridge. Its World War II, Korean, and Vietnam exploits are documented in exhibits, and general naval history is illustrated through models of ships, planes, and weapons. You can wander through the bridge wheelhouse, flight and hangar decks, chapel, and sick bay, and view the film *The Fighting Lady,* which depicts life aboard the carrier. Also at Patriots Point are the World War II destroyer *Laffey,* the World War II submarine *Clamagore,* and the cutter *Ingham.* Patriots Point is open daily from 9am to 6:20pm April to October, until 5pm November to March. Admission is $16 for adults, $13 for seniors 63 and over and military personnel in uniform, $9 for kids 6 to 11. Adjacent is the fine 18-hole public Patriots Point Golf Course. For further information, call ℂ **843/884-2727** or visit www.patriotspoint.org.

ORGANIZED TOURS

BY HORSE & CARRIAGE   **Old South Carriage,** 14 Anson St. (ℂ **843/723-9712;** www.oldsouthcarriagetours.com), offers narrated horse-drawn-carriage tours through the Historic District daily from 9am to dusk. A 1-hour carriage tour spans a distance of 2½ miles, covering 30 blocks of the Historic District. The cost is $21 for adults and $13 for children 3 to 11.

BY MULE TEAM   **Palmetto Carriage Tours,** 40 N. Market St., at Guignard Street (ℂ **843/723-8145;** www.carriagetour.com), uses mule teams instead of the usual horse and carriage for its guided tours of Old Charleston. Tours originate at the Big Red Barn behind the Rainbow Market. The cost is $20 for adults and seniors and $12 for children 4 to 11. It operates daily from 9am to 5pm.

BY BOAT   **Spiritline Cruises,** 360 Concord St., Ste. 201 (ℂ **800/789-3678** or 843/722-2628; http://spiritlinecruises.com), offers a **Harbor and Fort Sumter**

Tour by boat, departing daily from the City Marina and from the Patriots Point Maritime Museum. This is the only tour to stop at Fort Sumter, target of the opening shots of the Civil War. The fare is $16 for adults, $15 for seniors, $10 for children 6 to 11, and free for children 5 and under. The operator also has an interesting **Charleston Harbor Tour,** with daily departures from Patriots Point. The 2-hour cruise passes the Battery, Charleston Port, Castle Pinckney, Drum Island, Fort Sumter, and the aircraft carrier *Yorktown,* and sails under the Cooper River Bridge and on to other sights. Prices are the same as those for the Harbor and Fort Sumter Tour.

WALKING TOURS   Charlestonians are proud to talk about the historical quirks of their city, and as such, several tour operators compete for your walking tour business. A well-recommended staple is **Charleston Strolls** (✆ 843/766-2080; www. charlestonstrolls.com), which conducts a 2-hour walking tour every day beginning at 10am that touches on the salient points of the city's sometimes bloody history. Admission is $18 per person, or else $10 for ages 7 to 12 (6 and under free).

Another well-recommended guided stroll through historic Charleston is the **Charleston Tea Party Walking Tour** (✆ 843/722-1779; http://charlestongateway. com). It lasts 2 hours and costs $25 for adults and $10 for children 12 and under. Departing year-round Monday to Saturday at 9:30am and 2pm, tours originate at the Kings Courtyard Inn, 198 Kings St. The tour goes into a lot of nooks and crannies of Charleston, including secret courtyards and gardens. Finally, you get that promised tea. Reservations are required.

Tours of Charleston's 18th-century **architecture** in the original walled city begin at 10am and 2pm, and tours of 19th-century architecture along Meeting Street and the Battery begin at 2pm. Departures are from in front of the Meeting Street Inn, 173 Meeting St. Tours last 2 hours and are given every day but Tuesday and Sunday. The cost is $20 for adults, $6 for children 7 to 12, and free for children 6 and under. For reservations, call ✆ 843/893-2327.

BEACHES & OUTDOOR PURSUITS

BEACHES   Three great beaches are within a 25-minute drive of the center of Charleston.

In the West Islands, **Folly Beach,** which had degenerated into a funky Coney Island–type amusement park, is making a comeback following a multimillion-dollar cleanup, but it remains the least pristine beach in the area. The best bathroom amenities are located here, however. At the western end of the island is the **Folly Beach County Park,** with bathrooms, parking, and shelter from the rain. To get here, take U.S. 17 East to S.C. 171 South to Folly Beach.

In the East Cooper area, both the **Isle of Palms** and **Sullivan's Island** offer miles of public beaches, mostly bordered by beachfront homes. Windsurfing and jet-skiing are popular here. Take U.S. 17 East to S.C. 703 (Ben Sawyer Blvd.). S.C. 703 continues through Sullivan's Island to the Isle of Palms.

Kiawah Island has the area's most pristine beach—far preferable to Folly Beach, to our tastes—and draws a more upmarket crowd. The best beachfront is at **Beachwalker County Park,** on the southern end of the island. Get there before noon on weekends; the limited parking is usually taken by then. Canoe rentals are available for use on the Kiawah River, and the park offers not only a boardwalk, but also bathrooms, showers, and a changing area. Take U.S. 17 East to S.C. 171 South (Folly Beach Rd.), and turn right onto S.C. 700 Southwest (Maybank Hwy.) to Bohicket Road, which turns into Betsy Kerrison Parkway. Where Betsy Kerrison Parkway dead-ends, turn left on Kiawah Parkway, which takes you to the island.

For details on the major resorts on Kiawah Island and the Isle of Palms, see "Kiawah Island & the Isle of Palms," later in this chapter.

BIKING   Charleston is basically flat and not traffic-clogged except on its main arteries at rush hour. Biking is a popular local pastime, and most of the city parks have biking trails. The most popular run is across the 2.5-mile, eight-lane Arthur Ravenel Jr. Bridge, which links downtown Charleston to the suburb of Mount Pleasant. For the best bike rentals, contact **Bike the Bridge** at 6 Vendue Range (© **843/853-BIKE** [853-2453]; www.bikethebridgerentals.com). Rentals begin at $15 for 3 hours or $25 per day.

Another deal is offered by **Charleston Cruiser Rentals** (© **843/754-0176**), which will deliver a rental bike to your hotel door. This outfitter offers a half-day rental for $20, going up to $30 for 8 hours.

The **Bicycle Shoppe,** 280 Meeting St. (© **843/722-8168;** www.thebicycle shoppecharleston.com), open Monday to Saturday 9am to 6pm and Sunday 1 to 5pm. Cruisers and hybrids range in price from $28 to $32 per day.

BOATING   A true Charlestonian is as much at home on the sea as on land. Sailing local waters is a popular family pastime. One of the best places for boat rentals is **Isle of Palms Marina,** Isle of Palms (© **843/886-0209;** www.iop.net/community/iop marina.aspx), where 18-foot boats, big enough for seven people, rent for around $240 for 4 hours, plus fuel. A larger boat, big enough for 10, goes for about $375 to $450 for 4 hours, plus fuel.

DIVING   Several outfitters provide rentals and ocean charters, as well as instruction for neophytes. At **Atlantic Coast Diving,** 426 W. Coleman Blvd., Mt. Pleasant (© **843/884-1500;** www.charlestondiving.com), you can rent both diving and snorkeling equipment. Diving equipment costs $50 per day. It's open Monday to Saturday from 10am to 6pm.

FISHING   Freshwater fishing charters are available year-round along the Low Country's numerous creeks and inlets. The waterways are filled with flounder, trout, spot-tail, and channel bass. Some of the best striped-bass fishing available in America can be found at nearby Lake Moultrie.

Offshore-fishing charters for reef fishing (where you'll find fish such as cobia, black sea bass, and king mackerel) and for the Gulf Stream (where you fish for sailfish, marlin, wahoo, dolphin, and tuna) are also available. Both types of charters can be arranged at the previously recommended **Isle of Palms Marina,** Isle of Palms (© **843/886-0209**). A fishing craft holding up to 10 people rents for $900 for 6 hours, including everything but food and drink. Reservations must be made 24 hours in advance.

Folly Beach Fishing Pier (© **843/588-3474;** www.ccprc.com) at Folly Beach is a wood pier, 25 feet wide, that extends 1,045 feet into the Atlantic Ocean. Facilities include restrooms, a tackle shop, and a restaurant. It's accessible to people with disabilities.

GOLF Charleston is said to be the home of golf in America. Charlestonians have been playing the game since the 1700s, when the first golf clubs arrived from Scotland. With 26 public and private courses in the area, there's a golf game waiting for every buff.

Wild Dunes Resort, Isle of Palms (© **888/778-1876** or 843/886-6000; www. wilddunes.com), offers two championship golf courses designed by Tom Fazio. The **Links ★★★** is a 6,387-yard, par-70 layout that takes the player through marshlands, over or into huge sand dunes, through a wooded alley, and into a pair of oceanfront finishing holes once called "the greatest east of Pebble Beach, California." The course has been ranked among the 100 greatest courses in the United States by *Golf Digest* and among the top 100 in the world by *Golf Magazine. Golf Digest* has also ranked the Links as the 13th-greatest resort course in America. The **Harbor Course** offers 6,402 yards of Low Country marsh and Intracoastal Waterway views. This par-70 layout is considered to be target golf, challenging players with 2 holes that play from one island to another across Morgan Creek. Greens fees at these courses can range from $85 to $165, depending on the season. Both courses are open daily 7am to 6pm year-round.

Your best bet, if you'd like to play at any of the other Charleston-area golf courses, is to contact **Charleston Golf, Inc.** (© **800/774-4444;** www.charlestongolfguide. com; Mon–Fri 8:30am–5pm). The company represents 17 golf courses, offering packages that range from $100 to $200 per person March to August. Off-season packages range from $75 to $150 per person. Prices include greens fees on one course, the use of a golf cart, a hotel room based on double occupancy, and taxes. Travel pros here will customize your vacation with golf-course selections and tee times; they can also arrange rental cars and airfares. Reservations must be made 1 week in advance.

HIKING The most interesting hiking trails begin around Buck Hall in **Francis Marion National Forest** (© **843/887-3257**), located some 40 miles north of the center of Charleston via U.S. 17-N. The site consists of 250,000 acres of swamps, with towering oaks and pines. Also in the national forest, **Buck Hall Recreation,** reached by U.S. 17/701 North from Charleston, has 15 camping sites ($15–$25 per night), plus a boat ramp and fishing. Other hiking trails are at **Edisto Beach State Park,** State Cabin Road, on Edisto Island (© **843/869-2156**).

TENNIS Charlestonians have been playing tennis since the early 1800s. Your best bet is the **Family Circle Tennis Center,** 161 Seven Farms Dr. (© **843/849-5300;** www.familycirclecup.com), which charges hourly rates ranging from $10 to $20 per person. Hours are Monday to Thursday 8am to 8pm, Friday 8am to 7pm, Saturday 8am to 5pm, and Sunday 9am to 5pm. The location is northeast of the center of Charleston, about a 10-minute drive from the airport.

SHOPPING

The densest and some say most appealing collection of upscale shops in the Carolinas is on King Street. The **Shops at Charleston Place,** 130 Market St. (www. charlestonplaceshops.com), is an upscale complex of top-designer clothing shops (Gucci, Montblanc, St. John, Lacoste, Ralph Lauren, and so on). A short stretch of trendy, youth-conscious boutiques known as Upper King Street Design District (http://littleworksofheart.typepad.com/upperkingcharleston) is where about a dozen avant-garde artisans ply their penchant for jewelry, millinery, and crafts.

Antiques

George C. Birlant and Co. If you're in the market for 18th- and 19th-century English antique furnishings, this is the right place. This Charleston staple prides itself on its Charleston Battery Bench, which is seen (and sat upon) throughout the Battery. The heavy iron sides are cast from the original 1880 mold, and the slats are authentic South Carolina cypress. It's as close to the original as you can get. Hours are Monday to Saturday 9am to 5:30pm. 191 King St. © **888/BIR-LANT** (247-5268) or 843/722-3842. www.birlant.com.

Livingston Antiques For nearly a quarter of a century, discriminating antiques hunters have patronized the showroom of this dealer. Both authentic antiques and fool-the-eye reproductions are sold. Hours are Monday to Saturday 10am to 5pm. 2137 Savannah Hwy. © **843/556-3502.** www.livingstonantiques.com.

Art

Gallery Chuma With some 2,900 square feet of exhibition space, this is the largest African-American art gallery in the South. The original pieces change every 2 months. On permanent display are the works of prominent artists, including Dr. Leo Twiggs and historical artist Joe Pinckney (prints only). Hours are Monday to Saturday 10am to 6pm. 43 John St. © **843/722-7568.** www.gallerychuma.com.

Lowcountry Artists In a former bookbindery, this gallery is operated by eight local artists, who work in oil, watercolor, drawings, collage, woodcuts, and other mediums. Hours are Monday to Saturday 10am to 5pm and Sunday noon to 5pm. 148 E. Bay St. © **843/577-9295.** www.lowcountryartists.com.

Waterfront Gallery Facing Waterfront Park, this gallery is the premier choice for the work of South Carolina artists. The works of 21 local artists are presented. For sale are pieces ranging from sculpture to oils. Hours are Monday to Thursday 11am to 6pm, Friday and Saturday 11am to 10pm, and Sunday noon to 5pm. 215 E. Bay St. (across from Custom House). © **843/722-1155.** www.waterfrontartgallery.com.

Wells Gallery Works by artists from the Low Country and all over the Southeast are on display at this Charleston gallery. Specializing in Low Country landscapes, the gallery also offers works by artists from all over the U.S. Prices range from $600 to $12,000. Hours are Monday to Saturday 10am to 5pm. 103 Broad St. © **843/853-3233.** www.wellsgallery.com.

Books

Preservation Society of Charleston Bookstore This shop features a collection of books about Charleston and the Low Country, as well as art books, Southern literature, and even early recordings of Low Country lore told in the Gullah dialect. Hours are Monday to Saturday 10am to 5pm. 147 King St. © **843/722-4630.** www.preservationsociety.org.

Candies

Lucas Belgian Chocolate This is one of the truly fine chocolatier shops in South Carolina, in business for more than 2 decades. In the Historic District near

Market Street, it sells imported Belgian chocolates, chocolate truffles, turtles, and clusters, among other mouthwatering confections. The store, in fact, features just about anything made of chocolate you might be seeking. Your purchases, incidentally, are beautifully wrapped. Hours are Tuesday to Saturday 10am to 6pm and Sunday 12:30 to 5:30pm. 73 State St. © **843/722-0461.**

Civil War Artifacts

CSA Galleries   This is one of the busiest and best-stocked Civil War and art gallery shops in the South. Its main specialty is Civil War prints, and it offers a full framing department. It also peddles gifts and collectibles, clothing, glassware, videos, books, music boxes, and a collection of specialty foods. Based in North Charleston, it happens to be owned by one of South Carolina's state senators, Glenn McConnell. Open Monday to Saturday 10am to 6pm. 5605 Rivers Ave., North Charleston. © **800/256-1861** or 843/747-7554. www.csagalleries.com.

Crafts & Gifts

Charleston Crafts   This is a permanent showcase for Low Country crafts artists who work in a variety of mediums, including metal, glass, paper, clay, wood, and fiber. Handmade jewelry is also sold, along with basketry, leather, traditional crafts, and even homemade soaps. Hours are Monday to Saturday 10am to 5:30pm. 87 Hasell St. © **843/723-2938.** www.charlestoncrafts.org.

Fashion

Ben Silver   One of the finer men's clothiers in Charleston, this is the best place to get yourself dressed like a member of fine society. The store specializes in blazers and buttons; it has a collection of more than 600 blazer-button designs that are unique in the city. The store features house names and designs only, so don't go looking for Ralph Lauren here. Hours are Monday to Saturday 9am to 6pm. 149 King St. © **843/577-4556.** www.bensilver.com.

Nancy's   Nancy's specializes in clothing for the woman who wants to be both active and stylish. Complete outfits in linen, silk, and cotton are sold, along with such accessories as belts and jewelry. Hours are Monday to Saturday 10am to 5:30pm. 342 King St. © **843/722-1272.** www.nancyscharleston.com.

Furnishings

The Shop of the Historic Charleston Reproductions   It's rare that a store with so much to offer is not-for-profit, but that's the case here. All items are approved by the Historic Charleston Foundation, and all proceeds benefit the restoration of Charleston's historic projects. Licensed-replica products range from furniture to jewelry. The pride of the store is its home-furnishings collection by Baker Furniture, an esteemed company based in Michigan. What makes this collection unusual is the fact that the pieces are adaptations of real Charleston antiques, made of mahogany, a rich dark wood with an authentic feel, that can only be found here.

If one of Charleston's iron designs around town has caught your eye, there's a chance that you'll find a replica of it in the form of jewelry. A collection of china from Mottahedeh is also featured. Hours are Monday to Saturday 10am to 5pm.

The store operates shops in several historic houses, and for slightly more than basic souvenirs, see its Francis Edmunds Center Museum Shop at 108 Meeting St.

(**843/724-8484;** www.heritagefederation.org). Hours are Monday to Saturday 10am to 5pm and Sunday 1 to 5pm. 105 Broad St. **843/723-8292.**

Jewelry

Croghan's Jewel Box   Here you'll find gift ideas for any situation, from baby showers to weddings. Estate jewelry and some contemporary pieces are featured. This store also sets diamonds for rings and pendants, and can even secure the diamond for you, with the price depending on the type of stone and grade that you choose. Hours are Monday to Friday 9:30am to 5:30pm and Saturday 10am to 5pm. 308 King St. **843/723-3594.** www.croghansjewelbox.com.

Dazzles   One-of-a-kind jewelry is sold here, along with the finest collection of handmade 14-karat-gold slide bracelets in town. Some of the jewelry is of heirloom quality. The staff will also help you create jewelry of your own design from a choice of stones. Hours are Monday to Wednesday 10am to 6pm, Thursday to Saturday 10am to 7pm, and Sunday noon to 5pm. Charleston Place, 226 King St. **843/722-5951.** www.dazzlesjewelry.com.

Geiss & Sons Jewelers   Jewelry here is custom designed by old world–trained craftspeople. This is a direct offshoot of a store opened by the Geiss family in Brazil in 1919. It's an official watch dealer for names such as Rolex, Bertolucci, and Raymond Weil. Hours are Monday to Friday 10am to 5pm. 116 E. Bay St. **843/577-4497.** www.geissjewelers.com.

Joggling Boards

Old Charleston Joggling Board Co.   Since the early 1830s, joggling boards have been a Charleston tradition. These boards are the creation of Mrs. Benjamin Kinloch Huger, a native who sought a mild form of exercise for her rheumatism. Mrs. Huger's Scottish cousins sent her a model of a joggling board, suggesting that she sit and gently bounce on the board. The fame of the device soon spread, and the board soon turned up in gardens, patios, and porches throughout the Charleston area. After World War II, joggling boards became rare because of the scarcity of timber and the high cost of labor, but the tradition was revived in 1970. The company also produces a joggle bench, a smaller replica of the joggling board. Hours are Monday to Friday 8am to 5pm. 652 King St. **843/723-4331.** www.oldcharlestonjogglingboard.com.

Perfume

Scents of Charleston   Favorite fragrances, some of them original and unique to this store, are found here, and prices (for the most part) are relatively reasonable. A fragrance that has endured virtually since the store was established in the 1980s is Southern Rain, evocative of lily of the valley, magnolia, and violet. The glycerin body cream is a bestseller, and the store is the exclusive sales outlet in Charleston for every scent, soap, and cream branded by Crabtree & Evelyn. It is open Sunday to Thursday 10am to 9pm and Friday and Saturday 10am to 10pm. 92 N. Market St. **800/854-8804** or 843/853-8837. www.scentsofcharleston.com.

Pharmacy

Pitt Street Pharmacy ★★   This time-honored old-fashioned pharmacy is pretty much as it was more than 7 decades ago. You can still get thick malted milk shakes like your grandfather enjoyed, or else mortar-and-pestle ground prescriptions—called "compounds" here. It's like wandering back in a time capsule when you order a cherry Coke float from the old soda fountain. If you drop in for lunch, you might order a grilled cheese sandwich. Oh, yes, you can also get almost any prescription filled as well. Hours are Monday to Saturday 9am to 6pm. The location is in the suburb of Mount Pleasant across the bridge from downtown Charleston. 111 Pitt St., Mount Pleasant. ✆ **843/884-4051.** www.pittstreetpharmacy.com.

Textiles

Lulan Artisans ★★ 🎒 This is the showcase of Eve Blossom, who is a specialist in modern textile design fused with Southeast Asian weaving techniques. Moving to Charleston from San Francisco, she opened this chic showcase for her products. Her weavers are master artisans, working in such countries as Cambodia, Vietnam, Thailand, even Laos, using centuries-old techniques to create intricate hand-woven textiles. Hours are Tuesday to Saturday 10am to 5pm. 469 King St. ✆ **843/722-0118.** http://lulan.com.

CHARLESTON AFTER DARK

The Performing Arts

Charleston's major cultural venue is the **Dock Street Theatre,** 133 Church St. (✆ **843/577-7183;** www.charlestonstage.com), a 463-seat theater. The original was built in 1736 but burned down in the early 19th century, and the Planters Hotel (not related to the Planters Inn) was constructed around its ruins. In 1936, the theater was rebuilt in a new location. It's the home of the **Charleston Stage Company,** a local not-for-profit theater group whose season runs from mid-September to May. Dock Street hosts performances ranging from Shakespeare to *My Fair Lady.* It's most active during the Spoleto Festival USA in May and June. The box office (✆ **843/577-7183**) is open Monday to Friday 10am to 5pm, Saturday 10am to 5pm and a half-hour before curtain, and Sunday from 10am to 3pm.

The **Robert Ivey Ballet,** 1910 Savannah Hwy. (✆ **843/556-1343;** www.robertiveyballet.com), offers both classical and contemporary dance, as well as children's ballet programs. The group performs at various venues throughout the Charleston area, with general-admission prices of $25 for adults and $15 for children.

Charleston Ballet Theatre, 477 King St. (✆ **843/723-7334;** www.charlestonballet.org), is one of the South's best professional ballet companies. The season begins in late October and continues into April. Tickets are $22 to $50.

The **Charleston Symphony Orchestra,** 14 George St. (✆ **843/723-7528;** www.charlestonsymphony.com), performs throughout the state, but its main venues are the Gaillard Auditorium and Charleston Southern University. The season runs from September to May.

The Club & Music Scene

Blind Tiger Pub Near Bay Street, this pub occupies a historic location, a bar having operated here since 1803. The name comes from the days when Charlestonians opened up illegal "parlors of consumption" before the days of speak-easies—these parlors were known as "blind tigers." The legend was that admission fees were paid to see the mythical beast known as a Blind Tiger, with "complimentary" cocktails served. Lawyers and businessmen in suits frequent the on-site Four Corners Café at lunch, but at night more casual attire is worn by the crowd, usually in the 30-to-40 age range. Live jazz or other music is played in the evening. Out back is a walled deck with subdued lighting and fountains. The bar is open Monday to Saturday 11:30am to 2am. 38 Broad St.© **843/577-0088.** www.btpub.com.

Chai's ★　This is the most talked about bar on Upper King Street. As such, it's a nocturnal centerpiece of a neighborhood that insiders refer to as Charleston's version of New York City's SoHo. The most popular night here, other than Friday and Saturday (when it's packed) is Wednesday, when reggae is the theme and all things Jamaican can help the evening rock and roll along. The color scheme is terra cotta, and there's an enlarged mural of Angkor Wat on one wall, but other than that, the main visual focus is on the rambling wooden bar where tapas are available. Mojitos are big here. It's open Monday to Saturday 5pm to midnight. 462 King St.© **843/722-7313.** www.eatatchais.com.

Henry's　One of the best places for jazz in Charleston, this club features a live band on Friday and Saturday. Otherwise, you get taped Top-40 music for listening and dancing. If you're a single man or woman with a roving eye, this is one of the hottest pickup bars in town. It attracts a mainly over-30 crowd. Happy hour, with drink discounts and free appetizers, is Monday to Friday from 4 to 7pm. Hours are Monday to Saturday 4pm to 2am and Sunday noon to 2am. 54 N. Market St.© **843/723-4363.** http://henryshousecharleston.com.

The Bar Scene

The Brick　Set in what was built in the 19th century as a warehouse, this neighborhood bar is lined with handmade bricks and capped with heavy timbers. It receives a wide medley of drinkers, everyone from college students to local dockyard workers, as well as a scattering of travelers from out of town. Appetizers and burgers are the only food served, but at least a dozen beers are on tap. Live music begins at 9:30pm Wednesday to Saturday. The tavern is open daily 5pm to 2am. 213 E. Bay St.© **843/720-7788.**

Club Habana　With the ambience of a private club, this two-story house from 1870 is where the Ernest Hemingway of today would head if he were in Charleston. Relax in one of three Gilded Age salons, each evocative of the Reconstruction era. The house specializes in exotic cigars and martinis, and serves appetizers, desserts, fruit and cheese plates, and even some miniature beef Wellingtons. When filming *The Patriot*, Mel Gibson made Habana his second home in the city. You pass through a well-stocked tobacco store downstairs to reach the club. Hours are Monday to Thursday and Sunday 4:30pm to midnight, Friday and Saturday 4:30pm to 2am. 177 Meeting St.© **843/853-5900.** www.clubhabana.com.

First Shot Lounge　Our preferred watering hole is this old standby, where we've seen such visiting celebs as Gerald Ford and Elizabeth Taylor (not together, of course) over the years. The bar is one of the most elegant in Charleston, a comfortable and smooth venue for a drink. If you get hungry, the kitchen will whip up some shrimp and grits for you. Hours are daily from 4 to 10:30pm. In the Mills House Hotel, 115 Meeting St.© **843/577-2400.** www.millshouse.com.

Roof Top at the Vendue Inn　If you like your drinks with a view, there is none more panoramic than the rooftop of the Vendue Inn (see "Where to Stay," earlier in this chapter). As you down your cocktails, you can take in a sweeping vista of Charleston that includes Waterfront Park, the Cooper River Bridges, and embattled Fort Sumter. Patronize this upmarket bar for your sundowner. From Sunday to Friday you can listen to live music, including jazz, reggae, and bluegrass. There's never a cover charge. Hours are daily 11:30am to 11pm. 19 Vendue Range. ℭ 800/845-7900. www.vendueinn.com.

Vickery's Bar & Grill   This is one of the most popular gathering places in Charleston for the younger crowd, especially students. It's also a good dining choice, with an international menu that includes jerk chicken and gazpacho. But the real secrets of the place's success are its 16-ounce frosted mug of beer for $2.50 and the convivial atmosphere. It's open daily from 11:30am to 1am. 15 Beaufain. ℭ 843/577-5300. www.vickerys.com.

Gay & Lesbian Bars

Déjà Vu II   Some people say this is the coziest and warmest "ladies' bar" in the Southeast. The owners have transformed what used to be a supper club into a cozy enclave with two bars, weekend live entertainment (usually by "all-girl bands"), and a clientele that's almost exclusively gay and 75% lesbian. The ambience is unpretentious and charming, and definitely does not exclude sympathetic patrons of any ilk. This is a late-night spot, but hours vary; call ahead. 4634 Prulley Ave., North Charleston. ℭ 843/554-5959. Cover varies.

Dudley's   If you happen to be gay, over 35, a wee bit jaded, and without any real interest in disco madness, Dudley's is the kind of mellow, laid-back gay bar that might appeal to you. Nobody dances, and there's a pool table in case you feel like hustling somebody. Open nightly from 9pm. 42 Ann St. ℭ 843/577-6779.

Patrick's Pub & Grill   If you like your men in leather, chances are, you'll find Mr. Right here. A gay pub and grill, right outside Charleston, this is a late-night venue for some of the hottest men in Charleston. Levi's take second place to leather. Hours are 6pm to 2am daily. 1377 Ashley River Rd. (Hwy. 61). ℭ 843/571-3435.

Late-Night Bites

Kaminsky's Most Excellent Café   Following a night of jazz or blues, this is a good spot to rest your feet and order just the power boost you need to make it through the rest of the evening. The handsome bar offers a wide selection of wines and is ideal for people-watching. Visitors who like New York's SoHo will feel at home here. The desserts are sinful, especially the Italian cream cake and the mountain chocolate cake. The cafe is open daily noon to 2am. 78 N. Market St. ℭ 843/853-8270. www.tbonz.com.

A SIDE TRIP TO EDISTO ISLAND ★

Isolated, and offering a kind of melancholy beauty, Edisto lies some 45 miles south of Charleston (take U.S. 17 W. for 21 miles; then head south along Hwy. 174 the rest of the way). By the late 18th century, Sea Island cotton had made the islanders wealthy, and some plantations from that era still stand. Today the island attracts families from Charleston and the Low Country to its white sandy beaches. Watersports include shrimping, surf-casting, deep-sea fishing, and sailing.

Edisto Beach State Park, State Cabin Road, sprawls across 1,255 acres, opening onto 2 miles of beach. There's also a signposted nature trail. Enjoy a picnic lunch under one of the shelters. The park has 75 campsites with full hookups and 28 with no hookups. Campsites cost $25 to $30 per night (the price is the same for RV hookups). Tent sites are $17 to $22 per night. Two restaurants are within walking distance of the campsite. Call © **843/869-2756** for reservations.

You can stay in a hotel in Charleston and commute here during the day.

Where to Dine

Barbecue fanciers—and what Southerner isn't one?—flock to **Po-Pigs BBQ Restaurant,** 2410 Hwy. 174 (© **843/869-9003**), for the finest barbecue on the island, with all the Southern fixin's. An all-you-care-to-eat barbecue buffet is a daily feature for only $7.50 for adults and $3.50 for children. In addition to the barbecue, you get grilled or fried chicken, liver hash, red rice, and an assortment of vegetables served the long-cooked Southern way, including turnip greens, field peas, and squash casserole. Hours are Wednesday to Saturday 11:30am to 9pm; no credit cards.

The Old Post Office SOUTHERN   This is the most prominent building that you're likely to see as you drive through the forests and fields across Edisto Island. About 5 miles from the beach, the restaurant was once a combination post office and general store, as its weathered clapboards and old-time architecture imply. Partners David Gressette and Philip Bardin, who transformed the premises in 1988, prepare a worthy compendium of Low Country cuisine and serve it in copious portions. Try island corn and crabmeat chowder, Orangeburg onion sausage with black bean sauce, scallops and grits with mousseline sauce, fried quail with duck-stock gravy, and "fussed-over" pork chops with hickory-smoked tomato sauce and mousseline.

Hwy. 174 at Store Creek.© **843/869-2339.** Reservations recommended. Main courses $15–$29. MC, V. Mon–Sat 5:30–10pm.

KIAWAH ISLAND ★ & THE ISLE OF PALMS ★

Kiawah Island

This eco-sensitive private residential and resort community sprawls across 10,000 acres located 21 miles south of Charleston. Named for the Kiawah Indians who inhabited the islands in the 17th century, it today consists of two resort villages: East Beach and West Beach. The community fronts a lovely 10-mile stretch of Atlantic beach; magnolias, live oaks, pine forests, and acres of marsh characterize the island.

Kiawah boasts many challenging golf courses, including one designed by Jack Nicklaus at Turtle Point that *Golf Digest* has rated among the top 10 courses in South Carolina. Golf architect Pete Dye designed a 2½-mile oceanfront course to host the 1991 PGA Ryder Cup match. *Tennis* magazine rates Kiawah as one of the nation's top tennis resorts, with its 28 hard-surface and Har-Tru clay courts. Anglers are also attracted to the island, especially in spring and fall.

For more information on golf and the beaches, see "Beaches & Outdoor Pursuits," earlier in this chapter.

The Sanctuary at Kiawah Island ★★★ The Sanctuary, one of the greatest resorts in the Southeast, opened in the summer of 2004. With its sweeping views of the Atlantic, this $125-million ultraluxury resort and spa lies just south of Charleston. It is nestled among majestic live oak stands along the island's 10-mile beachfront. It was constructed in the grand tradition of a seaside mansion, offering guests preferred tee times at the island's five championship golf courses. The sprawling resort features some of the largest and most luxurious guest rooms in America, with 90% of the rooms opening onto the water. In addition, the resort offers two oceanfront restaurants, plus other dining choices. The entrance to the resort is lined with some 150 transplanted live oak trees.

One Sanctuary Beach Dr., Kiawah Island, SC 29455. ⓒ **800/654-2924** or 843/576-1570. Fax 843/768-2736. www.kiawahresort.com. 255 units. $490-$860 double; from $1,300 suite. AE, DC, DISC, MC, V. **Amenities:** 12 restaurants; 4 bars; babysitting; 5 18-hole golf courses; exercise center; room service; sauna; spa; 28 tennis courts (lit as needed). *In room:* A/C, TV, hair dryer, Wi-Fi (free).

The Isle of Palms

A residential community bordered by the Atlantic Ocean and lying 10 miles north of Charleston, this island, with its salt marshes and wildlife, has been turned into a vacation retreat, but one that is more downscale than Kiawah Island. The attractions of Charleston are close at hand, but the Isle of Palms is also self-contained, with dining, an array of accommodations, and two championship golf courses. Charlestonians have been flocking to the island for holidays since 1898. I-26 intersects with I-526 heading directly to the island via the Isle of Palms Connector (S.C. 517). Seven miles of wide, white, sandy beach are the island's main attraction, and sailing and windsurfing are popular. The more adventurous will go crabbing and shrimping in the creeks.

WHERE TO STAY

Wild Dunes Resort ★★ ☺ A bit livelier than Kiawah Island, its major competitor, this complex is set on landscaped ground on the north shore. The resort sits on 1,600 acres of a private, gated community. The award-winning hotel has two widely acclaimed golf courses, plus an array of other outdoor attractions, including kayaking, a kids' camp, and more. Guests have a wide choice of options for accommodations, including the 93-room Boardwalk Inn, plus the Village at Wild Dunes, with some 160 quality rooms and suites with AAA's rating of four diamonds. The rest of the compound is formed by homes and villas ranging from 1 bedroom to 11, many of them oceanfront. All accommodations are just steps from the beach. The family recreation program is designed for ages 8 to 88.

5757 Isle of Palms (PO Box 20575), Charleston, SC 29413. ⓒ **888/778-1876** or 843/886-6000. Fax 843/886-2916. www.wilddunes.com. 600 units. $149-$339 double; from $200 1-bedroom villas. Golf packages available. AE, DC, DISC, MC, V. Free parking. **Amenities:** 4 restaurants; 3 bars; babysitting; 2 18-hole golf courses; exercise room; room service; sauna; 17 tennis courts (5 lit). *In room:* A/C, TV, hair dryer, Wi-Fi (in some; free).

WHERE TO DINE

The Boathouse at Breach Inlet ★ SEAFOOD Starting out as a ramshackle bait shop, this Low Country beach–style structure today is one of the finest seafood restaurants in the area. The decor, as might be expected, is nautical, with artifacts taken directly from hand-built wooden boats. Diners can select from a half-dozen different types of the freshest fish in the area, and they can also choose from an equal number of preparation styles, ranging from blackened to pesto. At lunch feast on some of the best sandwiches in the area, ranging from a shrimp or oyster po'boy to crab cake with chipotle aioli. At night the menu expands, featuring everything from crab fritters with a green Tabasco sauce to a Low Country egg roll with andouille, chicken, collards, and shrimp. The chef's specialties are Parmesan-crusted tilapia seared in brown butter or roasted local fresh fish flavored with basil and lemon. Also look for nightly specialties.

101 Palm Blvd., Isle of Palms. © **843/886-8000.** Reservations recommended. Main courses $17–$29. AE, DC, DISC, MC, V. Tues–Sat 11am–2pm; daily 5–10pm.

HILTON HEAD & THE LOW COUNTRY

12

Hilton Head is part of the Low Country, where much of the romance, beauty, and graciousness of the Old South survives. Broad white-sand beaches are warmed by the Gulf Stream and fringed with palm trees and rolling dunes. Graceful sea oats, anchoring the beaches, wave in the wind. The subtropical climate makes all this beauty the ideal setting for golf and for some of the Southeast's finest saltwater fishing. Somewhat more sophisticated and upscale than Myrtle Beach and the Grand Strand, Hilton Head's "plantations" offer visitors a leisurely lifestyle.

Although it covers only 42 square miles, Hilton Head feels spacious, a blessing because about 2.5 million resort guests visit annually. The lovely setting attracts artists, writers, musicians, theater groups, and craftspeople. The only downtown (of sorts) is Harbour Town, at the Sea Pines Resort, a Mediterranean-style cluster of shops and restaurants.

The island's recorded origins go back to visits from Spanish sailors in 1521, and its later "discovery" by an English sea captain, William Hilton, in 1663. By 1860, it boasted 24 plantations, most of them cultivating long-stem Sea Island cotton as well as indigo, rice, and sugar cane. On November 7, 1861, Hilton Head became the scene of the largest naval battle ever fought in American waters. More than 12,000 Union soldiers and marines invaded the island as part of a plan to blockade shipping in and out of nearby Charleston and Savannah. After the Civil War, and with the subsequent destruction of its cotton crops by the boll weevil, Hilton Head slid into obscurity, inhabited mostly by descendants of former slaves, who survived on small farms and as hunters and fishermen. An unusual result of the island's obscurity involved the survival of their language and culture, Gullah.

In 1956, Charles Fraser, son of one of the families that owned the island, embarked on an ambitious plan to develop it as a modern resort and residential community. Under Fraser, the Sea Pines Plantation (today the Sea Pines Resort) became a much-studied prototype of an ecologically desirable resort community, and was copied worldwide.

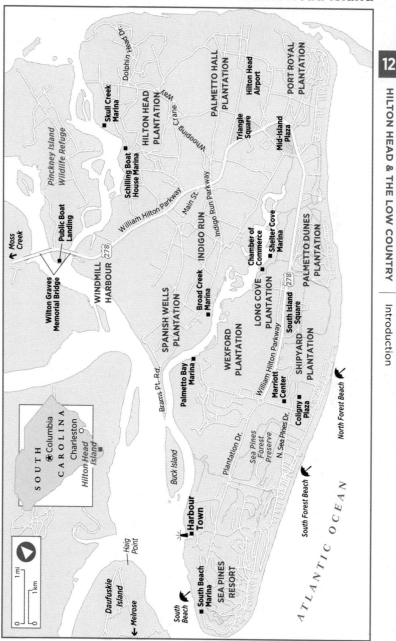

ESSENTIALS

GETTING THERE   Two separate airports service Hilton Head. They include the Hilton Head Airport (HHH), about 5 miles from the island's resorts, and the larger and busier Savannah/Hilton Head International Airport (SAV), which is 45 miles south of the island. At least a half-dozen airlines service either one or both of the airports from at least 17 destinations within North America. Those airlines include US Airways and US Airways Express, Delta Connection/Comair, United Express, AirTran, and Continental Express. If you're driving from other points south or north, use I-95 to reach the island (exit 8 off I-95). U.S. 278 leads over the bridge and runs the length of the island. It's 52 miles northeast of Savannah and directly on the Intracoastal Waterway.

  Yellow Cab (© 843/686-6666; www.yellowcabhhi.com) has two-passenger flat fares determined by zone, with an extra $2 charge for each additional person.

VISITOR INFORMATION   The official **Welcome Center** of the **Hilton Head Island–Bluffton Chamber of Commerce and Visitor & Convention Bureau** (© 800/523-3373 or 843/785-3673; www.hiltonheadisland.org) is located at 100 William Hilton Pkwy. and is open 8:30am until 5:30pm daily. You can pick up free vacation guides (or order them from the website) and free maps of the area. The staff can assist you in finding places of interest and activities and also offers video tours in several languages. The main chamber of commerce office is located at 1 Chamber Dr.

SPECIAL EVENTS   Scattered cultural events in February, including basket-weaving classes, art exhibitions, and storytelling, showcase the island's mysterious Gullah heritage as part of the annual **Gullah Celebration.** For more information call © 843/689-9314 or visit www.gullahcelebration.com. During the first week of March, the Hilton Head Hospitality Association sponsors **Winefest** (© 800/424-3387; www.hiltonheadhospitalityassociation.com), an annual outdoor wine tasting—the largest of its kind on the East Coast—that transforms even the most devoted beer drinkers into oenophiles and connoisseurs. Outstanding PGA golfers also descend on the island in mid-April for the **Verizon Heritage PGA Tour and Tournament** at the Harbour Town Golf Links at the Sea Island Resort (© 800/243-1107; www.verizonheritage.com). To herald fall, the **Hilton Head Celebrity Golf Tournament** (© 843/842-7711; www.hhcelebritygolf.com) is held on Labor Day weekend at various island golf courses. For 3 days straddling Halloween, Hilton Head's **Concours d'Elegance and Motoring Festival** (© 843/785-7469; www.hhiconcours.com) provides a venue for some of the most sought-after antique automobiles in the world.

BEACHES, GOLF, TENNIS & OTHER OUTDOOR PURSUITS

You can have an active vacation here any time of year; Hilton Head's subtropical climate ranges in temperature from the 50s (teens Celsius) in winter to the mid-80s (around 30°C) in summer. And if you've had your fill of historic sights in Savannah or Charleston, don't worry—the attractions on Hilton Head mainly consist of nature preserves, beaches, and other places to play.

The **Coastal Discovery Museum,** at historic Honey Horn, 70 Honey Horn Dr., and 100 William Hilton Pkwy. (© **843/689-6767** or 689-3033; www.coastaldiscovery. org), provides a concentrated dose of information about the Low Country's ecology, history, and sociology. In 1990, the Town of Hilton Head bought 68 acres of land-locked flatlands (Honey Horn) historically used to grow cash crops such as rice and indigo, as a means of protecting it from development as a shopping center. The site contains about a dozen historic buildings, a few of them from before the Civil War. Today, the site is administered by the Coastal Discovery Museum and used for municipally sponsored events such as picnics, concerts, charity drives, and sporting events. Guided tours go along island beaches and salt marshes or stop at Native American sites and the ruins of old forts or long-gone plantations. Children can search for sharks' teeth with an identification chart. The nature, beach, and history tours generally cost $12 for adults and $7 for children 4 to 12. The dolphin and nature cruise costs $19 per adult and $13 per child, and a kayak trip goes for $32 per adult and $28 per child 5 to 12. The museum's hours are Monday to Saturday 9am to 4:30pm and Sunday 11am to 3pm.

BEACHES *Travel + Leisure* ranked Hilton Head's **beaches ★★★** among the most beautiful in the world. The sands are extremely firm, providing a sound surface for biking, hiking, jogging, and beach games. In summer, watch for the endangered loggerhead turtles that lumber ashore at night to bury their eggs.

All beaches on Hilton Head are public. Most of the land inland from the beaches, however, is private property. Most beaches are safe, although there's sometimes an undertow at the relatively isolated northern end of the island. Lifeguards are posted only at major beaches, where concessions are usually available for the rental of chairs, umbrellas, and watersports equipment.

There are a number of public-access sites to popular beach areas. **Coligny Beach** at Coligny Circle at Pope Avenue and South Forest Beach Drive is the island's busiest strip of sand with toilets, sand showers, a playground, and changing rooms. **Alder Lane,** entered along South Forest Beach Road at Alder Lane, offers parking and is less crowded. Toilets are also found here. Off the William Hilton Parkway, **Dreissen Beach Park** at Bradley Beach Road has toilets, sand showers, and plenty of parking as well as a playground and picnic tables. Of the beaches on the island's north side, we prefer **Folly Field Beach,** on Starfish Road, which has more limited parking but offers toilets and sand showers. The Town of Hilton Head has made efforts to make many of the beaches wheelchair accessible.

BIKING Enjoy Hilton Head's more than 50 miles of bicycle paths. There are even bike paths running parallel to U.S. 278. Beaches are firm enough to support wheels, and every year, cyclists seem to delight in dodging the waves or racing the fast-swimming dolphins in the nearby water.

Most hotels and resorts rent bikes to guests. If yours doesn't, try **Hilton Head Bicycle Company,** off Sea Pines Circle at 112 Arrow Rd. (© **800/995-4319** or 843/686-6888; www.hiltonheadbicycle.com). The cost starts at $27 per week. Baskets, child carriers, locks, and headgear are supplied. The inventory includes cruisers, BMXs, mountain bikes, tandems, and bikes for kids. Hours are daily 9am to 5pm. The company also offers free delivery and pickup.

Another rental place is **Peddling Pelican** (© **843/785-3546;** www.pelican cruiser.com), offering beach cruisers, tandems, child carriers, and bikes for kids.

There's free delivery to any area hotel or resort. Cost is $15 for a full day, or $25 for 3 days. Hours are 9am to 6pm daily.

CRUISES & TOURS   To explore Hilton Head's waters, contact **Adventure Cruises, Inc.,** Shelter Cove Harbour, Ste. G, Harbourside III (© **843/785-4558;** www.hiltonheadisland.com/adventure). Outings include a 1¼-hour dolphin-watching cruise, which costs $20 for adults and $15 for children 3 to 12.

Another outfitter, **Drifter & Gypsy Excursions,** South Sea Pines Drive, South Beach Marina (© **843/363-2900;** www.hiltonheadboattours.com), takes its 65-foot *Gypsy,* holding 89 passengers, on dolphin-watching cruises, sightseeing cruises, and nature cruises. Call for more information to see what's happening at the time of your visit.

FISHING   No license is needed for saltwater fishing, although freshwater licenses are required for the island's lakes and ponds. The season for fishing offshore is April through October. Inland fishing is good between September and December. Crabbing is also popular; crabs are easy to catch in low water from docks, boats, or right off banks.

Off **Hilton Head** ★, you can go deep-sea fishing for amberjack, barracuda, shark, and king mackerel. **Drifter & Gypsy Excursions,** South Sea Pines Drive, South Beach Marina (© **843/363-2900;** www.hiltonheadboattours.com), features a 50-passenger, 60-foot drifter vessel that offers 3- to 5-hour offshore and inshore fishing excursions ranging in price from $54 to $64. The 32-foot *Boomerang* fishing boat is available for private offshore and inshore custom fishing charters lasting up to 8 hours.

Harbour Town Yacht Basin, Harbour Town Marina (© **843/671-2704;** www.harbourtownyachtbasin.com), has five boats available for rentals. *The Hero* and *The Echo* are 32-foot ships. Their rates for a group of six are $495 for 4 hours, $750 for 6 hours, and $990 for 8 hours. A smaller four-passenger inshore boat is priced at $425 for 4 hours, $650 for 6 hours, and $850 for 8 hours. *The Proving Ground* and *The Judith E* are six-passenger boats available for $550 for 4 hours, $800 for 6 hours, and $1,050 to $1,150 for 8 hours.

A cheaper way to go deep-sea fishing—only $47 per person—is aboard *The Drifter* (© **843/363-2900**), a party boat that departs from the South Beach Marina Village. Ocean-bottom fishing is possible at an artificial reef 12 miles offshore.

GOLF   With more than 20 highly challenging **golf courses** ★★★ on the island itself, and an additional 16 within a 30-minute drive, this is heaven for both professional and novice golfers. Wide, scenic fairways and rolling greens have earned Hilton Head the reputation of being the resort with the most courses on any number of the "World's Best" lists. To receive a copy of the island's *Golf Planner,* a guide to the golf courses and golf packages on Hilton Head Island, call © **888/465-3475.** For additional information about golf on Hilton Head, go to www.golfisland.com or www.hiltonheadgolf.net.

Most of Hilton Head's championship courses are open to the public, including the **George Fazio Course** ★ at Palmetto Dunes Oceanfront Resort (© **843/785-1130;** www.palmettodunes.com/george-fazio-golf-course.php), an 18-hole, 6,534-yard, par-70 course that *Golf Digest* ranked in the top 50 of its "75 Best American Resort Courses." The course has been cited for its combined length and keen accuracy. The cost is $58 to $130 for 18 holes, and hours are daily from 6:30am to 6pm.

Old South Golf Links ★★★, 50 Buckingham Plantation Dr., Bluffton (© 800/257-8997 or 843/785-5353; www.oldsouthgolf.com), is an 18-hole, 6,772-yard, par-72 course, open daily from 7:30am to 7pm. When it opened in 1992, it was recognized as one of the "Top 10 New Public Courses" by *Golf Digest,* which cited its panoramic views and setting ranging from an oak forest to tidal salt marshes. Greens fees range from $55 to $120. The course lies on Highway 278, 1 mile before the bridge leading to Hilton Head.

Hilton Head National Golf Club, Highway 278 (© 843/842-5900; www.golfhiltonheadnational.com/sites/courses/layout9.asp?id=446&page=13501), is a Gary Player Signature Golf Course, including a full-service pro shop and a grill and driving range. It's a 27-hole, 6,779-yard, par-72 course with gorgeous scenery that evokes Scotland. Greens fees range from $55 to $125, and hours are daily 7am to 6pm.

Island West Golf Club, Hwy. 278 (© 843/689-6660; www.islandwestgolf.net/golf/proto/islandwestgolf), was nominated in 1992 by *Golf Digest* as the best new course of the year. With its backdrop of oaks, elevated tees, and rolling fairways, it's a challenging but playable 18-hole, 6,803-yard, par-72 course. Greens fees are from $70, and hours are 7am to 6pm daily.

Robert Trent Jones Ocean Course at the Palmetto Dunes Oceanfront Resort (© 843/785-1138; www.palmettodunes.com) is an 18-hole, 6,710-yard, par-72 oceanfront course. The greens fees are $65 to $98 for 18 holes, and hours are daily 7am to 6pm.

HORSEBACK RIDING   Riding through beautiful maritime forests and nature preserves is reason enough to visit Hilton Head. We like **Lawton Stables** at the Sea Pines Resort, 190 Greenwood Dr. (© 843/671-2586; www.lawtonstableshhi.com), which offers trail rides for both adults and kids (kids 7 and under ride ponies instead of horses) through the Sea Pines Forest Preserve. The cost is $60 per person for a ride that lasts somewhat longer than an hour. Riders must weigh under 250 pounds. The stables are open Monday to Saturday 7:30am to 5:30pm. Reservations are necessary.

JOGGING   Our favorite place for jogging is Harbour Town at the Sea Pines Resort. Go for a run through the settlement just as the sun is going down. Later, you can explore the marina and have a refreshing drink at one of the many outdoor cafes. In addition, the island offers lots of paved paths and trails that cut through scenic areas. You can also jog on the new pedestrian paths along U.S. 278, the main artery.

KAYAK TOURS   Few other venues provide as close a view of the flora and fauna of the salt marshes as a kayak. **Outside Hilton Head** (© 800/686-6996 or 843/686-6996; www.outsidehiltonhead.com) offers well-orchestrated kayak tours of various Low Country waterways and salt marshes from at least two locations on island. Their busiest location is at 32 Shelter Cove Lane, Hilton Head, close to Shelter Cove Marina. Their 2-hour Dolphin Nature Kayak Tour costs $40 (half price for children 11 and under). The tour takes you through the salt-marsh creeks of the Calibogue Sound or Pinckney Island National Wildlife Refuge. The trip begins with instructions on how to control your boat.

A worthy competitor is **Marshgrass Adventures** (© 843/684-3296; www.marshgrassadventures.com), featuring sailing and kayak tours from a base at Broad Creek Marina. Every day between April and October, an experienced guide takes participants out on 2-hour kayak tours for sightings of egrets, herons, fish, crabs, and all manner of crawling critters. There's even the occasional spotting of dolphins from the low-slung, waterfront seat of your oared craft. The cost is $35 for adults and $20 for children 12 and under.

NATURE PRESERVES   The **Audubon-Newhall Preserve,** Palmetto Bay Road (no phone; www.hiltonheadaudubon.org/outings.htm), is a 50-acre preserve on the south end of the island. Here you can walk along marked trails to observe wildlife in its native habitat. Guided tours are available when plants are blooming. Except for a scattered handful of public toilets, there are no amenities. The preserve is open from sunrise to sunset, and admission is free.

The second leading preserve is also on the south end of the island. **Sea Pines Forest Preserve ★★**, Sea Pines Resort (© 843/363-4530; www.hiltonhead-sc. com/attractn/seapines.htm), is a 605-acre public wilderness with marked walking trails. Nearly all the birds and animals known to live on Hilton Head can be seen here. (Yes, there are alligators, but there are also less fearsome creatures, such as egrets, herons, osprey, and white-tailed deer.) All trails lead to public picnic areas in the center of the forest. The preserve is open from sunrise to sunset year-round. Maps and toilets are available.

SAILING   **Advanced Sail, Inc.** (© 843/686-2582; www.hiltonheadisland.com/ sailing), operating out of Palmetto Bay Marina, is a two-catamaran charter operator piloted by Captain John and his mate Jeanne. You can pack a picnic lunch and bring your cooler aboard for a 2½-hour trip—in the morning but more often during either the afternoon or at sunset. The cost for an excursion aboard the 53-foot-long *Pau Hana* is $35 for adults and $20 for children 11 and under. *Flying Circus,* measuring 30 feet in length, offers private 2-hour trips for up to six people priced at $250. Call for daytime special rates for fewer than six people.

H2O Sports, Harbour Town Marina (© 877/290-4386 or 843/671-4386; www. h2osportsonline.com), offers jet-skiing, parasailing, eco-tours, and water-skiing. We especially recommend their eco-tours (or "enviro," as they are called). Passengers head out on Zodiac inflatable boats for close encounters with wildlife, including dolphin sightings and bird-watching. Rates are $25 to $60 for adults and $20 to $50 for kids 12 and under.

SPA TREATMENTS   Hilton Head Island boasts a denser concentration of spas than virtually anywhere else in South Carolina. As such, you might be confronted with a barrage of publicity and brochures touting the virtue of various health-and-beauty farms, each offering a staggering array of treatments. They don't come cheaply though. We urge you to compare prices and treatment options, and then, if it's possible, to reserve your spa session as far in advance as possible, since space in each of them is limited. Your choices include the **Heavenly Spa** within the Westin (© 843/681-4000; www.starwoodhotels.com) and the **Spa Soleil** within the Marriott (© 843/686-8400; www.hiltonheadmarriott.com). You do not have to be a hotel guest to make a reservation. Spas less inclined to give priority to guests of any particular hotel or resort include **Faces Day Spa** (© 888/443-2237 or 843/785-3075; www.facesdayspa.com) and the **Sanctuary Day Spa** (© 843/842-5999; www.sanctuaryeurospa.com).

TENNIS   *Tennis* magazine ranked Hilton Head among its "50 Greatest U.S. Tennis Resorts." No other domestic destination can boast such a concentration of **tennis facilities ★★★**. Hilton Head has more than 300 courts that are ideal for beginning,

HILTON HEAD'S WONDERFUL wildlife

Hilton Head has preserved more of its wildlife than almost any other resort destination on the East Coast.

Hilton Head Island's **alligators** are a prosperous lot, and, in fact, the South Carolina Department of Wildlife and Marine Resources uses the island as a resource for repopulating state parks and preserves in which alligators' numbers have greatly diminished. The creatures represent no danger if you stay at a respectful distance.

Many of the large **water birds** that regularly grace the pages of nature magazines are natives of the island. The island's Audubon Society reports around 200 species of birds every year in its annual bird count, and more than 350 species have been sighted on the island during the past decade. The snowy egret, the large blue heron, and the osprey are among the most noticeable.

Other animals include **deer, bobcat, otter, mink,** and a few **wild boars.** At the Sea Pines Resort, on the southern end of the island, the planners set aside areas for a deer habitat back in the 1950s.

The **loggerhead turtle,** an endangered species, nests extensively along Hilton Head's 12 miles of wide, sandy beaches. Because the turtles choose the darkest hours of the night to crawl ashore and bury their eggs in the soft sand, few visitors meet these 200-pound giants.

Ever present is the **bottle-nosed dolphin,** usually called a porpoise by those unfamiliar with the island's sea life. The water off Port Royal Plantation, adjacent to Port Royal Sound, is a good place to meet up with the playful dolphins, as are Palmetto Dunes, Forest Beach, and all other oceanfront locations. Barring that, consider participating in either of the kayak tours as described under "Kayak Tours," above.

The Sea Pines Forest Preserve, the Audubon-Newhall Preserve, and the Pinckney Island National Wildlife Preserve, just off the island between the bridges, are of interest to nature lovers. The **Coastal Discovery Museum** (© 843/689-6767) hosts several guided nature tours and cruises. Tours, conducted weekdays, generally cost $12 for adults and $7 for children. Check the museum's Events Calendar online at www.coastaldiscovery.org for specific dates and times; you can even reserve your tour online in advance.

intermediate, and advanced players. The island has 19 tennis clubs, seven of which are open to the public. A wide variety of tennis clinics and daily lessons are available.

Sea Pines Racquet Club ★★★, at the Sea Pines Resort (© 866/561-8802 or 843/363-4495; www.seapines.com), has been ranked by *Tennis* magazine as a top-50 resort and has been the site of more nationally televised tennis events than any other location. Two hours of tennis are complimentary for guests of the hotel; otherwise, there's a $25-per-hour charge. The club has 23 clay courts (two are lighted for night play). Sea Pines' most visible competitor, with a long history of teaching tennis techniques and an equivalent number of courts and equivalent prices, is the **Van Der Meer Shipyard Tennis Resort,** 116 Shipyard Dr. (© 800/845-6138 or 843/785-8388; www.vandermeertennis.com).

Port Royal Racquet Club, Port Royal Plantation (© 843/686-8803; www.portroyalgolfclub.com), offers 10 clay and four hard courts. Charges are $25 per hour, and reservations should be made a day in advance. Clinics are $23 per hour. Private lessons are available for $58 per hour.

Bluffton, a town perched on the South Carolina mainland within a short drive of Hilton Head, is a 19th-century riverfront community that time has almost passed by.

Calhoun Street has the community's densest concentration of historic homes. But for a deeper insight into just how slow and sleepy this town really is, drop into the **Heyward House**, 70 Boundary St. at the corner of Bridge Street (📞 **843/757-6293;** www.heyward house.org/hh/index). The low-slung farmhouse design of Heyward House, originally built in 1840 and later enlarged prior to 1900, was inspired by earlier planters' homes in the British West Indies. It's open for guided tours Monday to Friday 10am to 3pm and Saturday 11am to 2pm. Tours cost $5 per person; students are charged only $2, and kids 9 and under enter free. A caretaker here will give you a free map for a self-guided walking tour of the town as well. The most impressive of the buildings is the much-weathered, Carpenter Gothic Episcopal Church of the Cross, 110 Calhoun St., at the edge of the May River.

For information about the somewhat limited appeal of Bluffton, contact the **Old Town Bluffton Merchant Society** at 📞 **843/815-9522** or visit www.oldtown bluffton.com.

Palmetto Dunes Tennis Center, Palmetto Dunes Resort (📞 **843/785-1152;** www.palmettodunes.com), has 23 clay and two hard courts (some lighted for night play). Hotel guests pay $25 per hour; nonguests pay $30 per hour.

WINDSURFING   Hilton Head is not recommended as a windsurfing destination. Finding a place to windsurf is quite difficult, but with the plethora of other sporting activities available, no one seems to mind. One windsurfer warns that catching a tailwind at the public beaches at the airport and the Holiday Inn could land you at the bombing range on Parris Island, the Marine Corps' basic-training facility.

Shopping

Hilton Head is browsing heaven, with more than 30 shopping centers spread around the island. Chief shopping sites include **Pineland Station** (Matthews Dr. and U.S. 278), with more than 30 shops and half a dozen restaurants, and **Coligny Plaza** (Coligny Circle), with more than 60 shops, food stands, and several good restaurants. We've found some of the best bargains in the South at **Tanger Outlet Stores I and II** (📞 **843/837-4339;** www.tangeroutlet.com), on Hwy. 278 at the gateway to Hilton Head. The outlet has more than 45 factory stores, including Ralph Lauren, Brooks Brothers, and J. Crew. The hours of most shops are Monday to Saturday 10am to 9pm and Sunday 11am to 6pm. Another desirable gaggle of upscale boutiques is the **Village at Wexford,** on Hilton Head Island's south end. Within, you'll find one of the most comprehensive purveyors of kitchen tools and tableware in the Low Country, **Le Cookery,** B-3 Wexford Village (📞 **843/785-7171;** www.lecookeryusa.com).

WHERE TO STAY

Since its debut, Hilton Head has tended to specialize in the rental of mostly upscale, oceanfront luxury homes and villas, and prices are higher than what's available in less desirable parts of South Carolina. In recent years, however, the roster of lodgings has expanded to include some simplified economy lodgings as well. The resort boasts more than 6,000 villas, 3,000 hotel or motel rooms, and at least 1,000 timeshare units. Most facilities offer discount rates between November and March, and golf and tennis packages are available year-round.

Very Expensive

The Inn at Palmetto Bluff ★★★ ☺ A jewel in the crown of the world-renowned Auberge Resorts, the Inn at Palmetto Bluff is an elegant, peaceful, relentlessly upscale resort on the May River. Guests can walk through the beautiful gardens, play golf on the Jack Nicklaus signature course, relax in the full-service spa, enjoy watersports like kayaking and fishing, enroll their children in the kids' camp, take art classes, or enjoy a beach excursion. There is a $25-per-day service fee per guest room to be able to use the fitness center, kayaks, canoes, and outdoor lap pool. Accommodations include cottages, cottage suites, and village homes. Exquisitely appointed, the cottages and cottage suites have vaulted ceilings, hardwood pine floors, fireplaces, screened porches, and water views. With two to four bedrooms, full kitchens, screened porches, and luxury bed linens, the village homes are ideal for families. The Inn at Palmetto Bluff offers four dining options: the elegant **River House Restaurant,** with river views; the **May River Grill** at the May River Golf Club; **Buffalo's,** in the Village; or dining in your own cottage.

476 Mount Pilla Rd., Bluffton, SC 29910. ℂ **866/706-6565** or 843/706-6500. Fax 843/706-6550. www.palmettobluffresort.com. 77 units, 42 cottages, 8 cottage suites, 27 village homes. $475–$950 cottage; $700–$1,100 cottage suite; from $1,100 village home. AE, DC, DISC, MC, V. **Amenities:** 3 restaurants; children's camp; exercise room; outdoor pool; spa. In room: A/C, TV, fridge, kitchen (in village home), Wi-Fi (free).

The Westin Hilton Head Island Resort & Spa ★★ Set near the relatively isolated northern end of Hilton Head Island on 24 landscaped acres, this hotel stands out as the most child- and pet-friendly blockbuster hotel on the island. Its Disney-esque design, including cupolas and postmodern ornamentation that looks vaguely Moorish, evokes fanciful Palm Beach hotels. If there's a drawback, it's the fact that its so obviously geared to families with children that romantically inclined couples without children in tow might not necessarily thrill to the family-friendly sweep of it all. Fortunately, there's an active and much-respected children's camp on-site for the care and attention of young'uns. Most of the guest rooms have ocean views, and are outfitted in modernized interpretations of the Low Country plantation style. The hotel is also home to the new Heavenly Spa by Westin, a full-service spa.

2 Grasslawn Ave., Hilton Head Island, SC 29928. ℂ **800/937-8461** or 843/681-4000. Fax 843/681-1096. www.starwoodhotels.com. 412 units. $169–$429 double; $450–$1,900 suite. Children 17 and under stay free in parent's room; children 4 and under eat free. Special promotions offered. AE, DC, DISC, MC, V. **Amenities:** 3 restaurants; bar; 3 18-hole golf courses; Jacuzzi; room service. In room: A/C, TV, hair dryer, minibar, Wi-Fi ($13 per day).

Expensive

Crowne Plaza Hilton Head Island Beach Resort ★ Tucked away in the Shipyard Plantation and designed as the centerpiece of that plantation's 800 acres, this five-story inn gives the Westin stiff competition. The golf course associated with the hotel has been praised by the National Audubon Society for its respect for local wildlife. Guest rooms are simple, yet the sheer beauty of the landscaping, the attentive service, and the well-trained staff (dressed in nautically inspired uniforms) go a long way toward making your stay memorable. The most glamorous restaurant is **Portz,** and a good middle-bracket choice is **Brella's,** serving both lunch and dinner. Certain nights in the premier bar, **Signals,** feature line dancing and shag dancing.

130 Shipyard Dr., Shipyard Plantation, Hilton Head Island, SC 29928. © **800/334-1881** or 843/842-2400. Fax 843/785-8463. www.cphiltonhead.com. 340 units. $199–$399 double; from $299 suite. AE, DC, DISC, MC, V. Free parking. **Amenities:** 2 restaurants; bar; bike rentals; exercise room; 2 pools (1 indoor); room service. *In room:* A/C, TV, hair dryer, minibar, Wi-Fi ($9.95 per day).

Disney's Hilton Head Island Resort ★★

This medium-scale, cost-effective, family-conscious resort is on a 15-acre island, inland from the coast, that rises above Hilton Head's widest estuary, Broad Creek. About 20 woodsy-looking buildings are arranged into a compound. Expect lots of pine trees and fallen pine needles, garlands of Spanish moss, plenty of families with children, and an ambience that's several notches less intense than that of hotels in Disney theme parks. Characters include Shadow the Dog (a golden retriever that is the resort's mascot) and Blue Crab, a storyteller, fisherman, and musician. Part of the fun is the many summer-camp-style activities for kids with or without their parents. Guest rooms usually contain mini-kitchens, suitable for feeding sandwiches and macaroni to the kids. **Tide Me Over** is a walk-up window serving Carolina cookery for breakfast and lunch. The resort runs a shuttle bus to and from a nearby beach at 15-minute intervals daily between 10am and 5pm.

22 Harbourside Lane, Hilton Head Island, SC 29928. © **800/500-3990** or 843/341-4100. Fax 843/341-4130. http://dvc.disney.go.com. 123 units. $165–$350 studio; $260–$1,100 villa. AE, DC, DISC, MC, V. **Amenities:** 2 restaurants; bar; babysitting; exercise room; 3 outdoor pools. *In room:* A/C, TV, hair dryer, kitchenette (in most), Wi-Fi ($11 per day).

Hilton Oceanfront Resort ★

This award-winning property isn't the most imposing on the island. Many visitors, however, prefer the Hilton because of its hideaway position, tucked at the end of the main road through Palmetto Dunes, and because its rooms are, on average, a bit larger than those within any other resort on the island. In addition, a $4-million renovation, completed in 2008, adds to its appeal. The low-rise design features hallways that open to sea breezes at either end. The guest rooms offer balconies that angle out toward the beach allowing sea views from all rooms. **HH Prime,** an upmarket steakhouse which looks a lot more glamorous at night than during the day, when it evokes an upscale coffee shop, is the resort's premier restaurant, although an on-site Pizza Hut serves less expensive fare. In 2007, the resort inaugurated a glossy, urban-looking bar and lounge, with live music.

23 Ocean Lane (PO Box 6165), Hilton Head Island, SC 29938. © **800/845-8001** or 843/842-8000. Fax 843/341-8033. www.hiltonoceanfrontresort.com. 323 units. $139–$349 double; $359–$609 suite. AE, DC, DISC, MC, V. Parking $8–$12. **Amenities:** 4 restaurants; 2 bars; exercise room; 2 outdoor pools; room service; spa. *In room:* A/C, TV, hair dryer, kitchenette, Wi-Fi ($11 per day).

Moderate

Hilton Head Marriott Resort & Spa ★★

Set on 2 acres of landscaped grounds and bordering the oceanfront, this supremely comfortable hotel is surrounded by the much more massive acreage of the Palmetto Dunes Oceanfront Resort (p. 292) and is just 10 minutes from the Hilton Head airport. But the hotel's 10-story tower of rooms dominates everything around it. Rooms are smaller and less opulent than you might expect of such a well-rated hotel, but all are comfortably furnished. Most open onto small balconies overlooking the garden or the ocean. The hotel's program of sports and recreation is among the best on the island, and the state-of-the-art spa (Spa Soleil) is the largest on Hilton Head Island.

In the Palmetto Dunes Oceanfront Resort, Hilton Head Island, SC 29938. ℭ **800/228-9290** or 843/686-8400. Fax 843/686-8450. www.marriott.com. 513 units. $179–$219 double; $324–$725 suite. AE, DC, DISC, MC, V. Valet parking $20; self-parking $11. **Amenities:** Restaurant; 2 bars; coffee shop; babysitting; 3 18-hole golf courses; health club; room service; 25 tennis courts. *In room:* A/C, TV, hair dryer, minibar, Wi-Fi ($9.95 per day).

Holiday Inn Oceanfront ★ ☺   The island's leading moderately priced hotel, and its oldest, with a history going back to 1970, this sprawling five-story building opens onto a crowded stretch of beach on the southern side of the island, directly across the road from the fast-food joints and souvenir shops of Coligny Plaza. The rooms are spacious and informally but comfortably furnished with rattan furniture and pastel colors. Unfortunately, the balconies are generally too small to actually walk out onto. Only a few of the rooms have actual sea views—most of them have views over parking lots and trees. In summer, planned children's activities are offered. Don't expect glamour, as the place is comfortable, crowded, and family invasive, with a crowded pool and barely enough parking. The staff, despite the many demands on their time, are genuinely concerned and helpful.

1 S. Forest Beach Dr. (PO Box 5728), Hilton Head Island, SC 29938. ℭ **800/423-9897** or 843/785-5126. Fax 843/785-6678. www.hiltonhead.com. 202 units. $129–$234 double. AE, DC, DISC, MC, V. Free parking. **Amenities:** Restaurant; outdoor bar; exercise room; outdoor pool; room service; Wi-Fi (free). *In room:* A/C, TV, hair dryer.

The Inn at Harbour Town ★★★   Set within the boundaries of the Sea Pines Resort, this postmodern and upscale inn provides the only conventional hotel accommodations within a resort that's otherwise devoted to rentals of villas or condominiums. In their development of this inn, Sea Pines demanded an exceptionally high staff-to-client ratio. The building's exterior (ca. 2001) is high style, buff colored, and postmodern. Inside, there's a richly upholstered, lushly paneled replica of an English-inspired country house, with heart pine floors. Although the inn isn't positioned directly beside the sea, shuttle buses haul guests back and forth, and its location within a very short walk from the waterways, restaurants, shops, and entertainment of Harbour Town and its marina more than make up for it. The hotel is proud of its four-diamond rating from AAA.

7 Lighthouse Lane, in the Sea Pines Resort, Hilton Head Island, SC 29928. ℭ **800/732-7463** or 843/363-8100. Fax 843/363-8155. www.seapines.com. 60 units. $139–$249 double. AE, DC, DISC, MC, V. **Amenities:** Bike rentals; concierge; exercise room; outdoor pool; room service; spa; 23 tennis courts (5 lit). *In room:* A/C, TV, fridge, hair dryer, Wi-Fi (free).

Main Street Inn ★★★ ⛅   Don't expect cozy Americana from this small, luxurious inn, as it's grander and more European in its motifs than its name would imply. Designed like a small-scale villa that you might expect to see in the south of France, it was built in 1996 in a format that combines design elements from both New Orleans and Charleston, including cast-iron balustrades and a formal semitropical garden where guests are encouraged to indulge in afternoon tea. Inside, you'll find artfully clipped topiary, French Provincial furnishings, and accommodations that are more luxurious and more richly appointed than those of any other hotel in Hilton Head. Overall, despite a location that requires a drive to the nearest beach, the hotel provides a luxe alternative to the less-personalized megahotels that lie nearby.

2200 Main St., Hilton Head Island, SC 29926. ☏ **800/471-3001** or 843/681-3001. Fax 843/681-5541. www.mainstreetinn.com. 33 units. $139–$199 double. Additional person $35 extra. Rates include breakfast. AE, DISC, MC, V. Free parking. **Amenities:** Breakfast room; outdoor pool; spa. *In room:* A/C, TV, hair dryer, Wi-Fi (free).

Inexpensive

Days Inn The Days Inn provides easy access to the beach, golf, tennis, marinas, and shopping. The rooms are wheelchair accessible and, although unremarkable, are a good value for expensive Hilton Head. Families save money by using one of the grills outside for a home-style barbecue, to be enjoyed at one of the picnic tables.

9 Marina Side Dr., Hilton Head Island, SC 29928. ☏ **800/329-7466** or 843/842-4800. Fax 843/842-5388. www.daysinn.com. 119 units. $89–$139 double; $129–$169 suite. Rates include continental breakfast. Senior discounts available. AE, DISC, MC, V. Free parking. **Amenities:** Breakfast room; outdoor pool. *In room:* A/C, TV, hair dryer, Wi-Fi (free).

Hampton Inn Hilton Head Island This is one of the two or three most sought-after motels on Hilton Head, especially by families and business travelers who don't mind its lack of resort-style amenities and its straightforward, cost-effective simplicity. It's 5 miles from the Graves bridge and the closest motel to the airport. Rooms in pastel pinks and greens are quite comfortable and well maintained. Some rooms have refrigerators. Local calls are free, and breakfast is included in the rates. A renovation in 2007 adds to its appeal.

1 Dillon Rd., Hilton Head Island, SC 29926. ☏ **800/HAMPTON** (426-7866) or 843/681-7900. Fax 843/681-4330. www.hamptoninn.com. 125 units. $124–$189 double. Children 17 and under stay free in parent's room. Rates include continental breakfast. AE, DC, DISC, MC, V. **Amenities:** Breakfast room; exercise room; outdoor pool. *In room:* A/C, TV, hair dryer, Internet (free), kitchen (in some).

The South Beach Marina Inn ★ 🎒 Of the dozens of available accommodations within the Sea Pines Resort, this 1986 clapboard-sided complex of marina-front buildings is the only place offering traditional hotel-style rooms by the night. With lots of nautical, seafaring charm, the inn meanders over a labyrinth of catwalks and stairways above a complex of shops, souvenir kiosks, and restaurants. It is especially known for being located immediately adjacent to the Salty Dog Cafe—one of the island's most popular eateries. Each one- or two-bedroom unit is cozily outfitted with country-style braided rugs, pinewood floors, and homespun-charm decor celebrating rural 19th-century America.

232 S. Sea Pines Dr. (in the Sea Pines Resort), Hilton Head Island, SC 29920. ☏ **800/367-3909** or 843/671-6498. www.sbinn.com. 17 units. $65–$179 1-bedroom; $87–$186 2-bedroom. AE, DISC, MC, V. Free parking. **Amenities:** Outdoor pool. *In room:* A/C, TV, hair dryer, kitchenette, Wi-Fi (free).

Villa Rentals

The **Vacation Company** (☏ **800/845-7018;** www.hiltonheadvacationrentals.com) has been in business for almost a quarter-century and specializes in the rental of homes and villas throughout the region. Its leading competitors include **Beach Properties of Hilton Head** (☏ **800/671-5155** or 843/671-5155; www.beach-property.com), **Hilton Head Vacation Rentals** (☏ **800/232-2463;** www.800 beachme.com), and **ResortQuest Vacation Home Network** (☏ **800/875-8726** or 843/785-7300; www.resortquesthiltonhead.com).

Two developments that we consider especially appealing are reviewed below.

Palmetto Dunes Oceanfront Resort ★ ☺ This relaxed and informal enclave of privately owned villas is set within the sprawling 1,800-acre complex of Palmetto

Dunes Plantation, 7 miles south of the bridge. Accommodations range all the way from one-bedroom condos, booked mostly by groups, to four-bedroom villas, each of the latter furnished in the owner's personal taste. This is the place for longer stays, ideal for families who want a home away from home when they're traveling. In fact, in 2003 it was ranked as the number-one family resort in the continental U.S. and Canada by *Travel + Leisure Family* and is still listed among the top 10. Villas are fully equipped and receive housekeeping service; they're located on the ocean, fairways, and lagoons. Each villa comes with a full kitchen, washer and dryer, living room and dining area, and balcony or patio. The resort opens onto a 200-slip marina.

Palmetto Dunes (PO Box 5606), Hilton Head Island, SC 29938. © **800/827-3006.** www.palmetto dunes.com. 500 units. $800–$3,500 per week condo or villa. Golf and honeymoon packages available. 2-night minimum stay. 50% deposit for reservations. AE, DC, DISC, MC, V. Free parking. **Amenities:** 20 restaurants; 12 bars; 3 18-hole golf courses; 28 outdoor pools; 25 tennis courts (8 lit). *In room:* A/C, TV, free Internet.

The Sea Pines Resort ★★★ Since 1955, this has been one of the leading condo developments in America, sprawling across 5,500 acres at the southernmost tip of the island. Lodgings vary—everything from one- to four-bedroom villas to opulent private homes that are available when the owners are away. An additional option is the separately recommended Inn at Harbour Town, a 60-room inn, which offers the only venue at Sea Pines Resort for rental of a conventional hotel room. The clientele here includes hordes of golfers because Sea Pines is the home of the Verizon Heritage golf tournament, a major stop on the PGA tour. If you're not a Sea Pines guest, you can eat, shop, or enjoy aspects of its nightlife.

Sea Pines (PO Box 7000), Hilton Head Island, SC 29938. © **866/561-8802.** Fax 843/842-1475. www. seapines.com. 500 units. $170–$340 1-bedroom villa; $300–$385 2-bedroom villa; $320–$600 3-bedroom villa. Rates are daily, based on 3-night stay. AE, DC, DISC, MC, V. **Amenities:** 12 restaurants; 12 bars; babysitting; 3 18-hole golf courses; exercise room; 2 outdoor pools; spa; 23 tennis courts (5 lit); watersports/rentals. *In room:* A/C, TV, free Internet, kitchen or kitchenette.

WHERE TO DINE

Hilton Head has the dubious distinction of having some of the most expensive restaurants in South Carolina. What on the island might be ranked as moderate would be considered very expensive in other parts of the state. There are more than 250 eateries of all price levels and styles. Here are some of the best of them.

Expensive

Alexander's ★ SEAFOOD/INTERNATIONAL One of the most visible independent restaurants (in other words, not associated with a hotel) on Hilton Head lies in a gray-stained, wood-sided building just inside the main entrance into Palmetto Dunes. The decor includes Oriental carpets, big-windowed views over the salt marshes, wicker furniture, and an incongruous—some say startling—collection of vintage Harley-Davidson motorcycles, none with more than 1,000 miles on them, dating from 1946, 1948, 1966, and 1993, respectively. Powerful flavors and a forthright approach to food are the rules of the kitchen. The chefs don't allow a lot of innovation on their menu—you've had all these dishes before—but fine ingredients are used, and each dish is prepared with discretion and restraint. Try the oysters Savannah or the bacon-wrapped shrimp, and most definitely have a bowl of Low Country seafood chowder. Guaranteed to set you salivating are the scallops encrusted with sun-dried tomatoes, and the bluefin crab cakes. Steak, duck, rack of lamb, and pork—all in familiar versions—round out the menu.

76 Queen's Folly, Palmetto Dunes. ⓒ **843/785-4999.** www.alexandersrestaurant.com. Reservations recommended. Main courses $23–$33. AE, DC, DISC, MC, V. Daily 5–10pm.

Old Fort Pub ★ INTERNATIONAL   Remote and isolated from the bulk of other Hilton Head eateries, and nestled within the upscale residential community of the Hilton Head Plantation on the island's northwest coast, this is one of the most consistently reliable and upscale restaurants in the Low Country. It is only a few paces from the ruin of what was commissioned by the Union army in 1862 as a fort (Fort Mitchell), and as such, some diners make it a point to traipse around the signposted footpaths. You'll dine within a building (ca. 1973) that evokes an interconnected series of clapboard-sided houses, amid candlelight and crisp napery, with views over salt marshes and estuaries. Chef Keith Josefiak prepares dishes which include Vidalia onion shoots and goat cheese tarts; spring asparagus "en croute" with prosciutto and roasted tomato vinaigrette; a succulent version of local bouillabaisse that just happens to include collards and tasso ham; crab cakes; and pork loin with chanterelles, Vidalia onions, and pistachio nuts.

65 Skull Creek Dr. ⓒ **843/681-2386.** www.oldfortpub.com. Reservations recommended. Main courses $24–$38. AE, DC, DISC, MC, V. Mon–Sat 5–10pm; Sun 11am–2pm (brunch).

Redfish Grill ★ INTERNATIONAL   One of the more talked-about restaurants on Hilton Head Island occupies a rambling villa that contains shopping as well as dining options. A popular pastime involves dropping into the on-site wine shop, selecting a bottle, and for a $10 corkage fee, drinking it with your meal. There are two postmodern, Asian-inspired dining rooms, or the wine shop has a few tables. The menu changes with the seasons, but might include Asian-style marinated tenderloin of beef with Thai cucumbers in a lettuce-leaf wrap; grilled sea bass with a wasabi cream sauce and soy glaze on a bed of udon noodles; seared jumbo scallops served with asparagus and lobster-studded macaroni and cheese; and two upscale and expensive burgers: One is made entirely with Kobe beef and accented with foie gras, pepper jack cheese, truffles, and port demi-glace; the other is crafted from chunks of Maine lobster mixed with shrimp. This restaurant lies in an isolated residential neighborhood inland from the sea, close to the Cross-Island Bridge.

8 Archer Rd. ⓒ **843/686-3388.** www.redfishofhiltonhead.com. Reservations recommended. Main courses $21–$34. AE, MC, V. Mon–Sat 11:30am–2pm and 5–10pm; Sun 5–10pm.

Moderate

All of these so-called moderately priced restaurants have expensive shellfish dishes. However, if you order from the lower end of the price scale, enjoying mainly meat and poultry dishes, you'll find platters that cost $20 or less. Helpings, for the most part, are generous, so you'll rarely need to order appetizers, which will keep your overall cost down.

Black Marlin Bayside Grill ★ SEAFOOD   Partly because of its location beside a marshy inland channel, a few steps from the most battered-looking boatyard and marina on Hilton Head Island, this is the most raffish of the "grand cuisine" restaurants of Hilton Head. Fun, with lots of salty cosmopolitan charm, and an insouciance that might remind you of Key West, it seems a world removed from the manicured, upscale conservatism of the island's secluded residential zones. Thomas Corey is the chef here, a refugee from the cold Northeast, and an expert at crafting flavor from the fresh seafood that arrives directly from fishermen every morning at dawn. Lunch fare includes meal-size salads and at least a dozen hungry-man's sandwiches, pastas, and fried seafood. Dinners are more ambitious, focusing on tuna carpaccio, tempura lobster, fish or shrimp tacos, crab-stuffed flounder, big slabs of steak, and between 7 and 10 dishes that appear only on a blackboard, based on the seafood haul brought in that day.

86 Helmsman Way, at the Palmetto Bay Marina. ☏ **843/785-4950.** www.blackmarlinhhi.com. Reservations not accepted. Main courses $13-$33. AE, DC, MC, V. Mon-Fri 11:30am-10pm; Sat-Sun 10am-2pm and 4-10pm.

Charlie's L'Etoile Verte ★★ INTERNATIONAL Outfitted like a tongue-in-cheek version of a Parisian bistro, our favorite restaurant on Hilton Head Island was also a favorite with former president Clinton during one of his island conferences. The atmosphere is unpretentious but elegant. The service is attentive, polite, and infused with an appealingly hip mixture of old- and new-world courtesy. Begin with roast portobello mushrooms and crab, and move on to tilapia sautéed in a Parmesan crust. End this rare dining experience with biscotti or a "sailor's trifle." The wine list is impressive.

8 New Orleans Rd. ☏ **843/785-9277.** www.charliesgreenstar.com. Reservations required. Main courses $24-$39 dinner. AE, DISC, MC, V. Tues-Sat 11:30am-2pm; Mon-Sat 5:30-9:30pm.

The Crazy Crab North ☺ SEAFOOD Usually crowded, especially in summer, this is the restaurant that's most likely to be patronized by locals, partly because an entire family can be fed here at relatively modest prices. In a modern, low-slung building near the bridge that connects the island with the South Carolina mainland, it serves baked, broiled, or fried versions of stuffed flounder; seafood kabobs; oysters; the catch of the day; and any combination thereof. She-crab soup and New England–style clam chowder are prepared fresh daily, children's menus are available, and desserts are a high point for chocoholics. There's a second branch of this restaurant with the same hours and virtually the same prices, at Harbour Town in the Sea Pines Resort (☏ **843/681-5021**).

U.S. 278 at Jarvis Creek. ☏ **843/681-5021.** www.thecrazycrab.com. Reservations not accepted. Main courses $14-$33. AE, DISC, MC, V. Daily 11:30am-10pm.

Harbour Town Grill ☗ AMERICAN For years, this woodsy-looking refuge of golfers and their guests was open only to members of the nearby golf club. Several years ago, however, it opened to the public at large, a fact that's still not widely publicized in Hilton Head and that sometimes seems to catch some local residents by surprise. Decorated with a simple, aggressively unpretentious style that's vaguely Scottish and punctuated with occasional pieces of golfing memorabilia, this small-scale affair has views over the 9th hole and room for only about 50 diners at a time. Inside, it's sporty looking and relatively informal during the day, when most of the menu is devoted to thickly stuffed deli-style sandwiches and salads named in honor of golf stars. Dinners are more formal and more elaborate, with good-tasting dishes such as local shrimp sautéed with ginger, Vidalia onions, and collard greens; roasted rack of American lamb with white beans, spinach, and rosemary; and an array of thick-cut slabs of meat that include beef, lamb, veal, and chicken.

In the Harbour Town Golf Links Clubhouse, Sea Pines. ☏ **843/363-8380.** www.seapines.com. Reservations recommended for dinner. Main courses $16-$38 dinner. AE, DC, DISC, MC, V. Daily 7am-3pm and 5-10pm.

Hudson's Seafood House on the Docks ★ SEAFOOD   Built as a seafood-processing factory in 1912, and an excellent choice if you're looking for an escape from the island's crowded southern tier, this restaurant still processes fish, clams, and oysters for local distribution, so you know that everything is fresh. If you're seated in the north dining room, you'll be eating in the original oyster factory. We strongly recommend the crab cakes, the steamed shrimp, and the especially appealing blackened catch of the day. Local oysters (seasonal) are also a specialty, breaded and deep-fried. Before and after dinner, stroll on the docks past shrimp boats, and enjoy the view of the mainland and nearby Parris Island. Sunsets here are panoramic. Lunch is served in the Oyster Bar.

1 Hudson Rd. (go to Skull Creek just off Square Pope Rd. signposted from U.S. 278). ✆ **843/681-2772.** www.hudsonsonthedocks.com. Reservations not accepted. Main courses $13–$23. AE, DC, MC, V. Daily 11am–2:30pm and 5–9pm.

Jump & Phil's Bar & Grill AMERICAN   Cozy and convivial, with dining tables positioned on three sides of a large rectangular bar that does a thriving business with 40- and 50-something owners of nearby homes and condos, this is the brainchild of entrepreneurs Jump and Phil, journalism majors who spent 20 years working in other restaurants before branching out on their own. Outfitted with early-20th-century Americana, some battered antiques, and dark paneling, the place identifies itself as headquarters for Hilton Head's Green Bay Packers fan club. Food is generously portioned, reasonably priced, and utterly unpretentious. Menu items include two-fisted versions of BLTs, Cuban sandwiches, chili dogs, tuna melts, barbecued pork, and burgers. More substantial fare includes grits with shrimp, fried oyster platters, chicken potpie, and grilled rib-eye steaks.

In the Hilton Head Plaza, Greenwood Dr. off Sea Pines Circle. ✆ **843/785-9070.** www.jumpand philshhi.com. Reservations not needed. Sandwiches $7–$12; main courses $11–$24. AE, DISC, MC, V. Daily 11:30am–2am.

The Old Oyster Factory ★ SEAFOOD/STEAK   Built on the site of one of Hilton Head's original oyster canneries, this always-popular landmark offers waterfront dining overlooking Broad Creek. At sunset, every table enjoys a panoramic view as diners sip their "sundowners." All the dishes here can be found on seafood menus from Maine to Hawaii. But the cuisine is truly palate friendly, beginning with such appetizers as a tangy kettle of clams steamed in a lemon-butter sauce, or else a delectable crab cake sautéed and served in a chili-garlic tartar sauce. Will it be oysters Rockefeller (baked with spinach and a béarnaise sauce) or oysters Savannah (shrimp, crabmeat, and smoked bacon)? Almond-crusted mahimahi is among the more tantalizing main courses, as are seafood pasta and broiled sea scallops. Those who don't eat seafood can opt for a chargrilled chicken breast or a steak.

101 Marsh Rd. ✆ **843/681-6040.** www.oldoysterfactory.com. Reservations not accepted. Main courses $17–$33. AE, DC, DISC, MC, V. Daily 5–10pm (closing times can vary).

Reilley's Grill & Bar ★ 🍴AMERICAN   It rarely advertises, so much of its business derives from locals, who come here after dark for hobnobbing, gossiping, or eating and drinking within the orbit of patriarch Tom Reilley, the island's ultimate foodie insider. If you can manage to pull yourself away from the mahogany and cherry-paneled bar, you'll discover that food items are the most fussed over and most sophisticated of any other eatery within Hilton Head Plaza. Examples include garlic chicken pasta; grilled loin of beef with peppers and onions; pork chops stuffed with spinach and mozzarella and served in a Gouda cream sauce; upscale salads such as a version with warm brie and spinach; sandwiches made with such ingredients as tilapia, croissants, meatloaf, and cheddar; and Asian-style chicken salad. There's also a roster of grills and a signature version of sirloin topped with an Irish whiskey peppercorn sauce and cheese grits.

In the Hilton Head Plaza, Greenwood Dr. off Sea Pines Circle. ℂ **843/842-4414.** www.reilleyshilton head.com. Reservations recommended for dinner. Main courses $10–$25. AE, MC, V. Daily 11am–2am.

Truffles Cafe ★ 🎒 INTERNATIONAL   It's no longer on the cutting edge of gastronomic newcomers to Hilton Head, but it's been around so long and garnered so many fans that it's one of our personal favorites on the island. Within the Sea Pines Center, this cafe has a dark, mostly black decor, with a large copper-topped bar, black banquettes, and a menu that somehow manages to please virtually everybody. Start with a spinach and artichoke dip or coconut fried shrimp, followed by baby back ribs or grouper that's grilled and topped with a basil-Parmesan glaze. You could also try Havana chicken with jack cheese and fresh tomato salsa or meatloaf that's grilled with a honey-flavored barbecue sauce and Vidalia onions. Don't confuse this place with the newer and somehow glossier Truffles Grill on Pope Avenue, between Coligny Circle and Sea Island Circle: The Grill is newer and trendier, but many restaurant insiders swear by the original. If you opt for a meal here, you'll have to pay a $5 charge to enter the Sea Island Resort itself. Most islanders recognize and acknowledge this, and accept that fact simply as the cost of doing business and living on Hilton Head Island.

Sea Pines Center, in the Sea Pines Resort. ℂ **843/671-6136.** www.trufflescafe.com. Reservations recommended for dinner. Main courses $12–$28. AE, DC, MC, V. Daily 11am–10pm.

Inexpensive

The British Open Pub BRITISH/AMERICAN   Except for the fact that the hardworking staff speaks with a Carolina accent, you might believe you've stumbled into a remote, woodsy-looking, and unpretentious corner of Britain. And if you opt for a meal here, you'll be in good company, since the town's mayor and a few of his cohorts have to some degree adopted the place as a regular hangout. Since it rarely advertises, prices remain low. Its name derives from the obsession of its owners with the minutiae of the U.K.'s most famous golf tournament. There's British ale on tap, plus ever-popular versions of fish and chips, lobster potpies, shepherd's pie, and meal-size salads. As for Carolina-inspired food, we recommend Chef Jason's twin crab-cake platter, or perhaps the baby back barbecued ribs. Frankly, this is one of the least touristed watering holes on Hilton Head Island, but the drinks are stiff enough to ensure that locals continue to patronize it in droves.

In the Village at Wexford Shopping Center. ℂ **843/686-6736.** www.britishopenpub.net. Reservations not accepted. Main courses $8–$16. AE, DC, MC, V. Mon–Sat 11am–10pm; Sun 9am–10pm.

One Hot Mama's American Grille ★ ☺ GRILL/BARBECUE   It's fun, it's whimsical, and its reasonably priced platters are served in a setting that evokes a mixture of a rock-'n'-roll cafe and a 1950s-era luncheonette. It's the least expensive of the eateries within "the Triangle" of Hilton Head Plaza, and the most child and family friendly. Food focuses on savory, grease-spattered ribs and barbecue dishes. The baby back barbecued ribs here are scrumptious, the pit-to-plate hand-pulled pork virtually addictive. Chargrilled steaks and chicken filets will make you call for more, and if you like fried chicken wings, this place serves them in almost 20 different variations, including a version with strawberry-jalapeño sauce. In case you're wondering who the Hot Mama is, she's Orchid, a hardworking entrepreneur whose prototype for this charming place migrated from nearby Bluffton in 2007.

In the Hilton Head Plaza, Greenwood Dr. off Sea Pines Circle. ℂ **843/682-MAMA** [682-6262]. www. onehotmamas.com. Reservations not accepted. Main courses $7.50–$23. AE, DC, MC, V. Daily 11:30am–midnight.

Santa Fe Cafe ★ MEXICAN   The best, most stylish Mexican restaurant on Hilton Head, the Santa Fe Cafe has rustic, Southwestern-inspired decor and cuisine that infuses traditional recipes with nouvelle flair. Live music adds to the allure. Menu items are often presented in colors as bright as the Painted Desert. Dishes might include tequila shrimp, herb-roasted chicken with jalapeño corn-bread stuffing and mashed potatoes laced with red chilies, grilled tenderloin of pork with smoked habañero sauce and sweet-potato fries, and worthy burritos and chimichangas. The quesadilla is one of the most beautifully presented dishes of any restaurant in town.

700 Plantation Center. ℂ **843/785-3838.** www.santafecafeofhiltonhead.com. Reservations recommended. Main courses $7–$14. AE, DISC, MC, V. Mon–Fri noon–2pm and 5–10pm; Sat–Sun 5–10pm.

Signe's Heaven Bound Bakery & Café SANDWICHES/PASTRIES   Sometime in the early '70s, Signe Gardo, a refugee from the snows of Connecticut, opted to open this bakery. Almost 3,000 wedding cakes and countless Danishes later, it's the oldest eatery under a single ownership on Hilton Head, with a roster of loyal clients. It lies in a relatively underpopulated neighborhood of private homes way, way off the island's beaten touristic track. Many come for breakfast, oohing and aahing over Signe's signature deep-dish French toast, her breakfast polenta, and her waffles. (Rachael Ray came here to film a feature story in 2007.) Lunches focus on a half-dozen salads, a spinach-and-feta *spanikopita* pie that might have been inspired by Zorba himself, tomato or crab-cake tarts, and a steaming ration of shrimp and grits. Simple tables on an outdoor deck (no view of the sea, alas) provide a place setting for your meal. Few guests can resist carting off any of the dozen or so homemade breads including Swiss pear, French oat and apricot, and Hilton Head sourdough bread. Equivalent cakes include a Forever Valentine and a version flavored with piña coladas, coconut, and pineapple cream.

93 Arrow Rd. ℂ **866/807-4463** or 843/785-9118. http://signesbakery.com. Reservations not accepted. Main courses $6–$9. AE, MC, V. Mon–Fri 8am–4pm; Sat–Sun 9am–2pm. Closed Sun Nov–Feb.

HILTON HEAD AFTER DARK

Hilton Head doesn't have Myrtle Beach's nightlife, but enough is here, centered mainly in hotels and resorts. Casual dress (but not swimming attire) is acceptable in most clubs.

Cultural interest focuses on the **Arts Center of Coastal Carolina,** in the Self Family Arts Center, 14 Shelter Cove Lane (ℂ **888/860-2787** or 843/842-ARTS [2787]; www.artshhi.com), which enjoys one of the best theatrical reputations in the Southeast. The Elizabeth Wallace Theater, a 350-seat, state-of-the-art theater, was added to the multiplex in 1996. The older Dunnagan's Alley Theater is located in a renovated warehouse. A wide range of musicals, contemporary comedies, and classic dramas are presented. Showtimes are 8pm Tuesday to Saturday, with a Sunday matinee at 2pm. Adult ticket prices range from $45 for a musical to $75 for a play. Tickets for children 16 and under are $18 to $35. The box office is open 10am to 5pm Monday to Friday and 10am to curtain time on performance days.

The island abounds in sports bars, far too many to document here. We recommend **Callahan Sports Bar & Grill,** 49 New Orleans Rd. (✆ **843/686-7665**), and **Casey's Sports Bar & Grill,** 37 New Orleans Rd. (✆ **843/785-2255**; www. caseyshhi.com).

Jazz Corner Tucked away into an obscure corner of the shopping center known as the Village at Wexford, this is the closest thing to a shadowy, romantic, and permissive jazz bar on Hilton Head. No other nightclub here attracts such a diverse and noteworthy collection of jazz artists. The best way to find out who's playing here is to visit its website for names and dates of upcoming gigs. Doors open nightly at 6pm, performances begin at 8pm, and intermissions are scheduled at 9:30pm. There's an on-site restaurant and a copious drink menu where many of the martinis are ultraoversize and designed for two drinkers. In the Village at Wexford, Unit C1. ✆ **843/842-8620.** www.thejazzcorner.com.

The Metropolitan Lounge Consider a martini or two within this very adult, sophisticated nightclub whose decor might be tactfully described as "bordello chic." Here, a sometimes outrageously good-looking female staff in stylish evening décol-letage will serve you anything you want from a huge martini list. Laura Moretti is the hardworking director of this urban and glossy-looking cocktail lounge, where live music provides an environment that actually celebrates adulthood. Martinis cost from $7 to $13. There is no cover charge. The lounge is open Tuesday to Saturday 8pm to at least 2am. In the Park Plaza Shopping Center, off Greenwood Dr., near the Sea Pines Traffic Round-about. ✆ **843/785-8466.**

Quarterdeck Our favorite waterfront lounge is the best place on the island to watch sunsets, but you can visit any time during the afternoon or evening until 2am. Try to go early and grab one of the outdoor rocking chairs to prepare yourself for nature's light show. There's dancing every night to beach music and Top-40 hits. Quarterdeck is open daily 11am to 2am. Harbour Town, Sea Pines Plantation. ✆ **843/671-2222.** http://quarterdeckrestaurant.com.

The Triangle & How Not to Get Lost Within It

Hilton Head's hottest nightlife spot goes by many names. In an area that resembles a shopping center without any shops, the compound is known variously as the Triangle, the Golden Triangle, the Bermuda Triangle, and most officially of all, **Hilton Head Plaza.** Set beside Greenwood Drive, very close to the Sea Pines Traffic Roundabout, it contains five of the busiest nightclub venues and restaurants on Hilton Head.

Ironically, these bars and restaurants spend relatively low amounts on advertising, relying as they do on grass-roots word of mouth for their ongoing success. The names of these bars and restaurants, arranged from the most formal to the least formal, are **Reilley's**

Grill & Bar, Jump & Phil's Bar & Grill, and **One Hot Mama's American Grille** (see reviews above). In a close tie for the grungiest, least formal, most youth oriented, and most raucous are the **Hilton Head Brew Pub** (✆ **843/785-3900**) and the **Lodge** (✆ **843/842-8966**). Of these two, we prefer the Lodge with its pool tables. But they're all so close together that if one place isn't to your liking, you can easily move on to the next one. The Brew Pub is open daily from 11am to 2am, while the Lodge is a nighttime-only affair, open daily from 7pm 'til sometime after midnight every night. None of these bars begin to get busy, however, until after dark.

SIDE TRIP TO BEAUFORT ★★

Some 30 miles north of Hilton Head Island, Beaufort (Low Country pronunciation is *Bew*-fort) is an old seaport with narrow streets shaded by huge live oaks and lined with 18th-century homes. The oldest house (at Port Republic and New sts.) was built in 1717. This was the second area in North America to be discovered by the Spanish (1520), the site of the first fort on the continent (1525), and the first attempted settlement (1562). Several forts have been excavated, dating from 1566 and 1577.

Beaufort has been used as a setting for several films, including *The Big Chill*. Scenes from the Paramount blockbuster *Forrest Gump,* starring Tom Hanks, and *The Prince of Tides* were also shot here.

If you're traveling from the north, take I-95 to exit 33, then follow the signs to the center of Beaufort. From the south, take I-95 to exit 8 and follow the signs. From Hilton Head, take U.S. 278 West, and after S.C. 170 North joins U.S. 278, follow S.C. 170 into Beaufort.

Beaufort Chamber of Commerce, 1106 Carteret St. (PO Box 910), Beaufort, SC 29901 (✆ 800/638-3525 or 843/525-8500; www.beaufortsc.org), has information and self-guided tours of this historic town. It's open daily 9am to 5pm. If your plans are for early to mid-October, contact the **Historic Beaufort Foundation,** PO Box 11, Beaufort, SC 29901 (✆ 843/379-3331; www.historicbeaufort.org), for dates and details regarding its 3 days of antebellum house and garden tours.

A tour called the **Spirit of Old Beaufort,** 103 West St. Extension (✆ 843/525-0459; www.thespiritofoldbeaufort.com), takes you on a journey through the old town, exploring local history, architecture, horticulture, and Low Country life. You'll see houses that are not accessible on other tours. Your host, clad in period costume, will guide you for 2 hours from Monday to Saturday at 10:30am and 2:30pm. The cost is $15 for adults and $8 for children 6 to 12. Tours depart from just behind the John Mark Verdier House Museum.

The **John Mark Verdier House Museum,** 801 Bay St. (✆ 843/379-6335), is a restored 1802 house partially furnished to depict the life of a merchant planter from 1800 to 1825. It's one of the best examples of the Federal period and was once known as the Lafayette Building because the Marquis de Lafayette is said to have spoken here in 1825. It's open Monday to Saturday from 10:30am to 3:30pm. Admission is $5, and children 5 and under are admitted free.

St. Helena's Episcopal Church, 507 New Castle St. (✆ 843/522-1712; www.sthelenas1712.org), traces its origin back to 1712. Visitors, admitted free Monday to Saturday from 10am to 4pm, can see its classic interior and visit the graveyard, where tombstones served as operating tables during the Civil War.

Where to Stay

The Beaufort Inn ★★   Built in 1897, this is the most appealing hotel in Beaufort and the place where whatever movie star happens to be shooting a film in town is likely to stay. The woodwork and moldings inside are among the finest in Beaufort, and the circular, four-story staircase has been the subject of numerous photographs and architectural awards. The guest rooms, each decorated in brightly colored individual style, are conversation pieces. Children 8 and older are welcome.

809 Port Republic St., Beaufort, SC 29902. ✆ 888/522-0250 or 843/521-9000. Fax 843/521-9500. www.beaufortinn.com. 21 units. $159–$199 double; $220–$299 suite; $350–$450 loft. Rates include full gourmet breakfast. AE, DISC, MC, V. No children 7 and under. **Amenities:** Room service. *In room:* A/C, TV, hair dryer, Wi-Fi (free).

Side Trip to Beaufort

HILTON HEAD & THE LOW COUNTRY

The Cuthbert House Inn ★★   One of the grand old B&Bs of South Carolina, this showcase Southern home was built in 1790 in classic style. The inn was remodeled shortly after the Civil War to take on a more Victorian aura, but its present owner, Sharon Groves, has worked to modernize it without sacrificing its grace or antiquity—such as the graffiti carved by Union soldiers on the fireplace mantel in the Eastlake Room. Guest rooms are elegantly furnished in Southern plantation style, and some have four-poster beds. The inn is filled with large parlors and sitting rooms, and has spacious hallways and 12-foot ceilings characteristic of Greek Revival homes. At breakfast in the conservatory, you can order such delights as Georgia ice cream (cheese grits) and freshly made breads.

1203 Bay St., Beaufort, SC 29902. ℂ **800/327-9275** or 843/521-1315. Fax 843/521-1314. www.cuthbert houseinn.com. 7 units. $150–$259 double; $199–$269 suite. Rates include full breakfast and afternoon tea or refreshments. AE, DISC, MC, V. Free parking. **Amenities:** Breakfast room; bike rentals. *In room:* A/C, TV, fridge, hair dryer, Wi-Fi (free).

Hilton Garden Inn ★   Of course, any Hilton Garden Inn is not as charming as the town's historic inns, but this is a find for those seeking a modern, well-maintained, affordable option. A mile from the historic district, it is convenient to the nearby military bases such as Parris Island, only 3 miles away. The bedrooms are standard motel style, but they are well equipped. A fresh breakfast is offered daily in the Great American Grill, and drinks are served in the cozy Pavilion Lounge. An on-site pantry sells ready-to-cook meals that can be prepared in the in-room microwave oven.

1500 Queen St., Beaufort, SC 29902. ℂ **843/379-9800.** Fax 843/379-9801. http://hiltongardenin. hilton.com. 115 rooms. $109–$229 double. AE, DC, DISC, MC, V. **Amenities:** Restaurant; bar; exercise room; outdoor pool; room service. *In room:* A/C, TV, Wi-Fi (free).

The Rhett House Inn ★★★   This inn is certainly very popular, at least with Hollywood film crews. Because it was a site for *Forrest Gump, The Prince of Tides,* and *The Big Chill,* chances are that you've seen it before. It's a Mobil and AAA four-star inn in a restored 1820 Greek Revival plantation-type home. Rooms are furnished with English and American antiques, and ornamented with Oriental rugs; eight contain whirlpools. The veranda makes an ideal place to sit and view the gardens. The inn is open year-round. Children 5 and older are welcome.

1009 Craven St., Beaufort, SC 29902. ℂ **888/480-9530** or 843/524-9030. Fax 843/524-1310. www. rhetthouseinn.com. 17 units. $159–$350 double. Rates include full breakfast, afternoon tea, and evening hors d'oeuvres. AE, DISC, MC, V. Free parking. No children 4 and under. **Amenities:** Breakfast room. *In room:* A/C, TV, hair dryer, minibar (in some), Wi-Fi (free).

Two Suns Inn   When this place was built in 1917, it was one of the grandest homes in its prosperous neighborhood, offering views of the coastal road and the tidal flatlands beyond. Every imaginable modern (at the time) convenience was added, including a baseboard vacuum-cleaning system, an electric call box, and steam heat. Later, it became housing for unmarried teachers in the public schools. Now it's a cozy B&B. Part of the inn's appeal stems from its lack of pretension, as a glance at the homey bedrooms with simple furnishings and neatly kept bathrooms will show. Children 12 and older are welcome.

1705 Bay St., Beaufort, SC 29902. ℂ **800/532-4244** or 843/522-1122. Fax 843/522-1122. www.twosuns inn.com. 5 units. $159–$199 double. Rates include full breakfast and afternoon cordials. AE, DISC, MC, V. Free parking. No children 11 and under. **Amenities:** Breakfast room. *In room:* A/C, TV, hair dryer, Wi-Fi (free).

Where to Dine

Emily's INTERNATIONAL   This is our favorite restaurant in Beaufort, a spot whose ambience and attitude put us in mind of Scandinavia. That's hardly surprising, because the bearded owner is an émigré from Sweden who feels comfortable in the South Carolina lowlands after years of life at sea. Some folks just go to the bar to sample tapas: miniature portions of tempura shrimp, fried scallops, stuffed peppers, and at least 50 other items. Menu items might include rich cream of mussel and shrimp soup, filet "black and white" (filets of beef and pork served with béarnaise sauce), duck with orange sauce, and a meltingly tender Wiener schnitzel. Everything is served in stomach-stretching portions.

906 Port Republic St. ✆ **843/522-1866.** www.emilysrestaurantandtapasbar.com. Reservations recommended. Tapas $8–$19; main courses $16–$30. AE, DISC, MC, V. Mon–Sat 4–10pm (main courses served starting at 6pm).

Panini's Cafe AMERICAN   Known for its savory stone-baked pizza, this Bay Street restaurant has a waterfront view from its terrace. The building was once a bank and later a movie theater, and what you see today has garnered several renovation awards for returning the building to its former grandeur. In addition to regular pizzas, you can also order a "Capri," the house specialty with spinach, sun-dried tomatoes, onions, feta cheese, extra-virgin olive oil, and mustard aioli. Lunch specialties include Mediterranean shrimp and grits with pancetta polenta and an olive tomato sauté, or the equally unique crab lasagna with mascarpone, spinach, artichoke, and tomato couli. Dinner main courses range from a delicious grilled lobster and shrimp carbonara with applewood smoked bacon, peas, asparagus, and a light Parmesan cream over capellini, to Spanish paella with shrimp, mussels, clams, red snapper, monkfish, chorizo saffron rice, tomatoes, onions, and garlic.

926 Bay St. ✆ **843/379-0300.** www.paniniscafe.net. Reservations recommended. Main courses $9–$13 lunch, $10–$22 dinner; tapas $8–$12. AE, DC, DISC, MC, V. Daily 11am–10pm. Closed Thanksgiving and Christmas.

Plums AMERICAN/SOUTHERN   Centrally located on Bay Street on the waterfront, Plums is one of Beaufort's favorite dining choices. Voted "Best Beaufort Restaurant" in 2006 by the *Island Packet* newspaper, this casual restaurant specializes in sandwiches, soups, and ice cream. While filming *The Prince of Tides* in Beaufort, Barbra Streisand claimed that Plums was her favorite place to come for a cool, refreshing dish of ice cream after a long day of working on the set. The chicken salad sandwich, with celery, toasted almonds, and tomato, is as delicious as Plums' Factory Creek Shrimp Roll, with shrimp, celery, lettuce, and spices, all piled high on a French roll. Quesadillas are another choice, as are heartier sandwiches such as the blackened catfish with spicy mayo or the Plum's Club with turkey, bacon, avocado, and curry mayo.

904½ Bay St. ✆ **843/525-1946.** www.plumsrestaurant.com. Reservations not required. Main courses $6.25–$9.95 lunch, $15–$23 dinner. AE, DC, MC, V. Daily 11am–5pm (soups, salads, sandwiches) and 5–10pm (pasta, seafood, sandwiches).

MYRTLE BEACH & THE GRAND STRAND

One of the top vacation destinations along the East Coast, the Myrtle Beach–Grand Strand area stretches 60 miles from the South Carolina state line at Little River south to Georgetown. Only 98 miles north of Charleston, the population might easily exceed half a million people on a summer day. The Grand Strand annually hosts as many as 14 million visitors, who also come for shopping, golfing, sightseeing, and live theater. Myrtle Beach has grown into a year-round destination—the Travel Channel has voted it the "Best Family Beach"—and South Carolina ranks second only to Florida as a destination.

Named for its abundance of crape myrtle trees, Myrtle Beach is the largest beach resort along the Grand Strand, with the greatest number of attractions, entertainment facilities, and restaurants. The tone is that of a family resort, and many hotels provide programs and diversions for children.

Boating and all the other watersports rank tops among things to do. Fishing is first-rate, whether you cast your line from the surf (permitted all along the beach), a public pier, or a "head boat," charter boats that are available at marinas up and down the Strand.

You can swing a golf club at any of 120 courses. Most motels and hotels offer guest-membership privileges, entitling their guests to packages or reduced greens fees. High season for golf is from February to November. There are also more than 200 public and private tennis courts along the Grand Strand.

Many North European tour groups are coming to the Grand Strand for its un-self-conscious charm and good value. While environmentalists are concerned that the development puts the region's natural beauty at risk—and longtime promoters fear that Myrtle Beach's family-friendly atmosphere may be threatened—corporate entrepreneurs continue pouring money into the area's popular attractions.

ESSENTIALS

GETTING THERE **Myrtle Beach International Airport,** on Harrelson Boulevard (© 843/448-1589), has scheduled air service via **Delta/ASA/ComAir** (© 800/221-1212; www.delta.com), **Continental**

Cutting Your Driving Time

If you're heading from Myrtle Beach to North Myrtle Beach, the opening of the 29-mile Conway Bypass has cut driving time by half an hour. The road brings to life the "Bridge to Nowhere," which for 3 years stood astride the Intracoastal Waterway without a road. The bypass, which is usually known simply as Route 17 or "the bypass," runs from south of Myrtle Beach, near Murrell's Inlet, to Myrtle Beach's northern fringe, near a collection of dinner theaters that include the Grand Ol' Opry and Dolly Parton's Dixie Stampede. Be careful not to confuse Route 17 (the bypass) with its more congested sibling, Business Route 17 (also known as the King's Hwy.), which runs in a north-south direction through the most congested neighborhoods of coastal Myrtle Beach.

(☎ 800/523-3273; www.continental.com), **Spirit Airlines** (☎ 800/772-7117; www.spiritair.com), **US Airways** (☎ 800/428-4322; www.usairways.com), and **Myrtle Beach Direct Air** (☎ 877/432-3473), which flies into Myrtle Beach from such unexpected places as Columbus, Ohio, and Plattsburg, New York, as well as Newark, New Jersey, and Pittsburgh, Pennsylvania.

The U.S. 17 Bypass runs north and south, about 2 miles inland from the Grand Strand's coastline. U.S. 17 Business (also known as the North or South King's Hwy.) runs about a half-mile inland from the coastline, through the most congested neighborhoods of Myrtle Beach. Direct access to most of the highway networks of inland South Carolina is via U.S. Highway 501, which runs eastward to Myrtle Beach from I-95.

Buses from **Greyhound** (☎ 800/231-2222; www.greyhound.com) and **Southeastern Stages** (☎ 404/591-2780; www.southeasternstages.com) arrive and depart from the **J & D Travel station,** 511 7th Ave. N (☎ 843/448-2472).

VISITOR INFORMATION   The **Myrtle Beach Area Chamber of Commerce** is at 1200 N. Oak St. (PO Box 2115), Myrtle Beach, SC 29578 (☎ 800/356-3016 or 843/626-7444 to order literature only; www.visitmyrtlebeach.com), open daily from 8:30am to 5pm. Two publications jampacked with specific area information are *Stay and Play* and the *Myrtle Beach Visitors' Guide,* both of which are available without charge from the chamber of commerce. Both magazines, as well as hundreds of brochures advertising regional pastimes, activities, bars, restaurants, and watersports facilities, are available from virtually every hotel and restaurant in town.

Warning: Although their borders blend almost imperceptibly, the communities of Myrtle Beach and North Myrtle Beach maintain distinctly different systems of numerating their roads and streets. Hundred-dollar cab fares have been racked up by passengers who weren't clear about which of the two communities they were going to.

THE BEACHES, THE LINKS & BEYOND

Family Kingdom Amusement Park and Water Park ☺   This is one of the declining numbers of sea-fronting amusement parks, replete with roller coasters, carousels, cotton candy, the largest Ferris wheel in South Carolina, and a beachfront water park that includes at least six water slides, lots of splashing fountains, and an

Myrtle Beach & the Grand Strand

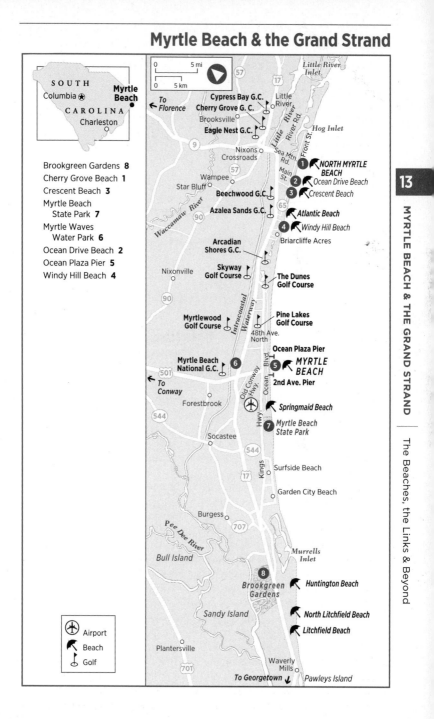

Brookgreen Gardens **8**
Cherry Grove Beach **1**
Crescent Beach **3**
Myrtle Beach
  State Park **7**
Myrtle Waves
  Water Park **6**
Ocean Drive Beach **2**
Ocean Plaza Pier **5**
Windy Hill Beach **4**

SOUTH
Columbia ✹   **Myrtle
CAROLINA   Beach**
  Charleston ○

To
← Florence

Cypress Bay G.C.   Little
Cherry Grove G. C.   River
  Brooksville ○
Eagle Nest G.C.

Nixons
Crossroads

Wampee ○
Star Bluff ○

Beechwood G.C.
Azalea Sands G.C.

Arcadian
Shores G.C.

Nixonville ○

Skyway
Golf Course

Myrtlewood
Golf Course

Myrtle Beach
National G.C.

← To
Conway

Forestbrook ○

Socastee ○

Burgess ○

Pee Dee River
Bull Island

Brookgreen
Gardens

Sandy Island

Plantersville ○

Waccamaw River

Intracoastal Waterway

Little River
Inlet

Little River Rd.
Sea Mtn. Rd.
Main St.
Front St.
Hog Inlet

❶ ↖ **NORTH MYRTLE
   BEACH**
❷ ↖ Ocean Drive Beach
❸ ↖ Crescent Beach

↖ Atlantic Beach
❹ ↖ Windy Hill Beach

Briarcliffe Acres

The Dunes
Golf Course

Pine Lakes
Golf Course

48th Ave.
North

Ocean Plaza Pier
❺ **MYRTLE
   BEACH**
2nd Ave. Pier

↖ Springmaid Beach
❼ Myrtle Beach
   State Park

Surfside Beach

Garden City Beach

Murrells
Inlet

❽ ↖ Huntington Beach

↖ North Litchfield Beach
↖ Litchfield Beach

Waverly
Mills ○

To Georgetown ↓ Pawleys Island

⊕ Airport
↖ Beach
⚲ Golf

13

MYRTLE BEACH & THE GRAND STRAND | The Beaches, the Links & Beyond interconnected series of lazy river–style swimming pools. A few of the park's attractions were salvaged from the Pavilion, a now-defunct venue that evokes nostalgia in the hearts of many local residents. The majority of the park's 30 rides, however, are high-tech enough to generate excitement, and traditional enough to still evoke memories of Clarence the Clown and spun-sugar candy.

300 S. Ocean Blvd. © **843/626-3447.** www.family-kingdom.com. Free admission to water park and amusement park; amusement park rides $1–$5.25 per person; all-day ride pass $24 for persons 48 in. and taller, $18 for persons shorter than 48 in.; 2-day combo pass for both amusement park and water park $33 per person. Combo pass can be used on two separate but consecutive days. Water park June–Aug daily 10am–6pm (some Sun open at 1pm). Amusement park daily Mar 21–Sept 27, usually 4pm–midnight.

The L.W. Paul Living History Museum ☺ Visits to this fun and educational working farm give a glimpse into the historical Southern farm life of yesteryear. Spread over 17 peaceful acres of land, multiple buildings re-create the goings-on of everyday farm work circa the early 1900s in a conscious attempt to preserve the region's cultural history. Visitors young and old are encouraged to participate in and observe hands-on activities from hanging leaves in the tobacco shed to dry, grinding cornmeal the old-fashioned way with a mule-powered mill, caretaking animals that range from chickens to pigs, making soap, blacksmithing, and more. A gift shop sells various snacks, treats, and refreshments, along with edible souvenirs such as handmade preserves. *Note:* Call ahead to make reservations to tour the farm outside of regular business hours.

2279 Harris Shortcut Rd, corner of Harris Short Cut Rd. and Hwy 701 N., Conway. © **843/365-3596.** www.horrycountymuseum.org. Tues–Sat 9am–4pm. Closed on government holidays.

MagiQuest ☺ Here's how it works: You (and presumably the children who accompany you) will select a magic wand, after which the adventures begin as you learn how to harness its power. Within a 20,000-square-foot space, you'll then do your magic upon more than 250 artifacts, producing the kinds of effects of which Harry Potter—at any stage of his development as a wizard—would be proud. The theme is medieval, Celtic, and mystical, with plenty of problems on-site for the solving, and lots of opportunities for the power of youth and truth to triumph over the forces of darkness and evil. Suspend disbelief, bring a sense of make-believe, and marvel at the way someone has found to harness the ongoing attraction for myths, lore, legend, the supernatural, and superheroes.

At Broadway at the Beach, 1185 Celebrity Circle. © **843/916-1800.** www.magiquest.com. Admission $26 adults and children. Discounts available for returning guests and for grandparents accompanying their grandchildren. May 22–Sept 6 daily 10am–10pm.

Myrtle Waves Water Park ☺ Myrtle Beach is *hot* in summer, so it's little wonder that June to August this park is jampacked with families escaping the heat. The state's largest water park has 1 million gallons and some 20 acres of curves, waves, and swerves. Some 200,000 visitors come annually for the more than 30 rides and various attractions, including an Ocean in Motion Wave pool; the LayZee River, a slow, 3-mph ride around the park; and Bubble Bay, a 7,000-foot leisure pool with a trio of cascading water umbrellas. Other amusements include a Saturation Station with splashes, slides, and waterfalls, including a Caribbean-themed "volcano"—the world's tallest tubular slides (10 stories high).

U.S. 17 Bypass at Mr. Joe White Ave. (10th Ave. N.). © **843/918-8725.** www.myrtlewaves.com. Admission $33 42 in. and over, $25 41 in and under. June to mid-Aug daily 10am–7pm; May and mid-Aug to early Sept Sat–Sun and some weekdays 10am–5pm. Call ahead for specific days.

NASCAR Speed Park ☺ The entrepreneurs of the park claim that "if you got any closer to the real thing, you'd have to hire a pit crew!" Opened in 1998, it's practically a Disneyland devoted to racing, complete with seven thrilling racetracks and such attractions as speed bumper boats, an indoor climbing wall, and kiddie rides. The most exciting track is a half-mile course featuring ⅝-scale Nextel Cup–style cars. (**Note:** Drivers must be 16 years old with a valid license.) All sorts of games, some 50 in all, are a feature of the Speed Dome Arcade, including side-by-side linked racing machines.

Hwy. 17 Bypass at 21st Ave. N. (across from Broadway at the Beach). ℂ **843/918-8725.** www.nascarspeedpark.com. Admission $33 ages 4 and over, free ages 3 and under. June–Aug daily 10am–11pm; Sept–May daily 10am to btw. 5pm and 8pm, depending on business and the season. Call ahead.

Ripley's Aquarium ★★ ☺ This is the most visited attraction in South Carolina, and deservedly so. In Broadway at the Beach, this aquarium—one of the greatest in America—was built at a cost of $40 million and is maintained in state-of-the-art condition. Visitors are surrounded on all sides by menacing 10-foot sharks as they travel through Dangerous Reef, a 750,000-gallon tank. The question always asked is why don't these monsters gobble up the other fish in the tank. The answer: They're so well fed they don't bother. Most of the habitats in the various holding tanks are saltwater. The only freshwater exhibit is the Rio Amazon, displaying fearsome piranhas, aruanas, and pacu. You can spend at least 4 hours here, enjoying such pleasures as Rainbow Rock, with its view of thousands of brilliantly colored fish from the Pacific. Children are drawn to the Sea-for-Yourself Discovery Center, an interactive, multimedia playground. Newly installed in 2008 is Pirates: Fact and Folklore, an exhibit about the privateers who once sheltered themselves in South Carolina's coves and inlets. Dive shows and marine education sessions are presented hourly.

At Broadway on the Beach, 1110 Celebrity Circle. ℂ **800/734-8888** or 843/916-0888. www.ripleysaquarium.com. Admission $19 ages 12 and over, $10 ages 6–11, $4 ages 2–5, free ages 1 and under. June–Aug daily 9am–10pm; Sept–May Sun–Thurs 9am–9pm, Fri–Sat 9am–10pm.

Beaches

Myrtle Beach sand is mostly hard packed and the color of brown sugar, to which it's often compared. During the resort's rapid growth during the 1980s and 1990s, city planners deliberately interspersed residential zones with commercial zones, thereby relieving clusters of honky-tonk with carefully landscaped communities of private homes and condos.

The beach has lifeguards and plenty of fast-food joints. Amazingly, there are no public toilets. South Carolina law, however, obligates hotels to allow beach buffs to use their facilities. (Many male beachgoers don't bother to go inside the hotels but use walls instead—a habit that has provoked endless local-newspaper comment.)

At the southern tier of the beach, **Myrtle Beach State Park,** 4401 South King's Hwy., Myrtle Beach (ℂ **843/238-5325;** www.myrtlebeachstatepark.net), offers 312 acres of pine woods and access to a sandy beach. Admission to the park is $4 for adults, $1.50 for children 6 to 15, and free for children 5 and under. Seniors (age 61 and over) who are residents of South Carolina pay an entrance fee of $2.50. The park contains toilets and picnic tables, and it's possible to fish from a pier for $4.50. The park is full of nature trails and offers 302 campsites, priced from $30 to $32 per night for full-service campsites, $28 to $30 per night for electrical (but not sewage and water) connections. Simple campsites with none of the above-mentioned hookups rent for $21 to $23 per night. The park is open March to November daily 6am to 10pm, off season daily 6am to 8pm.

Golf

Golfers can tee off at more than 100 **championship golf courses** ★★★ (www. mbn.com), making it possible to play a different course every day for 3 months straight. Many local courses host major professional and amateur tournaments. Some of the most visible tournaments attract huge interest locally: Examples include the PGA Tour Superstore World Amateur Handicap Championship, in late August; the Palmetto High Golf Championship, held in March and again in September, wherein golf teams from high schools throughout the country compete against each other; and the Veterans Golf Classic, a May event that's open only to active military personnel and qualified veterans.

Variety is a contributing factor to the success and popularity of Myrtle Beach and Grand Strand golf courses, which come in many shapes, sizes, and degrees of difficulty. Courses have been designed by some of the best-known names in golf: Jack Nicklaus, Arnold Palmer, Rees Jones, Tom Fazio, Gary Player, Don Ross, Dan Maple, Tom Jackson, and Pete and P. B. Dye.

Golf-course architects have taken care to protect the habitats of indigenous wildlife. Players find themselves in the midst of towering Carolina pines or giant live oaks draped in Spanish moss. Some courses overlook huge bluffs with the Atlantic Ocean or Intracoastal Waterway in the background. Some of the courses feature such unusual attractions as a private airstrip adjoining a clubhouse, a cable car that crosses the Intracoastal Waterway, and alligators lurking in water hazards. Some courses are built on the grounds of historic rice plantations, which offer Old South atmosphere.

Although golf is played year-round, spring and autumn are the busiest seasons. Many golf packages include room, board, and greens fees. For information, call **Myrtle Beach Golf Holiday** (© 800/845-4653; www.golfholiday.com).

Aberdeen Country Club, S.C. 9, North Myrtle Beach (© 843/399-2660 or 843/235-6061), is a 27-hole course designed by Tom Jackson, charging greens fees of $35 to $76. Along the banks of the Waccamaw River, this course has Bermuda greens, along with a pro shop and a practice area with a driving range.

Arcadian Shores, 701 Hilton Rd. (© 866/326-5275 or 843/449-5217; www. arcadianshores.com), an 18-hole, par-72 course opened in 1974, was created by noted golf architect Rees Jones. Just 5 miles north of Myrtle Beach off U.S. 17, the course has bent-grass greens winding through a stately live-oak grove. Electric carts are required, and greens fees are $37 to $65.

Azalea Sands, 2100 U.S. 17, North Myrtle Beach (© 800/253-2312 or 843/272-6191), opened in 1972. The 18-hole course features white-sand traps and blue lakes. Designed by architect Gene Hamm, it's a popular course for golfers of all handicaps. Greens fees range from $31 to $56.

Beachwood, 1520 U.S. 17, Crescent Section, North Myrtle Beach (© 800/526-4889 or 843/272-6168; www.beachwoodgolf.com), is another course designed by Gene Hamm. Opened in 1968, it has 18 holes, charging greens fees ranging from $38 to $63. It's a par-72 course with blue tees of 6,844 yards. The course annually hosts the Carolinas' PGA Senior's Championship and DuPont World Amateur.

Caledonia Golf Course and Fishing Club, Pawleys Island (© 800/483-6800 or 843/237-3675), is set atop what used to be a series of marshy rice paddies, and some of its links are graced with century-old oak trees. This golf course has an intelligent layout favored by pros, and a clubhouse whose architecture was inspired by an antique Low Country plantation house. Its only drawback is a location that's about a

30-minute drive south of Myrtle Beach. A flotilla of charter boats and deep-sea fishing pros are associated with this place as well. Greens fees range from $90 to $175.

Grande Dunes Golf Club ★★, 8700 Golf Village Lane (© **843/315-0333**), is one of the newer and better courses, set on a bluff overlooking the Intracoastal Waterway with panoramic views. Rated by *Golf Magazine* as one of the best courses in the nation, it is a par-72 course with numerous elevation changes and wide Bermuda grass fairways, including 34 acres of lakes. Greens fees are $82 to $152.

Legends ★★★, U.S. 501, Myrtle Beach (© **800/299-6187** or 843/236-9318; www.legendsgolf.com), designed by Pete Dye and Tom Doak, opened in 1990. The 54-hole, par-72 course charges greens fees of $67 to $121. Its Mooreland Course was ranked by *Golf Digest* as one of the top five new public courses in America in 1991. Dye's flair for deep bunkers, undulating fairways and greens, and signature bulkheads has transformed this course into one of the strongest challenges along the East Coast. The 42,000-square-foot Scottish-style clubhouse is an impressive entry to the course. Heathland, designed by Doak, has been called "the next best thing to visiting Scotland."

The 36-hole, par-72 **Myrtlewood Golf Club,** 1500 48th Ave. (U.S. 17 Business), North Myrtle Beach (© **800/283-3633** or 843/913-4516; www.myrtlewoodgolf. com), was designed by architect Arthur Hills. Bordering the Intracoastal Waterway, the PineHills course is the fourth oldest at Myrtle Beach, measuring 6,640 yards. Also at Myrtlewood, the Palmetto Course is one of the best in the area, with bentgrass putting greens. It stretches for 6,953 yards. Greens fees are $48 to $90.

Other Outdoor Pursuits

FISHING Because of the warming temperature of the Gulf Stream, fishing is good from early spring until around Christmas. You can pursue king mackerel, spadefish, amberjack, barracuda, sea bass, and Spanish mackerel, along with grouper and red snapper. Great fishing is available aboard any boat of **Captain Dick's,** Business Highway 17, at Murrells Inlet (© **866/557-FISH** [3474] or 843/651-3676; www. captdicks.com). Captain Dick's offers three charters that go as far as 60 miles offshore. The Sea Bass Fishing Adventure is a half-day trip that's usually conducted every Thursday between noon and 8pm. It's priced at $44 for adults and $26 for children 12 and under. The rates include rod and reel, bait, tackle, and license.

The Continental Shelf Fishing trip is an 8-hour trip that goes slightly farther out than the Sea Bass Adventure, in search of bigger fish. Rates are $62 for adults and $33 for children 12 and under, including rod and reel, bait, tackle, and license. Electric reels are available for $9. The All Day Gulf Stream trip is an 11-hour jaunt that departs at 6:30am in search of red snapper, grouper, triggerfish, and amberjack. The rate of $90 for adults and $56 for children 12 and under includes rod and reel, bait, tackle, and license. Electric reels are also available for this trip for an additional $12.

Once a month, between March and November, Captain Dick's hosts the Overnight Gulf Stream fishing expedition for the true fishing enthusiast. The cost of the 25-hour trip, which departs at 1:30pm on Saturday and returns at 2:30pm on Sunday, is $200. The rate includes rod and reel, bait, tackle, and license; an electric reel is an additional $12. On this trip, the price of the electric reel may well be worth it.

SAILING & KAYAKING **Captain Dick's,** Business Highway 17, at Murrells Inlet (© **866/557-FISH** [3474] or 843/651-3676), has cruises that offer stunning views of the Grand Strand. The Saltwater Marsh Explorer Adventure is a 2½-hour ecology trip that allows you to see marine life in its true element. Rates are $21 for adults and $15 for children 12 and under. The Cruising the Beach Ocean Sightseeing Cruise along the coast of Myrtle Beach wraps up the trip with a sunset at sea. Rates are $19 for adults and $11 for children ages 6 to 12 (free for children 5 and under).

You can rent kayaks and Hobie Cat sailboats at **Sail and Ski,** 515 Hwy. 501, Myrtle Beach (© **843/626-7245;** www.sailandskiconnection.com), from April to September. Usually rented only to experienced sailors, they cost $30 to $45 per hour. Escorted 2-hour kayak tours through local mangrove swamps are around $50 each.

TENNIS The **Myrtle Beach Public Courts,** 3200 Oak St., on Myrtle Beach (no phone), offer a trio of outdoor and asphalt courts next to the Myrtle Beach Recreation Center. A more elegant place to play is the **Kingston Plantation Sport & Health Club,** 9760 Kings Rd., Myrtle Beach (© **843/497-1610;** www.kingstonplantation. com). Such greats as Pete Sampras and Jimmy Connors have played these five hard-surface courts. There are also four clay courts. Courts cost $20 per hour.

Grand Dunes Tennis Club, U.S. 17 Bypass, across from Dixie Stampede, at Myrtle Beach (© **843/315-0218;** www.grandedunes.com), has 10 composition courts, eight of which are lighted for night play. Courts cost $30 for two people for 2 hours and $50 for four people for 2 hours. There's also an on-site pro shop and fitness room.

WATERSPORTS To rent jet skis and other watersports vehicles, contact **Myrtle Beach Watersports** (© **843/497-8848**). Their main office is at 5835 Dick Pond Rd., Myrtle Beach. Here the staff will refer you to any of four other locations along the Grand Strand.

Shopping

Cited by urban critics as one of the most appealing combinations of residential and commercial real estate that's ever been seen along South Carolina's coastal region, the recently inaugurated **Market Common,** 4017 Deville Street (© **843/839-3500;** www.marketcommonmb.com), has added a welcome touch of upscale class and charm to the strip-mall flavor of some other parts of Myrtle Beach. Designed with pedestrian-friendly streets, adequate parking, lots of stores, movie theaters, and restaurants, it resembles a self-contained village, a feeling that's reinforced by the dozens of private town houses and condos that occupy the upper floors of retail buildings.

Coastal Grand Mall (© **843/839-9100;** www.coastalgrand.com), South Carolina's largest shopping center, is at the intersection of Highway 17 Bypass and Highway 501. Containing four megasize department stores (Sears, Dillard's, Belk, and JCPenney), it also features dozens of specialty retail outlets along with at least a dozen restaurants and specialty food vendors. You can shop 'til you drop at outlets that range from Radio Shack to Victoria's Secret.

WHERE TO STAY

The Grand Strand is lined with hotels, motels, condominiums, and cottages. The highest rates are charged June 15 to Labor Day. Myrtle Beach is becoming more of a year-round destination, however, and you can find great off-season discounts in the winter. Golfers, in particular, take advantage of these low-cost rooms in the off season.

By and large, the double rooms in the recommended hotels and inns below have private bathrooms with tub/shower combinations, unless otherwise noted, and in some cases, they contain self-contained kitchens.

Very Expensive

Kingston Plantation ★★ This is the most desirable and one of the best-landscaped hotel and condominium complexes in Myrtle Beach. Set on 145 rolling acres of intensely manicured gardens, it combines a conventional hotel—the 20-story Embassy Suites—with a labyrinthine collection of individually owned one-, two-, and three-bedroom villas and condos. Be sure to specify your tastes in condo living, either when you reserve or at the time of check-in—some units are in soaring high-rises, others are low-slung town house–style accommodations. A few are free-standing, woodsy-looking buildings in their own right. Registration for every guest room within Kingston Plantation, regardless of its design and venue, is within the lobby of the above-mentioned Embassy Suites Hotel, which was extensively renovated during 2007 and 2008. Each of the conventional hotel rooms contains a kitchen, dining area, living room, and at least one bedroom, and is outfitted with a private balcony and a tasteful blend of light-grained woods and pale sand-and-sea colors. Residents of Embassy Suites benefit from slightly more intensive service rituals than those in the outlying condos and villas.

For such an enormous resort development, it's surprising to find only two restaurants, **Fish Eye Grill** (open for breakfast, lunch, and dinner) and the dinner-only **Omaha Steakhouse,** on the premises. Both are set on the ground floor of the high-rise Embassy Suites.

9800 Queensway Blvd., Myrtle Beach, SC 29572. ✆ **800/876-0010** or 843/449-0006. Fax 843/497-1017. www.kingstonplantation.com. 255 units, 600 condos and villas. $339 Embassy Suites; $99–$504 condo or villa. Children 18 and under stay free in parent's room. Rates include breakfast in Embassy Suites. AE, DC, DISC, MC, V. Take Hwy. 17 to the border of Myrtle Beach and N. Myrtle Beach. **Amenities:** 2 restaurants; 2 bars; exercise room; Jacuzzi; 11 outdoor pools; 9 tennis courts (lit). *In room:* A/C, TV, hair dryer, kitchenette, Wi-Fi ($9.95 per day).

Myrtle Beach Marriott Resort at Grande Dunes ★★★ Constructed at a cost of $50 million, this chain hotel is one of the most luxurious on the South Carolina coastline. Opening onto the beach, and designed with a distinct appreciation for the haciendas of Argentina with touches of Iberian baroque, this elegant tower lies 1 mile from the Carolina Opry and 10 miles from the international airport. The smartly modern guest rooms are midsize to spacious, each with a luxurious bathroom. Most units open onto ocean views, and nearly all have panoramic vistas of some sort. Because it is part of the 2,200-acre greater Grande Dunes community, a plantation-style residential and leisure development, the resort offers more amenities than many others in the Carolinas, including a championship golf course and a European spa with an indoor pool. The 15-story structure offers everything from an excellent on-site restaurant, Oceans on 82nd, with an international menu, to an array of in-room extras, ranging from voice mail to free coffee. There's a heavy-handed emphasis on the sale of timeshares within the surrounding resort, but in light of the spectacular swimming pool, the beachside location, and the overall sense of an ongoing fiesta, most visitors take it in stride.

8400 Costa Verde Dr., Myrtle Beach, SC 29572. ✆ **800/228-9290** or 843/449-8880. Fax 843/449-8669. www.marriott.com. 407 units. $130–$380 double; from $650 suite. AE, DC, DISC, MC, V. Parking $10. **Amenities:** 2 restaurants; 2 bars; babysitting; concierge; 2 pools (1 indoor); room service; spa. *In room:* A/C, TV, hair dryer, Wi-Fi ($13 per day).

Resort Quest Myrtle Beach at the Market Common ★ 🎁 This property originated in 2008, when the finishing touches were added to Myrtle Beach's Market

Common. Designed like a classy, self-contained, and very stylish village, it's a combination of private condos, restaurants, movie theaters, and shops that rose from land formerly designated as an air force base. Today, it's a destination in its own right, with some of the most appealing stores in Myrtle Beach. The upper floors of this development contain 81 privately owned, and usually plushly furnished, apartments, any of which are for rent. You'll be inland, about a mile from the nearest beach, but with plenty of parking and a sense of living within an upscale and immaculately landscaped village. Daily maid service is an option in your "vacation residence," if you're willing to pay extra for it.

1232 Farrow Pkwy., Myrtle Beach, SC 29577. *C* **877/869-5962** or 843/238-1614. www.resortquest myrtlebeach.com. 81 units. $236–$500 studio; $260–$570 1-bedroom apt; $350–$680 2-bedroom apt. 1-time mandatory cleaning charge $60–$80. 3-night minimum stay in summer; 2-night minimum stay in winter. AE, DISC, MC, V. *In room:* A/C, TV, Internet (free), kitchen.

Expensive

Anderson Ocean Club Resort ★★   Set amid the densest concentration of hotels in "downtown" Myrtle Beach, this oceanfront, ocher-colored, 22-story tower opened in 2008 to fanfare that immediately positioned it amid the most upscale properties at the resort. Its design and decor manage to evoke Andalusian Spain, Morocco, and (on the inside) baroque Sicily all at the same time. Thanks to a position near the Convention Center, it caters to lots of corporations, many of them from the Carolinas, for their annual sales and incentive meetings. Local gossip identifies the carved doors leading between this hotel's lobby and the street as among the most ornate and expensive in town.

2600 N. Ocean Blvd., Myrtle Beach, SC 29577. *C* **866/578-8494** or 843/213-5340. Fax 843/213-5341. www.oceanaresorts.com. 304 units. $60–$250 double; $77–$470 suite. AE, DC, DISC, MC, V. **Amenities:** Restaurant; bar; exercise room; 3 pools (1 indoor); spa. *In room:* A/C, TV, hair dryer, kitchen, Wi-Fi (free).

The Cypress Inn ★ 🛏   In the center of Conway, 15 miles northwest of Myrtle Beach, stands this oasis overlooking the Waccamaw River. Guests stroll along the river-walk where boats are tied up. This is one of the finer B&Bs along the coast of South Carolina. The good-size guest rooms are beautifully furnished, containing, among other offerings, Jacuzzi tubs, aromatic toiletries, and posh linens. Each room is individually decorated and has a different name, everything from the Wisteria Room to the Miss Marple Room, the latter inspired by the works of Agatha Christie.

16 Elm St., Conway, SC 29526. *C* **800/575-5307** or 843/248-8199. www.acypressinn.com. 12 units. $145–$235 double. Rates include breakfast. AE, DISC, MC, V. **Amenities:** Breakfast room. *In room:* A/C, TV/VCR, hair dryer, Wi-Fi (free).

The Island Vista ★★ ☺   This is one of the tallest, best-designed, best-managed, and most urban-stylish lodgings in Myrtle Beach. Rising 13 floors from an enviable stretch of beach within the Golden Mile area north of downtown Myrtle Beach, it is a world apart from the tacky congestion of the resort's downtown. Thanks to a Mediterranean–Art Deco design, the vibe is akin to what you might expect in a seaside Las Vegas. The sort you might find in a private mansion somewhere in the British West Indies, bedroom furnishings are plushly upscale. Throughout, you'll have huge-windowed views out over a wide expanse of beachfront. Notice the massive numbers of cypress planks the owner/designers of this place added to the public areas. Dug up from a local swamp, they're only some of the many thoughtful touches that permeate this genuinely appealing resort hotel. The resort's dining showcase, the **Cypress Room,** is separately recommended in "Where to Dine," below.

6000 N. Ocean Blvd., Myrtle Beach, SC 29577. ⓒ **800/854-5734** or 843/449-6406. www.island vistaresort.com. 149 units. $68–$185 studio; $85–$270 1-bedroom apt; $110–$385 2-bedroom apt; $206–$600 4-bedroom apt. AE, DC, MC, V. **Amenities:** Restaurant (see review, p. 316); bar; children's activities; 3 pools (all 3 indoor and outdoor). *In room:* A/C, TV, kitchen, minibar, Wi-Fi (free).

Moderate

The Breakers ★ ☺   This is a longtime family favorite whose growth over the past decades has paralleled that of Myrtle Beach itself. It consists of seven beachfront towers, six of them adjacent to each other, the seventh (the North Tower) within 6 blocks of the others. Boasting one of the best beachfront locations in Myrtle Beach, the complex is unified with a series of swimming pools whose interconnected waters include a scaled-down model of a pirate schooner, the surfaces of which double as sun-tanning space. You can book here on any number of plans, within a wide configuration of accommodations, from tastefully furnished guest rooms to efficiencies with kitchenettes, and even one- to three-bedroom suites. Extra beds in the form of fold-out sofas, Murphy beds, and twin sets of doubles make for flexible family units. Within this sprawling resort, a relatively stylish corner is the North Tower (ca. 1990), a soaring yellow-and-white boutique hotel with its own registration desk and some 140 condos, which join the rental pool of the Breakers whenever their individual owners are not on-site.

2006 N. Ocean Blvd. (PO Box 485), Myrtle Beach, SC 29578. ⓒ **800/952-4507** or 843/444-4444. Fax 843/626-5001. www.breakers.com. 650 units. $75–$276 double; $85–$592 suite. Ask about off-season rates. Children 16 and under stay free in parent's room. AE, DC, DISC, MC, V. Free parking. **Amenities:** 3 restaurants; 2 bars; exercise room; Jacuzzi; 14 pools (2 indoor); room service. *In room:* A/C, TV, hair dryer, kitchenette (in some), Wi-Fi (free).

The Caravelle Resort ★ ☺   One of Myrtle Beach's older hotels, this 6-decades-old, 15-story workhouse has a new lease on life. A renovation improved its standards, revved up its look, and brought it back into the spotlight. To a modern structure was added a variety of swimming pools, a "lazy river" for inner-tube rides, and facilities that might remind you of a children's summer camp. Overall, the rebuilt and reorganized Caravelle is a good, middle-of-the-road choice for families. It's north of the congestion of downtown Myrtle Beach, within the "Golden Mile" of hotels and upscale residential real estate. Its 2007 reorganization gathered as many as eight additional nearby buildings, many of them once-independent resort hotels in their own right, into its fold. Each guest room has a kitchen, so families can save money by making their own meals.

7000 N. Ocean Blvd., Myrtle Beach, SC 29577. ⓒ **888/854-0558.** www.thecaravelle.com. 632 units. $66–$260 double; $110–$421 suite. AE, DC, DISC, MC, V. **Amenities:** Restaurant; bar; indoor/outdoor pool complex. *In room:* A/C, TV, hair dryer, kitchen, Wi-Fi (free).

Hilton Myrtle Beach Resort ★★ ☺   This imposing high-rise is shaped like a Y, with guest rooms radiating from the central atrium. Thanks to the acres of private condos and houses that surround it, it's a more tranquil choice than other hotels in the bustling heart of Myrtle Beach. The guest rooms open onto the ocean and are furnished in a light, contemporary style, often with rattan pieces. There is an outdoor pool with a children's section and a separate toddlers' pool. A formal restaurant offers a Continental menu, or you can patronize the informal coffee shop. Entertainment is featured at the mezzanine-level bar, and light snacks are offered at the poolside cafe in good weather.

10000 Beach Club Dr., Myrtle Beach, SC 25972. ⓒ **800/HILTONS** (445-8667) or 843/449-5000. Fax 843/497-0168. www.hilton.com. 385 units. $99–$239 double; $139–$279 suite. AE, DC, DISC, MC, V. Parking $8. Take U.S. 17 for 9 miles north of Myrtle Beach to Arcadian Shores. **Amenities:** 2 restaurants; 2 bars; babysitting; children's activities; exercise room; Jacuzzi; 2 pools (1 indoor); 13 tennis courts (lit). *In room:* A/C, TV, kitchenette, Wi-Fi ($9.95 per day).

Landmark Resort ★   A huge U-shaped structure standing 15 stories tall amid the beach action, the Landmark is one of the Grand Strand's better examples of mid-priced accommodations, with the South's largest resort indoor-pool complex. Renovated to the tune of $11 million, the hotel has a West Indies–inspired lobby which makes a favorable impression, as do the gardenlike restaurant and bar. For more action, try the nightclub or the grill by the outdoor pool. In winter, the same pool is enclosed for year-round use. Each of the units has a tiny balcony and is equipped with one king-size bed or two double beds, well-kept bathrooms, refrigerators in kitchenettes that have granite countertops, and in some cases, ocean views. The lowest rates are available December and January.

1501 S. Ocean Blvd., Myrtle Beach, SC 29577. ⓒ **800/845-0658** or 843/448-9441. Fax 843/448-6701. www.landmarkresort.com. 552 units. $48–$177 double; $54–$199 suite. Additional person $8. Children 18 and under stay free in parent's room. Off-season discounts available. AE, DISC, MC, V. **Amenities:** Restaurant; bar; 9-hole miniature golf course; exercise room; 5 Jacuzzis; pool complex; room service. *In room:* A/C, TV, fridge, hair dryer, Wi-Fi (free).

Ocean Creek Resort ☺   One of the best-respected of the 1980s-era resorts along the beach, this first-class choice features studios and condos divided into about a half-dozen carefully landscaped complexes that sprawl across a spread of nearly 60 acres. Condominiums are categorized as studios, one bedrooms, two bedrooms, three bedrooms, lodge units, beachside towers, or tennis villas. The Beach Club on the ocean operates in summer.

10600 N. King's Hwy., Myrtle Beach, SC 29572. ⓒ **877/844-3800** or 843/272-7724. Fax 843/272-9627. www.oceancreek.com. 750 units, 345 available for short-term rental. $70–$195 studio or condo. AE, DISC, MC, V. Take U.S. 17 N. almost to N. Myrtle Beach. **Amenities:** Restaurant; bar; children's programs in summer; exercise room; Jacuzzi; 7 pools (1 indoor); 7 tennis courts (lit). *In room:* A/C, TV, hair dryer, kitchen (in most), Wi-Fi (free).

Ocean Reef Resort ☺   North of the bustling beach center, this oceanfront resort is better than most other moderately priced choices. It originated in the 1970s as a balconied, boxy-looking rectangle, but it was expanded in 2004 and 2006 with towers positioned on each end. The bar is Caribbean style, complete with bamboo, and the restaurant has tall windows opening onto ocean views. All the rooms and efficiency units are oceanfront and tropically inspired; most have two double beds, good-size bathrooms, and balconies. The best accommodations are the 51 suites (with whirlpool tubs).

7100 N. Ocean Blvd. (at 71st Ave. N.), Myrtle Beach, SC 29572. ⓒ **888/322-6411** or 843/449-4441. Fax 843/497-3041. www.oceanreefmyrtlebeach.com. 333 units. $49–$179 double; $79–$255 suite. Children 17 and under stay free in parent's room. Off-season discounts available. AE, DC, DISC, MC, V. Free parking. **Amenities:** Restaurant; bar; children's activities and water playground; exercise room; Jacuzzi; 3 pools (1 indoor); room service; sauna. *In room:* A/C, TV, hair dryer, kitchenette (in some), Wi-Fi (free).

Yachtsman Resort ⚑   Some 8 blocks from the Convention Center, this timeshare compound occupies a pair of 11-story towers. Most of the units are available for nightly rentals when the owners aren't in residence. Units are well furnished, albeit somewhat run-of-the-mill. Timeshares range from small studios to larger two-bedroom rooms. Each has a very small balcony, too narrow for a chair, but appropriate for anyone willing to stand. These drawbacks, coupled with an aging physical plant, set the stage for good value, especially in the peak of summer. Tour groups, golfers, and sometimes honeymooners book into the hotel.

1304 N. Ocean Blvd., Myrtle Beach, SC 29577. ✆ **800/955-2627** or 843/448-2214. Fax 843/626-8410. www.yachtsman.com. 160 units. $62–$164 per unit for up to 4 persons. AE, DISC, MC, V. Free parking. **Amenities:** Minigolf; 2 Jacuzzis; 2 outdoor pools. *In room:* A/C, TV, hair dryer, kitchen, Wi-Fi (free).

Inexpensive

Coral Beach Hotel ☺ Amid a cluster of other hotels about 1½ miles south of "downtown" Myrtle Beach, this angular white-sided hotel is a well-established favorite that is one of the resort's "best family accommodations." The staff works hard to convince its guests that nothing is too much for the care and amusement of children. There's a choice of up to 10 different swimming pools, an on-site bowling alley with eight lanes, and two separate dining outlets, one a full-service restaurant, the other a take-away grill within the bowling alley. The units are basic, but comfortably furnished with durable furniture. Each has sofa beds or Murphy beds, one or two TVs, and balconies.

1105 S. Ocean Blvd., Myrtle Beach, SC 29577. ✆ **800/556-1754** or 843/448-8421. Fax 843/626-0156. www.thecoralbeach.com. 310 units. $50–$210 double; $64–$279 suite. AE, DC, DISC, MC, V. Free parking. **Amenities:** Restaurant; bar; children's activities; exercise room; 4 Jacuzzis (3 indoor); 8 pools (2 indoor) and kiddie water park; spa. *In room:* A/C, TV, fridge, hair dryer, Wi-Fi (free).

Hampton Inn ⚑ This is the most appealing of the quartet of Hampton Inns in Myrtle Beach. It's well maintained, affordable, and stylish, with an Iberian-inspired design that emulates a blockbuster version of Spanish colonial and American mission. Best of all, it's the only hotel in Myrtle Beach that's within walking distance of the vast nightlife and entertainment complex, Broadway at the Beach. Rising eight floors, with an interior that was thoroughly renovated in 2008, it contains a seashell-colored, vaguely tropical decor, and an attentive, youthful staff well versed in the facilities at the nearby Broadway complex. Breakfast is the only meal served.

Broadway at the Beach, 1140 Celebrity Circle, Myrtle Beach, SC 29577. ✆ **800/HAMPTON** (426-7866) or 843/916-0600. Fax 843/946-6308. www.hamptoninn.com. 141 units. $109–$219 double. Children 17 and under stay free in parent's room. Rates include deluxe continental breakfast. AE, DC, DISC, MC, V. Free parking. **Amenities:** Breakfast room; bar; exercise room; Jacuzzi; 2 pools (1 indoor); sauna. *In room:* A/C, TV, fridge, hair dryer, Wi-Fi (free).

Serendipity Inn ★ This simple, Spanish-style inn on a quiet side street is about 900 feet from the beach. Originally built in the 1980s, and renovated two or three times since then, it contains rooms that are each decorated and furnished individually. A breakfast buffet includes fresh fruit, hard-boiled eggs, and hot breads, but other than that, no meals are served. You can cook your own steaks and such on the outdoor grill, which is shared by all guests.

407 71st Ave. N., N. Myrtle Beach, SC 29572. ✆ **800/762-3229** or 843/449-5268. www.serendipityinn. com. 15 units. $55–$109 double; $74–$149 suite. Rates include continental breakfast. Off-season discounts available. AE, DISC, MC, V. Take King's Hwy. (U.S. 17 N.) to 71st Ave. N., then turn east toward the ocean. **Amenities:** Breakfast room; babysitting; outdoor pool. *In room:* A/C, TV, hair dryer, kitchenette (in suite), Wi-Fi (free).

Camping

You'll find plenty of campsites along the Grand Strand, many on the oceanfront, and rates drop considerably after Labor Day. Most encourage families, and many don't allow any single person younger than 25. Set directly on the ocean, about halfway between Myrtle Beach and North Myrtle Beach, 430 sites are available at **Apache Family Campground,** 9700 Kings Rd., Myrtle Beach, SC 29572 (**©** **800/553-1749** or 843/497-6486; www.apachefamilycampground.com). Amenities include a swimming pool and recreation pavilion, water, electricity, shade shelters, modern bathhouses with hot water, sewer hookups, laundry, trading post, playground, public telephones, and ice. Reserve here year-round, except for the week of July 4th. Rates are $54 to $60, depending on the season.

WHERE TO DINE

Prices are no measure of quality here; dining costs are unexpectedly moderate at even the better restaurants.

Expensive

Collectors Cafe, Gallery & Coffee House ★ 🍴 MEDITERRANEAN   This unique fine-dining restaurant, art gallery, and coffeehouse is a culinary delight, as well as a feast for the eyes. Diners are seated in one of six rooms, which feature more than 100 original paintings, sculptures, and craftwork by 40 artists. In the afternoon, you can relax and listen to (recorded) music while you sip special blends of coffee or tea. Each of the paintings on display is for sale, so feel free to shop while you eat. If you arrive during dinner, we recommend Cuban-style black-bean cakes with fresh tomato jalapeño salsa, pan-fried scallops with tomato scallion sauce, grilled and spiced yellowfin tuna with mango salsa, or jumbo crab cakes with Thai-style cucumber salad and peanut sauce. A children's menu is available.

7740 N. King's Hwy. **©** **843/449-9370.** www.collectorscafeandgallery.com. Reservations recommended. Main courses $25–$35. AE, DC, DISC, MC, V. Mon–Fri 11:30am–2pm; Mon–Sat 5:30–10:30pm.

The Cypress Room in the Island Vista ★★ INTERNATIONAL   The dining room of one of Myrtle Beach's most upscale and up-to-date resorts isn't the flashiest restaurant in Myrtle Beach, but it's one of our favorites thanks to excellent and sophisticated food as well as an old-school emphasis on Southern good manners. Menu items are genuinely imaginative and surprisingly stylish: Think Hudson Valley foie gras with fresh seasonal fruit chutney, spiced pecans, and pomegranate molasses onions and a tomato cream sauce. The geometrically patterned cypress that sheathes the walls and ceiling was dredged out of a nearby swamp.

In the Island Vista Resort, 6000 N. Ocean Blvd. **©** **843/449-6406.** Reservations recommended. Main courses $16–$25. AE, DC, MC, V. Daily 5:30–9pm.

Greg Norman's Australian Grille ★ INTERNATIONAL/AUSTRALIAN   Although it no longer wields the novelty that it did when it first opened in 1999, this is still the most internationally hip, best designed, and most prestigious restaurant in Myrtle Beach. It's owned by one of the most visible pro golfers in the world, Australia-born Greg Norman, and is across a saltwater estuary from a Norman-endorsed golf course. It occupies what looks like a mock-medieval watchtower on the Rhine, with a soaring, flatteringly lighted, woodsy-looking interior designed by Norman's former wife. Norman generated additional news thanks to his marriage to—and eventual divorce from—tennis pro Chris Evert. There's a cigar bar on the premises, an impressive wine list, and a two-fisted, somewhat macho emphasis on nouvelle Australian cuisine. The best choices include any of the succulent cuts of steak or game fish, or the Australian lobster tails, poached in butter. Lunches are less formal, simpler, and less expensive.

At Barefoot Landing, 4930 Hwy. 17 S., N. Myrtle Beach. ✆ **843/361-0000**. www.shark.com/australian grille. Reservations recommended. Main courses $5–$10 lunch, $16–$30 dinner. AE, DISC, MC, V. Daily 11am–3pm and 4:30–10:30pm. Pub 4pm–midnight (happy hour 3–7pm).

The Library ★ CONTINENTAL/FRENCH On the northern perimeter of downtown Myrtle Beach, this is the most formal and classic restaurant along the Grand Strand, an area that is slowly becoming better known for classy food joints. Evoking a library, its walls are lined with old and new volumes which give the impression of genteel stability. Tables are covered in crisp white linens, a worthy setting for service rituals that focus on showy preparations on rolling trolleys. Serving dinner only, the Library is not particularly innovative in its array of seafood, duck, beef, chicken, and veal dishes, but only first-class ingredients are used. Start perhaps with such appetizers as soft-shell crabs or artichoke hearts, going on to a delightful version of Dover sole in champagne and almond sauce. Steak Diane, flambéed at tableside, is delicious.

1212 N. King's Hwy. (U.S. 17 Business). ✆ **843/448-4527.** www.thelibraryrestaurantsc.com. Reservations recommended. Main courses $18–$45. AE, DC, DISC, MC, V. Mon–Sat 5–10pm. Open on major holidays.

The Parsons Table ★★★ STEAKHOUSE One of the area's premier places to dine is in the former Little River Methodist Church in Little River, 25 miles north of the center of Myrtle Beach on Route 17. Since it opened in this abandoned 1885 church in the 1970s, it has been luring both locals and visitors with some of the best steaks and juicy roast prime rib in the region. Antique touches flourish throughout, including stained-glass windows and an original Tiffany lamp in the main dining hall. In addition to beef, lamb and succulent veal are also offered. Start with Maryland crab cakes or sesame-seared tuna flavored with wasabi, going on to the rib of beef, New York strip steaks, or Black Angus rib-eye. An array of other temptations are also offered including the fresh catch of the day. Other specialties include cashew-encrusted New Zealand rack of lamb or veal Marsala.

4305 McCorsley Ave., Little River. ✆ **842/249-3702.** Reservations required. Main courses $14–$28. AE, MC, V. Mon–Sat 4:30–9pm.

Moderate

Dick's Last Resort AMERICAN This is the most consistently irreverent restaurant along the Grand Strand, a fact that the owners proudly advertise in a large sign above the entrance. Most of the loyal fans of this place seem to revel in the ongoing banter provided by the waitstaff, members of whom compete for the role of sassiest, and/or most abrasive. In the equivalent of a wood-trussed airplane hangar with a scattering of motorcycles, an inventory of bras and panties hangs from rafters above the rough-hewed bar. The cavernous interior of the ample wraparound porches is usually mobbed with everyone from singles who swing to families with young children. Greasy food is served in huge portions—and sometimes in buckets. Expect pork that's grilled in half-slabs, full slabs, and a humongous portion known as the "full porker." Live music is usually presented between 7 and 11pm between June and October.

At Barefoot Landing, 4700 Hwy. 17 S., N. Myrtle Beach. (C) **843/272-7794.** www.dickslastresort.com. Reservations not accepted. Main courses $6–$18 lunch, $12–$30 dinner. AE, DC, DISC, MC, V. Daily 11:30am–11pm.

Hard Rock Cafe ☺ AMERICAN   Set a short distance north of Myrtle Beach's center, in the Broadway at the Beach shopping center, this nonstandard Hard Rock Cafe is designed like an ancient Egyptian pyramid, whose interior is for the most part covered with memorabilia from the great days of rock. True, there's a vintage motorcycle displayed in front, but no trademark Cadillac is suspended from the ceiling—which appeals to New Agers, who believe that cosmic and psychic forces are amplified beneath any pyramid. Adding to the Egyptian theme is an ornate stained-glass window depicting the mystical powers of Osiris. The most prized piece of rock memorabilia is a glittery, Liberace-style white cape, presumably worn in concert by the King (Elvis) himself. Menu items include the usual Americana: french fries, tacos, burgers, barbecued chicken, milkshakes, and banana splits. In midsummer, be prepared to wait up to 2 hours for a table.

In Broadway at the Beach, 1322 Celebrity Circle. (C) **843/946-0007.** Reservations not accepted. Main courses $9–$25; kids menu $6.50. AE, DC, DISC, MC, V. Daily 11am–midnight.

Joe's Bar & Grill ★ 🗿 AMERICAN   It's worth the drive to North Myrtle Beach to sample the fare at this plainly named restaurant with a rustic atmosphere. Joe's is known for its fresh fish and its homemade soups and sauces. With both downstairs and upstairs dining, it has a panoramic view of the saltwater marsh. Beef, veal, and seafood dominate the menu. The roast prime rib of beef is the best in the area, or you may prefer Low Country shrimp sautéed in a peppery butter sauce. Fish specials (look for the board) are from the Carolina coast. Service is excellent.

810 Conway St., N. Myrtle Beach. (C) **843/272-4666.** www.dinejoes.com. Reservations recommended. Main courses $14–$27. AE, DISC, MC, V. Daily 5–9:30pm. Closed for 3 weeks in Jan. Drive 15 miles north on U.S. 17; it's across from Barefoot Landing in N. Myrtle Beach.

Sea Captain's House ★   AMERICAN   Consistently crowded, and evocative of the kind of American colonial seafood restaurant you might expect on Cape Cod, this place originated in 1930 as a privately owned beachfront cottage. Today it retains a few of its original nostalgic touches, including a masonry fireplace that's lighted on cold evenings. More prevalent, however, is a sense of decent, well-managed modernity, with glassed-in views overlooking the sea. The menu is absolutely typical of coastal Carolina—and that's no put-down. When regional cuisine is done well, as it is here, it's excellent, especially the fresh coastal crab dishes, either served as an appetizer or in she-crab soup, or perhaps in a salad or else as sautéed crab cakes. Locals order the Low Country crab casserole topped with sherry. Any dish you order is likely to be decorated with hush puppies. A few poultry and meat dishes such as grilled pork chops are offered, but they're nothing special. Lunches focus on simpler versions of what's served at dinner, with an emphasis on soups, salads, and platters.

3002 N. Ocean Blvd. (C) **843/448-8082.** www.seacaptains.com. Reservations not accepted. Breakfast $6–$10; lunch platters, salads, and sandwiches $10–$14; lunch and dinner main courses $18–$25. AE, DISC, MC, V. Daily 7–10:30am, 11:30am–2:30pm, and 4:30–10pm.

Travinia Italian Kitchen ★ 🔥 MEDITERRANEAN   This is our choice of the five restaurants that occupy Market Common, Myrtle Beach's most appealing shopping mall and residential community. It's big, airy, and sophisticated, with authentic Italy-inspired flavors. This restaurant can be many things to many people—a friendly place for families as well as a warmly hospitable bar and grill. You are likely to have the single best bowlful of *pasta fagioli* (a traditional bean soup with pasta) outside of Italy. Menu items include "black truffle beggars purses" made from pasta, four different cheeses, black truffles, and sage-flavored butter sauce; veal saltimbocca which "jumps in your mouth"; flounder Parmesan served with lemon butter and capers; and "Vesuvio" Marsala, with angel-hair pasta, with either chicken or veal.

In the Market Common, Withers Preserve, 4011 Deville St. ✆ **843/233-8500.** Reservations accepted for 8 or more. Main courses $8–$12 lunch, $10–$21 dinner. AE, DC, DISC, MC, V. Mon–Thurs 11:30am–10pm; Fri–Sat 11:30am–11pm; Sun 11:30am–9pm.

Umi Pacific Grill ★ SEAFOOD   Named after the Japanese word for "tide," and set in the southernmost tier of North Myrtle Beach, this is one of the most appealing restaurants, with the most professional and intuitive service, of any restaurant along the Grand Strand. The cuisine is genuinely excellent, even experimental dishes that challenge your culinary radar. Stellar examples include seaweed-pineapple tuna, sesame seared scallops, Kobe filet mignon, well-choreographed versions of sashimi and sushi, and Alaskan halibut in a wasabi sauce.

959 Lake Arrowhead Rd., N. Myrtle Beach. ✆ **843/497-6016.** Reservations required for 10 or more. Main courses $6–$18. AE, DC, MC, V. Daily 11am–midnight.

Inexpensive

House of Blues ☺ AMERICAN/SOUTHERN   Many visitors come to this restaurant looking for a burger and a stiff drink, and leave with a newfound appreciation for American folk art. With virtually every inch of its interior plastered over with vernacular art by largely untrained Southern artists, this Grand Strand version of the House of Blues franchise is by far the most aesthetically interesting bar, restaurant, and musical venue in Myrtle Beach. Redolent of bourbon and live jazz, it's more urbanized and hip than the folk-art setting would imply. Culinary fare includes fish, burgers, salads, steaks, ribs, and all the Southern staples you can handle. There's a "Gospel Brunch" ("Have mercy and say yeah.") every Sunday from 9am to 2pm, with a buffet that's priced at $20 per person, $8.50 for children 6 to 12. No one will mind if you come here just to drink, mingle, gossip, and flirt. And, if you're interested in music, concerts are scheduled almost every night in the summer, with tickets priced from $15 to $85 each. Box office hours are from 11am to 6pm daily.

At Barefoot Landing, 4640 Hwy. 17 S., N. Myrtle Beach. ✆ **843/272-3000.** www.hob.com. Reservations not accepted. Breakfast buffet $7; main courses $10–$26. AE, DC, DISC, MC, V. Mon–Sat 8am–3pm and 4–10pm; Sun 9am–2pm (Gospel brunch) and 4–9pm (non-Gospel dinner).

The Ultimate California Pizza 🔥 ITALIAN   Its neon sign flashes prominently from a point just across from the largest cineplex in Market Common, promising (and delivering) filling and flavorful pizza meals to families at affordable prices. Pizza comes in three different sizes (small, medium, and family large), and includes versions with barbecued beef or pork or India-inspired tandoori chicken. A California white pie comes with four kinds of (you guessed it) white cheese and onions; or try a Thai chicken–style pizza with roasted red peppers and chopped peanuts or a

Mexican pizza with ground beef, guacamole, and sour cream. Or you can design your own pizza.

In the Market Common, 4003 Deville St. ℂ **843/839-9880.** www.ultimatecaliforniapizza.com. Reservations not accepted. Pastas, sandwiches, and submarine sandwiches $6–$8; pizzas $8–$20. DC, DISC, MC, V. Daily 11am–11pm.

THE GRAND STRAND AFTER DARK

Variety Shows & Theaters

The Alabama Theatre   The country-music supergroup Alabama unveiled this $7-million, 2,200-seat theater, located in an expanding waterside shopping complex, on the Fourth of July 1993. The theater features three kinds of shows. Alabama performs at least 10 shows a year; celebrities such as George Jones, the Lettermen, and Loretta Lynn fill in at about 20 others. Typical shows combine Opryland-style singing, dancing, and music on the other nights. Alabama began by singing for tips around Myrtle Beach before going on to sell millions of records.

Shows are daily at 7:30pm, and matinees are Saturday at 2pm, when business warrants it. *The South's Grandest Christmas Show* and *one: The Show* are presented November 1 to January 1. Celebrity concerts are booked for some Friday or Saturday nights, as announced.

Barefoot Landing, N. Myrtle Beach. ℂ **800/342-2262** or 843/272-1111. www.alabama-theatre.com. Tickets $20–$39 adults, $17 children 3–16, free for children 2 and under (in adult's lap). Christmas show tickets $40 adults, $20 children.

The Carolina Opry ★   Missouri-born musician-entrepreneur Calvin Gilmore has been called a better businessman than a guitarist. He's credited with starting the entertainment explosion in Myrtle Beach by launching this theater back in 1986 and thereby immediately spawning a host of imitators. In 1992, the original Carolina Opry moved into this new 2,200-seat facility, complete with its own recording studio. Shows offer a variety of music, including country, bluegrass, western swing, big band, patriotic, and show tunes, as well as comedy. An enduringly popular show, which keeps being revived year after year, is *Good Vibrations*, a program that celebrates, with verve, pop, and rock, the music of the '60s and '70s. The Christmas show is so popular that it's often sold out by June. Performances are daily at 8pm. Know in advance that the Carolina Opry is adjacent to the Dixie Stampede Dinner Theater (see below), and a battalion of parking supervisors will direct you to rigidly predesignated areas, depending on which theater you plan to visit.

N. King's Hwy. at U.S. 17. ℂ **800/843-6779** or 843/913-4000. www.carolinaopry.com. Tickets $34–$47 adults, $21 students, $16 children 3–16, free for children 2 and under. Christmas show tickets $38–$51 adults, $24 students and children 3–16, free for children 2 and under.

Dixie Stampede Dinner and Show   Owned by Dolly Parton's Dollywood Productions, this show house features a stable of trained horses that prance, jump, and pirouette in tandem with a rodeo and Civil War theme. Throughout, the show is permeated with a rather charming sense of humor about cultural differences between things Northern and things Southern. While you eat a four-course meal with your fingers, you're entertained by some 30 horses, riders, and singing Southern belles, each in period costume. Locals and visitors flock here to feast on chicken, ribs, and corn on the cob while cheering whichever side they're on—usually, the side of Dixie. Drinks (definitely nonalcoholic) are served in the Dixie Belle Saloon before the show. There are between one and four shows a day, year-round with the greatest frequency occurring during midsummer and the Christmas season. There are no shows in January.

3849 N. King's Hwy. at U.S. 17. ℂ **800/433-4401** or 843/497-9700. www.dixiestampede.com. Tickets $45 adults, $22 children 4–11, free for children 3 and under. No shows Jan.

Legends in Concert   Although the jokes are invariably cleaner, this is similar to what you might have seen in Las Vegas, a show that features impersonations of the biggest stars in the business, including Garth Brooks, Madonna, George Strait, Buddy Holly, Cher, Dolly, Reba, the Blues Brothers, and (inevitably) Elvis and Marilyn Monroe—the latter two being perhaps the easiest to imitate. Michael Jackson, the Beatles, Nat King Cole, Elton John, Judy Garland, John Lennon, and even Liberace get into the act. Singers, dancers, and a live band are featured.

301 U.S. 17, Surfside Beach. ℂ **800/960-7469** or 843/238-7827. www.legendsinconcert.com. Tickets $35–$40 adults, $15–$40 children 3–16, free for children 2 and under.

Medieval Times & Dinner Show   This family-entertainment spectacle, a branch with about a half-dozen equivalent shows scattered in family-friendly corners throughout the U.S., provides a sanitized look at the Middle Ages in a 1,300-seat arena. Before going into the arena, guests inspect the Hall of Banners & Flags and a Museum of Torture. Falconry, sorcery, and swordplay, along with some horsemen who are "gallant knights," add to guests' amusement. Guests consume a four-course banquet (without utensils) while watching the show. The highlight of the evening is a joust.

2904 Fantasy Way. ℂ **888/935-6878** or 843/236-4655. www.medievaltimes.com. Tickets $49 adults, $30 children 12 and under.

The Palace Theater   This domed, impressive-looking theater features at least three different shows throughout the year within two distinctly different showrooms. *Le Grande Cirque* is the headline show, featuring acrobats, jugglers, and circus performers from around the world. There is also a spirited and oft-reprised tribute to all things Celtic, in the form of *The Magical Spirit of Ireland,* in which a dozen Irish tenors and a bevy of Irish dancers pay tribute to the tragedies, the glories, and the poetry of Eire. From early November 'til early January, *Le Grande Cirque Christmas Special* rounds out the holiday season. Year-round, there are between one and three performances a day.

Within Broadway at the Beach, 1420 Celebrity Circle. ℂ **800/905-4228** or 843/448-0588. www. palacetheatremyrtlebeach.com. *Le Grande Cirque* tickets $35–$45 adults, $10 children 12 and under. Showtimes Mon–Sat 8pm; additional shows Wed 10am and Thursday 2pm.

The Club & Music Scene

Barefoot Landing, Highway 17 South (ℂ **843/272-3473;** www.bflanding.com), straddling the civic boundary between Myrtle Beach and North Myrtle Beach, has 13 restaurants; a variety-music venue known as the Alabama Theatre (see above), an endlessly popular nightclub (the House of Blues), and a reptilian theme park known as Alligator Adventure. Everything about this place, frankly, is well orchestrated except for parking, which, during peak seasons and weekends, is very, very hard to come by.

Broadway at the Beach (© 843/444-3200; www.broadwayatthebeach.com), by the Route 17 Bypass, between 22nd and 29th boulevards, is one of the best-accessorized, most glittery, and most-visited shopping, dining, and entertainment venues in South Carolina. It's a less glossy, and much less expensive, version of Disney World, but with very few of the rides and less emphasis on myths and legends. It sprawls across a vast acreage bisected with saltwater estuaries and lakes in the heart of town. Some of its most visible features include the most famous chain restaurant in town, the pyramid-shaped Hard Rock Cafe, as well as Margaritaville, Murray Brothers Caddy Shack, MagiQuest, and Ripley's Aquarium where fish swim in translucent turquoise waters behind a thick layer of Plexiglas. There are more than 100 shops, 20 restaurants and food outlets, a free-standing IMAX theater, a 16-screen conventional movie theater, a gaggle of theme-oriented bars (many with big-screen TVs for sports-watching), and a collection of late-night bars and dance clubs—each within a cluster known as Celebrity Circle—that includes everything from country-western line dancing to Latino salsa.

2001   With three clubs, and three very different diversions, this is a major stop on the Grand Strand's nightlife circuit where it's always party time. **Funky Town,** a tribute to the glory days of disco, comes complete with a "martini room." A crowd in their 20s and 30s dance the night away on an illuminated floor, as four huge video screens display hits from the 70s to the 90s.

The sound of hip-hop and techno emerge from **Club Touch,** with its sizzling beats and hot, sexy video walls. Its dance floor is one of the most vibrating along the Grand Strand. **Razzies Beach Club** has been around for a quarter of a century. Patrons dance the Shag and listen to golden oldies from an in-house band. Big names perform at the Wednesday Night Beach Party. 920 Lake Arrowhead Rd. © **843/449-9434.** Cover $10 after 9pm. Thursday to Saturday 8pm to 2am.

MURRELLS INLET: THE SEAFOOD CAPITAL OF SOUTH CAROLINA

11 miles S of Myrtle Beach; 11 miles N of Pawleys Island

Murrells Inlet ★ is often invaded by Myrtle Beach hordes in quest of a seafood dinner. Just take U.S. 17 (Business) south from Myrtle Beach, and prepare to dig in. This centuries-old fishing village has witnessed a parade of humanity, from Confederate blockade runners to federal gunboats, from bootleggers to today's pleasure craft. The island was also visited by Edward Teach, better known as Blackbeard. Drunken Jack Island lies off Murrells Inlet. During the 1600s, Blackbeard's ship allegedly left a sailor on the island by accident; when the ship returned 2 years later, the crew discovered the abandoned sailor's bones bleaching in the sun, along with 32 empty casks of rum.

In addition to its seafood restaurants (a few are recommended in this chapter), Murrells Inlet is the setting of Brookgreen Gardens, one of the most-visited attractions along the Grand Strand.

Brookgreen Gardens ★★

Halfway between Myrtle Beach and Georgetown on U.S. 17 (near Litchfield Beach), Brookgreen Gardens, 1931 Brookgreen Dr., in Murrell's Inlet (© **843/237-4218;** www.brookgreen.org), is a world-class sculpture garden and wildlife park that's a source of enormous civic pride to virtually everyone in the state. It occupies the low-lying flatlands of what functioned 200 years ago as a rice plantation. After the destruction of the original plantation house, the gardens were laid out in 1931 as a setting for the world's largest collection of American garden sculptures, each crafted between 1850 and the present. Archer Milton Huntington and his wife, the sculptor Anna Hyatt Huntington, planned the garden walks in the shape of a butterfly with outspread wings. All walks lead back to the central space, a contemporary building that occupies the site of the original plantation house. On opposite sides of this space are the Small Sculpture Gallery and the original plantation kitchen, now the site of one of the snack bars. An outstanding feature within the wildlife park is the Cypress Bird Sanctuary, a 90-foot-tall aviary housing species of wading birds within half an acre of cypress swamp. The curators of this garden recommend spending at least 2 hours wandering along its byways. Terrain is flat and makes for easy walking. The price of admission grants access to the park and garden for 7 consecutive days.

Admission is $12 for adults, $10 for seniors (65 and older) and students, $6 for children 4 to 12, and free for ages 3 and under. Hours are daily 9:30am to 5pm. Between June and August, it remains open 'til 9pm Wednesday to Friday. The gardens are closed December 4, 11, 18, and 25.

Where to Dine

Bovine's ★ STEAK/SEAFOOD/PIZZA   On the waterfront on the northern fringe of Murrell's Inlet, with large windows opening onto views over acres of marshland, this restaurant evokes the Southwest with its use of cowhide and mounted bulls' heads. In the heart of Seafood Row, Bovine's has made a name for itself with its wood-fired specialties. You can order honey-crust pizza from the brick oven, along with grilled or blackened rib-eye steak. Barbecued baby back ribs are roasted with bourbon, honey, shrimp and grits, tequila shrimp, and aged balsamic vinegar. Appetizers include crab gazpacho (a refreshing change) and Cajun oyster stew.

3979 Hwy. 17 Business. © **843/651-2888.** www.bovineswoodfired.com. Reservations recommended. Pizza $8–$16; main courses $16–$37. AE, DC, DISC, MC, V. Daily 4pm–midnight.

Capt. Dave's Dockside ★ ☺ SEAFOOD/SOUTHERN   Family owned and run since 1974, one of the area's best and most famous seafood restaurants offers dining indoors or on the patio outside overlooking the waterfront. Chef Richard ensures that the freshest seafood is featured as the catch of the day. Arrive early if you want to enjoy sundown at the waterfront **Gazebo Bar.** Start a meal with a bowl of Low Country steamed mussels or she-crab soup, either one a delight to the palate. Among the dinner specials are such sublime dishes as a *zuppa di pesce,* a kettle of fish with everything from lobster meat to clams, or grouper prepared in any of at least three different ways. Beef eaters can order a Black Angus New York strip steak. Each day a selection of homemade desserts is featured—count yourself lucky if it's New Orleans bread pudding with a Jack Daniel's sauce. A children's menu is also offered.

On the Waterfront (4037 Hwy. Business 17). © **843/651-5850.** www.davesdockside.com. Reservations recommended. Main courses $7–$29. AE, DISC, MC, V. Daily 11:30am–2:30pm and 4pm–midnight.

PAWLEYS ISLAND & LITCHFIELD

25 miles S of Myrtle Beach; 12 miles N of Georgetown

One of the oldest resorts in the South, **Pawleys Island** ★ has been a popular hide-away for vacationers for more than 3 centuries. Over the years, everyone from George Washington to Franklin Roosevelt to Winston Churchill has arrived. During the 18th century, rice planters made the island their summer home so that they could escape the heat and humidity of the Low Country and enjoy ocean breezes. Storms have battered the island, but many of the weather-beaten old properties remain, earning for the island the appellation of "arrogantly shabby."

This area of South Carolina is sometimes called Waccamaw Neck, a reference to a strip of land 30 miles long and 3 miles wide that extends from the Waccamaw River to the Atlantic Ocean. Both North Litchfield and Litchfield Beach lie between Murrells Inlet and Pawleys Island. (To get here from Myrtle Beach, take Hwy. 17 S.)

The beaches here are among the best maintained, least polluted, and widest along coastal South Carolina; however, access to public beach areas is severely limited.

Many visitors from Myrtle Beach come to Pawleys Island to shop for handicrafts, such as the famous Pawleys Island rope hammock. The best place to purchase one is the **Original Pawleys Island Rope Hammock** (© **800/332-3490** or 843/237-9122; www.hammockshop.com), 10880 Ocean Hwy. at Pawleys Island. It's open year-round Monday to Saturday from 9:30am to 6pm and on Sunday from noon to 5pm. At various plantation stores (known as the hammock shops), you'll find pewter, miniature doll furniture, clothing, candles, Christmas items, brass, and china.

Enjoying the Outdoors

Huntington Beach State Park ★, along Highway 17, 3 miles south of Murrells Inlet, across from Brookgreen Gardens (© **843/237-4440;** www.southcarolina parks.com), offers one of the best beaches along the Grand Strand. Entrance is $5 for adults, $3.25 for seniors, $3 for children 6 to 15, and free for children 5 and under. The 2,500-acre park has a wide, firm beach, which is slightly orange. Anna Hyatt Huntington and her husband, Archer, the creators of Brookgreen Gardens, once owned this coastal wilderness. The park is the site of their Iberian-style castle, Atalaya. In the park are 137 campsites, along with picnic shelters, a boardwalk, terrific birding, bike rentals, and toilets. Swimming in specially marked sections is excellent, as is fishing from the jetty at the north side of the beach, or crabbing along the boardwalk. Campsites are rented on a first-come, first-served basis, at a cost of $21 to $28 per day (price depends on sites with electricity and water). The park is open April to September daily 6am to 10pm, and in the off season Saturday to Thursday 6am to 6pm and Friday 6am to 8pm.

Caledonia Golf & Fish Club, 369 Caledonia Dr., Pawleys Island (© **800/483-6800** or 843/237-3675; www.fishclub.com), opened in 1993. Tees are marked by replicas of native waterfowl that inhabit the old rice fields. The centerpiece of the course is a clubhouse, a replica of a 1700s colonial plantation house. Architect Mike Strantz, a former assistant to Tom Fazio, took care to highlight the natural beauty of the area: huge, centuries-old live oaks; pristine natural lakes; scenic views of the old rice fields; and glimpses of native wildlife. Greens fees are $110 to $175.

Where to Stay

Litchfield Beach and Golf Resort ★ One of the largest developments along coastal South Carolina, this beautifully landscaped complex, known for its oak-lined vistas, sprawls across 4,500 acres, with 7 miles of private beach and some of the best tennis courts in the South. Often catering to groups, it offers a wide range of accommodations, including suites, condos, and cottages. Furnishings are hit-or-miss, described by one returning guest as being "residential beach stuff." The property is well maintained and forms its own private enclave away from the crowds of the Grand Strand. Many of the units have lake, ocean, and marshland views, complete with waterfowl. A restaurant on-site serves standard American food, and there's a grill at the golf club, plus a **Starbucks.**

14276 Ocean Hwy., Pawleys Island, SC 29585. ℂ **888/766-4633** or 843/237-3000. Fax 843/237-3282. www.litchfieldbeach.com. 300 units. $59–$549 suite or condo; $194–$750 2- to 4-bedroom cottage. 3-night minimum stay July–Aug. AE, DC, DISC, MC, V. Free parking. **Amenities:** Restaurant; bar; babysitting; health club; Jacuzzi; 3 18-hole golf courses; sauna; 17 tennis courts (lit). *In room:* A/C, TV, hair dryer, Wi-Fi (in some; free).

Litchfield Plantation Along the banks of the Waccamaw River, Litchfield Plantation is a stately manor house (ca. 1750) at the end of a quarter-mile avenue of live oaks, making it oft-photographed. A fine country inn, fully restored, it offers four suites. The Ballroom Suite, for example, occupies the north wing of the second floor. This suite includes a bedroom and fireplace, a bathroom with whirlpool, and a large living room (formerly the ballroom) with a Pullman-type kitchen area and a veranda overlooking the grounds. Rates include the use of a cabana, and a private beach club at Pawleys Island. There are numerous championship golf courses in the area. There's also a 31-acre equestrian center nearby. Children 5 and under are not permitted.

24 Avenue of the Oak (PO Box 290), Pawleys Island, SC 29585. ℂ **800/869-1410** or 843/237-5300. Fax 843/237-1688. www.litchfieldplantation.com. 38 units. $185–$540 plantation house room; $225–$525 villa. Rates include full breakfast. AE, DC, DISC, MC, V. No children 5 and under. **Amenities:** Restaurant; bar; outdoor pool; 2 tennis courts (lit). *In room:* A/C, TV, hair dryer, Wi-Fi (in some; free).

Pawleys Plantation Golf & Country Club ★★★ A group of elegant, regional-style structures border a nature preserve, offering a luxurious country-club aura for those discriminating clients who don't want to pile into a hotel or resort on overcrowded Myrtle Beach. Guests are housed in one-, two-, or three-bedroom luxury villas, each elegantly furnished with a living and dining room, outdoor patio, and full kitchen, plus a tiled bathroom. Many of the villas feature whirlpools, wet bars, and fireplaces. The villas, with screened-in porches and patios, open onto views of the Jack Nicklaus signature course. The location is 25 miles south of Myrtle Beach on Highway 17 and about an hour's drive north of Charleston. Some of the Low Country's best recreational facilities, such as outdoor pools and tennis courts, along with beautiful beaches, are found here. The elegantly appointed clubhouse's dining venues all serve first-rate cuisine.

70 Tanglewood Dr., Pawleys Island, SC 29585. ℂ **800/367-9959** or 843/237-6100. Fax 843/237-0418. www.pawleysplantation.com. 80 units. $110–$135 double; $114–$144 1-bedroom suite; $209–$234 2-bedroom suite; $259–$295 3-bedroom suite. AE, DISC, MC, V. **Amenities:** 3 restaurants; bar; 18-hole golf course; 2 outdoor pools (1 exclusive); room service; 2 tennis courts (lit). *In room:* A/C, TV, kitchen (in some), Wi-Fi (free).

Where to Dine

Frank's & Frank's Outback ★ ☺ LOW COUNTRY/INTERNATIONAL   Frank's has been a Grand Strand tradition since 1988. Its fans think that it's the best restaurant along the beach strip. Chef Pierce Culliton borrows inspiration wherever he finds it, from Arizona to Provence, from China to Thailand. Your seared tuna might arrive over black Thai rice and warm Asian slaw. The rack of lamb with rosemary-and-garlic-laced mushroom sauce is better than many versions of this dish we've sampled in France. With its painted tin ceilings and wood floors, Frank's is an intimate, cozy place. The menu changes every day, based on the chef's inspiration.

In back of the restaurant is **Frank's Outback,** the home of Frank Marlow's mother before its conversion. The candlelit restaurant is slightly less formal than the restaurant up front. In fair weather, tables are set outside in a garden under a canopy of trees.

10434 Ocean Hwy., Pawleys Island. ⓒ **843/237-3030** or 237-1581. www.franksandoutback.com. Reservations recommended. Frank's main courses $23–$39. Frank's Outback main courses $23–$42; pizza $14–$16; Children's Menu $7–$10. AE, DC, DISC, MC, V. Frank's Mon–Sat 5:30-10pm. Frank's Outback Tues–Sat 5:30-10pm.

GEORGETOWN ★★

28 miles S of Myrtle Beach

The lifestyle of pre–Revolutionary War days comes alive here. Named after George II, this enclave of only 11,000 people boasts more than 50 historic homes and buildings dating back as far as 1737. Masted ships sailed from this riverfront, bound for England with their cargoes of indigo, rice, timber, and "king cotton." You can take a leisurely stroll along the Harbor Walk, tour the antebellum homes, or dine at some of our favorite spots. Georgetown is rarely crowded with visitors. 12 miles from the Atlantic, this community is South Carolina's third-oldest city, and it has been rated among the 100 best small towns in America. When Elisha Screven laid out the town in 1729, he couldn't have known that it would become a lively shopping enclave.

Essentials

GETTING THERE   From Myrtle Beach, take U.S. 17 South. From I-95, take U.S. 521 into Georgetown. From Charleston, take U.S. 17/701.

VISITOR INFORMATION   Providing information about sights, accommodations, and tours, the **Georgetown Chamber of Commerce,** 531 Front St. (PO Box 1776), Georgetown, SC 29440 (ⓒ **800/777-7705** or 843/546-8436; www.georgetown chamber.com), is most helpful. The staff will also provide you with maps and brochures. It's open Monday to Friday 9am to 5pm.

Seeing the Sights

Harold Kaminski House Museum   A pre–Revolutionary War home (ca. 1760), this house is visited mainly for its collection of antiques, including a 15th-century Spanish wedding chest, a Chippendale dining table, and some excellent pieces from Charleston in the 1700s. Many of the interior architectural details, including moldings and the original floors, have been left intact. At one time, the house was occupied by Thomas Daggett, a Confederate sea captain. There's also a museum shop selling items related to the decorative arts and the history of Georgetown.

1003 Front St. ⓒ **843/546-7706.** Admission $10 adults, $8 seniors, $6 children 6–12, free for children 5 and under. Mon–Sat 9am–5pm. Closed holidays.

Prince George Winyah Episcopal Church   Built around 1750 with brick from English ships' ballast, this church was occupied by British troops during the Revolutionary War and by Union troops during the Civil War. The latter occupation resulted in a great deal of damage. The stained glass behind the rebuilt altar was once part of a slaves' chapel on a nearby plantation. In the churchyard is one of the state's oldest cemeteries, the most ancient marker dating back to 1767.

Broad and Highmarket sts. ⓒ **843/546-4358.** Free admission but donations welcome. Sanctuary tours Mar–Oct Mon–Fri 11am–4pm.

Rice Museum   This museum is easy to locate. It's in the Old Market Building, which local residents call "the town clock"—Georgetown's answer to Big Ben. The first building in town to be listed on the National Register of Historic Places, it houses a museum devoted to the once-flourishing rice trade. The museum is a repository of maps, artifacts, dioramas, and other exhibits, tracing the development of rice cultivation (which was long Georgetown's primary economic base) from 1700 to 1900. There's also a scale model of a rice mill.

633 Front St. ⓒ **843/546-7423.** www.ricemuseum.org. Admission $7 adults, $5 seniors, $3 students and children 6–21, free for children 5 and under with an adult. Mon–Sat 10am–4:30pm.

Organized Tours

Nell Morris Cribb, a Georgetown native who conducts tours wearing period dress, complete with a bonnet, provides personalized walking tours of the downtown Historic District. **Miss Nell's Tours** take in about 12 history-rich blocks, last about 1¼ hours, and cost $5 to $9 for adults (free for children 12 and under). Tours begin at HarborWalk Books, 723 Front St. (ⓒ **843/546-3975**). The tours are given Tuesday, Wednesday, and Thursday at 10:30am and 2:30pm and on Saturday and Sunday by appointment.

Outdoor Pursuits

CANOEING & KAYAKING   **Black River expeditions** can be arranged at Kensington Gardens, U.S. 701, 3 miles north of Georgetown (ⓒ **843/546-4840;** www.blackriveroutdoors.com), open Monday to Saturday 9am to 5:30pm. Half-day canoe rentals cost $35 a day, with kayaks going for $50.

GOLF   One of the popular Georgetown championship courses, **Wedgefield Plantation ★**, just north of Georgetown (ⓒ **843/546-8587** or 448-2124; www.wedgefield.com), is on the site of a former Black River plantation and has wildlife in abundance. It was designed by Porter Gibson, and *Golf Week*'s "America's Best" honored it as one of the top 50 golf courses in South Carolina in 1994. Greens fees are $25 to $60, including cart. The signature hole is the par-4 14th, with both tee and approach shots over water.

RIVER CRUISES   The *Carolina Rover* and the *Jolly Rover* (ⓒ **843/546-8822;** www.rovertours.com) set sail from Georgetown Harbor. The *Carolina Rover,* a 40-foot pontoon boat, offers a 3-hour trip including a docked stop on North Island. The 45-minute excursion to this rather remote island includes a nature walk and beach shelling. Trips leave at 9am, 1pm, and 5pm Monday to Saturday. It costs $25 for adults and $15 for children 11 and under. The *Jolly Rover,* an 80-foot topsail schooner, offers a 2-hour tour of Winyah Bay. On board is a storyteller in a pirate's costume, who relates tales about pirates and ghosts who have prowled the Carolina coast. Trips depart Monday to Saturday at 10am, 1pm, and 6pm. The 10am and 1pm tours are pirate adventures. The cost is $30 for adults and $20 for children 11 and under. Reservations are strongly recommended.

Where to Stay

Harbor House Bed & Breakfast ★   This top-rated B&B was created from a 1765 warehouse, opening onto views of the harbor. Immaculately restored, the Harbor House rents out generously sized bedrooms with fireplaces, Oriental carpets, family antiques, heart-pine floors, and deep colonial moldings. Some of the bedrooms contain king-size four-poster beds and all are named for famous ships that once sailed the waters of Winyah Bay. A Low Country breakfast is served, featuring the house specialty of shrimp and grits.

15 Cannon St., Georgetown, SC 29440. ℂ **877/511-0101** or 843/546-6532. www.harborhousebb.com. 4 units. $159–$189 double. MC, V. **Amenities:** Breakfast room; bikes. *In room:* TV, hair dryer, Wi-Fi (free).

The Shaw House Bed and Breakfast ★★   Nestled among pine trees overlooking miles of marshland, this recently upgraded colonial B&B has spacious rooms with impressive antiques that evoke the grandeur and culture of the Old South. Mary and Joe Shaw are the gracious innkeepers, and their knowledge of the area is encyclopedic. Your day begins with a full Southern breakfast that's probably more than you can eat. Historic walking tours and boat tours can be arranged.

613 Cypress Court, Georgetown, SC 29440. ℂ/fax **843/546-9663.** www.bbonline.com/sc/shawhouse. 3 units. $100 double. Additional person $10. Rates include full breakfast. AE, MC, V. **Amenities:** Breakfast room; Internet (free). *In room:* A/C, TV.

Where to Dine

The Rice Paddy SEAFOOD/AMERICAN   The Rice Paddy continues the Georgetown tradition of everything historic. This early-20th-century structure has a minimalist decor that relies on the effectiveness of its exposed-brick walls. The river side of the restaurant offers views of the Sampit River, and if you want to sit even closer to the river, an outdoor dining patio with awnings and ceiling fans seats up to 40 patrons comfortably. Cookery has flair and flavor, with a finesse and consistency that keep the most discriminating palates of Georgetown returning again and again. Main-course choices range from lump crab cakes to rack of lamb. The menu changes seasonally to take advantage of the freshest ingredients.

732 Front St. ℂ **843/546-2021.** www.ricepaddyrestaurant.com. Reservations recommended. Main courses $10–$37. AE, MC, V. Mon–Sat 11:30am–2:30pm and 6–10pm.

River Room SEAFOOD   This is about the best Georgetown gets in terms of seafood dining. Some dishes are a bit overcooked, but locals seem to prefer them that way. Guests are rewarded by waterfront views from cozy precincts; an equally inviting bar is decked out in wood and exposed brick. Diners are smartly dressed in a casual way. Daily specials might include seafood fettuccine or a soft-shell-crab sandwich. Grouper, crab cakes, and other seafood are regularly featured, and you can order such Low Country dishes as yellow grits sautéed with shrimp and sausage.

801 Front St. ℂ **843/527-4110.** www.riverroomgeorgetown.com. Reservations required. Main courses $9–$25. AE, MC, V. Mon–Sat 11am–2:30pm and 5–10pm.

Thomas Cafe LOW COUNTRY   This is the kind of cafe where Charles Kuralt might have come to talk with the locals. With only five tables, a few booths, and a handful of counter stools, it's real Americana. Your waitress might be a spry 80-year-old. Breakfast is a very filling event: grits or hash browns served with eggs, a Cajun omelet, or blueberry pancakes. At lunch, you can have selections like jambalaya, fried chicken, mashed potatoes, and fried green tomatoes. This is the Old South—plenty of hospitality but no nonsense.

703 Front St. ⓒ **843/546-7776.** www.thomascafe.net. Reservations not accepted. Breakfast $4–$9; plate lunches $5.50–$8.95; sandwiches $4.95–$8. MC, V. Mon–Sat 7am–2pm.

COLUMBIA & THE HEARTLAND

Moving inland, today's visitor comes face to face with vivid reminders of South Carolina's past, as well as with the New South. Industries such as textiles, chemicals, precision-tool making, and metalworks thrive alongside large farms producing dairy products, tobacco, soybeans, peaches, wheat, and cotton, plus large pine forests for an ever-growing paper industry.

Since the days of George Washington, who once visited Columbia, this area of South Carolina has been known for its equestrian tradition. Horses are ranked number three on the state's commodities list. Camden and Aiken are centers for training racehorses that compete on racetracks around the country. Camden's Springdale Race Course plays host to two major steeplechases each year: the Carolina Cup and the Colonial Cup. The latter event is run in November, with a purse of $100,000. Aiken stages its yearly Aiken Triple Crown on three consecutive Saturdays in the spring.

Most outdoor recreation is in Santee Cooper Country, which offers fishing, golf, camping, hunting, and boating, among other diversions. Lake Marion and Lake Moultrie draw anglers in search of catfish, striped bream, crappie, and, above all, bass—white, largemouth, and striped. There's no closed season for fishing.

The center is Columbia, the state capital, 3 miles from the geographic center of the state. It not only has its own attractions, but it's also a good base for exploring several historic Piedmont towns, including Camden and York.

COLUMBIA ★

120 miles NW of Charleston; 131 miles W of Myrtle Beach

Columbia, unlike many of America's older cities, has the orderly look of a planned community, with streets laid out like an almost-unbroken checkerboard and wide boulevards, giving it a graceful beauty. The city was created in 1786 as a compromise capital, located just 3 miles from the exact geographical center of the state, to satisfy both Low Country and Upstate factions. George Washington paid a visit to Columbia in 1791, just a year after the first General Assembly convened in the brand-new city.

It was here that a convention, held in the First Baptist Church, passed the first Ordinance of Secession in the Southern states on December 17, 1860. (Because of a local smallpox epidemic, however, it was actually signed in Charleston.) Columbia itself was little touched by battle until General Sherman arrived with his Union troops on February 17, 1865, and virtually wiped out the town by fire: An 84-block area and some 1,386 buildings were left in ashes. Although recovery during Reconstruction was slow, the city that emerged from almost-complete devastation is one of stately homes and public buildings, with government and education (seven colleges are located here) playing leading roles in its economy. Fort Jackson, a U.S. Army basic-training post on the southeastern edge of town, adds another element to the economic mix.

Long a well-patronized shopping village, **Five Points** contains restaurants, bars, galleries, specialty shops, and other establishments next to the University of South Carolina (USC). The increasingly hip part of town is **Congaree Vista,** which is giving the Five Points area competition as the place to hang out and patronize restaurants, bars, and galleries. The old warehouses around the Adluh Flour Mill have been turned into clubs and restaurants, and offices, condos, and private homes are springing up here.

Essentials

GETTING THERE   I-20 reaches Columbia from the northeast (connecting with I-95 running north and south) and southwest, I-26 from the southeast from Charleston (crossing I-95) and northwest, and I-77 from the north.

If you're flying, the **Columbia Metropolitan Airport** (© 803/822-5000; www.columbiaairport.com) is served by **Continental Airlines** (© 800/525-0280; www.continental.com), **Delta** (© 800/221-1212; www.delta.com), **US Airways** (© 800/428-4322; www.usair.com), and **United** (© 800/241-6522; www.united.com).

For **Amtrak** service, call © **800/USA-RAIL** (872-7245) or visit www.amtrak.com. **Greyhound** (© 800/231-2222; www.greyhound.com) and **Southeastern Stages** (© 404/591-2750; www.southeasternstages.com) run service to the **Columbia Greyhound Station,** 220 W. Broad St. (© **706/549-2255**), and the bus station (© 803/256-6465) at 2015 Gervais St., respectively.

VISITOR INFORMATION   The **Columbia Metropolitan Convention and Visitors Bureau** is at 1101 Lincoln St., Columbia, SC 29201 (© **800/264-4884** or 803/545-0001; www.columbiacvb.com). Its visitor center is open Monday to Friday from 9am to 5pm and Saturday from 10am to 4pm.

An excellent Web resource for information about South Carolina cities, including Columbia and surrounding points of interest, is **www.sciway.net**. It is the largest and most comprehensive site documenting South Carolina information on the Web. The site includes thousands of links to other South Carolina websites, as well as maps and other resources.

SPECIAL EVENTS   One of the country's best state fairs, the **South Carolina State Fair,** is held annually in early October on the fairgrounds at 1200 Rosewood Dr. (© **888/444-3247** or 803/799-3387; www.scstatefair.org), with shows, a carnival, food stalls, and entertainment, along with crafts, agricultural, and livestock exhibits.

Exploring the Area
THE STATE CAPITOL

The **State House,** at Main and Gervais streets (© **803/734-2430;** www.columbia southcarolina.com/statehouse.html), begun in 1855, was only half-finished when General Sherman bombarded Columbia in 1865. Today the west and south walls are marked with bronze stars where the shells struck. In the fire that wiped out so much of the city, the State House escaped destruction, but the architect's plans were burned. As a result, the dome is not the one that was originally envisioned. Despite that fact, the building, with its Corinthian granite columns, is one of the most beautiful state capitols in the U.S. The landscaped grounds hold memorial tablets and monuments; inside are portraits and statues of South Carolina's greats. A more recently dedicated African-American monument also stands on the grounds. The Confederate flag has come down from the dome, where its flying generated nationwide protest. (It's still displayed on the grounds, however, and its presence remains a temper-raising issue in South Carolina.) The State House is open Monday to Friday 9am to 5pm, Saturday 10am to 5pm, and the first Sunday in each month 1 to 5pm.

FOUR HISTORIC HOMES

At the **Historic Columbia Foundation,** 1616 Blanding St. (© **803/252-7742;** www.historiccolumbia.org), you can purchase tickets and get a tour map of the capital's most historic homes. Tickets for each property cost $6 for adults, $5 for seniors and students, $3 for children 6 to 17, and free for children 5 and under. A combination ticket to all four properties is $15 for adults; $12 for seniors 65 and older, military, and college students; $8 for children 7 to 17; and free for children 6 and under. Hourly tours are conducted Tuesday to Saturday 10am to 4pm and on Sunday 1 to 5pm, with tours starting every hour on the hour. On Tuesday to Saturday, the last tour is at 3pm; on Sunday, the last tour is at 4pm.

Woodrow Wilson's Boyhood Home ★, 1705 Hampton St., was built by the president's father in 1872. Much Wilson memorabilia remains, including the family's heirloom furnishings. The red-velvet music room and the plush parlor evoke the Victorian age. The 28th president lived here until 1875, leaving at age 14 when his family decided to move out of state. At press time the house was closed for restoration; check www.historiccolumbia.org to see if the house has reopened.

Hampton-Preston Mansion, 1615 Blanding St., was purchased by Wade Hampton and occupied by his family until 1865, when Union general J. A. Logan took it over. Much memorabilia of the antebellum period remains, including furnishings and decorative arts. The house dates from 1818. The Hamptons were once called "the Kennedys of the Old South," having grown rich from cotton instead of liquor.

Manns-Simons Cottage, 1403 Richmond St., is a small house from the early 1850s. It is the former abode of Celia Mann, an African-American slave who bought her freedom and walked from Charleston to Columbia. She'd earned money by working on the side as a midwife and started a church for blacks in her basement at the end of the Civil War. Today her former home houses a museum of African-American culture and an art gallery.

Robert Mills Historic House & Park is at 1616 Blanding St. Mills served seven presidents as the first federal architect, designing such landmarks as the Washington Monument, the U.S. Treasury Building, and the Old Patent Office in Washington, D.C. This is one of the few residences that he actually designed. It's rich in art and furnishings of the Regency and neoclassical periods.

> ### Why George Has a Broken Walking Stick
>
> When visiting the State House, note the statue of George Washington on the front steps with its broken walking stick. It was broken by Union soldiers when they invaded Columbia during the Civil War. The people of South Carolina, who have nothing if not long memories, decided to leave it the way the soldiers left it. The statue has been touched so many times since then that the stump of the cane is worn smooth.

More Attractions

Columbia Museum of Art ★   The museum's plaza has four quadrants: one containing an amphitheater, another a dining terrace, and two others designed to feature plants and sculptures. The dining section's fountains and pools create an ambience matched nowhere in Columbia. The museum entry is at the rear of the plaza. The museum houses a permanent collection of more than 5,000 items, including paintings, furniture, baroque and Renaissance sculptures, and works by native South Carolinians, including turn-of-the-20th-century photos. Of special interest are *The Seine at Giverny*, painted by Claude Monet, and *Nativity*, a painting by the great Sandro Botticelli. The Tiffany art glass is also of exceptional interest. Call the museum for a schedule of events.

Corner of Main and Hampton sts. *©* **803/799-2810.** www.columbiamuseum.org. Admission $10 adults, $8 seniors, $5 students, free for children 5 and under. Tues–Thurs and Sat 10am–5pm; Fri 10am–9pm (10am–5pm in Dec); Sun 1–5pm.

EdVenture ★ ☺   The South's largest children's museum isn't Disney World, but it's an adventure nonetheless for kids 12 and under. The attraction is hailed as a "turbo-charged learning and fun" center. One exhibit focuses on the topic of money, helping kids learn what money is, who invented it, and how it works in paperless commerce. One outdoor exhibit, Bubbleloosa!, explores the "science of bubbles." There's a cultural side here, too, with chances to learn about music, theater, and art, perhaps strange concepts to a generation raised at the TV set. Special features range from family outings to grandparents' day. At EdVenture's Imaginarium Theater, you can see original musical productions such as *Porcupine Saves the Dance*. Like Disney, the site also has its own magical castle. Carnival-like games and activities evoking an old-time country fair round out the exhibitions. There's watermelon for all, and even a bug lady telling you about "creepy crawlers."

211 Gervais St. *©* **803/779-3100.** www.edventure.org. Admission $9.50 adults and children, $8.50 seniors, free for children under 1. Mon–Sat 9am–5pm; Sun noon–5pm.

Governor's Mansion   This house was built in 1855 as an officers' quarters for Arsenal Academy. After General Sherman swept through town, this was the only building on the academy grounds left standing. South Carolina governors have lived here since 1868. Visitors get to see the state dining room, the private drawing rooms, and the library, each furnished with antiques, mostly 19th century. Many of these furnishings, including a railroad baron's bed, were made in the state. Portraits of the state's more famous governors hang in the Hall of Governors. The gardens can also be visited.

800 Richland St. (at Lincoln St.). *©* **803/737-1710.** www.scgovernorsmansion.org. Free admission. 20-min. guided tours by appointment only. Tues–Thurs 10–11am, by appointment only.

Riverbanks Zoo and Garden ★★★ ☺ Named one of the 10 great zoos in America, Riverbanks Zoo is known for its worldwide conservation work. The zoo is a refuge for many endangered species, including the American bald eagle, and shelters more than 2,000 animals. Animals live in natural habitats, and botanically significant trees and plants are labeled throughout the park. All kinds of domestic animals live at the **Farm,** including cows, goats, pigs, and chickens. The **Aquarium Reptile Complex** introduces the aquatic and reptilian creatures of South Carolina. The zoo continues to improve its physical geography and its animals, with the addition of **Gorilla Island** and the arrival of koalas. A 15-minute 3-D **Action Theater** is an interactive film experience for kids. Your admission ticket includes entrance to the **Botanical Garden** ★★, located across the river from the zoo, connected by a bridge that offers a panoramic view of the river. Named by HGTV as one of the "20 Great Botanical Gardens and Arboretums Across America," the Botanical Garden features more than 70 acres of gardens, ruins, scenic views, and natural plants and woodlands. The easiest way to get to the Botanical Garden is to hop aboard one of the free trams. Another one of the zoo's real treats is actually not inside the zoo grounds, but behind it—a place where you can picnic, swim, and revel in the mild rapids along the Saluda River. Wear your swimming trunks, and look for the rope that swings from a tree out over the river à la Tarzan.

500 Wildlife Pkwy. ✆ **803/779-8717.** www.riverbanks.org. Admission $9.75 adults, $8.75 seniors, $7.25 children 3–12, free for children 2 and under. Winter daily 9am–5pm; summer Mon–Fri 9am–5pm, Sat–Sun 9am–6pm.

South Carolina State Museum The state museum is housed in what was once the world's first all-electric textile mill. Each of the four floors is dedicated to one of four important areas: art, history, natural history, or science and technology. Hands-on exhibits, realistic dioramas, and laser displays make for exciting browsing through South Carolina's past, from prehistory to the present. Some of the decorative pottery on display was made by slaves. Look for the 1904 Oldsmobile "horseless carriage." Other exhibits focus on "king cotton" and slavery. One exhibit honors African-American astronauts, including Dr. Ronald McNair, a South Carolina native who was killed on *Challenger.*

301 Gervais St. ✆ **803/898-4921.** www.museum.state.sc.us. Admission $7 adults (ages 13–61), $5 seniors, $3 children 3–12, and free for children 2 and under. Tues–Sat 10am–5pm; Sun 1–5pm.

University of South Carolina The scenic 218-acre campus is covered with buildings dating from the early 1800s. The campus is filled with ancient oaks and magnolias. Note especially the historic Horseshoe, at the corner of Pendleton and Bull streets. It's worth half an hour or so to go by the **McKissick Museum** (✆ 803/777-7251; www.cas.sc.edu/mcks), located in a fine old building at the head of the Horseshoe. The museum features changing exhibitions on regional folk art, history, natural science, and fine art, and contains the university's collection of historic 20th-Century Fox Movietone newsreels.

Gregg, Pendleton, and Main sts. ✆ **803/777-7000.** www.sc.edu. Free admission. Museum Mon–Fri 8:30am–5pm; Sat 11am–3pm.

Nearby Attractions
EDISTO MEMORIAL GARDEN ★★

To reach Edisto Memorial Gardens, drive 45 miles southeast of Columbia on I-26 and take U.S. 601 South to Orangeburg. The 165-acre park, on U.S. 301, is located

State Farmers' Market

Serving Columbia since 1952, the 50-acre **State Farmers' Market** ★, 1001 Bluff Rd. (© 803/737-4664), is ranked in the top 10 in the nation for sales volume. Selling fruits and vegetables, as well as flowers and plants, the market has more than 500 open stalls, as well as wholesale and retail units. It also has four restaurants and a U.S. Post Office.

Don't worry about rain or inclement weather—a 100,000-square-foot drive-through building provides shelter to both sellers and buyers. The market is open Monday to Saturday 6am to 9pm and Sunday 1 to 6pm. It's across the street from the University of South Carolina's football stadium.

along the banks of the Edisto River, the world's longest black water river. The garden is one of three test gardens in the United States and is known especially for its experimentation in roses. Some 5,000 varieties bloom from mid-April until October. Other vegetation and trees include camellias, dogwoods, cherry trees, and thousands of azaleas that bloom from mid-March to mid-April. South Carolina's Festival of Roses, one of the 20 top festivals in the Southeast, is held here annually during the last weekend in April. The garden is open daily from dawn to dusk and admission is free.

THE SANTEE COOPER LAKES ★★

From Orangeburg, it's a short drive on U.S. 301 to I-95 North to Lake Marion and Lake Moultrie, known collectively as the Santee Cooper Lakes, which cover more than 171,000 acres. *Anglers, note:* Three world-record and eight state-record catches have been recorded here. These waters have been stocked with striped, largemouth, hybrid, and white bass; catfish; and other panfish. The lakes are ringed with fish camps, marinas, campgrounds, and modern motels.

You don't have to be an angler to enjoy this scenic region, however; you'll also find numerous golf courses, tennis courts, and wildlife sanctuaries. The best place for camping is Santee State Park, which offers 150 sites at two lakefront campgrounds on Lake Marion. Amenities include swimming, tennis, a boat ramp, fishing boats, a tackle shop, and nature programs (including a nature trail).

The **Santee-Cooper Counties Promotion Commission,** PO Drawer 40, Santee, SC 29142 (© 800/227-8510 or 803/854-2131 within South Carolina; www.santeecoopercountry.org), can furnish full details on recreational facilities and accommodations. For more on lakefront vacation cabins on Lake Marion, contact the Superintendent, **Santee State Park,** 251 State Park Rd., Box 79, Santee, SC 29142 (© 803/854-2408). In all cases, be sure to inquire about fishing and golf package deals. To reach the state park from Columbia, take I-26 East to U.S. 301 North to I-95 North; take exit 98 to Santee and head 3 miles northwest.

Columbia residents also go to **Santee Cooper Country** for 270 holes of golf. For a complete golf kit, contact Santee Cooper Country, PO Box 40, Santee, SC 29142 (© 800/227-8510 or 803/854-2131 within South Carolina).

Where to Stay

By and large, the double rooms in the recommended hotels and inns below have private bathrooms with tub/shower combinations, unless otherwise noted.

EXPENSIVE

Columbia Marriott ★   Close to the State Capitol, state offices, and the University of South Carolina, this upscale, 14-story downtown landmark (formerly Adam's Mark) is the capital's best. With its atrium design, the Marriott is clearly far superior to its major competitor, the Embassy Suites (at 200 Stoneridge Dr.). But it lacks the traditional charm of the Inn at Claussens (recommended below). The guest rooms now boast granite countertops and wireless Internet access. The restaurant menu has changed little from that of its previous ownership, offering regional and local fare. In the center of the city, the hotel is walking distance from local shopping, dining, and nightlife.

1200 Hampton St., Columbia, SC 29201. ✆ **800/593-6465** or 803/771-7000. Fax 803/758-2456. www.
marriottcolumbia.com. 300 units. $125–$185 double; $189–$215 suite. Children 17 and under stay free in parent's room. AE, DC, DISC, MC, V. Parking $10–$18. **Amenities:** Restaurant; bar; airport shuttle; fitness center; Jacuzzi; indoor pool; room service. *In room:* A/C, TV, hair dryer, Wi-Fi ($9.95).

The Whitney Hotel ★   Southeast of the center, this all-suite hotel is the premier motor hotel in the capital. It's about a 20-minute walk from the University of South Carolina and a mile from Five Points. It's an eight-floor stucco building, traditional in style from its classic marble lobby to its wood-trimmed lounge. All suites are tastefully furnished, with full kitchens with stoves, microwaves, and refrigerators. The suites also have washers and dryers, butler's tables, and balconies. The small staff is congenial, but the hotel is not quite as luxurious as it appears to be in its promotional material.

700 Woodrow St. (at Devine St.), Columbia, SC 29205. ✆ **800/637-4008** or 803/252-0845. Fax 803/771-0495. www.whitneyhotel.com. 74 units. $129–$149 1-bedroom suite; $149–$199 2-bedroom suite. Rates include full buffet breakfast. AE, DC, DISC, MC, V. Free parking. **Amenities:** Breakfast room; lounge; airport transportation; outdoor pool. *In room:* A/C, TV, hair dryer, kitchen, Wi-Fi (free).

MODERATE

Clarion Town House Hotel ★   In a tranquil area about 3 blocks from the State Capitol, this is a two-in-one complex, with a main six-floor building that forms the hotel proper, plus an adjoining, motel-like annex. The hotel was constructed on the site of the 1800s Minnaugh Mansion, General Sherman's headquarters when he marched on Columbia. The hotel is well maintained and charges moderate prices for top-grade (though not spectacular) midsize to spacious accommodations. The especially considerate staff is reflected in the basket of fresh cookies at reception. The hotel is noteworthy for its amenities.

1615 Gervais St., Columbia, SC 29201. ✆ **877/424-6423** or 803/771-8711. Fax 803/252-9347. www.
clariontownhouse.com. 163 units. $94–$114 double; $134–$145 suite. AE, DC, DISC, MC, V. Free parking.
Amenities: Restaurant; bar/lounge; outdoor pool; room service. *In room:* A/C, TV, Internet (free).

The Inn at Claussens ★ 🎁   Just 2 miles southeast of downtown, this is the premier inn of Columbia. It's in the fashionable Five Points district, near the University of South Carolina, and it offers far more charm than any other in the local landscape. The tastefully decorated rooms may have watermelon-color walls, pine armoires, Windsor chairs, and small patios; some have four-poster beds. Sherry and wine are offered in the lobby.

2003 Greene St., Columbia, SC 29205. ✆ **800/622-3382** or 803/765-0440. Fax 803/799-7924. www.
theinnatclaussens.com. 29 units. $130 double; $144–$170 suite. Rates include deluxe continental breakfast. AE, DC, DISC, MC, V. Free parking. **Amenities:** Breakfast room; lounge; Jacuzzi. *In room:* A/C, TV, hair dryer, Wi-Fi.

Where to Dine

Columbia has a host of restaurants, many with chain affiliations. The area around Five Points, close to the USC campus, is ideal for snacks, coffee, or something more substantial, as is the newly emerging Congaree Vista section.

EXPENSIVE

Hennessy's ★ CONTINENTAL   This converted hardware store provided us with our finest meal on our latest rounds in Columbia. The kitchen may not be particularly daring, but it's in capable hands, and the waitstaff is ready for the big time; it's that good. The food is nicely prepared and fresh tasting. Begin perhaps with such South Carolina favorites as Low Country seafood cocktail or the very enticing she-crab soup. Carnivores seeking "butcheries from the block" might opt for our favorite—an 8-ounce filet of beef tenderloin topped with blue cheese and served with a wild mushroom demi-glace. You can also order filet mignon marinated in teriyaki and flavored with ginger. Seafood fanciers are advised to sample the grouper encrusted with almonds and herbs and served with a lemon beurre blanc, or the jumbo shrimp Creole in a zesty tomato sauce.

1649 Main St. ⓒ **803/799-8280.** www.hennessyssc.com. Reservations recommended. Main courses $15–$25. AE, DISC, MC, V. Mon–Thurs 11:30am–2:30pm and 6–9:30pm; Fri 11:30am–2:30pm and 6–10pm; Sat 6–10pm.

MODERATE

California Dreaming AMERICAN   This large, popular restaurant in a restored 1902 depot is usually filled with both students and the uptown crowd. You just show up and wait for a seat because you won't have much luck trying to reserve a table. The freshly made salads are quite good, and the typical fare is prime rib or seafood. Barbecue ribs, homemade pasta, and Tex-Mex dishes are also featured. This place is renowned for its large portions. Don't miss the hot apple walnut cinnamon pie—a special recipe—topped with French vanilla ice cream for dessert.

401 S. Main St. (2 blocks south of Blossom St.). ⓒ **803/254-6767.** www.centraarchy.com/california dreaming_Col.php. Main courses $12–$26. AE, DC, DISC, MC, V. Sun–Thurs 11am–10pm; Fri–Sat 11am–11pm.

Motor Supply Company Bistro INTERNATIONAL   Despite its unappetizing name, this restaurant serves decent food. It's in an 1890s building, now listed on the National Register of Historic Places, that was once a motor-supply-parts warehouse and has been completely restored. You'd never suspect the building's former role as you sit at the oak German bar or a marble-topped English table. Outside is a sculpture garden, and diners can browse through the gift shop or art gallery inside. At night, the kitchen works harder than at lunch, turning out such well-prepared appetizers as grilled quail with balsamic barbecue and chicken *satay* with peanut sauce (definitely Thai influenced). Main dishes might include peppercorn-encrusted pink salmon with champagne beurre blanc, or filet of beef with crabmeat and hollandaise.

920 Gervais St. ⓒ **803/256-6687.** www.motorsupplycobistro.com. Reservations recommended. Main courses $12–$25. AE, DC, MC, V. Tues–Sat 11:30am–2:30pm and 6–10pm; Sun 11am–3pm and 5:30–9pm.

Mr. Friendly's New Southern Cafe ★★ NEW SOUTHERN   In the downtown business district, this award-winning bistro is hailed by many food critics as one of the finest and most innovative restaurants in South Carolina—and we concur. The chefs call their food "good old-fashioned, New Southern cuisine." That may seem a contradiction, but no matter. What matters is the taste and the freshness of the food platters offered, and in that regard, this casual place succeeds most admirably. Look

Maurice Bessenger's Piggie Park, 1600 Charleston Hwy. (✆ 800/MAURICE [628-7423] or 803/796-0200; www.mauricesbbq.com), may be the South's most controversial eatery. Fans claim Maurice's barbecue is the best in the South, while critics dismiss his sauce as a "gloppy mess." The sauce of this "Undisputed Barbecue King" is mustard based, so, to be called "yellow-bellied" means you've eaten his sauce. Good ol' Bubbas and Bubba-ettes file into this dive at the rate of 20,000 customers a week. So what's the rub? Maurice's politically incorrect views turn off many diners. He flies the South Carolina state flag and the Confederate flag over his joint. He doesn't have much good to say about "left-wing one worlders," and don't even ask him what he thinks of same-sex marriage! Even Lincoln comes under attack for issuing "illegal" executive orders. Plus, Maurice has a "racist past and approves of things that most Americans would find offensive—such as slavery," to quote a column by newspaper reporter John Monk. Many chains no longer carry Maurice's food products, but lots of folks simply bypass the loopy diatribes to get to the pig. A chopped barbecue and ribs platter begins at $10. Open daily 10am to 10pm.

for specialties on the ever-changing menu that focus on seafood delights and innovative wild game dishes. Some favorite dishes include pecan crab cakes with a sherry-laced cayenne mayonnaise, or a delectable grilled chicken breast with a sun-dried peach sauce (instead of sun-dried tomatoes, for a change). Their wine list has been ranked by *Wine Spectator,* and there is also a wide variety of microbrew beers.

2001-A Greene St. ✆ **803/254-7828.** www.mrfriendlys.com. Reservations not required. Main courses $17–$28. AE, DISC, MC, V. Mon–Thurs 11:30am–2:30pm and 5:30–10pm; Fri 11:30am–2:30pm and 5:30–10:30pm; Sat 5:30–10:30pm.

Travinia Italian Kitchen ★ 🍴 ITALIAN/MEDITERRANEAN   On the northeastern fringe of downtown Columbia, within a suburb that contains the Sand Hills Mall, this is one of four branches of one of the most appealing restaurant chains in South Carolina. Outfitted like a warmly decorated steakhouse, with one wall plastered with photos of Frank Sinatra and his Rat Pack, it offers supremely flavorful versions of Italian staples as well as relatively modern innovations on old-fashioned "mamma mias." Look for about a dozen kinds of pasta; well-flavored seafood, including crusted grouper served with macadamia nuts and seared ahi tuna; sirloin Marsala; and veal saltimbocca. Prices are reasonable, and the wine list is impressive—so much so that the chain as a whole has been cited in *Wine Spectator* magazine.

101 Sparkleberry Crossing Rd. ✆ **803/419-9313.** Reservations accepted for 8 or more. Main courses $9–$21 lunch, $12–$21 dinner. AE, DC, DISC, MC, V. Mon–Thurs 11:30am–10pm; Fri–Sat 11:30am–11pm; Sun 11:30am–9pm.

INEXPENSIVE

Adriana's Café & Gelateria COFFEE/DESSERT   This most quintessentially appealing coffeehouse in the area is frequented by university students who drop in either to chill out or warm up. Black-and-white art decorates the walls, and you sit at marble-topped tables on ice-cream-parlor chairs. The homemade desserts are delectable. Try the cheesecake, the velvety homemade gelato and sorbet, the yogurt, or one of the flavorful coffees.

721 Saluda Ave. ☏ **803/799-7595.** Reservations not accepted. Coffee $1.25–$3.75; desserts $2.35–$4.85; food $7.50–$13. AE, DISC, MC, V. Mon–Sat 8am–10pm; Sun 10am–4pm.

Lizard's Thicket ★ ☺ SOUTHERN/AMERICAN   If you aren't from the South and want to experience true home-style, stick-to-your-ribs, lip-smacking country food, then head here. With 11 locations scattered throughout the Columbia area, this restaurant is an annual winner of the *Metropolitan Columbia Magazine*'s "Best in State Country Cooking and Family Restaurant." The restaurant has printed menus, but it's more fun to pick your "meat and three's" from the huge menu boards located throughout the restaurant. We recommend the fried chicken, fried flounder, and country-fried steak. Vegetable options change seasonally, but staples include macaroni and cheese, Alabam' Slaw, green beans, fried okra, and squash. The "meat and three vegetable" lunch and dinner options include sweet Southern corn bread or rolls. For breakfast, your choices may include hearty combinations of eggs with grits or hash browns, toast, or thick homemade biscuits, along with bacon, sausage, or country ham (particularly good and salty here).

818 Elmwood Ave. ☏ **803/779-6407.** www.lizardsthicket.com. Main courses $8–$13 breakfast, $3.30–$8.30 lunch and dinner. AE, DC, DISC, MC, V. Daily 6am–10pm.

Yesterdays ★ ☺ SOUTHERN/AMERICAN   The neon cowboy in a bathtub over the entrance sets the tone for what you'll find inside this Old West–style tavern known for its good food and robust drinks. It's also the unofficial headquarters of the St. Patrick's celebration in Five Points. Everyone from students to politicians makes this their hangout. Run by locals, it attracts patrons with its casual tavern atmosphere and affordable prices. Tex-Mex, pastas, vegetarian selections, Cajun cookery—you get a little bit of everything here, even Confederate fried steak and stuffed yucca. It's also a great choice for families, with a special menu for the kiddies.

2030 Devine St. ☏ **803/799-0196.** http://yesterdayssc.com. Lunch specials $5.50–$8; dinner main courses $8.30–$14. AE, DISC, MC, V. Sun–Thurs 11:30am–midnight; Fri–Sat 11:30am–1am.

Columbia After Dark
PERFORMING ARTS
The **South Carolina Philharmonic** and the **Chamber Orchestra Association,** 1237 Gadsden St. (☏ **803/771-7937** or 254-7445 box office; www.scphilharmonic. com), perform concerts at various venues throughout Columbia and the surrounding area. The music runs from classical music to pop to jazz. The season lasts from September to May. Call for information about performances and tickets.

One of the best little regional theaters in South Carolina is **Trustus Theater ★**, 520 Lady St. (☏ **803/254-9732;** www.trustus.org), in the Congaree Vista neighborhood. Launched in the 1980s, the theater presents many regional premieres and develops new works in the regular season and its "late night series." All reserved seats are large armchairs, with a bowl of popcorn between every other seat and a place to put your drink (which the staff lets you bring in from the bar). Low-cost bleacher seats are available at every performance.

The **Workshop Theater of South Carolina,** 1136 Bull St. (☏ **803/799-4876;** www.workshoptheatre.com), which has a season lasting from October to March, produces musicals, comedies, and dramas. You can obtain ticket information from the box office from noon to 6pm on performance days only. For announcements of presentations, look in the local newspapers or call the theater.

The **Columbia Marionette Theatre,** 401 Laurel St. (© **803/252-7366;** www.columbiamarionettetheatre.org), offers shows for all ages every Saturday at 11am and 3pm. Tickets are $4 per person, free for children 2 and under. Productions include adaptations of classics, as well as original and innovative new shows.

Less than an hour's drive from Columbia is the historic **Newberry Opera House,** 1201 McKibben St. (© **803/276-5179** or 276-6264 box office; www.newberryoperahouse.com), in Newberry, South Carolina. The opera house has served the community for more than 100 years, primarily as a theatrical venue and movie theater. After the performance hall was turned into administrative offices in the 1950s, the historic building was in danger of being torn down until the Newberry Historical Society stepped in and saved this community treasure. It was placed on the National Register of Historic Places in 1970. After a $5.5-million renovation, the 426-seat theater is now equipped with state-of-the-art acoustics and lighting systems. Performances range from beach music to big band to Broadway and, of course, opera.

THE CLUB & BAR SCENE

It used to get very sleepy in Columbia after dark, but in the past few years, the town has been coming to life, thanks to the preponderance of young people. The best wine tavern and tapas bar is **Gervais & Vine,** 620A Gervais St. (© **803/799-8463**). Drop in to partake of the expanding list of tapas—Spanish for "small bites." If you order enough of them, these tapas can be a full meal. Bartenders also serve you more than five different wines by the glass. Other bars and nightspots include **Bailey's Sports Grille,** 115 Alton Court, across the street from the Columbiana Centre (© **803/407-3004**). Columbia's best sports bar, with big-screen TVs, attracts a macho crowd of good ol' boys. Food is served—and in such a spot, you expect ribs to be a specialty. **Damon's Clubhouse,** 900 Senate St. (© **803/758-5880;** www.ribsribsribs.com), is another sports bar with big TVs. Barbecue ribs are a specialty here as well. This lively place is popular with the college and Congaree Vista crowds.

An amusing late-night bar is **Group Therapy,** 2107 Green St. (© **803/256-1203**), which draws a diverse crowd. Even though it has a happy hour, it's best to go late at night. It's popular with the college crowd, many of whom drop in after their studies are done for the night. A neighborhood bar, **Hemingway's,** 7467 St. Andrews Rd. (© **803/749-6020**), has a real macho atmosphere, as befits its namesake. Its happy hour is the longest in town, extending from 4 to 8pm. Burgers and sandwiches emerge from the back, and live music and entertainment are presented every Friday and Saturday.

The gay hangout is **PT's 1109,** 1109 Assembly St. (© **803/253-8900**), which is a private club—but call for arrangements if you're visiting. Across from the State House, this is mainly a gentlemen's club, promising "gorgeous men, tasty beverages, upbeat music, and diverse customers." It's the home bar for a camp for kids dedicated to families of children affected by HIV, and it's also the home bar for the Carolina Bear Lodge. Cabaret is often presented, featuring such "Party Time Gals" as the "Lesbian Drag Queen of Columbia."

SIDE TRIPS FROM COLUMBIA

North-central South Carolina was the scene of several significant battles of the American Revolution. Camden was actually an important garrison for British general Lord Cornwallis, and the battle of Kings Mountain, many people believe, was the turning point of the Revolutionary War. Battles of another sort are regularly waged these days on Darlington's raceway here, as stock cars engage in fierce competition.

Lake Murray & Irmo

Ten miles from Columbia, this bustling suburb offers one of the crown jewels of South Carolina—**Lake Murray ★★**, a premier recreational area covering more than 500 miles of shoreline. When the 1½-mile-long earthen dam was constructed to create a lake in 1927 (completed in 1930), it was the largest earthen dam in the world. Owned by South Carolina Electric and Gas, the power-generating plant below the dam provides electricity for the entire Midlands region.

Offering boating, swimming, fishing, and a variety of watersports, Lake Murray is also recognized for hosting major fishing tournaments such as Bassmasters and the FLW tour. The swimming area on the Lexington side of the dam is open from the first week in April to the last weekend in September, daily 10am to 8pm. The cost is $3 per vehicle. A boat ramp area that also provides picnic tables is located on the Irmo side of the dam and is open 24 hours a day. A fishing pier is also available. The entrance fee is $3 per car. You must have a fishing license to fish on Lake Murray (age 16 and older), even from the pier. You can purchase a 7-day license for $11 on the Lexington side of the dam at **Lake World,** 1757 N. Lake Dr. (© **803/957-6548**). For more information about boat rentals, watersports equipment providers, or fishing guides, contact **Capital City/Lake Murray Country,** 2184 N. Lake Dr. (© **866/SC-JEWEL** [725-3935] or 803/781-5940; www.lakemurraymarinasc.com).

Named by *Travel + Leisure* magazine as one of the top 10 food festivals in the U.S., the **Okra Strut ★★** (© **803/781-6122;** www.irmookrastrut.com) draws 40,000 to 80,000 visitors to Irmo each fall. Held in late September or early October, the 2-day festival features food, arts and crafts, a parade, a street dance, rides, a petting zoo, a golf tournament, a cycling ride, and a 10km run across Lake Murray Dam. Proceeds of the festival benefit the community and provide scholarships and civic improvements.

Camden ★

The 24-mile drive northeast to Camden, via I-20 and U.S. 521, takes you straight back to this nation's beginnings. Founded by Irish Quakers in 1751, it's the state's oldest inland town. During the Revolutionary War, 14 battles raged within a 30-mile radius of here. Cornwallis held Camden until the British retreated in 1781, burning the town behind them. During the Civil War, another invader, General Sherman, brought his Union troops to burn the town once more because it had served the Confederates as a storehouse and as a hospital. Historic relics are everywhere you look.

Camden is equally well known for the training of fine thoroughbred horses; the internationally known **Colonial Cup** steeplechase, held at the nearby Springdale Course, draws huge crowds.

Make your first stop the **Kershaw County Chamber of Commerce,** 607 S. Broad (PO Box 605), Camden, SC 29020 (© **800/968-4037** or 803/432-2525; www.camden-sc.org). Pick up a guidebook and a self-guided driving tour of the 63 historic sites in the area. The chamber is open Monday to Friday from 9am to 5pm.

Historic Camden, 222 Broad St. (© **803/432-9841;** www.historic-camden.net), is a Revolutionary War park affiliated with the National Park Service. There are restored log houses with museum exhibits, fortifications, the Cornwallis House, a powder magazine, an 80-building model of the original town, and miniature dioramas depicting military actions between 1780 and 1781. The guided tour includes a narrated slide presentation and access to all museums. The park is open Tuesday to Saturday from 10am to 5pm and on Sunday from 1 to 5pm. Admission is $5 for adults, $4 for seniors, $3 for students 6 to 18, and free for children 5 and under. Self-guided tours are free.

Nearby **Goodale State Park** (✆ **803/432-2772**), 2 miles north of Camden on Old Wire Road (off U.S. 1), offers lake swimming and fishing, with pedal and fishing boats for rent. Bring along a picnic, and wander the nature trail.

WHERE TO STAY

The Greenleaf Inn at Camden ★   This inn in Camden's historic district consists of two separate houses. Our favorite is the Thomas McLean House, a lovely Victorian home from 1890. Its four comfortable and spacious guest rooms with high ceilings and four-poster beds have the aura of plantation-style living. Lodgings are almost equal in comfort at the Joshua Reynolds House, which has three rooms upstairs, and three rooms on the ground floor; in 1805, this converted building used to be a general store. Rooms are elegantly furnished and large, some opening onto a classic Southern veranda.

1308 Broad St., Camden, SC 29020. ✆ **800/437-5874** or 803/425-1806. Fax 803/425-5853. 10 units. $109–$159 double. Rates include full breakfast. AE, DISC, MC, V. Free parking. **Amenities:** Restaurant; bar; room service. *In room:* A/C, TV, hair dryer, Wi-Fi.

WHERE TO DINE

The Mill Pond Steakhouse ★ INTERNATIONAL   One of the finest restaurants in the heartland, this establishment attracts diners from miles away. Constructed in the 1890s, it's listed on the National Register of Historic Places. It has Early American decor and offers a view overlooking the millpond. The chef chooses prime, rigorously fresh ingredients and, with the help of a skillful staff, fashions dishes that are often sublime. The menu typically includes such traditional favorites as fried green tomatoes and other Southern delicacies.

84 Boykin Mill Rd., Boykin. ✆ **803/425-8825.** www.themillpondsteakhouse.com. Reservations required. Main courses $19–$37. MC, V. Tues–Sat 5–10pm. Take U.S. 521 S. to S.C. 261 to Boykin, 10 miles south of Camden.

Darlington

Stock-car fans in the thousands invade Darlington (70 miles northeast of Columbia via I-20 and U.S. 52/401) in May for NASCAR's **Dodge Charger 500** race. The **Darlington County Chamber of Commerce,** 38 Public Sq., Darlington, SC 29540 (✆ **888/427-8720** or 843/339-9511; www.visitdarlingtoncounty.org), can furnish detailed information on racing as well as on sightseeing in this area. Hours are Monday to Friday 9am to noon and 2 to 5pm.

If you arrive between the year's two main races, hike over to the **NMPA Stock Car Hall of Fame/Joe Weatherly Museum** (✆ **843/395-8821;** www.darlington raceway.com) at the Darlington Raceway, 1 mile west of town on S.C. 34. It holds the world's largest collection of stock cars. Hours are 9am to 5pm daily, and admission is $5 (free for kids 12 and under).

LOCAL FISH CAMPS

This is fish-camp country. Very often, you'll find down-home fish dinners (all you can eat for practically nothing) in rustic cafes on unpaved side roads. Stop at a gas station, grocery store, or some other local shop, and just ask; everybody has a favorite, and it's often worth a detour. A good place to begin your search is Route 6 (Porter Rd.). The best time to show up is on a Friday or Saturday night.

York ★

York is at the heart of South Carolina's northern Piedmont. To get here from Columbia, take I-77 North to Rock Hill, then S.C. 5 about 15 miles northwest to York. The Department of the Interior has granted York one of the largest historic districts in the United States. The restored downtown area is filled with specialty shops—in all, 180 historical structures and landmarks. Get a detailed map from the **Greater York Chamber of Commerce,** 23 E. Liberty St. (PO Box 97), York, SC 29745 (✆ **803/ 684-2590;** www.greateryorkchamber.com), open Monday to Friday from 9am to 5pm.

Nearby **Historic Brattonsville,** 1444 Brattonsville Rd., McConnells (✆ **803/ 684-2327**), is a restored Southern village of 18th- and 19th-century buildings. To reach it, take U.S. 321 South from York or S.C. 322 from Rock Hill. Restorations include a dirt-floor backwoodsman's cabin, a 1750s frontier home, an authentic antebellum plantation home, hand-hewn log storage buildings, and a brick slave cabin. It's open Monday to Saturday 10am to 5pm and Sunday 1 to 5pm. Admission is $6 for adults, $5 for seniors, $3 for children 5 to 17, and free for children 4 and under. Several buildings on the site were used to film the Mel Gibson Revolutionary War epic, *The Patriot.*

Kings Mountain

Just across the border from North Carolina, **Kings Mountain Military Park** (✆ **864/936-7921;** www.nps.gov/kimo) marks the site of the Revolutionary War battle that was crucial to the eventual colonial victory. The park is on I-85, 20 miles northeast of Gaffney; from York, take S.C. 5 northwest for about 20 miles.

The southern Appalachians were virtually undisturbed by the war until 1780, when British major Patrick Ferguson, who had threatened to "lay the country waste with fire and sword," set up camp here with a large Loyalist force. In spite of wave after wave of British bayonet charges, the ill-trained and outnumbered colonists converged on Kings Mountain and kept advancing on Ferguson's men until they took the summit. You can see relics and a diorama of the battle at the visitor center. It's open every day of the year (except Thanksgiving Day, Christmas Day, and New Year's Day) from 9am to 5pm (Sat–Sun 9am–6pm Memorial Day to Labor Day); admission is free.

AIKEN: THOROUGHBRED COUNTRY

60 miles SW of Columbia; 17 miles E of Augusta

The international horse set hangs out in the country around Aiken at the Georgia–South Carolina border, where horse training and racing are major preoccupations. There's even a stoplight just for horses on Whiskey Road. Nearly a thousand horses winter and train in this area, and Aiken has two racetracks, as well as polo grounds.

The fame of Aiken began in the 1890s, when rich Northerners flocked here in winter, often erecting lavish mansions. The horsy set amused themselves with horse shows, fox hunts, and lavish parties.

Essentials

GETTING THERE From Columbia, take I-20 West for 55 miles to either exit 22 (Hwy. 1) or exit 18 (Hwy. 19). Both routes lead into downtown Aiken. From Augusta (Georgia), take I-20 East, getting off at either exit 18 or 22.

VISITOR INFORMATION The **Aiken Chamber of Commerce,** 121 Richland Ave. E. (© **803/641-1111;** www.aikenchamber.net), is open Monday to Friday from 8am to 5pm.

Seeing the Sights

The 3 weekends of horse racing in March that make up the **Aiken Triple Crown** are the highlight of the year. Call **Thoroughbred Country** (© **888/834-1654** or 803/649-7981; www.tbredcountry.org) to find out about the many sporting activities.

Even nonhorsy folks, however, will delight in the lovely old homes in the town's Historic District. The **Aiken County Historical Museum,** 433 Newberry St. SW (© **803/642-2015;** www.aikencountysc.gov), occupies part of a former millionaire's estate. Of special interest are Native American artifacts, a 1930s drugstore from a little South Carolina town that no longer exists, a 19th-century schoolhouse, and a full miniature circus. Admission is by donation. Hours are Tuesday to Friday 10am to 5pm and Saturday and Sunday 2 to 5pm.

Hopeland Gardens, 100 Dupree Place (at the corner of Whiskey Rd.; © **803/642-7631**), are the pride of Aiken, graced with weeping willows, fountains, and shimmering ponds. The grounds hold the **Thoroughbred Racing Hall of Fame** (www.aikenracinghalloffame.com) in a restored carriage house. A touch-and-scent trail has plaques in both standard type and Braille to identify plants and to lead visitors, blind or sighted, to a performing-arts stage. Open-air concerts are given here Monday evenings in summer, and theatrical productions are offered periodically. Admission is free. The gardens are open daily from 10am to dusk; the Hall of Fame is open June to August Saturday and Sunday from 2 to 5pm.

The 2,200-acre **Hitchcock Woods,** 404 S. Boundary Ave., close to the center of town, is one of the best places to go riding in South Carolina. You'll even see some locals taking carriage drives. If you want to go riding, call one of the local centers and discuss your needs and requirements. The best outfitter is the **Black Forest Equestrian Center,** 4343 Bank Mill Rd. (© **803/642-0438;** www.black forestfarm.com).

Where to Stay

Aiken is an easy day trip from Columbia, but when special events are on (horse races; the Masters Golf Tournament in neighboring Augusta, Georgia; and so on), rates in the Aiken area often go up.

The Briar Patch Bed & Breakfast ★ ◉ Listed on the National Register of Historic Places, this is Aiken's finest B&B. It's very small, however, so reservations are important. Because it is a few blocks from the polo grounds and 2 miles from the racetracks, it attracts the horse set. The two guest units were created from a horse stable, and the bedrooms were once a tack room. The guest units are separated from the main house and furnished with Early American antiques. Both units have fireplaces and well-kept private bathrooms. Golfers enjoy privileges nearby.

544 Magnolia Lane SE, Aiken, SC 29801. ℃ **803/649-2010.** 2 units. $85 double. Rate includes continental breakfast. No credit cards. **Amenities:** Breakfast room; lounge. *In room:* A/C, TV, no phone.

Hotel Aiken   The main part of this hotel dates from 1929 and offers spacious, tastefully decorated rooms with high ceilings typical of the era. More modern but less interesting standard-size rooms are in the motel, offering modest comfort. Maintenance is excellent, and all rooms have well-kept bathrooms.

235 Richland Ave., Aiken, SC 29801. ℃ **877/817-6690** or 803/648-4265. Fax 803/649-6910. www.hotelaiken.com. 68 units. $90–$105 double; $65–$75 courtyard room; $175–$335 master room. Rates include continental breakfast. AE, DISC, MC, V. **Amenities:** Restaurant; bar; fitness center (nearby); outdoor pool. *In room:* A/C, TV, hair dryer, Wi-Fi (free).

Willcox Inn ★★   This 1897 inn, with its English-country-house decor and antique furnishings, is one of the premier inns of South Carolina. Six two-story columns line the front porch in the style of the antebellum South. Guest rooms are individually decorated, often with four-poster beds and ornamental fireplaces, and a liberal use of Second Empire furnishings. Each room has a marble bathroom the size of a compact car. The Vanderbilt Suite contains a 6-foot-long tub. All rooms are nonsmoking. The inn's **Pheasant Room** is also the top restaurant in Aiken. Well-prepared dishes are drawn from a changing repertoire of creative Continental fare based on seasonally fresh produce. Have a drink in the **Polo Pub,** which displays artifacts such as fly rods, cricket bats, and polo mallets.

100 Colleton Ave. (at the corner of Whiskey Rd.), Aiken, SC 29801. ℃ **877/648-2200** or 803/648-1898. Fax 803/643-0971. www.thewillcox.com. 22 units. $185–$240 double; $425–$525 suite. Continental breakfast included with room rate. AE, DC, DISC, MC, V. Free parking. **Amenities:** Restaurant; bar; babysitting; exercise room; room service; spa. *In room:* A/C, TV, hair dryer, Internet (free), minibar.

Where to Dine

Linda's Bistro ★ 🍴 STEAKS/SEAFOOD   Come here for the best steaks and seafood in the heart of historic downtown Aiken. Wine-tasting dinners are a special feature here (call and see if one is scheduled at the time of your visit). The menu is seasonally adjusted to showcase the best produce. The service is peerless, and most of the ingredients are fresh from the country. Delightful appetizers include roasted leek and lobster tart or fresh jumbo lump crabmeat with ginger mayo. The main courses never get overly elaborate but deliciously combine flavors, as in the seared Chilean sea bass with roasted tomatoes and basil, or the creamy risotto à la Linda with roasted garlic shrimp, sweet Italian sausage, and Asiago cheese.

135 York St. ℃ **803/648-4853.** www.lindasbistro-aiken.com. Reservations required. Main courses $20–$40. AE, MC, V. Mon–Sat 5:30–10pm.

Aiken After Dark

The repertoire at the **Aiken Community Playhouse,** Washington Center for the Performing Arts, 124 Newberry St. (℃ **803/648-1438;** www.aikencommunity playhouse.com), mainly sticks to the standard road-show fare, from *Smokey Joe's Café* to *Steel Magnolias.* On Friday and Saturday, performances are at 8pm, with a Sunday matinee at 3pm. Tickets are $17 for adults, $15 for seniors (60 and over), $12 for students, and $5 for children 11 and under.

THE UPSTATE

The northwestern region of South Carolina in the foothills of the Blue Ridge Mountains was originally known as the "back country" because it was "in back" of Charleston. Over the years, this land of scenic wonders, with miles of peaks, waterfalls, mountain hamlets, and unspoiled forests, became known as the Up Country (also Upcountry). Here, American patriots trounced vastly superior British forces at the Cowpens, one of the decisive battles of the Southern campaign during the Revolutionary War.

Today the region generally referred to as the Upstate offers a wide variety of attractions and outdoor activities: 90 festivals throughout the year, more than 500 historic sites, 12 state parks, and numerous recreational opportunities.

The nation's second-largest hot-air-balloon festival, Freedom Weekend Aloft, is held Memorial Day at the Anderson Sports and Entertainment Center in Greenville. Another favorite is the Collectors' Market on the Green (antiques and pottery), staged in Pendleton in mid-September. For the history buff, the Cowpens National Battlefield Weekend, featuring 18th-century living-history and tactical demonstrations, is held in mid-January on the anniversary of the battle.

Plantations, parks, churches, and homes of former notables abound. The entire Pendleton District is on the National Register of Historic Places. One of the first separate African-American congregations established in South Carolina after the Civil War is in Greenville. Spartanburg is the site of historic 1765 Walnut Grove Plantation. But the region isn't asleep in the past; it's also a modern center of international business, especially in Greenville and Spartanburg.

THE UPSTATE'S GREAT OUTDOORS

The landscape is scenic, with more than 50 waterfalls and countless forested hills, and the moderate climate is ideal for a wide range of activities. There are numerous campgrounds, 12 state parks, golf courses, lakes, and hiking trails. You can even do a little ice-skating, although it's indoors at the Pavilion in Greenville.

The best places to enjoy unspoiled nature are the state parks and the areas surrounding the region's lakes, which offer lush vegetation and abundant wildlife. One of the most popular spots is Lake Hartwell, where you can fish, camp, picnic, boat, hike, or swim. Another excellent choice is Oconee State Park, where a mountain lake offers cool swimming on a hot day.

Golf courses include the Verdae Greens Golf Club in Greenville. Campgrounds vary from primitive to RV sites with hookups and all amenities. Several are located along the Cherokee Scenic Highway, including the campsites at Caesars Head, Keowee-Toxaway, and Lake Hartwell state parks.

Anglers can do their fishing free at state parks on reservoir lakes, park lakes, and rivers. Savvy locals prefer to head for the larger lakes, such as Jocasse and Hartwell.

Hikers flock to the Foothills Trail, which offers some of the most rugged and scenic territory in the Southeast. The 85-mile trail begins at Table Rock State Park and concludes at Oconee State Park. There are many lonesome trails for equestrians, especially Rocky Gap Trail in the Sumter National Forest, which joins up with the Willis Knob Horse Trail in Georgia. The Rocky Gap portion is 13 miles, but if you continue into Georgia, the total length is 26 miles.

PENDLETON ★

130 miles NW of Columbia; 68 miles W of Spartanburg; 35 miles W of Greenville

If you can choose only one destination, make it **Pendleton ★**, the Upstate's most historic town. The whole town is on the National Register of Historic Places—it's one of America's largest such designated districts—and Pendleton offers nearly 50 buildings that are worth looking at, many of which are open to the public. The town is also an important shopping center for antiques.

The Cherokee Indians occupied this land until September 1776, when the South Carolina militia forces demolished their towns and property to quell an uprising. After this carnage, the Cherokees were forced to sue for peace and ended up surrendering their land to the state. Originally known as Pendleton County, the area was later designated the Pendleton District. In April 1790, land was purchased to establish the courthouse town of Pendleton. It was named after Judge Henry Pendleton for his efforts in fighting for Upstate rights. Although the village began with predominantly Scots-Irish immigrants, it soon became a summer retreat for wealthy Low Country families trying to escape the mosquitoes and humidity of the coast. It's just a stone's throw from Clemson University, which in 2000 was named *Time* magazine's "Public College of the Year."

Essentials

GETTING THERE   From Greenville, drive west on I-85 to exit 19B (Hwy. 76/28). Take Highway 28 7 miles into Pendleton. From Spartanburg, follow I-85 west also to exit 19B. From Columbia, take I-26 west to I-385 west. Continue westbound on I-385 to Greenville and follow the directions above.

The nearest rail station is in Clemson, 5 miles north of Pendleton. For **Amtrak** schedules, contact them at ℂ **800/USA-RAIL** (872-7245) or www.amtrak.com.

The closest bus transit is in Anderson, 15 miles south of Pendleton. For schedules and fares, call **Anderson Electric City Transit** (ℂ **864/231-7625**) or **Greyhound Bus Lines** (ℂ **864/224-4381**). After arrival, passengers have to take a taxi to Pendleton.

VISITOR INFORMATION   **Hunter's Store,** 125 E. Queen St. (ℂ **800/862-1795** or 864/646-3782), is the home of the tri-county **Pendleton District Historical, Recreational, and Tourism Commission** (ℂ **800/862-1795** or 864/646-3782; www.discoversouthcarolina.com). Here you will find cassette-tape tours, maps, and information on the entire district; locally handmade arts and crafts; and books on the area. The commission is open Monday to Friday 9am to 4:30pm. It is closed on holidays.

Seeing the Sights

Ashtabula Plantation ★ Lewis Ladson Gibbes of Charleston built this house in the late 1820s. *Ashtabula* is the Indian word for "fish river." When the Gibbes family sold the property, it was advertised as "the most beautiful farm in the Upstate." The property eventually fell into the hands of the Mead Corporation, which turned it into a tree farm. In 1961, Mead gave the house and 10 acres to the Foundation for Historic Restoration. The house has been restored and furnished with antiques dating back to the early to mid–19th century. A scrapbook about life at Ashtabula, kept by Mrs. O. A. Bowen in the 1860s, is on display.

S.C. Hwy. 88. ✆ **864/646-7249.** Admission $5 adults, $2 children 6-14. Tues–Thurs and Sun 1–4pm.

Woodburn Plantation West of town, this four-story house was built in the early 1830s by Charles Cotesworth Pinckney, lieutenant governor of South Carolina in 1833. One of the plantation's other notable owners was Dr. John Bailey Adger, a Presbyterian minister who translated the Bible into modern Armenian. He expanded the house to its current form. In 1966, the plantation was given to the Historic Foundation to be restored and operated as a museum. The four-story structure includes antiques from the 19th century, high ceilings, and columned porches.

U.S. Hwy. 76. ✆ **864/646-7249.** Admission $5 adults, $2 children 6-14. Apr–Oct Sun 2–5pm.

Where to Stay

American House on the Hill In lieu of suitable accommodations in Pendleton, visitors often drive on Route 88 east from Pendleton to the town of Piedmont. After 28 miles you approach this efficiently run B&B where the owners house you in well-maintained and comfortably furnished bedrooms, each of which is individually decorated. Rooms have various names, the best accommodation being the Williams-McDavid Room. Breakfast is generous and freshly prepared.

W. Georgia Rd. (¼ mile west of Hwy. 25), Piedmont, SC 29673. ✆ **866/338-1180** or 864/243-0003. 4 units. $65–$99 double. AE, DC, MC, V. **Amenities:** Breakfast room. *In room:* A/C, TV, Wi-Fi (free).

Where to Dine

1826 on the Green SOUTHERN This is Pendleton's front porch restaurant, on the Village Green in the center of historic Pendleton. The chefs are noted for offering one of the finest Southern cuisines in the area. Ever had deep-fried pickle spears with portobello mushrooms as a starter? You can here, though you may find the crab cake or raspberry baked Brie more tempting. Racks of pork ribs are prepared fresh daily, or else you may go for one of the pastas, such as penne made with roasted garlic and tossed in blue cheese butter cream with strips of blackened chicken breast. Lighter fare such as sandwiches and salads is featured at lunch, along with the soup of the day and sweet potato fries on the side.

105 Exchange St. ✆ **864/646-5500.** Reservations recommended. Sandwiches $9.95; main courses $17–$23. MC, V. Wed–Fri 11:30am–1:30pm; Wed–Sat 5–10pm.

Shopping

Antiquing is the favorite activity in Pendleton. In addition to the following shops, a famous antiques-and-pottery show, the Collectors' Market on the Green, is held in the fall, sometime between mid-September and mid-October. Dealers from the Carolinas and Georgia gather on the village green to sell their antiques, collectibles, and handmade pottery. Dates depend on the Clemson University football schedule; the market is scheduled for when there is no home game.

Grandma's Antiques At the corner of Broad and Queen streets, this shop offers a wide range of antiques, excluding furniture. The inventory includes crystal, china, toys, kitchenware, silver, tools, and jewelry. Hours are Monday to Saturday 10am to 5pm. 204 E. Queen St. © **864/646-9435.**

Pendleton Place Antiques This shop offers a selection of primitive antiques, furniture, crystal, glassware, dolls, and collectibles, including Hummel pieces. The owner, Jim Pruitt, is often out doing estate appraisals, so you should call ahead to see whether the store is open. Hours are Monday, Tuesday, and Saturday 10am to 4pm. 651 S. Mechanic St. © **864/646-7673.**

GREENVILLE

102 miles NW of Columbia

Lying halfway between Charlotte and Atlanta, Greenville is an inviting Upstate city with tree-lined streets in the foothills of the Blue Ridge Mountains. It's been called the textile center of the world and is known for turning out not only clothing nylon, but also chemicals. It makes a good hub for exploring the Upstate and the forested parks in the area.

Greenville began as a trading post in the 1700s. During the antebellum era, the area was a resort for plantation owners from the Low Country, but it later moved on to textiles. The textile industry began in the 1820s, but mills were not built here until the 1870s. The 1882 Huguenot Mill was advertised as being "an electric plant that makes plaid cloth," but the textile connection is long gone. Today the town is the home of the Metropolitan Arts Council, Upstate Visual Arts, the Historic Greenville Foundation, and the Peace Center for the Performing Arts.

Essentials

GETTING THERE Highway I-26 runs from Columbia to Spartanburg; I-85 reaches the city from the northeast and southwest.

The nearest airport is in Spartanburg (© **864/877-7426**; www.gspairport.com).

Amtrak stops daily at 1120 W. Washington St. Call © **800/USA-RAIL** (872-7245) for schedules and fares, or search www.amtrak.com.

For local **Greyhound** and **Trailways** bus information, call © **864/235-4741.**

VISITOR INFORMATION The **Greater Greenville Convention and Visitors Center,** 631 S. Main St. (PO Box 10527), Greenville, SC 29601 (© **800/351-7180** or 864/233-0461; www.greatergreenville.com), is located in the lobby of City Hall. You'll find a selection of more than 200 brochures on area attractions, facilities, and events, along with maps and souvenirs. Open Monday to Friday 8:30am to 5:30pm.

Seeing the Sights

Greenville is enjoying an active downtown revitalization. In addition to the Peace Center (which has been around for more than a decade but is the city centerpiece), several festivals draw people downtown on a regular basis year-round: **Art in the**

Park in September, **Fall for Greenville** in October, and **First Night,** the alcohol-free New Year's Eve celebration.

Beattie House   Listed on the National Register of Historic Places, this Italianate-style house was built in 1834 by Mr. and Mrs. Fountain Fox Beattie. It contains Victorian furnishings and architectural details such as the delicate turnings and brackets. Over the years, the house had two wings added on and was moved twice. It's now the center of the Greenville Women's Club.

8 Bennett St. 𝄁 **864/233-9977.** Free admission. Mon–Fri 9:30am–4:30pm by appointment.

Bob Jones University Museum & Gallery   This nondenominational Christian liberal-arts institution is often denounced in the national media as a center of right-wing extremism. Remember those headlines when George W. Bush was seeking the presidential nomination of his party and spoke at this forum? Founded in 1927 by Dr. Bob Jones, Sr., the school emphasizes "Christianity with culture." The Gallery of Sacred Art, begun in 1951, contains 30 rooms displaying representative works of European religious painting from the 14th through 19th centuries, including works by such masters as Botticelli, Titian, Tintoretto, Veronese, Murillo, Gerard David, Rubens, Van Dyck, Rembrandt, and Cranach. The museum also houses collections of Russian icons, Renaissance furniture, and vestments made for the Imperial Chapel in Vienna, as well as the Bowen Bible Lands Collection of items that are relevant to biblical times.

1700 Wade Hampton Blvd. 𝄁 **864/770-1331.** www.bjumg.org. Admission $5 adults, $4 seniors, $3 students, free for children 6–12. Museum and art gallery Tues–Sun 2–5pm.

Christ Episcopal Church   The church is a Gothic Revival structure with a cruciform shape and a 130-foot brick spire. Home of the oldest congregation in the city, this church was organized in 1820 by summer people from Charleston. The cornerstone was laid in 1852. The site of the original sanctuary is where the circular fountain and flower bed now lie.

10 N. Church St. 𝄁 **864/271-8773.** www.ccgsc.org. Free admission. Mon–Fri 8:30am–4:30pm.

Falls Park ★   After a long and seedy decline, Falls Park is once again the centerpiece of recreational life in Greenville. Enter the park at Main Street and West Camperdown Way or at East Camperdown Way and Falls Street. Falls Park is centered around the beautiful Reedy River Falls. Today 20 landscaped acres showcase the falls, and a 355-foot-long, 12-foot-wide suspension bridge spans the river, allowing dramatic views of the upper falls and the gardens below. The park now includes two amphitheaters to host annual performances, including Shakespeare plays and concerts. Bring a picnic basket to enjoy on the grounds or else dine at one of the park's two restaurants: **Mary's** (𝄁 **864/298-0005**) or the **Overlook Grill** (𝄁 **864/ 271-9700**).

Falls Park 8 (heart of downtown Greenville). 𝄁 **864/467-4355.** www.fallspark.com. Free admission. Daily 7am–9pm.

Greenville County Museum of Art   Begun in the 1930s as a small regional art gallery, this museum is now recognized as having one of the best collections of regional art in the country. The collection surveys the highlights of American art, primarily through works created in the South or by Southern natives. Among the artists represented are Washington Allston, John Gadsby Chapman, Martin Johnson

Heade, George P. A. Healy, John Ross Key, Georgia O'Keeffe, William Tylee Ranney, Helen Turner, and Catherine Wiley. Of exceptional interest is the **Andrew Wyeth: Greenville Collection** ★★, recently expanded to 32 pieces of art, including an example from every major period of the fabled artist's career. In addition, the museum has an impressive collection of contemporary art that includes works by such artists as Romare Bearden, Hans Hofmann, Jasper Johns, Lee Krasner, and Andy Warhol.

420 College St. ℂ **864/271-7570.** www.greenvillemuseum.org. Free admission. Tues–Wed and Fri–Sat 11am–5pm; Thurs 11am–8pm; Sun 1–5pm.

Sports & Outdoor Pursuits

GOLF   C. P. Willimon owns and designed **Bonnie Brae Golf Club,** 1316 Fork Shoals Rd. (ℂ **864/277-9838**). The 6,484-yard course is a par 72, offering Bermuda greens and fairways. The greens fees are $31 Monday to Friday and $40 on Saturday and Sunday. Carts are included. Hours are daily from sunrise to sunset.

A 9-hole option is the **Donaldson Golf Club,** 1074 Perimeter Rd. (ℂ **864/277-8414;** www.golflink.com). Originally part of Donaldson Air Force Base, this public facility offers three par-36 courses: the 3,197-yard Blue Course, the 3,050-yard White Course, and the 2,799-yard Red Course. Greens fees are $13 Monday to Thursday and $16 Friday to Sunday. Hours are daily dawn to dusk. Carts are included.

Verdae Greens Golf Club, 650 Verdae Blvd. (ℂ **864/676-1500;** www.verdae greens.com), is an 18-hole, 6,757-yard, par-72 course. Set in a pine forest, the Penncross Bentgrass greens and Bermuda fairway were designed by Willard C. Byrd and Associates. Greens fees are $31 to $50 Sunday to Friday and $36 to $58 on Saturday. Carts are included. Hours are daily 7am to 7pm.

SPECTATOR SPORTS   Clemson and Furman universities offer a plethora of sporting events, including football, baseball, basketball, and soccer. For **Clemson Tigers** information, call ℂ **888/253-6766.** For the **Furman Paladins,** dial ℂ **864/294-2061** for sports information and ℂ **864/294-3099** for tickets.

Baseball fans can enjoy the **Greenville Drive,** a South Atlantic League club of the Boston Red Sox that plays at the West End Field downtown. Tickets cost $5 to $8. For schedules and ticket information, call ℂ **864/240-4500.**

SWIMMING   For swimmers, there are outdoor pools at **Lakeside Park** and **Northside Park.** There is also an indoor pool at West Side Park. For information, call ℂ **864/295-0032.**

TENNIS   More than 50 outdoor public courts are scattered throughout the county. For information, call the **Greenville County Recreation District** (ℂ **864/288-6470**). The **Pavilion** offers use of indoor and outdoor courts free, unless you want to reserve the court for a specific time—then the fee is $2 per court, per hour. Hours are daily 6am to 10pm.

Where to Stay

EXPENSIVE

Embassy Suites Resort Hotel Greenville Golf Resort & Conference Center ★   As you walk into the atrium of this all-suite hotel on the Verdae Greens Golf Club, you'll feel that you have stepped into a minipark featuring plant-lined walkways and bubbling pools and fountains. The nine-story hotel offers comfortably furnished two-room suites decorated with a contemporary flair. At the **Café Verdae,**

American and Southern cuisine such as baked Gulf snapper and prime rib is served in a casual, relaxed atmosphere. As sunlight turns into moonlight in the atrium, you can unwind with a drink at the **19th Green.**

670 Verdae Blvd., Greenville, SC 29607. © **800/EMBASSY** (362-2779) or 864/676-9090. Fax 864/676-0669. http://embassysuites.hilton.com. 268 units. $119–$199 suite; $700–$850 presidential suite. Rates include cooked-to-order breakfast and nightly manager's reception. AE, DC, DISC, MC, V. Take I-385 to the Roper Mountain Rd. exit (exit 37) or the N. Laurens Rd. exit off I-85. Free parking. **Amenities:** Restaurant; bar; babysitting; concierge; 18-hole golf course; exercise room; 2 pools (1 indoor); room service; sauna; 2 tennis courts (lit). *In room:* A/C, TV, hair dryer, Wi-Fi ($9.95 per day).

Hilton Greenville ★   In a commercial area on the east side, 3½ miles north of town, this nine-story concrete-and-green-glass hotel offers bright and airy rooms appointed with brass and floral accents, as well as cozy furnishings such as chaise longues and love seats. The concierge level features added extras such as complimentary continental breakfast, evening hors d'oeuvres with honor-bar service, and the morning paper delivered to your room Monday to Friday. The restaurant, **Vercitti,** offers Northern Italian specialties and seafood and steaks. In the **Lobby Lounge,** you can enjoy a quiet evening with a pianist playing in the background.

45 W. Orchard Park Dr., Greenville, SC 29615. © **800/HILTONS** (445-8667) or 864/232-4747. Fax 864/235-6248. www.hilton.com. 256 units. $110–$180 double; $130–$199 junior suite; $300–$330 suite. Children stay free in parent's room. AE, DC, DISC, MC, V. From I-85, take I-385 to Haywood Rd. exit (exit 39). Free parking. **Amenities:** Restaurant; bar; exercise room; Jacuzzi; indoor pool; room service; sauna. *In room:* A/C, TV, hair dryer, Wi-Fi ($9.95 per day).

Hyatt Regency Greenville ★   In the heart of Greenville's entertainment-and-commercial district, this eight-story hotel caters to a predominantly business clientele and is the prime choice in town; we prefer it to the Hilton (see above). Patrons enter through a parklike setting created in the eight-story atrium lobby with lush plants and trees, lampposts, and a cascading waterfall. Rooms are comfortably furnished with a rather standardized decor. The most desired unit is the Brooks Suite, featuring such luxuries as a whirlpool with stereo system, walk-in wet bar, grand piano, and full entertainment center. For dining and entertainment, the **Provencia** restaurant offers Italian cuisine. The **Commons Bar** is a cigar lounge with piano music, open until 1am.

220 N. Main St., Greenville, SC 29601. © **800/633-7313** or 864/235-1234. Fax 864/232-7584. http://Greenville.hyatt.com. 328 units. $149–$279 double; $349–$550 suite. AE, DC, DISC, MC, V. Parking $5–$15. **Amenities:** Restaurant; bar; babysitting; concierge; outdoor pool; room service. *In room:* A/C, TV, hair dryer, Wi-Fi ($10 per day).

The Westin Poinsett ★★   In 1925, this was one of the grandest hotels in the area. In 2002, it came back, newly restored and outfitted with 21st-century conveniences. A favorite with both business travelers and visitors, the new Poinsett proudly boasts "heavenly beds," and we agree. Covered by eiderdowns, these luxurious beds are the finest of any hotel in the area. Not only are the beds comfortable, but so are the rooms, furnished in a tasteful, often elegant style, with first-class tiled bathrooms. You don't even have to leave the premises at night: Enjoy live entertainment in the **Piano Bar and Lounge** and excellent regional food in the restored **Spoonbread** restaurant.

120 Main St., Greenville, SC 29601. © **864/421-9700.** Fax 864/421-0460. www.starwoodhotels.com. 200 units. $149–$219 double; $235–$280 suite. Children 17 and under stay free in parent's room. AE, DC, DISC, MC, V. **Amenities:** Restaurant; bar; exercise room; room service. *In room:* A/C, TV, hair dryer, Wi-Fi ($10 per day).

MODERATE

Pettigru Place ★ 🏨   Fred and Sherry Smith own this B&B, which is listed on the National Register of Historic Places. It's on a tree-lined street in the Pettigru Historic District near downtown Greenville. You enter through a small garden into the Georgian Federalist–design house, built in the 1920s. Each of the rooms is individually decorated, ranging from the Chantilly, with its Victorian decor, to a tribute to *Out of Africa* in the Brass Giraffe, which features a 12-inch brass shower head for that rainforest effect. The most desirable is the Carolinian, appointed with Charlestonian decor in shades of blue and green, a king-size sleigh bed, whirlpool tub with hand shower, and private porch. Breakfast is served communally in the dining room and includes home-baked breads and a daily chef's special from the oven.

302 Pettigru St., Greenville, SC 29601. ℂ **877/362-4644** or 864/242-4529. Fax 864/242-1231. www. pettigruplace.com. 5 units. $119–$199 double; $195 suite. Rates include breakfast. AE, DC, DISC, MC, V. **Amenities:** Breakfast room; lounge. *In room:* A/C, TV, hair dryer, Wi-Fi (free).

Where to Dine

Locals swear by Sunday brunch at the **Embassy Suites,** 670 Verdae Blvd. (ℂ **864/676-9090**), where $24 per adult, $22 per senior, and $12 per child 6 to 12 (free for 5 and under) will get you shrimp on ice, Belgian waffles, smoked salmon, eggs Benedict, omelets, carving stations of prime rib and ham, and more. The best Chinese takeout in town is at the obviously named **China,** 2117 Old Spartanburg Rd., on the east side of town (ℂ **864/322-0405**), a family-run spot that serves up deliciously fresh standards like dumplings, General Tso's chicken, and shrimp with garlic sauce. And for a drive-by caffeine fix, head over to **Liquid Highway,** 14 Halton Rd., at Congaree Road (ℂ **864/281-9130**), a drive-through coffee bar serving excellent coffee, muffins, and smoothies (the beans are for sale, too). Don't forget to check out **Barley's Taproom & Pizzeria** and **Blue Ridge Brewing Company,** two downtown bars that serve great food as well (see "Greenville After Dark," below).

City Range Steakhouse Grill STEAKHOUSE/SEAFOOD   This lodgelike building looks out of place (and at least a few time zones too far east) in the parking lot of a strip mall. But many believe this is the best steakhouse in town. A large stone fireplace sits in the center of this rustic, open restaurant; the decor runs to wood beams, earth tones, and framed antique photos. Not surprisingly, steaks, chops, and other grilled items dominate the menu—though you might not have room for the meat after filling up on the killer garlic rolls and house-special Dusty Martinis, augmented with olive juice and blue cheese–stuffed olives. If you take a shine to the tangy house steak sauce, buy a bottle on your way out the door.

615 Haywood Rd. (across from Haywood Mall). ℂ **864/286-9018.** www.cityrange.com. Reservations not accepted. Main courses $16–$27. AE, DC, DISC, MC, V. Mon–Thurs 11am–10pm; Fri 11am–11pm; Sat noon–11pm; Sun 11:30am–9pm.

Coffee Underground AMERICAN   Owners Dana Lowie and Stephen Taylor gave birth to Greenville's only alternative coffeehouse after a trip to Seattle left them pining for a similar java experience at home. This cozy basement space in the heart of downtown is a great spot to relax any time of day or night. In addition to a diverse selection of coffee drinks, teas, and chais (Asian-style spiced teas), Coffee Underground serves bistro-style food at dinner, beginning with such appetizers as fried green tomatoes or crab cakes. For a main course, try the pork tenderloin with caramelized pears in a light pear brandy cream sauce or else stuffed chicken breast with herbed goat cheese and a wild rice pilaf.

1 E. Coffee St., at Main St. *C* **864/298-0494.** www.coffeeunderground.biz. Main courses $9.85–$13. AE, DISC, MC, V. Mon–Thurs 7am–11pm; Fri 7am–midnight; Sat 8am–midnight; Sun 8am–10pm.

Soby's ★ MODERN SOUTHERN Back in 1997, owners David Williams (a chef) and Carl Sobocinsky (an architect) bought and gutted this building, a down-at-the-heels shoe store, and transformed it into a stylish, award-winning restaurant. Restored wide-plank blond floors and brick walls complement a curving, hand-tooled bar and an airy, minimalist mezzanine to create a fusion of old and new. The menu, similarly stylistic, puts a new spin on old favorites: crab cakes with rémoulade, dressed up with haricots verts, mashed potatoes, and creamed hominy, and fried green tomatoes layered with jalapeño-pimento cheese. Wine is serious business here; the cellar holds over 5,000 bottles, and the restaurant hosts a regular schedule of wine-themed dinners. Soby's now also serves Sunday brunch.

207 S. Main St. *C* **864/232-7007.** www.sobys.com. Reservations accepted. Main courses $15–$28; Sun brunch $18 adults, $5 children 5–10, free for children 4 and under. AE, DC, DISC, MC, V. Mon–Thurs 5:30–10pm; Fri–Sat 5:30–11pm; Sun 11:30am–1pm and 5–9pm.

Stax's The Peppermill ★★ CONTINENTAL This is Greenville's best dining room, serving a finely tuned cuisine with market-fresh ingredients. A table on its terrace on a summer evening is one of the best places to spend an evening in this city. Some local critics call Stax's the state's finest cuisine, but the chefs of Charleston would challenge that claim. In spite of its ability to seat as many as 275 diners, the service is impeccable. It takes some time to read the 1,200-bottle wine list.

Try the chilled seafood appetizer of shrimp, oysters, and blue crab. The savory Southwestern cheesecake is also a tempting appetizer, served with scallions and a chipotle beurre blanc. The chefs are known locally for their steaks and chops, with a divine Kobe rib-eye steak. The fresh fish and shellfish are without equal in the area, including stone crab claws in season and a sushi-grade ahi tuna. For something elegant, opt for chargrilled ostrich with black truffles and a foie gras terrine. Care and attention go into the side dishes, none finer than young green beans with pecan butter.

30 Orchard Park Dr. *C* **864/288-9320.** www.staxs.net. Reservations recommended. Main courses $16–$28. AE, DC, DISC, MC, V. Mon–Fri 11:30am–2pm; Mon–Sat 5:30–10pm.

Trio ★ AMERICAN/ITALIAN In the heart of downtown Greenville, Trio is a restaurant you can feel comfortable bringing a client to for lunch and a place where your entire family can enjoy a relaxed meal. Gas lanterns light the open brick-lined cafe, where wood-fired pizzas are the specialty of the house, and sauces are made from scratch daily. Appetizers include a savory lobster ravioli with a spicy cream sauce, topped with tri-colored peppers, and traditional bruschetta served with an artichoke dip. If pizza is not your style, then opt for one of the fine pasta dishes, rotisserie chicken meals, or the superb seafood trio: Prince Edward Island rope-cultured mussels, Gulf shrimp, and large sea scallops sautéed in either a chardonnay cream reduction or marinara sauce, served with angel-hair pasta. There are 20 different wine varieties served by the glass. A children's menu is also available.

22 N. Main St. *C* **864/467-1000.** www.triocafe.com. Reservations not required. Main courses $7.95–$19. AE, DC, DISC, MC, V. Mon–Thurs 11:30am–10pm; Fri–Sat 11:30am–11pm.

People in Greenville drive down to Abbeville to attend performances at the **Abbeville Opera House,** Town Square (℘ **864/366-2157**; www.the abbevilleoperahouse.com). It's known for the high caliber of its productions—everything from plays to musicals. Built in 1908, and one of the most famous opera houses in the South, it used to feature headliners on the vaudeville circuit, including Fanny Brice (the inspiration for *Funny Girl*) and Jimmy Durante. Its summer opera season runs from early June to late August or mid-September, with performances on Friday and Saturday at 8pm, plus a Saturday matinee at 3pm. The winter season begins in early October, running until the end of April. In winter, shows are offered only on Friday and Saturday at 8pm, with a Saturday matinee at 3pm. Tickets cost $17 for adults, $16 for seniors (65 or older) and children 12 and under. The box office is open Monday to Friday from 10am to 2pm. Abbeville is 50 miles south of Greenville off I-185 south. Call ahead for exact directions.

Greenville After Dark

PERFORMING ARTS

Bi-Lo Center   This $63-million facility replaced the older Greenville Memorial Auditorium as the city's venue for Broadway touring shows, rock concerts, rodeos, basketball, ice shows, and art exhibits. It's also the home of the city's minor-league hockey team, the Greenville Grrrowls. Carrying the corporate name of a local grocery chain, the arena opened in September 1998, with Janet Jackson and Pearl Jam filling the 16,000-seat arena to capacity. 650 N. Academy St. ℘ **864/241-3800.** www.bilocenter.com.

Peace Center for the Performing Arts   This complex includes a 2,100-seat concert hall, a 400-seat theater, a 200-seat cabaret, a 1,500-seat amphitheater, and a full-service restaurant. Broadway shows and chamber music are offered and international dance companies, local groups, and star entertainers perform here. Call ahead for tickets and times, which vary. 300 S. Main St. ℘ **800/888-7768** or 864/467-3000. www.peacecenter.org.

The Warehouse Theatre   At Greenville's professional resident theater, the intimate setting is arranged so that all seats are within five rows of the stage. Performances include classical as well as new and innovative theater. Dress is casual. Call ahead for prices and times. 37 Augusta St. ℘ **864/235-6948.** www.warehousetheatre.com.

BARS & CLUBS

The number of bars, restaurants, and pubs that have sprung up in downtown Greenville is a firm testament to the neighborhood's revitalization. **Soby's** (p. 355) has a thriving bar scene. **Coffee Underground** (p. 354) serves beer, wine, and cordials in addition to coffee and tea, and offers a regular schedule of comedy acts, live folk music, and alternative films in its 60-seat theater.

Barley's Taproom & Pizzeria   As if the 27 beers on tap (including a few unusual microbrews) weren't enough of a reason to come to Barley's, it also serves excellent pizzas, with toppings both nouveau (sun-dried tomato, artichoke) and traditional (pepperoni, sausage, and such). There's never a cover to hear live music, which ranges from rock to bluegrass to blues. They've recently expanded into the upstairs space, adding pool tables and several dartboards. 23 W. Washington St. ✆ **864/232-3706.** www.barleystaproom.com.

Blue Ridge Brewing Company   The large copper tanks nested in the picture window out front should be your first indication that this place is all about the beer. Five house brews are standard; a roster of others changes seasonally. The food's not bad, if a little pricey for a brewpub, with a menu heavy on wild game, steak, and a few fresh seafood choices thrown in. Tables are large enough to accommodate big groups, and live bands perform several times a week. 217 N. Main St. (next to Fuddruckers). ✆ **864/232-4677.** www.blueridgebrewing.com.

Bubba Annie's   This beer joint—and that's the best way to describe Bubba Annie's—has the best wings in town. The decor can only be described as "All Things Bulldog." This reflects both the owner's interest in the breed and his collegial affiliation (he went to the University of Georgia, where the Dawg is the official mascot). 996 Batesville Rd. ✆ **864/297-0007.**

ALONG THE CHEROKEE FOOTHILLS SCENIC HIGHWAY ★

The Cherokee Foothills Scenic Highway, S.C. 11, curves 130 miles through the heart of South Carolina's Blue Ridge Mountain foothills. It stretches in an arc from I-85 at Gaffney, near the North Carolina border, almost to the Georgia border at Lake Hartwell State Park, where it links up once more with I-85. The "scenic" in this highway's name is best justified at spring-blossom time or when autumn leaves are coloring, but it can't compare with the more dramatic Blue Ridge Parkway of Virginia and North Carolina. Once, the highway was known as the Keowee Path or Cherokee Path. The highway offers access to 10 state parks and several historic sites. For information and a detailed route map, contact the **South Carolina State Park System,** 1205 Pendleton St., Columbia, SC 29201 (✆ **803/734-0156,** 866/224-9339, or 803/734-0156; www.southcarolinaparks.com).

The route begins in Gaffney at the **Peachoid,** the town's water tower (painted to resemble a peach), at exit 92 off I-85. After you turn onto the highway, you begin a journey through peach country. Peach orchards and stands line the road, selling peaches, tomatoes, cucumbers, and other produce in season. Many of the stands have been in operation for a good number of years, including one that was started more than 30 years ago.

Soon after entering the highway, you come to **Cowpens National Battlefield,** 11 miles west of I-85 near the Highway 11/Highway 110 intersection, Chesnee (✆ **864/461-2828;** www.nps.gov/cowp). On January 17, 1781, Daniel Morgan led his army of tough Continentals and backwoods militia to a brilliant victory over a larger and better-equipped force of British regulars under the command of the much-hated dragoon Banastre Tarleton. This crucial battle contributed to the eventual defeat of the British at Yorktown. The battle took place over an area of just 150 acres; today's park sprawls over 843 acres. In the park, a 3-mile loop takes you around the battlefield and its historical markers. The park also offers a 1.25-mile walking trail. In the visitor center are exhibits and memorabilia. A free 22-minute audiovisual program, *Daybreak at the Cowpens,* is presented every half-hour. The park and visitor center are open daily from 9am to 5pm, except for major holidays.

Detours off the route lead to various points of interest. The last covered bridge in South Carolina is **Campbell's Bridge,** built in 1909. To reach it, head 4 miles down Route 14 at Gowensville, then go west half a mile on Route 414. The oldest bridge in the state is believed to be the **Poinsett Bridge,** built in 1820. The stone-arched structure crosses the Middle Saluda River where it overlooks the clear, running water and kudzu-covered countryside. To reach this spot, take Route 25 north until you come to the signposted turnoff.

Other points of interest include **Glassy Mountain,** with its 1,000-foot sheer rock face; **Symmes Chapel** (better known as "Pretty Place"), atop Standing Stone Mountain and offering one of the most scenic overlooks; **Raven Cliff Falls,** where a wooden deck has been built to allow visitors to view a waterfall that plunges 800 feet into a gorge; **Sassafras Mountain,** the state's highest peak, at 3,548 feet; and **Stumphouse Mountain Tunnel,** begun in the 1850s to link Charleston to the Midwest, but abandoned at the onset of the Civil War. All these sites are signposted on the highway.

ATLANTA

Atlanta is the gateway to the New South. Bustling and ever growing—not always attractively—Georgia's capital is the 13th-largest metropolitan area in the United States. If only Rhett and Scarlett could see it now—or, better yet, if only General Sherman could rise from the grave to witness the phenomenal growth of a city that he was able to burn to the ground but whose spirit he couldn't destroy.

Atlanta has enlarged its rail system, brought in six interstate highways, and acquired an airport to rival Chicago's O'Hare. Some 450 of the Fortune 500 corporations have offices or home offices here.

Atlanta remains the showcase of the New South. It's filled with the homes of the rich and famous (everybody from Ted Turner to Elton John) and is the Promised Land to immigrants from as far away as Vietnam and as close as the Caribbean and (especially) Mexico.

Ever since Atlanta was selected as the site of the 1996 Summer Olympic Games and the 2000 Super Bowl, the city's face has changed. Massive construction began in the early 1990s with the $215-million, 70,500-seat Georgia Dome, and continued in 1994 and 1995 with the creation of a $50-million, 60-acre Centennial Park, the heart of the public area for the games. The hard work and construction were not wasted when the Olympics left town. Centennial Park is used for leisure by Atlantans today; the $169-million Olympic Village became housing for Georgia Tech and Georgia State University; the $170-million Olympic Stadium, scaled down to become Turner Field, is the home of the Atlanta Braves; and the Olympic Cauldron still stands in remembrance of the games. The city's major sports and entertainment facility, the Philips Arena, opened in late 1999 and hosts the Atlanta Hawks NBA team and the Atlanta Thrashers NHL expansion team. The Thrashers join the Atlanta Braves and the Atlanta Hawks as the crown jewels in mogul Ted Turner's sports empire.

All this commerce with the outside world has energized the city's cultural life. More than ever before, there are concerts and cabarets, art galleries and avant-garde "happenings," and the many late-night diversions of "Hotlanta." The influx of restaurants featuring international cuisine has put Atlanta on the gastronomic map, but has made it harder and harder to find fried chicken, country ham, hot biscuits, and grits. Locals like to boast that Atlanta has arrived—and they'll be happy to take you by the hand and prove it.

ORIENTATION

Getting There

BY PLANE   Atlanta's **Hartsfield-Jackson Atlanta International Airport** (✆ **800/897-1910;** www.atlanta-airport.com) has the largest passenger terminal complex *in the world*. It's the home of **Delta** (✆ 800/221-1212; www.delta.com) and is served by dozens of other international and domestic carriers, including **American** (✆ 800/433-7300; www.aa.com), **United** (✆ 800/241-6522; www.united.com), and **US Airways** (✆ 800/428-4322; www.usairways.com).

The Atlanta **airport shuttle** (✆ **866/545-9633** or 404/524-3400) connects the airport with downtown and major hotels between 6am and midnight, for a $17 fare downtown, $19 midtown, and $21 Buckhead. **MARTA's** (Metropolitan Atlanta Rapid Transit Authority; ✆ **404/848-5000;** www.itsmarta.com) rapid-rail trains run from 4:45am to 1am, with a downtown fare of $2. Taxi fare to downtown is $30 for one passenger, $32 for two passengers, and $34 for three. *Warning:* Be sure the taxi driver knows how to get to where you want to go before you leave the airport.

BY CAR   Atlanta is accessible by car via three interstate highways: I-75, which runs north-south between Tennessee and Florida; I-85, which runs northeast-southwest between South Carolina and Alabama; and I-20, which runs east-west between South Carolina and Alabama. I-285, more commonly known as the Perimeter Highway, circles the Atlanta metropolitan area.

BY TRAIN   Amtrak trains arrive at the **Brookwood Railway Station,** 1688 Peachtree St. (✆ **800/USA-RAIL** [872-7245]; www.amtrak.com), providing daily service to and from Washington, D.C., New York, Boston and intermediate points to the northeast, and New Orleans and intermediate points to the southwest. This is a very central location, within easy reach of most downtown or midtown hotels.

BY BUS   Buses arrive downtown at the **Greyhound Bus Terminal,** 232 Forsyth St. (✆ **404/584-1731**). In addition to service from **Greyhound** (✆ **800/231-2222;** www.greyhound.com), low-cost carriers such as **Chinatown Bus** (✆ **888/988-2739;** www.chinatown-bus.org) and **Southeastern Stages** (✆ **404/591-2780;** www.southeasternstages.com) link Atlanta to many other cities and often offer amenities such as free Wi-Fi. For more deals, be sure to check out **www.gotobus. com/chinatownbus**.

Visitor Information

The **Atlanta Convention and Visitors Bureau (ACVB),** 233 Peachtree St. NE, Ste. 100, Atlanta, GA 30303 (✆ **404/521-6600;** www.atlanta.net), can supply a wealth of information on sightseeing, accommodations, dining, cultural happenings, and special interests. The ACVB also offers the "Atlanta Passport," a vacation packet filled with coupons, discounts, and an events calendar.

After your arrival, stop by one of the helpful **ACVB visitor information centers,** at Hartsfield-Jackson Atlanta International Airport, in the Lenox Square Shopping Center (Buckhead), at 3393 Peachtree Rd., or in Underground Atlanta at 65 Upper Alabama St.

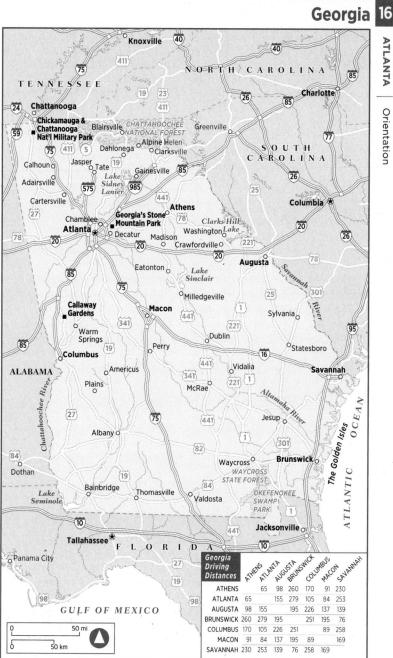

Georgia Driving Distances	ATHENS	ATLANTA	AUGUSTA	BRUNSWICK	COLUMBUS	MACON	SAVANNAH
ATHENS		65	98	260	170	91	230
ATLANTA	65		155	279	105	84	253
AUGUSTA	98	155		195	226	137	139
BRUNSWICK	260	279	195		251	195	76
COLUMBUS	170	105	226	251		89	258
MACON	91	84	137	195	89		169
SAVANNAH	230	253	139	76	258	169	

Neighborhoods in Brief

Downtown Atlanta's commercial center is home to numerous gleaming skyscrapers, the most outstanding of which is Peachtree Center. Underground Atlanta, the Georgia World Congress Center, department stores (Macy's and so on), the downtown branch of the High Museum of Art (in the Georgia-Pacific Center), Grant Park (with its zoo and Cyclorama), and the state capitol are all here. Adjacent to central downtown is the Martin Luther King, Jr., Historic District, a predominantly black neighborhood that bred and nurtured the revered civil rights leader. The safest downtown streets (particularly after dark) are in the well-traveled "hotel corridor"—bordered by Ellis, Courtland, Baker, and Peachtree streets. Private security officers and Atlanta police carefully patrol this area.

Midtown North of downtown, the midtown area extends roughly from Ponce de Leon Avenue to 26th Street. Major attractions include the Woodruff Arts Center (housing the High Museum of Art), the Alliance Theatre, the Atlanta Symphony Orchestra, and the Fox Theatre.

Ansley Park Adjacent to midtown and designed by Frederick Law Olmsted around the turn of the 20th century, this is chiefly a residential area of landscaped greenery. It also houses Colony Square, a complex of shops, restaurants, and offices.

Buckhead About 6 miles north of downtown is Atlanta's affluent district, the setting of gorgeous mansions surrounded by landscaped gardens, posh shops and boutiques, some of the city's top hotels and restaurants, and two top-of-the-line shopping centers—Lenox Square and Phipps Plaza. It's also well known for its bar and restaurant scene. Even the "border" of Buckhead is easily marked by the first of a long stretch of bars you'll see as you drive through.

Virginia-Highland Northeast of downtown, this is to Atlanta what Greenwich Village is to New York—an area of quirky little shops, bookstores, sidewalk cafes, art galleries, bistros, and some of the liveliest bars in the city.

Little Five Points Just beyond Virginia-Highland, Little Five Points is centered around the junction of Euclid and Moreland avenues. The Victorian homes here became the renovation craze of city residents and now shine in their original glory. This is also where you'll find the Jimmy Carter Presidential Center and Library.

Inman Park East of downtown is Atlanta's quintessential example of restoration. Inman Park is Atlanta's first planned community and one of the nation's first garden suburbs. During the mid-1900s, the area became depressed and was abandoned until the early 1970s. Inman Park is now one of Atlanta's most prestigious neighborhoods. Its streets are lined with shady willow trees and authentic Victorian-style homes. But the neighborhood is most noted for its annual tour of homes and its walking tours conducted by the Atlanta Preservation Society.

Sweet Auburn West of Inman Park is Atlanta's famed Sweet Auburn district. This area is noted for being the center of African-American nightlife during a time when African Americans were restricted by white-owned businesses. The neighborhood's Auburn Avenue was once hailed as the richest black street in America. Today Auburn Avenue is the center of Atlanta's African-American heritage and features the King Center; the Martin Luther King, Jr., National Historic Site; King's birth home; and Ebenezer Baptist Church, where King and his father preached.

Decatur This charming village dating from 1823 is clustered around the courthouse square, a 15-minute drive east of downtown. Decatur has the huge, bustling Dekalb Farmer's Market and is also the setting for a variety of cultural events and festivals. In recent years, it has been a popular destination for immigrants, prompting national publications such as *USA Today* to recognize that Atlanta's immigrant population growth is outpacing that of the rest of the country, especially in the number of Asian immigrants. The

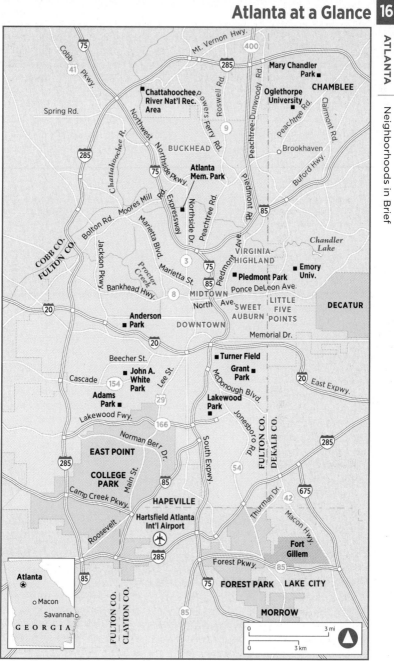

neighboring community of Chamblee has been referred to as "Little Hanoi."

Vining Set to the northwest of Buckhead, inside the Beltway, this leafy, pleasant

neighborhood's buildings and homes mostly date from the 1950s. Recently, it's been the site of a residential and commercial building boom, and the focus of lots of attention.

Getting Around

BY PUBLIC TRANSPORTATION

Sprawling Atlanta covers 6,000 square miles. Neighborhood "hopping" is most often done by car since public transportation is not only limited, but also very often inconvenient and time-consuming.

BY SUBWAY The **Metropolitan Atlanta Rapid Transit Authority** (MARTA; ✆ **404/848-5000;** www.itsmarta.com) is Atlanta's rapid-rail system, with 36 stations. It extends south to the airport, and east-west and north-south lines intersect at the Five Points Station in downtown. **BATMA** (Buckhead Area Transportation Management Association) operates free electric shuttle buses between Lenox and Buckhead, the two MARTA train stations in the district. MARTA operates Monday to Friday 4:45am to 1am, Saturday 5:15am to 12:45am, and Sunday 6am to 12:45am; the fare is $2. There are token vending machines at all stations, and transfers are free. For schedule and route information, call ✆ **404/848-5000** Monday to Friday from 6am to 11pm, and on Saturday, Sunday, and holidays from 8am to 10pm.

BY BUS **MARTA** also operates some 150 bus routes, which connect with all rapid-rail stations. You must have exact change—no pennies—for the $2 fare, and transfers are free. The transit authority now operates the Atlanta Tourist Loop, linking major hotels with some of the city's top attractions, including the Georgia Aquarium; the Martin Luther King, Jr., Historic District; the CNN Center; and Underground Atlanta. The user-friendly shuttle travels in a single clockwise loop every half-hour, picking up passengers at specially designated stops. Toohey's Trolleys also operates a shuttle service, ferrying riders in a 2¼-mile loop between the Georgia Aquarium and Underground Atlanta. For route and schedule information, call the MARTA number listed above. MARTA can also tell you when special shuttle buses run from downtown to major sports events. MARTA also provides transportation services for persons with disabilities; call ✆ **404/848-5112** for details.

BY CAR It's possible to reach most major Atlanta sites by transit system (MARTA), but a car is preferable, with a few caveats.

Parking isn't usually a problem (though it can be expensive downtown during conventions and sporting events), but traffic often is. (There's even a column in the local newspaper devoted to traffic information and difficulties.) Rush hour—roughly 7 to 9am and 4:30 to 6:30pm—can be vicious, especially when you're traveling into town in the morning or out of town in the afternoon on any of the interstates. Besides the commuter traffic, there are travelers passing through Atlanta on their way to points north, south, east, and west. Atlanta drivers are generally courteous, but they tend to travel at breakneck speeds well above the posted limit, so it's wise to avoid the interstates—especially I-285, which supports a lot of truck traffic—during peak hours.

All of the major car-rental companies are, of course, represented here and are reachable via toll-free numbers. These include **Avis** (✆ **800/331-1212;** www.avis. com/car-rental/avisHome/home.ac), **Budget** (✆ **800/527-0700;** www.budget.com/ budgetWeb/home/home.ex), **Dollar** (✆ **800/800-4000;** www.dollar.com), **Hertz** (✆ **800/654-3131;** www.hertz.com/rentacar/reservation/gaq/index.jsp?bsc=t&target Page=reservationOnHomepage.jsp), and **Thrifty** (✆ **800/367-2277;** www.thrifty.com).

AAA services are available through **AAA Auto Club South,** 4540B Roswell Rd., Atlanta, GA 30342 (✆ **404/843-4500**).

BY TAXI   Atlanta's taxis can be a major problem. Many are dirty, mechanically suspect, and manned by drivers unfamiliar with the city. Be sure the fare is settled before you set off. Fares operate on a set schedule downtown and in Buckhead: a flat rate of $8 for one passenger, $2 each for additional passengers. For all other destinations, a single passenger pays $2.50 for the first ⅛ mile and 25¢ for each additional ⅛ mile. You pay $21 per hour for waiting time and $5 for use of additional space for luggage. Taxis usually cannot be flagged down on the streets, but must be called or be met at major hotels or the airport. One of the most reliable companies is **Yellow Cab Company** (✆ **404/521-0200**). If you have a complaint about taxi service, call ✆ **404/658-7600.**

[FastFACTS] ATLANTA

American Express
There is an American Express Travel Service office at 3384 Peachtree Rd., Lenox Plaza (✆ **404/262-7561**). The office is open Monday to Friday 9am to 5:30pm and Saturday 10am to 4pm.

Babysitters   Friend of the Family (✆ **770/725-2748;** www.afriend.com) is a reliable firm with carefully screened, age-21-and-over sitters, some of whom speak foreign languages. Twenty-four-hour advance notice is recommended, and you may interview a sitter before making a commitment.

Camera Repair   Try **Wolf Camera,** 3141 Piedmont Rd. (✆ **404/869-1116**), open Monday to Friday 9am to 7pm, Saturday 10am to 6pm, and Sunday 12:30 to 5:30pm.

Currency Exchange
There's a currency exchange service at the airport. In the city, downtown major banks provide the service. Try **Bank of America,** 35 Broad St. NW (✆ **404/893-8282**).

Dentists   A free referral service is operated by the **Georgia Dental Association of Atlanta** (✆ **404/636-7553;** www.gadental. org), open Monday to Friday 8am to 5pm.

Doctors   For physician referrals, contact the **Georgia State Medical Board** (✆ **404/656-3913**). See also "Hospitals," below.

Drugstores   They're plentiful around the city. **RiteAid Drugs,** 1512 Piedmont Ave. (✆ **404/876-2263**), is open daily 8am to 10pm.

Emergencies   Call ✆ **911.**

Eyeglasses   LensCrafters, in the Lenox Square Mall, 3400 Woodlake Dr. in Buckhead (✆ **404/239-0784;** www.lenscrafters. com), is open Monday to Saturday from 10am to 9pm and on Sunday from noon to 6pm.

Hospitals   Twenty-four-hour emergency rooms are at the **Atlanta Medical Center,** 303 Parkway Dr. NE (✆ **404/265-4000**), and at **Grady Memorial Hospital,** 80 Jesse Hill Jr. Dr. (✆ **404/616-0600**).

Newspapers & Magazines   The *Atlanta Journal-Constitution* is the major daily newspaper. Others include the *Atlanta Business Chronicle* and the *Atlanta Daily World. Atlanta* magazine is an excellent reference for information on current cultural, entertainment, and sightseeing activities. Other periodicals include *Atlanta Now* and *Where* magazine. The *Southern Voice* serves the gay, lesbian, bisexual, and transsexual community; and *Creative Loafing* is to Atlanta what the *Village Voice* is to New York, with concert, movie, and theater listings—an insider's guide to what is going on in the city.

Post Office   The main post office is Atlanta Post Office, 3900 Crown Rd., Atlanta, GA 30321 (© **404/684-2308** or 800/275-8777 for general information).

Safety   More than 80% of the city's crimes are property crimes, including thefts from parked cars. Purse snatchings and muggings are commonplace, especially after dark. After the business clients leave the downtown and midtown areas, it becomes a venue for drug dealers and hookers. But there is improvement. Since the end of the Olympics, crime in Atlanta has dropped off thanks to a program that features a battalion of Atlanta Ambassadors. They are unarmed security guards—clad in pith helmets and white uniforms—that act as the eyes and ears of the Atlanta police force. Concentrated in the downtown area and paid for by a cooperative association of local business owners, they've gone a long way to discourage crime in downtown Atlanta.

Taxes   In addition to the 7% state sales tax, there is a 7% hotel and motel tax. Combined, they make a significant difference in your final hotel bill.

Toilets   In addition to bus, rail, and air terminals, there are public toilets at Underground Atlanta and at Peachtree Center.

Transit Information   Dial © **404/848-5000.**

Weather   Call © **770/603-3333.**

WHERE TO STAY

B&Bs are available in Atlanta in grand style or in modest houses and are located all over the city. Contact **Bed & Breakfast Atlanta,** 790 North Ave., Ste. 202, Atlanta, GA 30306 (© **800/96-PEACH** [967-3224] or 404/875-0525; www.bedandbreakfast atlanta.com). Rates run $95 to $110 per night, including a continental breakfast, with some exceptional lodgings in the $110-to-$250 range. There's a $5 booking fee, and major credit cards are accepted.

Downtown Atlanta

VERY EXPENSIVE

The Ritz-Carlton Atlanta ★★★   A premier state-of-the-art hotel in the heart of the business district, this is downtown Atlanta's finest, dating from 1984. It has more personal style and glamour than the Atlanta Hilton or Hyatt Regency. Less ostentatious than its Buckhead counterpart, this hotel is more intimately geared to the day-to-day bustle of business-oriented Atlanta. It's richly decorated with silks, tapestries, Persian carpeting, and 18th- and 19th-century paintings. Guest rooms are restful refuges in traditional style, with bay windows and luxurious marble bathrooms. Both the 24th and 25th floors have been set apart as "the Club," where guests enjoy a private lounge with complimentary refreshments and the services of a concierge.

Beyond the clublike, intimate lounge is an elegant dining room, the **Atlanta Grill,** where gourmet lunches and dinners, with a special fitness cuisine menu, are accompanied by piano music. The lobby lounge serves lighter fare.

181 Peachtree St. NE (at Ellis St.), Atlanta, GA 30303. © **800/241-3333** or 404/659-0400. Fax 404/688-0400. www.ritzcarlton.com. 444 units. $289–$339 double; $339–$2,500 suite. AE, DC, DISC, MC, V. Valet parking $29. MARTA: Peachtree Center. **Amenities:** 2 restaurants; bar; babysitting; concierge; exercise room. *In room:* A/C, TV/DVD, hair dryer, minibar, Wi-Fi ($9.95 per day).

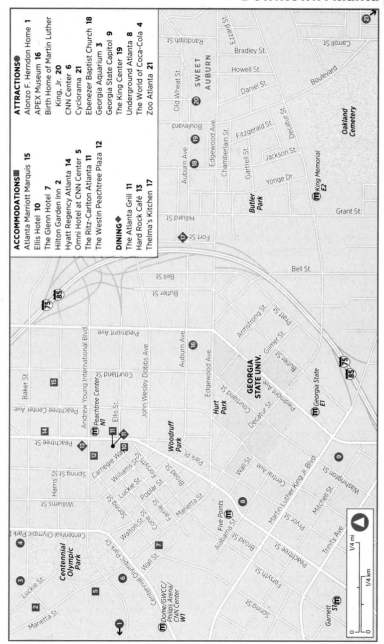

ATTRACTIONS●
Alonzo F. Herndon Home **1**
APEX Museum **16**
Birth Home of Martin Luther King, Jr. **20**
CNN Center **6**
Cyclorama **21**
Ebenezer Baptist Church **18**
Georgia Aquarium **3**
Georgia State Capitol **9**
The King Center **19**
Underground Atlanta **8**
The World of Coca-Cola **4**
Zoo Atlanta **21**

ACCOMMODATIONS■
Atlanta Marriott Marquis **15**
Ellis Hotel **10**
The Glenn Hotel **7**
Hilton Garden Inn **2**
Hyatt Regency Atlanta **14**
Omni Hotel at CNN Center **5**
The Ritz-Carlton Atlanta **11**
The Westin Peachtree Plaza **12**

DINING◆
The Atlanta Grill **11**
Hard Rock Café **13**
Thelma's Kitchen **17**

EXPENSIVE

Atlanta Marriott Marquis ★★   The futuristic design of this Marriott is evident the moment you walk into the seemingly infinite atrium, softened with greenery and sculpture. Fifty stories tall, this hotel rises dramatically toward the sky, and is more luxurious than the Hyatt. The guest rooms are in soothing shades, each with a king-size bed or two doubles. Two of the six club levels feature upgraded rooms, although all of them have club-level privileges. At the garden level is a bevy of restaurants, including a sidewalk cafe. **Allie's American Grille** is casual, with all-American fare, and the **Atrium Express** offers gourmet sandwiches, salads, and soups. There's also a piano bar on this floor, plus a noisy sports bar.

265 Peachtree Center Ave. (btw. Baker and Harris sts.), Atlanta, GA 30303. © **888/855-5701** or 404/521-0000. Fax 404/586-6299. www.marriott.com. 1,757 units. $159–$229 double; from $389 suite. Children 11 and under stay free in parent's room. AE, DC, DISC, MC, V. Parking $28–$32. MARTA: Peachtree Center. **Amenities:** 2 restaurants; 2 bars; babysitting; concierge; exercise room; 2 pools (1 indoor); room service. *In room:* A/C, TV, hair dryer, minibar, Wi-Fi ($13 per day).

Ellis Hotel ★   Like the phoenix, the Ellis Hotel has risen from the ashes (of the legendary Winecoff Hotel in downtown Atlanta). Originally constructed in 1913, the Winecoff was the site of one of the deadliest fires in U.S. history. It was billed as the first "fire-proof" hotel because of its brick construction, but 119 people perished when a fire on the third floor spread through the entire building. The long-awaited redevelopment of this property has turned the landmark into a luxury boutique hotel enhanced by state-of-the-art technology and design. The hotel owners poured $28 million into the restoration, creating sleek and comfortable bedrooms. Guests sit on a balcony overlooking Peachtree Street, Atlanta's "main street."

176 Peachtree St., NW, Atlanta, GA 30303. © **866/455-1154.** Fax 404/525-7872. www.ellishotel.com. 140 units. $179–$199 double; $199–$219 junior suite. AE, MC, V. MARTA: Peachtree Center. Parking: $23. **Amenities:** Restaurant; bar; concierge; exercise room; room service. *In room:* A/C, TV, CD player, hair dryer, Internet (free), minibar, MP3 docking station.

The Glenn Hotel ★★   A historic downtown building at the corner of Spring and Marietta streets has been converted into a beguiling boutique hotel next to the CNN Center. The hotel has become a favorite of everybody from rock stars to visiting dignitaries. For its theme and decor, it borrows from both Manhattan and Miami's South Beach. Modern Southern-inspired furnishings are used throughout, and the rooms are midsize to spacious. A first for Atlanta is the high-rise rooftop alfresco terrace bar (reserved for hotel guests). The ground floor contains the 140-seat **BED Atlanta** restaurant, serving some of the finest food in the downtown area. CNN anchorpeople are often seen dining here. The most luxurious lodging is the Jezebel Penthouse Suite, named after an old Bette Davis movie about the South.

110 Marietta St., NW, Atlanta, GA 30303. © **866/40GLENN** (404-5366) or 404/521-2250. Fax 404/521-2256. www.glennhotel.com. 110 units. $159–$269 double; $209–$359 suite. AE, DC, DISC, MC, V. Parking $27. MARTA: Omni or Dome. **Amenities:** Restaurant; bar; concierge; exercise room; room service. *In room:* A/C, TV, CD player, hair dryer, minibar, Wi-Fi (free).

Hilton Garden Inn ★   Near the Georgia Aquarium, this first-class hotel is part of the Legacy Property Group and a showcase of their mixed-use Park Pavilion, encompassing a complex of restaurants, retail space, and parking. At the crossroads of Centennial Olympic Park, the hotel draws a great deal of traffic from nonguests patronizing its dining facilities, which include the Sky Bar and Restaurant with spectacular views, plus an American grill, and, the chief draw, a Boston-like seafood restaurant and oyster bar. The midsize guest rooms are first-rate, with streamlined furnishings and extremely comfortable beds.

275 Baker St., Atlanta, GA 30313. ℭ **404/577-2001.** Fax 404/577-2002. www.hiltongardeninn.com. 242 units. $149–$279 double. AE, DC, MC, V. Parking $18–$24. MARTA: Omni/Dome/GWCC. **Amenities:** Restaurant; 2 bars; concierge; exercise room; room service. *In room:* A/C, TV, fridge, hair dryer, Internet (free).

Hyatt Regency Atlanta ★★   The first of Atlanta's superhotels, the Hyatt—flanked by two 23-story towers and standing near the Atlanta Mart—launched the chain's atrium look in 1967 when it was first designed by noted architect John Portman. The most desirable rooms are the posh executive rooms on the 21st and 22nd floors of the main building. Expense-account junkies like the rooms in the 24-floor International Tower overlooking the atrium and opening onto panoramic views of Atlanta. Guests are also accommodated in the 22-floor Radius Tower. At lobby level is the hotel's bistro-style restaurant, **Avanzare Steaks.**

265 Peachtree St. NE (btw. Baker and Harris sts.), Atlanta, GA 30303. ℭ **800/233-1234** or 404/577-1234. Fax 404/588-4137. http://atlantaregency.hyatt.com. 1,260 units. $109–$229 double; $159–$249 suite. Children 18 and under stay free in parent's room. AE, DC, DISC, MC, V. Parking $27. MARTA: Peachtree Center. **Amenities:** Restaurant; bar; concierge; exercise room; large outdoor pool; room service. *In room:* A/C, TV/DVD, hair dryer, minibar, Wi-Fi ($13 in rooms; free in suites).

Omni Hotel at CNN Center ★   Next to the Georgia World Congress Center and the Philips Arena (since 1999 the sports home of the NBA Atlanta Hawks and the NHL Atlanta Thrashers), this 15-story modernistic megastructure houses CNN headquarters. In its way, it's the most anonymous hotel in Atlanta, designed as part of a huge commercial complex that disguises the fact it is a hotel at all. Its soaring, marble-covered, split-level lobby and tastefully luxurious guest rooms send a contemporary message. Glass elevators climb to the top floors, where some rooms have balconies overlooking the lobby. The well-furnished guest rooms have well-maintained bathrooms. A VIP floor for the ultimate in luxury and service attracts CNN newshounds.

100 CNN Center (at Techwood Dr. and Marietta St.), Atlanta, GA 30335. ℭ **888/444-6664** or 404/659-0000. Fax 404/525-5050. www.omnihotels.com. 1,070 units. $159–$379 double; from $775 suite. AE, DC, DISC, MC, V. Parking $30. MARTA: Omni. **Amenities:** Restaurant; bar; concierge; outdoor pool; room service. *In room:* A/C, TV, hair dryer, minibar, Wi-Fi ($9.95 per day).

The Westin Peachtree Plaza ★★   Atlanta's most famous contemporary hotel is also the tallest, with 73 soaring floors. A bank of 18 elevators will carry you to the roof with its revolving restaurant, a grand spectacle for a special evening on the town. If you're not afraid of heights, you'll reach your room in a glass elevator that goes up the side of the building. Try to get a room high up, as the view becomes panoramic. Executive Club rooms are the most desirable; color-coordinated fabrics, light-wood furniture, and well-designed contemporary bathrooms add to the lavish ambience.

A refined American cuisine is served at the **Sun Dial Restaurant,** where a 360-degree cityscape comes into view. Three ground-level bars dispense potent libations.

210 Peachtree St. NE (at International Blvd.), Atlanta, GA 30303. ℭ **800/937-8461** or 404/659-1400. Fax 404/589-7424. www.starwoodhotels.com. 1,068 units. $115–$295 double; from $400 suite. Children 17 and under stay free in parent's room. AE, DC, DISC, MC, V. Valet parking $30; self-parking $23. MARTA: Peachtree Center. **Amenities:** 2 restaurants; 2 bars; concierge; exercise room; 2 pools (1 indoor); room service. *In room:* A/C, TV, hair dryer, minibar, Wi-Fi ($15 per day).

Midtown Atlanta

VERY EXPENSIVE

Four Seasons Hotel Atlanta ★★★ ☺ It's as opulent and plush as its nearest rival, the Buckhead branch of the Ritz-Carlton, but to its growing legion of fans, the Four Seasons is even better, with a midtown location that's increasingly favored as a venue for hip Atlantans. It occupies the bottom 19 floors of a granite-sheathed tower that soars 53 floors above midtown Atlanta—the upper floors contain private, and very upscale, condominiums. Managed by the Four Seasons chain, it has the most attentive and sophisticated staff, and the most impressive and dramatic lobby, of any hotel in Georgia. Guest rooms are as plush as you'd expect from this top-notch chain, each room with marble trim, ultracomfortable chaise longues, and all the electronic extras you'll need to conduct business or enjoy a holiday away from home. This is one of the most welcoming hotels for families with children in Atlanta, with a special program that includes cookies and milk upon check-in.

75 14th St. (btw. Peachtree and W. Peachtree sts.), Atlanta, GA 30309. ✆ **800/819-5053** or 404/881-9898. Fax 404/873-4692. www.fourseasons.com. 244 units. $300–$500 double; from $650 suite. Discounts available. Children 15 and under stay free in parent's room. AE, DC, DISC, MC, V. Parking $30. MARTA: Arts Center. **Amenities:** Restaurant, Park 75 (see review, p. 378); bar; babysitting; concierge; state-of-the-art health club; Olympic-size indoor pool; room service. *In room:* A/C, TV/DVD, CD player, hair dryer, minibar, Wi-Fi ($13 per day).

EXPENSIVE

Indigo ★ 🎁 This boutique hotel has been so stylishly redesigned that it's completely wiped away its former role as a Days Inn, except for the cramped bathrooms. It is the most pet friendly in Georgia, with special services for those who arrive with their animal companions. In summer, portions of the martini sales from a Canine Cocktail Hour are donated to local animal care causes. Directly across from the historic Fox Theatre, the hotel offers midsize and beautifully furnished guest rooms, with hardwood floors and oversize beds, along with high-quality linens and cozy duvets.

683 Peachtree St. (btw. Third St. and Ponce de Leon Ave.), Atlanta, GA 30308. ✆ **404/8INDIGO** (846-3446). Fax 404/873-4245. www.ichotelgroup.com. 139 units. $169–$319 double. AE, DC, DISC, MC, V. Self-parking $18. MARTA: North Ave. **Amenities:** Restaurant; bar; exercise center. *In room:* A/C, TV, hair dryer, Wi-Fi (free).

Shellmont Inn ★ Named after the carved seashell adorning the front of this elaborate Victorian from 1891, the Shellmont is a stylish and historically authentic period house, with wicker-laden verandas. Elaborate restoration has filled it with discreetly concealed modern luxuries as well as a historically appropriate collection of Oriental carpets; stained, leaded, and beveled glass; hand-painted stenciling; wall coverings and draperies; furnishings; fresh flowers; and 1890s accessories. Only breakfast is served, featuring seasonal specialties. From the back garden, where there are verandas and a fishpond, you'll swear you're in a small town in the Georgia countryside. The largest guest room is the suite, originally conceived as the servants' quarters.

821 Piedmont Ave. NE (at 6th St.), Atlanta, GA 30308. ✆ **404/872-9290.** Fax 404/872-5379. http://shellmont.com. 5 units. $175–$250 double; $225–$275 suite; $245–$350 cottage. Rates include full breakfast. AE, DC, DISC, MC, V. Free parking. MARTA: North Ave. or Midtown. **Amenities:** Breakfast room; concierge. *In room:* A/C, TV/DVD, hair dryer, Wi-Fi (free).

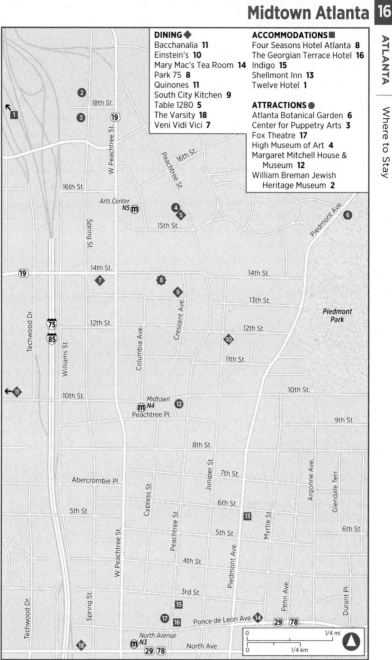

DINING ◆
Bacchanalia **11**
Einstein's **10**
Mary Mac's Tea Room **14**
Park 75 **8**
Quinones **11**
South City Kitchen **9**
Table 1280 **5**
The Varsity **18**
Veni Vidi Vici **7**

ACCOMMODATIONS ■
Four Seasons Hotel Atlanta **8**
The Georgian Terrace Hotel **16**
Indigo **15**
Shellmont Inn **13**
Twelve Hotel **1**

ATTRACTIONS ●
Atlanta Botanical Garden **6**
Center for Puppetry Arts **3**
Fox Theatre **17**
High Museum of Art **4**
Margaret Mitchell House &
  Museum **12**
William Breman Jewish
  Heritage Museum **2**

Twelve Hotel ★★ This all-suite luxury boutique hotel is in Atlantic Station, the largest live/work/play "village" in the Southeast. It's like living in a modern luxury condo, with the concrete and high ceilings in the bedrooms evoking an urban loftlike aura. Track lighting, elegantly comfortable beds, in-room computers, sleek furnishings, and marble counters are grace notes. The hotel has a high-tech system it calls "Ghost" (Guest Hotel Operating System Terminal), which lets you call room service, the maid, or the concierge desk; order a car from the valet service; and a lot more. On-site is the finest restaurant at Atlantic Station, **Lobby at Twelve** (*☎* **404/961-7370**), which is known for its regional Southern cuisine.

361 17th St., Atlanta, GA 30363. *☎* **404/961-1212.** Fax 404/961-1221. www.twelvehotels.com. 102 units. $169–$229 1-bedroom suite; $259–$399 2-bedroom suite. AE, MC, V. Valet parking $25. MARTA: Arts Station, then free shuttle to Atlantic Station. **Amenities:** Restaurant; bar; concierge; exercise room; outdoor pool. *In room:* A/C, TV, hair dryer, kitchenette, Wi-Fi (free).

MODERATE

The Georgian Terrace Hotel ★★ ☺ An Atlanta landmark since 1911, this fabled hotel dodged the wrecking ball and was beautifully restored in 2001. It now receives guests as it did in 1939 when Clark Gable and Vivien Leigh stayed here to attend the premiere of *Gone With the Wind* at the Fox Theatre across the street. Listed on the National Register of Historic Places, the hotel is graced with soaring pillars, French windows, and marble floors. The guest rooms have been modernized in grand comfort, with elegant furnishings, and queen-size "Dream Beds" with crisp white European-style duvet covers. The luxury suites are among the best in town; otherwise, the finest rooms are on the two club floors. The staff caters to children, with such extras as video games. Other options are studios (the smallest) or else two- or three-bedroom suites, the latter with kitchens and washers/dryers.

659 Peachtree St. (north of Ponce de Leon Ave.), Atlanta, GA 30308. *☎* **800/651-2316** or 404/897-1991. Fax 404/724-0642. www.thegeorgianterrace.com. 318 units. $139–$179 1-bedroom suite; $209–$649 2-bedroom suite; $339 3-bedroom suite. AE, DC, DISC, MC, V. Valet parking $30; self-parking $25. MARTA: North Ave. **Amenities:** Restaurant; bar; exercise room; room service. *In room:* A/C, TV, hair dryer, kitchenette, Wi-Fi (free).

Buckhead
VERY EXPENSIVE

Grand Hyatt Atlanta ★★ This is one of the most distinctive hotels in Atlanta, an award-winning combination of bold postmodern and Chippendale, with attention paid to aesthetic detailing. Grand Hyatt is a striking 24-story monolith with a massive motor entrance that some visitors compare to a set design for *The Wizard of Oz*.

The **Cassis** restaurant is international in scope, specializing in a range of food that covers all shores of the Mediterranean. English-style afternoon teas are served in the lobby, and a jazz trio sometimes entertains in the bar.

3300 Peachtree Rd., Atlanta, GA 30305. *☎* **800/233-1234** or 404/237-1234. Fax 404/504-2576. http://grandatlanta.hyatt.com. 438 units. $329–$399 double; from $429 suite. AE, DC, DISC, MC, V. Parking $17–$30. MARTA: Buckhead. **Amenities:** 2 restaurants; bar; babysitting; concierge; outdoor pool; room service. *In room:* A/C, TV, hair dryer, minibar, Wi-Fi ($9.95 per day).

Ritz-Carlton Buckhead ★★★ The Ritz-Carlton is the most sumptuous and elegant hotel in Atlanta. A 22-story tower soaring above Buckhead, it's awash in oiled paneling, tapestries, marble and hardwood, theatrical bouquets of spotlighted flowers, antiques, and a museum's worth of valuable paintings. It's been likened to Claridge's in London. The staff is artful, polite, soft-spoken, and efficient.

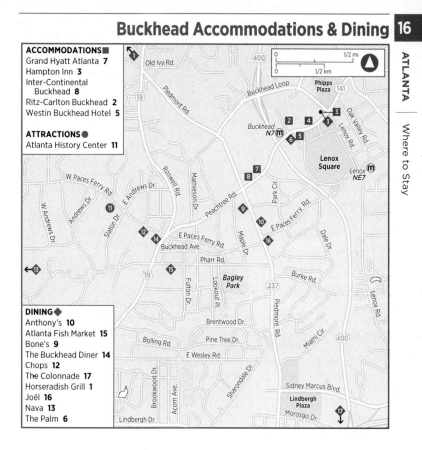

ACCOMMODATIONS■
Grand Hyatt Atlanta **7**
Hampton Inn **3**
Inter-Continental
 Buckhead **8**
Ritz-Carlton Buckhead **2**
Westin Buckhead Hotel **5**

ATTRACTIONS●
Atlanta History Center **11**

DINING◆
Anthony's **10**
Atlanta Fish Market **15**
Bone's **9**
The Buckhead Diner **14**
Chops **12**
The Colonnade **17**
Horseradish Grill **1**
Joël **16**
Nava **13**
The Palm **6**

The **Dining Room** is one of the most sought-after restaurants in Atlanta. There's also a deli with an attendant espresso bar, and both a cafe and a bar with a frequently blazing fireplace.

3434 Peachtree Rd. NE, Atlanta, GA 30326. ℭ **800/241-3333** or 404/237-2700. Fax 404/239-0078. www.ritzcarlton.com. 517 units. $319–$389 double; from $389 suite. AE, DC, DISC, MC, V. Parking $30. MARTA: Buckhead. **Amenities:** 3 restaurants; bar; babysitting; concierge; exercise room; indoor pool; room service. *In room:* A/C, TV/DVD, hair dryer, minibar, Wi-Fi ($13 per day).

Westin Buckhead Hotel ★★ Here's a hotel that would ordinarily stand head and shoulders above the others. But in Buckhead, the Westin is hard-pressed to keep up with the Joneses—in this case, the Ritz-Carlton. Still, it's first-class all the way, and the European-feel guest rooms and suites are the largest in Buckhead. The marble bathrooms feature oversize tubs and makeup and shaving mirrors. The suites are especially luxurious, with VCRs and glass-block bathing areas; the presidential suite houses a fireplace and a terrace with a Jacuzzi.

The **Palm** (see "Where to Dine," later in this chapter) is patterned after the famous all-American steakhouse, the Palm Restaurant, launched in New York in 1926.

3391 Peachtree Rd. NE (btw. Lenox and Piedmont roads), Atlanta, GA 30326. © **800/253-1397** or 404/365-0065. Fax 404/365-8787. www.starwoodhotels.com. 376 units. $244–$459 double; from $549 suite. Children 17 and under stay free in parent's room. AE, DC, DISC, MC, V. Valet parking $30. MARTA: Lenox. **Amenities:** Restaurant; bar; concierge; well-equipped health club; room service; spa. *In room:* A/C, TV/DVD, hair dryer, minibar, Wi-Fi ($11 per day).

EXPENSIVE

Inter-Continental Buckhead ★★★   International flair and Southern hospitality meet in the elliptical three-story lobby of this deluxe hotel. Traditional decor is given a modern twist, with hardwood floors and Italian marble laid in puzzlelike patterns. Bedrooms are midsize to spacious and come in a wide variety of offerings, including standard, double, or single-bed rooms, or executive suites. Furnishings are sleek, streamlined, and immensely comfortable. Nonguests like to come here to patronize the hotel's very-Parisian, 24-hour restaurant, **Au Pied de Cochon.** The signature dish, roasted pigs' feet with béarnaise sauce, is evocative of the old Les Halles in Paris.

3315 Peachtree Rd., NE, Atlanta, GA 30326. © **404/946-9000.** Fax 404/946-9001. www.ichotels group.com/intercontinental/en/gb/locations/atlanta. 422 units. $171–$294 double; from $570 suite. AE, DC, MC, V. Parking $20–$30. MARTA: Buckhead. **Amenities:** Restaurant; 2 bars; state-of-the-art health club; indoor pool; room service. *In room:* A/C, TV/DVD player, hair dryer, minibar, Wi-Fi ($13 per day).

The Mansion on Peachtree ★★★   The skyline of Buckhead is forever altered by this slender 42-story, eight-sided tower designed by the noted American architect Robert Stern. An ultraluxury hotel and development, it offers 127 elegant and spacious guest rooms alongside 45 residential units. Luxury is the theme here, with guest rooms featuring marble bathrooms, plush furnishings, and French doors opening onto private balconies. In the tower is an 80-seat restaurant serving haute cuisine and complemented by a library/lounge bar. A specialty restaurant occupies a separate mansion fronting Peachtree Street. The spa with its outdoor relaxation deck and lap pool is the finest facility in an Atlanta hotel.

3376 Peachtree Rd., Atlanta, GA 30326. © **404/995-7500.** Fax 404/995-7501. www.rwmansionon peachtree.com. 127 units. $209–$429 double; from $599 suite. AE, DC, MC, V. Parking $30. MARTA: Buckhead. **Amenities:** 2 restaurants; 2 bars; concierge; state-of-the-art health club; room service; spa. *In room:* A/C, TV/DVD, CD player, hair dryer, minibar, Wi-Fi ($9.95 per day).

INEXPENSIVE

Hampton Inn   This hotel is no better than most standard Hampton Inns—it's strictly chain format. But what makes it special are its price and location in upscale Buckhead. Staying in this neighborhood and living well for a reasonable tab brightens the glow of this place. Guest rooms are medium in size and come with all the usual Hampton Inn equipment such as free newspapers. The hotel has a pool and can arrange temporary visits to a nearby health club. An adjacent restaurant is open daily from 11am to 11pm.

3398 Piedmont Rd. NE, Atlanta, GA 30305. © **800/426-7866** or 404/233-5656. Fax 404/237-4688. http://hamptoninn.hilton.com. 154 units. $129–$169 double. Children 17 and under stay free in parent's room. Rates include full breakfast. AE, DC, DISC, MC, V. MARTA: Lindbergh. **Amenities:** Breakfast room; outdoor pool. *In room:* A/C, TV, hair dryer, Internet (free).

Virginia-Highland

1890 King-Keith House Bed & Breakfast ★★ 📖   One of Atlanta's most photographed houses, King-Keith House is on the National Register of Historic Places. This Queen Anne–style house dates from 1890, when it was constructed by hardware

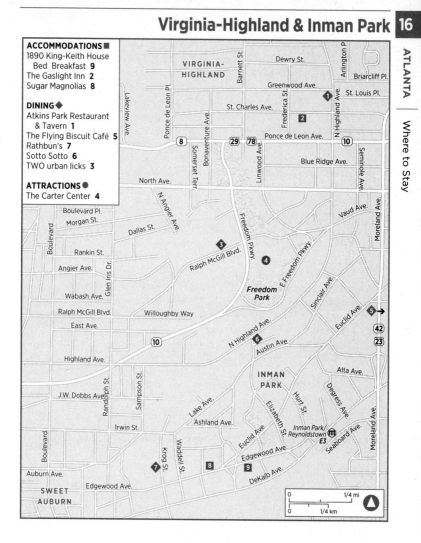

ACCOMMODATIONS ■
1890 King-Keith House
  Bed Breakfast 9
The Gaslight Inn 2
Sugar Magnolias 8

DINING ◆
Atkins Park Restaurant
  & Tavern 1
The Flying Biscuit Café 5
Rathbun's 7
Sotto Sotto 6
TWO urban licks 3

ATTRACTIONS ●
The Carter Center 4

magnate George King. The guest rooms are beautifully furnished, generally with antiques, and the 12-foot ceilings and carved fireplaces evoke oak-shaded Inman Park of another time. Rooms are spacious, each with a private bathroom, although two are in the hallway but not shared with other guests. The best rooms here are the downstairs suite with a Jacuzzi, private sitting room, and stained-glass and Empire furnishings, and the cottage out back, with its vaulted ceilings. It, too, has a Jacuzzi for two and is ideal for a honeymoon or a getaway. Guests also enjoy the inn's private gardens.

889 Edgewood Ave. NE, Atlanta, GA 30307. ✆ **800/728-3879** or 404/688-7330. Fax 404/584-8408. www.kingkeith.com. 6 units, including separate cottage. $120–$240 double. Rates include breakfast. AE, DISC, MC, V. Free parking. MARTA: Inman Park. **Amenities:** Breakfast room. *In room:* A/C, TV, hair dryer, Wi-Fi (free).

The Gaslight Inn ★★ 🎁 The most appealing B&B in Virginia-Highland is this 1913 Craftsman-style house that's set above a steeply sloping front garden, behind a commodious front porch. In the 1990s, it was enlarged and renovated, and a well-proportioned annex was added, separated from the main house by a garden illuminated by flickering gas-fired lanterns. Guest rooms, especially the suites, are outfitted like private apartments. Four of the six contain working kitchens; the remaining two have access to a kitchen right outside their doors. Breakfast is a high point of the day here: It's served in an early-20th-century dining room accented with a Craftsman-style fireplace and fine paintings. Morning coffee and afternoon wine are offered by the staff, as well as information about attractions and diversions.

1001 St. Charles Ave., Atlanta, GA 30306. ✆ **404/875-1001.** Fax 404/876-1001. www.gaslightinn.com. 8 units. $115–$165 double; $169–$235 suite. Rates include continental breakfast. AE, DC, DISC, MC, V. Free parking. Bus: 2 (Ponce) or 16 (Noble). **Amenities:** Breakfast room. *In room:* A/C, TV, hair dryer, Wi-Fi (in some; free).

Sugar Magnolia ★ 🎁 In a historic district of Atlanta, this 1892 Victorian house was originally constructed by a Southern colonel but was turned into a B&B of charm and beauty by its owners, Jim Emshoff and Debi Starnes. The oasis lives up to its name, with a three-story turret, six fireplaces, oval beveled windows, hand-painted plasterwork, and a grand staircase fit for an entrance by Scarlett O'Hara. A nonsmoking house, the inn rents individually styled and commodious guest rooms, including one called the Royal Suite, with a king-size brass bed in a curtained alcove and a rooftop deck with a waterfall garden. The cottage suite has a fully equipped galley kitchen and a vaulted ceiling with skylight, along with a Jacuzzi and open-loft bedroom with a double bed. The delightful Aviary guest room is furnished with antiques and a fireplace, and this seven-sided room has a painted ceiling of clouds and birds.

804 Edgewood Ave. NE, Atlanta, GA 30307. ✆ **404/222-0226.** Fax 404/681-1067. www.sugarmagnolia bb.com. 4 units. $120–$140 double; $150–$160 suite. Rates include full continental breakfast. MC, V. MARTA: Inman Park. **Amenities:** Breakfast room. *In room:* A/C, .TV, hair dryer, Wi-Fi (free).

Stone Mountain

Marriott Stone Mountain Park Inn ★ ☺ This low-rise, neocolonial inn was originally built in 1965 for visitors interested in staying as close as possible to the massive bas-reliefs of Stone Mountain's northern face. Set inside the park boundaries, about 16 miles east of the city, it offers guest rooms outfitted with reproductions of 18th-century country furniture. Don't expect a mountain view: Many guest rooms overlook the forest or the hotel's inner courtyard, and you must stand on the plantation-style front porch to catch a glimpse of the laser-light show illuminating the mountain. Views are even better from the hotel's lawns, and better still across the highway. The in-house restaurant, the **Mountain View,** features a revolving series of all-you-can-eat buffets. This is an especially good choice for families, who can enjoy the many recreational opportunities of the park.

1058 Robert E. Lee Dr., Stone Mountain Park, Stone Mountain, GA 30083. ✆ **800/228-9290** or 770/469-3311. Fax 770/876-5009. www.marriott.com. 92 units. $139–$259 double. AE, DC, DISC, MC, V. Parking free at the hotel, but a $10 fee for parking and entering Stone Mountain Park. **Amenities:** Restaurant; bar; 18-hole golf course; exercise room; outdoor pool. *In room:* A/C, TV, fridge, hair dryer, Wi-Fi ($13 per day).

Decatur

Emory Inn ★ 🎁 Owned by Emory University, this hotel lies east of midtown and Buckhead, a 10-minute drive from the center of activity. It's also close to the famous

Centers for Disease Control and Prevention. You'll think you're in the country: The inn lies in a secluded corner of the university grounds tucked away among trees. Guest rooms are handsomely and comfortably furnished. Guests can explore walking trails at the nearby Hahn Woods Nature Preserve.

1641 Clifton Rd. NE (btw. Briarcliff and N. Decatur roads), Atlanta, GA 30329. ✆ **800/933-6679** or 404/712-6000. Fax 404/712-6235. www.emoryconferencecenter.com. 107 units. $149 double. Rate includes continental breakfast. AE, DC, DISC, MC, V. Free parking. Bus: 6. **Amenities:** Restaurant; health club (on campus); heated indoor pool (on campus); outdoor pool; 12 tennis courts (lit); Wi-Fi (free). *In room:* A/C, TV, hair dryer.

Palmetto

Serenbe Bed & Breakfast ★★ ☺
Only 32 miles south of Atlanta, Steven and Marie Nygren's inn lies on a 350-acre farmstead, where you can hand-feed the cows and chickens, fish from a lake, or top off a perfect day with a moonlit canoe ride. For families with children, it is a total delight, complete with marshmallow roasts at a bonfire. The house itself is nearly a century old. Each handsomely furnished guest room comes with a private bathroom, one with a Jacuzzi tub. Rag rugs, knotty pine floors, beds piled high with decorative pillows, and lace curtains at the windows make it ultrahomey. You can also rent a two-bedroom cottage with its own kitchen and living room. Guests enjoy a full country breakfast complete with such delights as fried green tomatoes, cheese grits, and homemade biscuits.

10950 Hutcheson Ferry Rd., Palmetto, GA 30268. ✆ **770/463-2610.** Fax 770/463-4472. www.serenbe. com. 18 units, 1 cottage. $130–$255 double; $360–$380 cottage. Rates include farm breakfast. No credit cards. Free parking. Call for directions. **Amenities:** Babysitting; bike rentals; outdoor pool. *In room:* A/C, TV, hair dryer, Wi-Fi (in some; free).

WHERE TO DINE

Underground Atlanta, bounded by Peachtree, Wall, Alabama, Pryor, and Central streets and by Martin Luther King Jr. Drive (✆ **404/523-2311;** www.underground-atlanta.com; see "Attractions," later in this chapter), is home to a dozen "food courts" and nightclubs centered around Kenny's Alley, most open nightly until midnight.

Downtown

EXPENSIVE

The Atlanta Grill ★★ STEAKS Stylish, well organized, and urbane, this downtown Atlanta steakhouse evokes some of the Southern charm of New Orleans, thanks to an elaborate iron balcony that juts over the sidewalk of one of the busiest sections of Peachtree Street. Inside, flickering gas lanterns and photos of Old Atlanta's political and debutante parties usually evoke dialogues from the most taciturn of local residents. Although meals here are impeccable, this is not a fine-dining enclave. Instead, the hotel that contains it refers to it as a steakhouse with extremely refined service rituals, leaving the culinary finesse to the restaurant within the Ritz-Carlton in Buckhead instead. Menu items include cuts of juicy steak, prime beef, lobster macaroni with cheese, and buttermilk-marinated fried green tomatoes. For lunch you might begin with a mint julep soup made with chilled Georgia peaches or else a seared crab cake. At night, the menu expands with such Southern-influenced dishes as molasses-grilled pork tenderloin, or tomato stone-ground grits cake with baby summer squash.

In the Ritz-Carlton, 181 Peachtree St., Atlanta. ℭ **404/659-0400.** www.ritzcarlton.com. Reservations recommended. Main courses $25–$53. AE, DC, MC, V. Restaurant daily 11:30am–2:30pm and 5:30–10pm. Bar daily 3pm–1am. MARTA: Peachtree Center.

MODERATE

Hard Rock Cafe AMERICAN   This enduring favorite can still pack 'em in on a good night. The music is loud and raucous, the hamburgers aren't bad, and the banana splits evoke those halcyon days of James Dean and Marilyn Monroe.

215 Peachtree St. NE (at International Blvd.). ℭ **404/688-7625.** www.hardrockcafe.com. Reservations not accepted. Main courses $9–$29. AE, DC, DISC, MC, V. Sun–Thurs 11am–midnight; Fri–Sat 11am–1am. MARTA: Peachtree Center.

Midtown

VERY EXPENSIVE

Quinones ★★★ MODERN SOUTHERN   You may—just may—have your best gourmet experience in Atlanta at this little 36-seat dining room below its sibling restaurant, Bacchanalia (see below). One of the finest dining experiences in town, it's expensive but worth it. Owners Anne Quatrano and Clifford Harrison offer an ever-changing 10-course tasting menu, based on market-fresh ingredients. Against a backdrop of antique mirrors, hand-blown Venetian glass chandeliers, and plush furniture, guests enjoy an innovative re-creation of classic dishes using farm-fresh produce, including local fish and poultry, along with the choicest cuts of meat.

1198 Howell Mill Rd. ℭ **404/365-0410.** www.starprovisions.com. Reservations required. Fixed-price 10-course menu $125, with wine pairings $195. AE, MC, V. Fri–Sat 6–9:30pm. Closed Christmas Eve to New Year's Eve and 2 weeks in summer. MARTA: Midtown.

EXPENSIVE

Bacchanalia ★★ CONTEMPORARY AMERICAN   Posh, upscale, and artfully contrived to appeal to the entertainment needs of Atlanta's thousands of upscale consumers, this establishment combines a stylish and sought-after restaurant with a series of boutique-style food shops. The setting, in what was built in the 1920s as a meatpacking plant, is an unlikely spot for Anne Quatrano and Clifford Harrison's fine dining, brought all the way from the California Culinary Academy. Portions are small in size but big on flavor. Try the Kumamoto oysters on the half shell from Washington State, or the sautéed veal sweetbreads with braised baby artichokes. Full-flavored main courses, inspired by what looks good at the market and by the whims of the chef, include sautéed turbot with baby red kale, pan-seared breast of duck with caramelized apples and turnips, and braised short ribs of Kobe beef with a potato purée. Save room for dessert, especially the blood orange and rosemary soup with a sheep's milk yogurt sorbet, or the ginger soufflé given added zest by a lemon sauce.

1198 Howell Mill Rd. ℭ **404/365-0410.** www.starprovisions.com. Reservations recommended. Main courses $12–$16; fixed-price 4-course dinner $75. AE, DC, MC, V. Mon–Sat 6–10pm. MARTA: 10th St.

Park 75 ★★★ NEW AMERICAN   It's chic, it's sexy, and the food that's dished up by the international staff is among the very best in the Southeast. Come here for an insight into the New American cuisine that the Four Seasons chain is promoting with verve, and for a meal you're likely to remember long after it's finished. The setting evokes a dignified-looking pavilion where subtle depictions of lattices and garden ornaments don't interfere with the visual appeal of absolutely superb cuisine. Fish and meats are combined into artful and unexpected combinations that, while sophisticated, never dip into the purely experimental. Menus and wines change frequently and seasonally. Depending on when you arrive, offerings might include a carpaccio of Kobe beef with juniper-flavored foie gras and braised arugula, a succulent version of loin of lamb with *cèpe* mushrooms and golden tomatoes, and roasted free-range chicken baked with Oregon truffles. The fixed-price menus come in both vegetarian and meat-based versions.

In the Four Seasons Hotel Atlanta, 75 14th St. (btw. Peachtree and W. Peachtree sts.). ℂ 404/253-3853. www.fourseasons.com/atlanta. Reservations recommended. Main courses $28–$52; 3–4 course fixed-price dinner $65–$100. AE, DC, DISC, MC, V. Mon–Sat 11:30am–2pm and Tues–Sat 6–10pm. MARTA: Arts Center.

Table 1280 ★★ INTERNATIONAL   Part of the Renzo Piano extension to the Woodruff Arts Center, this popular choice has elegant minimalism in two soaring rooms with striking art installations. At night it seems to glow like an aquarium. It's not just the dramatic setting but the finely honed cuisine that lures serious foodies. The menu bursts with freshness and originality, beginning with such starters as snapper seviche with watermelon or sweet corn soup with a black-pepper crème fraîche. Main courses are often surprising delicacies such as Magret duck breast with braised pork belly or sirloin of lamb with an Israeli couscous salad. One dessert inspired by Southern cooking is corn-bread pudding with black-pepper ice cream. You can also patronize a Tapas Lounge serving a variety of fresh small plates.

At Woodruff Arts Center, 1280 Peachtree St. NE. ℂ 404/897-1280. www.table1280.com. Reservations required. Main courses $21–$28. AE, MC, V. Tues–Fri 11am–3pm; Tues–Thurs 5–9:30pm; Fri–Sat 5–10:30pm. MARTA: Arts Center.

MODERATE

Veni Vidi Vici ★★ ITALIAN   Hailed by everyone from *Wine Spectator* to *Gourmet* magazine, this is a creative citadel of a finely honed Italian cuisine. Executive chef Jamie Adams has an extraordinary palate and knows how to bring authentic Italian flavors to American plates, partly by using impeccably market-fresh ingredients. Among the selection of appetizers, our favorite is the crispy Maine calamari with lemon and capers in a tangy tomato aioli. Adams also serves a baked stuffed Vidalia onion with Scamorza cheese. The handmade pasta dishes are truly succulent: The Italian-style linguine, served with a traditional white clam sauce, is the best we've ever had in Atlanta. We gravitate to the rotisserie-meat dishes prepared in the exhibition rotisserie kitchen, including the duck served with beans and sautéed spinach.

41 14th St. (btw. E. Peachtree and Spring sts.). ℂ 404/875-8424. www.buckheadrestaurants.com. Reservations recommended. Main courses $12–$18 lunch, $21–$34 dinner. AE, DC, DISC, MC, V. Mon–Thurs 11:30am–10pm; Fri 11:30am–11pm; Sat 5–11pm; Sun 5–10pm. MARTA: Arts Center.

INEXPENSIVE

Einstein's AMERICAN   The setting of this place is a clapboard-sided bungalow (ca. 1904) on a quiet street of midtown, close to some of the neighborhood's tallest towers. Partly because the owner is the godson of the late physicist and partly because scientists appreciate their nuances, you're likely to see several of Einstein's equations decorating blackboards near the bar, sometimes misstated in ways that, during our visit, provoked lots of arguments among this restaurant's clients. You can dine inside, in a woodsy-looking bar, or outside, on an open-air front terrace, elbow to elbow with many other residents of this rather liberal neighborhood. The food is well prepared and tasty without being spectacular. Try the grilled pork chop with a pepper and cream sauce, or freshly prepared filet of salmon with a savory barbecue pepper sauce. A signature dish is Einstein's shrimp with a mustard sauce enhanced by mango and orange.

1077 Juniper St. (C) **404/876-7925.** www.einsteinsatlanta.com. Reservations recommended. Sandwiches and burgers $5–$13; main courses $9–$28. AE, DC, DISC, MC, V. Mon–Thurs 11am–11pm; Fri 11am–midnight; Sat 9am–midnight; Sun 9am–11pm. MARTA: Midtown.

Mary Mac's Tea Room ★ ☺ SOUTHERN   This landmark follows the tradition of "Southern hospitality with damn Yankee efficiency," a slogan launched in 1945. In a midtown storefront, some 2,000 hungry diners, including lots of families and local politicos, are served daily. Since Jimmy Carter used to drop in for lunch, it's always been a tradition that governors visit for meals. The food is fine if you like the slightly overcooked down-home Southern style. The fried chicken and country ham are really good here, as are the fresh but long-cooked vegetables and the straight-from-the-oven breads. Your best bet might be a sautéed rainbow trout from the North Georgia mountains. For dessert, who would order anything but the fresh peach cobbler made with Georgia peaches?

224 Ponce de Leon Ave. NE (at Myrtle St.). (C) **404/876-1800.** www.marymacs.com. Reservations required for 10 or more. Main courses $9.45–$18. AE, DISC, MC, V. Daily 11am–9pm. MARTA: North Ave.

South City Kitchen NEW SOUTHERN   Although many critics have found its new-style Southern cookery inconsistent, most Atlantans salute this choice in a renovated two-story building. Fireplaces on both floors burn on nippy nights to make it cozy and inviting. If the weather's fair, patio dining is possible. Try the buttermilk-fried chicken or the sautéed scallops and shrimp over creamy, stone-ground grits. The secret of South City's pork chops is that they're apple-smoked, making them a real winner. Also good are the shredded barbecue pork on jalapeño bread and the corn bread with creamy lump crab. The grilled swordfish on a bed of homemade grits with Monterey Jack cheese left us cold, but a taste of pork porterhouse with grilled apples, parsnips, and pepper jelly warmed our souls.

1144 Crescent Ave. NE (btw. 13th and 14th sts.). (C) **404/873-7358.** www.southcitykitchen.com. Reservations recommended. Main courses $16–$29; Sun brunch $8–$17. MC, V. Mon–Thurs 11am–3:30pm and 5–10pm; Fri–Sat 11am–3:30pm and 5–10:30pm; Sun 11am–3:30pm (brunch) and 5–10pm. MARTA: Arts Center or Midtown.

The Varsity ☺ AMERICAN   This local legend offers enough *Grease* for the Broadway show and 80 roadside versions. The world's largest drive-in restaurant, opened in 1928 by Frank Gordy, is run nowadays by his daughter, Nancy Simms, and her children. Some 16,000 people a day dine at this Atlanta institution—on hot dogs, hamburgers, french fries, and 300 gallons of chili. Service is fast both carside and inside, with seats and stand-up eating counters, and prices are definitely low. Hot dogs are called "dawgs," and hamburgers are "steaks." If you order them plain, just add "naked" to the front of the name—"nekkid dawg" or "nekkid steak," and so on. *Insider's tip:* If you want a cheeseburger, be sure to ask for pimento cheese. It's a mess, but you've never had anything like it.

61 North Ave. (at Spring St.). (C) **404/881-1706.** www.thevarsity.com. Reservations not accepted. Main courses $1.20–$7. MC, V. Sun–Thurs 10am–11:30pm; Fri–Sat 10am–12:30am. MARTA: North Ave.

Buckhead
VERY EXPENSIVE

Bone's ★★ STEAK/SEAFOOD   Yes, that's Ted Turner at the next table, and where else would former president George H. W. Bush eat when he's in Atlanta? In an atmosphere one food critic called "boardroom frat house," this is just the type of place to get that juicy rib-eye steak weighing in at 16 ounces. Fresh Maine lobster is flown in daily, and the corn-fed beef is butchered and cut into steaks on the premises. Grits fritters are favored by locals, who invariably end their meal with Georgia pecan pie and vanilla-bean ice cream. A cigar humidor can be brought to your table at your request after dinner. One female CEO from New York found the service by the waiters "sexist."

3130 Piedmont Rd. NE (half a block below Peachtree Rd.). ✆ **404/237-2663.** www.bonesrestaurant.com. Reservations required. Main courses $15–$49 lunch, $27–$55 dinner. AE, DC, DISC, MC, V. Mon–Fri 11:30am–2:30pm and 5:30–10pm; Sat 5:30–11pm; Sun 5:30–10pm. Closed major holidays. MARTA: Buckhead.

The Palm ★ STEAK   The emphasis in this two-fisted, upscale tavern is macho friendliness, macho portions, and a kind of bustling unpretentiousness. Its namesake in Manhattan was established in 1926 by two Italian immigrants who wanted to name a restaurant after their hometown (Parma), and the result was a trattoria whose mistranslated name was "the Palm," which was transformed into an all-American steakhouse. Despite a sense that the place is a bit less glamorous than it was a few years ago, the Palm survives and thrives. The Palm's menu is deceptively simple—six different preparations of veal, massive steaks, and chops; pastas and salads that would appeal to a vegetarian; and shellfish (including succulent 3-lb. lobsters and four preparations of clams). Lunchtime choices include less-expensive items like sirloin burgers, grilled chicken sandwiches, crab cakes, and Caesar salads with chicken strips.

In the Buckhead Westin, 3391 Peachtree Rd. (btw. Lenox and Piedmont roads, just south of Lenox Sq.). ✆ **404/814-1955.** Reservations recommended. Main courses $16–$48 lunch, $24–$86 dinner. AE, DC, MC, V. Mon–Sat 11:30am–11pm; Sun noon–10pm. MARTA: Buckhead.

EXPENSIVE

Chops ★ STEAK/SEAFOOD   This 1930s-era macho enclave of good steaks is another jewel in the crown of restaurateur Pano Karatassos. Chops is the most informal restaurant in his chain, which includes the Atlanta Fish Market and Veni Vidi Vici. Business types, media stars, and locals flock to this handsome, clubby place, with its low lighting, roomy banquettes, and tri-level seating. The Chops Lobster Bar, on the lower level, is the best in Atlanta, and large live Maine lobsters are flown in daily. But the fame of the kitchen rests on its chops and steaks, specially aged and selected from corn-fed beef. The Chops porterhouse for two (weighing in at 3 lb.) is enough to satisfy two gargantuan appetites. Mega steaks aside, save room for some of Chops' homemade ice cream: The banana white-chocolate fudge is to die for, as is the chocolate black-bottom pie. Most of the wines are reasonable in price unless you're tempted by a $3,000 bottle.

70 W. Paces Ferry Rd. (at Peachtree Rd.). ✆ **404/262-2675.** www.buckheadrestaurants.com. Reservations strongly recommended for dinner. Main courses $12–$40 lunch, $28–$92 dinner. AE, DC, MC, V. Mon–Thurs 11:30am–2:30pm and 5:30–11pm; Fri 11:30am–2:30pm and 5:30pm–midnight; Sat 5:30pm–midnight; Sun 5:30–10pm. MARTA: Buckhead.

Nava ★ CONTEMPORARY/SOUTHWESTERN   It's Atlanta's most sophisticated Southwestern restaurant, with a colorful theme directly inspired by the pueblos, cactus branches, and adobe houses of the Painted Desert. Appetizers include a fire-roasted adobe quail with citrus honey, a green chili lobster-sauce taco, and tortilla-crusted shrimp rellenos. Main courses have flair and are spicy, especially the wood-roasted pork tenderloin with a tamarind-bean glaze that seems in perfect harmony, as does the giant shrimp with a mango glaze and white-bean enchiladas. Save room for the raspberry crème brûlée. The service here is first-rate.

3060 Peachtree Rd. ⓒ **404/240-1984.** www.buckheadrestaurants.com. Reservations required. Main courses $8.95–$23 lunch, $16–$32 dinner. AE, DC, DISC, MC, V. Mon–Fri 11:30am–2:30pm and 5:30–11pm; Sat 5–11pm; Sun 5:30–10pm. MARTA: Buckhead.

MODERATE

Atlanta Fish Market ★★ SEAFOOD/SUSHI   This is the best seafood place in Atlanta, and we don't want to have an argument about that. Even Madonna agrees that the pecan-crusted catfish and the Carolina mountain trout are the best. The jazzy, 475-seat dining room has been compared to an old Southern train station. It's the creation of Pano Karatassos, sometimes known as "Kingfish." Some locals may be taken aback by the grilled halibut over creamy grits, garnished with shards of apple-smoked bacon, but they're quickly won over. Also try the New Orleans seafood gumbo to start—it contains crabmeat, spicy sausage, shrimp, and a peppery oceanic stock. For dessert, a wise choice is the pineapple-macadamia upside-down cake. The extensive menu is changed daily.

265 Pharr Rd. (btw. Peachtree Rd. and N. Fulton Dr.). ⓒ **404/262-3165.** www.buckheadrestaurants. com. Main courses $11–$33 lunch, $15–$48 dinner. AE, DC, DISC, MC, V. Sun–Thurs 11:30am–10pm; Fri–Sat 11:30am–11pm. MARTA: Buckhead.

The Buckhead Diner ★ AMERICAN   Since reservations aren't accepted, you may find yourself waiting in line with Elton John. Even though the place sounds like a hash house for truckers, it's one of the hottest spots in Atlanta. A highly theatrical venture, it has a gleaming stainless-steel exterior adorned with neon. Inside, try the crisp, spicy barbecued oysters served over creamy succotash with a Cajun rémoulade on the side, or butternut squash soup—the city's best. The veal and wild-mushroom meatloaf is a bit overrated, but not the seared calamari with a hot red sauce. For dessert, the coconut sorbet or the chocolate-chip crème brûlée will convince you that you've visited no meat-and-taters roadside diner.

3073 Piedmont Rd. (at E. Paces Ferry Rd.). ⓒ **404/262-3336.** www.buckheadrestaurants.com. Reservations not accepted. Main courses $9.95–$24 lunch, $15–$29 dinner. AE, DC, DISC, MC, V. Mon–Sat 11am–midnight; Sun 10am–10pm. MARTA: Lenox.

Horseradish Grill ★ SOUTHERN CUISINE   Overhyped but satisfying seems to be the consensus about this brash restaurant named for its equestrian art, not the root vegetable. Try the maple-smoked Georgia quail. Those inevitable pork chops are moist and made even more delectable with a cheddar-cheese macaroni side dish and cucumber salad. Grilled lamb chops also appear on the menu, as does the catch of the day. Naturally, turnip greens are served, as is cornmeal-battered catfish with home fries.

4320 Powers Ferry Rd. ⓒ **404/255-7277.** www.horseradishgrill.com. Reservations recommended. Main courses $9–$16 lunch, $18–$36 dinner. AE, DISC, MC, V. Mon–Thurs 11:30am–2:30pm and 5:30–9pm; Fri 11:30am–2:30pm and 5–10pm; Sat 5–10pm; Sun 11am–2:30pm and 5–9pm. MARTA: Buckhead.

INEXPENSIVE

Café Sunflower CONTINENTAL/VEGETARIAN   This upscale vegetarian restaurant lies on the Sandy Springs strip. The kitchen takes its inspiration from Mexican, Asian, and Mediterranean cuisine. Against a decor described as Williams-Sonoma, the service is more polite than efficient. The spring rolls are stuffed with shredded vegetables, rice noodles, and tofu, and a red-pepper hummus is served with pita triangles and a medley of crunchy raw vegetables. The quesadilla arrives stuffed with black beans, brown rice, tomato, cheese, and corn, a taste sensation in spite of the too-watery salsa. Eggplant and wood-ear mushrooms are delectable in a garlic-ginger sauce, but forget the house salad. Another good choice is curried vegetables on a bed of couscous spiked with raisins and cashews. Instead of wine or beer, you can order freshly squeezed carrot juice.

5975 Roswell Rd. (at Hammond Dr.). © **404/256-1675.** www.cafesunflower.com. Reservations recommended. Main courses $6.50–$12 lunch, $13–$17 dinner. AE, DISC, MC, V. Mon–Fri 11:30am–2:30pm and 5–9pm; Sat noon–2:30pm and 5–9:30pm. MARTA: Sandy Springs.

The Colonnade ✦ SOUTHERN   An Atlanta favorite since 1927, this friendly joint lies between Wellborne Drive and Manchester Street. Like a cheerful American restaurant of the 1950s, it offers great value and attracts the family trade with its down-home cookery and gargantuan portions. Inexpensively priced steaks, chops, seafood, and the inevitable Southern fried chicken round out the menu, along with vegetables boiled all day long. One regular comes here every day to order sugar-cured ham with red-eye gravy. Some of the menu items might lead to arterial overload, but fans of the Colonnade aren't complaining.

1879 Cheshire Bridge Rd. NE (near Piedmont Rd.). © **404/874-5642.** www.colonnadeatl.com. Reservations not accepted. Main courses $12–$22. No credit cards. Mon–Thurs 5–9pm; Fri 5–10pm; Sat noon–10pm; Sun 11:30am–9pm. MARTA: Lindbergh; then bus 27.

North Atlanta
EXPENSIVE

Anthony's ★★★ NEW AMERICAN   Only a 15-minute drive from the center of Atlanta, Anthony's is on 3 wooded acres in an antebellum plantation from 1797. You have a choice of a dozen different dining rooms, graced with seven fireplaces. A special feature is the glass-enclosed porch. Anthony's is often a venue for special events such as weddings. The chef shops for fresh, quality ingredients that he fashions into various culinary temptations, beginning with appetizers that range from crab cakes with a Creole mustard cream sauce to fried green tomatoes layered with goat cheese and a red onion confit. Main course selections are classics, including the chef's select cuts of beef or game, which can be grilled and served with various sauces. One delight is a Dijon-crusted jumbo domestic lamb rack served with a mint demi-glace. Hopefully, the pumpkin-seed-and-coriander-crusted grouper will be on the menu.

3109 Piedmont Rd. NE. © **404/262-7379.** www.anthonysfinedining.com. Main courses $28–$62. AE, DC, MC, V. Mon–Sat 6–11pm. Bus: 5.

MODERATE

Abattoir ★★ 🍴 SOUTHERN   This restaurant is definitely for the carnivore. Its claim to fame is its "whole animal" approach to cuisine—that is, it uses every functional part of the animal. Offal is a special feature, including roast pork belly, or tripe flavored with cilantro. To avoid wasting any part of the animal, the chef features dishes redolent of head cheese, innards, feet, and tongue. Try the beer-braised rabbit or the lamb's tongue with pea sprouts. Chef owners Anne Quatrano and Clifford Harrison claim "we are a meatcentric restaurant, committed to using local ingredients to create one-of-a-kind culinary experiences."

1170 Howell Mill Rd. © **404/892-3335.** Reservations required. Main courses $18–$29. AE, MC, V. Tues–Sat 5–11pm. Bus: 1 or 12.

Miller Union ★ 🏛 SOUTHERN Chef Steven Satterfield believes that chefs and farmers should be "married," so to speak, and bases his menu on the harvests of the week. In this rustic setting in a mid-century warehouse, Miller Union has been one of the keystones in gentrifying the Westside. The chef strives, and succeeds, in preserving the natural flavors of his farm-fresh ingredients. On the third Tuesday night of each month, a special family supper is offered: a prix-fixe three-course menu costing $30. A typical menu might include a seasonal soup, local lettuce with bacon dressing, Darby Farms chicken with fried okra and scallion spoonbread, followed by a blackberry cobbler and vanilla ice cream. Specialties on offer include a farm-fresh egg baked in celery cream, or chicken liver mousse on cranberry walnut toast.

999 Brady Ave. ✆ **678/733-8550.** www.millerunion.com. Reservations required. Main courses $12–$27. AE, DC, MC, V. Tues–Sat 11:30am–2:30pm; Mon–Thurs 5–10pm; Fri–Sat 5–11pm. Bus: 12.

INEXPENSIVE

Holeman & Finch ★ 🏛 SOUTHERN Owner and "gastro-preneur" Linton Hopkins runs one of the friendliest and most convivial joints in town. At 10pm every night a portable bullhorn announces "burger time," and these juicy treats often disappear within 5 minutes. Some items never go off the menu; other newcomers are described as "neo-Southern," including delicacies such as crawfish beignets or griddled hen-of-the-woods mushrooms with Anson Mills polenta. Plates are often shared, as in a Chinese restaurant. Some items are way down South, including a crisp pig ear, or glazed veal sweetbreads with soft grits and sorghum. How many restaurants do you know that offer bacon caramel popcorn on the menu as a dessert? A drink special of the house is a Johnny Ryall, a surprising combination made from cherry liqueur, Peychaud's bitters, grapefruit juice, and Miller High Life.

2277 Peachtree Rd. ✆ **404/948-1175.** Reservations recommended. Main courses $9–$14. AE, MC, V. Mon–Sat 5pm–1:30am; Sun 11:30am–3pm. Bus: 110.

Virginia-Highland

EXPENSIVE

TWO urban licks ★★★ SOUTHERN/AMERICAN Good, homemade food and a unique and eclectic atmosphere combine to create one of the best dining experiences in Atlanta. Fire is the theme running throughout, most dramatically showcased in the 14-foot flame-licked rotisserie. The stainless-steel wine wall, housing 42 barrels of wine, is yet another spectacle in this ultramodern restaurant. Executive chef and part owner Scott Serpas is a South Louisiana boy with a unique style and a gift for the culinary arts. His slow-roasted meats and fresh fish are reason to cross town for what *Bon Appétit* hailed as one of the 50 hottest restaurants in the United States. The juicy barbecue beef brisket won our devotion, and the duck from the rotisserie tasted as good as some of the better offerings in New York's Chinatown. Frogs' legs are given the buffalo-wings treatment with hot sauce and blue cheese. Don't tell Mom, but Serpas makes a better warm chocolate fudge cake, served with a white chocolate mousse and vanilla ice cream. Every Sunday at 6pm, a "Low Country Boil" is featured. Live blues music is offered 5 nights a week.

820 Ralph McGill Blvd. ✆ **404/522-4622.** www.concentrichospitality.com. Reservations not required. Main courses $19–$28. AE, DC, MC, V. Mon–Thurs 5:30pm–midnight; Fri–Sat 5:30pm–1am; Sun 5:30–10pm. MARTA: Edgewood.

MODERATE

Atkins Park Restaurant and Tavern ★ 🎒 TRADITIONAL AMERICAN/ CAJUN   With a long and colorful history, this is the city's oldest continuously licensed tavern, with good and affordable family dining. It attracts the chicken wings crowd: Many drinkers come here for the late-night munchies and the beer. Weekend brunch is another popular time, attracting a faithful coterie of Virginia-Highland residents. In fair weather, opt for a table on the patio. Popular food items for the breakfast crowd include buttermilk biscuits and gravy, even Southern fried chicken. The sandwiches can be appropriately described as bulging. The locals dig into the earthy gumbo and jambalaya dishes, though we prefer the crusted Georgia mountain trout. For dinner, things get a little more elaborate, with dishes like drunken pork tenderloin (marinated in bourbon), or a thick-cut pork chop stuffed with goat cheese and served with toasted pecans. A special kids' menu is featured.

794 N. Highland Ave. NE. 🕜 **404/876-7249.** www.atkinspark.com. Reservations not needed. Main courses $7–$11 lunch, $13–$20 dinner. AE, DC, DISC, MC, V. Mon–Sat 11am–3am; Sun 11am–midnight. Bus: 16.

INEXPENSIVE

The Flying Biscuit Cafe ★ SOUTHERN   This cozy Candler Park favorite enjoys renown all over the Atlanta area for its all-day breakfasts and weekend brunches. It made its reputation by serving what are arguably the best biscuits in Georgia. We recommend you pair the biscuits with a jar of cranberry apple butter.

The restaurant decor features oddly matched vinyl tablecloths and funky accessories. The fare is strictly down-home, including "love cakes"—three black-bean and cornmeal cakes sautéed and topped with a tomatillo salsa, sour cream, feta cheese, and spears of red onion. The most popular dish is turkey meatloaf and "pudge." Pudge is based on an old family recipe for mashed potatoes, sun-dried tomatoes, basil, and olive oil. For breakfast, we prefer the orange-scented French toast with raspberry compote and crème Anglaise, but the long-enduring favorite of most diners is the Flying Biscuit breakfast: two large farm-fresh eggs served with the cafe's signature free-range chicken breast sausage. A three-course dinner special with wine costs just $25 on Friday. Kids 11 and under eat free from the children's menu Monday to Wednesday after 5pm.

The Biscuit also has a more convenient midtown location at 1001 Piedmont Ave. (🕜 **404/874-8887**), which charges the same prices and keeps the same hours.

1655 McLendon Ave. at Clifton Rd. 🕜 **404/687-8888.** www.flyingbiscuit.com. Breakfast $5.95–$11; dinner specials after 5pm $9.95–$18. AE, MC, V. Daily 7am–10pm. MARTA: Midtown.

Inman Park

Rathbun's ★★ MODERN AMERICAN   If Elvis were still alive, we know he'd head straight to this transformed 19th-century warehouse for its banana-and-peanut-butter cream pie. You might go for it, too, and if you're a true Southerner, you can't resist oysters served two ways—lemon-grass stewed and cornmeal fried. In a setting where the industrial 1800s meets the 21st century, an innovative menu of small plates and "second mortgage plates" reinvent Southern delicacies, as *Bon Appétit* has already discovered. For the small plates we went for the sambal-tossed crispy calamari and the mussels on sourdough toast—and were glad we did. For a main, how many places today serve grilled chicken livers with fig molasses? Locals really go for this dish, though you may prefer the enticing monkfish *picatta*. On one occasion we dug into the crispy duck breast with a Thai risotto and green curry essence—and sang its praise.

112 Krog St. ⓒ **404/524-8280.** www.rathbunsrestaurant.com. Reservations recommended. Main courses $17–$40. AE, DC, MC, V. Mon–Thurs 5–10pm; Fri–Sat 5–11pm. MARTA: Inman Park/Reynoldstown.

Sotto Sotto ★ TUSCAN/PIEMONTESE/EMILIA-ROMAGNOLA The best and most appealing restaurant in Inman Park occupies the unpretentious premises of what was built around 1900 as a low-slung row of brick-fronted stores. In 1999, Stefano Volpi and a team of culinary entrepreneurs from Turin and Milan inserted a stylish minimalist decor of glowing hardwoods and immaculate napery, and added a high-tech, open-to-view kitchen where a team of chefs supervises batteries of bubbling pastas and sauces. Today the Northern Italian ambience is as authentic and accurate to the European motif as anything you're likely to find in Atlanta. Superbly prepared menu specialties include wood-roasted whole fish (either pompano, trout, or snapper) flown in ultrafresh from Florida, risotto with seafood, and a succulent version of scallops braised with arugula, white beans, and truffle oil. A favorite pasta is tortelli di Michelangelo, stuffed with a mixture of minced veal, pork, and chicken, served with brown butter and sage sauce. Most wines here are Italian, including goodly numbers of Barolos, Brunellos di Montalcino, and Barbarescos.

313 N. Highland Ave. ⓒ **404/523-6678.** www.sottosottorestaurant.com. Reservations recommended. Main courses $19–$34. AE, DC, MC, V. Mon–Thurs 5:30–11pm; Fri–Sat 5:30pm–midnight; Sun 5:30–10pm.

Sweet Auburn

Thelma's Kitchen ★ SOUL FOOD/SOUTHERN Between downtown and Little Five Points, this is the legendary soul-food kitchen of Atlanta founded by Thelma Grundy. If you attended grade school in Appalachia in the 1940s and ate in the cafeteria, you'll know what to expect in ambience, complete with plastic tablecloths. Smothered collards, rousing rutabagas, great catfish, greasy fried chicken, rice and gravy, creamy limas, sweet potato pie, country-fried steak, barbecued ribs, corn bread, pineapple upside-down cake—you get the culinary picture. Local attorneys nearby flock here for lunch, as do what one habitué called "slide-rule types from Tech and grimy transmission surgeons." He added, "Just tell your readers everything is finger-lickin' good." Rib-eye steak is the most expensive item on the menu, but everything is cheap, including the specials of the day.

302 Auburn Ave., Sweet Auburn. ⓒ **404/688-5855.** Reservations not needed. Main courses $7–$13. MC, V. Mon–Fri 8am–6pm; Sat 8am–8pm.

College Park

Brake Pad AMERICAN The foodies of Atlanta are no longer staying in their own neighborhoods, but heading out to all the suburbs, including College Park, south of downtown, for eating and drinking. Brake Pad is a bona fide neighborhood bar, attracting a *Cheers* crowd. Converted from a former gas station (how chic), the place, in the words of its chef, Seth Trattford, is an "upscale burger joint." Of course, you get supersize burgers and fries, but also such delightful surprises as the best fish taco plate in Atlanta. Grilled tilapia comes with smoky grilled corn and chipotle aioli. Ever had chicken banana egg rolls with a spicy chili sauce? If you crave something more traditional, the quesadillas are to die for. Anglophiles go for the Newcastle beer, but our gang ordered pitchers of Harp.

3403 Main St., College Park. ℂ **404/766-1515.** www.brakepadatlanta.com. Reservations not needed. Main courses $4.50-$8.75. AE, MC, V. Sun-Thurs 11am-midnight; Fri-Sat 11am-1am.

Nearby Dining

For locations of the following two restaurants, see the "Buckhead Accommodations & Dining" map on p. 373.

Canoe ★★ CONTEMPORARY AMERICAN   Canoe is on the city's outskirts in Cobb County—of Newt Gingrich fame. Tables at this hip and fashionable restaurant open onto the Chattahoochee River. After World War II, the locale was famous as a dance hall for "big dresses, big hair, senior proms, and *East of Eden* scenes." Today the much-gentrified pair of connected Quonset huts housing the restaurant have been upgraded. Canoe's appetizers are among the most sophisticated in the city. Sure, they serve catfish, but it comes with a toasted-pistachio green-curry sauce. The chef is known for his light pastas and risottos, one an outstanding pumpkin tortellini with roasted pine nuts and a spicy lamb ragout. The standing menu includes crispy duck with spicy greens and caramel-ginger sauce, slow-roasted pork with Gorgonzola polenta and a spicy escarole, and bacon-wrapped sturgeon with whipped potatoes and sage butter. The waiters warn you to save room for dessert.

4199 Paces Ferry Rd. NW. ℂ **770/432-2663.** www.canoeatl.com. Reservations strongly recommended. Main courses $11-$16 lunch, $15-$30 dinner. AE, DC, DISC, MC, V. Mon-Fri 11:30am-2:30pm and 5:30-10pm; Sat 5:30-11pm; Sun 11am-4pm and 5:30-9:30pm.

Five Seasons Brewing Company ★ 🏮 AMERICAN/JAPANESE   When you tire of grits and collards, head for Sandy Springs, just north of Buckhead, for some unique dishes as well as the highest-quality handcrafted beers in Georgia. The signature beer is Seven Sisters, named after the original seven breweries in Munich that hosted Oktoberfest. It's deep amber, soft, and rich, with a malty finish. The menu's blend of Japanese dishes with stateside grill fare comes as a surprise and a refreshing change to the palate. Our favorite appetizers are the fried blue-crab fingers with a honey-mustard aioli, and the calamari with orange-chili dipping sauce. Grilled pizza is a regular feature. The meats are well handled, to judge by the chargrilled Black Angus New York strip with asparagus, or the lamb tenderloin. The chef uses textural contrasts to good effect in dishes like miso-marinated sea bass with sesame spinach. Some sides appear here and nowhere else, such as a sweet-onion spaetzle.

5600 Roswell Rd., Ste. 21, The Prado. ℂ **404/255-5911.** www.5seasonsbrewing.com. Reservations recommended. Main courses $8-$12 lunch, $12-$25 dinner. AE, DC, DISC, MC, V. Mon-Wed 11am-10pm; Thurs 11am-10:30pm; Fri-Sat 11am-11pm; Sun noon-10pm. MARTA: Medical Center Station.

ATTRACTIONS

Sit in the tourist office in Atlanta, and, within an hour, at least three visitors will come by and ask for directions to "Tara" or "Twelve Oaks." Regrettably, these places never existed in real life, only in Margaret Mitchell's imagination. Even the movie theater where *Gone With the Wind* premiered in 1939 was gutted by fire in the early 1980s. A marble skyscraper sits on the site where Clark Gable and Vivien Leigh launched the film. But even with no Tara, Atlanta has a great deal to offer.

Birth Home of Martin Luther King, Jr. ★   This Queen Anne–style house is where Martin Luther King, Jr., was born on January 15, 1929. He was the oldest son of a Baptist minister and a music teacher. King lived at this modest house until he was 12. It has been restored to its appearance when young Martin lived here. Even the linoleum is an authentic reproduction, and a good deal of King memorabilia is displayed. Be warned that in summer, tickets to the house often run out because of the crowds.

501 Auburn Ave. (at Hogue St.). © **404/331-6922.** www.nps.gov/malu/index.htm. Free admission (obtain tickets at 449 Auburn Ave.). Daily 9:30am–5:30pm. Closed major holidays. MARTA: Five Points; then bus 3.

The Carter Center ★ This center, opened in 1986, is the 30-acre site from which former U.S. president Jimmy Carter works to advance peace and human rights, efforts for which he won a Nobel Prize in October 2002. Its work in democratization and development, global health, and urban revitalization has touched the lives of people in some 65 countries. The center is 2 miles east of the center of downtown Atlanta, with the skyline as a dramatic backdrop. On the same grounds is the Jimmy Carter Library and Museum, housing millions of documents, photos, gifts, and memorabilia of Carter's career and his years in the White House. You can even view a full-scale reproduction of the Oval Office and use interactive video geared to both children and adults. Displays of gifts received by then-president and Mrs. Carter range from silver, ivory, and crystal from heads of state, to paintings and peanut carvings from around the world. *Presidents,* a 30-minute film, looks at the crises and triumphs that marked his administration.

1 Copenhill, 441 Freedom Pkwy. © **404/865-7100.** www.jimmycarterlibrary.org. Admission $8 adults, $6 seniors, free for children 16 and under. Mon–Sat 9am–4:45pm; Sun noon–4:45pm.

CNN Center ★ In the heart of Atlanta, the CNN Center anchors the city's dynamic entertainment, news, sports, and business core and is adjacent to the Georgia Dome and the Georgia World Congress Center. It houses CNN, Headline News, and CNN International studios, and offers guided **studio tours** of these facilities daily. Group tours can also be arranged.

The center also features more than 40 one-of-a-kind retail stores. The **Turner Store,** on the ground level in the Atrium, has merchandise from all of broadcasting's networks and properties. Visitors can create their own CNN news tape by reading the day's top stories in the **Turner Studio** from a teleprompter while sitting behind an actual CNN anchor desk. Through the magic of chroma-key, you can have your photo taken on the pitcher's mound with your favorite Braves players, relax with Scarlett O'Hara and Rhett Butler in a scene from *Gone With the Wind,* or choose from more than 40 other backgrounds.

Visitors can continue their Turner adventure at the **Braves Clubhouse Store** on the ground level in the Atrium, which holds the largest collection of official Braves merchandise in Atlanta. The store is open 7 days a week 9:30am to 7pm, with extended hours on Braves' and Hawks' game days, and for Georgia Dome special events.

The **Atrium** has a variety of eateries in its international food court, where visitors can sit down for a quick meal.

1 CNN Center (at Marietta St. and Techwood Dr.). © **404/827-2300.** www.cnn.com/studiotour. CNN studio tours $13 adults, $12 seniors 65 and over, $9 children 4–12, $30 VIP tour. Tours given every 10 min. Reservations highly recommended at least 1 day in advance. Children 3 and younger not allowed on tours. CNN Center daily 9am–5pm. Turner Store and Studio daily 9:30am–7pm. Closed major holidays. MARTA: Omni, Dome, or GWCC.

Ebenezer Baptist Church   From 1960 to 1968, this Gothic Revival–style church, founded in 1886 and completed in 1922, became a center of world attention. Martin Luther King, Jr., served as copastor of the church during the civil rights struggle. Martin Luther King, Sr., a civil rights leader before his son, was also a pastor here. In early 1999, the National Park Service assumed a 99-year lease on the church and will oversee it as a living museum, with guided weekday tours, periodic church services, and a monthly choir performance.

400–407 Auburn Ave. ⓒ **404/688-7300.** www.historicebenezer.org. Free admission, donations welcome. Mon–Sat 9am–6pm; Sun 1–5pm. MARTA: King Memorial; then a long 8-block walk. Bus: 3 from Peachtree St.

Fox Theatre   This Moorish-Egyptian extravaganza, with its minarets and onion domes, began life as a Shriners' temple. It became a movie theater when movie mogul William Fox, after 2 years of extensive work on the block-long structure, threw open its doors to the public. Its exotic lobby was decorated with lush carpeting; in the auditorium itself, a skyscape was transformed to sunrise, sunset, or starry night skies as the occasion demanded, and a striped Bedouin canopy overhung the balcony. The Great Depression came hot on the heels of the Fox's opening, however, and in 1932, bankruptcy forced its closing. In the 1940s, it was brought to life again with the installation of a huge panoramic movie screen, but decline closed its doors once more in the 1970s. The Fox was slated for demolition, but Atlantans raised $1.8 million to save their treasured old movie palace. Restored to its former glory, it now thrives as a venue for live entertainment.

660 Peachtree St. NE. ⓒ **404/881-2100.** www.foxtheatre.org. Tours $10 adults, $5 children. Tours given Mon, Wed, and Thurs 10am; Sat 10 and 11am. MARTA: North Ave.

Georgia Aquarium ★★★   The greatest attraction to open in the South in 2006 is the world's largest aquarium. It holds 8 million gallons of water in which 100,000 fish, from sea otters to whale sharks, swim. Built with a $200-million gift from Home Depot, the aquarium is perhaps the best in the world and the centerpiece of the Downtown Atlanta revival. Across from the CNN Center, the aquarium is next to Centennial Olympic Park. The World of Coca-Cola Museum opened next door in 2007. In less than a year, the aquarium has become the number-one attraction in Atlanta.

The tanks teem with creatures, both fish and marine mammals, including California sea lions, Beluga whales, the African black-footed penguin, and even such curious animals as the Australian leafy sea dragon. The giant Pacific octopus is a creature to behold.

Georgia sea life isn't ignored, either, as several large habitats feature the state's sea turtles and the fish off Gray's Reef, an underwater area off the Georgia coast that has been designated a National Marine Sanctuary. In residence are whales, the most endangered mammal on the planet, captured right off the Georgia coast, where they were spending the winter giving birth to the largest babies on earth.

One section on freshwater river mysteries highlights such exotica as the electric fishes of Africa and South America. Nearby, kids can safely enter a tank filled with piranha and get a close-up look at the razor-sharp teeth of these deadly predators. Other features include a 4-D theater with unique special effects. You not only see a jellyfish floating, but can also feel the tingling tentacles brushing against your face.

225 Baker St. ☏ **404/581-4000.** www.georgiaaquarium.org. Admission $30 adults, $26 seniors 65 and over, $22 children 3-12. Theater $5.50 adults, $4 children 3-12. Parking $10. Sun–Fri 10am–5pm; Sat 9am–6pm. MARTA: Omni or Dome.

Georgia State Capitol   Writer Colin Campbell saw the 1884 capitol building as "weird, colorful, relentlessly Southern; a super attic of flags, paintings, two-headed snakes, scale models, stuffed animals, and weapons." Its gold-topped dome rises 237 feet above the city. Besides a hall of fame (with busts of famous Georgians) and a hall of flags (U.S., state, and Confederate), it houses the **Georgia State Museum of Science and Industry,** with collections of Georgia minerals and Indian artifacts, dioramas of famous places, and fish and wildlife exhibits. Visit in late January and February to hear Georgia legislators at work.

Capitol Sq. ☏ **404/656-2846.** www.sos.georgia.gov. Free admission. Mon–Fri 8am–5pm. Sept–May tours at 10am, 10:30am, 11am, 1pm, 1:30pm, and 2pm; June–Aug tours at 10am, 11am, 1pm, and 2pm. Closed major holidays. MARTA: Georgia State.

Georgia's Stone Mountain Park ★   A monolithic gray granite outcropping (the world's largest), carved with a massive Confederate memorial, Stone Mountain is a distinctive landmark on Atlanta's horizon and the focal point of its major outdoor recreation area—3,200 acres of lakes and beautiful wooded parkland.

Over half a century in the making, Stone Mountain's neoclassical carving—90 feet high and 190 feet wide—is the world's largest piece of sculpture. Originally conceived by Gutzon Borglum, it depicts Confederate leaders Jefferson Davis, Robert E. Lee, and Stonewall Jackson galloping on horseback throughout eternity. Borglum started work on the mountain sculpture in 1923; after 10 years, he abandoned it because of insurmountable technical problems and rifts with its sponsors. (He went on to South Dakota, where he gained fame carving Mount Rushmore.) It wasn't until 1963, when the state purchased the mountain and its surroundings for a park, that work resumed under Walter Kirtland Hancock and Roy Faulkner. The memorial was completed in 1970.

The best view of the mountain is from below, but you can ascend a walking trail up its moss-covered slopes, especially lovely in spring when they're blanketed in wildflowers, or take the narrated tram ride to the top. Trams run about every 20 minutes in both directions.

A highlight at Stone Mountain is **Lasershow,** a spectacular display of laser lights and fireworks with animation and music. It begins in April Friday to Sunday at 9:30pm; from early May to Labor Day, it can be seen nightly at 9:30pm. Don't miss it.

Other major park attractions include the **Stone Mountain Scenic Railroad,** which chugs around the 5-mile base of Stone Mountain. The ride takes 25 minutes. Trains depart from Railroad Depot, an old-fashioned train station with an attractive restaurant on-site. The *Scarlett O'Hara,* a paddlewheel riverboat, cruises 363-acre Stone Mountain Lake. The **Antique Auto & Music Museum** is a jumble of old radios, jukeboxes, working nickelodeons, Lionel trains, and carousel horses, along with classic cars.

The 19-building **Antebellum Plantation** is a major sightseeing attraction in itself. Self-guided tours are assisted by hosts in period dress. Highlights include an authentic 1830s country store; the 1845 Kingston House; clapboard slave cabins; the 1790s Thornton House, elegant home of a large landowner; the smokehouse and well; a doctor's office; and the 1850 neoclassical Tara-like Dickey House, formal gardens, and kitchen garden. It takes at least an hour to tour the entire complex (a map is provided at the entrance). Often there are crafts and cooking demonstrations, medicine shows, storytellers, or balladeers on the premises.

Confederate Hall, an information center, houses a large narrated exhibit called The War in Georgia, a chronological picture story of the Civil War.

Additional activities are golf (on a top-rated 36-hole course designed by Robert Trent Jones and John LaFoy), miniature golf, tennis on 15 hard-surface courts (the site of the tennis competition for the 1996 Summer Olympic Games), sunbathing on a sizable lakefront beach with wonderful water slides, hiking 20 acres of wildlife trails with natural animal habitats and a petting zoo, boating, biking, fishing, and more. Also located in the park is the **Evergreen Conference Resort,** a 249-room state-of-the-art conference facility.

Hwy. 78 E., Stone Mountain (16 miles east of downtown on U.S. 78). (C) **800/317-2006.** www.stonemountainpark.com. Tickets (for all major attractions) $27 adults, $21 children 3–11. Park year-round 6am–midnight. Major attractions fall–winter daily 10am–5pm; spring–summer Sun–Thurs 10am–6pm, Fri–Sat 10am–8pm. Parking $10 per day, $35 per year. Attractions closed for Christmas, but park is open. MARTA: Avondale; then transfer to a bus to Stone Mountain Village.

The King Center ★ Martin Luther King, Jr.'s, commitment to nonviolent social change lives on at this memorial and educational center under the direction of his son, Dexter Scott King. On the premises is an information counter where you can find out about all Auburn Avenue attractions.

The center works with government agencies and the private sector to reduce violence within the community and among nations. It provides day care for low-income families, assists students in developing leadership skills in nonviolence, and holds workshops on topics such as hunger and illiteracy. Its library and archives house the world's largest collection of books and other materials documenting the civil rights movement, including Dr. King's personal papers and a rare 87-volume edition of *The Collected Works of Mahatma Gandhi,* a gift from the government of India. Equally important, it is King's final resting place, a living memorial to an inspiring leader, which is visited by tens of thousands each year, including heads of foreign governments.

Visitors are given a self-guided tour brochure. The tour begins in the exhibition hall, where memorabilia of King and the civil rights movement are displayed. Here you can see his Bible and clerical robe, a handwritten sermon, a photographic essay on his life and work, and, on a grim note, the suit he was wearing when a deranged woman stabbed him in New York City, as well as the key to his room at the Lorraine Motel in Memphis, Tennessee, where he was assassinated. In an alcove off the main exhibit area is a video display on King's life and works. Additional exhibits—including a room honoring Rosa Parks and another honoring Gandhi—are in **Freedom Hall.**

Outside in Freedom Plaza, Dr. King's white marble crypt rests, surrounded by a five-tiered reflecting pool, a symbol of the life-giving nature of water. An eternal flame burns in a small circular pavilion directly fronting the crypt.

An important part of a visit is the **Screening Room,** where four excellent half-hour videos play continuously throughout the day. They show many of Dr. King's most stirring sermons and speeches, including "I've been to the mountaintop" and "I have a dream"—speeches that are as much a part of America's heritage as the Gettysburg Address.

449 Auburn Ave. (btw. Boulevard and Jackson sts.). (C) **404/526-8900.** www.thekingcenter.org. Free admission. Daily 9am–5pm. Closed Thanksgiving, Christmas, and New Year's Day. MARTA: Five Points; then bus 3.

Underground Atlanta   Right in town, 4 blocks of Atlanta's history lie beneath newer city streets. Underground Atlanta is the city's birthplace, where the Zero Mile-post of the Western & Atlantic Railroad was planted in 1837. In post–Civil War days, railroad viaducts were built over its rococo buildings, and they lay deserted for the better part of a century. Restoration of the crumbling area has resulted in an authen-tic picture of Atlanta in the 1800s. During the mid-1980s the historic city beneath a city was closed for massive redevelopment, and in 1989 it reopened with more than 100 establishments, including shops, restaurants, and nightspots. Regrettably, it is looking a bit seedy these days, as souvenir shops and fast-food joints take over.

Bounded by Peachtree, Wall, Alabama, Pryor, and Central sts. and by Martin Luther King Jr. Dr. *C* **404/523-2311.** www.underground-atlanta.com. Free admission. Mon–Sat 10am–9:30pm; Sun 11am–7pm (clubs and restaurants stay open until midnight or beyond). MARTA: Five Points, with a pedestrian tunnel linking it directly to the Underground.

The World of Coca-Cola ★   It has been called "the world's most popular prod-uct." It's been called a lot of other things, too, including "the Devil's Drink." But Coca-Cola—its recipe still a secret—has been consumed by people all over the world and has endured, even surviving Shirley Temple singing "Sweet Coca-Cola Bush." A three-floor pavilion exhibits memorabilia of the world's most famous drink, from endorsements by fabled stars of yesterday (including those *It Happened One Night* actors, Clark Gable and Claudette Colbert) to campy commercials by the Supremes. The pavilion boasts the most innovative outdoor neon sign ever created for a com-pany—an 11-ton extravaganza hanging 18 feet above the entrance. In all, there are more than 1,000 exhibits, including a 1930s vintage soda fountain, complete with a soda jerk. Coke World moved in 2007 to larger and better headquarters next to the Georgia Aquarium. The new site features a contemporary glass-and-stainless-steel design on one side, dominated by a 27-foot "frosted" replica of its famous contoured bottle encased in a 90-foot cylinder. The location includes more than 4 acres of out-door space, including a reflecting pool and a plaza shared with the aquarium.

Adjacent to Centennial Olympic Park. *C* **800/676-COKE** (2653) or 404/676-5151. www.woccatlanta. com. Admission $15 adults, $13 seniors, $10 children 3–12, free for children 2 and under. Mon–Sat 9am–6pm; Sun 11am–6pm; last admission at 5pm. Closed major holidays. MARTA: Omni.

Museums

Atlanta History Center ★★   From the Civil War and the burning of Atlanta to the civil rights movement of Martin Luther King, Jr., it's all here on vivid display in this vast museum. There's even a collection of memorabilia from Margaret Mitchell. There are frequently changing exhibits as well—everything from *Gone With the Wind* to Atlanta's first black millionaire.

On the grounds is **Swan House and Gardens,** the finest residential design of architect Philip Trammell Schutze. This classical home was constructed in 1928 by the Edward H. Inman family, heirs to a cotton fortune. It's listed on the National Register of Historic Places. Also on the grounds is a "plantation plain" home (ca. 1840), the **Tullie Smith Farm.** Here you can see how Georgia farmers lived in the mid-1800s right before the Civil War.

130 W. Paces Ferry Rd. (at Slaton Dr.). *C* **404/814-4000.** www.atlantahistorycenter.com. Admission $17 adults, $13 seniors and students 13 and over, $11 children 4–12, free for children 3 and under. Mon–Sat 10am–5:30pm; Sun noon–5:30pm. MARTA: Lenox; then bus 23 to Peachtree St. and W. Paces Ferry Rd., then a 3-block walk.

Under the auspices of the National Park Service is the Martin Luther King, Jr., National Historic Site, an area of about 10 blocks around Auburn Avenue, established in 1980 to "preserve the birthplace and boyhood surroundings of the nation's foremost civil rights leader." It includes the **Birth Home of Martin Luther King, Jr.**, and **Ebenezer Baptist Church**, where King, his father, and his grandfather were ministers. Other Auburn Avenue attractions, not under National Park Service auspices, include the **King Center** (where King is buried) and the **APEX Museum** (135 Auburn Ave.; ✆ 404/523-2739; www.apexmuseum.org), a museum that explores the history of the African-American experience in America. A **visitor center** at 449 Auburn Ave., across from the King Center, provides a complete orientation to area attractions and includes a theater for audiovisual and interpretive programs, exhibits, and a bookstore. Guided tours of the area (including those of the Birth Home) originate here. The visitor center is fronted by a beautifully landscaped plaza with a reflecting pool and outdoor amphitheater for park service programs.

Cyclorama For a panorama of the Battle of Atlanta, see this 42-foot-high, 356-foot-circumference, 1880s painting with a three-dimensional foreground and special lighting, music, and sound effects. When you see the monumental work, you'll know why Sherman said, "War is hell." One of only three cycloramas in the United States, it has recently been fully restored—an artistic and historical treasure that many visitors to Atlanta miss, erroneously thinking it "strictly for kids." There are 15 shows daily.

800 Cherokee Ave., in Grant Park. ✆ **404/624-1071** or 658-7625. Admission $8 adults, $7 seniors, $6 children 6–12, free for children 5 and under. Tues–Sat 9:15am–4:30pm; Sun 12:15–3:30pm. Closed major holidays. MARTA: Five Points; then bus 97 (Georgia Ave.).

Fernbank Museum of Natural History ★ This is the largest museum of the natural sciences in the Southeast, a $43-million complex that abuts 65 acres of virgin forest. Opened in 1992, it has a permanent exhibition, A Walk Through Time in Georgia, taking visitors through more than a dozen galleries that explore Georgia's scenic wonders. Spectrum of the Senses comprises some 65 displays shown on a rotating basis. Adventures here include stepping inside a life-size kaleidoscope and viewing IMAX Theater films on a six-story screen.

767 Clifton Rd. (off Ponce de Leon Ave.). ✆ **404/378-0127** or 929-6300 recorded info. www.fernbank museum.org. Museum $15 adults, $14 students and seniors, $13 children, free for children 2 and under. IMAX $13 adults, $12 seniors and students, $11 children. Combination museum and IMAX $23 adults, $21 seniors and students, $19 children. Mon–Sat 10am–5pm; Sun noon–5pm. MARTA: North Ave.; then bus 2 to Clifton Rd.

Fernbank Science Center This is a planetarium, observatory, and museum all rolled into one. Next to the 65-acre Fernbank Forest, it's a branch of the Fernbank Museum of Natural History (see above). Many visitors who've seen all the exhibits come for the 1.5-mile forest trail, showcasing some of the state's most popular trees, such as magnolias and dogwoods. Inside you can see the original *Apollo 6* space capsule and a spacesuit, as well as a replica of the Okefenokee Swamp (see chapter 21 for details on the real one). The greenhouse, 2½ miles from the center, is open only on Sunday and presents changing workshops and lectures.

156 Heaton Park Dr. NE (at Artwood Rd., off Ponce de Leon Ave.). (✆) **678/874-7102.** http://fsc.fern bank.edu. Center free admission. Planetarium show $4 adults, $3 seniors and students, children 4 and under not admitted. Museum Mon–Wed 8:30am–5pm; Thurs–Fri 8:30am–10pm; Sat 10am–5pm; Sun 1–5pm. Planetarium show Thurs 8pm; Fri 3pm and 8pm; Sat–Sun 1:30pm and 3pm (also Tues–Fri 11am and 1:30pm in summer). Observatory Thurs–Fri at 8pm (or dusk–10:30pm). Forest trails Mon–Fri 9am–5pm; Sat 10am–5pm; Sun 2–5pm. Closed major holidays. Take North Ave. east and make a left onto Piedmont. Make a right onto Ponce De Leon Ave. and follow this road for 4½ miles. Take a left onto Artwood Rd. and then a right on Heaton Park Dr.

High Museum of Art ★★★   This little gem of a museum is one of the finest in Georgia, but sensitive Atlantans warn that it shouldn't be oversold to visitors. The building itself, designed in 1983 by Richard Meier at a cost of $20 million, has been called an "architectural masterpiece." You'll find first-rate traveling exhibitions along with the museum's permanent collection. Part of the Woodruff Arts Complex, the museum houses some 10,000 works, including a painting by one of our favorites, John Singer Sargent. Many are by artists like Mattie Lou O'Kelley and Howard Finster, with roots in Georgia. There's also an extensive sub-Saharan African art collection. We visit at times just to view the Virginia Carroll Crawford Collection of American Decorative Arts, covering changing tastes from 1825 to 1917. The museum has greatly expanded its space with the addition of three buildings designed by Italian architect Renzo Piano. The expansion has more than doubled the museum's size.

In the Woodruff Arts Center, 1280 Peachtree St. NE. (✆) **404/733-4400** or 733-HIGH (4444) 24-hr. information. www.high.org. Admission $18 adults, $15 seniors and students, $11 children 6–17, free for children 5 and under. Tues–Wed and Fri–Sat 10am–5pm; Thurs 10am–8pm; Sun noon–5pm. Closed major holidays. MARTA: Arts Center.

Margaret Mitchell House   Margaret Mitchell is the author of *Gone With the Wind*, the bestselling book in the world next to the Bible, and this is her former home. A suspicious fire damaged the house in 1994, and on May 12, 1996, just 40 days before its scheduled reopening, arson struck again. Daimler-Benz, Germany's largest industrial group, came to the rescue, and the property was rebuilt and opened to the public. Although Margaret Mitchell hated the place and called it "the dump," her turn-of-the-20th-century house is once again a major tourist attraction, even though the author would probably have been horrified to see millions of people traipsing through the place where she lived and wrote and created characters like Scarlett O'Hara and Rhett Butler.

Atlanta's first city landmark and listed on the National Register of Historic Places, the house was dedicated on May 16, 1997, about a year after the second fire on the property. You can experience a 40-minute anecdotal guided tour that shares the life story of this amazing author and the impact her book and the movie made upon the world. A new *Gone With the Wind* Museum opened here in late 1999, exhibiting the Herb Bridges collection of *Gone With the Wind* movie memorabilia, to coincide with the 60th anniversary of the movie's premiere in 1939. You can see props, scripts, posters, and even seats from the Loew's Grand Theatre, the Atlanta theater where the movie premiered. More people have seen *Gone With the Wind* than any other motion picture ever produced, including *Harry Potter*.

The house and adjacent visitor center contain exclusive photographs and archival exhibits, including the original typewriter on which Mitchell crafted her novel, her

1937 Pulitzer Prize, original movie posters from around the world, and other exhibits. Mitchell lived here in this small apartment from 1925 to 1932.

990 Peachtree St. (at 10th St.). ✆ **404/249-7015.** www.gwtw.org. Admission $13 adults, $10 seniors and students, $8.50 children 4-12, free for children 3 and under. Public tours daily 9:30am–5pm (last tour begins at 4pm). MARTA: Midtown.

Michael C. Carlos Museum of Emory University   Only a tenth of this museum's holdings are ever on display, so Atlantans return again and again. As an out-of-towner, you can count on something interesting even if it's only a small piece of the Carlos pie. Beautiful objects from the ancient Mediterranean, stunning art from Africa, and pre-Columbian art are among its rich collections. There are also special shows mounted from the museum's vast holdings, including exquisite drawings—some as old as the 1600s. There's nothing in Georgia to equal this collection. The 1916 Beaux Arts building housing the museum is listed on the National Register of Historic Places.

Kilgo St. (near the junction of Oxford and N. Decatur roads on the Main Quadrangle of the Emory campus). ✆ **404/727-4282.** www.carlos.emory.edu. Admission $8 adults; $6 students, seniors, and ages 6-7; free for kids 5 and under. Tues–Sat 10am–4pm; Sun noon–4pm. Closed major holidays. Bus: 6 or 36.

William Breman Jewish Heritage Museum   An unusual museum for the South, this is the most expansive museum of its type in the entire Southeast. It focuses on Jewish heritage but places a spotlight on the Jewish experience in Atlanta itself. Its permanent exhibit, Creating Community: The Jews of Atlanta from 1845 to the Present, shows how Jews not only settled into Atlanta, but also contributed to the community. Some of the exhibits tell sad tales, such as the 1913 Leo Frank case. Frank was wrongfully accused of murder and was lynched by a mob, although his sentence was commuted by Georgia's governor. Exhibits also document anti-Semitic attacks in Atlanta, such as the 1958 bombing of the Temple on Peachtree Street. Documents, photographs, and memorabilia re-create the Jewish saga. There are programs with hands-on activities for younger children.

1440 Spring St. NW, in the Selig Center at 18th St. ✆ **678/222-3700.** www.thebreman.org. Admission $10 adults, $7 seniors, $5 students, $1 children 3-6, free for children 2 and under. Mon–Thurs 10am–5pm; Fri 10am–3pm; Sun 1–5pm. Closed major holidays. MARTA: Arts Center.

The Wren's Nest ☺   Atlanta had another famous writer aside from Margaret Mitchell. Joel Chandler Harris, the creator of the wily deeds of his fictional African characters, Br'er Rabbit and Br'er Fox, lived in this house from 1881 until his death in 1908. The house, since 1913 the oldest museum in Atlanta, is an 1870s Queen Anne–style farmhouse with a Victorian facade added in 1884. Its 10 rooms have been restored, with the original books, furniture, and family heirlooms such as a stuffed great horn owl, a gift from Theodore Roosevelt. A storyteller comes in every Saturday at 1pm to thrill kids of all ages with stories of Uncle Remus and other Harris characters.

1050 Ralph David Abernathy Blvd. ✆ **404/753-7733.** www.wrensnestonline.com. Admission $8 adults, $7 seniors and students, $5 children 4-14, free for children 3 and under. Tues–Sat 10am–2:30pm. MARTA: Bus 71 from West End Station.

An Antebellum Cemetery

Oakland Cemetery ★   Margaret Mitchell, one of the most famous authors ever to emerge from the Deep South, is buried here. Many other famous personages are also here, including golfing great Bobby Jones. The cemetery is an 88-acre Victorian site founded 10 years before the Civil War. It later became the burial place for nearly 50,000 soldiers, both Confederate and Union. This is actually an outdoor museum of funerary architecture, including both classic and Gothic Revival mausoleums. People often bring a picnic lunch and eat ham sandwiches among the dead. The visitor center distributes a self-guided walking-tour map and brochure for $2.

248 Oakland Ave. SE (main entrance at Oakland Ave. and Martin Luther King Jr. Dr.). ℂ **404/688-2107.** www.oaklandcemetery.com. Free admission. Daily sunrise–sunset. Visitor center Mon–Fri 9am–5pm. Guided tours $10 adults; $5 seniors, students, and children. Mar 18–Nov 26 tours Sat 10am and 2pm; Apr 8–Oct 22 tours also Sat 6:30pm, Sun 2 and 6:30pm. MARTA: King Memorial.

The Historic Home of the Richest Black Man in Atlanta

Alonzo F. Herndon Home ★ 📷   Although born into slavery in 1858, only 2 years before the Civil War, Herndon was an industrious man. By 1895, he was the richest black man in Atlanta and had founded the Atlanta Life Insurance Company, the nation's largest black-owned insurer. With his newly acquired wealth, he built this lavish mansion in the Beaux Arts neoclassical style, complete with a colonnaded entrance, and furnished it with antiques and art he'd amassed over a lifetime. The building stands at the Vine Street edge of the Morris Brown campus.

587 University Place (btw. Vine and Walnut sts.). ℂ **404/581-9813.** www.nps.gov. Free admission. Tours $5 adults, $3 students and children 16 and under. Tours by appointment only. Closed major holidays. MARTA: Vine City.

Parks & Gardens

Encompassing 21 acres of downtown Atlanta real estate, **Centennial Olympic Park** ★ (ℂ **404/223-4412** or 222-PARK [7275]; www.centennialpark.com), built for the 1996 Olympics, is at the junction of International Boulevard, Techwood Drive, and Baker and Marietta streets. It was designed as a "landscape quilt" and creates a green "lung" in the center of one of Atlanta's most congested neighborhoods. The energy present during the games has long since subsided, but Atlantans still frequent the park, with its outdoor amphitheater, reflecting pool, and the Olympic rings fountain. A marker notes the site of the bomb blast that claimed two lives in July 1996. Undaunted by the bombing, people were waiting in line for the park to reopen after the mishap, and that spirit still holds true today. You can stroll among the gardens or put on your bathing suit and jump into the geyserlike fountains—an activity for which they were designed. Twice daily, the fountains spurt water in synchronized patterns, arching gracefully in time to the marching tunes that were played during the 1996 Olympics. Hours of these water spectaculars vary—call the park number listed above for exact showtimes. Admission to the park is free; it is open daily from 7am to 11pm.

Another highlight is **Atlanta Botanical Garden,** at Piedmont Avenue and the Prado, in Piedmont Park (ℂ **404/876-5859;** www.atlantabotanicalgarden.org). Sprawling across 30 acres, this garden is Atlanta's most tranquil urban retreat, embracing a 15-acre hardwood forest. A highlight is the glass-walled Dorothy Chapman Fuqua Conservatory, which opened in 1989. Admission is $15 for adults; $12 for seniors, students, and kids 3 to 17; free for children 2 and under. It's open April to October Tuesday to Sunday 9am to 7pm (open until 9pm on Thurs in May) and November to March Tuesday to Sunday 9am to 5pm.

Especially for Kids

The Atlanta Botanical Garden (see above) has added a children's garden loaded with child-friendly instructions about plants and other data.

Center for Puppetry Arts ☺ Don't miss this place even if you're not traveling with kids. It offers puppet shows, workshops, and a museum containing puppets from all around the world. A video with the late Jim Henson as host provides an overview of puppetry and takes visitors around the world to meet masters of the art. The puppet shows are sophisticated and riveting, full-stage productions with elaborate scenery. Some are family oriented; others, with nighttime showings, are geared toward adults. Call ahead to find out what's on; reservations are essential.

1404 Spring St. NW (at 18th St.). ✆ **404/873-3089** or 873-3391 box office. www.puppet.org. Museum admission $8 (free Thurs 1–3pm). Combination ticket for the museum, show, and workshop $16–$22 ages 2 and up. Tues–Sun 9am–5pm. Closed holidays. MARTA: Arts Center.

Six Flags Over Georgia ☺ This theme park is one of the best of its kind in the country. Set on 88 fun-filled acres, it incorporates more than 100 rides, a multitude of shows, and several restaurants. Hours and prices are subject to change daily, so it's a good idea to call or go online to check.

7561 Six Flags Pkwy. ✆ **770/739-3400.** www.sixflags.com. Admission $45 adults, $30 children 48 in. tall and under. Parking $15–$45. Admission includes all rides and shows except amphitheater concerts. Apr to Labor Day opening times range from 9–10am and closing times range from 5–10pm daily; Sept Sat 10am–8pm, Sun 11am–7pm; Oct Sat 10am–10pm, Sun 10:30am–7pm. Closed Nov–Mar. Take I-20 W. for 12 miles; the park is just off the highway.

Zoo Atlanta ★★ ☺ This absolutely delightful 40-acre zoo is an exciting and creatively run facility, with animals housed in large, open enclosures that simulate their natural habitats. The zoo gained new prestige in 1999 when it became the home of a pair of giant pandas, Lun Lun and Yang Yang, both on loan from China for the next 10 years. **Flamingo Plaza** is the first habitat you'll see upon entering the zoo. Farther on, **Masai Mara** houses rhinos, lions, and African elephants. The lushly landscaped **Ford African Rain Forest** centers on four vast gorilla habitats separated by moats. Sumatran tigers (a highly endangered species) and orangutans live in the **Asian Forest** section, an Indonesian tropical rainforest with clusters of bamboo and a waterfall. A zoo train travels through the **Children's Zoo** area, a peaceful enclave with a playground and children's petting zoo. There are shops and snack bars throughout the zoo, and tree-shaded picnic areas in Grant Park. Free animal shows in the Kroger Wildlife Theater are presented Memorial Day to Labor Day Tuesday to Sunday at 11am, 1:30pm, and 2:30pm; after Labor Day to Memorial Day Saturday and Sunday 11am, 1:30pm, and 2:30pm.

800 Cherokee Ave. (in Grant Park). ✆ **404/624-WILD** (9453). www.zooatlanta.org. Admission $20 adults, $16 seniors, $15 children 3–11, free for children 2 and under. Daily 9:30am–5:30pm. Admission booth closes 4:30pm. Closed Thanksgiving and Christmas. Take I-75 S. to I-20 E. Get off at the Boulevard exit and follow the signs to Grant Park. MARTA: Five Points; then bus 97. A MARTA bus labeled "Zoo Shuttle" runs from Five Points June–Sept.

ORGANIZED TOURS

The most intriguing tours in Atlanta are those found at the **Atlanta Preservation Center,** 327 St. Paul Ave. (✆ **404/688-3350** or 688-3353; www.preserveatlanta. com). The center offers seven 1½- to 2-hour guided walking tours, each costing $10 for adults, $5 for seniors and students, and free for children 4 and under. Most tours are offered only from March to November and many are specialized; call for details. For example, the Historic Downtown Tour surveys the city's architecture; the Inman Park Tour visits the city's first garden suburb; the Sweet Auburn Tour surveys the stamping grounds of Martin Luther King, Jr.; Walking Miss Daisy's Druid Hills explores the neighborhood of the film *Driving Miss Daisy.*

OUTDOOR PURSUITS

BIKING Although it may be a bit crowded, **Piedmont Park** is best for biking because it's closed to traffic. Enter the park on Piedmont Avenue between 10th and 14th streets. Bikes can be rented at **Skate Escape,** across the park at 1086 Piedmont Ave. (© **404/892-1292;** www.skateescape.com). It rents single-speed bikes for $6 per hour or $25 per day, with mountain bikes going for $40 per day or $125 a week, including a helmet. A Georgia license or a major credit or charge card is required as a deposit. Skate Escape is open Monday to Friday 11am to 6:30pm and Saturday and Sunday 11am to 6pm.

BOATING **Lake Lanier Islands Beach and Water Park,** 7000 Holiday Rd., Lake Lanier Islands (© **800/840-LAKE** [5253] or 770/932-7200; www.lakelanier islands.com), includes in its entry fee use of canoes, paddleboats, and sailboats. To reach it from Atlanta, a distance of 45 miles, take I-85 North to I-985 (exit 45); get off I-985 at exit 1 and turn left at the end of the ramp, following the signs. This family retreat is part of a larger resort complex with golf courses, homes, campgrounds, and freshwater marinas. It contains more than half a dozen water slides, a wave pool, and a tropical lagoon designed exclusively for children. It is open Memorial Day to Labor Day Sunday to Friday from 10am to 6pm and Saturday from 10am to 7pm. Admission is $26 for adults and seniors, $16 for children. Parking costs $10. *Note:* Children must be 42 inches or more to enter the water park.

CAMPING The **Family Campground,** PO Box 778, at Stone Mountain, GA 30086 (© **800/385-9807** or 770/498-5710), about 16 miles from Atlanta, has 400 wooded sites for RVs and tents. There are full hookups for RVs, LP gas, showers, a laundry area, a supply store, and a restaurant. There's also minigolf, swimming, boating, fishing, and other recreational activities. Rates for two campers at tent sites are $42 to $58, plus $2 for each additional person. Full hookup costs $40 to $720. Take I-285 to the Stone Mountain exit, then drive 7½ miles east on Ga. 78 to Stone Mountain Park.

CANOEING At the **Chattahoochee Nature Center,** 1990 Island Ford Pkwy., in Dunwoody (© **770/992-2055;** http://chattnaturecenter.com), you can take canoe trips Thursday to Sunday from June to August at 6pm. The trips cost $30 per person for ages 6 and up. The sunset trip goes on a 2½-hour educational adventure led by an experienced naturalist, who will point out beavers, otters, herons, ospreys, wildflowers, and a variety of wetland plants. No prior canoeing experience is necessary, and life jackets (furnished on-site) are required. The center is open Monday to Saturday 9am to 5pm and Sunday noon to 5pm. It's closed New Year's Day, Thanksgiving, and Christmas.

FISHING The **Fish Hawk,** 3095 Peachtree Rd. (© **800/331-8919** or 404/237-3473; www.thefishhawk.com), sells Georgia fishing licenses costing $3.50 for 1 day or $9 for 3 or more days. After supplying you with quality tackle and other gear, it will direct you to the best places to fish along the Chattahoochee River, in the North Georgia mountains, or at Lake Lanier, with its 38,000-acre reservoir. The store is open Monday to Friday from 9am to 6pm and on Saturday from 9:30am to 5pm. Other information can be obtained from the **Georgia Department of Natural Resources,** Wildlife Resources Division, 2123 U.S. 278 SE, Social Circle, GA 30025 (© **770/918-6418;** www.gofishgeorgia.com).

GOLF   The best course is Georgia's **Stone Mountain Park Golf Course,** in Stone Mountain Park (© **770/465-3278**), with its 36-hole greens designed by Robert Trent Jones. This challenging course is 16 miles east of the center of Atlanta. Greens fees are $49 to $55, including a cart. It's open daily from 7:30am to dusk.

RUNNING   Most joggers prefer Piedmont Park in spite of its overcrowding, although the Chattahoochee National Recreation Area is more scenic. Serious runners should contact the **Atlanta Track Club,** 3097 Shadowlawn Ave. (© **404/231-9064;** www.atlantatrackclub.org).

SWIMMING   Dozens of Atlanta hotels have their own swimming pools. Public swimming is available at **Piedmont Park.** If you'd like to swim in climate-controlled conditions, contact **Martin Luther King, Jr., Natatorium,** 70 Boulevard Dr. (© **404/658-7330**), open Monday to Friday from 6:30am to 7:45pm and on Saturday from 9am to 4:45pm. Admission is $4 for adults, $2 for children 5 to 16, and free for children 4 and under.

TENNIS   The best courts are those at the **Bitsy Grant Tennis Center,** 2125 Northside Dr., between I-75 and Peachtree Battle Avenue (© **404/609-7193;** www.bitsytennis.com), leased from the Atlanta Parks and Recreation Department. Offered are six outdoor clay courts plus 10 outdoor hard courts, all of which are lighted. No reservations are accepted—it's strictly first-come, first-play. Facilities include a pro shop, showers, and lockers. The cost is $6 to $7 per person per hour for the clay courts or $3 to $5 per person per hour for the hard courts. Hours are Monday to Thursday 9am to 9pm, Friday 9am to 7pm, Saturday 9am to 4pm, and Sunday 9am to 6pm.

SHOPPING

Think of Atlanta as a great shopping bazaar. There's nothing in the American Southeast to equal it. It consists of mall after endless mall—each packed with goodies.

If you're downtown and looking for a souvenir, head for **Underground Atlanta,** but if your tastes are more refined, it's the mall for you. For high fashion—and high prices, too—head for **Buckhead,** 8 miles north of the center. Here the main shopping district centers around Lenox Square Mall and Phipps Plaza, and there are at least 200 specialty stores in the Greater Buckhead area. In Buckhead, seek out **Bennett Street,** a 2-block strip off Peachtree on the southern periphery. A warehouse district at the time of the Civil War, the street today is loaded with galleries and boutiques, selling art, antiques, decorative accessories, whatever. At the intersection of West Paces Ferry and Peachtree roads is **Buckhead West Village,** another healthy concentration of shops, ideal for strolls.

If you'd like something a little more imaginative, go to **Virginia-Highland,** which has been referred to as "New York's SoHo a decade ago." The neighborhood, near the junction of Highland Avenue at Virginia Avenue and Ponce de Leon Avenue, offers five different art galleries, at least 30 restaurants, a scattering of artsy cafes, and endless rows of stores devoted to clothing, flea-market junk, antiques, jewelry, and everything from high to low camp.

For "New York's downtown a decade ago," meander your way to **Little Five Points,** Atlanta's resident art community. Discover eclectic items from hard-to-find books to jazz vinyl records you thought were a part of the past, plus clothes and jewelry to adorn any aspiring rock star. Its mythical center is at the junction of North and Moreland avenues, just east of downtown Atlanta.

For the antiques buff, one of the densest concentrations of such stores is near the T-junction of Peachtree Road and Broad Street, in the northern suburb of **Chamblee,** 17 miles from central Atlanta.

If you're yearning for granite countertops in your kitchen, or access to some of the most prestigious designers and antiques dealers in Atlanta, chances are good that you'll find them within the cluster of entrepreneurs at **Miami Circle.** Set in the heart of Buckhead, off Piedmont Avenue, it's a premier resource for anyone buying or building a house in any of Atlanta's affluent neighborhoods.

Antiques

Atlanta is home to several permanent antiques shop clusters that sell everything from arts and crafts to old and custom furniture. The vendors who peddle here are often from around the country and appear only once or twice a year—the result is a revolving roster of hawkers whose wares are always fresh, however often you shop here. Markets are usually held on weekends and mostly only once a month, so call ahead for details.

Get here first—on Thursday during setup—for the best finds. However, for the best deals, bargain on Sunday, usually the last day of the sale. Many dealers aren't interested in taking their things back home, so you may be able to talk them down. The best streets for permanent year-round shopping for antiques and flea-market discoveries are **Bennett Street** and **Miami Circle** at Buckhead.

Lakewood 400 Antiques Market   This market is by far the largest and most diverse in the area. With more than 1,500 dealer spaces, you'll find something, ranging from old reproductions to books, cookware, linens, custom furniture, pottery, and sculpture. But this only scratches the surface. The market is open the third weekend of every month—Friday 9am to 5pm, Saturday 9am to 6pm, and Sunday 10am to 5pm. Admission is $3, except on Thursday ("early buyer day"), which is $5. The location is at 1321 Atlanta Hwy., Cumming. ⓒ **770-889-3400.** www.lakewoodantiques.com. Lies a mile north of exit 13 on Georgia Hwy. 9.

Art Galleries

Art Station   Established in 1985, this well-recommended art gallery occupies the premises of what was once a garage for trolley cars. It sells works by regional and some national and international artists. 5384 Manor Dr., Stone Mountain. ⓒ **770/469-1105.** www.artstation.org. Bus: 120 to Manor Dr.

Books

Barnes & Noble   This popular flagship of seven Atlanta locations, south of the Lenox Square Mall, has everything. When you've chosen among the wealth of books, the cafe invites you to relax with your book or newspaper. Book signings and other events are frequent. 2900 Peachtree Rd., Buckhead. ⓒ **404/261-7747.** www.barnesandnoble.com. MARTA: Lenox.

art COMES TO CASTLEBERRY HILL

Sometime in the 1990s artists began to renovate Castleberry Hill, a district of postbellum warehouses. Today the district is a booming and artist-driven community, and many long-abandoned factories are now filled with galleries, shops, eateries, and bars. The two best galleries are the **Marcia Wood Gallery,** 263 Walker St. (✆ **404/827-0030;** www.marciawoodgallery.com), and **Studio Clout,** 144 Walker St. (✆ **404/688-2787;** www.studioclout.com). Each of these galleries exhibits paintings by some of the South's most talented and up-and-coming artists. For the best lunch in the area stop in at **No Más! Cantina** at 180 Walker St. (✆ **404/574-5678;** www.nomascantina.com), to enjoy some exquisite Mexican food.

Borders   This upper-Buckhead location affords you the opportunity to sip a *caffe latte* while you peruse your next book. It's one of five Borders locations, whose late hours are a hit with the working reader. 3637 Peachtree Rd. NE. ✆ **404/237-0707.**

Department Store

Belk   Belk is the country's largest privately owned mainline department store. It's a favorite of frugal shoppers, and carries a wide range of brand-name fashions for men, women, and children. It's also known for shoes, leather goods, and a large array of cosmetics. In Phipps Plaza, 3500 Peachtree Rd. NE. ✆ **404/814-3200.** www.belk.com. MARTA: Lenox.

Fashion

Mitzi & Romano   Local designers are showcased here in a series of sexy "cocktail dresses," as we used to call them back in the '50s. Their accessories are "of-the-moment," including Hervé Chapelier bags, chunky leather belts, and Kate Spade handbags. 1038 N. Highland Ave. NE. ✆ **404/876-7228.** Bus: 16.

Mooncake Clothing Co.   Like its whimsical name, this clothing outlet takes us back to the nostalgic '70s for its vintage jewelry, flowing scarves, and floppy hats. This retro-style clothing only looks old: It's actually new but based on vintage designs. 1019 Virginia Ave. NE. ✆ **404/892-8043.**

Susan Lee   Its specialty is women's dresses, suitable for the office, evening wear, or cocktail hour, and no matter how hard you look, you won't find a shred of sportswear. 56 E. Andrews Dr., Buckhead. ✆ **404/365-0693.** MARTA: Buckhead.

Versace   It sells more of the garments by the house of Gianni Versace, for both men and women, than many of that designer's other outlets. It's unusual in enjoying exclusivity for all of Georgia, and for maintaining under one roof every line ever produced by the award-winning house. In Phipps Plaza, 3500 Peachtree Rd. NE. ✆ **404/814-0664.** MARTA: Lenox.

Food

Atlanta State Farmer's Market ★   The largest food outlet in the Southeast, this market covers 146 acres. About half the vendors sell wholesale only; the other half sell to the public, purveying meats, poultry, plants, flowers, fruits, vegetables, and a staggering variety of home-canned jams, pickles, and relishes. Most vendors don't accept credit cards. Open 24 hours daily. Closed Christmas Day. 16 Forest Pkwy., Forest Park. ✆ **404/675-1782.** www.farmersmarketonline.com. Take I-75 S to exit 78, a 15-min. drive south of downtown Atlanta.

Dekalb Farmer's Market   Strictly speaking, because all the stalls are owned by the same entrepreneur, this is not a farmer's market at all. Instead, it's one of the largest, best-stocked, and most atmospheric grocery stores in Atlanta, rustically outfitted like your fantasy version of a country fair. 3000 E. Ponce de Leon Ave., Decatur. ✆ **404/377-6400.** www.dekalbfarmersmarket.com.

Gifts

The Fickle Manor   This boutique is filled with fun gifts, art, jewelry, accessories, and designer items created by such trendy fashionistas as Jill Stuart and David & Goliath. 1402 N. Highland Ave. NE, Ste. 4, Atlanta. ✆ **404/541-0960.** Bus: 16.

Jewelry

Richters   Specializing in antique jewelry, this is one of the most unusual stores in town, a compendium of Grandmother's grandest things—don't expect the baroque jewels worn by the grand duchess of Austria. The owners stress that this is not a museum, and that almost everything displayed was made during the 20th century. Pieces incorporate Edwardian, Art Deco, and the "retro" styles of the 1950s. 2300 Peachtree Rd., Buckhead. ✆ **404/355-4462.** www.atlantaantiquedealers.com. MARTA: Lenox.

Malls & Shopping Centers

Atlantic Station ★   This 138-acre site provides homes for 10,000 people as well as sidewalk cafes, movie theaters, first-class restaurants, and a vast array of retailers and shops. Formerly the home of Atlanta Steel Company, the new site is in the northwest section of the Midtown market and includes 11 acres of public parks. Many of the names are familiar to shoppers, including Ann Taylor, Dillard's, Gap, Old Navy, and the city's first IKEA (though its cafe and restaurant serves sweet tea and grits instead of Swedish meatballs). 17th St. (west of I-75). ✆ **404/733-5000.** www.atlanticstation. com. MARTA: Arts Center Station; then free shuttle bus to Atlantic Station.

Lenox Square Mall   North of Atlanta's commercial core, near the upscale district of Buckhead, this began as a small cluster of merchants in 1959, but has been expanded at least four times since then. Today it incorporates a modern hotel (the JW Marriott), half a dozen movie theaters, two dozen restaurants, and a bewildering array of at least 200 shops. 3393 Peachtree Rd. NE, at Lenox Rd. ✆ **404/233-6767.** www.simon.com. MARTA: Lenox.

Phipps Plaza ★   This is the most upscale shopping mall in Atlanta. A short drive north of downtown in Buckhead, it was enlarged in 1992. Today its two largest tenants (Lord & Taylor and Saks) function as "anchors" at the opposite ends of passageways incorporating some of the most elegant boutiques in the Southeast. There's also a food court, a handful of tony restaurants, and a movie theater with more than a dozen screens. 3500 Peachtree Rd. NE, at the Buckhead Loop. ✆ **404/262-0992.** www.simon.com. MARTA: Lenox.

Underground Atlanta   On the site of Atlanta's original antebellum core, this complex manages to fulfill the roles of living-history museum, nightlife venue, and shopping mall all rolled into one ongoing carnival. (For more information on Underground Atlanta, see "Attractions," earlier in this chapter.) 50 Upper Alabama St., btw. Peachtree St. and Central Ave. ✆ **404/523-2311.** www.underground-atlanta.com. MARTA: Five Points.

ATLANTA AFTER DARK

Most hotels and motels distribute free the publications *Where, Key: This Week in Atlanta* and *After Hours*. The Saturday edition of the *Atlanta Constitution* has a "Weekend" section to fill you in further. Should you *still* be at a loss as to how to spend an evening, take yourself to Kenny's Alley at Underground Atlanta.

The Bar Scene

Atkin's Park One of the most frequented Virginia-Highland taverns, this is called "the *Cheers* of the neighborhood." It attracts 25- to 35-year-olds. Photographs of the city's tumultuous history decorate the walls. The patio, with a decor of brick, brass, and wood floors, is a little small for dining, but it's extremely lively on weekends. Music is country, pop, Top 40, and rock—and is it ever loud. 794 N. Highland Ave. NE. ✆ **404/876-7249.** www.atkinspark.com.

Eddie's Attic Believe it or not, the once-sleepy Decatur area is becoming a magnet on the after-dark circuit. A favorite spot here, Eddie's Attic showcases up-and-coming singer-songwriters as well as big names—the Indigo Girls got their start here. The attic is divided into a trio of sections, including the main bar for music lovers; the Billy Pilgrim of tomorrow may be appearing on the small stage here. Rowdier areas are the poolroom and the covered patio. A pub menu is available for those with the munchies. 515 N. Mcdonough St., Decatur, next to the old courthouse on the square. ✆ **404/377-4976.** www.eddiesattic.com. Cover $4–$10. MARTA: Decatur.

Halo Lounge Stylishly remodeled in the basement of the Biltmore Hotel, this bar is one of the most fashionable and beautiful in the city. Unusual for Atlanta, it draws a mixture of both gay and straight patrons (Thurs is the most popular night for the gay crowd). Candy-colored lawn furniture is spread around the interior. You'll see some of the city's sexiest people at the backlit onyx bar, ordering one of the 17 single-malt scotches. Some of the coolest DJs in town spin tunes here. 817 W. Peachtree St. NW. ✆ **440/962-7333.** www.halolounge.com. MARTA: Midtown.

Manuel's Tavern This is the hangout for local politicos. Jimmy Carter shows up every now and then, ordering a Moosehead, whereas his Secret Service boys order Atlanta's favorite hometown drink, Coca-Cola. Since 1956, the tavern has been serving its burgers, steaks, and hot dogs to the local gang. Dress is always casual. 602 N. Highland Ave. NE. ✆ **404/525-3447.** www.manuelstavern.com.

Moe's & Joe's Offering a cool refuge from the blazing Atlanta heat, this is one of the most nostalgia-packed bars in Atlanta. Set at the street corner that gave Virginia-Highland its name, it has thrived here since 1947, amid a collection of sports memorabilia that grows every year. Lots of liquor has been swilled here since its debut (it sells more Pabst Blue Ribbon than any other bar in the Southeast), and it's so genuinely friendly and indulgent that you might quickly adopt it as your local hangout. Menu items include a roster of predictable bar platters, including burgers and barbecue chicken wings. 1033 N. Highland Ave. at the corner of Virginia Ave. ✆ **404/873-6090.** www.moesandjoes.com.

Park 75 Lounge ★★ Sheathed in a zillion dollars' worth of russet-colored marble and richly figured mahogany, this is the most appealing and opulent hotel bar in Atlanta. A magnet for a clientele that includes lots of well-heeled residents of nearby homes and condominiums, it offers a staggering array of single-malt scotches, rare wines by the glass, vintage ports, and two-fisted cocktails that are poured tableside by a hip, well-trained, and endlessly indulgent staff. Light platters and desserts are served as well, in a setting that evokes the best aspects of a discreet but chic private club in London. In the Four Seasons Hotel Atlanta, 75 14th St. (btw. Peachtree and W. Peachtree sts.). ℂ **404/881-9898.** www.fourseasons.com/atlanta.

Sun Dial ★   This bar and restaurant atop the Westin Peachtree not only makes the best chocolate martinis in town, but also offers the most spectacular view, a glittery panorama taking in everything from the Georgia Dome to the new aquarium. The revolving bar attracts chic young Atlantans who drop in here after work to sip cocktails and catch up on the latest gossip. You may want to stick around for dinner to delight in such dishes as pan-seared halibut with a mustard sabayon or grilled center-cut beef tenderloin with roasted garlic. In the Westin Peachtree Plaza, 210 Peach St. ℂ **404/589-7506.** MARTA: Peachtree Center.

GAY & LESBIAN BARS

Bulldog & Co.   Named after the canine pet of the entrepreneur who founded the place in 1978, it's a gay-lifestyle staple for men ages 30 and over who, while not addicted to leather, don't flinch at it, either. Inside you'll find five or six bars, depending on the season, and a crowd that runs from the Marlboro Man to look-alikes for Denzel Washington and Billy Dee Williams. 893 Peachtree St. NE. ℂ **404/872-3025.** Cover $2 for nonmembers.

The Heretic   Come here for hot music, a big dance floor, and the proximity of hundreds of ripped glistening men, fresh from the gym and/or the most recent circuit party. Most of the clients are under 35 and hail from virtually everywhere on the North American mainland. Depending on the night of your arrival, there might be a high percentage of leather and uniforms, even a bit of latex, especially every Wednesday and Sunday after 10pm. 2069 Cheshire Bridge Rd. ℂ **404/325-3061.** www.hereticatlanta. com. Cover $4–$10 Fri–Sat after 11pm.

My Sister's Room   In the heart of gay-friendly East Atlanta Village, this is perhaps the best women's club in Georgia. It's the home of the largest Thursday hip-hop ladies night in Atlanta, featuring the best in lesbian musicians and performance artists. Women from all walks of life gather here. Open Wednesday to Saturday 8pm to 2am (Fri–Sat until 3am). 1271 Glenwood Ave. ℂ **678/705-4585.** www.mysisters room.com.

3 Legged Cowboy   This is self-styled, with some degree of accuracy, as the most kickin' country and western bar in the South. Cowboys dance with cowboys, or even cowgirls. Gay, straight, and all the in-betweens keep this joint rocking. The place evokes home on the range even though the setting is urban. Tight jeans, Stetsons, and boots are the preferred dress code, and no one will mind if you accessorize with chaps and spurs, too. 931 Monroe Dr. ℂ **404/876-0001.**

The Club & Music Scene

COMEDY CLUBS

Punchline Comedy Club   Some of the best touring comics in America play here in the Balconies Shopping Center and have been doing so for the past 18 years. Jerry Seinfeld has appeared here. The club is small, and most tables have a good view. Shows run Wednesday to Sunday. 280 Hildebrand Dr. NE. ℂ **404/252-5233.** www.punchline. com. Cover $10–$30, higher for big-name acts.

COUNTRY & ROCK

Dark Horse Tavern Opened in 1989, this Virginia-Highland tavern features a restaurant and bar, with the original railing used on the set of *Gone With the Wind*. The tavern is decorated with hunter-green walls and an antique brass bar and grill with saddles and bridles. The music offers everything from jazz to rockabilly and pop, but rock dominates. Both Atlanta and national bands perform in the downstairs bar. 816 N. Highland Ave. NE. 𝓒 **404/873-3607.** www.darkhorseatlanta.com. Cover $3–$10 for bands.

DANCE CLUBS

Compound ★★ This is the hottest club in Atlanta. We plebeians had to wait in line as Usher and Drew Barrymore were led inside and assigned to the VIP lounge. There's even a VIP suite with bed and shower. This large nightclub in the West Midtown section was once the home of a classic-car dealership. Today it attracts all the visiting celebrities to its stylish precincts, which features several courtyards, "a mist garden," and various lounges. We prefer Thursday nights, which are very international, featuring Latin rhythms, among other music. The on-site dance club Ride is a whirlwind of 21 flatscreen TVs and exploding colors powered by a kinetic lighting system. The club is open only Thursday to Saturday nights. 1008 Brady Ave. NW. 𝓒 **404/898-1702.** www.compoundatl.com. Cover $10–$50.

Johnny's Hideaway This ballroom, frequented by everybody ages 35 to 65, is just a local tavern during the day. The Big Band sounds of the 1940s, including Glenn Miller, live on here, as do the golden sounds of 1950s rock 'n' roll, including the music of Macon-born Little Richard. This is a good place for the single visitor, either male or female. Chances are, if you're lookin' good, you'll be asked to dance. A silver ball still rotates above the dance floor in the grand old tradition. Two big-screen TVs provide further divertissement. 3771 Roswell Rd. 𝓒 **404/233-8026.** www.johnnyshideaway.com.

JAZZ & BLUES

Blind Willie's Live Blues Club This is one of the best live blues clubs in Atlanta. Opened in 1986, it has a simple interior of old brick walls and wooden floors and is dimly lighted. Sometimes nationally known acts are booked here, and Cajun entertainment is often featured. It's open Monday to Saturday at 7pm. 828 N. Highland Ave. NE. 𝓒 **404/873-2583.** www.blindwilliesblues.com. Cover $5–$10.

Café 290 Jazz and blues, along with some R&B, form the background in this club, drawing a crowd that ranges in age from 30 to 50. At the back is a sports bar with televised games and pool tables. But most patrons come here for the music. Reservations are needed on Friday and Saturday. Fine dancing is also a feature here, or you can enjoy intimate, candlelit dining. The cuisine is Continental, and a specialty is hand-carved steaks. Only fresh ingredients are used, and meals cost $12 to $30. 290 Hildebrand Dr. NE. 𝓒 **404/256-3942.** www.cafe290atlanta.com. Cover $5–$10 for those not dining at the restaurant.

Dante's Down the Hatch Dante's design has created the illusion of a pirate ship tied up to an old Mediterranean wharf. In the wharf section there's jazz, classical, and flamenco guitar until 8pm nightly. As for the "crew," most have been aboard for a long time, and all really make you feel cared for. Dante himself is always on hand to see that you have a good time. This is really a jazz supper club, with many intimate seating areas, the most romantic being the semiprivate cabins on the lower "deck." A trio plays traditional jazz later in the evening, and classical folk guitarists perform on weekend nights. Across from the Lenox Square Mall, 3380 Peachtree Rd., Buckhead. ☎ **404/266-1600.** www.dantesdownthehatch.com. Cover $10 on the ship deck, none on the wharf.

The Performing Arts

BALLET The **Atlanta Ballet** ★ performs at the historic Fox Theatre, 660 Peachtree St. NE, at Ponce de Leon Avenue (☎ **800/982-2787** box office or 404/873-5811; www.atlantaballet.com). The Atlanta Ballet, under artistic director John McFall, is the oldest in the nation, now in its 70th year. McFall creates excitement with new sets, costumes, and choreography. Ticket prices range from $25 to $120. Take MARTA to North Avenue.

CLASSICAL MUSIC The **Atlanta Symphony Orchestra** ★★★, performing in the Woodruff Arts Center, 1280 Peachtree St. NE, at 15th Street (☎ **404/733-4800** or 733-5000 box office; www.atlantasymphony.org), celebrated its 50th anniversary in 1995. Under the musical directorship of Yoel Levi, it's acclaimed especially for the 200-voice Atlanta Symphony Orchestra Chorus, formerly the Robert Shaw Chorus.

The season runs from September to May and includes the master series and the light classics series. The master series features world-acclaimed guest artists. Light classics are likely to dip into such fun shows as *Broadway's Hottest Tickets*. The **Chastain Summer Concerts** ★ are held in 7,000-acre Chastain Park Amphitheater between June and August. It's the custom to bring an elaborate picnic to the event. Artists such as the Beach Boys perform here. Holiday concerts are also performed at Christmas and other times.

Ticket prices vary but are generally $25 to $68 for the master series, $20 to $45 for the light classics series, and $22 to $45 for the Chastain Summer Concerts. To reach the Woodruff Arts Center, take MARTA.

OPERA The **Atlanta Opera** ★★ (☎ **800/356-7372** box office or 404/881-8885; www.atlantaopera.org) is under the artistic leadership of Dennis Hanthorn. Founded in 1979, the opera company has earned national recognition. The Atlanta Opera presents four fully staged productions each season at the Cobb Energy Centre, 2800 Cobb Galleria Pkwy., Atlanta. Four performances of each opera are staged. Tickets range from $25 to $130, with seniors and students granted 50% discounts on the day of the performance if any tickets are available (tickets are generally extremely difficult to obtain). The season lasts from late May to Labor Day. Take MARTA to North Avenue.

SPECIAL EVENTS Major cultural and entertainment events are often presented at the 2,750-seat John A. Williams Theatre, part of the **Cobb Energy Performing Arts Center,** 3 blocks from the Cobb Galleria Center, 2800 Cobb Galleria Pkwy. (☎ **770/916-2800;** www.cobbenergycentre.com). The program features Broadway shows, ballet, concerts, family performances, opera, and other events. The avant-garde design features a pedestrian-friendly entry park with green space, walking paths, botanical gardens, plazas, and fountains. Tickets and information are available from Ticketmaster. Take the Cobb Community Transit bus to the Arts Center.

THEATER In the Little Five Points District, **7 Stages,** 1105 Euclid Ave. (☎ **404/523-7647** or 522-0911; www.7stages.org), is the leading producer of new and contemporary plays in Atlanta. It's also a venue for performances by international touring theater companies. Performances run Wednesday to Sunday in the newly renovated theater. Tickets cost $10 to $36 for most productions, with discounts offered to seniors and students. Take MARTA to Inman Park.

Alliance Theatre Company, at the Woodruff Arts Center, 1280 Peachtree St. NE (© **404/733-5000** box office or 733-4650; www.alliancetheatre.org), is the largest resident professional theater troupe in the Deep South. It produces about 10 plays a year, ranging from a musical of *The Color Purple* to love stories like *Guardsmen.* Such famous actors as Jane Alexander often appear with this group. Ticket prices range from $20 to $60. The season runs September to May, with occasional productions staged in summer. Take MARTA to the Arts Center.

ATHENS, THE ANTEBELLUM TRAIL & AUGUSTA

I f you looked for antebellum Georgia around Atlanta, you were in the right church but the wrong pew. The state's pre–Civil War moonlight-and-magnolias romance lives on, and you'll find it some 60 to 100 miles east of Atlanta in charming old towns with patriotic names like Madison and Milledgeville, two classic antebellum towns that Sherman didn't burn. And although the cities of central Georgia that lie along the Antebellum Trail are cut off from the mountains or the seashore, they are at the doorstep of some of the state's most mammoth lakes.

This area also encompasses two of the most famous cities of Georgia, Athens and Augusta. Athens, called "the Classic City," is the home of the University of Georgia, and lies in a setting beside the Oconee River. Many of its restored and still-occupied antebellum houses make it a worthwhile stopover. Augusta, founded in 1736, is today famed as the headquarters of the Masters Golf Tournament the first full week in April.

ATHENS ★

85 miles NW of Augusta; 58 miles E of Atlanta

Just below the foothills of the Blue Ridge Mountains, near the confluence of the North and Middle Oconee rivers, lies the city of Athens amid the rolling red-clay hills of North Georgia.

Athens's fame grew because of the University of Georgia (UGA; www.uga.edu), which covers 605 acres and includes 313 buildings in the center. The university was incorporated in 1785, making it America's first state-chartered college. Abraham Baldwin, one of Georgia's four signers of the U.S. Constitution, was named president. Today the University of Georgia is ranked among the nation's top research institutions, and boasts America's 19th-largest library and many nationally recognized programs of study, including pharmacy, business, and journalism. More than 30,000 students attend the university.

Athens, the Antebellum Trail & Augusta

In the last 2 decades, Athens has gained national attention for its music scene as well. This is where R.E.M., the Indigo Girls, and the B-52s got their start. They occasionally return to Athens to play local clubs, but their presence is felt philanthropically through donations to local homeless shelters and AIDS organizations. The town continues to have a booming music scene; for the latest music news and concert information, see "Athens After Dark," p. 413.

Essentials

GETTING THERE   From Atlanta, take I-85 northwest to Highway 316, which leads the rest of the way to Athens. From Augusta, take I-20 West to Atlanta, cutting northwest on Highway 78 into Athens via Washington.

US Airways (© **800/428-4322;** www.usairways.com) offers flights only between Athens and Charlotte, North Carolina. Planes land at **Athens–Ben Epps Airport** (© **706/613-3420;** www.athensairport.net).

Greyhound (© **800/231-2222;** www.greyhound.com) and **Southeastern Stages** (© **404/591-2750;** www.southeasternstages.com) run service to the **Athens bus station,** 220 W. Broad St. (© **706/549-2255**).

VISITOR INFORMATION   **Athens Welcome Center,** 280 E. Dougherty St. (© 706/353-1820; www.visitathensga.com), is open 10am to 6pm Monday to Saturday and 2 to 5pm on Sunday.

SPECIAL EVENTS   The best time to visit is during the **Historic Homes Tour,** the last weekend in April. Sponsored by the Athens-Clarke Heritage Foundation, this is one of the most attended events in East Georgia. For information, call © 706/353-1801 or visit www.achfonline.org.

Seeing the Sights

Athens begins Georgia's antebellum trail and showcases several buildings of note, many centered around the University of Georgia.

Taylor-Grady House, 634 Prince Ave. (© 706/549-8688; www.taylorgrady house.com), a Greek Revival home constructed in the 1840s by Gen. Robert Taylor, planter and cotton merchant, is open year-round. Filled with period furniture, it has 13 columns said to symbolize the original 13 states. Henry W. Grady, a native of Athens, lived here from 1865 to 1868. As managing editor of the *Atlanta Constitution,* he became a spokesperson for the New South. Admission is $3. Hours are Monday to Friday from 9am to 5pm, closed 1 to 2pm. *Tip:* Call ahead, as the house is sometimes booked for private events.

Athens's **Double Barreled Cannon** is the only one of its kind in the world and is among the most unusual relics preserved from the Civil War. It was designed by John Gilleland and built at a local foundry in 1863. The concept was to load the cannon with two balls connected by a chain several feet in length. When fired, the balls and chain would whirl out, bola style, and cut down the unfortunate enemy soldiers caught in the path of this murderous missile. It stands on the City Hall lawn at College and Hancock avenues.

Tree That Owns Itself, at Dearing and Finley streets, is another Athens landmark. William H. Jackson, a professor at the University of Georgia, owned the land on which a large oak stood. He took such delight in the shade of the tree that he willed the tree 8 feet of land surrounding its trunk. The original tree blew down in a windstorm in 1942. The local garden club planted a sapling on the land in 1946, grown from one of the acorns from the original tree. Locals refer to the tree as "the world's most unusual heir and property owner."

The main campus of the **University of Georgia** ★ extends 2 miles south from "the arch" at College Avenue and Broad Street. For information, call © 706/542-3000 or visit www.uga.edu/visit. The current campus was established in 1801. John Milledge, late governor of the state, purchased and gave the board of trustees the chosen tract of 633 acres on the banks of the Oconee River. The view from the hill on which the 1832 Chapel now stands reminded Milledge of the Acropolis in Athens, and the hill was named after its Greek forebear, the classical center of learning. The school produced its first graduating class in 1804. Later funds were raised for the first permanent structure on campus, Old College (1806), which still stands today.

The **State Botanical Garden of Georgia** ★, 2450 S. Milledge Ave. (© 706/542-1244; www.uga.edu/botgarden), encompassing 313 acres, is a "living laboratory" in teaching and research that is open to the public. Its three-story conservatory features a display of tropical and semitropical plants. Along the garden's 5 miles of nature trails are diverse ecosystems, with many plants labeled. There are nearly a dozen specialty gardens. The garden lies a mile from U.S. 441, about 3 miles from the university campus. Admission is free; it's open daily 8am to sunset. A visitor center and the conservatory are open Tuesday to Saturday 9am to 4:30pm and on Sunday 11:30am to 4:30pm. Grounds open daily April to September 8am to 8pm and October to March 8am to 6pm.

The **Georgia Museum of Art,** 90 Carlton St. (℗ **706/542-4662;** www.uga.edu/gamuseum), is the official state art museum, offering an extensive collection of American paintings, prints, and drawings in a new 52,000-square-foot facility. It is currently closed through early 2011, though scheduled events are still open to the public during the closure; call or check the website for the calendar of events.

Founders Memorial Garden and Houses, 325 S. Lumpkin St. on the University of Georgia campus (℗ **706/542-4776;** www.uga.edu/gardenclub/foundersgarden. html), became the first garden club in the United States, founded in 1891 by 12 Athens women. Set on 2½ acres, it offers varying landscapes and the seasonal foliage of a Southern garden. Plantings range from the native to the exotic, and the gardens are a particular delight in spring when the azaleas burst into bloom. The boxwood garden evokes the formality of bygone ages, and the camellia walk is notable. Admission is free, and the garden is open during daylight hours.

Outdoor Pursuits

Sandy Creek Nature Center, half a mile north of the Athens bypass, off U.S. 441, offers some 200 acres of woodland and marshland, with a live animal exhibit. It has many nature trails for hikers, and on-site is a cabin nearly 2 centuries old. For more information, call ℗ **706/613-3615** or visit www.sandycreeknaturecenter.com.

Visitors can enjoy **Sandy Creek Park** (℗ **706/613-3631;** www.sandycreekpark. com), north on U.S. 441 (signposted). It offers a beach, fishing, playgrounds, softball, volleyball, and shelters for picnics. Paddleboats and canoes can be rented. April to September, hours are Tuesday to Sunday 7am to 9pm. Off-season hours are Tuesday to Sunday 8am to 6pm. Admission is $2.

Where to Stay

In addition to the listings below, there's a **Holiday Inn Athens** at 197 E. Broad St. (℗ **800/HOLIDAY** [465-4329] or 706/549-4433; www.hi-athens.com).

The Colonels on Angel Oaks Farm ★★ 🏠 The most atmospheric place to stay in the area is here at this beautifully restored mansion that dates from the year the Civil War was declared. Less than a 15-minute drive from the center of historic Athens, the farm stands on a 30-acre pastoral estate. Many motorists touring the antebellum trail stop off here, especially equestrian enthusiasts. Many of the furnishings came from a Belgium château dating from 1794. Bedrooms are period pieces that still contain their original doors, woodwork, and heart-pine floors. A special feature is a sunken garden with beautiful flowers and brickwork. Your hosts are Beth and Marc, both retired lieutenant colonels.

3890 Barnett Shoals Rd., Athens, GA 30605. ℗ **706/559-9595.** www.thecolonels.net. 10 units. $115–$195 double; $200–$380 suite. Additional person $20. MC, V. **Amenities:** 2 breakfast rooms. *In room:* TV, Wi-Fi (free).

Microtel Inn This small-scale chain hotel is one of the most comfortable and best-run in town. It also offers superb value. Bedrooms are well maintained, functional in styling, and the free continental breakfast will fortify you until lunch. Because the inn rises only two floors you probably won't mind the lack of an elevator.

The location is convenient, at the Junction U.S. 78 business route (Broad St.) and the SR 10 Loop.

105 Ultimate Dr., Athens, GA 30605. ℂ **800/771-7171** or 706/548-5676. Fax 706/613-5153. www.microtelinn.com. 60 units. $49–$69 double. Rates include breakfast. AE, DISC, MC, V. **Amenities:** Breakfast room; snack shop. *In room:* A/C, TV, fridge, hair dryer, Wi-Fi (free).

Rivendell Bed & Breakfast ★★   Although it was built in 1989, this inn contains many architectural features that make you think it's much older. Set on the Oconee River on 11 acres of forested private land, it's the finest inn in the area. It contains lofty beamed ceilings, two fireplaces crafted from large stones, antiques collected from around the world, and big windows opening onto views of the surrounding countryside. There are walking paths for woodland strolls, with many nice places to stop for picnicking. Complimentary tea and sherry are provided in the afternoon.

3581 S. Barnett Shoals Rd. (10 miles southeast of Athens), Watkinsville, GA 30677. ℂ **706/769-4522.** Fax 706/769-4393. www.negia.net/~rivendel. 4 units. $85–$100 double. Rates include full breakfast. MC, V. Drive 8 miles south on U.S. 441, then 5 miles west on Barnett Shoals Rd. No children 10 and under. **Amenities:** Breakfast room; lounge. *In room:* A/C, Wi-Fi (free).

Where to Dine

East West Bistro FUSION   This place, which opened in 1995 on the main street in Athens, is all the rage. Upstairs, dining is more formal, in a classically styled room where the fare of Northern Italy is sometimes prepared with zest and flavor, though the other dishes are uneven, at best. Depending on the night, many dishes merit a rave, whereas others, such as shrimp and mussels tossed with spaghetti in a mild red-curry cream sauce, don't make it. Try fresh-grilled yellowfin tuna with a parsley caper butter or chicken breast breaded with shaved ginger and orange instead. Downstairs is the largest selection of tapas in Athens, including carpaccio and a Thai ratatouille crepe. Main dishes range from jerk chicken to salmon in rice paper.

351 E. Broad St. ℂ **706/546-9378.** www.eastwestbistro.com. Reservations recommended. Sandwiches and pastas $8.50–$12; main courses $6–$14. AE, DISC, MC, V. Mon–Thurs and Sun 11am–10pm; Fri–Sat 11am–11pm.

Farm 225 ★★ 🍽 SOUTHERN/MEDITERRANEAN   Its food is farm fresh, and its chefs sail the Mediterranean for their culinary influence but definitely have a Southern drawl in the kitchen. The menu changes daily and manages to be both elegant and simple at the same time. Most of the ingredients come from their own Full Moon Farms nearby. Many of their recipes have emerged from grandmother's attic. They bake their own pastries, cure meats, and even can their own preserves and pickles. In addition, the restaurant also uses meat and poultry from their livestock operation, Moonshine Meats. Begin perhaps with fried green tomatoes with pimento cheese or the famous Swiss dish *raclette,* made with potatoes. Main courses likely to tempt are shrimp and grits, or a North Carolina wahoo with leeks and local squash. Always on the menu is their famous burger made from staff-raised beef.

255 W. Washington St. ℂ **706/549-4660.** Reservations recommended. Main courses $14–$21. AE, MC, V. Tues–Thurs 5:30–10pm; Fri–Sat 5:30–10:30pm; Sun 11am–2pm.

Five & Ten ★★ SOUTHERN/CONTINENTAL   For the most imaginative food offered by any restaurant reviewed in this chapter, partake of the viands featured at Hugh Acheson's place. He calls his own food "contemporary American with inspirations from Italy and France." The self-trained Acheson has risen to the top of the list among the chefs of Athens. The bright, contemporary restaurant in Five Points,

1 mile south of the University of Georgia, has an enclosed patio for alfresco dining, plus a long metallic bar with wooden accents. We take delight in his specialty, Frogmore stew, a modern version of a Low Country "boil" with shrimp, sausage, potatoes, corn, and other vegetables. Almost any dish you order at Five & Ten (so-called because the building used to be a five-and-dime store) is likely to be good. We've enjoyed the pork tenderloin with roasted pepper, asparagus, and potatoes, and especially the red grouper served with a scallion broth, braised endive, and leek-flecked mashed potatoes. The desserts are the best in town and include a delightful blueberry cinnamon tart with cinnamon ice cream and warm maple syrup.

1653 S. Lumpkin St. ℂ **706/546-7300.** www.fiveandten.com. Reservations required. Main courses $17–$32. AE, DISC, MC, V. Sun–Thurs 5:30–10pm; Fri–Sat 5:30–11pm; Sun 10:30am–2:30pm (brunch).

Last Resort Grill MODERN SOUTHERN   This is the most artsy haunt in town, attracting a mostly college crowd. Although its days as a center for avant-garde music are over, it's still a place to find out what's happening in town. We prefer the booths in the bar area, although other patrons like the courtyard, with its open end protected by ornate grillwork. In chilly weather, a gas heater blasts away. The chefs really try hard, and many of their dishes are among the best in town, but it's a hit-or-miss affair. Check out the blackboard specialties, or try your luck and sample grilled salmon with Charlestonian grits, chicken stuffed with cheese and covered with a honey-praline sauce, or chipotle pork chops grilled and marinated.

174–184 W. Clayton St. ℂ **706/549-0810.** www.lastresortgrill.com. Reservations not accepted. Main courses $4.50–$18. AE, DISC, MC, V. Mon–Thurs 11am–3pm and 5–10pm; Fri–Sat 11am–3pm and 5–11pm; Sun 10am–3pm and 5–10pm.

Athens After Dark

To find out who's playing and what's on, pick up *Flagpole,* Athens's arts, entertainment, and events weekly, free at many shops, restaurants, bars, and clubs; or go online to **www.athensmusic.net** for the latest band information. Another good barometer of what's happening is the UGA student newspaper, the *Red and Black.* Remember that this is a college town, so the nightlife scene is much hotter during the school year. Most of the music clubs and bars present nightly live bands September through June only, shrinking their offerings to just the weekends in the summer.

Make a pilgrimage to the famous **40 Watt Club,** 285 W. Washington St. (ℂ **706/549-7871;** www.40watt.com), the little joint that launched the B-52s and R.E.M. Although you can still hear up-and-coming local bands, these days the 40 Watt is more geared toward national bands, such as Luscious Jackson or the Lemonheads. They also run a late-night disco several times a week, as does the **Georgia Theatre,** 215 Lumpkin St., at the corner of Clayton Street (ℂ **706/549-9918;** www.georgia theatre.com). A former movie theater, it gives local college-rock bands (along with a smattering of blues and Southern rock) the chance to jam long into the night. Oh, and that skinny guy in the corner may just be Michael Stipe.

Our favorite bar in town by far, however, is the **Globe,** 199 N. Lumpkin St. at Clayton Street (ℂ **706/353-4721;** www.globeathens.com). In the mix are students, an occasional filmmaker, and a cross-cultural selection of anyone from hip latter-day rebels to necktie-toting salesmen. It's like an English pub, with the largest selection of exotic beers in Athens—more than 150 brands. It also has a collection of 50 kinds of single-malt whiskeys. There's also wine, port, and sherry, served by the glass, and nine boutique bourbons.

MADISON ★

52 miles E of Atlanta; 73 miles W of Augusta; 21 miles N of Eatonton

Madison, off I-20, an hour's drive east from Atlanta, was once populated by wealthy merchants and cotton planters who erected houses that were fine examples of Federal and Greek Revival architecture. Antebellum travelers called it "the wealthiest and most aristocratic village between Charleston and New Orleans." Late in 1864, with Atlanta in flames, Gen. William T. Sherman's Union juggernaut reached Madison's outskirts. Happily for us, they were met by former U.S. senator Joshua Hill, a secession opponent who'd known Sherman in Washington, and the town was spared.

Today thousands of visitors come to see the oak-lined streets, historic homes, parks, gardens, churches, galleries, and antiques shops. The Historic District was recognized by the Department of the Interior as one of the finest such districts in the South.

Essentials

The **Madison Chamber of Commerce,** PO Box 826, 115 E. Jefferson St. (© **800/ 709-7406** or 706/342-4454; www.madisonga.org), has information about the area. It's open Monday to Friday 8:30am to 5pm, Saturday 10am to 5pm, and Sunday 1 to 4pm.

Seeing the Sights

Stop first at the **Madison-Morgan Cultural Center,** 434 S. Main St., U.S. 441 (© **706/342-4743;** www.mmcc-arts.org). The redbrick schoolhouse (ca. 1895) features a history museum on the Piedmont region of Georgia, an 1895 classroom museum, art galleries with changing exhibits, and an auditorium for presentations. Programs range from Shakespeare to chamber orchestras to gospel singing. Hours are Tuesday to Saturday 10am to 5pm and Sunday 2 to 5pm. Admission is $3 for adults, $2 for students, $2.50 for seniors, and free for children 5 and under.

Pick up a self-guided walking-tour map and other information at the center, and stroll past the majestic Greek Revival, Federal, Georgian, neoclassical, and Victorian homes lining Main Street, Academy Street, Old Post Road, and the courthouse square. You'll find plenty of places to buy antiques and handicrafts.

You can relax outdoors at **Hard Labor Creek State Park** (© **706/557-3001** or 557-3006 golf course; www.gastateparks.org/info/hardlabor), near Madison. Leave town via I-20 West and take exit 49 into Rutledge, then drive 2 miles on Fairplay Road to the park. *Golf* magazine rates the park's 18-hole course as one of the finest public courses in America. You can also swim at a sand beach, fish for bass and catfish, and hike the 5,000 wooded acres. The park has 51 campsites with electricity, water, restrooms, and showers for $25 to $50 a night. There are also 20 fully furnished two-bedroom cottages available for $115 to $125 per night. A Michael J. Fox movie, *Poison Ivy,* was filmed here in the mid-1980s.

Where to Stay

The Brady Inn ★ 🏚 The restored Victorian cottages of the Brady Inn lie in the center of the Historic District (they were once two private homes linked by a walkway). Rooms are tastefully furnished, often with antiques, and the breakfast is most generous. All rooms also have well-kept bathrooms with tub/shower combinations. You get old-fashioned hospitality here, along with a good night's sleep.

250 N. Second St., Madison, GA 30650. © **866/770-0773** or 706/342-4400. www.bradyinn.com. 7 units. $125–$175 double; $200–$350 suite. Rates include full breakfast. AE, MC, V. **Amenities:** Breakfast room; lounge. *In room:* A/C, TV, fridge (in some), Wi-Fi (free).

Madison Oaks Inn & Gardens ★ 🎁 In a beautifully restored Greek Revival mansion, this elegant B&B lies only half a mile from the historic town square. If you want a relaxing weekend away from the bustle of Atlanta, this place is for you. Owners Dianne and Roger Simmons rent out four exquisitely furnished rooms, all with an antique aura but with modern amenities. A communal gourmet breakfast is one of the highlights of a stay here, as all the food is homemade and individually prepared. The pool, hammock, and lovely gardens await you. The inn does not accept children.

766 East Ave., Madison, GA 30650. © **706/343-9990.** www.madisonoaksinn.com. 4 units. $185–$250 double. Rates include full breakfast. MC, V. No children. **Amenities:** Breakfast room; outdoor pool. *In room:* A/C, TV, hair dryer.

Where to Dine

Old Colonial Restaurant 🍴 SOUTHERN This is the busiest restaurant in Madison. The site it occupies, close to the town's main square, comprises an early-18th-century tavern that later functioned as a bank and a storefront. The staff manages to be friendly, helpful, and restrained all at the same time. Don't expect grand cuisine: Lunches and dinners are copious portions served summer-camp cafeteria style. If you like candied yams, pork chops, and collard greens, come on in. Corn bread is served with everything.

108 E. Washington St. © **706/342-2211.** Breakfast $5–$9; lunch and dinner main courses $6.50–$11. AE, DISC, MC, V. Mon–Sat 5:30am–8:30pm.

EATONTON

21 miles S of Madison; 22 miles N of Milledgeville; 47 miles NE of Macon; 75 miles SE of Atlanta

Home of Br'er Rabbit and the Uncle Remus Tales, this town, filled with antebellum architecture, is a sleepy old place of tree-lined streets and historic homes. Eatonton is not only the original home of Joel Chandler Harris, who created the Uncle Remus Tales, but also of Alice Walker, author and Pulitzer Prize winner for *The Color Purple*.

Essentials

To get here from Madison, take Highway 441 South. The **Eatonton-Putnam Chamber of Commerce,** 105 S. Washington St. (© **706/485-7701;** www.eatonton. com), dispenses information Monday to Friday 8:30am to 5pm.

Seeing the Sights

Uncle Remus Museum, Highway 441 South (© **706/485-6856;** www.uncleremus. com), lies in Turner Park, 3 blocks south of the courthouse. It has a kid-pleasing collection of memorabilia about Br'er Rabbit, Br'er Fox, and Harris's other storybook critters. The museum is open Monday to Saturday 10am to 5pm (closed 1 hr. for lunch) and Sunday 2 to 5pm. Admission is $1 for adults and 50¢ for children 7 and younger. Closed Tuesday from November to March.

 Bronson House, 114 N. Madison Ave. (© **706/485-6442**), is the home of the Eatonton/Putnam Historical Society. Constructed in 1822 by Thomas T. Napier, it was purchased in 1852 by Andrew Reid, who was the first patron of Joel Chandler

Harris. The author lived with his mother in a tiny cottage in back of the mansion. Several rooms of the Greek Revival mansion have been restored, displaying local memorabilia. The house can be visited on Saturday and Sunday from 1 to 5pm, but call for an appointment. Admission is $2.50.

Where to Stay

The Lodge on Lake Oconee ★   Nestled on the shore of Lake Oconee, this is one of the best bets for lodging in the area, its well-furnished bedrooms opening onto waterfront views. The resort is also convenient to golfing, boating, and fishing. It's also a short drive to the Oconee National Forest and the Hard Labor Creek State Park. Bedrooms are configured with either queen-size beds, one king-size bed, or suites with two queen-size beds and a living room. This is a favorite with families since children's suites are also offered for parents who want a respite from their brood.

930 Lake Oconee Pkwy., Eatonton, GA 31024. ✆ **877/OCONEE1** or 706/485-7785. Fax 706/485-3996. www.thelodgeonlakeoconee.com. 81 units. $129–$159 double; $179–$189 suite. Rates include breakfast. MC, V. **Amenities:** Breakfast room; boat rentals. *In room:* A/C, TV, fridge, hair dryer, Wi-Fi (free).

Where to Dine

Bone Island Grill at Crooked Creek Marina SOUTHERN/CARIBBEAN   In a scenic location at the marina, this is a favorite among boaters and visitors, and it also does a good business serving local diners. The menu is market fresh and well-prepared. The chef lodged time in Key West, and many of the dishes show the influence of the Florida Keys, such as the mahimahi sandwich with spicy mayonnaise served at lunch. Fresh appetizers are offered at noon along with poultry, vegetable, and shrimp salads. A good selection of sandwiches is also featured, as well as a fried green tomato BLT on Cuban bread. Dinner is far more substantial, beginning with such appetizers as fried oysters. Two of the best main courses are the seafood gumbo with rice or corn bread or else the pan-sautéed fresh red snapper with a lemon butter sauce. Hush puppies are always on the menu.

Crooked Creek Marina, 208 Crooked Creek Dr. ✆ **706/485-9693.** No reservations taken. Main courses $50–$22. MC, V. Fri–Sat 11am–4pm; Wed–Thurs 5–10pm; Fri–Sat 4pm–12:30am.

MILLEDGEVILLE

20 miles S of Eatonville; 30 miles NE of Macon; 90 miles SE of Atlanta

This town ranks along with Madison and Washington in historic sights. Carved from Native American territories in 1803, Milledgeville was the capital of Georgia until 1868, when the seat was moved to Atlanta. Milledgeville was miraculously spared by General Sherman and today remains a treasure-trove of antebellum architecture.

Essentials

From Eatonton, follow U.S. 441 South into Milledgeville. The Welcome Center of the **Milledgeville-Baldwin County Convention & Visitors Bureau** is at 200 W. Hancock St. (✆ **800/653-1804** or 478/452-4687; www.milledgevillecvb.com). It's open Monday to Friday 8:30am to 5pm and Saturday 10am to 4pm.

Seeing the Sights

Old Governors Mansion, 120 S. Clark St. (✆ **478/445-4545;** www.gcsu.edu/mansion), a pink marble Palladian beauty, has been exquisitely restored and refurbished as the home of the president of Georgia College. ... antiques-rich public rooms. The mansion was the home of Geor... 1839 to 1868. This National Historic Landmark house is an ... Greek Revival architecture. Guided tours begin on the hour from ... 10am to 4pm and on Sunday 2 to 4pm. Admission is \$10 for ... \$2 for students, and free for children 5 and under.

The mansion is on the campus of **Georgia College & State University,** 231 w. Hancock St. (✆ **478/445-5004;** www.gcsu.edu), a former women's college that dates from 1889 and today is home to some 5,500 students. The college occupies four 20-acre plots. You may want to stroll about the campus.

At the college's **Ina Dillard Russell Library,** on Clark Street (✆ **478/445-0988**), you can visit the Flannery O'Connor Room, but check its status before coming here. As this guide went to press, it was closed for renovations. O'Connor, distinguished author of *The Violent Bear It Away* and *A Good Man Is Hard to Find,* lived in Milledgeville. You can also visit **Memory Hill Cemetery** (www.friendsof cems.org/memoryhill), the oldest burial ground in the city, where the author is buried.

O'Connor fans should also visit **Andalusia—Flannery O'Connor's Farm ★**, 2628 N. Columbia Street/Hwy. 441 (✆ **478/454-4029;** www.andalusiafarm.org), outside of town. It is free and open to the public Monday, Tuesday, and Saturday 10am to 4pm. The author lived at her family's farm from 1951 until her death from lupus in 1964. The memorabilia-filled farmhouse is 4 miles northwest of Milledgeville on the west side of U.S. Highway 441. Visitors can see the 544-acre estate, complete with the main house, main barn, even smaller barns, three tenants' houses, and water tower, plus a man-made pond. The white two-story, plantation-style main house (ca. 1850) is listed on the National Register of Historic Places.

The easiest way to see the town is to take a **Historic Guided Trolley Tour.** The 2-hour tour explores the major sights in the town, including the old governor's mansion and the former state capitol building (ca. 1807). Tours depart from the Welcome Center (see "Essentials," above) Monday to Friday at 10am and Saturday at 2pm. Cost of the tour is \$10 for adults, \$5 for children 6 to 16, and free for children 5 and under.

Nearby, you can visit **Lake Sinclair,** north on U.S. 441, a 15,330-acre lake with 417 miles of shoreline. It was created when the Oconee River was impounded and today it is a venue for fishing and boating. There's a marina, and camping is possible. Call ✆ **478/452-1605** for more information.

Where to Stay

Antebellum Inn ★ Innkeeper Jane Lorenz welcomes you to her well-restored 1890 Greek Revival home in the heart of the Antebellum Trail in the center of Milledgeville, just a block from the Georgia College & State University campus. The Old Governor's Mansion is just down the street. The inn has two old-fashioned parlors and five spacious guest rooms. Individually furnished guest rooms have beds covered with tasteful linens and down comforters. Several of the well-kept bathrooms have antique claw-foot tubs. The town's best B&B breakfast is served in an elegant dining room. If you'd like to recapture the feel of Georgia's former capital, find a rocking chair on the wraparound porch. The grounds are beautifully landscaped.

200 N. Columbia St., Milledgeville, GA 31061. ✆ **478/453-3993.** www.antebelluminn.com. 5 units. \$109–\$149 double. AE, DISC, MC, V. **Amenities:** Breakfast room; outdoor pool. *In room:* A/C, hair dryer, Wi-Fi (free).

eville Days Inn ⚓ This modest motel is preferred over its major com-
, the 169-room Holiday Inn out on U.S. 441 North. Days Inn is a two-story inn
d with Southern comfort. Its guest rooms are strictly functional, but they're well
aintained, with good beds and spacious bathtubs with tub/shower combinations.

2551 N. Columbia St., Milledgeville, GA 31061. © **800/329-7466** or 478/453-8471. Fax 478/453-8482.
www.daysinn.com. 95 units. $51–$65 double. Rates include continental breakfast. Children 11 and under
stay free in parent's room. AE, DC, DISC, MC, V. Pet $10. **Amenities:** Breakfast room; lounge; exercise room;
Jacuzzi; outdoor pool; room service; 2 tennis courts (lit). *In room:* A/C, TV, fridge, hair dryer, Wi-Fi (free).

Where to Dine

Bo Jo's Boardwalk Café SOUTHERN/STEAK/SEAFOOD   A local eatery, this
regional cafe is known for its helpful staff and large portions. Residents come here for
steak and fresh seafood—often fried—and plenty of good-tasting Southern favorites
like fried chicken. Dress is informal, and there is also a full bar on-site. The cafe is at
the junction of U.S. Business Route 44 and U.S. 441 Bypass.

3021 N. Columbia St. © **478/453-3234.** Reservations not needed. Main courses $6–$24. MC, V. Mon-
Sat 4–10pm.

WASHINGTON

42 miles S of Athens; 150 miles E of Atlanta; 60 miles NW of Augusta

Founded in 1773, and the first city incorporated in the name of George Washington,
the city of Washington is one of the three most important antebellum towns in Georgia, ranking along with Madison and Milledgeville. It was not visited by General
Sherman on his notorious burning spree known as The March to the Sea, and, as a
result, still contains a wealth of antebellum architecture.

Washington was settled by Southern planters, mainly from Britain, who in time
rebelled against British rule. At the nearby Battle of Kettle Creek, 8 miles southwest
of town on Kettle Creek, off GA. 44, the settlers destroyed the British stranglehold
on Georgia.

Heard's Fort, later Washington, became the temporary capital of Georgia in 1789.
The cotton gin was perfected by Eli Whitney at Mount Pleasant plantation, just east
of Washington.

In the closing hours of the Civil War, Jefferson Davis and members of his cabinet
fled here to sign the last official papers to dissolve the Confederacy. The site was the
Heard House, which no longer stands, although a marker on the main square in
Wasington indicates where this historic event took place.

ESSENTIALS

GETTING THERE   Take I-20 East from Atlanta to exit 59, turning left to Washington; from Augusta, take I-20 West to exit 59, turning right for Washington.

VISITOR INFORMATION   The **Washington-Wilkes Chamber of Commerce,**
29 W. Square (tel. **706/678-5111;** www.washingtonwilkes.org) is open Monday to
Friday 9am to 5pm.

SEEING THE SIGHTS

Robert Toombs House State Historic Site ★   This restored home was the
residence of that unreconstructed Confederate statesman and soldier, Robert
Toombs, former brigadier general in the Confederate army who served briefly under

President Jefferson Davis (a man he despised) as Secretary of State of the Confederacy. On May 11, 1865, Yankee troops arrived at his home with orders to hang the former leader from an oak tree on his front yard. His wife, Julia stalled the troops until her husband could escape on horseback.

He fled into the Georgia Mountains and became a fugitive in his own country, eventually escaping to Cuba where he made his way to Paris, there to live a bitter life. He returned home just before Christmas in 1866, upon learning of the death of his last living child, Sallie. He refused a presidential pardon from Andrew Johnson. "A pardon?" Toombs asked. "I have done nothing to ask forgiveness for, and I have not pardoned *them* yet!" He spent his remaining years denouncing the "carpetbag rule" of the Reconstruction South, participated in state politics, and was a major force in rewriting the Georgia Constitution. Twenty years after the end of the Civil War, Toombs died at the age of 75.

The frame Federal-style house with a Greek Revival portico is filled with Toombs memorabilia and antique furniture. The house was originally built in 1797 but went through five architectural face-lifts: Federal, Plantation Plain, Greek Revival, Victorian, and Neoclassical. Relatives of the Toombs family lived here until 1973, when the state purchased the house and hired Edward Neal, a Columbus architect, to restore it as it was at the time of General Toombs death in 1885. Visitors can view a dramatic film, portraying the elderly Toombs relating his sad story to a young reporter.

216 E. Robert Toombs Ave. Tel. 706/678-2226. www.gastateparks.org/info/rtoombs. Admission $3 adults, $2 children 6-18, free for children 5 and under. Tues-Sat 9am-5pm.

Callaway Plantation ★ This early-American building outside Washington, across from the town's small airport, is designated to illustrate life in the various periods of history of the area. A working plantation, the complex includes a red-brick Greek Revival mansion from 1869. There's also a gray-framed "Federal plainstyle" house circa 1790, with period furnishings. Exhibits include the old kitchen, a formal parlor, and a dignified but rather bleak series of upstairs bedrooms. Accompanied by a local guide, you can also visit several outbuildings.

5 miles west on U.S. 78 Tel. 706/678-7060. http://callaway.washingtongeorgia.net. Admission $4 adults, $2 children. Tues-Sat 10am-5pm, Sun by appointment.

Washington-Wilkes Historical Museum The rich history of Washington comes alive at this museum housed in a white clapboard antebellum house circa 1836. Much Civil War memorabilia is exhibited, along with utensils and agricultural equipment. The house has been splendidly restored and furnished. Look for the Confederate gun collection and artifacts of Native Americans.

308 E. Robert Toombs Ave. Tel. 706/678-2105. www.historyofwilkes.org. $3 adults; $2 children 5-12; 4 and under free. Tues-Sat 10am-5pm, Sun 12:30-3:30pm.

WHERE TO STAY

Jameson Inn This is the leading motel in Washington. Crisply modern and inviting, it is the best-maintained and best-managed inn in the county. Designed in a two-story mall with distinct references to 18th-century colonial architecture, it offers comfortable bedrooms with good beds and adequate-size baths, and a two-story format that emulates a drive-up motel but with considerably more grace. Bedrooms are cozy and clean, outfitted with wood-grained furniture and tidy bathrooms featuring shower-tub combinations. *Note:* Rates can go up considerably around the Masters golf tournament.

115 Ann Denard Dr., Washington, GA 30673. Tel. 706/678-7925. Fax 706/678-7962. www.jamesoninns.com. 43 units. $59 double. Rates include continental breakfast. AE, DC, DISC, MC, V. Amenities: Breakfast room; Internet (free). In room: A/C, TV, hair dryer.

WHERE TO DINE

Washington Jockey Club SOUTHERN   On the historic town square, this restaurant and bar is a bastion of good southern cooking, including Joe Barnett's award-winning shrimp and grits, once featured on Martha Stewart's show. The dish combines sautéed wild Georgia shrimp with cheesy grits and a spicy sauce topped with country ham. Some of the recipes are from the Washington Jockey Club's archives; the club opened in 1798.

Start with such delights as fried green tomatoes or sweet potato shillings (instead of regular french fries). Main course delights include hand-cut, tender filet mignon, fried oysters, or perhaps a Jockey Club ribeye, a 14-ounce steak seasoned with the house's special sauce.

5 E. Square. Tel. 706/678-1672.. Reservations recommended. Main courses $9.95-$23.95. MC, V. Fri-Sat 11am-2pm; Mon-Sat 5-9pm.

CRAWFORDVILLE

45 miles SE of Athens; 90 miles E of Atlanta; 55 miles W of Augusta; 20 miles SE of Washington

The moment you arrive in sleepy Crawfordville, you may experience déjà vu. If you're a moviegoer, you probably have seen the Main Street of Crawfordville many times. Locals have dubbed it the Tinseltown of East Georgia. It's been used in a number of films—*Summer of My German Soldier, A 1940s tale* with Kristy McNichol, *Coward of the County* with Kenny Rogers and Dan Biggers, *Paris Trout* with Dennis Hopper and Barbara Hershey, and *Passion for Justice*, with Jane Seymour portraying a newspaper editor. It's also been used as a backdrop for *Carolina Skeltons*, with Lou Gosset Jr. and Bruce Dern, and *Neon Bible*, with Gena Rowlands.

Since the days of the Depression, no one could afford to make any improvements on the Main Street, so it exists today as a living monument to the early 1930s.

Crawfordville is only 2 miles off I-20, about midway between Atlanta and Augusta. Take exit 55 and go north on Highway 22 for 2 miles. Go east on U.S. 278 one mile to Crawfordville.

SEEING THE SIGHTS

The town's major attraction is the **A.H. Stephens State Historic Park** (✆ 706/456-2602), site of **Liberty Hall** (✆ 706/456-2221). The park is named for A.H. Stephens, vice president of the Confederacy and former governor of Georgia. He lived at Liberty Hall from 1834 until his death in 1883. The home has been restored, and is very much as it was in the Georgia hero's day. Some of the antiques on display were used by the Stephens family, and the former vice president's bedroom is furnished with original pieces. Stephens was imprisoned at Fort Warren for part of 1865, at the end of the Civil War. Small in stature and frail in health, he seldom weighed more than 90 pounds.

Adjacent to Liberty Hall is an impressive **Confederate Museum** (✆ 706/456-2221), housing uniforms of men in gray, along with a display of muskets, swords, documents, letters, diaries, and more than 300 other items related to the Civil War and Stephens. The exhibit is one of the finest collections of Confederate artifacts in Georgia. The museum is open Tuesday to Saturday from 9am to 5pm and Sunday from 2 to 5pm. Admission is $3 for adults and $1.50 for children 12 and under.

The park, which is open daily from 7am to 10pm and charges no admission, offers boating, fishing, hiking, camping, biking, and walking opportunities. It has two lakes along with outdoor cooking and even dance facilities. Many area residents hunt here, mainly for deer, although wild turkey and squirrels are targets as well. The park stretches across 1,200 acres, with 25 tent and trailer sites. It has an Olympic-size swimming pool and embraces the 18-acre Lake Buncombe, with public fishing. The lake is stocked with bass and brim. The smaller 2 ½-acre Lake Liberty—stocked with catfish—also offers public fishing. Historic nature trails cut through the park.

WHERE TO DINE

Do not rush to get the editors of *Bon Appétit* on the phone. One old-timer told us that the food served today in Crawfordville was exactly as he recalls it from when he was young here in 1914. But for good, simple, filling fare that's as American as apple pie, you've come to the right place.

Heavy's Barbecue BARBECUE Since 1970, this isolated homestead has ladled up platters of barbecue every weekend to travelers from as far away as Atlanta. During deer-hunting season, you will think you have arrived on the set of a remake of *Deliverance*. It occupies a rustic log-and-plank-sided cabin straight out of summer camp, with a thick stone chimney belching up the smoke that seasons the limited array of menu items. Order at the battered countertop, then carry your selection to one of the three dining rooms. Each has enough accountrements to stock a museum of local folklore, including a selection of stuffed animals and antique farm implements. Your host is William Grant ("Heavy"), who is assisted by members of his extended family. Take the chance, especially if you're with children, to wander around the compound, whose buildings include cooped-up chickens, roosters, and peacocks, a pond with its own gazebo, and old fashioned houses. Some folks drive hours out of the way for a taste of Heavy's.

2155 Sparta Rd. SE, 4 miles south of Crawfordville. (© **706/456-2445**). Sandwiches $3.50-$4.50; platters $5.75-$9.75. MC, V. Fri-Sun 9am–9pm.

AUGUSTA ★

139 miles E of Atlanta; 122 miles N of Savannah

Home to one of the world's most prestigious men's professional golf tournaments, the Masters, Augusta is a Southern city of charm and grace. Lying along the banks of the Savannah River, it stands about halfway between Savannah and Atlanta.

Augusta is the state's second-oldest city, dating from 1736, when it was marked off for settlement by Gen. James E. Oglethorpe, founder of Georgia. It was a major winter resort, attracting the Yankee wealthy, such as John D. Rockefeller. Except at the time of the Masters Tournament, Augusta doesn't attract vacationers like it did in its heyday, but that's beginning to change.

Essentials

GETTING THERE Augusta lies off I-20, the main route from Atlanta, on the west bank of the Savannah River.

Bush Field Airport (© 706/798-3236; http://ags.skyharbors.com) lies just a 15-minute drive from the center of Augusta. Fifty commercial flights wing their way into the airport daily. Connections are possible via **Delta** (© 800/221-1212; www.delta.com) or **US Airways** (© 800/428-4322; www.usair.com) from both Atlanta and Charlotte.

Buses run by **Greyhound** (© 800/231-2222; www.greyhound.com) and **Southeastern Stages** (© 404/591-2750; www.southeasternstages.com) arrive downtown at the **Southeastern Stage bus terminal,** 1128 Greene St. (© 706-722-6411).

VISITOR INFORMATION   The **Augusta Metropolitan Convention & Visitors Bureau,** 1450 Greene St. (© 800/726-0243 or 706/823-6600; www.augustaga.org), is open Monday to Friday 8:30am to 5pm.

SPECIAL EVENTS   It seems that half the world—at least, the golfing half—focuses on Augusta the first full week in April for the nationally televised **Masters Golf Tournament ★★★**, a tradition since 1934 and now the most prestigious golf tournament in the world. Hotel space is at a premium then, and prices for rooms soar to whatever the market will bear. Call © 706/667-6000 or go to www.masters.org for more information.

Seeing the Sights

The major attraction is **Riverwalk ★**, the tree-lined paths at the edge of the Savannah River, between 5th and 10th streets, which are resplendent with greenery and seasonal flowers. Riverwalk includes 5 blocks of unique development, including a full-service, 67-slip marina. It boasts a 1,700-seat amphitheater that plays host to various performances throughout the year. It's perfect for a moonlit stroll or an afternoon spent picnicking, shopping, and enjoying one of the city's many festivals. You can see the river from both bi-level and tri-level platforms, with historical markers along the way.

Although it's not a grand attraction, you can visit the **Boyhood Home of Woodrow Wilson,** 419 7th St. (© 706/722-9828; www.wilsonboyhoodhome.org), which has been restored and opened to the public. The future president lived here from 1860 to 1870 during the years his father served as pastor of the First Presbyterian Church. Admission is $5 for adults, $4 for seniors, and $3 for students and children, and hours are Tuesday to Saturday 10am to 5pm. (Last tour departs at 4pm.)

Confederate Powderworks, along the Augusta Canal on Goodrich Street, is a 168-foot-tall chimney, all that remains of the second-largest powder factory in the world, which operated between 1862 and 1865. It is the only permanent structure begun and completed by the Confederate government, and it once consisted of 26 buildings.

The best way to introduce yourself to Augusta is to contact **Historic Augusta Tours** (© 706/724-4067; www.augustaga.org), which conducts tours every Saturday from 1:30 to 3:30pm. The tour leaves from the Museum of History Building at 5 Reynolds St. Reservations are required by noon the Friday before. Cost is $10 for adults and $5 for children.

Ezekiel Harris House   Constructed by Ezekiel Harris, a leading Augusta tobacco merchant, this 1797 house re-creates the heyday of the late 18th century, when locals grew rich trading in tobacco. The planter's house is filled with period furnishings.

1822 Broad St. © **706/737-2820.** Admission $2 adults and seniors, $1 children 6–17, free for children 5 and under. Sat 10am–5pm; Tues–Fri by appointment.

Gertrude Herbert Institute of Art   This Federal-style house was built in 1818 for Augusta mayor Nicholas Ware at the cost of $40,000—a tidy sum back then. It now serves as an art institute, a center not only for art classes, but for changing exhibitions open to the public.

506 Telfair St. ✆ **706/722-5495.** www.ghia.org. Free admission; donations accepted. Tues–Fri 8:30am–5pm.

Meadow Garden   This Sand Hill cottage (ca. 1791) was the home of George Walton, youngest original signer of the Declaration of Independence and twice Georgia governor. It is the oldest documented house in Augusta and the first historic preservation project in the state.

1320 Independence Dr. (near the intersection of 13th St. and Walton Way). ✆ **706/724-4174.** www.historicmeadowgarden.org. Admission $4 adults, $3.50 seniors, $1 children. Mon–Fri 10am–4pm. Last tour leaves at 3:30pm.

Morris Museum of Art   This museum features period galleries that display more than 2,000 works spanning 1790 to the present. The museum, which hosts changing exhibitions quarterly, also has a museum shop and a visitor-orientation gallery. Admission is free on Sunday.

Riverwalk and 1 Tenth St. ✆ **706/724-7501.** www.themorris.org. Admission $5 adults; $3 seniors, students, and military; free for children 6 and under and for all on Sun. Tues–Sat 10am–5pm; Sun noon–5pm.

National Science Center's Fort Discovery ★ ☺   This is a hands-on science, technology, and communications center that attracts families and student groups from all over Georgia. There are some 250 interactive exhibits, and traveling exhibitions, such as Inventions of Leonardo da Vinci, are presented throughout the year. On-site is a science store selling replications of the most popular custom exhibits.

7th Street. ✆ **800/325-5445** or 706/821-0600. www.nscdiscovery.org. Admission $8 adults, $6 seniors and children 4–7, free for children 3 and under. Thurs–Sat 10am–5pm.

St. Paul's Episcopal Church   The fourth structure to be built on this site, the St. Paul's you see today was built after a fire destroyed much of the downtown area in 1915. The first St. Paul's was constructed in 1750 as part of Fort Augusta, constructed by the British in 1739. The Celtic Cross, used to designate the site, still stands. The cemetery next to the church was used during colonial days up through 1819, and many notable Georgians are buried here.

605 Reynolds St. ✆ **706/724-2485.** www.saintpauls.org. Free admission. Guided tours by appointment only. Mon–Thurs 9am–4:30pm; Fri–Sat 9am–noon. Sun service 7:45am, 9am, and 11am.

Golf & Other Outdoor Pursuits

Golf is king in Augusta, but unfortunately, the famous tournament course at Augusta National isn't open to the public. We recommend **Goshen Plantation,** 1601 Goshen House Club Dr. (✆ **706/793-1035;** www.goshenplantation.com), one of the most beautiful and challenging courses in the Central Savannah River Area (CSRA). It has well-bunkered greens and demanding par 3s, 4s, and 5s, and requires you to use every club in your bag. It also has a fully stocked pro shop and the restaurant On the Green. Greens fees are $32 to $37, and hours are daily 7:30am to dusk.

Augusta Canal (✆ **888/659-8926** or 706/823-0440; www.augustacanal.com), stretching across two counties from the center of Augusta to Evans-to-Locks Road in Columbia County, is the setting for an array of activities, including bicycling, fishing, canoeing, hiking, running, walking, and picnicking. Visit **Savannah Rapids Park** (📞 706/868-3349; www.savannahrapids.com) for easy access to the canal. For canoe rentals, call 📞 **706/738-8500.**

Thurmond Lake, north on Washington Road (about 20 miles from the center of Augusta), offers 1,200 miles of shoreline bordering Georgia and South Carolina. One of the largest inland bodies of water in the South, it has some of the best outdoor sports around, including swimming, sailing, water-skiing, fishing, hunting, and just plain sunbathing. The lake is surrounded by a 70,000-acre park. A Visitor and Information Center (www.georgialakeinfo.com/thurmond) is located at the South Carolina end of the dam off Highway 221.

Where to Stay

If you can't get a room in town for the Masters, try for lodgings in Aiken, South Carolina (see chapter 14).

Doubletree Hotel Augusta ★★   The renovated hotel, with its airy atrium lobby, is ideal for the business traveler or the vacationer seeking first-class accommodations in a conventional hotel. Rising six floors, it is about 2 miles from the Augusta Mall and some 10 miles from downtown attractions. The hotel facilities are the best in the area, with a heated indoor pool. Guest rooms are spacious and elegantly decorated, from the granite countertops to the cherrywood vanities. The most desirable rooms come with "jetted" bathtubs, microwaves, and refrigerators.

2651 Perimeter Pkwy., Augusta, GA 30909. 📞 **706/855-8100.** Fax 706/860-1720. www.augusta. doubletree.com. 179 units. $109–$134 double; $134–$349 suite. AE, DC, MC, V. **Amenities:** 2 restaurants; bar; exercise room; 2 pools (1 indoor); room service. *In room:* A/C, TV, hair dryer, Wi-Fi (free).

Marriott Hotel & Suites ★   This chain hotel enjoys the best location in town; its well-furnished but standard rooms open onto the Savannah River and historic River-walk. Frommer's readers Michael Barnas and Phyllis Feingold-Barnas likened the spacious second-floor concourse of the hotel to a trip back to the "Castle of Versailles, with its sweeping marbled floor length, chandelier after chandelier ceiling, and profusion of flower-filled oversize vases." Augustino's serves only fair Italian dishes, and an adjoining lounge offers big-screen sports. The staff will direct guests to 19 premium golf courses in the area, challenges to both novices and pros alike.

2 Tenth St., Augusta, GA 30901. 📞 **800/868-5354** or 706/722-8900. Fax 706/823-6513. www.marriott. com. 372 units. $109–$139 double; $229–$259 suite. AE, DC, DISC, MC, V. **Amenities:** Restaurant; bar; exercise room; Jacuzzi; 2 pools (1 indoor); room service. *In room:* A/C, TV, hair dryer, kitchenette (in some), Wi-Fi (free).

The Partridge Inn ★   During Augusta's heyday as a winter resort—roughly from 1889 to 1930—the Partridge Inn was known as the city's grande dame. The resort's fame faded when Henry Flagler extended the railroad to Florida and the Great Depression hit. By the early 1980s, the hotel was slated for demolition. Fortunately, it was saved, and in 1988, after a major restoration, it reopened. Today's accommodations come in an almost dizzying array of combinations, from standard double to queen- and king-size beds, and some rooms offer views or kitchenettes.

2110 Walton Way, Augusta, GA 30904. 📞 **800/476-6888** or 706/737-8888. Fax 706/731-0826. www.partridgeinn.com. 144 units. $119–$169 double. AE, DC, DISC, MC, V. **Amenities:** Restaurant; bar; exercise room; outdoor pool; room service. *In room:* A/C, TV, hair dryer, kitchenette (in some), Wi-Fi (free).

Where to Dine

Calvert's ★★ AMERICAN   Since it opened in 1977, Calvert's has emerged as the best restaurant in Augusta. In the Surrey Center, the elegant restaurant lures with its dark paneling and candlelit tables. Traditional cuisine is based, whenever possible, on fine local ingredients. The crab cakes are made with Virginia fried ham, a zesty concoction, as is the velvety blend of shrimp, clams, and spinach into a seafood bisque perked up with a touch of Pernod. The main courses are impressive in their wise simplicity and superb cooking technique. Especially notable is the leek-wrapped salmon with a grilled shrimp skewer and a lemon white butter, or pan-seared duck breasts with a black-cherry port sauce. Desserts are made fresh daily.

475 Highland Ave. ✆ **706/738-4514.** www.calvertsrestaurant.com. Reservations recommended. Main courses $25–$35. AE, DISC, MC, V. Tues–Sat 5–10pm.

French Market Grille ★ LOUISIANA   In a faux French-market atmosphere located in a shopping center, this restaurant is often hailed as the best in Augusta. It's good, but we give our vote to Calvert's (see above). Po'boys are featured at lunch and might be stuffed with everything from spicy chicken to soft-shell crab. Recommended is the chef's crab chop à la Charles (crabmeat bound by white sauce, with the added flavors of green onions and other seasonings). The *étouffée* (choice of either shrimp or crawfish) was suitably spicy, Cajun style. The desserts, including pecan praline pie and New Orleans bread pudding, have been voted "best desserts in Augusta" by *Augusta Magazine* several years in a row.

425 Highland Ave. ✆ **706/737-4865.** www.frenchmarketaugusta.com. Reservations not accepted. Main courses $18–$32. AE, DISC, MC, V. Mon–Thurs 11:30am–10pm; Fri–Sat 11:30am–11pm.

La Maison Restaurant & Veritas Wine & Tapas ★ FRENCH/AMERICAN   In a Southern Revival home, this elegant choice for dining is perhaps the finest in Augusta in terms of cuisine, ambience, and service. Its special feature is a wine bar and tapas lounge, recognized by *Wine Spectator* for its excellence. This is the finest choice in Augusta for a romantic dinner. Appetizers are often typical, though excellent: French appetizers such as snails in garlic butter, and delightful surprises such as smoked ostrich carpaccio with arugula and vine-ripened tomatoes misted with truffle oil. Chef Heinz's signature dishes (and we endorse them with enthusiasm) include rack of lamb with fresh herbs and an apricot teriyaki glaze, and Dover sole sautéed in butter with grapes and almonds. The five-course light dinner is the best value in the city.

404 Telfair St. ✆ **706/722-4805.** www.lamaisontelfair.com. Reservations recommended. Main courses $17–$43. AE, DC, DISC, MC, V. Mon–Sat 6–9:30pm.

Old McDonald Fish Camp, Inc. ★ 🐟 SEAFOOD   When locals from Augusta hanker for catfish and hush puppies and all those good things, they head right to this old fish camp. It's known for serving the best catfish in the area, although you can also order ocean perch, fried shrimp, scallops, crabs, oysters, and even fried gator. One feature is a Low Country boil, with shrimp, sausage, potatoes, corn, and coleslaw. The Thursday-night special is an all-you-can-eat fry of catfish, fish filet, and perch filet—a real bargain. It's a family favorite, even if the fish is often overcooked—hey, that's the way the locals like it.

355 Currytown Rd., N. Augusta. ✆ **803/279-3305.** www.oldmcdonaldfishcamp.com. Main courses $12–$20. MC, V. Thurs 5–9pm; Fri 5–9:30pm; Sat 4–9:30pm. Take I-20 E. to exit 1 in South Carolina, turn left, and go 5 miles.

Veranda Grill in the Partridge Inn ★ 🔥 STEAKHOUSE/SEAFOOD/SOUTH-ERN Dining at the legendary Partridge Inn has long been an Augusta tradition. The chef, Dominic Simpson, brings a fresh innovative approach to certified Angus beef, fresh seafood from the coast, and old-time Georgia favorites. A breakfast buffet is offered every morning with freshly prepared dishes or else a la carte choices such as blackened shrimp with roasted peppers and tasso gravy over creamy grits. The lunch buffet is the best in Augusta, or you can order menu favorites such as she-crab bisque followed by grilled pesto chicken breast. At night the chef really shines with his beef dishes, including grilled hangar steak and seared venison medallions on a butter bean and country ham ragout.

In the Partridge Inn, 2110 Walton Way. ✆ **706/737-8888.** Reservations recommended. Breakfast $12 buffet, $7.95–$11 main courses; lunch $21 buffet, $12–$14 main courses; dinner main courses $18–$27; Sun brunch $26. AE, DC, DISC, MC, V. Sun–Thurs 6am–10pm; Fri–Sat 6am–11pm.

NORTH GEORGIA

Within 70 to 120 miles of Atlanta, North Georgia may be one of the South's best-kept travel secrets. City dwellers can hike through national forests, scale Georgia's highest peak, canoe and swim in mountain lakes, and return home at dusk, or stay over in a comfortable lodging or campground.

Tennessee, Alabama, and Georgia meet in the "TAG Corner" on the Cumberland Plateau. The TAG (Tennessee-Alabama-Georgia) Corner is a terrain of sheer-walled canyons, limestone caves, boulder-littered fields, streaming waterfalls, and mesa-topped mountains that has been compared to a landscape in the West. The first European visitors claimed they had rediscovered Eden when they first came upon the area. It's amazing how little known these Georgia mountains are—even today. Yet, the mountain chain, occupying some two-thirds of North Georgia, consists of the Blue Ridge Mountains frontal range to the east and the Cohutta Mountains to the west.

Northwest Georgia is also filled with remnants of the Civil War (called "the War of Northern Aggression" in these parts) and with artifacts left over from ancient aboriginal civilizations. You'll also be introduced to traditional Appalachian culture, Georgia style. Arts and crafts, including pottery making, basket weaving, and quilting, are still practiced in the region. And at all local festivals and even on the front porch on a Saturday night, the sound of bluegrass music still fills the air.

Dahlonega (see later in this chapter) and its environs are the premier "gateways" to the area. The best parks to visit include Amicalola Falls, Unicoi, and Vogel.

THE GREAT OUTDOORS IN NORTH GEORGIA

As one naturalist said of North Georgia, "scenic touring is about any road you want to travel." Of course, some trails and scenic highways are more memorable than others. Just north of Helen and within easy reach of Blairsville, the **Richard Russell Scenic Highway** (Ga. 348) is one we always travel, with mountain vistas up to 3,644 feet.

If you don't like to hike, you can see much of the panorama of North Georgia from your car by taking Ga. 52, the highway between Chatsworth and Ellijay (the latter called the apple capital of the state). This road offers scenic previews of **Fort Mountain State Park,** about 7 miles east of Chatsworth (© **800/ 864-7275** or 706/422-1932; www.gastateparks.org/info/fortmt), and the **Cohutta Wilderness.**

Much of North Georgia is encompassed by **Chattahoochee National Forest ★★,** a vast region of some 750,000 acres, including the Georgia Blue Ridge Mountains to the north. Elevations range from 1,000 to some 5,000 feet. It's a vacationer's paradise, with some two dozen picnic areas, the same number of camp-sites, six swimming beaches, and 10 protected wilderness areas. The forest offers such natural attractions as **Anna Ruby Falls,** 6 miles north of Alpine Helen; the **Appalachian National Scenic Trail; Vogel State Park,** south of Blairsville; and **Amicalola Falls State Park,** with the state's highest waterfall, outside Dahlonega.

For information about exploring this vast forest, write to the **U.S. Forest Service,** 1755 Cleveland Hwy., Gainesville, GA 30501 (© **770/297-3000;** www.fs.fed.us).

In contrast, the **Cohutta Wilderness** alone covers 37,000 acres or some 60 square miles spilling over into Tennessee. When an area called Hemp Top was added in 1986, the region became the third-largest mountain wilderness in the East. Fishers claim that the Cohuttas have the best trout streams in the south. Hikers and anglers alike are seen along the banks of the Conasauga River and Jack's River. Walking trails follow the old logging roads of the 1920s. Hikers and backpackers should take 17-mile Jack's River Trail, which virtually crosses the wilderness going northwest to southeast.

For detailed information about this vast wilderness, call © **706/695-6736** and speak to the U.S. Forest Service in advance of your trip. Always check road conditions before venturing into such wild terrain—roads may be closed in bad weather.

Of course, the most famous trail in the area—in fact, America's most fabled scenic trail—is the **Appalachian Trail ★★★** (© **304/535-6331;** www.appalachiantrail. org), beginning at Georgia's Springer Mountain and crossing 14 states until it finally comes to an end some 2,100 exhausting miles later in Katahdin, Maine. Hikers usually leave Georgia in April, arriving in Maine in September or even as late as October, when they earn the right to call themselves a "2,000 Miler." The trail runs across Georgia for 79 miles before reaching the border of North Carolina.

Among our favorite state parks in Georgia is **Cloudland Canyon State Park.** The terrain is rugged, but the park has modern outdoor amenities, such as a swim-ming pool and a tennis court. The 2,120-acre scenic park lies near the village of Rising Fawn, on the west side of Lookout Mountain. Gulch Creek, a deep gorge, slices through the park, with elevations ranging from 800 to 1,800 feet. It has some 75 camping sites and lots of ideal spots for a picnic.

The park lies on Ga. 136, 8 miles east of Trenton and I-59, and 18 miles northwest of La Fayette. It's open daily 7am to 10pm year-round. For additional information, contact **Cloudland Canyon State Park,** Department of Natural Resources, 122 Cloudland Canyon Rd., Rising Fawn, GA 30738 (© **706/657-4050;** www.gastate parks.org).

Lookout Mountain (© **800/825-8366** or 706/820-2531; www.lookoutmountain. com) sprawls more than 100 miles, ignoring state lines and spilling into Tennessee, Alabama, and Georgia. Two towns—both named Lookout Mountain—lie on each side of the border. Lookout Mountain is accessible by I-24 from Chattanooga heading toward Georgia.

CHICKAMAUGA & CHATTANOOGA NATIONAL MILITARY PARK ★★

110 miles N of Atlanta

The country's oldest (1890) and biggest military park stretches across an 8,000-acre site 9 miles south of Chattanooga on U.S. 27. Ranking along with Gettysburg and Vicksburg, the national historic shrine consists of multiple sites, principally Chickamauga Battlefield, Lookout Mountain Battlefield, and Moccasin Bend National Archeological District.

On September 19 and 20, 1863, a Confederate force of 66,000 men met by accident a Union force of 58,000. The 2-day battle left 36,000 casualties. It marked the greatest success of Confederate armies in the west, although the advantage was not seized.

Some 80 miles of hiking trails cut through the valley and 1,500 historical markers, tablets, artillery pieces, and monuments mark the movement of troops. At the **visitor center** (© **706/866-9241**), on the northern entrance to the battlefield, self-guided audiotape tours are available. A slide show recounts the battle hour by hour. The center is open daily from 8:30am to 6pm Memorial Day to Labor Day, closing at 4:45pm for the rest of the year. Admission is free to the park. To reach it, exit I-75 at Ga. 2 and go west for 6 miles to Highway 27 (exit 141), at which point you head south to the park, a mile from the town of Fort Oglethorpe.

Where to Stay

Since accommodations are scarce in the area, you may want to drive toward the Tennessee border. Just across the state line is Chattanooga's full range of accommodations, bars, restaurants, and nightclubs.

Chattanooga Choo Choo ★★   This gets our vote for one of the most unusual hotels in the state. From 1909 to 1970, all trains to points south passed through Chattanooga's famous terminal. A group of investors in 1973 saved the landmark from demolition and created a magnificent 85-foot free-standing dome to crown the station, the main point of this 24-acre property. Exceptional accommodations were installed in the 48 original Pullman cars, including roomy suites. Accommodations are handsomely and comfortably furnished and well accessorized, including such features as a hot tub, large vanity with two sinks, and a separate shower unit. On-site is the Station House Restaurant, featuring succulent steaks, barbecue ribs, and fresh seafood, along with singing servers. Also on-site is a museum of 120 locomotives, plus 1,000 freight cars, and 80 passenger cars.

140 Market St., Chattanooga, TN 37402. © **800/TRACK-29** (872-2529) or 423/266-5000. www. choochoo.com. 363 units. $150 double; $190 suite. Rates include breakfast. AE, DC, DISC, MC, V. **Amenities:** 4 restaurants; 2 bars; cafe; concierge; exercise room; 2 pools (indoor); room service. *In room:* A/C, TV, fridge (in some), hair dryer, Wi-Fi (free).

The Stonefort Inn ★★   In the heart of the downtown area, this is one of Tennessee's most elegant B&Bs. The inn makes for a romantic getaway in a historic landmark. Inside the boutique hotel is a blaze of colors—harvest yellow, rich maple sugar brown, deep coral, and periwinkle blue. Because of the ceiling height in some of the bedrooms, they appear cavernous. Each room is individually decorated, and much remains from the original construction, including arched nooks, heart-pine stairwells, and balconies. Bathrooms are a special feature, often containing classic tiles, two-person jetted tubs, and French showers. Among the furnishings in the bedrooms, the old and new have been skillfully combined. Stonefort is not suited for children under 12.

120 E. 10th St., Chattanooga, TN 37402. ✆ **888/945-7866** or 423/267-7866. www.stonefortinn.com. 16 units. $120–$145 double; $135–$155 suite. Rates include breakfast. AE, DC, DISC, MC, V. **Amenities:** Breakfast room. *In room:* A/C, TV/VCR, Wi-Fi (free).

ADAIRSVILLE

60 miles N of Atlanta

An hour's drive north of Atlanta will deliver you to northwest Georgia's most romantic retreat. The Barnsley Gardens, which lay in ruins for half a century, are now restored and part of a luxury resort funded by Prince Hubertus Fugger of Babenhausen, Germany. Before 1999, it was easy to skip Adairsville, until the German prince and his princess opened the sprawling 1,300-acre resort, nestled in the foothills of the Blue Ridge Mountains. Even if you're not a guest, you can dine at one of its restaurants, including a Bavarian beer garden, or else explore its 19th-century ruins, small museum, and 160-year-old formal gardens.

Essentials

GETTING THERE By car, take I-75 north from Atlanta for 60 miles, getting off at exit 306. Go west on Route 140 for 10 miles, following the signs to Barnsley Gardens.

Exploring the Gardens

Barnsley Gardens ★★ (✆ **877/773-2447**) are the only Andrew Jackson Downing–inspired gardens in the South. Downing, a renowned 19th-century architect, was the original designer of the White House grounds and the Washington Mall. The gardens themselves were planned in the late 19th century by Godfrey Barnsley, a cotton baron who built an Italian-style manor house and English gardens for his wife, Julia, in the foothills of the Blue Ridge Mountains. The estate boasts the largest private collection of conifers in the Southeast, with 88 species of pines. A museum in the manor's kitchen wing contains artifacts from the Civil War and memorabilia tracing the history of the ill-fated Barnsley family.

The museum and garden are open daily. Hours for the museum are 9am to 5:30pm and for the garden are 6am to 6pm. Admission is $10 for adults, $8 for seniors, and $5 for children.

Barnsley Inn & Golf Resort ★★★ Prince Fugger wanted his guests to feel as if they were visiting the country estate of a friend. The 19th-century pedestrian village is in keeping with Godfrey Barnsley's original vision. All 45 buildings, including 33 guest cottages, reflect architect Andrew Jackson Downing's drawings.

Guests can stay in one- to seven-bedroom cottages, each with a private porch with rocking chairs. Suites have wood-burning fireplaces, heart-pine floors, 12-foot ceilings, and custom-made king-size sleigh or poster beds dressed in Egyptian linens. Guest rooms are warm and homelike with antiques, plus original prints by Princess Alexandra, once a noted botanical photographer for *National Geographic*. Dining is among the finest in the area, with chefs providing interpretations of Southern

WILL THE REAL scarlett o'hara PLEASE STAND UP?

Julia, the daughter of cotton baron Godfrey Barnsley, was named after her mother and is said to be the inspiration for Margaret Mitchell's tempestuous character Scarlett O'Hara in *Gone With the Wind*. Detailing her Reconstruction struggles to hold on to the Barnsley estate in a letter to a friend, Julia wrote, "With God as my witness, I will never go hungry again." Of course, that is one of the most famous lines in the film.

Mitchell had read a book called *St. Elmo*, which was written about Julia in the 1860s, and in the process of researching *Gone With the Wind*, the Atlanta novelist interviewed Julia's daughter, Addie. It turns out that Julia might not have gone hungry, but her family fortune didn't improve. In 1906, a tornado blew the roof off the manor, forcing the family to live in the kitchen wing. The final blow came in 1935, when Preston Saylor, great-grandson of Godfrey and a successful prizefighter, shot and killed his brother in the manor during a dispute over control of the property. He was convicted of murder and sent to prison.

Descendants of Godfrey and Julia continued to live on the estate until it was auctioned off in 1942. The manor fell into a state of disrepair, and it was in this ruinous state that Prince Hubertus Fugger of Bavaria and his wife, Princess Alexandra, found it when they decided to buy it in 1988.

classics. The German royals have installed a Bavarian beer garden, and Barnsley also boasts one of the most spectacular spas in the state.

To add to the accolades, *Golf News* has proclaimed the **Barnsley Golf Course** the "Best Resort Course" in Georgia. The par-72, 18-hole course was designed by Jim Fazio, with one of the most difficult par 3s in the country. It stretches 5,450 yards (the red tees) to 7,200 yards (the pro tees) through the foothills of the Blue Ridge Mountains. Greens and cart fees are seasonal, varying from $75 to $125 for 18 holes.

597 Barnsley Gardens Rd., Adairsville, GA 30103. (C) **877/773-2447** or 770/773-7480. Fax 770/773-1779. www.barnsleyresort.com. 87 units. $299–$556 suite; $600–$2,903 2- to 7-bedroom cottages. AE, DC, MC, V. Pets permitted in some cottages. **Amenities:** 2 restaurants; bar; children's programs; exercise room; outdoor pool. *In room:* A/C, TV, minibar, Wi-Fi (free).

JASPER

60 miles N of Atlanta

As Georgia towns go, even some state residents draw a blank at the mention of Jasper. Yet Jasper contains one of the most famous inns in the northern part of the state. The town makes an ideal base for exploring the northwest corridor of Georgia on day trips.

Jasper is one of the marble centers of Georgia—in fact, marble quarried here was used in the Lincoln Memorial and the U.S. Capitol in Washington, D.C. A Marble Festival in early October highlights tours of the quarries, with music, food, and arts and crafts.

Essentials

GETTING THERE From Atlanta, drive along I-75 North to I-575, which turns into Highway 515 going north. Continue along Highway 515 North until you reach Highway 53 North, which will take you into the center of Jasper.

VISITOR INFORMATION   Contact the **Pickens Chamber of Commerce,** 500 Stegall Dr., Jasper, GA 30143 (*(©)* **706/692-5600;** www.pickenschamber.com). The chamber distributes information about the Jasper area. Hours are Monday to Friday from 9am to 5pm.

Where to Stay & Dine

The Woodbridge Inn ★★   Known for the quality of its food and lodging, this is the most famous inn in Northwest Georgia. It's in an antebellum setting with mountain vistas in all directions. The three-level lodge was designed to take in the views— patios and balconies open off the guest rooms. Some of the upper-level rooms have spiral staircases leading to sleeping lofts. The lodge is completely modern, having been reconstructed after a fire. People drive from miles away, even from Atlanta, to sample the food here. Both European and American dishes are offered, everything from veal Oscar to oysters Rockefeller. All the food is fresh, and dishes are individually prepared. Save room for dessert, especially the lemon cream pie.

44 Chambers St., Jasper, GA 30143. *(©)* **706/253-6293.** Fax 706/253-9061. www.woodbridgeinn.net. 18 units. $60–$80 double. AE, DC, DISC, MC, V. **Amenities:** Outdoor pool. *In room:* A/C, TV, Wi-Fi (free).

DAHLONEGA ★

70 miles NE of Atlanta

Dahlonega is a Cherokee word meaning "precious yellow." In 1828, according to legend, a trapper named Benjamin Parks stubbed his toe on a rock and uncovered a vein of gold here that quickly brought prospectors streaming into these hills. A town called Dahlonega suddenly appeared—America's first mining boomtown. The gold craze changed Cherokee culture forever.

Although prospecting hasn't been a major industry since the Civil War, enough gold is still around to periodically releaf the dome of Georgia's State Capitol, and to intrigue visitors who come here to pan for it.

Essentials

GETTING THERE   From Atlanta, take Highway 19/S.R. 400 North to S.R. 60, which you follow north for another 5 miles to reach Dahlonega.

VISITOR INFORMATION   The **Dahlonega Chamber of Commerce,** 13 S. Park St. (*(©)* **800/231-5543** or 706/864-3711; www.dahlonega.org), is open daily from 9am to 5:30pm. The staff distributes information about scenic attractions, state parks, and gold panning in the area.

Seeing the Sights

Dahlonega's Public Square sports a rustic look. Old galleried buildings and stores have been turned into shops purveying gold-panning equipment, gold jewelry, mountain handicrafts, antiques, ice cream, and fudge. It's very touristy but preserves a quaint charm in spite of the hordes who sometimes descend on summer days, mostly families with lots of kids in tow.

Formerly the Lumpkin County Courthouse, the **Dahlonega Courthouse Gold Museum,** Public Square (*(©)* **706/864-2257**), is in the center of the town square. Artifacts, coins, and tools from the nation's first major gold rush are shown, and a 27-minute film chronologically documents the feverish era. Besides being a gold miners' haven, this old museum is the state's third-oldest standing courthouse. It's also the second-most-visited Georgia historical site. The hours of operation are Monday to Saturday 9am to 5pm, and Sunday 10am to 5pm. Admission is $5 for adults, $4.50 for seniors, $3.50 for children 6 to 17, and free for children 5 and under.

You can take a tour and pan for gold at **Consolidated Gold Mines,** 185 Consolidated Gold Mines Rd. (© **706/864-8473;** www.consolidatedgoldmine.com). At the turn of the 20th century, it boasted the largest and most-advanced gold mine east of the Mississippi River, covering more than 7,000 acres, with some 200 tunnels. Tours into illuminated tunnels take about 40 minutes and are conducted by miners. Look for the 250-foot vertical shaft. The mine also offers a chance to pan for gold. It's open daily from 10am to 5pm, until 4pm in winter. Admission is $13 for adults and $9 for children 4 to 14. Take Highway 400 North from Dahlonega to Highway 60, turn left, and follow the signs.

Where to Stay

The Smith House   The owners, the Welch family, are known mainly for their restaurant (see "Where to Dine," below). With the Smith House, they offer plenty of mountain hospitality, if you don't mind staying at a place overrun with visitors. Originally built atop a rich vein of gold ore in 1884, it was turned into an inn in 1922, although the original owners wouldn't recognize today's bustling place. The inaugural $4.50-a-night rooms are long gone, too. The original rooms are furnished in a cozy, 19th-century style, and all have been authentically remodeled. One section of the little two-story hotel was originally a carriage house. This is very much a country inn, with rocking chairs on the front porch.

84 S. Chestatee St., Dahlonega, GA 30533. © **800/852-9577** or 706/867-7000. Fax 706/864-7564. www.smithhouse.com. 16 units. $139–$229 double. AE, MC, V. **Amenities:** Restaurant, The Smith House (see review, below); outdoor pool. *In room:* A/C, TV, hair dryer, Wi-Fi (free).

STAYING NEARBY

Forrest Hills Mountain Resort & Conference Center ★ 📷   Surrounded by the mountains of North Georgia, this adults-only retreat is a luxurious hideaway. It offers deluxe B&B rooms in the main lodge, and 12 bi-level luxury suites in the resort's Mountain Laurel Inn. But its special attraction is its rustic cottages, many ideal for a honeymoon, with hot tubs and large canopied beds. Fireplaces and well-kept bathrooms with tub/shower combinations add to the allure. The cottages have a woodland setting best enjoyed from porch swings. The 140 wooded acres border Chattahoochee National Forest and are about 4 miles from Amicalola Falls State Park; there are many hiking and bridle trails. Make reservations as far in advance as possible.

135 Forrest Hills Rd. (PO Box 510), Dahlonega, GA 30533. © **800/654-6313** or 706/864-6456. Fax 706/864-0757. www.foresths.com. 45 units. $79–$158 B&B double; $199–$250 Mountain Laurel Inn suite; $129–$249 cottage. Rates include full breakfast and candlelight dinner. AE, DISC, MC, V. 10 miles west on Ga. 52, then right onto Wesley Chapel Rd. **Amenities:** Restaurant; Jacuzzi; pool; Wi-Fi (free). *In room:* A/C, TV, no phone.

Where to Dine

The Smith House 🍴 SOUTHERN   In North Georgia, this large family-style restaurant—a tradition since 1922—is called "pig-out heaven." A lavish array of Southern food, along with homemade Smith House rolls, relishes, and desserts, is served at shared tables. This is true mountain cookin'—and plenty of it, all you can eat. Many dishes are based on 100-year-old recipes. Continuously replenished platters arrive, including angel biscuits, sweet-baked country-fried steak, and lots and lots of Southern fried chicken. Everything tastes better with the homemade corn bread, especially the Southern-style vegetables that include fried okra, black-eyed peas, rice and gravy, and candied yams. No one saves room for dessert, but everyone eats it anyway—banana fritters, strawberry shortcake, fruit cobbler, whatever.

84 S. Chestatee St. ✆ **706/867-7000.** www.smithhouse.com. Reservations not accepted. All-you-can-eat lunch and dinner Tues–Fri $15–$18, Sat–Sun $18. AE, MC, V. Tues–Fri 11am–3pm and 4–7:30pm; Sat 11am–8pm; Sun 11am–7:30pm.

BLAIRSVILLE

105 miles NE of Atlanta

You don't come here to visit this mountain town itself, but you can use it as a center for exploring—including Georgia's highest point, offering a panoramic view of the whole northern part of the state. Blairsville is set in a national forest.

The **Sorghum Festival** is held the first 3 weekends in October. Crafts are displayed, canned goods are sold, and cane is converted to sweet sorghum syrup before your eyes, with lots of free samples. Square dancing, greased pole climbing, and other contests typical of the mountain folk are followed by country music and more dancing.

Essentials

GETTING THERE   Driving from Atlanta, take I-75 North to I-575 and continue north on this highway until you reach Highway 515. Go north on Highway 515 to reach Blairsville.

VISITOR INFORMATION   The **Blairsville Chamber of Commerce,** 78 Blue Ridge Hwy., in Blairsville (✆ **877/745-5789** or 706/745-5789; www.blairsville chamber.com), is open Monday to Friday from 9am to 5pm and Saturday 10am to 1pm, distributing maps and brochures about the area.

Exploring the Area

Brasstown Bald ★★, Georgia's highest mountain, is set in a national forest with an observation tower atop its 4,784-foot summit. Here you'll have a 360-degree view across ridges into four different states. After parking, you can walk up the half-mile paved road or else take a bus to the top. There is no steeper half-mile walk in all of Georgia! At the top you can see a video explaining the legend and lore of the mountain. There's access to four hiking trails, ranging from .5 to 6 miles in length, and picnic tables are available. The surrounding area is home to a wide variety of plants and animals.

The park is open May to mid-November Monday to Friday 10am to 5pm, and Saturday and Sunday 10am to 5pm. In April, it is open only Saturday and Sunday 10am to 5pm. Admission is $4 for parking. The bus ride to the top and back costs $3 for all ages. For more information, write **Brasstown Ranger District,** 1881 Hwy. 515, Blairsville, GA 30512 (✆ **706/745-6928**). There is also the **Visitor Information Center** at the park (✆ **706/896-2555**) that is open daily 10am to 5pm.

To reach the mountain from Blairsville, take U.S. 19/129 South for 8 miles. Turn left or east onto Ga. 180 and go 12 miles to Ga. 180 Spur, where you turn left, or north. Another 3 miles leads to the Brasstown Bald parking lot.

Vogel State Park ★ is Georgia's second-oldest state park and one of its most frequented. In the heart of the North Georgia mountains at the foot of Blood and Slaughter mountains, it sprawls across 240 acres cut through with nature trails. It has a 22-acre lake, Lake Trahlyta, named for a Cherokee princess. You can swim (there's a bathhouse) or fish for bass, trout, and bream. The park hosts festivals, like Old Timer's Day in August.

Campsites are available with power and water hookups, hot showers, and laundry facilities. A tent costs $19 to $25. Cottages, 35 in all, are comfortably furnished and have wood-burning fireplaces. Prices range from $90 to $155.

At an elevation of 2,500 feet, park temperatures are cool, even in July and August. The park is open year-round daily from 7am to 10pm. It's 11 miles from Blairsville on U.S. 19/129. For more information, write **Vogel State Park,** 7485 Vogel State Park Rd., Blairsville, GA 30512 (© **706/745-2628;** www.gastateparks.org/info/vogel).

Richard Russell Scenic Highway is south of Blairsville, via U.S. 19/129, and east on Ga. 180. This 14-mile scenic mountain drive, with elevations ranging from 1,600 to 3,000 feet, offers panoramic views at every turn. The drive is especially popular in fall, when hardwoods blaze with colors. At the 3,500-foot Tesnatee Gap, the highway crosses the Appalachian Trail. The road crosses the Blue Ridge and forms the northern perimeter of the eastern half of Raven Cliffs Wilderness.

Where to Stay

Blood Mountain Cabins and Country Store   These cabins stand near the breezy top of Blood Mountain at a 3,000-foot elevation, and the Appalachian Trail crosses U.S. 19/129 only yards away. Summers here are the coolest in Georgia, and winter will send you seeking a seat close to the stove. The owners, Colley and George Case, can be found in their general store, dispensing information on the area and selling freshly brewed coffee. Cabins are furnished in a rustic style and—at least, in spring—don't match their natural setting when all the rhododendrons and azaleas burst into flame. Each cabin has a bedroom and an additional sleeping loft, plus a fireplace, ceiling fan, fully equipped kitchen, well-kept up-to-date bathroom, and a spacious deck with country rockers for taking in that view of Blood Mountain.

12829 Gainesville Hwy., Blairsville, GA 30512. ©/fax **800/284-6866** or 706/745-9454. www.blood mountain.com. 14 units. $79–$99 cabin for 4. 2-night minimum. DISC, MC, V. 13 miles south of Blairsville along U.S. 19/129. **Amenities:** Lounge. In room: A/C, TV, no phone.

Misty Mountain Inn and Cottages   This pet-friendly Victorian-style farmhouse in a bucolic setting is both a B&B and an inn, offering rooms with private bathrooms, fireplaces, and balconies, plus a cottage cluster with wood-burning fireplaces and kitchenettes. Rooms are furnished in a country-rustic style, and maintenance is high. Two cabins have whirlpool tubs, and all have well-kept bathrooms. Family cottages sleep five to eight, although two are suitable for only two guests. Hiking trails nearby include the Appalachian Trail, and Brasstown Bald Mountain is less than 10 miles away. White-water rafting is within a short drive, as are trout-filled mountain streams.

55 Misty Mountain Lane at Town Creek Rd., Blairsville, GA 30512. © **888/647-8966** or 706/745-4786. Fax 706/781-1002. www.jwww.com/misty. 10 units. $90 B&B room; $110 cottage. B&B rates include breakfast. MC, V. **Amenities:** Breakfast room; lounge. In room: A/C, TV, Wi-Fi (free).

ALPINE HELEN ★

85 miles NE of Atlanta

Once a quiet Appalachian village, Helen has been turned into a bit of Bavaria in the Georgia hills. Main Street buildings have red roofs, flower boxes, balconies, and murals. You can shop for sweaters, porcelains, cuckoo clocks, and Christmas ornaments; enjoy wurst and beer to oompah music at an outdoor beer garden; and, in September and October, join the revelry of Oktoberfest.

Essentials

GETTING THERE From Atlanta, drive north on I-85 to exit 45 near Gainesville. From here, take Highway 985/365 North for some 20 miles to Highway 384. After that, go for another 20 miles to Highway 75, then turn right for the final 3 miles into Helen.

VISITOR INFORMATION Alpine Helen Convention and Visitors Bureau, 726 Brucken St. (a half-mile from downtown), right off Main Street (© **800/858-8027** or 706/878-2181; www.helenga.org), dispenses information and provides maps and brochures of attractions in the area. Hours are Monday to Saturday from 9am to 5pm and Sunday from 10am to 4pm.

Exploring the Area

The best time to be here is for a special event, such as the Hot Air Balloon Festival, which kicks off the race to the Atlantic Ocean in late May (lasting until June), and Oktoberfest, a pale imitation of the real one in Munich. This beer-drinking fest in alcohol-shy Georgia begins in mid-September and continues to mid-October.

After you've seen all the shows and bought all those beer mugs and lederhosen you don't really need, you can do some serious exploring in the environs of Helen, which many visitors find more alluring than the overly commercialized town itself.

Outdoor Pursuits

Alpine tubing is the most popular outdoor sport here. If the day is hot, more people can be seen tubing on the Chattahoochee River than buying beer steins. The river runs right through Helen, and tube-rental outfits abound all along the banks. There are some rapids here, but they're rather brief, so even small children go tubing. We prefer **Cool River Tubing** (© **800/896-4595** or 706/878-2665; www.coolrivertubing.com), which will take you on a 2-hour float and bring you back to your starting point. The cost is $5 per person.

Sunburst Stables, 9 miles east of Helen on Ga. 255 in the Sautee Valley (© **800/806-1953** or 706/947-7433; www.sunburststables.com), offers 25 miles of scenic wooded trails year-round. You can even go riding in winter, perhaps spotting a deer cavorting through the forest. Various types of rides are offered, including a 2-day overnight ride and a 3-hour sunset ride. The stables are set on 60 acres and adjoin the Chattahoochee National Forest. The outfit also offers hayrides.

Advance reservations are required; the hourly rate is $35 per person. No children 7 and under are allowed. When making a reservation and agreeing upon the time, give them your height, weight, and experience in riding. A major credit card (American Express, Discover, MasterCard, or Visa) is required to hold a reservation. A weight limit of 240 pounds is imposed.

Where to Stay

Helendorf River Inn Tucked away on a side street, in the Teutonic-looking heart of the village, this hotel sports Bavarian-style frescoes on its stucco surfaces that look oddly incongruous in the Georgia heat. It's one of the town's enduring hotels, with one of the most central locations. Despite its folkloric exterior, it's remarkable for what it doesn't offer: The lobby is cramped and unimaginative, and there's no bar. You'll find an ersatz kind of folklore, a staff with a laconic mountain drawl, and a wide variety of accommodations. The most appealing overlook the Chattahoochee River, which runs against one foundation of the building. Some rooms have hints of alpine coziness, and many have private balconies. Suites contain Jacuzzis and fireplaces.

33 Munichstrasse St., Helen, GA 30545. © **800/445-2271** or 706/878-2271. Fax 706/878-2271. www. helendorf.com. 99 units. $54–$114 double; $150–$199 suite. MC, V. **Amenities:** Restaurant; indoor pool. *In room:* A/C, TV, kitchenette (in some), Wi-Fi (free).

Hofbrau Riverfront Hotel This is a faux German-style guesthouse. At any minute, you expect to see a ruby-cheeked innkeeper emerge to wish you *guten appetit.* Its restaurant, the **Hofbrauhaus,** is one of the best and most famous in Helen (see "Where to Dine," below). Families enjoy the shaded patio with its porch swings, and guests stroll down to watch the flow of the river. The guest rooms are simply furnished but comfortable, each well maintained. Couches and TVs are found in the lounge.

9001 N. Main St., Helen, GA 30545. © **800/830-3977** or 706/878-2184. www.riverfronthotel.com. 38 units. Double Sun–Thurs $79–$129; Fri–Sat $99–$159; suite Sun–Thurs $139–$159, Fri–Sat $169–$179. Children 11 and under stay free in parent's room. AE, DC, DISC, MC, V. **Amenities:** Restaurant, The Hofbrauhaus (see review, p. 438); bar; outdoor pool; room service. *In room:* A/C, TV, fridge, hair dryer (on request), Wi-Fi (free).

The Lodge at Smithgall Woods ★ 🎁 This elegant mountain retreat stands in the midst of a 5,555-acre conservation area, attracting a well-heeled clientele who enjoy its seclusion and the country charm of a private mountain estate. In peace and seclusion, the guest rooms are located in five different cottages that all open onto panoramic views. The rooms are well furnished and exceedingly comfortable, all with private bathrooms with tub/shower combinations. Each is individually decorated with antiques, well-chosen fabrics, and Oriental rugs, the ambience both rustic yet elegant. The lodge also opens onto one of the finest trout streams in Georgia and, as such, the chef's specialty is mountain trout. In addition to fishing, activities include hiking, biking, birding, and nature walks.

61 Tsalaki Trail, Helen, GA 30545. © **800/318-5248** or 706/878-3087. Fax 706/878-0301. http:// gastateparks.org/core/item/page.aspx?s=14181.0.9.5646. 14 units. $189–$399 double. Rates include all meals Sat–Sun. AE, DC, DISC, MC, V. **Amenities:** Dining area; lounge. *In room:* A/C, TV, Wi-Fi (free).

Stovall House ★ Nestled amid a copse of trees at the summit of a hill, this veranda-ringed farmhouse was built in 1837 as the centerpiece of a 300-acre plantation. It was converted into a B&B in 1983 by Hamilton ("Ham") Schwartz, a hardworking schoolteacher and soccer coach from Philadelphia. Guest rooms are high ceilinged and outfitted with an eclectic mix of antiques. They include old-fashioned beds, which might not be as comfortable as the ones you're used to, but which compensate with their charm. Top-floor rooms have skylights.

Dinner is a celebration of well-flavored food. Served Thursday to Saturday 5:30 to 8:30pm, menu items include a "phyllo of the day" (including a version filled with ham, broccoli, and cheddar), chicken stuffed with cream cheese and herbs, scaloppini of pork, and at least two versions of fresh mountain trout. Full dinners are a bargain, starting from about $20 per person.

1526 Hwy. 255 N., Sautee, GA 30571. © **706/878-3355.** www.stovallhouse.com. 5 units. $98 double. Rate includes continental breakfast. Discount of 10% Dec–Mar. AE, MC, V. 5 miles southeast of Helen on Hwy. 255. **Amenities:** Restaurant; lounge. *In room:* A/C, no phone, Wi-Fi (free).

Unicoi State Park and Lodge ⚓ On a pristine lake in the midst of 1,063 acres of woodland, this state lodge, built in 1972, stands in the heart of the park. Warm and wood beamed, it offers fully equipped and rather rustic cottages tucked into the wooded hillsides. Some of the guest rooms need refurbishing, but the price is right. The cottages lie along the lake and farther up Smith Creek. The lodge has an excellent cafeteria-style dining room serving three meals a day at modest prices. Even if you're not staying here, consider a stopover for an all-you-can-eat buffet.

Unicoi State Park (PO Box 849), Helen, GA 30545. © **800/573-9659** or 706/878-2201. Fax 706/878-1897. www.gastateparks.org/info/unicoi. 100 units, 30 cottages. $70–$130 double; $105–$139 cottage. AE, DC, DISC, MC, V. **Amenities:** Restaurant; bar; bike rentals; outdoor pool; 4 tennis courts (lit); Wi-Fi (free). *In room:* A/C, TV, hair dryer, kitchenette (in some).

Where to Dine

The Hofbrauhaus INTERNATIONAL By virtue of its name alone, this is the most famous restaurant in Helen, with a Teutonic-derived schmaltz that can be endearing in a rather corny way. It sits at the edge of the Chattahoochee and caters to a hard-core battalion of serious beer drinkers, especially during Oktoberfest. Most of the time, however, the place is a family-trade enclave. The menu is divided into six categories that cover a wide cross section of the world's cuisines. There's Italian (chicken cacciatore), French (frogs' legs Provençal and steak *au poivre*), seafood (chargrilled swordfish), German/Bavarian (Wiener schnitzel), and American (fried Georgia mountain trout or prime rib of beef). All main courses include soup, salad, vegetable, roll, and butter.

9001 N. Main St. © **706/878-2248.** Reservations recommended. Main courses $10–$25. AE, DC, DISC, MC, V. Restaurant Mon–Thurs and Sun 4–9pm; Fri–Sat 4–10pm. Bar/lounge daily 3pm–1am.

Shopping

Betty's Country Store It's the most folkloric large grocery store in Georgia, stocked with all the inventory you'd expect in a modern grocery chain, yet permeated with the old-time aura of an early-20th-century general store. Its central core was built in 1937, but even the more recent enlargements feature a decor as rough-hewed as a log cabin in the Georgia mountains, while the completely concealed amenities are as modern as the computer age. Overall, the place is a conversation piece and a bit of a tourist attraction in its own right, a setting right out of the *Old Farmer's Almanac*. It's open daily 7am to 9pm. 15 Yonah St. © **706/878-2943.**

Nora Mill Granary At first glance, you might bypass this rustic plank-sided building as little more than a battered tourist emporium, on the main road about 2 miles south of Helen. Actually, it's one of the most famous sites in the region, visited by schoolchildren as a slice of Americana, and sought after by engineers eager for a glimpse of its old-time grinding wheels. It was built in 1876 as a water-driven mill powered by the flowing waters of the Chattahoochee River. Today you can sample grits and oatmeal, which bubble away on a massive antique stove, or buy burlap minibags of grits, stone-ground flour (buckwheat, rye, and whole-wheat), pancake

mix, and bread mix. A gift store next door sells cookbooks, candy, and crafts. Both enterprises are open Monday to Saturday 9am to 5pm, Sunday 10am to 5pm. 7107 S. Main St., Helen. ✆ **800/927-2375** or 706/878-2375. www.noramill.com.

The Old Sautee Store　　Four miles from Helen, this 130-year-old country store is as much a museum as it is a store. In fact, a museum can be found in a section of the store where the post office used to be. The Old Sautee Store has the largest collection of old-store memorabilia in all of Georgia, including items of merchandise not for sale. It's also a Scandinavian specialty shop: Astrid Fried still remembers her native Norway and will show you her personally selected imports, including ski sweaters and hand-carved trolls; Scandinavian crystal and dinnerware; Norwegian pewter, gold, and enamel jewelry; and gourmet foods. The store is listed on the National Register of Historic Places. Admission is free. Hours are Monday to Saturday from 10am to 5:30pm and Sunday noon to 5pm. Ga. 17 and Ga. 255, Sautee-Nachoochee. ✆ **888/463-9853** or 706/878-2281. www.oldsauteestore.com.

RABUN COUNTY

In northeast Georgia, 2 hours north of Atlanta on Highway 444, Rabun County is one of the gems of the Deep South. From Atlanta, take I-85 north to I-985, then continue to its end at Highway 441. Proceed 30 miles north into the heart of Rabun County, with its Blue Ridge Mountains scenery galore.

With cascading waterfalls, lakes, mountain vistas, and fish-filled streams, Rabun is one of the vacation meccas of Georgia. Bordering both Carolinas, it is filled with outdoor adventures—though not necessarily those depicted in the famous film *Deliverance* with Burt Reynolds, which was shot here.

The Chattahoochee National Forest covers more than 60% of the county, including wilderness areas like the Wild and Scenic Chattooga River, consistently rated among the top 10 white-river runs in America. Attractions range from Tallulah Gorge, called "the Grand Canyon of the South," to Rabun Bald, with its panoramic vistas.

Tallulah Falls & Gorge ★

This land of waterfalls and gorges was a fashionable resort with several upmarket hotels until 1913. But the construction of the Georgia Power Hydroelectric Dam changed the fate of the community, and the area became a bit of a ghost town.

At 600 feet, Tallulah Gorge is one of the deepest and most panoramic in the east. The Cherokees believed it was inhabited by a race of "little people" and that those who ventured inside never came out.

Hiking in the gorge is very strenuous. The recreational center is at the 300-acre **Terrora Park and Visitor Center** (✆ **706/754-7970**), with picnic areas, 50 campsites with water and electrical hookups, a beach for swimming, a playground, a bathhouse, and tennis courts, along with several nature trails. Office hours are 8am to 5pm. For the campsites, call ✆ **706/754-7979.** Nightly campsite rentals cost $16 for campers with tents, $18 for those with RVs. **Terrora Park** is immediately north of the bridge over Tallulah Gorge on the west side of U.S. 441 in the town of Tallulah Falls.

Lake Rabun

About 5 miles from Tallulah Falls and some 20 miles from Alpine Helen, in Chattahoochee National Forest, **Lake Rabun Recreation Area** has camping sites, a fishing pier, a boat dock, hiking trails, a public beach, and picnic areas. For information

about the area, call the **National Forest Tallulah Ranger District** at ✆ **706/782-3320.** The lake is also the site of one of the area's best-known hotels.

WHERE TO STAY

Lake Rabun Hotel ★ 🛏 This is a real, old-fashioned place where "nobody puts on fancy airs." First built in 1922, it still has no telephones, air-conditioning, or TVs in the guest rooms. As a getaway, it's been called "Georgia's sweetest secret garden." Some of the hotel's original rhododendron and twisted laurel are still here, a little worse for wear, but mellow. Quilts on the beds and tiebacks holding the ruffled curtains add to the old-time charm. Most of the guest rooms have sinks, but outside bathrooms are shared. Guests gather informally around the big, old fireplace in the great room. The food is good and home-cooked. Canoes are available if you'd like a closer look at the lake.

35 Andrea Lane (PO Box 10), Lakemont, GA 30552. ✆ **706/782-4946.** www.lakerabunhotel.com. 8 units. $99–$179 double. Rates include continental breakfast. AE, DISC, MC, V. **Amenities:** Restaurant/bar; lounge. *In room:* No phone, Wi-Fi (free).

Mountain City

The mountain is Black Rock Mountain, setting of **Black Rock Mountain State Park,** so named for its dark granite cliffs. It's the highest state park in Georgia, at 3,640 feet in elevation, embracing some 1,500 acres. On a clear day, views extend for 80 miles. To reach the park, leave Mountain City and go 3 miles north of Clayton via U.S. 441. The park is open daily from 7am to 10pm year-round. It offers 48 tent and trailer sites, 11 walk-in campsites, and 10 rental cottages, plus a playground and a 17-acre lake. Campsites rent for $28, with cottages going for $110 to $130. There are six scenic overlooks and a 10-mile trail system. For more information, contact Black Rock Mountain State Park, PO Box A, Mountain City, GA 30562 (✆ **706/746-2141;** www.gastateparks.org).

WHERE TO STAY

York House ★ This is the oldest B&B in Georgia. Today John and Judy Hurlburt are the innkeepers with panache, maintaining the collections of oak, cherry, and pinewood furniture that have furnished the place since the early part of the century, and upgrading the accommodations with nostalgic charm and modern style. In 1903, scenes from *The Great Train Robbery* were filmed here, and the building is listed on the National Register of Historic Places. A kitchen is available in the main house for guest use. Call ahead to discuss the inn's policy on children.

416 Yorkhouse Rd., Rabun, GA 30568. ✆ **800/231-YORK** (9675) or 706/746-2068. Fax 706/746-0210. www.yorkhouseinn.com. 12 units. $89–$124 double. Rates include country breakfast. MC, V. **Amenities:** Breakfast room; lounge. *In room:* A/C, TV, no phone.

Dillard

There's one good reason to come here: to eat. Dillard lies along Highway 441, 2 miles south of the North Carolina border, about a 2-hour drive north from Atlanta. It's Southern hospitality all the way here, especially at Dillard House.

WHERE TO DINE

Dillard House ★ 🍴 SOUTHERN The family-style meals served here are famous all over Georgia. More than five million hungry eaters have devoured food at the Dillard House since 1915. Country-cured ham, Southern fried chicken, tons of

fresh vegetables, old-fashioned corn bread, pan-fried trout, and all the relishes and desserts you could ever want burden the tables. No one in history has ever left here hungry. You can also lodge at **Dillard House Hotel,** which has been restored and furnished in part with antiques. It has 85 rooms, costing $59 to $169. Eight suites with kitchenettes cost $109 to $199. Guests have the use of a swimming pool and tennis courts, and can also go on horseback rides at the Dillard House Stables.

Old Dillard Rd., U.S. 441/23 (PO Box 10), Dillard, GA 30537. Ⓒ **800/541-0671** or 706/746-5348. www. dillardhouse.com. Reservations required for 15 or more. Lunch $16–$20; dinner $19–$25. AE, DC, DISC, MC, V. Daily 7:30–10:30am and 11:30am–8pm.

MACON & THE SOUTHWEST

S outhwest Georgia is the land of peach orchards, pecan groves, and Jimmy Carter. It's also a land of giant textile mills, pulp and paper plants, and manufacturing centers for automobiles, metal, chemicals, and furniture that bear the definite stamp of the New South.

Macon, the cherry tree capital of Georgia, is only 84 miles southeast of Atlanta and might easily be your gateway to the state's southwest. Home of rock legend Little Richard and birthplace of Southern poet Sidney Lanier, Macon is filled with white-columned antebellum buildings on the National Register of Historic Places.

After visiting the historic heartland of Georgia, you can cut southwest through two very different tourist districts, which Georgia dubs "Presidential Pathways" and "Plantation Trace." The first honors two presidents: Franklin Roosevelt, who sometimes lived at Warm Springs, and Plains's own Jimmy Carter. Steeped in history, this land is one of rolling hills and green forests. It also encompasses Pine Mountain, the gateway to the 2,500-acre Callaway Gardens—the most beautiful natural setting in Georgia. Along Plantation Trace, Native Americans and frontier soldiers have given way to farmers and timber barons. Its pocket of posh is Thomasville, which in the 1880s became the center for winter sunshine for the wealthy from the North.

MACON ★

84 miles SE of Atlanta

Only Savannah tops Macon for its striking old buildings. What comes as a huge surprise to visitors, though, is that Macon has 170,000 cherry trees—and they're a remarkable sight in late March when in bloom. Compare Washington, D.C.'s, famous Cherry Blossom Festival (with a mere 3,000 trees), and you'll understand how perfumed that time of year is in Macon.

The original city planners designed Macon in 1823 as a "city in a park." Today that heritage has been preserved. Wide avenues are lined with grand, stately mansions, many built before the Civil War during the cotton boom. It's more than just a river town, with its many cultural offerings—such as the Georgia Music Hall of Fame, Georgia Sports Hall of Fame, and Grand Opera House—and educational institutions, such as Macon College, Mercer University, and Wesleyan College, the world's

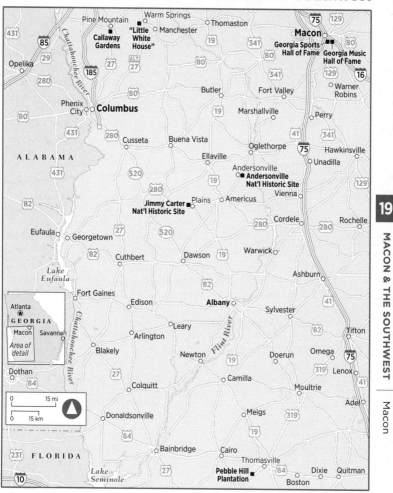

first college for women. Also, a $36-million revitalization project was launched in 1999. Through this expenditure, much of the original charm of Macon was restored.

As you'll see below, Macon has a wealth of historic sites, a handful of delightful places to stay, and the hospitality for which the South is known.

Essentials

GETTING THERE Drive on I-75 South from Atlanta, exiting at the signposted exits.

Greyhound (© **800/231-2222;** www.greyhound.com) offers regular service to Macon. The **greyhound bus terminal** is at 65 Spring St. (© **478/743-2868**).

VISITOR INFORMATION   If you're traveling south toward Macon on I-75, there's a **welcome center** (© **478/994-8181**) and rest area north of the city, open daily from 8:30am to 5:30pm. When you get into town, the **Downtown Macon Welcome Center,** 450 Martin Luther King Jr. Blvd., Macon, GA 31201 (© **800/ 768-3401** or 478/743-3401; www.maconga.org), at the foot of Cherry Street in the historic Macon Terminal Station, will provide you with information. It's open Monday to Saturday from 9am to 5pm.

SPECIAL EVENTS   The **Cherry Blossom Festival** ★ is traditionally held around the last 10 days in March. During that time, 500 activities are held around the city. You'll find everything from hot-air ballooning to a giant parade with marching bands and floats. Many events are held in the city parks. The residential areas are filled with thousands of Yoshino cherry trees. For more information, contact the Macon Cherry Blossom Festival, Inc., 794 Cherry St. (© **478/751-7429;** www. cherryblossom.com).

Seeing the Sights

The **Downtown Macon Welcome Center** (see "Essentials," above) is in the Macon Terminal Station, which dates back to 1916, when it hosted more than 100 trains a day. The welcome center offers three different discounted "Around Town" combination tickets, which admit you to several attractions in town. The **Historic Macon Combination Ticket** gives you free passage aboard the downtown trolley plus admission to the Cannonball House, Hay House, Sidney Lanier Cottage, St. Joseph's Catholic Church, Georgia Music Hall of Fame, Georgia Sports Hall of Fame, Historic Douglass Theatre, and Tubman African American Museum; the cost is $32 for adults, $17 for children ages 5 to 18, and free for children 4 and under. The **Historic Macon Downtown Tour** includes the Georgia Music Hall of Fame, Georgia Sports Hall of Fame, Historic Douglass Theatre, and Tubman African American Museum; the cost is $18 for adults, $8.50 for children ages 5 to 18, and free for children 4 and under. Almost 25 stops are included in this walking tour. The **Historic Macon Intown Tour** gives you free passage on the in-town trolley plus admission to the Cannonball House, the Hay House, the Sidney Lanier Cottage, and St. Joseph's Catholic Church; the cost is $17 for adults, $9 for children ages 5 to 18, and free for children 4 and under. The welcome center sells tickets Monday through Saturday from 9am to 5pm.

At **Central City Park,** a 250-acre recreational area, you can enjoy ongoing events. Dr. Martin Luther King, Jr., made his only major speech in Georgia in 1957 at the **Steward Chapel of the African Methodist Episcopal Church,** 887 Forsyth St. (© 478/742-4922). **Ocmulgee National Monument,** at 1207 Emery Hwy., is a memorial to native peoples on the site of an ancient Indian settlement and burial grounds. It's open daily, and admission is free.

Georgia Music Hall of Fame ★   When it comes to music, few states can lay claim to the number of influential acts that Georgia has produced. Opened in 1996, the Georgia Music Hall of Fame has since inducted into the hall such music greats as Ray Charles, Little Richard, Otis Redding, the Allman Brothers Band, James Brown, Lena Horne, Gladys Knight, Johnny Mercer, Ronnie Milsap, Curtis Mayfield, Isaac Hayes, and Chet Atkins. The tradition of music continues with more current acts like R.E.M. and the B-52s, two bands who introduced the "alternative" genre to the music industry. The 12,000-foot exhibit hall includes a virtual Tune Town, re-creating a Georgia village at twilight, with such exhibits as Gospel Chapel, the Soda Fountain, and the Skillet Licker Cafe. Music, photos, instruments, and memorabilia can be found at every turn, including the shoes that Otis Redding was wearing the day he died in a plane crash, as well as a classic James Brown costume. A delightful children's wing, the Billy Watson Music Factory, opened in late 1999, with interactive drums, keyboards, and the like.

200 Martin Luther King Jr. Blvd. ✆ **888/GA-ROCKS** (427-6257) or 478/751-3334. www.georgiamusic. org. Admission $8 adults, $6 seniors, $3.50 children 4-17, free for children 3 and under. Tues–Sat 9am–5pm; Sun 1–5pm.

Grand Opera House   The Academy of Music was constructed in 1884 and later became known as the Grand Opera House. Such old-timers as Sarah Bernhardt, Will Rogers, the Gish sisters, Dorothy Lamour, and Burns and Allen have performed here. With seating for 1,057, it also boasts one of America's largest stages—big enough to accommodate a production of *Ben-Hur* with its stage machinery and treadmills for the chariot races. Around Christmas each year, the Allman Brothers Band performs a homecoming concert for a small crowd of friends, family, and fans.

400 Poplar St. ✆ **478/301-5470.** www.thegrandmacon.com. Tickets $25–$70. Box office Mon–Fri 10am–5pm.

Hay House ★   If you see nothing else in Macon, see the Hay House. Built between 1855 and 1860 for the then-exorbitant cost of $100,000, this extravagant Italian Renaissance Revival home belonged to William Butler Johnston, the keeper of the Confederate treasury. The restored interiors here are nothing short of spectacular—stained glass, ornate period furnishings, Carrara marble, and *trompe l'oeil* wall paintings. Its infrastructure was ahead of its time as well, with a cleverly designed ventilation system, hot and cold running water, and central heating. An ongoing restoration is uncovering original hand-painted decorative walls. The house is a registered National Historic Landmark.

934 Georgia Ave. ✆ **478/742-8155.** www.hayhouse.org. Admission $8 adults, $7 seniors, $4 students, free for children 6 and under. Tues–Sat 10am–4pm; Sun 1–4pm. Closed holidays and Sun July–Aug and Jan–Feb.

Rose Hill Cemetery   This beautiful 68-acre cemetery alongside the Ocmulgee River was landscaped in 1840, making it one of the oldest surviving public cemeteries in the country. Terraced hills and cypress trees give it a grandeur not unlike that of the Forum in Rome. Among those buried here are Confederate generals, Georgia politicians and entrepreneurs, beloved pets, and two members of the Allman Brothers Band, who died within a year of each other in motorcycle accidents at the same Napier Street intersection.

Riverside Dr. ✆ **478/751-9119.** http://rosehillcemetery.org. Free admission. Daily 8:30am–sunset.

Sidney Lanier Cottage   This 1842 Victorian cottage is the birthplace of Sidney Lanier, one of Georgia's most famous citizens, a poet who is best known for "The Marshes of Glynn." The wedding gown of Lanier's wife, Mary Day, is on display; Scarlett O'Hara would have been pea green with envy over the bride's ultratiny waist. The house is outfitted in furnishings of the period and is home to the Middle Georgia Historical Society.

935 High St. ✆ **478/743-3851.** www.historicmacon.org. Admission $5 adults, $4 seniors and military, $3 children 6–18, free for children 5 and under. Mon–Sat 10am–4pm. Closed holidays.

Tours

Stop at the Downtown Macon Welcome Center (see "Essentials," above) for a self-guided tour map, or download it yourself from the welcome center's website (www.maconga.org). You can also arrange, through the welcome center, **customized group tours** with professional guides, or you can buy an "Around Town" combination ticket. The ticket gives you admission to several attractions (see "Seeing the Sights," above).

Organized tours are offered by the popular **Around Town Tours,** 450 Martin Luther King Jr. Blvd. (© **800/768-3401;** www.maconga.org), which offers tours of three antebellum homes. Tours are given Monday to Saturday between 9am and 5pm, and costs $18 for adults and $8.50 for children 5 to 18, including admission prices. It's advised that you arrive at least 15 minutes prior to tour departure.

Where to Stay

Along I-75 are many chain hotels and motels, including Howard Johnson, Comfort Inn, Holiday Inn, and Hampton Inn. Off I-475 are Ramada Inn, Travelodge, and Holiday Inn. A good value choice is **Courtyard by Marriott,** 3990 Sheraton Dr. (© **888/391-8725** or 478/477-8899; www.marriott.com).

1842 Inn ★★★ The 1842 Inn is reason enough to come to Macon. It's truly special and is one of our favorite inns south of the Mason-Dixon line. This inn is romantic, upscale, and charming. You're likely to find a working fireplace in your room, along with antiques, expensive fabrics, four-poster beds, and maybe even a whirlpool. But what makes this place truly memorable are the lovely members of the staff, who have been here for years and epitomize warm-as-toast Southern hospitality. Complimentary evening hors d'oeuvres are served in one of the parlor rooms. The inn has no restaurant (look for on-site dining facilities in the future), but travelers arriving late can arrange to have a meal from one of the local restaurants waiting for them in their room or on the candlelit patio. Across the courtyard is a 1900 Victorian cottage with equally elegant rooms. Come to Macon and add your name to the list of celebrities (including Dr. Ruth and Barbara Walters) who have stayed here.

353 College St., Macon, GA 31201. © **877/452-6599** or 478/741-1842. Fax 478/741-1842. www.1842inn. com. 19 units. $189–$279 double. AE, DC, MC, V. Take exit 52 off I-75, then go 4 blocks to the center of the Historic District. **Amenities:** Bar, breakfast room; lounge. *In room:* A/C, TV, hair dryer, Wi-Fi (free).

Ramada Plaza Macon ★★ Elegantly decorated and well-appointed, this first-class hotel lies in the historic downtown, with an outdoor pool and sun deck, even a nightclub where you can dance the evening away. The hotel offers spacious and rather beautifully furnished guest rooms spread over 16 floors. Rollaway beds are provided for parents who share their room with young children. Business travelers like the work desk with a lamp, and clothes hounds appreciate the separate hanging closet. A first-rate cuisine is served in both of the restaurants.

108 First St., Macon, GA 31201. © **800/272-6222** or 478/746-1461. Fax 478/738-2460. www.ramada. com. 298 units. $89–$139 double; $140–$270 suite. AE, DC, DISC, MC, V. Valet parking $10; self-parking free. **Amenities:** 2 restaurants; bar; exercise room; outdoor pool; room service; sauna. *In room:* A/C, TV, hair dryer, Wi-Fi (free).

Where to Dine

Macon has a growing number of upscale restaurants, but if it's down-home Southern cooking you want, you won't be disappointed. Barbecue lovers can opt for

Satterfield's, on 120 New St. (✆ **478/742-0352;** www.satterfieldscatering.com), where you can snack on homemade boiled peanuts while you wait for your order of good barbecue, Brunswick stew, and long-cooked vegetables.

The Back Burner Restaurant ★ NOUVELLE CONTINENTAL   Chef Christian Losito has brought serious food to Macon at this charming cottage off Ingleside Avenue. The Nice, France, native offers a changing menu that may include a Chilean halibut in a champagne-and-shallot sauce, rack of lamb in a Dijon-thyme sauce, or grilled shrimp over penne pasta in a mushroom-wine sauce. Lunchtime soups and salads are fresh and innovative. The restaurant is broken into intimate, low-ceilinged rooms, each painted a different handsome color; nice linens and flowers complete the sunny picture.

2242 Ingleside Ave. ✆ **478/746-3336.** www.backburnermacon.com. Main courses $7–$12 lunch, $15–$21 dinner. AE, DC, DISC, MC, V. Mon–Sat 11:30am–2pm and 6–9:30pm.

CALLAWAY GARDENS ★★★

70 miles S of Atlanta

One of the most beautiful spots in the South, Callaway Gardens embraces 14,000 acres of gardens, woodlands, and lakes, with wildlife and outdoor activities. Some 750,000 visitors are attracted to this site annually, especially in spring when its Azalea Trail displays some 700 colorful varieties. But every season brings something new into bloom, from rhododendron and holly trails to wildflowers.

Callaway Gardens at Pine Mountain was begun back in the 1930s. Cason Callaway, head of one of Georgia's most prosperous textile mills, set about rebuilding the soil, nurturing and importing plant life, building the largest man-made inland beach in the world, and providing inn and cottage accommodations—and opened it all to citizens of modest means.

Essentials

GETTING THERE   From Atlanta, take I-85 South to I-185, continue on I-185 South to exit 14, and then turn left on U.S. 27 and drive 11 miles to Callaway Gardens. Driving north on either I-185 or I-85, exit east on Ga. 18 to Pine Mountain, and then turn right on U.S. 27 and enter Callaway Gardens.

Seeing the Gardens

Callaway Gardens, at Pine Mountain (✆ **800/225-5292** or 706/663-2281; www.callawaygardens.com), include floral and hiking trails and acres of picnic grounds. Special events abound, particularly the Spring Celebration. In May, Callaway plays host to the Masters Waterski Tournament. July 4th is the occasion of the sunrise-to-sunset Surf and Sand Spectacular, giving way to the Sky High Balloon Festival over Labor Day weekend. The Fall Festival celebrates the beauty of the chrysanthemums, and Fantasy in Lights at Christmas is a brilliant ride through the gardens with a display of lights and music.

The park has many attractions. The **Cecil B. Day Butterfly Center ★,** a $5.3-million center, ranks with the world's foremost conservatories in London, Melbourne, and Tokyo. The octagonal conservatory houses more than 1,000 free-flying butterflies and numerous birds. The conservatory includes a 12-foot waterfall and lush tropical foliage.

The **John A. Sibley Horticultural Center,** one of the most advanced garden and greenhouse complexes in the world, encompasses 5 acres with 20,200 square feet of indoor floral displays, plus 30,675 feet of greenhouse space. Floral displays integrate indoor and outdoor settings.

Mr. Cason's Vegetable Garden, started in 1960, was the last major project initiated by Mr. Callaway. On 7½ acres, gardeners demonstrate scientific, educational, and practical applications of fruit and vegetable cultures. A trio of large terraces in a semicircular design, the vegetable garden produces more than 400 varieties of crops that range from traditional Southern fruits and vegetables to wildflower test plots. The PBS show *Victory Garden* films its Southern segments from here.

The **Ida Cason Callaway Memorial Chapel,** in the English Gothic style, was built to honor Mr. Callaway's mother, Ida Cason. It was dedicated in 1962 by Dr. Norman Vincent Peale. It's patterned much like a rural wayside chapel of the 16th and 17th centuries.

The park is open daily from 9am to 6pm, with extended summer hours. Admission is $18 for adults, $9 for children 6 to 12, and free for children 5 and under.

Outdoor Pursuits

BEACH RESORT **Robin Lake Beach,** on a 65-acre lake, is the largest inland man-made white-sand beach anywhere in the world. It offers a center for children with a large outdoor playground, as well as miniature golf, badminton, and rides on a riverboat. In summer, a show is presented by Florida State University's Flying High Circus. A trail stretches nearly a mile around the lake with 20 fitness stations. Robin Lake Beach is a virtual miniresort, with sand, surf, and dozens of activities. Admission is $18 for adults, $9 for children 6 to 12, and free for children 5 and under. The beach is open daily from 9am to 6pm in summer. It is closed from Labor Day until the first of June.

BIKING Callaway Gardens has 7½ paved miles for bikers who'd like to see the gardens up close instead of from a car. The Discovery Bicycle Trail is a family favorite. It begins at Bike Barn near the beach parking lot at Robin Lake, where you can rent bikes and helmets (some bikes are equipped with child safety seats). A ferry is available near the end of the trail at the boat dock to transport riders across Mountain Creek Lake back to their starting point. The Bike Barn rents bikes daily from 8am to 6pm, charging $14 for 2 hours and $20 for a half-day.

FISHING Fishing is available on Mountain Creek Lake, where two persons can rent a boat for $45 per half-day or $60 per full day.

GOLF Callaway's well-groomed courses, hailed by *Golf Digest* and *Golf* magazine, are set in the midst of clear lakes, lush landscaping, and wooded shores. **Mountain View,** designed by Dick Wilson, is viewed as the best by many golfers. Tight, tree-lined fairways are characteristic of this championship course. At hole no. 15 (par 5), the threat of water looms over both tee and approach shots. This hole is ranked as one of the most difficult par 5s by *USA Today.* The first course built here, **Lake View** was designed only in part by Dick Wilson. Mr. Callaway himself provided the inspiration for this course, whose challenge lies in its 9 water holes. The par-70 course is known for its no. 5 with its island tee and serpentine bridge over Mountain Creek Lake to the green in front of the Gardens Restaurant. Mountain View is the most expensive course to play, at a cost of $100, while Lake View goes for $80. Call ✆ **800/225-5292** to make reservations for either course.

TENNIS *Tennis* magazine awarded Callaway a "Top 50" national rating. Nine courts are hard surfaced, and eight have Rubico surfaces. Two glass-walled racquetball courts and a pro shop are also located in Callaway's sports complex.

Where to Stay

Callaway Gardens Resort ★★ In 1951, as the success of Callaway Gardens attracted visitors from around the country, Cason Callaway engaged Holiday Inn to build a motel on gently sloping terrain across the highway from the gardens. Eventually, Callaway acquired the property and enlarged it. It now encompasses the **Mountain Creek Inn,** the **Cottages at Callaway Gardens,** the **Villas at Callaway Gardens,** and the **Lodge and Spa at Callaway Gardens.**

Adjacent to the resort's freshwater beach, rustic two-bedroom cottages contain fireplaces, kitchens, and lots of modern luxuries. Popular with families, they're what you'd expect at an outdoor camping retreat: They have endured their share of wear and tear. More stylish are the villas; all have kitchens, relatively formal furnishings, fireplaces, screened-in verandas, and a greater emphasis on style and comfort.

The Lodge and Spa offers deluxe guest rooms and suites, with private balconies opening onto the forest. This first-class lodge is furnished with an eclectic mix of furnishings, some in the style of an elegant Southern estate. In the beautiful landscaping is a swimming pool with a cabana-style bar. The spa features 13 treatment rooms, with "nature-based massages" and nourishing facials. The fitness center features the latest equipment and also has a yoga studio.

17800 U.S. 27 south, Pine Mountain, GA 31822. (*) **800/CALLAWAY** (225-5292) or 706/663-2281. Fax 706/663-5090. www.callawaygardens.com. 900 units. $79–$167 double; $189–$900 suite; $252–$617 2- to 4-bedroom villa. Honeymoon, sports, and monthly packages available. AE, DC, DISC, MC, V. **Amenities:** 7 restaurants; 2 bar lounges; babysitting; concierge; 2 18-hole golf courses; exercise room; 3 pools (1 indoor); room service; 10 tennis courts (lit). *In room:* A/C, TV, hair dryer, Wi-Fi (free).

Magnolia Hall Bed & Breakfast ★ 📷 Open year-round, this B&B lies 5 miles from the entrance to Callaway Gardens. An 1890s Victorian home, it's surrounded by an acre of land with azaleas, tea olives, camellias, and the namesake magnolias. Potted ferns and cushioned wicker evoke the Deep South. Antiques-filled rooms, a grand piano in the sitting room, and high ceilings add grace notes. Guest rooms are spacious and contain well-kept bathrooms. This is not necessarily a place for kids.

127 Barnes Mill Rd. (PO Box 326), Hamilton, GA 31811. (*) **877/813-4394** or 706/628-4566. Fax 706/628-5802. www.magnoliahallbb.com. 5 units. $115–$135 double. Additional person $30 extra. Rates include breakfast. AE, MC, V. **Amenities:** Breakfast room; 2 lounges. *In room:* A/C, TV, hair dryer, no phone, Wi-Fi (free).

Valley Inn Resort ☺ There's nothing special here, but as motels go, it's one of the best of the lot. Families, especially in summer, like this small resort set on 52 acres near a lake. Guest rooms are comfortably furnished. Some contain kitchens, and all contain well-kept bathrooms. You can park your RV in the Travel Trailer Park or rent a two-bedroom mobile home unit that sleeps up to six. All rooms are nonsmoking.

14420 Hwy. 27, Hamilton, GA 31811. (*) **800/944-9393** or 706/628-4454. 20 units. $59 double; $105 1-bedroom cottage; $125 2-bedroom cottage. AE, DC, DISC, MC, V. **Amenities:** Cafe; lounge; outdoor pool. *In room:* A/C, TV, kitchenette (in some).

White Columns Motel One mile from Callaway Gardens, this small family-owned-and-operated white-columned motel is a favorite budget choice in the area. There's a large swing on an old magnolia tree on the front lawn, a great place to spend a lazy summer afternoon. Rooms are basic but clean and comfortable, and have been recently "fixed up." Within walking distance of the motel are two good and moderately priced restaurants.

Hwy. 27 S. (PO Box 531), Pine Mountain, GA 31822. ℂ **800/722-5083** or 706/663-2312. Fax 706/663-2311. www.whitecolumnsmotel.com. 14 units. $60–$79 double. Rates include continental breakfast. MC, V. *In room:* A/C, TV, fridge, hair dryer, kitchenette (in some), Wi-Fi (free).

Where to Dine

The Country Kitchen SOUTHERN   First things first: Don't come here looking for health food. Despite that, its premises (a stone-built roadside country store about a mile south of the Callaway Gardens entrance, near the top of Pine Mountain) are usually mobbed with families looking for a taste of wholesome country nostalgia. The setting is rustic and woodsy. Menu items include chicken or country ham with biscuits and gravy, an array of vegetables, burgers, and club sandwiches. Dessert might be a portion of muscadine ice cream. If you need grits to get your day started right, have them along with "Mama's pancakes" or a country omelet.

Hwy. 27, near Callaway Gardens. ℂ **706/663-2281.** Breakfast platters $6.25–$9.50; main courses $8–$13. AE, DISC, MC, V. Daily 8am–8pm.

The Gardens ITALIAN/INTERNATIONAL   The Gardens occupies a sprawling and immensely atmospheric building whose stout timbers and rambling verandas resemble a grange in eastern France or Germany. Our favorite tables are perched on a balcony overlooking a landscape of golf fairways and a pond that has a serpentine bridge zigzagging across its waters. The menu emphasizes grilled steaks, seafood, and chops, and the kitchen prepares this fare exceedingly well.

Hwy. 27, at Callaway Gardens. ℂ **706/663-2281.** Reservations recommended. Main courses $12–$19. AE, DC, DISC, MC, V. Tues–Sat 5–9pm.

The Plantation Room 🍴 SOUTHERN   The buffets here celebrate culinary traditions of the Old South. Vegetables are the freshest in summer, when they come to your table just hours after being picked from Mr. Cason's vegetable garden. If you've never eaten corn just pulled from the stalk, you'll find how different it is from store-bought corn pulled days or weeks before. It can get very crowded here, especially on Friday nights when the theme is seafood.

At Callaway Gardens. ℂ **706/663-2281.** Buffet $11 breakfast, $13 lunch, $17–$25 dinner. AE, DISC, MC, V. Daily 6:30–10:30am, 11:30am–2pm, and 5:30–9pm.

WARM SPRINGS & FDR'S LITTLE WHITE HOUSE ★★

17 miles E of Callaway Gardens; 65 miles S of Atlanta

If you take Ga. 190 East and follow the signs, you'll be directed to Warm Springs, forever associated with the legacy of Franklin D. Roosevelt, who died here on April 12, 1945. Most visitors—some 110,000 a year—come to visit the "Little White House." Warm Springs village is also an attraction. After Roosevelt's death, it became a virtual ghost town, but today the village is alive with 65 shops selling antiques, crafts, and collectibles.

The **Franklin D. Roosevelt State Park,** off U.S. 27, is one of the largest in Georgia's state system, with many historic buildings, the King's Gap Indian Trail, a swimming pool, and fishing and camping facilities. For more information, contact the Superintendent, 2970 Ga. 190 E. (© **800/864-7275** or 706/663-4858; www.gastate parks.org).

Essentials

GETTING THERE   Take I-85 South from Atlanta to Alt. U.S. 27 South, which you follow into Warm Springs.

To reach Warm Springs from Callaway Gardens, take U.S. 27 North into the town of Pine Mountain. At the intersection of U.S. 27 and Ga. 18, take Ga. 18 East to Ga. 194, and proceed on Ga. 194 East until it joins Alt. U.S. 27. Stay on Alt. U.S. 27/Ga. 194 South into Warm Springs.

VISITOR INFORMATION   **Warm Springs Welcome Center,** 1 Broad St. (PO Box 578), Warm Springs, GA 31830 (© **800/337-1927** or 706/655-3322; www. warmspringsga.ws), is open Monday to Saturday 10am to 5pm, dispensing information and maps of the village.

Seeing Roosevelt's Little White House

This home, which came to be called the **"Little White House,"** a quarter of a mile south of Warm Springs on Ga. 85 West (© **706/655-5870;** www. georgiastateparks. org/littlewhitehouse), was built in 1932 for $8,738—a modest outlay for a man of Franklin Roosevelt's wealth. This tiny place was once the occasional nerve center of the commander in chief of the nation during the greatest war of all time.

FDR discovered Warm Springs in 1924. He had contracted polio in 1921 and came here for the beneficial effect of the healing waters. Two years later, he bought the springs, hotel, and some cottages and started a foundation to develop facilities for helping paralytic patients from all over the country. Today the house is much as he left it when he died here in 1945. It's open daily from 9am to 4:45pm. Admission is $8 for adults, $7 for seniors, $5 for children 6 to 18, and free for children 5 and under.

Also on-site is the **FDR Memorial Museum** (© **706/655-5870**). FDR memorabilia is displayed in a modern 12,000-square-foot museum constructed on one level, with special care taken to provide entry for persons who suffer disabilities. The unfinished portrait of FDR that Elizabeth Shoumatoff was painting on the day the president died is on display here (see "An Unfinished Portrait," below).

The house is open daily 9am to 4:45pm (closed Thanksgiving, Christmas Day, and New Year's Day.). Admission is $6 for adults, $5 for children 6 to 18, and $1 for children 5 and under.

Where to Stay

Hotel Warm Springs Bed and Breakfast Inn ★   This hotel, built in 1907, thrived when the region's economy boomed because of the presence of FDR throughout the war years. Gerrie Thompson, its owner since 1988, can recite a guest list that includes the queen of Mexico; the king and queen of Spain; the president of the Philippines; armies of journalists, Cabinet members, and Secret Service agents—and a screen legend named Bette Davis. Despite some half-hearted attempts at redecoration, this artfully dowdy period piece from another age evokes the languor and sultriness of the 1940s in the Deep South. Some of the guest rooms contain old-fashioned oak furniture made in the factory Eleanor Roosevelt established in Val-Kill, New York, to

Although never completed, one of the world's most famous portraits rests in Warm Springs in FDR's Little White House. He was posing for it shortly before he died on April 12, 1945. In some respects, Elizabeth Shoumatoff's portrait symbolizes Roosevelt's unfinished life, and his unfinished (and unprecedented) fourth term that was filled out by Harry S Truman. Roosevelt, plagued by ill health, would have continued to face monumental decisions that year if he'd lived. He would have presided over the defeat of the Nazi armies and been faced with the decision of whether or not to drop the atomic bomb (which he'd ordered built) on Japan. After that fateful spring day, Truman had to make those decisions in FDR's place.

The president's ashen pallor and his tired, drawn face are captured in the unfinished portrait, revealing the stress FDR felt at the end of the most destructive war in history. His wife, Eleanor, arrived in Warm Springs shortly after midnight on the day of his death. When she wrote about that night in *This I Remember,* Mrs. Roosevelt chose not to mention that Lucy Mercer Rutherford, FDR's sweetheart, was with him when he died. However, she later wrote: "All human beings have failings, and all human beings have needs and temptations and stresses." It is Roosevelt's humanity that we remember.

relieve unemployment during the Great Depression. Sitting rooms and a high-ceilinged breakfast room are located on the second and third floors. All rooms are nonsmoking.

47 Broad St., Warm Springs, GA 31830. $\copyright$ **800/366-7616** or 706/655-2114. www.hotelwarmspringsbb.org. 14 units. $65–$110 double; $120–$160 suite. Rates include breakfast. AE, DISC, MC, V. **Amenities:** Breakfast room; lounge. *In room:* A/C, TV, hair dryer, Wi-Fi (free).

Where to Dine

Bulloch House Restaurant SOUTHERN   Set on a leafy hillside, a 10-minute walk from the center of town, Bulloch House occupies the genteel premises of a house originally built in 1892. Citizens from virtually every walk of life file by the buffets, plate in hand. There are five different homey, dowdy dining areas. One is a front porch overlooking the road, although most diners remain in the air-conditioned interior. Menu items celebrate deep-fried, local cookery and always include fried green tomatoes, fried fish, fried chicken, fried okra, butterbeans, turnip greens, potatoes, biscuits, bread, and copious amounts of iced tea. No alcohol of any kind is served. It's very much a family-fry operation.

47 Bulloch St. $\copyright$ **706/655-9068.** Buffet $7.95 lunch, $12 dinner. MC, V. Daily 11am–2:30pm; Fri–Sat 5–8:30pm.

PLAINS: JIMMY CARTER'S HOMETOWN

80 miles SE of Callaway Gardens; 85 miles SW of Macon; 10 miles W of Americus

This aptly named town with a population of 716 is both plain and sited on the plains. Humble though it is, Plains, Georgia, is closely identified with Jimmy Carter as his hometown. "Jimmy," as he is called locally, was—and still is—a man of the people, the most approachable president in recent history, and a Nobel Prize winner, to boot.

You'll know Plains by the little green-and-white train depot, its water tower brightly painted with the Stars and Stripes. A small-town charm still clings to Plains and its people. The early-1900s buildings are much as they were before the Depression shut them down (most were warehouses until Jimmy brought business back to town).

Essentials

GETTING THERE   From Macon, take I-75 South to Cordele; exit there onto U.S. 280 and head west through Americus to Plains. From Callaway Gardens, take U.S. 27 to Pine Mountain, turn left on Ga. 18 to I-185, and then take I-185 South through Columbus to U.S. 280; head south (or east) on U.S. 280 into Plains.

VISITOR INFORMATION   If you stand in the middle of the street, you can almost see the whole town, including Billy Carter's former service station, which used to sell beer to newspeople when Billy was alive. For a do-it-yourself walking or driving tour to points of interest, stop in at the **Georgia Visitor Center,** east of Plains at 1763 Hwy. 280 W. (✆ **229/824-5373;** www.plainsgeorgia.com), open daily from 8:30am to 5:30pm. The staff there will furnish maps and brochures.

Seeing the Sights

The **Jimmy Carter National Historic Site ★** (✆ **229/824-4104;** www.nps.gov/jica) is 77 acres administered by the U.S. Department of the Interior. An old-fashioned railway depot from 1888 is the headquarters of the visitor center—it also served as Carter's campaign headquarters in 1976 and again in 1980 when he lost to Ronald Reagan. The depot is filled with campaign memorabilia and is open daily (except Thanksgiving, Christmas, and New Year's Day) from 9am to 5pm. Admission is free. An information booklet costs $1.25.

The one-story, ranch-style brick **Carter home** is on Woodland Drive; when the Carters are in residence, the Secret Service is stationed in booths at this entrance and at the one on Paschal Street (you can get a pretty good look at it by walking and driving west on Church St.). Then there's the **Plains Methodist Church,** at the corner of Church and Thomas streets, where Jimmy asked Rosalynn for their first date. When he's in town, Jimmy teaches Sunday school at **Maranatha Baptist Church.** Visitors are invited—check the notice in the window of Hugh Carter's Antiques on Main Street. **Archery,** a 2½-mile drive west of town on U.S. 280, is where Jimmy Carter lived as a child when his father operated a country store.

In 2001, the Depression-era **Jimmy Carter Boyhood Farm,** signposted off Route 280 West (✆ **229/824-4104**), opened to the public. The last living occupant of the one-story, white-frame house, the former U.S. president himself, was an adviser to the restorers of the house. The former president took such an interest that he spent 2 days supervising the reconstruction of a privy in back of the house. He wanted it to be as "authentic" as memory served him. The farm has been restored to its appearance in 1937 before electricity was put in.

Mr. Carter lived in the house from 1928 to 1942 until he went off to college. The historic site lies 2½ miles west of Plains and 120 miles south of Atlanta. Visitors can explore the former Carter home, a reconstructed barn, a small farm store, a windmill, a buggy shed, a pump house, and a blacksmith shop on 15 acres of what originally was a 360-acre farm. Several walking trails are along the property. Hours are daily from 9am to 5pm, and admission is free.

Where to Stay

Plains Historic Inn & Antiques ★★★   After being the most powerful man in the world for years, what's left but to sit on a swing on the front porch and welcome visitors to Plains and your B&B? When Jimmy Carter and his wife, Rosalynn, saw hundreds of tourists coming each day, the couple decided to convert the upstairs portions of two buildings into guest rooms, each themed to a specific decade. Carter himself helped with the carpentry, aided by a group of prison inmates in white uniforms who were even invited to the grand opening. Naturally, the 1970s are represented with a presidential suite. Other rooms are authentically furnished from the 1920s to the 1980s, and even include vintage magazines. All rooms are nonsmoking.

Guests share a public room and a balcony overlooking the historic square where Carter once had his campaign headquarters. Below, two old storefronts have been converted into an antiques mall. Few guests miss the opportunity to have a cup of coffee and some boiled peanuts at the adjacent Plains Coffee Shop. And for the rarest treat in this entire guide, on some afternoons "Mister Jimmy and Miz Rosalynn" drop in to join guests on the front porch for afternoon tea and to discuss politics.

106 Main St., Plains, GA 31780. ✆ **229/824-4517.** www.plainsinn.net. 7 units. Double Sun–Fri $75, Sat $85; presidential suite Sun–Fri $89, Sat $110. AE, MC, V. **Amenities:** Lounge. *In room:* A/C, TV, hair dryer, Wi-Fi (free).

Where to Dine

Do as the Carters do and head for nearby Americus—notably, the **Grand Dining Room at the Windsor Hotel,** 125 W. Lamar St. (✆ **888/297-9567** or 229/924-1555). This high-ceilinged, historic restaurant reigns in a town filled with rustic, down-home contenders. Expect the most generous luncheon buffet available. Dinners showcase upscale versions of Caesar salad garnished with shrimp or chicken, quail stuffed with rice and served with a brandy-cream sauce, and a delectable version of pork Normandy, stuffed with apples and served with an apple-brandy sauce. Main courses cost $13 to $26.

A Side Trip to Andersonville

Just 21 miles northeast of Plains (take U.S. 280 to Americus, then Ga. 49 North) is the site of the most infamous of Confederate prison camps, Andersonville. It was built to hold 10,000 but at one time had a prisoner population of more than 32,000, struggling to survive on polluted water and starvation rations. Nearly 15,000 prisoners died here. The commander, Capt. Henry Wirtz, although powerless to help the situation, was tried and hanged after the Civil War on charges of having conspired to murder Union prisoners. Today you can visit the **Drummer Boy Civil War Museum** (✆ **229/924-2425**), open August to mid-September Thursday to Sunday 1 to 5pm and mid-September to November and February to July Thursday to Saturday 10am to 5pm and Sunday 1 to 5pm. You'll see slide shows of the camp's sad history, as well as the remains of wells and escape tunnels. Legend says that **Providence Springs** gushed up in answer to the prayers of prisoners during the drought of 1864. **Andersonville National Historic Site** (✆ **229/924-0343;** www.nps. gov/ande) is open daily from 8am to 5pm; admission is free.

After visiting the historic site, browse the antiques shops in the adjacent village of Andersonville. Stop by the **Andersonville Guild Welcome Center** (✆ **229/924-2558;** www.andersonvillegeorgia.com) in the old train depot and meet Peggy

Sheppard, a gregarious, transplanted New Yorker who spearheaded the village's rejuvenation. The center is open daily from 9am to 2pm.

Andersonville National Historic Site and National Prisoner of War Museum ★ This museum was dedicated in April 1998 by a host of senators, including John McCain, R-Arizona, a prisoner of war in Vietnam for 5 years, and Georgia governor Zell Miller. The museum is adjacent to the site of one of the two deadliest Civil War POW encampments, and its 10,000 square feet contain artifacts in tribute to the 800,000 soldiers who have suffered as POWs, from the American Revolution to the Persian Gulf War. The $5.8-million structure was built from private funds raised by POW veterans, with $3.6 million coming from the state and federal governments. There are stories of prisoners in Japanese camps who lost 55 pounds during their stay, and tales of brothers who were imprisoned together, with only one surviving.

Adjacent to the museum is the notorious Confederate POW camp, Andersonville (see above). When its inmate population was heaviest during the last 14 months of the Civil War, the mortality rate was 29%, partly because of the heat, since Northerners were not acclimated to the Southern weather. The camp's Union counterpart in Elmira, New York (known as Hellmira), had a mortality rate of 24% during its lifetime, conversely because of the cold; many Southerners froze to death. Visitors are allowed to walk the grounds, and an audiocassette or CD tour of the grounds is available for $1.

Ga. 49, Andersonville. ☏ **229/924-0343.** www.nps.gov/ande. Free admission to museum and site; donations accepted. Museum daily 8:30am–5pm. Site daily 8am–5pm. From I-75 North or South, take exit 127 at Montezuma/Hawkinsville. Travel west along Ga. 26, continuing south on Ga. 49. The park entrance will appear on your left just outside Andersonville.

THOMASVILLE ★★

45 miles W of Valdosta; 35 miles NE of Tallahassee; 230 miles S of Atlanta

From the 1800s to the early 1900s, Thomasville was one of the world's most fashionable places, hailed by *Harper's Magazine* in 1887 as "the best winter resort on three continents." After the Civil War, when much of the South was embittered and in ruins, a remarkable and progressive group of civil leaders began building resorts that attracted the wintering wealthy. Few other places in the South wanted to encourage the "damn Yankees" at the time. Regrettably, every one of the grand hotels that once flourished here has disappeared, victims of fires, rot, termites, and the opening of nearby Florida as a holiday destination. Many of the Victorian homes of the town, however, remain intact, attracting architectural enthusiasts from around the state.

Considering that the wealth of North America's Gilded Age once disported itself here, Thomasville remains relatively obscure. Yet at various times, the world press has descended on the area, notably when President Eisenhower used to play golf here, and when Jacqueline Kennedy was discovered hiding out here following the assassination of her husband.

Historic Thomasville remains unique in the South today as the centerpiece of a county containing approximately 70 enormous plantations encompassing some 300,000 acres. Only the post–Civil War prosperity of the town's 19th- and early-20th-century tourism allowed these estates to survive intact. Throughout the rest of the South, plantations were broken up, subdivided, sold for back taxes, allowed to fall into decay, and, in a later age, turned into housing developments. Regrettably, of the many that survive, only one is open to the public.

Essentials

GETTING THERE   From Tallahassee, drive northeast along Highway 319. From Atlanta, take I-75 South to the junction with Route 122 to Tifton, exiting onto Highway 319 southwest into Thomasville.

VISITOR INFORMATION   The welcome center for the **Thomasville Tourism Authority,** at 144 E. Jackson St. (© **866/577-3600** or 229/228-7977; www.thomasvillega.com), is one of the most helpful in Georgia. It's open Monday to Friday from 8am to 5pm and Saturday from 10am to 3pm. The **Thomasville Genealogical, History & Fine Arts Library** (© **229/226-9640;** http://home.rose.net/~glibrary) is also maintained by the city; admission is free. Hours are Monday to Friday 9am to 5pm, Saturday 9am to 4pm.

Seeing the Sights

The town's mascot is **"the Big Oak,"** at the corner of North Crawford and East Monroe streets, in back of the Federal Courthouse and the post office. It's at least 3 centuries old and has been a respected member of the National Live Oak Society since 1936. If anyone attempted to cut it down or harm it in any way, the townspeople would rise up in revolt. The giant is 68 feet tall with a limb spread of 162 feet and a circumference of 24 feet.

Lapham-Patterson House ★   This example of Victorian architecture, declared a National Historic Landmark in 1975, is known for its fish-scale shingles, Asian-style porch decorations, long-leaf pine inlaid floors, and double-flue chimney with walk-through stairway and cantilevered balcony. Built between 1884 and 1885, it was the winter cottage for a prosperous shoe merchant, C. W. Lapham of Chicago. As a survivor of the Great Chicago Fire, Lapham wanted to make his winter cottage as safe as possible. This explains why, in the 19 rooms in this cottage, there are 45 doors, 26 of them exterior. All of the 53 windows open from the bottom up and the top down.

626 N. Dawson St. © **229/225-4004.** Admission $5 adults, $4.50 seniors, $2.50 children 18 and under. Tues–Sat 9am–4pm; Sun 2–4pm.

Pebble Hill Plantation ★ 🏛   They called her "Miss Pansy," and she was a local legend, greatly admired by Jimmy Carter. Her name was Elisabeth Ireland Poe (1897–1978), and she was the last of the Hanna dynasty, which owned Pebble Hill. A sportswoman, she was also a patron of the arts, a grand hostess, and a collector, and upon her death she willed that her home should be open to the public for a glimpse into an elegant past. Hers is the only plantation home in Thomas County open to the public. Established in the 1820s, the house was almost destroyed by fire in the 1930s but was rebuilt under the direction of architect Abram Garfield, son of the nation's 20th president.

5 miles southwest of Thomasville via U.S. 319. © **229/226-2344.** www.pebblehill.com. Admission grounds $5 adults, $2 children 2 to 12; main house $10 adults, $4 children. Children 1 and under not admitted. Tues–Sat 10am–5pm; Sun 1–5pm. Last tour at 3:45pm.

Thomas County Museum of History   This is the best place for learning about the extraordinary "Winter Resort Era" that began in Thomasville in the 1880s. Although all the grand Victorian hotels are gone, photographs on display show their remarkable architecture. Along with memorabilia of Thomasville from this era are exhibits of historic plantations, restored 19th-century buildings, antique women's dresses, and vintage automobiles. Out back is an antique bowling alley. The museum also offers guided hour-long bus tours of Thomasville for $50.

725 N. Dawson St. © **229/226-7664.** Admission $5 adults, $1 children 6–18, free for children 5 and under. Mon–Sat 10am–5pm.

Where to Stay

1884 Paxton House Inn ★★ This is the finest, best-furnished, and most meticulously maintained bed-and-breakfast hotel in Thomasville, the one most often cited as a role model and learning forum for anyone considering going into the B&B trade. It's in a dignified Victorian house within an upper-class neighborhood, 4 blocks east of the town center. It contains a museum-quality collection of porcelain, acquired over many decades, which decorates virtually every corner of a tasteful and elegant decor, inspired by 18th- and early-19th-century models. Ms. Susie Sherrod is the innkeeper. Breakfasts are lavish affairs, featuring eggs Benedict or orange-flavored French toast, served with meticulous Southern charm.

445 Remington Ave., Thomasville, GA 31792. © **229/226-5197.** Fax 229/226-9903. www.1884 paxtonhouseinn.com. 9 units. $165–$190 double; $185–$275 suite. Rates include breakfast. AE, MC, V. **Amenities:** Breakfast room; lounge; health club; Jacuzzi; indoor lap pool; 8 tennis courts. *In room:* A/C, TV, hair dryer, Wi-Fi (free).

Jameson Inn ★ 🍴 Although part of a small chain, this is one of the best and most affordable places to stay in town. Bedrooms are generous in size and attractively furnished with quality pieces that give comfort and a bit of style. You have a choice of premium rooms, which are grabbed up first, or interior corridor units. Bathrooms are first-rate, with granite counters and brushed-nickel faucets. The hotel is filled with thoughtful extras such as express check-in and check-out services, homemade Belgian waffles at breakfast, an extensive cable line-up, and a complimentary *USA Today.* There's a large shopping center across the street, and several restaurants are nearby.

1470 Remington Ave., Thomasville, GA 31792. © **866/538-0187.** 40 units. $80 double. Rates include continental breakfast. AE, MC, V. **Amenities:** Breakfast lounge; exercise room; outdoor pool. *In room:* A/C, TV, fridge, hair dryer, Wi-Fi (free).

Where to Dine

Plaza Restaurant 🍴 GREEK/AMERICAN In the center of town, this well-established dining room is the place the local B&B ladies recommend when their

---

> ### Where *Gone With the Wind* Was First Screened

On the site of the elegant Historic Coalson Plantation, in Thomasville, the first actual screening of *Gone With the Wind* took place. It was held at the plantation's on-site theater, built in 1934. The Hanna family, who owned the estate at the time, had built the theater to resemble a river showboat. John Whitney, a major investor in the film, was a neighbor of the Hannas. He obtained a copy of the film after its final editing in 1939 and asked the Hannas if it could be shown at their little theater for a private screening before the official Atlanta premiere.

guests ask for the best place to eat in town. Restaurants come and go around Thomasville, but this one has built a loyal clientele and makes new friends every year. Whether it's breakfast, lunch, or dinner, the Plaza is open to serve you—just don't expect innovative cuisine. What you get is good, solid fare. For lunch, we opt for the tantalizing Greek salad. Many guests come for the oyster sandwich, a Southern favorite. Dinners are more elaborate, including a succulent pasta with seafood. The usual array of steaks, chicken, and seafood is prepared well with fresh ingredients. Thursday night is Greek Night, when the national dish of that country, moussaka, is often featured.

217 S. Broad St. (©) **229/226-5153.** Breakfast $2.95-$10; lunch buffet $7; main courses $4.95-$40. AE, DISC, MC, V. Mon–Sat 7am–2pm and 5–9pm (10pm Fri–Sat).

SAVANNAH

I f you have time to visit only one city in Georgia, make it Savannah. The movie Forrest Gump may have put the city squarely on the tourist map, but nothing changed the face of Savannah more than the 1994 publication of John Berendt's Midnight in the Garden of Good and Evil. The impact has been unprecedented, bringing in countless millions in revenue as thousands flock to see the sights from the mega bestseller. In fact, Savannah tourism has increased some 46% since publication of what's known locally as "The Book." Even after all this time, some locals still earn their living off The Book's fallout, hawking postcards, walking tours, T-shirts, and, in some cases, their own careers, as in the case of Lady Chablis, the black drag queen depicted in The Book who played herself in the Eastwood film.

The free spirit, the passion, and even the decadence of Savannah resemble that of Key West or New Orleans more than they do the Bible Belt, down-home interior of Georgia. Yet, Savannah—pronounce it with a drawl—conjures up all the clichéd images of the Old South: live oaks dripping with Spanish moss, stately antebellum mansions, mint juleps sipped on the veranda, magnolia trees, peaceful marshes, horse-drawn carriages, ships sailing up the river (though no longer laden with cotton), and even General Sherman, no one's favorite military hero here.

20

Today the economy and much of the city's day-to-day life still revolve around port activity. For the visitor, however, it's Old Savannah, a beautifully restored and maintained historic area, that's the big draw. More than 800 of Old Savannah's 1,100 historic buildings have been restored, using original paint colors—pinks and reds and blues and greens. This "living museum" is now the largest urban National Historic Landmark District in the country—some 2½ square miles, including 20 1-acre squares that still survive from Gen. James Oglethorpe's dream of a gracious city.

ORIENTATION

Getting There

BY PLANE   **Savannah Hilton Head International Airport** is about 8 miles west of downtown just off I-16. **American** (✆ 800/433-7300; www.aa.com), **Delta** (✆ 800/221-1212; www.delta.com), **United** (✆ 800/241/6522; www.united.com), and **US Airways** (✆ 800/428-4322; www.usairways.com) have flights from Atlanta and Charlotte, with connections from other points.

BY CAR   From the north or south, I-95 passes 10 miles west of Savannah, with several exits to the city, and U.S. 17 runs through the city. From the west, I-16 ends in downtown Savannah, and U.S. 80 also runs through the city from east to west. AAA services are available through the **AAA Auto Club South,** 712 Mall Blvd. (✆ **800/222-4357;** www.aaany.com).

BY TRAIN The **train station** is at 2611 Seaboard Coastline Dr. (✆ **912/234-2611**), some 4 miles southwest of downtown; cab fare into the city is around $5. For **Amtrak** schedule and fare information, contact ✆ **800/USA-RAIL** (872-7245) or visit www.amtrak.com. Reservations are required.

BY BUS Greyhound (✆ **800/231-2222;** www.greyhound.com) and **Southeastern Stages** (✆ **404/591-2750;** www.southeasternstages.com) offer regular service to Savannah. The **bus station** is at 610 W. Oglethorpe Ave. (✆ **912/232-8186**).

Visitor Information

The **Savannah Information Visitor Center,** 301 Martin Luther King Jr. Blvd., Savannah, GA 31401 (✆ **912/944-0455**), is open Monday to Friday 8:30am to 5pm and Saturday and Sunday 9am to 5pm. The staff is friendly and efficient. The center offers an audiovisual presentation ($5 adults, $2 children), organized tours, and self-guided walking, driving, or bike tours with excellent maps, cassette tapes, and brochures.

Tourist information is also available from the **Savannah Area Convention & Visitors Bureau,** 101 E. Bay St., Savannah, GA 31402 (✆ **877/SAVANNAH** [728-2662] or 912/644-6401; www.savannahvisit.com).

City Layout

Every other street—north, south, west, and east—is punctuated by greenery. The grid of **21 scenic squares** was laid out in 1733 by Gen. James Oglethorpe, the founder of Georgia. The design—still in use—has been called "one of the world's most revered city plans." It's said that if Savannah didn't have its history and architecture, it would be worth a visit just to see the city layout.

Bull Street is the dividing line between east and west. On the south side are odd-numbered buildings, on the north side even numbered.

Neighborhoods in Brief

The Historic District The Historic District—the real reason to visit Savannah—takes in both the riverfront and the City Market, described below. It's bordered by the Savannah River and Forsyth Park at Gaston Street and Montgomery and Price streets. Within its borders are more than 2,350 architecturally and historically significant buildings in a 2½-square-mile area. About 75% of these buildings have been restored.

Riverfront In this popular tourist district, River Street borders the Savannah River. Once lined with warehouses holding King Cotton, it has been the subject of massive urban renewal, turning this strip into a row

of restaurants, art galleries, shops, and bars. The source of the area's growth was the river, which offered a prime shipping avenue for New World goods bound for European ports. In 1818, about half of Savannah fell under quarantine during a yellow-fever epidemic. River Street never fully recovered and fell into disrepair until its rediscovery in the mid-1970s. The urban-renewal project stabilized the downtown and revitalized the Historic District. Stroll the bluffs along the river on the old passageway of alleys, cobblestone walkways, and bridges known as **Factor's Walk.**

City Market Two blocks from River Street and bordering the Savannah River, the City

Market was the former social and business mecca of Savannah. Since the late 18th century, it has known fires and various devastations, including the threat of demolition. But in a major move, the city of Savannah decided to save the district. Today former decaying warehouses are filled with restaurants and shops offering everything from antiques to collectibles, including many Savannah-made products. And everything from seafood and pizza to French and Italian cuisine is served here. Live music often fills the nighttime air. Some of the best jazz in the city is presented here in various clubs. The market lies at Jefferson and West Julian streets, bounded by Franklin Square on its western flank and Ellis Square on its eastern.

Victorian District The Victorian District, south of the Historic District, holds some of the finest examples of post–Civil War architecture in the Deep South. The district is bounded by Martin Luther King Jr. Boulevard and by East Broad, Gwinnett, and Anderson streets. Houses in the district are characterized by gingerbread trim, stained-glass windows, and imaginative architectural details. In all, the district encompasses an area of nearly 50 blocks, spread across some 165 acres. The entire district was added to the National Register of Historic Places in 1974. Most of the two-story homes are wood frame and were constructed in the late 1800s on brick foundations. The district, overflowing from the historic inner core, became the first suburb of Savannah.

GETTING AROUND

The grid-shaped Historic District is best seen on foot—the real point of your visit is to take leisurely strolls with frequent stops in the many squares.

BY CAR Though you can reach many points of interest outside the Historic District by bus, your own wheels will be much more convenient, and they're absolutely essential for sightseeing outside the city proper.

All major car-rental firms have branches in Savannah and at the airport, including **Hertz** (✆ **800/654-3131** or 912/964-9595 at the airport; www.hertz.com); **Avis** (✆ **800/331-1212;** www.avis.com), with locations at 422 Airways Ave. (✆ 912/964-1781) and at the airport (✆ 912/964-0234); and **Budget** (✆ **800/527-0700;** www.budget.com), with offices at 7070 Abercorn St. (✆ 912/966-1771) and the airport (✆ 912/354-4718).

BY BUS You'll need exact change for the $1 fare, plus $1 for a transfer. For route and schedule information, call **Chatham Area Transit (CAT)** at ✆ **912/233-5767.**

BY TAXI The base rate for taxis is $2, with a $1.80 additional charge for each mile. For 24-hour taxi service, call **Adam Cab Co.** at ✆ **912/927-7466.**

[FastFACTS] SAVANNAH

American Express
The American Express office has closed, but card-holders can obtain assistance by calling ✆ **800/221-7282.**

Dentist Call **Abercorn South Side Dental,** 11139 Abercorn St. (✆ **912/925-9190**), for complete dental care and emergencies Monday to Friday 8:30am to 3pm.

Drugstores Drugstores are scattered throughout Savannah. A good choice is **CVS,** 12012 Abercorn St. (✆ **912/925-5568**), open Monday to Friday 8am to 10pm, Saturday 8am to

6pm, and Sunday 10am to 6pm.

Emergencies Dial ℂ **911** for police, ambulance, or fire emergencies.

Hospitals There are 24-hour emergency-room services at **Candler General Hospital,** 5353 Reynolds St. (ℂ **912/819-6000**), and at **Memorial Medical Center,** 4700 Waters Ave. (ℂ **912/350-8000**).

Newspapers The *Savannah Morning News* is a daily filled with information about local cultural and entertainment events. The *Savannah Tribune* and the *Herald of Savannah* are geared to the African-American community.

Police In an emergency, call ℂ **911.**

Post Office Post offices and sub-post offices are centrally located and open Monday to Friday 8am to 4:30pm. The main office is at 3601 Montgomery St. (ℂ **912/234-8935**).

Safety Although it's reasonably safe to explore the Historic and Victorian districts during the day, the situation changes at night. The clubs along the riverfront, both bars and restaurants, report very little crime. However, muggings and drug dealing are common in the poorer neighborhoods of Savannah.

Taxes Savannah has a 6% sales tax. It tacks a 6% accommodations tax (a room or occupancy tax) on your hotel bill.

Transit Information Call **Chatham Area Transit** at ℂ **912/233-5767.**

Weather Call ℂ **912/964-1700.**

WHERE TO STAY

The undisputed stars here are the charming small inns in the Historic District, most in restored old homes that have been renovated with modern conveniences.

Because many of Savannah's historic inns are in converted former residences, price ranges can vary greatly. Advance reservations are necessary in most cases, since many of the best properties are quite small.

By and large, the double rooms in the recommended hotels and inns below have private bathrooms with tub/shower combinations, unless otherwise noted.

Along the Riverfront

EXPENSIVE

Hyatt Regency Savannah ★ There was an outcry from Savannah's historic preservation movement when this place went up in 1981. Boxy and massively bulky, and fully renovated in 2006, it stands in unpleasant contrast to the restored warehouses flanking it along the legendary banks of the Savannah River. Today it is grudgingly accepted as one of the biggest and flashiest hotels in town. It has a soaring atrium as well as glass-sided elevators. The comfortable rooms, often with paper-thin walls, are international and modern in their feel, all with good-size bathrooms and some with balconies overlooking the atrium. Room prices vary according to their views—rooms without a view are quite a bargain. Chances are, you'll find better food by dining outside the hotel at one of the independent restaurants recommended (see "Where to Dine," later in this chapter).

2 W. Bay St., Savannah, GA 31401. ℂ **800/223-1234** or 912/238-1234. Fax 912/944-3678. www.hyatt.com. 351 units. $169–$409 double; $400–$600 suite. AE, DC, DISC, MC, V. Parking $18. **Amenities:** Restaurant; bar; exercise room; indoor pool; room service. *In room:* A/C, TV, hair dryer, Wi-Fi ($9.95 per day).

Marriott Riverfront Hotel ★ At least the massive modern bulk of this place is far enough from the 19th-century restored warehouses of River Street not to clash with them aesthetically. Towering eight stories, with an angular facade sheathed in orange and yellow brick, it doesn't quite succeed at being a top-rated luxury palace,

Savannah Accommodations & Dining

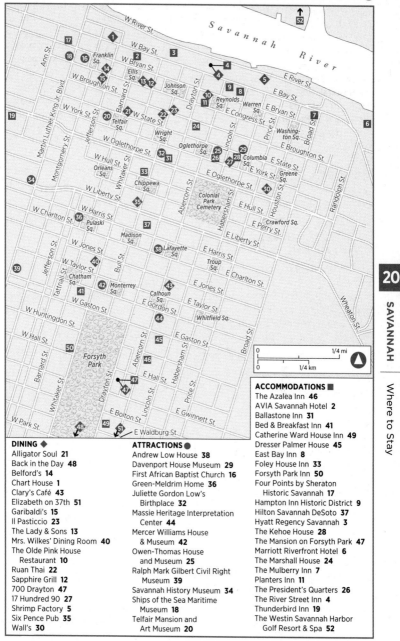

ACCOMMODATIONS ■

The Azalea Inn **46**
AVIA Savannah Hotel **2**
Ballastone Inn **31**
Bed & Breakfast Inn **41**
Catherine Ward House Inn **49**
Dresser Palmer House **45**
East Bay Inn **8**
Foley House Inn **33**
Forsyth Park Inn **50**
Four Points by Sheraton
  Historic Savannah **17**
Hampton Inn Historic District **9**
Hilton Savannah DeSoto **37**
Hyatt Regency Savannah **3**
The Kehoe House **28**
The Mansion on Forsyth Park **47**
Marriott Riverfront Hotel **6**
The Marshall House **24**
The Mulberry Inn **7**
Planters Inn **11**
The President's Quarters **26**
The River Street Inn **4**
Thunderbird Inn **19**
The Westin Savannah Harbor
  Golf Resort & Spa **52**

DINING ◆

Alligator Soul **21**
Back in the Day **48**
Belford's **14**
Chart House **1**
Clary's Café **43**
Elizabeth on 37th **51**
Garibaldi's **15**
Il Pasticcio **23**
The Lady & Sons **13**
Mrs. Wilkes' Dining Room **40**
The Olde Pink House
  Restaurant **10**
Ruan Thai **22**
Sapphire Grill **12**
700 Drayton **47**
17 Hundred 90 **27**
Shrimp Factory **5**
Six Pence Pub **35**
Wall's **30**

ATTRACTIONS ●

Andrew Low House **38**
Davenport House Museum **29**
First African Baptist Church **16**
Green-Meldrim Home **36**
Juliette Gordon Low's
  Birthplace **32**
Massie Heritage Interpretation
  Center **44**
Mercer Williams House
  & Museum **42**
Owen-Thomas House
  and Museum **25**
Ralph Mark Gilbert Civil Right
  Museum **39**
Savannah History Museum **34**
Ships of the Sea Maritime
  Museum **18**
Telfair Mansion and
  Art Museum **20**

20

SAVANNAH | Where to Stay

463

but nonetheless it attracts lots of corporate business and conventions to its comfortable, modern rooms, which aren't style setters but are generous in space. The Magnolia Spa has on-site facilities.

100 General McIntosh Blvd., Savannah, GA 31401. ⓒ **800/228-9290** or 912/233-7722. Fax 912/233-3765. www.marriott.com. 397 units. $179–$259 double; from $239 suite. Children 12 and under stay free in parent's room. AE, DC, DISC, MC, V. Parking $18 per day. **Amenities:** 4 restaurants; 2 bars; exercise room; Jacuzzi; 2 pools (1 indoor); room service; spa. *In room:* A/C, TV, hair dryer, Wi-Fi ($13 per day).

The Westin Savannah Harbor Golf Resort & Spa ★ Savannah's largest hotel is in a 16-story blockbuster format that rises somewhat jarringly from what were until the late 1990s sandy, scrub-covered flatlands on the swampy far side of the river. Deriving the bulk of its business from corporate groups who arrive for large conventions throughout the year, it's the largest of the four large-scale hotels that dominate the city's convention business. Yet despite a worthy collection of contemporary art that accents the labyrinth of high-ceilinged public rooms here, there's something just a bit sterile, even lifeless, about this relatively anonymous hotel. Despite its isolated position, the hotel is served by cross-river shuttle ferries that deposit clients into the center of the River Street bar-and-restaurant frenzy. The most elaborate guest rooms are on the two top floors and contain extras and comforts designated as Club Level. Otherwise, rooms are comfortable but bland.

1 Resort Dr. (PO Box 427), Savannah, GA 31421. ⓒ **800/WESTIN-1** (937-8461) or 912/201-2000. Fax 912/201-2001. www.westinsavannah.com. 403 units. $249–$419 double; from $450 suite. AE, DC, DISC, MC, V. From I-95 and Savannah International Airport, take exit 17A to I-16 toward Savannah. Follow sign for Rte. 17–Talmadge Bridge. Take the Hutchinson Island exit onto Resort Dr. Resort fee of $20 covers parking and the Internet (see below). **Amenities:** 4 restaurants; 3 bars; babysitting; 18-hole golf course; exercise room; Internet (included in resort fee; see above); Jacuzzi; outdoor pool; room service; sauna. *In room:* A/C, TV, hair dryer, minibar.

MODERATE

The River Street Inn ★★ ☺ When Liverpool-based ships were moored on the nearby river, this building stored massive amounts of cotton produced by upriver plantations. After the boll weevil decimated the cotton industry, it functioned as an icehouse, a storage area for fresh vegetables, and the headquarters of an insurance company. Its two lowest floors, built in 1817, were made of ballast stones carried in the holds of ships from faraway England. The building was later converted into some of the most comfortable and well-managed hotel rooms in town. In 2007, the owners poured nearly $2.5 million into renovations, as part of an ongoing effort to keep this charming, well-located inn a viable competitor. If night-crawls among the bars and restaurants of River Street are a priority, there is no other hotel better positioned than this one.

124 E. Bay St., Savannah, GA 31401. ⓒ **800/253-4229** or 912/234-6400. Fax 912/234-1478. www.riverstreetinn.com. 86 units. $139–$189 double. Children 13 and under stay free in parent's room. AE, DC, DISC, MC, V. Parking $8. **Amenities:** 2 restaurants; exercise room. *In room:* A/C, TV, hair dryer, Wi-Fi (free).

In the Historic District
VERY EXPENSIVE

Ballastone Inn ★★ This glamorous inner-city B&B occupies a dignified 1838 building separated from the Juliette Gordon Low Birthplace (home of the founder of the Girl Scouts of America) by a well-tended formal garden; it's richly decorated with all the hardwoods, elaborate draperies, and antique furniture you'd expect. For a brief period (only long enough to add a hint of spiciness), the place functioned as a bordello *and* a branch office for the Girl Scouts (now next door). It has an elevator, unusual for Savannah B&Bs, but no closets (they were taxed as extra rooms in the old days and so never added). It also has many truly unusual furnishings—cachepots filled with scented potpourri, and art objects that would thrill the heart of any decorator. A full-service bar is tucked into a corner of what was originally a double parlor. Each suite has a Jacuzzi tub as well as a private dressing area.

14 E. Oglethorpe Ave., Savannah, GA 31401. *©* **800/822-4553** or 912/236-1484. Fax 912/236-4626. www.ballastone.com. 16 units. $179–$335 double; $335 suite. Rates include full breakfast, afternoon tea, and evening hors d'oeuvres. AE, MC, V. Free parking. No children 15 and under. **Amenities:** Breakfast room; spa. *In room:* A/C, TV, hair dryer, Wi-Fi (free).

The Kehoe House ★★★   The Kehoe was built in 1892. In the 1950s, after the place had been converted into a funeral parlor, its owners tried to tear down the nearby Davenport House (see "Exploring Savannah," later in this chapter) to build a parking lot. The resulting outrage led to the founding of the Historic Savannah Association and the salvation of most of the neighborhood's remaining historic buildings.

Today the place functions as a spectacularly opulent B&B, with a collection of fabrics and furniture that's almost forbiddingly valuable. However, it lacks the warmth and welcome of the Ballastone Inn (see above). Breakfast and afternoon tea are part of the ritual that has seduced such former clients as Tom Hanks, who stayed in room no. 301 during the filming of parts of *Forrest Gump*. The rooms are spacious, with 12-foot ceilings, and each is tastefully furnished with English period antiques. Amenities include a concierge and twice-daily maid service with turndown. All rooms are nonsmoking. Ghostly goings-on within this inn, incidentally, are prominently featured as a standard part of the nightly ghost walks (p. 482).

123 Habersham St., Savannah, GA 31401. *©* **800/820-1020** or 912/232-1020. Fax 912/231-0208. www. kehoehouse.com. 13 units. $175–$215 double. Rates include full breakfast, evening tea, and hors d'oeuvres. AE, DC, DISC, MC, V. **Amenities:** Breakfast room. *In room:* A/C, TV, hair dryer, Wi-Fi (free).

The Mansion on Forsyth Park ★★★   This is the most opulent and spectacular boutique hotel in Savannah. Its core, known as the Kayton Family Mansion, was built in 1888 of terra-cotta bricks in a high-ceilinged, neo-Romanesque style. This place is international and more of a (tasteful) version of a Las Vegas blockbuster hotel than anything else in southeastern Georgia. Part of its allure derives from the rotating series of more than 400 paintings that sheath the walls of both the public areas and the upper hallways. Expect a plush environment with gilded cove moldings; Beaux Arts marble statues of, among others, turn-of-the-20th-century rococo goddesses at their baths; lavish antique chandeliers; and Versace copies of 19th-century French armchairs upholstered in faux zebra or leopard skin. The hotel's focal point is a courtyard and a small but artfully postmodern swimming pool. Bedrooms are avant-garde and plush, and among the most spacious in Savannah.

700 Drayton St., Savannah, GA 31401. *©* **888/213-3671** or 912/238-5158. Fax 912/721-1123. www.mansion onforsythpark.com. 126 units. $169–$300 double; from $400 suite. AE, DC, DISC, MC, V. Parking $20. **Amenities:** Restaurant, 700 Drayton (see review, p. 472); 2 bars; exercise room; outdoor pool; room service; spa. *In room:* A/C, TV, minibar, Wi-Fi (free).

EXPENSIVE

AVIA Savannah Hotel ★★★   This is arguably the best boutique hotel in town. You get taste, comfort, and all the modern conveniences with a heavy dose of Southern charm. The bedrooms are among the town's finest, with fresh, elegant Italian cotton linens, spacious bathrooms, terry bathrobes, in-room laptop safes, blackout drapes, personal climate control—and a lot more. The gourmet AVIA Kitchen and Wine Bar serves a deluxe breakfast and small plates in the evening. The terrace is a social magnet, with plenty of outdoor living space and intimate seating nooks, private cabanas, a fire pit, and a welcoming pool.

14 Barnard St., Savannah, GA 31401. © **866/644-2842** or 912/233-2116. www.aviahotels.com. 151 units. $179–$209 double; $199–$289 suite. AE, DISC, MC, V. Parking $16–$20. **Amenities:** Wine bar; concierge; exercise room; spa. *In room:* A/C, TV, hair dryer, minibar, MP3 docking station, Wi-Fi (free).

The Azalea Inn ★ 🎁
The furnishings of this B&B are a little richer, its colors a bit more evocative, and its decor more appealingly cluttered than those of many of its nearby competitors. The setting is an Italianate house (ca. 1889) set less than 2 blocks east of Forsyth Park, within a "historically correct" garden laid out as a garden might have been in Victorian times, contrary to the modernity of its swimming pool. It was originally built for Capt. Walter Coney, an army officer whose fortune derived from a then-flourishing maritime supply company. Rooms are furnished with period antiques, and each has its own distinctive Victorian-era decor. Especially appealing is the Gentleman's Parlor, a ground-floor guest room once dominated by men discussing manly things, which still carries a hint of bourbon and cigars. More frilly and feminine is the Magnolia Room, while the Cotton Exchange guest room features a massive four-poster bed and a deck overlooking the swimming pool.

217 E. Huntingdon St., Savannah, GA 31401. © **800/582-3823** or 912/236-6080. Fax 912/236-0127. www.azaleainn.com. 10 units. $199–$300 double; $275–$400 2-bedroom suite. Rates include full breakfast. AE, DISC, MC, V. **Amenities:** Outdoor pool. *In room:* A/C, TV, hair dryer, Wi-Fi (free).

Catherine Ward House Inn ★ 🎁
It isn't as spectacular or desirable as it was when it was newer, but the restoration of this house has won several civic awards, and it's so evocative of Savannah's "carpenter Gothic" Victorian revival that Clint Eastwood inserted a long, graceful shot of its exterior in *Midnight in the Garden of Good and Evil*. Built by a sea captain for his wife (Catherine Ward) in 1886 in a location a short walk from Forsyth Park, it offers one of the most lavishly decorated interiors of any B&B in Savannah, but at prices that are significantly less than those offered at better-known B&Bs a few blocks away. Leslie Larson, the owner and innkeeper, maintains a policy that discourages children 13 and under. A garden in back encourages languid sun-dappled dialogues. Each midsize guest room is richly decorated.

118 E. Waldburg St., Savannah, GA 31401. © **800/327-4270** or 912/234-8564. Fax 912/231-8007. www. catherinewardhouseinn.com. 9 units. $139–$249 double. Rates include full breakfast. AE, DISC, MC, V. **Amenities:** Breakfast room. *In room:* A/C, TV, hair dryer, Wi-Fi (free).

Foley House Inn ★
Decorated with all the care of a private home, this small B&B occupies a brick-sided house built in 1896. Its owners doubled its size in the early 1990s by acquiring the simpler white-fronted house next door, whose pedigree predates its neighbors by half a century. All rooms are neatly furnished. The staff will regale you with tales of the original residents of both houses. Breakfast and afternoon hors d'oeuvres, tea, and cordials are served in the two houses' connected gardens. The inn has earned AAA's rating of four diamonds and has been featured on HGTV's *Great Homes Across America* and some of the TV features of Turner South. Enjoy homebaked sweets every afternoon in the parlor wing and homemade appetizers from 6 to 7pm.

14 W. Hull St., Savannah, GA 31401. ℂ **800/647-3708** or 912/232-6622. Fax 912/231-1218. www.foleyinn.com. 19 units. $199–$354 double. Rates include full breakfast, afternoon hors d'oeuvres, wine, and cordials. AE, MC, V. No children 11 and under. **Amenities:** Breakfast room. *In room:* A/C, TV, hair dryer, Wi-Fi (free).

Four Points by Sheraton Historic Savannah ★

This tasteful and well-managed newcomer is in Savannah's Historic District, close to the emerging shopping district known as Ellis Square. The five-story, brick-fronted inn is a winner, thanks to a location only 3 blocks from Broughton Street. Guest rooms are comfortable, contemporary, and unfussy, appropriate nests for explorations of the Historic District without the lack of privacy you'll sometimes experience in a smaller inn or B&B.

520 W. Bryan St., Savannah, GA 31401. ℂ **912/790-1000.** Fax 912/721-1270. www.fourpoints.com/historicsavannah. 127 units. $95–$210 double; $175–$285 suite. AE, DC, DISC, MC, V. **Amenities:** Restaurant; piano bar; exercise room; rooftop pool. *In room:* A/C, TV, fridge (in some), Wi-Fi (free).

Hilton Savannah DeSoto ★

The name of this well-managed commercial hotel still evokes a bit of glamour—built in 1890, this hotel was for many generations the city's grandest. In 1967, thousands of wedding receptions, Kiwanis meetings, and debutante parties later, the building was demolished and rebuilt in a bland, angular, modern format. The renovated guest rooms are conservatively modern, and reached after you register in a stone-floored lobby whose decor was partly inspired by an 18th-century colonial drawing room. Despite the absence of antique charm, many guests like this place for its polite efficiency and modernism.

15 E. Liberty St. (PO Box 8207), Savannah, GA 31401. ℂ **800/445-8667** or 912/232-9000. Fax 912/232-6018. www.desotohilton.com. 246 units. $109–$279 double; $209–$509 suite. AE, DC, DISC, MC, V. Valet parking $17; self-parking $13. **Amenities:** 2 restaurants; bar; babysitting; exercise room; room service. *In room:* A/C, TV, hair dryer, Wi-Fi (free).

The Mulberry Inn ★ ☺

Locals point with pride to the Mulberry as a sophisticated adaptation of what might've been a derelict building into a surprisingly elegant hotel. Built in 1868 as a stable and cotton warehouse, it was converted in 1982 into a simple hotel, and in the 1990s it received a radical upgrade and a dash of decorator-inspired Chippendale glamour. Today its lobby looks like that of a grand hotel in London, and the rooms, though small, have a formal decor (think English country-house look with a Southern accent). The hotel's brick-covered patio, with fountains, trailing ivy, and wrought-iron furniture, evokes the best aspects of New Orleans.

601 E. Bay St., Savannah, GA 31401. ℂ **877/468-1200** or 912/238-1200. Fax 912/236-2184. www.savannahhotel.com. 145 units. $99–$309 double. Children 17 and under stay free in parent's room. AE, DC, DISC, MC, V. Parking $12. **Amenities:** Restaurant; exercise room; Jacuzzi; outdoor pool; room service; Wi-Fi (free). *In room:* A/C, TV, fridge, hair dryer.

The President's Quarters ★

This hotel combines the coziness of a B&B with the advantages of a small and elegant inn. Its design of labyrinthine hallways is quirky enough to be within a much-renovated private home. It's composed of two interconnected 1850s-era brick-built town houses whose modern-day gazebo and walled garden jut out into Oglethorpe square. This is the only B&B in Savannah with enough on-site parking for all of its guests, and with a working fireplace in every room. Each guest room is named after a U.S. president. Breakfast is a big deal here, served in a somewhat cramped dining room with old-fashioned accessories. Complimentary wine and hors d'oeuvres are presented every evening between 5:30 and 6:30pm.

225 E. President St., Savannah, GA 31401. ✆ **800/233-1776** or 912/233-1600. Fax 912/238-0849. www. presidentsquarters.com. 16 units. $189–$239 double; $329 suite. AE, DC, MC, V. Free parking. **Amenities:** Breakfast room. *In room:* A/C, TV, hair dryer, minibar (in suite), Wi-Fi (free).

MODERATE

Dresser Palmer House   This major investment in period restoration was built as two separate houses sharing an Italianate facade. In 1997, a lavish reunification of the two houses was undertaken. Today the unified building bears the distinction of having the city's longest and most stately front porch (called a gallery in Savannah) and inner ceilings that are almost dizzyingly high. Each guest room is beautifully furnished, and most are equipped with a well-maintained bathroom containing a tub/shower combination. The breakfasts are social events, each featuring a different dish, like curried eggs or Southern grits casserole. Wine and cheese are served daily from 5:30 to 7pm.

211 E. Gaston St., Savannah, GA 31401. ✆ **800/671-0716** or 912/238-3294. www.dresserpalmerhouse. com. 16 units. $169–$319 double. AE, DISC, MC, V. **Amenities:** Breakfast room. *In room:* A/C, TV, Wi-Fi (free).

East Bay Inn   Though the views from its windows might be uninspired, the East Bay is near the bars and attractions of the riverfront. It was built in 1853 as a cotton warehouse; green awnings and potted geraniums disguise the building's once-utilitarian design. A cozy lobby contains Chippendale furnishings and elaborate moldings. The guest rooms have queen-size four-poster beds and reproductions of antiques. The inn frequently houses tour groups from Europe and South America. In the cellar is **Skyler's** (✆ **912/232-3955**), an independently managed restaurant specializing in European and Asian cuisine. Midafternoon tea, wine, and cheese are a highly visible social ritual within this inn's daily schedule. The entire building is strictly nonsmoking.

225 E. Bay St., Savannah, GA 31401. ✆ **800/500-1225** or 912/238-1225. Fax 912/232-2709. www.east bayinn.com. 28 units. $159–$259 double. Rates include continental breakfast. AE, DC, DISC, MC, V. **Amenities:** Breakfast room. *In room:* A/C, TV, hair dryer, Wi-Fi (free).

Forsyth Park Inn ★   One of the grandest houses on the western flank of Forsyth Park is this frame place built in the 1890s by a sea captain (Aaron Flynt, also known as Rudder Churchill). A richly detailed staircase winds upstairs from a paneled vestibule, and the Queen Anne decor of the formal salon extends through the rest of the house. Guest rooms have oak paneling and oversize doors that are testimonials to turn-of-the-20th-century craftsmanship. The more expensive guest rooms, including one in what used to be the dining room, are among the largest in town. Home-baked breads and pastries are a staple of the breakfasts.

102 W. Hall St., Savannah, GA 31401. ✆ **866/670-6800** or 912/233-6800. Fax 912/233-6804. www. forsythparkinn.com. 11 units, 1 cottage with kitchenette. $195–$295 double; $245 cottage. Rates include full breakfast. AE, DISC, MC, V. **Amenities:** Breakfast room. *In room:* A/C, TV, Internet (free).

Hampton Inn Historic District ☺   This is one of the most appealing of the city's middle-bracket large-scale hotels. Opened in 1997, it rises seven redbrick stories above the busy traffic of historic Bay Street, across from Savannah's Riverwalk and some of the city's most animated nightclubs. Its big-windowed lobby was designed to mimic an 18th-century Savannah salon, thanks to the recycling of heart-pine flooring from an old sawmill in central Georgia and the use of antique Savannah bricks. Comfortably formal seating arrangements, a blazing fireplace, and an antique bar add cozy touches. The guest rooms are simple and comfortable, with wall-to-wall carpeting, midsize tiled bathrooms, and flowered upholstery. On the roof are a small pool and a sun deck supplemented by an exercise room on the seventh floor. There's no restaurant, but many eateries are a short walk away.

201 E. Bay St., Savannah, GA. ℭ **800/426-7866** or 912/721-1600. Fax 912/721-1610. www.hampton-inn. com. 154 units. $107–$249 double. AE, DC, DISC, MC, V. Parking $8. **Amenities:** Breakfast room; rooftop pool; Wi-Fi (free). *In room:* A/C, TV, hair dryer.

The Marshall House   Some aspects of this hotel—especially the second-story cast-iron veranda—might remind you of a 19th-century hotel in the French Quarter of New Orleans. It originally opened in 1851 as the then-finest hotel in Savannah. In 1864 and 1865, it functioned as a Union army hospital before housing such luminaries as Conrad Aiken and Joel Chandler Harris, author of *Stories of Uncle Remus*. After a ratty-looking decline, it closed—some people thought permanently—in 1957. In 1999, it reopened as a "boutique-style" inn. Despite the fact that this place has some of the trappings of an upscale B&B, some aspects evoke a busy commercial motel. Guest rooms succeed at being mass-production-style cozy without being particularly opulent. Seven of the largest and most historically evocative rooms in the hotel are on the second floor, overlooking noisy Broughton Street, and are prefaced with wrought-iron verandas with wrought-iron furniture. The bar has exposed brick, a very Southern clientele, and green leather upholstery. The restaurant **45 Bistro** (ℭ **912/234-3111**), set beneath the glassed-in roof of what used to be the hotel's rear stable yard, serves Southern and international cuisine.

123 E. Broughton St., Savannah, GA 31401. ℭ **800/589-6304** or 912/644-7896. Fax 912/234-3334. www.marshallhouse.com. 68 units. $109–$219 double; $249–$279 suite. Rates include continental breakfast. AE, DC, DISC, MC, V. **Amenities:** Restaurant; bar. *In room:* A/C, TV, hair dryer, Wi-Fi (free).

Planters Inn   This small European-style inn is more businesslike than the average Savannah B&B. Built adjacent to Reynolds Square in 1912 as a seven-story brown brick tower, it boasts a lobby with elaborate millwork and a scattering of Chippendale reproductions. The guest rooms are comfortably outfitted with four-poster beds and flowery fabrics; they're rather dignified and formal. Each contains a neatly kept bathroom with a tub/shower combination. The Planters Inn isn't associated with the well-recommended Planters Tavern (which stands next door and is separate).

29 Abercorn St., Savannah, GA 31401. ℭ **800/554-1187** or 912/232-5678. Fax 912/232-8893. www. plantersinnsavannah.com. 59 units. $119–$239 double. Rates include continental breakfast and evening wine reception. AE, DC, MC, V. Parking $14. **Amenities:** Breakfast room. *In room:* A/C, TV, hair dryer, Wi-Fi (free).

INEXPENSIVE

Bed & Breakfast Inn ★ 🍴   Adjacent to Chatham Square, in the oldest part of historic Savannah, this is a dignified stone-fronted town house built in 1853. You climb a gracefully curved front stoop to reach the cool, high-ceilinged interior, outfitted with a combination of antique and reproduction furniture. The accommodations are good-size, comfortable, and tastefully furnished.

117 W. Gordon St. (at Chatham Sq.), Savannah, GA 31401. ℭ **888/238-0518** or 912/238-0518. Fax 912/233-2537. www.savannahbnb.com. 18 units. $99–$209 double. Rates include full breakfast. AE, DISC, MC, V. **Amenities:** Breakfast room. *In room:* A/C, TV, hair dryer, Wi-Fi (in some; free).

Fairfield Inn by Marriott   This reliable budget hotel offers standard but comfortably appointed guest rooms with large, well-lighted desks and well-kept bathrooms.

Health-club privileges are available nearby, as are several good, moderately priced restaurants.

2 Lee Blvd. (at Abercorn Rd.), Savannah, GA 31405. © **800/228-2800** or 912/353-7100. Fax 912/355-5290. www.marriott.com. 135 units. $99–$129 double. Rates include continental breakfast. Children 17 and under stay free in parent's room. AE, DC, DISC, MC, V. Free parking. From I-16, take exit 34A to I-516 east, then turn right on Abercorn St. and go right again on Lee Blvd. **Amenities:** Breakfast room; outdoor pool. *In room:* A/C, TV, hair dryer, Wi-Fi (free).

Thunderbird Inn ✦   Although it's within a 5-minute walk from the edge of Savannah's Historic District, the Sputnik-era architecture of this "hip hotel" makes it seem a world away. Originally built in 1964, it had degenerated into an outmoded, sun-beaten relic—like something you'd expect along a dusty, sun-blasted stretch of Route 66—until a radical overhaul turned its former seediness into something approaching high camp. Expect geometric patterns of bright, Mondrian-inspired primary colors, an indulgent staff of Australian or perhaps European hipsters at the reception desk, and a punk-rock perspective that's refreshing when compared to the historicity and propriety of Savannah's Historic District.

611 W. Oglethorpe Ave., Savannah, GA 31401. © **866/324-2661** or 912/232-2661. www.thethunderbird inn.com. 42 units. $79–$339 double. Rates include continental breakfast. AE, DC, DISC, MC, V. **Amenities:** Breakfast room; Wi-Fi (free). *In room:* A/C, TV, fridge.

WHERE TO DINE

Savannah is known for the excellence of its seafood restaurants. They're among the best in Georgia, rivaled only by those in Atlanta. The best dining is in the Historic District, along River Street, bordering the water.

Some of Savannah's restaurants, like Elizabeth on 37th, are ranked among the finest in the entire South. And others, like Mrs. Wilkes' Dining Room, are places to go for real Southern fare.

Along or Near the Waterfront

Chart House ★ STEAK/SEAFOOD   Overlooking the Savannah River and Riverfront Plaza, "the home of the mud pie" is part of a nationwide chain—and one of the better ones. It's housed in a building that predates 1790, reputed to be the oldest masonry structure in Georgia and once a sugar-and-cotton warehouse. You can enjoy a view of passing ships on the outside deck, perhaps ordering an appetizer and a drink before dinner. The bar is one of the most atmospheric along the riverfront. As in all Chart Houses, the prime rib is slow roasted and served *au jus*. The steaks from corn-fed beef are aged and hand-cut on the premises before being chargrilled. The most expensive item is lobster. You may prefer one of the fresh catches of the day, which can be grilled to your specifications.

202 W. Bay St. © **912/234-6686.** www.chart-house.com. Reservations recommended. Main courses $18–$44. AE, DC, DISC, MC, V. Mon–Fri 5–10pm; Sat 11am–10:30pm; Sun 11am–9pm.

The Lady & Sons ★★ 🛏 SOUTHERN   Paula Deen started this place in 1989 with $200, the help of her sons, and a 1910 structure. Her namesake first cookbook, *The Lady & Sons Savannah Country Cookbook,* is an ongoing bestseller, and Paula also hosts a top-rated cooking show, *Paula's Home Cooking,* on the Food Network. Lunches are busy with a loyal following; dinners are casual and inventive. Menu items like crab cakes (one Maryland visitor claimed they were the best he'd ever eaten), crab burgers, and several creative varieties of shrimp best exhibit Paula's style. The locals love her buffets, which are Southern to the bone and feature fried chicken, meatloaf, collard greens, beef stew, "creamed" potatoes, and macaroni and cheese. The aphrodisiac dish has to be the raw oyster shooters, each served in a shot glass. Paula's signature dish is chicken potpie topped with puff pastry. Be careful not to fill up on the cheese biscuits and hoecakes that constantly land on your table. If for some reason you don't want a glorious glass of syrup-sweet tea, you'd better ask for unsweetened. In 2007, Paula Deen and Co. established a cookware store (p. 485) in a space immediately adjacent to the restaurant.

102 W. Congress St. ⓒ **912/233-2600.** www.ladyandsons.com. Reservations recommended for dinner. Main courses $19–$28; all-you-can-eat buffet $18; Sun buffet $16. AE, DISC, MC, V. Mon–Thurs 11am–3pm and 5–9pm; Fri–Sat 11am–3pm and 5–10pm; Sun 11am–5pm (buffet only).

Shrimp Factory 🐟 SEAFOOD   The exposed old brick and wooden plank floors form a setting for harborside dining in a cotton warehouse (ca. 1850). Lots of folks drop in before dinner to watch the boats pass by, perhaps enjoying a Chatham Artillery punch in a souvenir snifter. Yes, the place is touristy, never more so than when it welcomes tour buses. A salad bar rests next to a miniature shrimp boat, and fresh seafood comes from local waters. A specialty, pine bark stew, is served in a little iron pot with a bottle of sherry on the side; it's a potage of five types of seafood simmered with fresh herbs but minus the pine bark. Other dishes include peeled shrimp, shucked oysters, live Maine lobsters, sirloin steaks, and various fish filets.

313 E. River St. (2 blocks east of the Hyatt). ⓒ **912/236-4229.** www.theshrimpfactory.com. Reservations not accepted. Main courses $21–$35. AE, DC, DISC, MC, V. Mon–Thurs 11am–10pm; Fri–Sat 11am–11pm; Sun noon–10pm.

In the Historic District
VERY EXPENSIVE
Il Pasticcio NORTHERN ITALIAN   This restaurant is one of the city's most popular dining spots. In a postmodern style, with big windows and a high ceiling, it has a definite big-city style. A rotisserie turns out specialties. Many locals come here just for the pasta dishes, all homemade and served with savory sauces. Begin with carpaccio (thinly sliced beef tenderloin) or a tricolor salad of radicchio, endive, and arugula. Main dishes are likely to feature veal Marsala, angel-hair pasta with shellfish, or a mixed-grill seafood platter or grilled fish steak with tricolor roasted sweet peppers. There's a more upscale, much more expensive steakhouse immediately upstairs from this place.

2 E. Broughton St. (corner of Bull and Broughton sts.). ⓒ **912/231-8888.** www.ilpasticciosavannah. com. Main courses $28–$45. AE, DC, DISC, MC, V. Mon–Thurs 5–10pm; Fri–Sat 5–11:30pm; Sun 5–9:30pm.

Sapphire Grill ★ AMERICAN/LOW COUNTRY   One of the city's most consistently stylish restaurants evokes a low-key, counterculture bistro, but its cuisine is grander and more cutting edge than its industrial-looking decor and its level of hipness would imply. Christopher Nason is the owner and the most talked-about chef of the moment in Savannah, preparing what he defines as a "coastal cuisine" based on seafood hauled in, usually on the day of its preparation, from nearby waters. If you opt for a table here, you won't be alone: Scads of media and cinematic personalities will have preceded you. Launch your repast with endive, rocket, and baby field lettuce with sesame cream sauce and confit of tomato and Stilton cheese, or barbecue wild halibut with sweet corn broth. Each day the chef serves a tasting menu that includes an appetizer, salad, main course, and confections.

110 W. Congress St. ✆ **912/443-9962.** www.sapphiregrill.com. Reservations recommended. Main courses $19–$36; 6-course tasting menu $100, with wine $145. AE, DC, MC, V. Sun–Thurs 6–10:30pm; Fri–Sat 5:30–11:30pm.

700 Drayton ★★★ INTERNATIONAL   This is the culinary showplace of the most plush and sybaritic hotel to open in Savannah in years. It occupies the oldest section—a brick-built mansion from 1888—of the Mansion on Forsyth Park (see "Where to Stay," earlier in this chapter). Inside, scattered over two floors of the echoing, high-ceilinged interior, are 150 seats and six dining rooms, each of which contains remnants and reminders (including the working fireplaces) of the building's original role as a private home. The well-chosen menu is market inspired and one of the most seductive in Savannah, as evoked by the fried green tomatoes served with baked goat cheese, grilled pork chops stuffed with tomatoes and thyme, pecan-crusted rack of New Zealand lamb in a balsamic syrup, pan-roasted Gulf Coast grouper with a shrimp fricassee, and the most upscale version of tuna tartare we've seen. The steakhouse New York strip came as an imaginative and delightful surprise; it was Gorgonzola-crusted with caramelized shallots and a blackberry compote. Skewered shrimp with grits are served in a saffron-flavored shellfish sauce. Even if you're famished, we recommend a before-dinner drink at **Casimir's Bar,** which lies on the building's second floor.

In the Mansion on Forsyth Park, 700 Drayton St. ✆ **912/721-5002.** www.700drayton.com. Reservations recommended. Main courses $24–$35. AE, DC, DISC, MC, V. Daily 7–11am, 11:30am–2pm, and 5–9:30pm.

EXPENSIVE

The Olde Pink House Restaurant ★★ SEAFOOD/SOUTHERN   Built in 1771 and sheathed with a layer of pink stucco, this house has functioned as a private home, a bank, a tearoom, and headquarters for one of Sherman's generals. Today its interior is severe and dignified, with stiff-backed chairs, bare wooden floors, and an 18th-century aura similar to what you'd find in Williamsburg, Virginia. In 2008, a renovation and enlargement added the Planters Tavern, within an antique cellar room outfitted with a generously proportioned bar. Richly steeped in the traditions of the Low Country, its cuisine includes sautéed local shrimp with country ham and grits cake, crispy scored flounder with apricot sauce, steak *au poivre,* black grouper stuffed with blue crab and drenched in white onion and butter sauce, and grilled tenderloin of pork served with collard greens and yams. You can enjoy your meal in the rather formal and spartan-looking candlelit dining rooms or within the more permissive, less-formal decor of Planters Tavern.

23 Abercorn St. ✆ **912/232-4286.** Reservations recommended. Main courses $18–$35. AE, MC, V. Daily 5–10pm.

17 Hundred 90 INTERNATIONAL   In the brick-lined, low-ceilinged cellar of Savannah's oldest inn (which seems to be showing its age a bit these days), this place evokes a seafaring tavern along the coast of New England. Many visitors opt for a drink at the woodsy-looking bar in a separate back room before heading down the slightly claustrophobic corridor to the nautically inspired dining room. Students of paranormal psychology remain alert to the ghost rumored to wander through this place, site of Savannah's most-famous 18th-century suicide. Lunch might include the quiche of the day, Southern-style crab cakes, and a choice of salads and sandwiches.

Dinners are more formal, featuring crab bisque, snapper Parmesan, steaks, and bourbon-flavored chicken. The cooking is of a high standard.

307 E. President St. ✆ **912/236-7122.** www.17hundred90.com. Reservations recommended. Main courses $23–$38. AE, DISC, MC, V. Mon–Fri 11:30am–3pm and 6–10pm; Sat–Sun 6–10pm.

INEXPENSIVE

Back in the Day ★ 🍴 BAKERY This bakery is beloved by locals, and it might make an offbeat luncheon stopover. All its products are made from scratch, including "homespun" desserts and hearth breads using quality ingredients. At lunch you can order one of the best sandwiches in town. The "Hum Bee" features a house-made butterbean hummus, or you can order the Madras curry chicken sandwich on ciabatta. Specialty items include blackberry pie bar or orange coconut scones.

2403 Bull St. ✆ **912/495-9292.** www.backinthedaybakery.com. Sandwiches $6.50–$7.50. AE, MC, V. Tues–Fri 7:30am–4pm; Sat–Sun 8am–3pm.

Clary's Café ★ 🍴 AMERICAN Clary's Café has been a Savannah tradition since 1903, though the ambience today, under the direction of Jan Wilson, is decidedly 1950s. The place was famous long before it was featured in *Midnight in the Garden of Good and Evil* in its former role as Clary's drugstore, where regulars like eccentric flea-collar inventor Luther Driggers breakfasted and lunched. John Berendt is still a frequent patron, as is the fabled Lady Chablis. Begin your day with the classic "hoppel poppel" (scrambled eggs with chunks of kosher salami, potatoes, onions, and green peppers) and go on from there. Fresh salads, New York–style sandwiches, and stir-fries, along with Grandmother's homemade chicken soup and flame-broiled burgers, are served throughout the day, giving way in the evening to chicken potpie, stuffed pork loin, or planked fish (a fresh filet of red snapper—broiled, grilled, or blackened).

404 Abercorn St. (at Jones St.). ✆ **912/233-0402.** Breakfast $5–$13; main courses $5.95–$12. AE, DC, DISC, MC, V. Mon–Fri 7am–4pm; Sat–Sun 8am–4pm.

Masada Café ★ 🍴 SOUTHERN The South has a well-established tradition of pairing church and food, so it shouldn't come as a great surprise that some of the best down-home Southern cooking is at a buffet annex to the United House of Prayer for All People. Part of a group of eateries founded by Charles ("Sweet Daddy") Grace, this tile-floored cafeteria in the back of the church offers filling lunches and early suppers. The fried chicken with a peppery bite is among the best in town. Try such sides as tender pole beans or stewed squash, or a heavenly macaroni and cheese, which is crusty and cheesy but not overly rich. On any day expect soul-food classics, which you might consume to the shouts of "Hallelujah" coming from the front.

2301 W. Bay St. ✆ **912/236-9499.** Reservations not needed. Main courses $8.75–$10. No credit cards. Tues–Sat 11am–3pm; Sun 11am–6pm.

Mrs. Wilkes' Dining Room ★ ☺ SOUTHERN Remember the days of the boardinghouse, when everybody sat together and belly-busting food was served in big dishes in the center of the table? Before her death in late 2002 at the age of 95, Sema Wilkes had served breakfast and lunch to locals and travelers in just that manner since the 1940s. Bruce Willis, Demi Moore, and Clint Eastwood are on the long list of celebrities who've dined here. The tradition continues. Expect to find a line of people patiently waiting for a seat at one of the long tables in the basement dining room of this 1870 brick house with curving steps and cast-iron trim.

Mrs. Wilkes believed in freshness and planned her daily menu around the seasons. Your food will be a reflection of the cuisine Savannah residents have enjoyed for generations—fried or barbecued chicken, red rice and sausage, black-eyed peas, corn on the cob, squash and yams, okra, corn bread, and collard greens.

107 W. Jones St. (west of Bull St.). ℭ **912/232-5997.** www.mrswilkes.com. Lunch $16. No credit cards. Mon-Fri 11am-2pm.

Ruan Thai 🍴 THAI   This is the Savannah branch of a three-member chain that does a roaring business in other parts of coastal South Carolina and Georgia. It occupies a high-ceilinged former storefront along Savannah's main downtown shopping corridor—a welcome alternative to a constant dose of regional cuisine. Menu items come in whatever degree of spiciness you specify, and might include spring rolls; satay skewers with peanut sauce; and your choice of chicken, pork, beef, shrimp, tofu, or vegetables prepared with ginger sauce, garlic sauce, or various curries. An ongoing favorite is lemon-grass chicken topped with peanut sauce and served with rice.

17 W. Broughton St. ℭ **912/231-6667.** Reservations not necessary. Main courses $8-$25. AE, MC, V. Mon-Fri 11am-3pm and 4:30-10pm; Sat-Sun noon-11pm.

Six Pence Pub AMERICAN   There's a lot about this woodsy-looking place that emulates an 18th-century pub in England, and, except for the (much-appreciated) air-conditioning, the Americanized menu, and the Southern accents of the staff, you might, for a moment or two, think you're in the U.K. It's always been popular as a centrally located neighborhood restaurant, but its main claim to fame comes from its inclusion as the set, several years ago, for a scene in *Something to Talk About*, when the character played by Julia Roberts (dressed in a nightgown) confronts the character played by Dennis Quaid about infidelity. As befits Savannah gossip, locals still talk about it.

The bar offers 37 kinds of beer, 10 of them on tap, and the salads served here are fresh, large, and big enough for a meal. Also look for juicy burgers, various kinds of spaghetti, fried fresh fish and shrimp, well-stuffed sandwiches, marinated pork roasts, and such old English staples as shepherd's pie and bangers and mash.

245 Bull St. ℭ **912/233-3151.** www.sixpencepub.com. Reservations not necessary. Salads, sandwiches, and platters $7.50-$15. AE, MC, V. Daily 11:30am-1am. Bar daily 11:30am-2am.

Wall's ☺ BARBECUE   This is the first choice for anyone seeking the best barbecue in Savannah. Southern barbecue aficionados have built-in radar to find a place like this. Once they see the plastic booths, bibs, Styrofoam cartons, and canned drinks from a fridge, they'll know they've found home. Like all barbecue joints, the place is aggressively casual. Spare ribs and barbecue sandwiches star on the menu. Deviled crabs are the only nonbarbecue item, though a vegetable plate of four nonmeat items is also served.

515 E. York Lane (btw. York St. and Oglethorpe Ave.). ℭ **912/232-9754.** Main courses $7-$11. No credit cards. Thurs-Sat 11am-9pm. Closed mid-July to mid-Aug.

In & Around the City Market
EXPENSIVE

Alligator Soul ★ NEW SOUTHERN   We've had readers who adore this place, sinking right into its agreeable bar area and cozy dining room. Others view it as a heavy-handed, theme-ridden, and overpriced bastion of Southern Redneckism appealing shamelessly to local chauvinism and a yearning for the Old South. The best way to choose is to drop in for a cocktail at its bar. Meals mingle local ingredients with updated versions of time-tested recipes. Examples include fried green tomatoes with chipotle mayonnaise and bacon-flavored macaroni and cheese with shrimp. Main courses include all manner of oversize grilled steaks as well as "a big 'ol" grilled pork chop stuffed with apricot sausage and garnished with bourbon-braised Georgia peaches. A particularly scrumptious dessert is the house version of banana beignets served with roasted banana ice cream and candied pecans.

114 Barnard St. (C) **912/232-7899.** www.alligatorsoul.com. Reservations recommended. Main courses $23–$32. AE, DC, DISC, MC, V. Daily 5:30–10pm.

Belford's ★ LOW COUNTRY This restaurant keeps alive the tradition of offering good food in the area of the old city market. The setting is nostalgic, with hardwood floors, brick walls, high ceilings, and a patio. The cooks prepare a daily crab stew that is excellent, along with such other favorites as fried green tomatoes, fried calamari, or crab cakes, the latter served with a spicy tomato jam and lemon aioli. A trio of pastas is featured daily, our favorite being the lobster and wild mushroom ravioli served with a spicy calamari salad and a balsamic brown butter sauce.

For your main course, the array of delights may include potato-wrapped grouper with a prosciutto-enhanced beurre blanc sauce. The hazelnut red snapper is also a temptation, served with prawns and lump crabmeat in a hazelnut-liqueur sauce and a side of apple chutney. Shrimp, greens, 'n grits is a favorite, with smoked bacon, green onions, and a chardonnay butter sauce.

315 W. St. Julian St. (C) **912/233-2626.** www.belfordssavannah.com. Reservations recommended. Breakfast buffet $7.95; lunch $8–$19; dinner $14–$34; Sun brunch $6–$17. AE, DC, DISC, MC, V. Mon–Sat 8–11am, 11:30am–3pm, and 5:30–10pm; Sun 11:30am–3pm and 5:30–10pm. Closed Thanksgiving, Christmas Eve (night), and Christmas Day.

MODERATE

Garibaldi's SEAFOOD/ITALIAN Many of the city's art-conscious students appreciate this Italian cafe because of the fanciful murals adorning its walls. (Painted by the owner's daughter, the theme is "the jungles of Italy.") If you're looking for a quiet, contemplative evening, we advise you to go elsewhere—the setting is loud and convivial during the early evening and even louder later at night. Designed as a fire station in 1871, it boasts the original pressed-tin ceiling.

Menu items include roasted red peppers with goat-cheese croutons on a bed of wild lettuces, crispy flounder with an apricot-shallot sauce, artichoke hearts with aioli, about a dozen kinds of pasta, and a repertoire of Italian-inspired chicken, veal, and seafood dishes. Daily specials change frequently but sometimes include duck Garibaldi, king-crab fettuccine, and a choice of lusciously fattening desserts.

315 W. Congress St. (C) **912/232-7118.** www.garibaldisavannah.com. Reservations recommended. Main courses $13–$40. AE, MC, V. Mon–Thurs and Sun 5–10:30pm; Fri–Sat 5pm–midnight.

In the Victorian District
VERY EXPENSIVE

Elizabeth on 37th ★★ MODERN SOUTHERN This restaurant is frequently cited as the most glamorous and upscale in town. It's housed in a palatial neoclassi-cal-style 1900 villa ringed with semitropical landscaping and cascades of Spanish moss. The menu items change with the seasons and manage to retain their gutsy originality despite an elegant presentation. They may include roast quail with mustard-and-pepper sauce and apricot-pecan chutney, herb-seasoned rack of lamb, or broiled salmon with mustard-garlic glaze. You might begin with grilled-eggplant soup, a culinary first for many diners. There's also an impressive wine list. The desserts are the best in Savannah.

105 E. 37th St. ☎ **912/236-5547.** www.elizabethon37th.net. Reservations required. Main courses $28–$38; 7-course fixed-price menu $90. AE, DC, DISC, MC, V. Daily 6–9pm.

Dining Nearby

Johnny Harris Restaurant AMERICAN   Started as a roadside diner in 1924, Johnny Harris is Savannah's oldest continuously operated restaurant. The place has a lingering aura of the 1950s and features all that great food so beloved back in the days of Elvis and Marilyn: barbecue, charbroiled steaks, and seafood. The barbecue pork is especially savory, and the prime rib is tender. Colonel Sanders never came anywhere close to equaling the fried chicken here. Guests can dine in the "kitchen" (an area with a view into the slow-cooking barbecue pits) or in the main dining room, where you can dance under the "stars." The place will make you nostalgic.

1651 E. Victory Dr. (Hwy. 80). ☎ **912/354-7810.** www.johnnyharris.com. Reservations recommended. Main courses $7–$12 lunch, $12–$23 dinner. AE, DC, DISC, MC, V. Mon–Thurs 11:30am–9:30pm; Fri–Sat 11:30am–10:30pm.

EXPLORING SAVANNAH

Black History Sights

Savannah boasts the **First African Baptist Church,** 23 Montgomery St., Franklin Square (☎ 912/233-2429; www.theoldestblackchurch.org), the first such church in North America. It was established by George Leile, a slave whose master allowed him to preach to other slaves when they made visits to plantations along the Savannah River. Leile was granted his freedom in 1777 and later raised some $1,500 to purchase the present church from a white congregation. The black congregation rebuilt the church brick by brick, and it became the first brick building in Georgia to be owned by African Americans. The pews on either side of the organ are the work of African slaves. Sunday-morning worship is at 8:30 and 11:30am.

Ralph Mark Gilbert Civil Rights Museum, 460 Martin Luther King Jr. Blvd. (☎ 912/231-8900; www.savcivilrights.com), close to the Savannah Information Visitor Center, opened in 1996. It's dedicated to the lives and services of African Americans and their contributions to the civil rights movement in Savannah. Dr. Gilbert died in 1956 but was a leader in early efforts to gain educational, social, and political equity for African Americans in Savannah. Hours are Tuesday to Saturday 9am to 5pm. Admission is $8 for adults, $6 for seniors, and $4 for children.

Forts

About 2½ miles east of the center of Savannah via the Islands Expressway stands **Old Fort Jackson,** 1 Fort Jackson Rd. (☎ 912/232-3945), Georgia's oldest standing fort, with a 9-foot-deep tidal moat around its brick walls. In 1775, an earthen battery was built here. The original brick fort was begun in 1808 and manned during the War of 1812. It was enlarged and strengthened between 1845 and 1860, and saw its greatest use as headquarters for the Confederate river defenses during the Civil War. Its arched rooms, designed to support the weight of heavy cannons mounted above, hold 13 exhibit areas. The fort is open daily 9am to 5pm, with cannon firings scheduled for 10am, 2pm, and 4pm. Admission is $6 for adults; $5.50 for students, seniors, and children 6 to 18; admission is free for children 5 and under.

Fort McAllister, Richmond Hill, 10 miles southwest on U.S. 17 (✆ **912/727-2339**), on the banks of the Great Ogeechee River, was a Confederate earthwork fortification. Constructed in 1861–62, it withstood nearly 2 years of bombardments before it finally fell on December 13, 1864, in a bayonet charge that ended General Sherman's infamous March to the Sea. A visitor center with historic exhibits, walking trails, and campsites is open daily 8am to 5pm. Admission is $5 for adults, $3.50 for seniors and children 6 to 18, and free for children 5 and under.

Fort Pulaski (✆ **912/786-5787;** www.nps.gov/fopu), a national monument, is 15 miles east of Savannah off U.S. 80 on Cockspur and McQueen islands at the very mouth of the Savannah River. It cost $1 million and took 25 tons of brick and 18 years of toil to finish. Completed in 1847 with walls 7½ feet thick, it was taken by Confederate Georgia forces at the beginning of the war. However, on April 11, 1862, defense strategy changed worldwide when Union cannons, firing from more than a mile away on Tybee Island, overcame the masonry fortification. The fort was captured in just 30 hours by Union forces. The effectiveness of rifled artillery (firing a bullet-shaped projectile with great accuracy at long range) was clearly demonstrated. The new Union weapon marked the end of the era of masonry fortifications. The fort was pentagonally shaped, with galleries and drawbridges crossing the moat. You can still find shells from 1862 embedded in the walls. There are exhibits of the fort's history in the visitor center. It's open daily (except Christmas) from 9am to 5pm. Admission is $3 for adults and free for those 15 and under.

Historic Homes

Andrew Low House After her marriage, Juliette Low (see Juliette Gordon Low Birthplace, below) lived in this 1848 house, and it was here where she actually founded the Girl Scouts. She died on the premises in 1927. The classic mid-19th-century house facing Lafayette Square is made of stucco over brick with elaborate ironwork, shuttered piazzas, carved woodwork, and crystal chandeliers. William Makepeace Thackeray visited here twice (the desk at which he worked is in one bedroom), and Robert E. Lee was entertained at a gala reception in the double parlors in 1870.

329 Abercorn St. ✆ **912/233-6854.** www.andrewlowhouse.com. Admission $8 adults; $4.50 students, children 6-12, and Girl Scouts; free for children 5 and under. Mon–Wed and Fri–Sat 10am–4:30pm; Sun noon–4:30pm. Closed major holidays.

Davenport House Museum This is where seven determined women started the whole Savannah restoration movement in 1954. They raised $22,500, a tidy sum back then, and purchased the house, saving it from demolition and a future as a parking lot. They established the Historic Savannah Foundation, and the whole city was spared. Constructed between 1815 and 1820 by master builder Isaiah Davenport, the Davenport House is one of the truly great Federal-style houses in the United States, with delicate ironwork and a handsome elliptical stairway.

324 E. State St. ✆ **912/236-8097.** www.davenporthousemuseum.org. Admission $8 adults, $5 children 6-18, free for children 5 and under. Mon–Sat 10am–4pm; Sun 1–4pm. Closed major holidays.

Green-Meldrim Home This impressive house was built on Madison Square for cotton merchant Charleston Green, but its moment in history arrived when it became the Savannah headquarters of Gen. William Tecumseh Sherman at the end of his

1864 March to the Sea. It was from this Gothic-style house that the general sent his now infamous (at least, in Savannah) Christmas telegram to President Lincoln, offering him the city as a Christmas gift. Now the Parish House for St. John's Episcopal Church, the house is open to the public. The former kitchen, servants' quarters, and stable are used as a rectory for the church.

14 W. Macon St. ℂ **912/233-3845.** Admission $8 adults, $2 children. Tues and Thurs-Fri 10am–4pm; Sat 10am–1pm.

Juliette Gordon Low Birthplace   Juliette Gordon Low—the founder of the Girl Scouts—lived in this Regency-style house. It's now maintained both as a memorial to her and as a Girl Scout national center. The Victorian additions to the 1818–21 house were made in 1886, just before Juliette Gordon married William Mackay Low.

10 E. Oglethorpe Ave. ℂ **912/233-4501.** www.juliettegordonlowbirthplace.org. Admission $8 adults, $7 children 6–18, free for children 5 and under. Mon–Sat 10am–4pm; Sun 11am–4pm. Closed major holidays and some Sun Dec–Jan.

Owen-Thomas House and Museum ★   Famed as a place where Lafayette spent the night in 1825, this house evokes the heyday of Savannah's golden age. It was designed in 1816 by English architect William Jay, who captured the grace of Georgian Bath in England and the splendor of Regency London. The place has been called a "jewel box." You can visit not only the bedchambers and kitchen, but also the garden and the drawing and dining rooms. Adapted from the original slave quarters and stable, the Carriage House Visitors' Center opened in 1995.

124 Abercorn St. ℂ **912/233-9743.** Admission $15 adults, $5 students, $3 children 6–12, free for children 5 and under. Mon noon–5pm; Tues–Sat 10am–5pm; Sun 1–5pm.

Telfair Mansion and Art Museum ★   The oldest public art museum in the South, housing a collection of both American and European paintings, the Telfair Mansion and Art Museum was designed and built by William Jay in 1818. He was a young English architect noted for introducing the Regency style to America. The house was built for Alexander Telfair, son of Edward Telfair, the governor of Georgia. A sculpture gallery and rotunda were added in 1883, and Jefferson Davis attended the formal opening in 1886. William Jay's period rooms have been restored, and the Octagon Room and Dining Room are particularly outstanding.

121 Bernard St. ℂ **912/232-1177.** www.telfair.org. Admission $15 adults, $5 students, $4 children 5–12, free for children 4 and under. Mon noon–5pm; Tues–Sat 10am–5pm; Sun 1–5pm.

Kid Stuff

Massie Heritage Interpretation Center   Here's a stop in the Historic District for the kids. Geared to school-age children, the center features various exhibits about Savannah, including such subjects as the city's Greek, Roman, and Gothic architecture; the Victorian era; and a history of public education. Other exhibits include a period costume room and a 19th-century classroom, where children can experience a classroom environment from days gone by.

207 E. Gordon St. ℂ **912/201-5070.** www.massieschool.com. Admission $5 for adults, $3 children 11 and under. Mon–Fri 9am–4pm.

Literary Landmarks

Long before John Berendt and his *Midnight in the Garden of Good and Evil,* there were other writers associated with Savannah.

A VISIT TO THE MURDER HOUSE

A landmark building, paid for by Gen. Hugh W. Mercer, great-grandfather of Johnny Mercer, the Mercer Williams House was completed around 1868. It became known as "the envy of Savannah." Decades later, it was rumored that Jacqueline Onassis wanted to purchase it for use as a private home.

Mostly its fame was promulgated by the John Berendt book *Midnight in the Garden of Good and Evil.* It was here, in May 1981, as related in the book, that the wealthy homosexual antiques dealer Jim Williams fatally shot his lover, that blond "walking streak of sex," Danny Hansford, age 21. The Mercer Williams House was also the setting where Williams gave his legendary Christmas parties each year. In January 1991, Williams died of a heart attack at the age of 59 in the same room where he'd shot Hansford.

For years, heirs to Williams's estate have been downplaying its prurience and emphasizing, with much justification, Williams's role as a bon vivant and the savior of at least 60 historic houses in and around Savannah. The estate has agreed, for a fee, to open the house for tours.

Buy your ticket in the carriage house behind the Mercer Williams House, inside a gift shop loaded with objects of which Jim, the decorator, might have approved, and a few that he might have found sappy and sentimental. You'll be ushered into one of an ongoing series of tours, each lasting about 30 or 35 minutes. Tours depart from the carriage house and gift shop, at the compound's back entrance (430 Whitaker St.).

Don't think for a second that questions about Williams's sexuality, his promiscuity, or the murder will be engaged. Guides firmly advise before tours even begin that these are AAA Tours (including only questions about art, architecture, and antiques). Photos are rigidly forbidden, and a strong-willed guide will emphatically urge you "not to touch, drool on, dribble on, or engage the furniture or art objects in any way."

You'll learn that the Mercer family commissioned the design of the house but no member ever actually lived here; that a "dry moat" surrounds the house, allowing for light and air to enter the lower floors; that there's a ballroom on the second floor, but because of fire codes, no one is allowed upstairs.

The house has been used as the setting for movies, including Clint Eastwood's film *Midnight in the Garden of Good and Evil,* *Swamp Thing,* and *Return of Swamp Thing.* The Mercer Williams House is gorgeously furnished in a style that befits a sophisticated millionaire. It is not an authentic re-creation of a Federalist or mid-Victorian home, thanks to the presence of comfortable 20th-century sofas, personalized photos, art objects, and the "eclectic" vision of its style setter.

The tour's main benefit is that it makes you realize that Jim Williams was a helluva guy and a helluva benefactor to the Savannah that has so richly profited from his efforts ever since.

The **Mercer Williams House Museum** is at 929 Bull St. ((℃) **912/236-6352;** www.mercerhouse.com). Admission is $13 for adults and $8 for students with ID (both college and grad school). Tours run every 40 minutes daily from 10:30am to 4:10pm.

Chief of these is **Flannery O'Connor** (1925–64), one of the South's greatest writers, author of *Wise Blood* (1952) and *The Violent Bear It Away* (1960). She is also known for her short stories, including the collection *A Good Man Is Hard to Find* (1955). She won the O. Henry Award three times. Between October and May, an

MARTINIS IN THE CEMETERY

All fans of *Midnight in the Garden of Good and Evil* must pay a visit to the now world-famous **Bonaventure Cemetery,** 330 Bonaventure Rd. (📞 **912/651-6843**), on the low-lying eastern edge of the city. Filled with obelisks and columns and dense shrubbery and moss-draped trees, it's open daily 8am to 5pm. You get here by taking Wheaton Street east out of downtown to Skidaway to Bonaventure Road. (You don't want to approach it by boat like Minerva the "voodoo priestess" and John Berendt did—and certainly not anywhere near midnight.)

This cemetery lies on the grounds of what was once a great oak-shaded plantation, built by Col. John Mulryne. In the late 1700s, the mansion caught fire during a formal dinner party; reportedly, the host quite calmly led his guests from the dining room and into the garden, where they settled in to finish eating while the house burned to the ground in front of them. At the end, the host and the guests threw their crystal glasses against the trunk of an old oak tree. It's said that on still nights you can hear the laughter and the crashing of the crystal. In The Book, Mary Harty calls the ruins the "scene of the Eternal Party. What better place, in Savannah, to rest in peace for all time—where the party goes on and on."

It was at the cemetery that John Berendt had martinis in silver goblets with Miss Harty, while they sat on the bench gravestone of poet **Conrad Aiken.** She pointed out to the writer the double gravestone bearing the names of Dr. William F. Aiken and his wife, Anna, parents of Conrad. They both died on February 27, 1901, when Dr. Aiken killed his wife and then himself. The Aikens are buried in Lot #78H. Songwriter **Johnny Mercer** is also buried here in Lot #49H.

But not **Danny Hansford,** the blond hustler of the book. You can find his grave at Lot #6, Block: G-8 in the Greenwich Cemetery, next to Bonaventure. After entering Bonaventure, turn left immediately and take the straight path to Greenwich. Eventually, you'll see a small granite tile:

DANNY LEWIS HANSFORD
MARCH 1, 1960
MAY 2, 1981

Incidentally, **Jim Williams** is buried in Gordon, Georgia, a 3½-hour drive northwest of Savannah.

association dedicated to her holds readings, films, and lectures about her and other Southern writers. You can visit the **Flannery O'Connor Childhood Home,** 207 E. Charlton St. (📞 **912/233-6014**). The house is open only Saturday and Sunday from 1 to 4pm. Admission is free.

Conrad Aiken (1889–1973), the American poet, critic, writer, and Pulitzer Prize winner, was also born in Savannah. He lived at 228 (for the first 11 years of his life) and at 230 E. Oglethorpe Ave. (for the last 11 years of his life). In *Midnight in the Garden of Good and Evil,* Mary Harty and John Berendt sipped martinis at the bench-shaped tombstone of Aiken in Bonaventure Cemetery (see "Martinis in the Cemetery," below).

Museums

Savannah History Museum Housed in the restored train shed of the old Central Georgia Railway station, this museum is a good introduction to the city. In the theater, *The Siege of Savannah* is replayed. An exhibition hall displays memorabilia from every era of Savannah's history.

303 Martin Luther King Jr. Blvd. © **912/238-1779.** www.chsgeorgia.org. Admission $5 adults, $4.50 seniors and children 7–11, free for children 6 and under. Mon–Fri 8:30am–5pm; Sat–Sun 9am–5pm.

Ships of the Sea Maritime Museum   This museum has intricately constructed models of seagoing vessels, from Viking warships to nuclear-powered ships. In models ranging from the size of your fist to 8 feet in length, you can see such famous ships as the *Mayflower* and the *Savannah*, the first steamship to cross the Atlantic. More than 75 ships are in the museum's ship-in-a-bottle collection, most of them constructed by Peter Barlow, a retired British Royal Navy commander.

41 Martin Luther King Jr. Blvd. © **912/232-1511.** www.shipsofthesea.org. Admission $8 adults, $6 children 8–12, free for children 7 and under. Tues–Sun 10am–5pm. Closed major holidays.

ORGANIZED TOURS

If it's a *Midnight in the Garden of Good and Evil* tour you seek, then you've obviously come to the right place. Virtually every tour group in town offers tours of the *Midnight* sites, many of which are included on their regular agenda. Ask any of the tour groups. **Note:** Some tour outfits will accommodate only groups, so if you're traveling alone or as a pair, be sure to make that known when you make your tour reservations.

A delightful way to see Savannah is by horse-drawn carriage. An authentic antique carriage carries you over cobblestone streets as the coachman spins a tale of the town's history. The 1-hour tour ($20 for adults, $10 for children 5–11) covers 15 of the 20 squares. Reservations are required. Contact **Carriage Tours of Savannah** (© **912/236-6756;** www.carriagetoursofsavannah.com).

Old Town Trolley Tours (© **912/233-0083;** www.oldtowntrolley.com) operates tours of the Historic District ($25 for adults, $10 for children 4–12), with pickups at most downtown inns and hotels, as well as a 1-hour **Haunted History** tour detailing Savannah's ghostly past (and present). Call ahead to make reservations for all tours.

Savannah Walks, Inc., from a headquarters at Abercorn Street just south of Reynolds Square (© **912/238-WALK** [9255]; www.savannahwalks.com), offers three well-orchestrated walks. The most mainstream is the Savannah Stroll, a well-articulated ramble through the city's most central parks and thoroughfares, offering an anecdotal introduction to the city's history, lore, and legend. They also have a tour focusing on Savannah's triumphs, torments, and despair during the War between the States. Both tours last 90 minutes and are offered twice daily, at 10am and 1pm. After dark, the venue gets spookier, with a Savannah Ghost Tour, a 90-minute exposure of the city's flair for the macabre, with departures at 7:30pm and 9:30pm. When business warrants, there is a tour at 5:30pm as well. Each of the tours requires an advance reservation, and costs $16 for adults and $7 for children 6 to 14. Your guide might be a part-time student at Savannah College of Art and Design (SCAD) or an older, long-term resident of the city, but the likelihood is high that he or she will have some dramatic flair and a gift for oratory as well.

Gray Line Savannah Tours (© **866/374-8687**) has joined forces with **Historic Savannah Foundation Tours** to offer narrated bus tours of museums, squares, parks, and homes. Reservations must be made for all tours, and most have starting points at the visitor center and pickup points at various hotels. Tours cost $15 per person.

Riverboat Cruises are offered aboard the *Savannah River Queen*, operated by the River Street Riverboat Co., 9 E. River St. (© **800/786-6404** or 912/232-6404; www.savannah-riverboat.com). You get a glimpse of Savannah as Oglethorpe saw it back in 1733. You'll see the historic cotton warehouses lining River Street and the statue of Florence Martus, known as Savannah's Waving Girl, as the huge modern freighters see it when they arrive daily at Savannah. Fares are $19 for adults and $11 for children 12 and under.

Ghost Talk Ghost Walk takes you through colonial Savannah on a journey filled with stories and legends based on Margaret Debolt's book *Savannah Spectres and Other Strange Tales*. If you're not a believer at the beginning of the guided tour, you may be at the end. The tour starts at Reynolds Square. For information, call © **912/233-3896.** Hours for tour departures can vary. The cost is $10 for adults and $5 for children 12 and under.

Low Country River Excursions, a narrated nature cruise, leaves from the Bull River Marina, 8005 Old Tybee Rd. (U.S. 80 E.). Call © **912/898-9222** for information. Passengers are taken on the 1993 40-foot pontoon boat *Natures Way,* for an encounter with the friendly bottle-nosed dolphin. Both scenery and wildlife unfold during the 90-minute cruise down the Bull River. Trips are daily noon, 2pm, and sunset spring through fall, weather permitting. Fares are $15 for adults, $12 for seniors, and $10 for children 11 and under. There's a 30-passenger limit.

20 OUTDOOR PURSUITS

BIKING   Savannah doesn't usually have a lot of heavy traffic except during rush hours, so you can bicycle up and down the streets of the Historic District, visiting as many of the green squares as you wish. There's no greater city bicycle ride in all the state of Georgia. In lieu of a local bike-rental shop, many inns and hotels provide bikes for their guests.

CAMPING   The **Savannah Oak RV Resort,** 805 Fort Argyle Rd. (© **912/748-4000;** www.savannahoaks.net), is 2½ miles west of I-95, 4½ miles west of U.S. 17, and 12 miles from the Savannah Historic District on the banks of the Ogeechee River. Facilities include full hookups, LP gas service, a store, self-service gas and diesel fuel, a dump station, hot showers, laundry facilities, and a pool. The rate is $39 for an RV hookup.

Open year-round, **Skidaway Island State Park** (© **912/598-2300;** www.gastateparks.org/info/skidaway) offers 87 camping sites with hookups for $28. On arrival, you purchase a $5 parking pass valid for your entire stay. The grounds include 1- and 3-mile nature trails, grills, picnic tables, a pool, a bathhouse, and laundry facilities. Also open year-round, the **River's End Campground and RV Park,** Polk Street, Tybee Island (© **912/786-5518;** www.riversendcampgroundga.com), consists of 128 sites featuring full hookups, with groceries and a beach nearby. Tent sites cost $30 to $34 per day and RV sites $39 to $55 per day.

DIVING   The **Diving Locker-Ski Chalet,** 74 W. Montgomery Cross Rd. (© **912/927-6603;** www.divinglockerskichalet.com), offers a wide selection of equipment and services for various watersports. Scuba classes cost $225 for a series of weekday evening lessons and $240 for a series of lessons beginning on Friday evening. A full scuba-gear package, including buoyancy-control device, tank, and wet suit, is included. It's open Monday to Friday 10am to 6pm and Saturday 10am to 5pm.

FISHING **Amicks Deep Sea Fishing,** 6902 Sand Nettles Dr. (℃ **912/897-6759;** www.amicksdeepseafishing.com), offers daily charters featuring a 41-foot 1993 custom-built boat. The rate is $120 per person and includes rod, reel, bait, and tackle. Bring your own lunch. Beer and soda are sold on board. Reservations are recommended, but if you show up 30 minutes before the scheduled departure, there may be space available. The boat departs at 7am and returns at either 3 or 5pm.

GOLF **Bacon Park,** Shorty Cooper Drive (℃ **912/354-2625;** www.baconpark golf.com), is a 27-hole course with greens fees of $21 to $23 for an 18-hole round, including cart. Golf facilities include a lighted driving range, putting greens, and a pro shop. It's open daily dawn to dusk.

Henderson Golf Club, 1 Henderson Dr. (℃ **912/920-4653;** www.henderson golfclub.com), includes an 18-hole championship course, a lighted driving range, a PGA professional staff, and golf instruction and schools. The greens fees are $39 Monday to Friday and $48 Saturday and Sunday. It's open daily 7am to 7pm.

Or try the 9-hole **Mary Calder,** 1201 West Lathrop Ave. (℃ **912/238-7100**), where the greens fees, including cart, are $28 per day Monday to Friday and $30 per day Saturday and Sunday. It's open daily 7am to 8pm (or 5:30pm in winter).

JOGGING "The most beautiful city to jog in"—that's how the president of the Savannah Striders Club characterizes Savannah. The historic avenues indeed provide an exceptional setting for your run. The convention and visitors bureau can provide you with a map outlining three of the Striders Club's routes: Heart of Savannah YMCA Course, 3 miles; Symphony Race Course, 5 miles; and Children's Run Course, 5 miles.

NATURE WATCHES Explore the wetlands with **Palmetto Coast Charters,** 1 Billy Sasser Rd., Tybee Island (℃ **912/786-5403;** www.boatcharterssavannah.com). Charters include trips to the Barrier Islands for shell collecting and watching for otter, mink, birds, and other wildlife. The captain is a naturalist and a professor, so he can answer your questions. Palmetto also offers dolphin-watching, usually conducted daily 4:30 to 6:30pm, when the shrimp boats come in with dolphins following behind. The cost is $150 for up to six people for a minimum of 2 hours, plus $50 for each extra hour.

RECREATIONAL PARKS **Bacon Park** (see "Golf," above, and "Tennis," below) includes 1,021 acres, with archery, golf, tennis, and baseball fields. **Daffin Park,** 1001 E. Victory Dr. (℃ **912/351-3851**), features playgrounds, tennis, basketball, baseball, a pool, a lake pavilion, and picnic grounds. Both parks are open daily May to September 8am to 11pm and October to April 8am to 10pm.

Located at Montgomery Cross Road and Sallie Mood Drive, **Lake Mayer Park** (℃ **912/652-6780**) consists of 75 acres featuring a multitude of activities, such as public fishing and boating, lighted jogging and bicycle trails, a playground, and pedal-boat rentals.

SAILING **Sail Harbor,** 606 Wilmington Island Rd. (℃ **912/897-2896;** www. sailharbormarina.com), features the Catalina 25 boat, costing $150 per full day, with an extra day costing $125. It's open Tuesday to Saturday 10am to 6pm and Sunday 12:30 to 5:30pm.

TENNIS **Bacon Park** (see "Golf," above; ℃ **912/351-3850**) offers 16 lighted courts open Monday to Friday 8:30am to 9pm, and Saturday 9am to 1pm. **Forsyth Park,** at Drayton and Gaston streets (℃ **912/351-3850**), has four courts open daily

7am to 9pm. Both parks charge $5 per hour. Use of the eight lighted courts at **Lake Mayer Park,** Montgomery Cross Road, is free. They are open daily 8am to 11pm.

SHOPPING

River Street is a souvenir shopper's delight, with some 9 blocks (including River-front Plaza) of interesting shops, offering everything from crafts to clothing. The **City Market,** between Ellis and Franklin squares on West St. Julian Street, boasts art galleries, boutiques, and sidewalk cafes along with a horse-and-carriage ride. Book-stores, boutiques, and antiques shops are located between Wright Square and For-syth Park.

   Oglethorpe Mall, at 7804 Abercorn St., has more than 100 specialty shops and four major department stores, as well as restaurants and fast-food outlets. The **Savannah Mall,** 14045 Abercorn St., is Savannah's newest shopping center, with two floors of shopping, plus a food court with its own carousel. The anchor stores are Dillard's, Parisian, and Belk.

   ShopSCAD, 340 Bull St. (✆ **912/525-5180;** shopscadonline.com), is a store opened by the Savannah College of Art and Design's president in 2003. A raging suc-cess, it now has satellite shops at the college's other locations in Atlanta and Lacoste, France. Amy Zurcher, who is the managing director of the gallery, frequently displays works made by alumni, who create everything gift-worthy, from jewelry, bags, and dolls to housewares.

Antiques

Alex Raskin Antiques   This shop offers a wide array of antiques of varying ages. The selection includes everything from accessories to furniture, rugs, and paintings. 441 Bull St. (in the Noble Hardee Mansion), Monterey Sq. ✆ **912/232-8205.**

J.D. Weed & Co.   This shop prides itself on providing "that wonderful treasure that combines history and personal satisfaction with rarity and value." If you're look-ing for a particular item, just let the staff know and they'll try to find it for you. 102 W. Victory Dr. ✆ **866/308-1933** or 912/234-8540. www.jdweedco.com.

Art & Sculpture

Desotorow Gallery   A nonprofit organization, this is a gallery operated by current and recent art students, who stage the most avant-garde exhibitions in town. The studio is in an up-and-coming section of Savannah, called "Starland," and is filled with galleries and studios. Exhibitions are forever changing—one, for example, featured painted big box radios. 2427 De Soto Ave. ✆ **912/220-0939**. www.desotorow.org.

Gallery 209   Housed in an 1820s cotton warehouse, this gallery displays two floors of original paintings by local artists, sculpture, woodworking, fiber art, gold and silver jewelry, enamels, photography, batiks, pottery, and stained glass. You'll also find a wide selection of limited-edition reproductions and notecards of local scenes. 209 E. River St. ✆ **912/236-4583.** www.gallery209savannah.com.

John Tucker Fine Arts   This gallery offers museum-quality pieces by local artists as well as by those from around the world, including Haitian and Mexican craft-speople. In a restored 1800s home, this gallery features 19th- and 20th-century landscapes, marine-art paintings, portraits, folk art, and still lifes. 5 W. Charlton St. ✆ **912/231-8161.** www.johntuckerfinearts.com.

Morning Star Gallery This gallery features the works of more than 80 artists. Pieces include hand-thrown pottery, metalwork, paintings, prints, woodworks, jewelry, and glass (hand-blown and leaded). 60 Jasper St. ✆ **912/233-4307.**

Village Craftsmen This collection of artisans offers a wide array of handmade crafts, including hand-blown glass, needlework, folk art, prints, restored photographs, and hand-thrown pottery. 223 W. River St. ✆ **912/236-7280.** www.thevillagecraftsmen.com.

Books

Book Warehouse This store offers more than 75,000 titles, including fiction, cookbooks, children's books, computer manuals, and religious tomes. Prices begin at less than a dollar, and all proceeds are donated to Emory University for cancer research. 11 Gateway Blvd. ✆ **912/927-0824.**

E. Shaver, Bookseller Housed on the ground floor of a Greek Revival mansion, E. Shaver features 12 rooms of tomes. Specialties include architecture, decorative arts, regional history, and children's books, as well as 17th-, 18th-, and 19th-century maps. 326 Bull St. ✆ **912/234-7257.**

Candy & Other Foods

Plantation Sweets Vidalia Onions Outside Savannah, check out the Vidalia onion specialties offered by the Collins family for more than 50 years. Sample one of the relishes, dressings, or gift items as well. Call for directions. Rte. 2, Cobbtown. ✆ **800/541-2272** or 912/684-2272. www.plantationsweets.com.

River Street Sweets Begun more than 20 years ago as part of the River Street restoration project, this store offers a wide selection of candies, including pralines, bear claws, fudge, and chocolates. Included among the specialties are more than 30 flavors of taffy made on a machine from the early 1900s. 13 E. River St. ✆ **800/793-3876** or 912/234-4602. www.riverstreetsweets.com.

Savannah's Candy Kitchen Chocolate-dipped Oreos, glazed pecans, pralines, and fudge are only a few of the delectables at this confectionery. Staff members are so sure you'll be delighted with their offerings that they offer a full money-back guarantee if you're not satisfied. 225 E. River St. ✆ **800/443-7884** or 912/233-8411. www.savannah candy.com.

Cookware

The Paula Deen Store In 2007, the Paula Deen group took over what had previously functioned as a pub and transformed it into a shop selling the cookbooks and gadgets you'll need to cook like a pro and emulate the award-winning TV technique of Savannah's most famous chef. It's immediately adjacent to Ms. Deen's restaurant (p. 470), within tempting view of the line that forms prior to mealtimes. 108 W. Congress St. ✆ **866/957-2852** or 912/233-2600.

Gifts & Collectibles

Charlotte's Corner Featuring local items, this shop offers a wide array of gifts and souvenirs. The selection encompasses children's clothing, a few food items, Sheila houses, and Savannah-related books, including guidebooks and Southern cookbooks. 1 W. Liberty St. (at Bull St.). ✆ **912/233-8061.**

The Christmas Shop   This shop keeps the Christmas spirit alive all year with a large selection of ornaments, Santas, nutcrackers, and collectibles. Collectors will appreciate the various featured lines, including Department 56, Polonaise, Christina's World, and Patricia Breen. 307 Bull St. ℰ **912/234-5343.** www.thechristmasshop. homestead.com.

Household Decoration

Arcanum Antiques Interiors ★ 🎁   This shop in the historic district lives up to its namesake, Arcanum, specializing in unusual, often bizarre, decorative artifacts from around the world. The silver mint-julep cups are a popular item, and you can even purchase a crystal ball here, or perhaps a neoclassical urn with brass snake handles or some jewelry made from semiprecious gemstones. 346 Whitaker St. ℰ **912/236-6000.** www.arcanumsavannah.com.

Jewelry & Silver

Levy Jewelers   This downtown boutique deals mainly in antique jewelry. It offers a large selection of gold, silver, gems, and watches. Among its other items are crystal, china, and gift items. 101 E. Broughton St. ℰ **800/237-5389** or 912/233-1163. www.levyjewelers.com.

Simply Silver   The specialty here is sterling flatware, ranging from today's designs to discontinued items of yesteryear. The inventory includes new and estate pieces along with an array of gift items. 236 Bull St. ℰ **912/238-3652.**

Markets

The Paris Market and Brocante ★   The owners, Paula and Taras Danyluk, were inspired by some of the world's most famous bazaars and flea markets, including the Marché aux Puces in Paris, but also the markets of Cairo, Alexandria, and India. They sell treasures they have gathered from their travels—London wharves, the markets of Hungary, and other "hidden corners" around the globe. The merchandise is forever changing, so you never know what treasures to expect. 36 W. Broughton St. ℰ **912/232-1500.** www.theparismarket.com.

SAVANNAH AFTER DARK

River Street, along the Savannah River, is the major after-dark venue. Many night owls stroll the waterfront until they hear the sound of music they like, then follow their ears inside. In summer, concerts of jazz, Big Band, and Dixieland music fill downtown **Johnson Square** with lots of foot-tapping sounds that thrill both locals and visitors. Some of Savannah's finest musicians perform regularly on this historic site.

Bars, Pubs & Coffeehouses

American Legion Post ★ 🎁   Perhaps the most unusual bar to patronize is actually at the American Legion Post, south of Forsyth Park, in a historic Gothic Revival facade featuring fortresslike elements. In 1942, this was the local home of the Eighth Air Force. Not just war veterans, but clients of various ages patronize this surprisingly shimmery, mirrored establishment. Thursday is ladies night, from 4pm to midnight, featuring $1 beers, and Fridays men get $1 beers from 6 to 8pm. Open Monday to Saturday 4pm to midnight. 1108 Bull St. ℰ **912/233-9277.**

Bernie's   This bar and grill, conveniently located on the riverfront, is in one of the city's pre–Civil War cotton warehouses and has the ambience of an old portside pub. The bar offers live music, televised sports, and extended weekend hours. The bartenders claim their bloody mary is the best on River Street, and it's presented in a Mason jar and topped with pickled okra. If you're hungry, a light menu features seafood, burgers, and sandwiches. It's open Monday to Thursday 11am to midnight, Friday and Saturday 11am to 3am, and Sunday noon to midnight. 115 E. River St. © **912/236-1827.**

Gallery Espresso   Facing Chippewa Square, on the site of what used to be a Victorian storefront, this artsy, New Age, bohemian enclave evokes the hippie heyday of the 1960s. If you can find an available seat on any of the battered, artfully mismatched sofas and armchairs, you might be tempted to remain in place a long, leisurely time. There's no table service—you order your espresso, salads, desserts, pastries, and ice cream directly from the countertop and display cases in back. Some of the macramé items, weavings, and ceramics are for sale, and scattered throughout are free copies of the city's various student magazines and culture guides. The only alcohol served is wine, priced from $6 to $8 per glass. Open Monday to Friday 7:30am to 10pm and Saturday and Sunday 8am to 11pm. 234 Bull St. © **912/233-5348.** www.galleryespresso.com.

Kevin Barry's Irish Pub   The place to be on St. Patrick's Day, this waterfront pub rocks all year. Irish folk music will entertain you as you choose from a menu featuring such Irish fare as beef stew, shepherd's pie, and corned beef and cabbage. Many folks come here just to drink, often making a night of it in the convivial atmosphere. It's open Monday to Saturday 11am to 2am and Sunday noon to 1am. 117 W. River St. © **912/233-9626.** www.kevinbarrys.com.

Mellow Mushroom   Don't expect grandeur here. A member of a Georgia-based restaurant chain, it appeals to a funky, irreverent, and sometimes raucous crowd of college students and faded counterculture aficionados from yesterday. Decor includes rambling murals painted with an individualized—and subjective—iconography that might require an explanation from a member of the cheerful waitstaff. There's the cut-off front end of a VW Beetle near the entrance; a limited menu that focuses almost exclusively on pizzas, salads, and calzones; and a die-hard emphasis on cheap beer, especially Pabst, which sells by the pitcher. Expect lots of SCAD (Savannah College of Art and Design) students, a battered and dimly lighted interior, recorded (not live) music, and a vague allegiance to the hard rock, hard drugs, and hard sex fantasies of the early 1970s. Open daily 11am to 10pm. 11 W. Liberty St. © **912/495-0705.** www.mellowmushroom.com.

Mercury Lounge   The venue is as hip, counterculture, and artfully kitsch as anything you might have expected in Manhattan, with the added benefit of a reputation for the biggest martinis (10 oz.) in town. You'll find the most comfortable bar stools anywhere (they're covered in faux leopard or zebra), live music most nights, and, when a band is not performing, a jukebox. Everything is congenially battered, with enough rock and musical memorabilia to please the curators of a rock-'n'-roll hall of fame. It's open daily from 3pm to 3am. 125 W. Congress St. © **912/447-6952.** www.mercury lounge.com.

Savannah Smiles   Near River Street and in back of the Quality Inn, this piano bar not only encourages audience participation, it requires it. A pair of talented musicians duels for the audience's attention as they play old-time favorites. Request a song, and the musicians will do the rest. Savannah Smiles won city awards for best new bar in 2001 and best overall bar in 2002. There are several shows of dueling pianos Wednesday to Saturday, and karaoke on Sunday. The bar is open Wednesday through Saturday 7pm to 3am and Sunday 7pm to 2am. 314 Williamson St. ⓒ **912/527-6453.** Cover varies from $5 (on Wed ladies get in free).

17 Hundred 90 Lounge This is Savannah's haunted pub. The ghost of Anna Powers, who killed herself by jumping out of the third-floor window onto a brick courtyard, has been spotted wandering about at night. She committed suicide after falling in love with a married sea captain who sailed away. If you don't mind ghosts, this is a cozy bar attached to one of Savannah's most acclaimed restaurants. Happy hour with hors d'oeuvres lasts from 4:30 to 8:30pm. It's open daily noon to midnight. 307 E. President St. ⓒ **912/236-7122.** www.17hundred90.com.

GAY & LESBIAN BARS

Chuck's Bar Most of the bars along Savannah's River Street are mainstream affairs, attracting goodly numbers of tourists, some of whom drink staggering amounts of booze and who seem almost proud of how rowdy they can get. In deliberate contrast, Chuck's usually attracts local members of Savannah's counterculture, including lots of gay folk, who rub elbows in a tucked-away corner of a neighborhood rarely visited by locals. The setting is a dark and shadowy 19th-century warehouse, lined with bricks, just a few steps from the Jefferson Street ramp leading down to the riverfront. Hours are Monday to Wednesday from 8pm to 3am and Thursday to Saturday 7pm to 3am. 305 W. River St. ⓒ **912/232-1005.**

Club One ★★ Club One defines itself as the premier gay bar in a town priding itself on a level of decadence that falls somewhere between New Orleans's and Key West's, and it's the hottest and most amusing spot in town. Patrons include lesbians and gays from the coastal islands, visiting urbanites, and cast and crew of whatever film is being shot in Savannah at the time (Demi Moore and Bruce Willis are two stars who have showed up here). There's also likely to be a healthy helping of voyeurs who've read *Midnight in the Garden of Good and Evil.*

You pay your cover at the door, showing ID if the attendant asks for it. Wander through the street-level dance bar, trek down to the basement-level video bar for a (less noisy) change of venue, and (if your timing is right) climb one floor above street level for a view of the drag shows. There, a bevy of artistes lip-sync the hits of Tina Turner, Gladys Knight, and Bette Midler. The bar is open daily 5pm to 3am. Shows are nightly at 10:30pm and 12:30am. 1 Jefferson St. ⓒ **912/232-0200.** www.clubone-online. com. Cover (after 9:30pm) $10 for those 18–20, $5 for those 21 and older.

Dinner Cruises

The ***Savannah River Queen,*** a replica of the boats that once plied this waterway, is a 350-passenger vessel operated by the River Street Riverboat Co., 9 E. River St. (ⓒ **800/786-6404** or 912/232-6404; www.savannah-riverboat.com). It offers a 2-hour cruise with a prime rib or fish dinner and live entertainment. Reservations are necessary. The fare is $49 for adults and $28 for children 12 and under. Departures are usually daily at 7pm, but the schedule might be curtailed in the colder months.

About 10 miles south of downtown Savannah is the charming community of **Isle of Hope** ★. First settled in the 1840s as a summer resort for the wealthy, it's now a showcase of rural antebellum life. To reach Parkersburg (as it was called in those days), citizens traveled by steamer down the Wilmington River or by a network of suburban trains. Today you can reach Isle of Hope by driving east from Savannah along Victory Drive to Skidaway Road. At Skidaway, go right and follow it to LaRoche Avenue. Take a left and follow LaRoche until it dead-ends on Bluff Drive. This is the perfect place for a lazy afternoon stroll. The short path is home to authentically restored cottages and beautiful homes, most enshrouded with Spanish moss cascading from the majestic oaks lining the bluff. A favorite of many local landscape artists and Hollywood directors, Bluff Drive affords the best views of the Wilmington River.

As you head back toward Savannah, drive down Skidaway Road. On your left is **Wormsloe Plantation,** 7601 Skidaway Rd. (✆ **912/353-3023;** www. wormsloe.org). Wormsloe, the home of Noble Jones, isn't much more than a ruin. After you enter the gates, you proceed down an unpaved oak-lined drive, and the ruins lie less than half a mile off the road. Dr. Jones was one of Georgia's leading colonial citizens and a representative to the Continental Congress. Wormsloe has also been home to forts and garrisons during the Civil and Spanish-American wars. It's open Tuesday to Sunday 9am to 5pm. Admission is $5 for adults and $3.50 for students 6 to 18; children 5 and under are admitted free.

Live Music

Planters Tavern   This is Savannah's most-beloved tavern, graced with a sprawling and convivial bar, a pair of fireplaces, and a decor of antique bricks and carefully polished hardwoods. Because it's in the cellar of the Olde Pink House Restaurant, many guests ask that platters of food be served at their tables. Otherwise, you can sit, drink in hand, listening to the melodies emanating from the sadder-but-wiser pianist. Foremost among the divas who perform is the endearingly elegant Gail Thurmond, one of Savannah's most legendary songstresses, who weaves her enchantment Tuesday to Sunday. In the Olde Pink House Restaurant, 23 Abercorn St. ✆ **912/232-4286.**

The Performing Arts

Savannah Symphony Orchestra has city-sponsored concerts in addition to its regular ticketed events. Spread a blanket in Forsyth Park and listen to the symphony perform beneath the stars, or be on River Street on the Fourth of July when the group sends rousing strains echoing across the river.

The orchestra is one of two fully professional orchestras in the state of Georgia, and its regular nine-concert masterworks series is presented in the Savannah Civic Center's **Johnny Mercer Theater,** Orleans Square (✆ **912/651-6556;** www. savannahcivic.com), which is also home to ballet, musicals, and Broadway shows. Call to find out what's being presented at the time of your visit. Tickets range from $15 to $100.

20

SAVANNAH

Savannah After Dark

Savannah Theatre, Chippewa Square (© **912/233-7764;** www.savannahtheatre. com), presents contemporary plays. Tickets are usually $33 for adults, $31 for seniors and students, and $16 for children 17 and under.

Late September brings the 5-day **Savannah Jazz Festival** www.savannahjazz festival.org), with nationally known musicians appearing around the city.

he Golden Isles are ideal for naturalists, with miles and miles of private secluded
ches, plus acres of ancient forests. More than 200 species of birds are sighted
lly, especially on Little St. Simons.

Temperature and climate make the islands a year-round destination. Spring arrives
ly in March, with air temperatures ranging from 50° to 80°F (10°–27°C) and
ter temperatures at 66°F (19°C). Summer heat is moderated by coastal breezes.
mperatures range from 72° to 90°F (22°–32°C), with water temperatures at 80°F
17°C). Fall arrives in mid-October and is marked by clear days, with temperatures
eraging 68°F (20°C). Winter is brief and mild, with daytime highs in the 60s (teens
Celsius), lows in the 40s (single digits Celsius), and water temperatures averaging
50°F (10°C).

The Golden Islands are also the gateway to Okefenokee Swamp Park, one of the
most forbidding yet lovely places in America. Boating excursions into the swamp
allow close encounters with alligators. A 111-acre lake attracts water-skiers, anglers,
and boaters. Nearby Stephen C. Foster State Park offers cabins and campsites along
with signposted nature trails and canoe rentals.

SAPELO ISLAND ★

The fourth largest of Georgia's barrier islands, Sapelo Island is filled with the diverse
wildlife of the forested uplands as well as a salt marsh and a complex beach-and-
dunes system. The island is reached from the Sapelo ferry dock, 8 miles northeast of
Darien off Ga. 99. Educational tours of this undeveloped barrier island are conducted
year-round by the Georgia Department of Natural Resources.

Taking in everything from maritime forests to marshes, the **R. J. Reynolds State
Wildlife Refuge** encompasses 8,240 acres. Some 5,900 of these acres have been
designated as the **Sapelo Island National Estuarine Research Reserve.**

Guale Indians, Spanish missionaries, English freebooters, and French royalists
called this island home before Thomas Spalding purchased the south end of the
island in 1802. In the antebellum years, Spalding (1802–51) refined the Georgia Sea
Island cotton and sugar industries, and designed and constructed an octagonal tabby
sugar mill in 1809. (Tabby is a mixture of equal parts of oyster shell, sand, water, and
lime.)

In 1912, Howard E. Coffin purchased the island from Spalding's heirs. Coffin
undertook a complete rebuilding of **South End House,** Spalding's plantation mansion, which dated from 1810. By 1928, the house was ready to entertain President
and Mrs. Coolidge, and later President and Mrs. Hoover in 1932. In February 1929,
Charles A. Lindbergh landed on the island and visited the Coffins. The house was
purchased in 1934 by the tobacco heir Richard J. Reynolds. Twenty years later, Reynolds donated the dairy complex of the farm to the University of Georgia for use as a
marine research laboratory. Jimmy Carter used the mansion during his administration
in 1980.

Today the island has some 400 acres of private property, concentrated in a hamlet
known as Hog Hammock, whose residents are descended from slaves from Spalding's
plantation days. Interpretive programs include marsh and beach walks, bird and
wildlife observation, and special historical tours. Salt-marsh vegetation includes
needlerush, sea oxeye, salt grass, glasswort, and cordgrass. You'll see osprey feeding in
the Duplin River and hear the call of the clapper rail, a marsh bird. The island is
inhabited by such species as raccoons, feral cows, white-tailed deer, and a variety of

THE GOLDEN ISLES & THE OKEFENOKEE SWAMP

G eorgia's barrier islands extend along the Atlantic coast from Ossabaw Island near Savannah all the way down to Cumberland Island, near Florida. Although some have been developed, others, such as Cumberland and Little St. Simons, still linger in the 19th century. Some are accessible only by boat.

This 150-mile-long stretch of Georgia coast is semitropical and richly historic. The scenic Georgia portion of U.S. 17 goes past broad sandy beaches, creeks and rivers, and the ruins of antebellum plantations. The major highlights are the "Golden Isles"—principally Jekyll Island, Sea Island, and St. Simons Island. Cumberland Island, the newest National Seashore, is still under development.

Brunswick is the gateway to the Golden Isles. Sea Island and St. Simons are just across the F. J. Torras Causeway (which passes over the famous Marshes of Glynn, immortalized by local poet Sidney Lanier). Jekyll Island is south of town, across the Lanier Bridge, then south on Ga. 520.

The islands became world famous for their Sea Island cotton, grown on huge plantations supported mainly by slave labor. The last slaver, the *Wanderer*, (illegally) landed its cargo of Africans on Jekyll Island as late as 1858. The plantations languished and finally disappeared in the post–Civil War period.

In the late 1880s, the Golden Isles got into the resort business when a group of Yankee millionaires discovered Jekyll Island. They bought it for $125,000 and built "cottages" with 15 to 25 rooms and a clubhouse large enough to accommodate 100 members. In 1947, second-generation members of the Jekyll Island Club sold the exclusive Millionaires' Village to the state of Georgia for $675,000. Many of the cottages are open to visitors today, and all the attractions that drew the wealthy are now public property.

Sea Island was purchased back in 1927 by Howard Coffin, who built a causeway from St. Simons to reach the 5-mile-long barrier island. His world-famous resort, the Cloister, opened in October 1928.

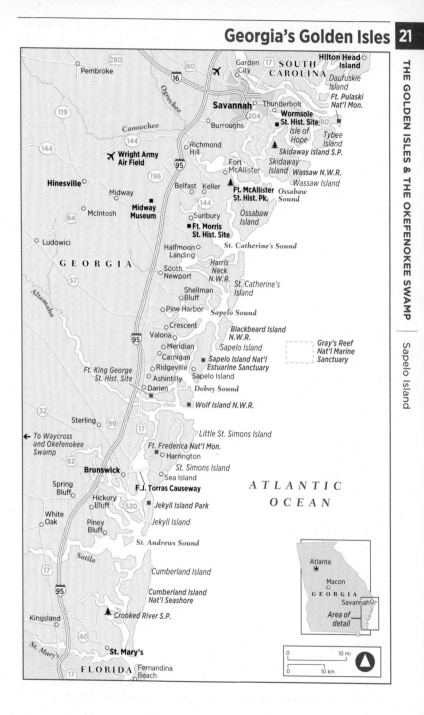

snakes, including the eastern diamondback rattler and the cottonmouth. Chachalacas, a Mexican species of bird introduced to the island as a game bird, might also be spotted.

A 30-minute ferryboat ride from the mainland aboard the **Sapelo Queen** takes visitors to the island. Guides accompany guests on the half-day bus tour, including a marsh walk. The ferry leaves Wednesday and Friday at 8:30am, returning at 12:30pm, and Saturday at 9am, returning at 1pm. An extended tour is conducted the last Tuesday of each month March to October 8:30am to 3pm. The tour costs $10 for adults and $6 for children 6 to 18, including the boat ride. Reservations are required. To make a reservation, contact the **Sapelo Visitors Center,** Landing Road, in Meridian, Georgia, just outside of Darien, Georgia (© **912/437-3224;** www.sapelonerr.org).

BRUNSWICK

75 miles S of Savannah; 15 miles S of Darien

The gateway to the Golden Isles is a sleepy town not quite awake to the tourism potential of its antique houses, palms, flowering shrubs, and moss-draped live oaks. Brunswick has always been an important port, with a natural harbor that can handle oceangoing ships. In World War II, with Nazi U-boats prowling the Atlantic, Brunswick's shipyard began to construct "Liberty Ships," stronger, larger cargo vessels. Beginning in 1943, these 447-foot vessels slipped down the ways at the feverish rate of some four a month. Today, instead of Liberty Ships, you'll find a large fleet of shrimp boats—the town bills itself as the "shrimp capital of the world."

At some point, you'll want to sample **Brunswick stew** in the town of its origin (although the citizens of Brunswick County, Virginia, would beg to differ). It is made basically with a combination of meats and flavored with an array of vegetables such as tomatoes, potatoes, okra, lima beans, and corn. In the old days, cooks would make it with squirrel, rabbit, or what virtually amounted to roadkill ("or anything else you could catch in the woods," as one local diner told us), all simmering in the same pot—but preparations are less exotic today. A good time to sample the versions is during the **Brunswick Stewbilee,** a Brunswick stew cook-off held here the second Saturday in October from 11:30am to 3pm.

Essentials

GETTING THERE From Savannah, head west, following the signs to I-95; you'll take the highway south until the Brunswick turnoff.

Six miles north of Brunswick, **Glynco Jetport** (© **912/264-9200;** www.glynco manningaviation.com) is served by **Delta ASA** (© **800/221-1212** or 912/267-1325; www.delta.com), an affiliate of Delta. It offers flights to the Brunswick area from Atlanta. At the small airport, car rental agencies are available, including **Avis** (© **912/638-2232;** www.avis.com) and **Hertz** (© **912/265-3645;** www.hertz.com).

VISITOR INFORMATION The **Brunswick–Golden Isles Visitors Bureau** operates a welcome center located at I-95 southbound, between exits 42 and 38 (© **912/264-0202;** www.bgivb.com), and two visitor centers: one on U.S. 17 at the F. J. Torras Causeway in Brunswick (© **912/264-5337**), and another in the Old Casino Building on St. Simons Island (© **912/638-9014**). The friendly staff of each can give you area information. If you come without hotel reservations, they can book a room for you at one of more than 20 nearby hotels and motels. Hours are daily 9am to 5pm.

Seeing the Sights

The welcome center will provide you with a free map indicating the main points of interest, which include the waterfront off Bay Street, with its bustling docks and fleet of shrimp boats. Oceangoing freighters are often seen here.

The **Lanier Oak,** along U.S. 17, off Lanier Boulevard, is said to be the tree where the Georgia poet Sidney Lanier was inspired to write "The Marshes of Glynn." Another tree, the 9-century-old **Lover's Oak,** at Albany and Prince streets, is also a source of pride for the town.

After dark, the big attractions are the dinner and casino cruises aboard the *Emerald Princess* (© **800/842-0115;** www.emeraldprincesscasino.com). Bookings can be made at the **Golden Isles Cruise Lines,** 1 St. Andrews Court in Brunswick (© **912/ 265-3558**). This 200-foot luxury cruiser offers dining, dancing, and live entertainment on one level, and a full casino with slot machines, poker, blackjack, craps, and roulette on another level. After departure, the ship sails out past the 3-mile limit, where the casino then opens for business. Cruises depart from Golden Isles Cruise Lines docks at the Brunswick Landing Marina (Newcastle and K sts.).

Reservations are not required, but you should make them anyway just to be on the safe side. The rate is $10 per person. Cruise hours are Monday to Thursday 7pm to midnight, Friday and Saturday 7pm to 1am, and Sunday 1 to 6pm. A special Saturday-morning departure leaves at 11am and returns at 4pm. All cruises offer a full meal at sea, with music, dancing, and games such as scavenger hunts. Call ahead for special summer deals.

Where to Stay

Brunswick Manor ★★ This is the most imposing, most impressive, and most elegant B&B in Brunswick. It was built in 1886 by an entrepreneur from Ohio who moved, carpetbagger style, to manage the local bank and establish a nearby cooperage. The house is an eclectic and rather masculine brick-sided Victorian, with many Eastlake features and the most elaborate Corinthian portico (a later addition) of any house in Brunswick. Inside, a collection of Empire and Federal furniture, a greenhouse-style hot tub, and a collection of miniature electric trains demonstrate the personal flair of the owners, Harry and Claudia Tzucanow. Guest rooms are tastefully outfitted, especially the nautically stylish Romance of the Seas room. The least expensive rooms are in the clapboard-sided Victorian house next door.

825 Egmont St., Brunswick, GA 31520. © **912/265-6889.** Fax 912/265-7879. www.brunswickmanor. com. 4 units. $100 double; $110 suite. Rates include full breakfast and afternoon tea. MC, V. **Amenities:** Breakfast room; Jacuzzi. *In room:* A/C, TV, fridge, hair dryer.

WatersHill Bed & Breakfast ★ Some of the most old-fashioned hospitality in Brunswick is found at this restored 1860s Victorian house. It's an exceedingly comfortable place, with guest rooms named after the mothers and grandmothers of the present owners. The B&B is among the most conveniently located in town, right in the center of the historic old section. Breakfast is one of the best in the area.

728 Union St., Brunswick, GA 31520. © **912/264-4262.** Fax 912/265-6326. www.watershill.com. 5 units. $85–$125 double. Rates include breakfast. AE, DISC, MC, V. **Amenities:** Breakfast room; lounge. *In room:* A/C, TV.

Where to Dine

Mack's Barbecue Place ★ 🔥 BARBECUE   Mack's occupies a 1960s building of no architectural charm and lies beside the grimy commercial edges of Highway 17, on the heavily trafficked outskirts of town. Despite its lack of visual appeal, the place serves the best barbecue in the Golden Isles. Notice the neatly arranged cords of oak firewood stacked in the parking lot. The domain is maintained with an iron grip by members of the Wilson family. The interior resembles that of an uninspired steakhouse beside a thruway, enhanced with a smoking chamber that gobbles firewood and looks like a hybrid between a blast furnace and a locomotive. The menu is limited to fabulous sandwiches and platters of barbecued pork, beef, chicken, turkey, ribs, and hamburgers, accompanied by salad, coleslaw, fried mushrooms, onion rings, and corn. And you've got to have Brunswick stew on the side. No alcohol is served.

2809 Glynn Ave. 🕐 **912/264-0605.** Sandwiches $3.50–$6.50; main courses $7–$11; country buffet $8. AE, DISC, MC, V. Mon–Sat 10:30am–9pm.

Spanky's SEAFOOD/AMERICAN   Set between the coastal highway and the sea, this place is like a sprawling, clapboard-sided seafood restaurant and saloon in New England. It's rather chaotic and always buzzing with locals. Avoid the place during peak dinner hours on Friday and Saturday, when you might not get a seat. The food is delicious: There is a wide selection of seafood, burgers, Mexican platters, and steaks, including an especially tasty chicken Reuben sandwich. Seafood platters are served with hush puppies, of course, and there's a superb version of Brunswick stew, which a chef obviously labors over.

1200 Glynn Ave. 🕐 **912/267-6100.** Burgers, salads, and sandwiches $6–$8.95; platters $16–$18. AE, DISC, MC, V. Sun–Thurs 11am–9:30pm; Fri–Sat 11am–10:30pm.

ST. SIMONS ISLAND ★★

80 miles S of Savannah; 10 miles E of Brunswick

The largest of the Golden Isles, St. Simons is also the most popular for its beaches, golf courses, scenery, and numerous tennis courts. Through tunnels of ancient oaks, you can bike and drive the length of St. Simons, finding treasures at every turn. It's very much a vacation haven for families.

Essentials

GETTING THERE   Take I-95 to Ga. 25 (the Island Pkwy.) or U.S. 17 to Brunswick, where signs direct visitors across the F. J. Torras Causeway to St. Simons Island.

VISITOR INFORMATION   The **St. Simons Island Visitors Center & Chamber of Commerce,** 530 Beachview Dr. W. (🕐 **912/638-9014;** http://comecoast awhile.com), offers maps and information, particularly on beaches. It's open daily 9am to 5pm.

Seeing the Island

The best way to introduce yourself to the island is via **St. Simons Trolley Island Tours** (🕐 **912/638-8954**), which acquaints you with 400 years of history and folklore, taking 1½ hours and costing $20 for adults and $10 for children 4 to 12; tours for children 3 and under are free. Tours depart March 15 to Labor Day daily at 11am and 1pm and daily at 11am during off season.

The island's chief attraction is **Fort Frederica National Monument** (✆ 912/638-3639; www.nps.gov/fofr), on the northwest end of the island (signposted). Go first to the National Park Service Visitor Center, where a film and displays explain the role of the fort. There isn't much left; about all you'll see of the original construction is a small portion of the king's magazine and the barracks tower, but archaeological excavations have unearthed many foundations. The fort was constructed in 1736 by Gen. James Oglethorpe. On the grounds is a gift shop, and walking tours can be arranged. Admission is $3 per person, free for children 15 and under. It's open from 9am to 5pm daily.

Christ Church, 6329 Frederica Rd., at the north end of the island, was built in 1820. It was virtually destroyed when Union troops camped here during the Civil War, burning the pews for firewood and butchering cattle in the chapel. In 1886, Anson Greene Phelps Dodge, Jr., restored the church as a memorial to his first wife, who had died on their honeymoon. The serene white building nestled under huge old oaks is open every day from 2 to 5pm during daylight saving time, 1 to 4pm at other times. There's no admission charge.

St. Simons Island Lighthouse Museum, 101 12th St. (✆ 912/638-4666; www.saintsimonslighthouse.org), is a restored lightkeeper's house from 1872. You can climb its 129 steps for a panoramic view of the Golden Isles. Inside are exhibits devoted not only to the lighthouse, but also to the Golden Isles in general. But you go more for the view than the nautical exhibits. Admission is $6 for adults, $3 for children 6 to 12, and free for children 5 and under. Hours are Monday to Saturday 10am to 5pm and Sunday 1:30 to 5pm.

Scattered from end to end on St. Simons are ruins of the plantation era: the **Hampton Plantation** (where Aaron Burr spent a month after his duel with Alexander Hamilton) and **Cannon's Point** on the north; **West Point, Pines Bluff,** and **Hamilton Plantations** on the west along the Frederica River; **Harrington Hall** and **Mulberry Grove** in the interior; **Lawrence, St. Clair, Black Banks,** the **Village,** and **Kelvyn Grove** on the east; and the **Retreat Plantation** on the south end. There's a restored chapel on West Point Plantation made of tabby, with mortar turned pink from an unusual lichen. Locals say it reflects blood on the hands of Dr. Thomas Hazzard, who killed a neighbor in a land dispute and built the chapel after being so ostracized that he would not attend Christ Church.

Beaches, Golf & Other Outdoor Pursuits

St. Simons not only attracts families looking for a beach, but it's also heaven for golfers, with 99 holes. One golfer we met who's played every hole said that each one presents a worthy challenge. Other sports are boating, inshore and offshore fishing, and water-skiing. Jet-skiing, charter fishing, scuba diving, and cruising can also be arranged at **Morning Star Marinas at Golden Isles,** 206 Marina Dr. (✆ 912/634-1128; http://morningstarmarinas.com), on the F. J. Torras Causeway.

Neptune Park, at the island's south end, has miniature golf, a playground, picnic tables under the oaks, and pier fishing. There's beach access from the park.

BEACHES You'll find two white-sand public beaches here, foremost of which is the **Massingale Park Beach,** Ocean Boulevard. It has a county-maintained beach with a picnic area and a bathhouse. It's open with a lifeguard on duty June 1 to Labor Day, daily from 11am to 4pm. Parking is free in designated areas, and drinking is allowed on the beach but only from plastic containers (no glass). Fishing is free from the beach but allowed only from 4 to 10pm.

Another public beach is the **Coast Guard Station Beach,** East Beach Causeway, also family oriented, with a bathhouse and showers. Lifeguards are on duty from June 1 to the Labor Day weekend, daily from 11am to 4pm. Parking is free in designated areas, and fishing is permitted during nonswimming hours from 4:30 to 10pm. Drinking is allowed on the beach from plastic containers only.

Further information about beaches can be obtained from the **Glynn County Recreation Department** (© 912/554-7780; www.glynncounty.org).

BIKE RENTALS **Ocean Motion,** 1300 Ocean Blvd. (© **800/669-5215** or 912/638-5225), suggests that you explore St. Simons by bike and will provide detailed instructions about the best routes. The island is relatively flat, so biking is easy. Beach cruisers are available for men, women, and kids, with infant seats and helmets. Bike rentals cost $12 for 4 hours and $16 for a full day.

FISHING Your best bet is **Golden Isles Charter Fishing,** 104 Marina Dr., Golden Isles Marina Village (© **912/638-7673;** www.goldenislesfishing.com), which offers deep-sea fishing and both offshore and inshore fishing. Capt. Mark Noble is your guide.

GOLF It's golf—not tennis—that makes St. Simons Island a star attraction. Foremost among the courses is the for-guest-use-only **Sea Island Golf Club ★★★**, 100 Retreat Ave. (© **912/638-5118;** www.seaisland.com), owned by the Cloister of Sea Island. At the end of the "Avenue of Oaks" at historic Retreat Plantation, the club consists of a number of courses: the Retreat Course (9 holes, 3,260 yd., par 36), the Plantation Course (18 holes, 6,549 yd., par 72), the Seaside Course (9 holes, 3,185 yd., par 36), and the Ocean Forest (18 holes, 7,011 yd., par 72).

The club opened in 1927 and offers dramatic ocean views, adding a measure of excitement to the game. Its greatest fans mention it with the same reverence as St. Andrews, Pebble Beach, or Ballybunion. Former president George H. W. Bush liked the courses so much that he once played 36 holes a day. Seaside and Retreat are the most requested 9s, with Seaside definitely the most famous of all—known for the 414-yard no. 7. *Golf Digest* has called this hole one of the best in golf and among the toughest in Georgia. A drive has to clear a marsh-lined stream and avoid a gaping fairway bunker.

Greens fees are $150 to $175, with the cart and the caddie fee included. Clubs rent for $65. The state-of-the-art Golf Learning Center on the grounds can help improve even an experienced golfer's game. Professional instruction is available for $95 to $110 per half-hour. Also on the grounds are a pro shop, clubhouse, and restaurant. The course is open daily from 7am to 7pm.

The **Retreat Golf Club,** 100 Kings Way (© **912/638-3611;** www.seaisland.com), is an 18-hole, par-72 course of 6,200 yards—also for hotel guests only. Known for its Low Country architecture, it hosts several popular tournaments every year. The demanding course, designed by Joe Lee, features narrow fairways lined by lagoons and towering pines. Greens fees for Cloister guests are $200 to $250; cottage guests at Sea Island pay the same. Professional instruction is available for $100 to $300 per hour through arrangements made at the clubhouse and pro shop. There's also a restaurant on the premises. Play is available daily 7am to 7pm.

Sea Palms Golf & Tennis Resort, 5445 Frederica Rd. (© **800/841-6268** or 912/638-3351; www.seapalms.com), offers outstanding golf on its Tall Pines/Great Oaks (18 holes, 6,500 yd., par 72), Great Oaks/Sea Palms West (18 holes, 6,200 yd., par 72), and Sea Palms West/Tall Pines (9 holes, 2,500 yd., par 72) courses. Some holes nestle alongside scenic marshes and meandering tidal creeks. Reserved tee times are recommended, and cart use is required. The courses are open daily 7am to 7pm, charging greens fees of $69 and $59 after 1pm, with cart rental included. Professional instruction costs $50 for a 30-minute session, $80 for an hour.

NATURE TOURS The **Ocean Motion Surf Co.,** 1300 Ocean Blvd. (© 912/638-5225), offers nature tours by kayak of the island's marsh creeks and secluded beaches. Featured are a 2-hour dolphin nature tour for $45 and a 4-hour wildlife tour, by request only, for $85.

SAILBOAT RENTALS **Barry's Beach Service, Inc.,** at the King and Prince Beach Hotel, 420 Arnold Rd. (© 912/638-8053), arranges hourly, half-day, or full-day sailboat rentals, along with sailing lessons (by experienced instructors) and sailboat rides. Kayak rentals, tours, and instruction are also available.

TENNIS There are two public tennis courts on the island. The **Mallory Park Courts,** Mallory Street, has two lighted courts open year-round, and admission is free. **Epworth Park,** on Lady Huntington Drive, has two courts open 24 hours but they are not equipped with lights; it, too, is free.

Where to Stay

In addition to the accommodations listed below, private cottages are available for weekly or monthly rental on St. Simons. You can get an illustrated brochure with rates and availability information from **Parker-Kaufman Realtors,** 22 Beachway Dr., Jekyll Island, GA 31527 (© 888/453-5955; www.parker-kaufman.com). The office is open Monday to Friday 9am to 5pm and on Saturday 9am to 1pm. Vacation rental cottages can range from one to four bedrooms. Rentals begin at $625 per week in summer, lowered to as little as $490 per week off season.

Best Western Island Inn This unassuming, brick-sided motel was built in the late 1980s, about 2½ miles from the nearest beach. The efficiencies have a kitchenette, and the guest rooms are no-nonsense, unfrilly, and economical. All rooms have well-kept bathrooms. About a dozen of them can be connected with adjoining rooms to allow families to create their own live-in arrangements.

301 Main St., St. Simons Island, GA 31522. © **800/673-6323** or 912/638-7805. Fax 912/634-4720. www. bestwesternstsimons.com. 61 units. $85–$119 double; $129–$139 suite. Children 17 and under stay free in parent's room. Rates include continental breakfast. AE, DC, DISC, MC, V. **Amenities:** Breakfast room; lounge; Jacuzzi; outdoor pool. *In room:* A/C, TV, hair dryer, Wi-Fi (free).

King and Prince Beach Resort ★ This is a midsize oceanfront resort founded in 1932 by partners who were evicted from the Jekyll Island Club. Today's reincarnation of five Spanish-style buildings is a venue for frequent corporate conventions. The resort has grown and expanded over the years, and in time has attracted many famous guests. But Hugh Hefner and his Playboy bunnies haven't been seen romping around since the 1950s. The original 70 guest rooms are still here but have been restored. Even better are the newer and larger rooms with expanded bathrooms, some offering private patios or balconies. Darker woods evoke a decidedly English influence, but other brighter appointments suggest a West Indian plantation style. The condo apartments have kitchenettes.

201 Arnold Rd., St. Simons Island, GA 31522. © **800/342-0212** or 912/638-3631. Fax 912/638-7699. www.kingandprince.com. 188 units. $174–$309 double; $351–$919 villa. AE, DC, MC, V. **Amenities:** Restaurant; bar; babysitting; exercise room; 5 pools (1 indoor); room service; 2 tennis courts. *In room:* A/C, TV, hair dryer, kitchenette (in some), Wi-Fi (free).

The Lodge at Sea Island Golf Club ★★   Golfers who have stayed at some of the greatest resorts in California and the Carolinas justifiably rave about this resort. A great golfing experience and first-rate accommodations combine to form this smoothly operating lodge. It doesn't pretend to have the grandeur of its sibling, the Cloister on Sea Island (see later in this chapter), but for a luxurious, casual retreat, it's hard to beat, attracting not only golfers, but also small corporate groups. Attached to one of America's premier golf clubs, the lodge has been created in the spirit of one of those private clubs in Newport or the Hamptons. Set on beautiful grounds, it overlooks Rees Jones's Plantation Golf Course, often from a private balcony with views of the fairways and ocean. An English manor-house decor prevails throughout. Whether in the hotel or in the cottages, the guest rooms are spacious and beautifully furnished, with deluxe bathrooms.

100 Retreat Ave., St. Simons Island, GA 31522. ✆ **800/SEA-ISLAND** (732-4752) or 912/634-4300. Fax 912/634-3909. www.seaisland.com. $300–$750 double; $1,600 suite; call for cottage pricing. AE, DC, DISC, MC, V. **Amenities:** 4 restaurants; 2 bars; babysitting; 3 18-hole golf courses; exercise room; Jacuzzi; room service; sauna; spa. *In room:* A/C, TV, hair dryer, Wi-Fi (free).

Saint Simons Inn ★ 📖   Standing in the shadow of the old lighthouse, this condo hotel is for the connoisseur of offbeat lodgings. Don't be put off by the word *condo*. The inn operates like a regular hotel, except that each condo is individually owned by a person who renovates and decorates it to his or her own tastes. That means that each condo is unique, the most elegant being the penthouse, of course. When the owners aren't in residence, the units are rented to the general public. In a setting of palmettos and live oaks, the inn has an outdoor pool. This is an ideal place for a romantic weekend. All the condos are equipped with microwaves and refrigerators.

609 Beachview Dr., St. Simons Island, GA 31522. ✆ **912/638-1101.** Fax 912/638-0943. www.stsimons inn.com. 35 units. $149–$179 double; $289 penthouse. Rates include continental breakfast. AE, DISC, MC, V. **Amenities:** Outdoor pool. *In room:* A/C, TV, kitchenette, Wi-Fi (free).

Sea Gate Inn   Its charms and advantages are often underestimated because of its low-rise format, unpretentious entrance, and location near other, much larger hotels. Despite that, this is a well-maintained, respectable hotel whose condo units are divided into two buildings separated from one another by a quiet road that runs parallel to the sea. The more desirable (and expensive) of the two is the Ocean House, a 1985 annex built on stilts. The less-expensive, and less-desirable, guest rooms are clustered around a swimming pool, roadside-motel style. All units, each a suite, offer modest kitchenettes. Otherwise, Sea Gate lacks general amenities. The hotel, incidentally, was named after an old-fashioned ferryboat that used to ply the waters between Brunswick and St. Simons Island.

1012 Beachview Dr., St. Simons Island, GA 31522. ✆ **800/562-8812** or 912/638-8661. www.seagateinn. com. 48 units. $199–$490 suite. DISC, MC, V. *In room:* A/C, TV, kitchen.

Sea Palms Golf & Tennis Resort ★★   This place imitates the older and more upscale resorts nearby. Sprawled over 800 landscaped acres, it combines aspects of a retirement community with a family-friendly resort. Most people stay 3 to 5 days. After registering in a woodsy bungalow near the entrance, you'll be waved off toward your room, to which you carry your own bags. If you're looking for maximum isolation, this place might be appropriate; otherwise, you might feel it's too anonymous. Each suite contains a kitchenette. There's a golf course on the premises and views over some beautiful marshland from many of the simply furnished units. The nearest good beach is about 4 miles away.

5445 Frederica Rd., St. Simons Island, GA 31522. ℂ **800/841-6268** or 912/638-3351. Fax 912/634-8029. www.seapalms.com. 154 units. $149–$169 double; $219–$338 1- or 2-bedroom suite. Children 17 and under stay free in parent's room. Golf, tennis, and honeymoon packages available. AE, DC, MC, V. **Amenities:** Restaurant; bar; babysitting; 27-hole golf course; exercise room; 2 outdoor pools; 3 tennis courts (lit). *In room:* A/C, TV, hair dryer, kitchenette (in suite), Wi-Fi (free).

Where to Dine
EXPENSIVE

Colt & Alison ★★ INTERNATIONAL   At the Sea Island Golf Club, this restaurant was built on the ruins of a cow barn of a plantation great house that burned down. The elegant restaurant, with its high-back leather chairs and cozy banquettes, opens onto panoramic views of the Plantation Course's 18th hole. In chilly weather, you can relax by a wood-burning fireplace. Tableside preparations are a feature of the staff, who create everything from steak *au poivre* to bananas foster in front of you. Chefs specialize in the best dry-aged beef on the island, along with fresh seafood. Start with the colossal shrimp cocktail or goat cheese fritters with marinated green tomatoes and smoked pecan dressing. For a main course, you can opt for various beef dishes, the herb-crusted rack of lamb, or the Southern-fried Maine lobster tails with a Jack Daniel's honey glaze. You can also dine nearby at the Oak Room (see below).

In the Lodge at Sea Island Golf Club, 100 Retreat Ave. ℂ **800/732-4752,** ext. 4353. Reservations required. Main courses $34–$52. AE, DC, MC, V. Wed–Mon 6–9:30pm. Closed Tues.

Oak Room ★ INTERNATIONAL   The sibling of Colt & Alison (see above) invites you into its oak-lined publike atmosphere with hand-painted murals, an outdoor terrace, wood-burning fireplace, and leather ceilings, opening onto views of the Plantation Golf Course. The so-called tavern menu is one of the best in East Georgia. Don't expect pub grub. Instead you're treated to such appetizers as blue crab and jalapeño hush puppies with a Cajun rémoulade or else seared foie gras with toasted corn bread and dandelion jelly. One salad is composed of buttermilk fried oysters. For your main, sample the braised pork shanks with a Parmesan polenta or the braised free-range chicken with Yukon gold potato dumplings in a chervil sauce.

In the Lodge at Sea Island Golf Club, 100 Retreat Ave. ℂ **800/732-4752,** ext. 4353. Reservations recommended. Main courses $21–$35. AE, DC, MC, V. Daily 11:30am–2:30pm and 6–10pm.

MODERATE

Delaney's Bistro AMERICAN   Local chef Tom Delaney's loyal following includes both islanders and visitors. He aims to appeal to a wide culinary taste and, in general, succeeds. In his low-rise building, Delaney offers an array of food ranging from fresh seafood to certified Black Angus beef. The menu at lunch is light, including the usual pastas, sandwiches, and salads, as well as grilled shrimp salad and sautéed crab cakes. Tom is more ambitious at night. You might begin with a pâté of foie gras or baked goat cheese before selecting a main course such as a mixed grill (beef, veal, and lamb chop in a cabernet sauce) or veal Hannah (scaloppine topped with wild mushrooms and crab). Desserts are made fresh daily.

3415 Frederica Rd. ℂ **912/638-1330.** www.delaneysbistro.com. Reservations recommended. Main courses $9–$12 lunch, $17–$29 dinner. AE, DC, DISC, MC, V. Tues–Sat 11am–2pm and 6–10pm.

Gnat's Landing AMERICAN   This is a laid-back Key West–style place in the heart of Redfern Village. It's a family favorite in large part because of the on-site pizzeria and a kiddie menu that includes fried shrimp and chicken fingers. The joint's irreverent tone is set by its slogan: "If you like home cookin', stay home." The array of freshly made salads is among the best on the island, including a tarragon chicken salad made with chunks of chicken breast, grapes, and pecans. The real specialty of the house, worth a trip over here, is Mrs. Slappy's Seafood Gumbo. Devotees have fallen in love with this savory treat, and Gnat's Landing now ships it across the nation. Their St. Simons Stew (actually, a Brunswick stew) isn't bad, either. A wide selection of sandwiches is sold, but seafood dominates the menu. We go for the savory deviled crab.

310 Redfern Village. ✆ **912/638-7378.** www.gnatslanding.com. Reservations not needed. Main courses $3.95-$24. AE, DISC, MC, V. Mon-Sat 11:30am-2:30pm and 5:30-10pm.

INEXPENSIVE
Bennie's Red Barn ✦ STEAKS/SEAFOOD   Established in 1954, the place has a Southern folksiness, almost a hillbilly kind of charm. Menu items include an uncomplicated medley of food to please everyone's Southern grandmother, including fried or broiled fish, chicken, and shrimp. Steaks are sizable slabs, wood-fire-grilled and appropriately seasoned. Dinners include house salad, potato, rolls, and tea or coffee. If you're a biscuit-and-gravy kind of diner, you've arrived.

5514 Frederica Rd. ✆ **912/638-2844.** www.benniesredbarn.com. Reservations recommended Fri-Sat. Main courses $12-$32. AE, DISC, MC, V. Daily 6-10pm.

The Crab Trap ☺ SEAFOOD   For the family in pursuit of coleslaw, hush puppies, and fried shrimp, the Crab Trap is the island's most popular seafood restaurant and a good buy. Forget fancy trappings—the place is downright plain. Fresh seafood is offered daily, and you can order it fried, broiled, blackened, or grilled. Appetizers include oysters on the half shell and crab soup. Boiled crab is the chef's specialty, and the seafood platter is big enough for three. For those who aren't turned on by crabs and shrimp, steaks in various cuts are also available. Heaps of battered fries come with most dishes. That hole in the middle of your table is for depositing shrimp shells and corncobs. Dress as if you're going on a summer fishing trip.

1209 Ocean Blvd. ✆ **912/638-3552.** Main courses $8.95-$27. AE, MC, V. Sun-Thurs 5-10pm; Fri-Sat 5-10:30pm. Closed Thanksgiving and Christmas.

LITTLE ST. SIMONS ISLAND ★
20-min. boat ride from St. Simons Island

The ideal place to savor the wild beauty of Georgia's coast is still untouched by commercial development. Reached only by boat, Little St. Simons Island—6 miles long and 2 to 3 miles wide—remains one of the last privately owned islands off the Georgia coast. The current owners have welcomed family and friends since the early 1900s, but in 1978 it was opened to the general public, with only a few accommodations.

The island is a haven for naturalists and for those seeking a secluded getaway. (But be warned that mosquitoes are a serious problem in summer.) Activities on Little St. Simons include shelling, swimming, and sunbathing along 7 miles of secluded beaches; and hiking (watch out for snakes) and horseback riding through acres of ancient forest. There are also canoeing and fishing in the island's many rivers and creeks, plus bird-watching of at least 200 species. Guests can learn about the local ecosystems by joining naturalists on explorations.

Essentials

GETTING THERE   Take I-95 to Ga. 25 (the Island Pkwy.) or U.S. 17 to Brunswick, where signs direct visitors across the F. J. Torras Causeway to St. Simons Island. Once on the island, follow the signs to the Hampton River Club Marina. At the marina, on the north end of St. Simons, a ferryboat departs daily at 10:30am and again at 4:30pm, taking visitors to Little St. Simons. It's privately owned, so unless you're a guest, you are not even allowed to ride the ferry.

VISITOR INFORMATION   All information is supplied directly by the lodge (see below).

Where to Stay & Dine

The Lodge on Little St. Simons Island ★ 🏕   The all-inclusive lodge is for those seeking a Robinson Crusoe type of vacation. It's surprisingly exclusive, but unlike luxury resorts such as Fripp Island, it doesn't have plush upholstery and dramatic architecture. If you like life summer-camp style, this eco-friendly hotel is for you. Simple guest rooms, cooled by ceiling fans, are in the 1917 Hunting Lodge in the main house (which contains the dining room); the 1930s Michael Cottage (a two-bedroom cottage at the forest's edge); and the 1980s Cedar Lodge and River Lodge, each a cottage with four private guest rooms sharing a sitting room with a fireplace and screened porch.

You pour your own drinks at a makeshift bar in the corner of a communal living room with hunting trophies from another era. Hearty, homey meals are served family style in the main dining room, and the staff will be happy to prepare a picnic lunch for you. The menu features locally caught seafood and such Southern staples as fried chicken and barbecue. An array of activities await you here, including biking, boating, fishing, hiking, horseback riding, and bird-watching. Guests have free use of the lodge's recreational equipment.

PO Box 21078, Little St. Simons Island, GA 31522. Ⓒ **888/733-5774** or 912/638-7472. Fax 912/634-1811. www.littlestsimonsisland.com. 15 units. $600–$675 double; $675–$2,500 2-, 3-, and 4-bedroom cottage. Rent the entire lodge (up to 30 persons) $8,000–$8,500. Rates include all meals and beverages. Additional person $150–$250 extra. AE, DISC, MC, V. **Amenities:** Restaurant; bar; bikes; outdoor pool. *In room:* A/C, ceiling fan, no phone, Wi-Fi (free).

SEA ISLAND ★★

11 miles E of Brunswick

Since 1928, Sea Island has been the domain of the Cloister hotel (see below). Today, in addition to the hotel, it's home to some of the most elegant villas and mansions in the Southeast. Most of Sea Island's homes are second homes to CEOs and other rich folk. Some can be rented if you can afford it; prices range from $720 to $1,770 a day. Call **Sea Island Cottage Rentals** (Ⓒ **800/SEA-ISLAND** [732-4752]; www.sea islandcottages.com).

The island was acquired by Ohio-based Howard Earle Coffin, an automobile executive, in 1925. Still owned by Coffin's descendants, the Cloister combines 10,000 acres of forest, lawn, and marshland, plus 5 miles of beachfront. Many day visitors who can't afford the high prices of the Cloister come over for a scenic drive along Sea Island Drive, called "Millionaire's Row"—there's no tollgate.

Essentials

GETTING THERE   From Brunswick, take the F. J. Torras Causeway to St. Simons Island and follow Sea Island Road to Sea Island.

VISITOR INFORMATION   There is no welcome center. Information is provided by the Cloister, but the staff prefers to cater to registered guests.

Where to Stay & Dine

The Cloister ★★★   Georgia's poshest hotel retreat, set amid the most elaborate landscaping on the coast, is a vast compound between the Atlantic Ocean and the Black Banks River. It takes in about 50 carefully maintained buildings, some of them massive and others on neighboring St. Simons Island. Everyone from honeymooners to golfers checks in here. The hotel offers gorgeous suites and deluxe guest rooms, all with 24-hour butler service. Other perks include 500-thread-count Italian sheets, Bulgari toiletries, Turkish stone bathrooms with deep-soaking tubs, and Wi-Fi.

Sea Island, GA 31561. © **800/SEA-ISLAND** (732-4752) or 912/638-3611. Fax 912/638-5159. www.sea island.com. $525–$750 double; $1,350–$2,000 suite; $5,000 ultimate suite. Golf, tennis, and honey-moon packages available. AE, DC, DISC, MC, V. **Amenities:** 4 restaurants; 2 bars; babysitting; 3 18-hole golf courses; exercise club; room service; spa; 8 tennis courts (4 lit). *In room:* A/C, TV, hair dryer, minibar, Wi-Fi (free).

JEKYLL ISLAND ★★★

9 miles S of Brunswick

Once a winter playground for the Rockefellers, Pulitzers, Goulds, Morgans, and Cranes, Jekyll Island is the smallest of the state's coastal islands, with 5,600 acres of highlands and 10,000 acres of marshlands. Today it's no longer the exclusive enclave it once was, and is open to all those attracted by its miles of beautiful white-sand Atlantic beaches and holes of championship golf. It also has far better tennis complexes than St. Simons Island. Families come here for a wealth of outdoor activities.

Essentials

GETTING THERE   From Brunswick, take U.S. 17 South to the turnoff for Jekyll Island. Head east across the Jekyll Island Causeway, paying a daily parking rate of $3 per vehicle to enter the island.

VISITOR INFORMATION   The **Jekyll Island Visitors Center,** 901 Jekyll Island Causeway (© **877/4-JEKYLL** [453-5955] or 912/635-3636; www.jekyll island.com), is open daily from 9am to 5pm, dispensing maps, brochures, and other helpful information. You can also get information from the **Brunswick–Golden Isles Visitors Bureau** (http://comecoastawhile.com).

Seeing the Sights

The best way to see the **Historic District** ★★—the former enclave of the million-aires of America's Gilded Age, who built what they called "cottages" here—is to take a guided historical tour departing daily on the hour from 10am to 3pm from the **Museum Orientation Center** (© **912/635-4036**) on Stable Road. The tour lasts 1½ hours, costing $16 for adults, $7 for children 6 to 12, and free for children 5 and under. Highlights of the tour include **Indian Mound** (or Rockefeller) **Cottage** from 1892 and the **du Bignon Cottage** from 1884.

On your own, you can view the Goodyear Cottage in the district, housing the Jekyll Island Arts Association (✆ 912/635-3920; www.jekyllcitizens.org)—with a gift shop and a free monthly exhibition. Admission is free, and it's open daily noon to 4pm. Also in the district, **Mistletoe Cottage** (✆ 912/635-4036) showcases the work of the nationally renowned, late Jekyll Island sculptor, Rosario Fiore, and is open Saturday and Sunday 2 to 4pm.

Last, Jekyll Island is also home to **Horton's Brewery Site,** Georgia's first brewery, signposted on the northwest end of the island. It was started by General Oglethorpe, who evidently knew how to put first things first for his settlers. This two-story ruin, dating from 1742, is one of the oldest standing structures in the state. It was mainly constructed of tabby, a building material made of crushed oyster shells that is native to coastal Georgia. Very near the brewery stand the ruins of a home built in 1738 by William Horton, one of Oglethorpe's captains.

Summer Waves, 210 S. Riverview Dr. (✆ 912/635-2074; www.summerwaves. com), offers 11 acres of watersports with more than a million gallons of water. It features rides and attractions ranging from a totally enclosed speed flume that jets riders over three breathtaking humps, to a ride over the rolling waves in the Frantic Atlantic wave pool. You can also hang on around the twisting turns of the Hurricane Tornado and Force 3 slides. For toddlers, there's the Pee Wee Puddle—fun in only a foot of water. Admission is $20 for those 48 inches or taller, and $16 for children under that height. Children 3 and under enter free. Open the weekend before Memorial Day to December 31, Sunday to Thursday 10am to 6pm and Friday and Saturday from 10am to 8pm.

Outdoor Pursuits

If you have a car, take the South Jekyll Loop to survey the scene before concentrating on specifics. Drive south on North Beachview Drive to view some of the island's 10 miles of public beaches with public bathhouses and picnic areas. Your loop around the island's southern end will include the **South Dunes Picnic Area.** Continue around onto South Riverview Drive, passing **Summer Waves** and the **Jekyll Harbor Marina,** until you return to Fortson Parkway.

BEACHES There are three public beaches on the island, all open daily round-the-clock and free to the public. Those choosing to swim off Jekyll Island do so at their own risk, as there are no lifeguards on duty. The **St. Andrew Picnic Area,** reached beyond Summer Waves, the water park along South Riverview Drive, is one of the best beaches at the southeastern tip of the island. It has an adjacent picnic area, but no bathhouse or showers available. **South Dunes Beach,** with a picnic area and showers, is north of St. Andrew and is reached along South Beach Drive. Farther along, **Central Dunes** has showers but no picnic area. Saltwater fishing is allowed on the public beaches, and no license is required.

BIKING Because of its flatness, Jekyll Island is relatively easy to explore by bike. Rentals are available from **Barry's Beach Service** (✆ 912/638-8053), 420 Arnold Rd. Bikes (including lock and helmet) rent for $12 for 4 hours, $16 for a full day, and $49 for 1 week.

FISHING Freshwater fishing is allowed with a Georgia license, which costs $3.50 and is available at most hardware or sporting-goods stores. No license is required for saltwater fishing.

GOLF   Three championship 18-hole courses await golfers on Jekyll Island, plus one historic 9-hole course. The **Great Dunes Golf Course,** Beach View Drive (© **912/635-2170**), is a small 9-hole course patterned after the course at St. Andrews, Scotland. It offers some holes that were part of the original course laid out in 1898 when only millionaires played golf here. The course was remodeled as an authentic links course in the 1920s by Walter J. Travis. A 3,023-yard, par-36 course, it's open daily from 7am to 6pm. There are a small pro shop and clubhouse on the grounds. Greens fees are $61. No professional instruction is available.

Jekyll Island Golf Courses, 322 Captain Wylly Dr. (© 912/635-2368; www. golfjekyllisland.com), consists of three separate courses: **Oleander** (18 holes, 6,241 yd., par 72), **Pine Lake** (18 holes, 6,760 yd., par 72), and **Indian Mound** (18 holes, 6,282 yd., par 72). Dick Wilson's Oleander is consistently ranked among the state's best courses, and the *Atlanta Constitution* called its 12th hole "the most demanding par 4 of any daily fee course in the state." Pine Lakes was designed by Clyde Johnson and is the longest and tightest layout on Jekyll Island. Tree-lined fairways dogleg both left and right as they wind through the island's interior. Indian Mound was designed by Joe Lee with wide fairways and large, sloping greens. All courses prefer that you reserve tee times, and charge $61 greens fee. Clubs are available for $7 to $21. Play is daily from 7am to 6pm for all three courses. A clubhouse, restaurant, and pro shop are on the grounds. Professional instruction is available for $60 to $250 per hour.

TENNIS   Jekyll Island Tennis Center ★★, 400 Captain Wylly Dr. (© **912/635-3154**), was ranked by *Tennis* magazine as one of the nation's top municipal tennis complexes. Its 13 clay courts, seven of them lighted for night play, are favored because of low-impact conditions and cooler court temperatures. The center is open daily 9am to 6pm. Ball machines can be rented for $24 per hour, and the court fee is $10 per hour. Professional instruction is available for $40 to $50 per hour. There's a pro shop on the grounds, plus a restaurant and showers.

Where to Stay

Jekyll Island cottage rentals are available through **Parker-Kaufman Realtors,** 22 Beachview Dr. (PO Box 13126), Jekyll Island, GA 31527 (© **888/453-5955** or 912/635-2512; www.parker-kaufman.com). The realtor offers 105 individual properties ranging from a small one-bedroom apartment to a six-bedroom home. Rental prices start at $730 per week in winter, rising to $4,700 per week in the busy summer months. Reservations for summer rentals are accepted as early as December 1. The office is open Monday to Saturday 9am to 5pm.

Motel rooms are available at **Ocean Side Inn and Suites,** 711 Beachview Dr. (© **866/5JEKYLL** [553-5955] or 912/635-2211; www.oceansideinnandsuites.com).

Jekyll Island Campground, North Beachview Drive (© **866/658-3021** or 912/635-3021; www.jekyllisland.com), is managed by the Jekyll Island Authority and is the only island campground in the Golden Isles. On its 18 wooded acres are 220 sites, nestled among live oaks and pines. The facilities include bathhouses, showers, laundry facilities, camping equipment, pure tap water, a grocery store, garbage pickup, LP gas, and bike rentals. Tent sites cost $21 to $48. Stay 6 nights and get your seventh night free.

Jekyll Island Club Hotel ★★★   This is the undisputed star of Jekyll Island accommodations, steeped in the history of the Gilded Age. A rambling, turreted 1880s monument, it was conceived as a private club for millionaires. In 1987, long after its decline during World War II, the property was restored to its deliberately understated turn-of-the-20th-century grandeur. The guest rooms are high-ceilinged and outfitted in the garnet, sapphire, and emerald tones of the building's original construction. Some are awkwardly shaped, but all are very comfortable and nostalgic. Don't expect easy access to the beach.

371 Riverview Dr., Jekyll Island, GA 31527. © **800/535-9547** or 912/635-2600. Fax 912/635-2818. www. jekyllclub.com. 157 units. $259–$449 suite. Meal plans are available. Discounts around 25% Labor Day to early May. Children 17 and under stay free in parent's room. AE, DC, DISC, MC, V. **Amenities:** 3 restaurants; 2 bars; babysitting; 3 18-hole golf courses; 1 9-hole golf course; outdoor pool; room service. *In room:* A/C, TV, hair dryer, minibar, MP3 docking station, Wi-Fi (free).

Jekyll Oceanfront Resort & Spa ★ ☺   This is the largest oceanfront hotel on Jekyll Island, set on about 15 flat, sandy acres whose focal point is a rectangular swimming pool. It sits near the island's northern tip and is designed in a vaguely Iberian motif of white walls and terra-cotta roofs rising amid pine trees. An expanse of lawn and a breakwater composed of a ribbon of massive boulders separate the compound from the sea. Guests walk over a raised boardwalk to reach the sands. The guest rooms are furnished in a rather bland style. The management rather grandly refers to its units as "villas"; they're more like duplex-style town houses, each of which abuts similar units to the left and right. On the hotel premises is a bar and restaurant, the **Italian Fisherman.**

975 N. Beachview Dr., Jekyll Island, GA 31527. © **800/736-1046** or 912/635-2531. Fax 912/635-2332. www.jekyllinn.com. 260 units, 75 1- and 2-bedroom town houses. $139–$199 double; $259–$319 1- or 2-bedroom town house. AE, DC, DISC, MC, V. **Amenities:** Restaurant; 2 bars; babysitting; children's playground; exercise center; outdoor pool; room service; Wi-Fi (in lobby; free). *In room:* A/C, TV, hair dryer.

Villas by the Sea ★   This is the most northerly and, after the Jekyll Island Club Hotel, one of the most upscale accommodations on Jekyll Island. Not a conventional hotel, it's a compound of condominium-style apartments scattered among 10 two-story buildings in a 17-acre forest. The 2,000 feet of ocean frontage is longer than that of any other hotel on the island. You'll have to cross a raised boardwalk bridging a lawn and a rocky breakwater to reach it. The villas are privately owned, which means they are individually furnished, and they are spacious one-, two-, or three-bedroom vacation condos. The condos contain kitchens, a separate living and dining area, plus private patios or balconies. Minisuites without full kitchens are also available for rent. On-site is the **Surf Steakhouse,** plus the **Riptides Lounge,** offering live entertainment.

1175 N. Beachview Dr., Jekyll Island, GA 31527. © **866/920-1263** or 912/635-2521. Fax 912/635-2569. www.jekyllislandga.com. 176 units. $169–$199 1-bedroom condo; $249–$269 2-bedroom condo; $329 3-bedroom condo; call for minisuite pricing. Discounts offered for stays of 1 week or more. AE, DC, DISC, MC, V. **Amenities:** Restaurant; bar; outdoor pool. *In room:* A/C, TV, hair dryer, kitchen (in condo), Wi-Fi (free).

Where to Dine

Blackbeard's ☺ SEAFOOD/AMERICAN   This restaurant occupies a large, modern building set on a sandy and barren stretch of beach down the island's eastern coast. Its menu items include shrimp, oysters, deviled crabs, scallops, and such fish filets as flounder. Steak, grilled chicken, and burgers are staples around here, and your sandwich choice might be oysters on a hoagie roll, turkey, or "crabby crabmeat."

The food is standard fare but rather tasty and sold at a fair price. The kitchen also offers a children's menu.

200 N. Beachview Dr. ☎ **912/635-3522.** Main courses $18–$25. AE, DISC, MC, V. Mon–Thurs 11am–4pm and 5–9pm; Fri–Sun noon–3:30pm and 5–10pm. Closed Christmas.

The Grand Dining Room ★★ INTERNATIONAL Graciously formal and steeped in nostalgia, this place reigns as one of the Golden Isles' most elegant. Its design incorporates a double row of columns, soaring windows, and furniture evocative of an English country house. Our preferred spot for a drink is on the cluster of sofas adjacent to a pianist, who performs highly digestible music throughout the dinner hour. Menu items include fresh catch of the day, prepared in any of five different ways; chicken Atlantis (sautéed with crabmeat, shrimp, and cream sauce); scaloppine of veal with sun-dried tomatoes and artichoke hearts; and grilled lamb chops. The cuisine is first-rate, using the finest ingredients of any restaurant on the island.

In the Jekyll Island Club Hotel, 371 Riverview Dr. ☎ **912/635-2600.** Reservations recommended. Jacket preferred for men. Main courses $24–$35. AE, DC, DISC, MC, V. Mon–Sat 7am–2pm and 6–9pm; Sun 10:45am–2pm (brunch) and 6–9pm; Victorian tea daily 4–5:30pm.

Latitude 31 ★ SEAFOOD/INTERNATIONAL The leading seafood restaurant on Jekyll Island occupies a clapboard-sided house built on stilts above the tidal flats, adjacent to the wharves servicing the Jekyll Island Club Hotel. J. P. Morgan used the site as a mooring for his yacht *The Corsair*. At the time, the building was a warehouse for storing supplies and ice. Today it's evocative of a 19th-century seafront building in Scandinavia, with a pale and airy interior, and a simple decor that the Shakers would have appreciated. The bar, whose view extends over the mud flats, is appealing. Menu items include bacon-wrapped tenderloin of beef, catch of the day (served grilled, baked, broiled, sautéed, or blackened), seafood crepes, and several preparations of fresh-off-the-boat shrimp.

Jekyll Wharf. ☎ **912/635-3800.** Main courses $18–$35. DC, DISC, MC, V. Tues–Sun 5:30–10pm.

McCormick's Grill AMERICAN Golfers can lunch here daily in a bright, airy room overlooking the Jekyll Island Golf Courses greens. Trimmed in oak, the large room with an adjoining bar recalls Florida in its decor. You won't find grand cuisine here, just salads, soups, and sandwiches. From the grill comes a half-pound burger prepared as you like it, and you can also order a grilled chicken-breast sandwich or a super sub served on a hoagie, including ham, turkey, salami, cheese, and other ingredients.

Golf Clubhouse, Captain Wylly Rd. ☎ **912/635-4103.** Main courses $4.95–$8.95. AE, DISC, MC, V. Daily 7:30am–3:30pm.

Zachry's Seafood Restaurant ★ 👜 SEAFOOD This local favorite sits in the midst of a collection of launderettes, convenience stores, and gift shops, in a shopping center across the street from the convention center. Part of its success derives from the Zachry's ownership of their own shrimp boat (the *Miss Angie*), which guarantees an almost-constant supply of fresh seafood. Menu items include stuffed jalapeño peppers served with marinara sauce, deep-fried or boiled shrimp, trout, deviled crab, stuffed broiled flounder, and combination platters. This is real good, finger-lickin' coastal Georgia home cookery, with loads of authentic flavor.

44 Beachview Dr. ☎ **912/635-3128.** Platters $18; main courses $4.50–$19. DISC, MC, V. Easter to late Aug Sun–Thurs 11am–9pm, Fri–Sat 11am–10pm; late Aug to Easter daily 11am–8pm. Closed 2 weeks at Christmas.

CUMBERLAND ISLAND ★

7 miles NE of St. Marys

Nowhere else on the East Coast are peace and unspoiled natural surroundings so perfectly preserved as at Cumberland Island. Since 1972, most of this island has been a National Seashore administered by the National Park Service.

Cumberland Island reached the peak of its prestige in the Gilded Age when Carnegie steel barons used the island as a retreat. Their uninhabited mansion, Plum Orchard, is still standing, although badly deteriorating. Not only the Carnegies wielded power here, but also the Rockefellers and even the Candlers of Atlanta (founders of Coca-Cola). The island was the top-secret site of the 1996 wedding of John Kennedy, Jr., and Carolyn Bessette. After the publicity generated in the aftermath of that wedding, Cumberland became famous around the world.

To visit Cumberland Island, just 16 miles long and 3 miles across at its widest point, is to step into a wilderness of maritime forest, salt marshes alive with waving grasses, sand dunes arranged by wind and tide into a double line of defense against erosion, and wide, gleaming sand beaches. It is to enter a world teeming with animal life, where alligators wallow in marshes, white-tailed deer bound through the trees, wild pigs snuffle in the undergrowth, armadillos and wild turkeys roam freely about, more than 300 species of birds wheel overhead, and wild horses canter in herds.

Essentials

GETTING THERE   The only public transportation to the island is via the ferry from St. Marys on the mainland. (Get to St. Marys on Ga. 40 from I-95 or U.S. 17.) You must reserve passage on the ferry; contact the National Park Service, **Cumberland Island National Seashore,** PO Box 806, St. Marys, GA 31558 (✆ **912/882-4335;** www.nps.gov/cuis). There are two trips daily from March 1 to September 30 every day except Tuesday and Wednesday in winter. In summer, book as far in advance as possible. The fare is $17 for adults, $15 for seniors, and $12 for children 12 and under plus a $4 park fee.

If you plan to stay overnight, the best way to reach Cumberland is by the Greyfield Inn ferry, the *Lucy R. Ferguson,* which maintains a regular schedule to Fernandina Beach, Florida. Reservations are necessary and must be made through the Greyfield Inn (see "Where to Stay & Dine," below). We strongly urge that you bring your bicycle, since there's no public transportation on the island. You can, however, safely leave your car in the Fernandina Beach parking lot across from the police station.

There's an airstrip for small planes near the Greyfield Inn, and air-taxi arrangements can be made from Jacksonville or St. Simons Island (call the inn for details).

VISITOR INFORMATION   Information is available from the Greyfield Inn (see "Where to Stay & Dine," below).

Exploring the Island

Don't look for a swimming pool, tennis courts, or a golf course—Cumberland's attractions are a different sort, straight out of *The Prince of Tides.* The inn is just a short walk from those high sand dunes and a wild, undeveloped beach. Beachcombing, swimming, shelling, fishing, and exploring the island are high on the list of activities.

No signs are left of the Native Americans who lived here beginning some 4,000 years ago, nor of the Franciscan missionaries who came to convert them during the 1500s. No ruins exist of the forts built at each end of the island by Gen. James

If you are a day-tripper who would prefer not to dine at Greyfield Inn (see below), you can assemble the makings of a picnic at the **Riverside Café** in St. Marys (© **912/882-3466**). It lies directly across from the ferry terminal where boats depart for Cumberland, and you can't miss it.

Oglethorpe in the 1700s, and the only thing that remains of his hunting lodge is its name, Dungeness. What you will find as you poke around this island are the ruins of Andrew Carnegie's own massive mansion, **Dungeness** (which burned in 1959); the **Greene-Miller cemetery,** which still holds inhabitants from Revolutionary War times through the Civil War era; and the **Stafford plantation house.** Down the lane a bit are **"the Chimneys,"** a melancholy post–Civil War ruin (ask at the inn for the full story), and **Plum Orchard,** another Carnegie mansion, fully furnished but unoccupied and now the property of the U.S. Park Service.

Where to Stay & Dine

Greyfield Inn ★★ 🏚 Cumberland's one hotel is no less enchanting than the island itself. The only commercial building (if you can call it that) in the area is this three-story plantation mansion with a wide, inviting veranda set in a grove of live oaks. Built shortly after the turn of the 20th century as a summer retreat by Thomas Carnegie (Andrew's brother and partner), Greyfield has remained family property ever since. Guests today are treated very much as family visitors were in years past: The extensive and very valuable library is open; the furnishings are those the family has always used; the bar is an open one, operated on an honor system; and you dine at the long family table, adorned with heirloom silver candlesticks. You're at liberty to browse through old family photo albums, scrapbooks, and other memorabilia scattered about the large, paneled living room (if the weather is cool, a fire is lighted in fireplaces in the living room and dining room). If beachcombing or exploring is what you have in mind for the day, the inn will pack a picnic lunch for you. The guest rooms vary in size, but all are nonsmoking; some bathrooms are shared and still hold the original, old-fashioned massive fittings. Reservations must be made well in advance. Bring your cellphone if you need to stay in touch—the hotel has only a radio-telephone for emergencies.

Cumberland Island, GA. Mailing address: PO Box 900, Fernandina Beach, FL 32035. © **866/401-8581** or 904/261-6408. Fax 904/321-0666. www.greyfieldinn.com. 16 units, 10 with bathroom. $395–$595 double. Rates include all meals. 50% deposit required. AE, DISC, MC, V. No children 5 and under. **Amenities:** Dining room; bar. *In room:* A/C, hair dryer, no phone.

THE OKEFENOKEE SWAMP ★★

8 miles S of Waycross

This swamp is one of the largest preserved freshwater wetlands in the United States. Naturalists have hailed the wetlands as "the most beautiful and fantastic landscape in the world." It's unique on earth—it was once part of the ocean floor—and encompasses some 650 square miles, measuring 40 miles in length and 20 miles in width. The Creek Indians called it "land of the trembling earth" because of its many floating islands.

Okefenokee is one of the most ecologically intact swamps in North America. It takes in everything from tupelo stands to vast open prairies. A few acres fall within the northeastern corner of Florida. Runoff is discharged into the Suwanee and St. Marys rivers.

The swamp was inhabited as early as 2000 B.C. Many Native Americans, displaced from their homelands, settled here in the 1700s and 1800s. Beginning in 1909, the Hebard Lumber Company harvested some half a billion cubic yards of timber—most of it cypress—from the land before they went out of business in 1927. Virgin tracts of cypress still remain, however, and some trees are 6 centuries old. Conservation-minded advocates persuaded Franklin Roosevelt to designate the swamp a refuge area in 1937. Further protection came in 1974 when Congress added Okefenokee to the National Wilderness Preservation System. This system occupies some 90% of the swamp, home to such wildlife as alligators, deer, and bobcats. The swamp's bay trees bloom from May to October, with a distinctive white flower.

Exploring the Swamp

Before heading in, you can visit the **Okefenokee Heritage Center,** 2 miles west of Waycross (birthplace of actor Burt Reynolds) on U.S. 82 (© **912/285-4260;** www.okefenokeeheritagecenter.org). Here you can see a restored 1912 steam locomotive and depot, an "operating" 1890 print shop, and the restored 1840 Gen. Thomas Hilliard House, plus exhibits on local history. The center is open Tuesday to Saturday 10am to 4:30pm. Admission is $3, free for children 4 and under.

At the same site, the **Southern Forest World** (© **912/285-4056**) is a museum depicting the development and history of the South's forest industry. The collection includes a logging train, tools and other artifacts, and forestry-related relics, as well as a variety of audiovisuals. Hours are the same as those of the Heritage Center. Admission is $2 for adults ages 5 to 54, $1.50 for seniors 55 and over, and free for children 4 and under.

Okefenokee Swamp Park   The park—at the swamp's northern perimeter, on Cowhouse Island—can occupy a day of your time. It offers boat tours (included with admission), canoe rentals, interpretive programs, an outdoor museum, marked trails, and even a serpentarium with reptile shows. Take a cypress boardwalk into the swamp to a 90-foot-high observation tower. You'll see lots of the swamp's most famous residents, a collection of cruising Georgia alligators. There are no overnight facilities, but food and beverages are sold.

Waycross, GA 31501. © **912/283-0583.** www.okeswamp.com. Admission $12 adults, $11 seniors 62 and over and children 3–11, free for children 2 and under. Daily 9am–5:30pm. Take I-95 to exit 296 at Brunswick and then U.S. 82 west toward Waycross; at the intersection with Ga. 177, go left for 11 miles to the park entrance.

Stephen C. Foster State Park ★   On the western edge of Okefenokee, 18 miles from Fargo, this is an 80-acre island park with a sprawling forest of black gum and cypress. As a refuge, it forms one of the thickest terrains of vegetation in the Southeast. In the mirrorlike black waters live some 55 species of reptiles, 37 species of fish, more than 40 species of mammals, and some 225 species of birds. The park has a half-mile nature trail and some 25 miles of day-use waterways. Canoes and motorboats can be rented, or you can take boat tours lasting 1 to 1½ hours. Minnie's Lake and Big Water can also be visited. Picnicking and camping are permitted. Two-bedroom cabins are also available for rent: $70 a night Sunday to Thursday, going up to

$90 on Friday and Saturday. Campsites with running water and electricity, including showers, go for only $18 to $22 a night. (For reservations, contact the superintendent at the address and phone number below.) Park gates close between sunset and sunrise to discourage wildlife poachers. Groceries can be obtained at stores in Fargo.

Georgia Department of Natural Resources, Rte. 1, Fargo, GA 31631. © **800/864-7275** or 912/637-5274. www.gastateparks.org. Admission $3 per person. Mar to Labor Day daily 6:30am–8:30pm; off season daily 7am–7pm. Take I-95 to exit 6 at Brunswick and then U.S. 82 west to Waycross; there, head west on U.S. 84 to Homerville, and turn left onto U.S. 441 South to Fargo; at the intersection with Ga. 177, go left and follow the signs to the park.

Suwanee Canal Recreation Area ★   Run by the U.S. Fish and Wildlife Service, this recreation area offers some of America's finest birding and freshwater fishing. The area provides entry to the prairies of Mizell, Chase, Grand, and Chesser, the last the site of a century-old farmstead. Small lakes and "gator holes" are sprinkled throughout the area. The visitor information center provides an orientation film and offers exhibits of the swamp's flora and fauna. Take a boardwalk over the water to a 40-foot observation tower. Several interpretive walking trails and picnic sites are available. The 12-mile-long canal results from a failed attempt in the 1880s to drain the swamp. The U.S. Fish and Wildlife Service provides overnight and 2- to 5-day canoe trips, but reservations are essential. Canoe rentals begin at $25 for day trips, $16 for the second day. The Canal Recreation Concession rents everything from canoes to boats, from sleeping bags and Coleman stoves to portable toilets. It also rents bicycles for $10 per day.

U.S. Fish and Wildlife Service, Okefenokee National Wildlife Refuge, Rte. 2, Box 3330, Folkston, GA 31537. © **912/496-7156.** Admission $5 per car. 1:15pm tours $16 adults, $10 children 5–11, free for children 4 and under. Mar–Sept 10 daily 6am–7:30pm; off season daily 7am–5:30pm. Take I-95 to exit 2 and go west along Ga. 40 to Folkston; there, turn onto Ga. 23/121 south for 7 miles, then turn right onto Spur Ga. 121 and follow the signs for 4 miles to the recreation area.

FAST FACTS: THE CAROLINAS & GEORGIA

NORTH CAROLINA

Many fast facts presented here for North Carolina also pertain to South Carolina and Georgia. A more limited selection of South Carolina–specific fast facts and Georgia-specific fast facts follows.

Area Codes   North Carolina has various area codes: **828** for Asheville and Banner Elk; **919** for Chapel Hill, Durham, and Raleigh; **704** for Charlotte; **252** for the Outer Banks; **910** for Wilmington; and **336** for Winston-Salem.

ATMs   These are found in every city and town of the tri-state area, especially at banks, but at many other outlets as well, including convenience stores.

Automobile Organizations   Motor clubs will supply maps, suggested routes, guidebooks, accident and bail-bond insurance, and emergency road service. The **American Automobile Association (AAA)** is the major auto club in the United States. If you belong to a motor club in your home country, inquire about AAA reciprocity before you leave. You may be able to join AAA even if you're not a member of a reciprocal club; to inquire, call AAA (✆ **800/222-4357;** www.aaany.com). AAA is actually an organization of regional motor clubs, so look under "AAA Automobile Club" in the White Pages of the telephone directory. AAA's nationwide emergency road service telephone number is ✆ 800/AAA-HELP (222-4357).

Business Hours   **Banks:** Monday to Friday 9am to 3pm (some are also open Sat 9am–noon). Most banks and other outlets offer 24-hour access to automated teller machines (ATMs). **Stores:** Monday to Saturday 10am to 6pm, and some also on Sunday from noon to 5pm. **Malls** usually stay open until 9pm Monday to Saturday, and department stores are usually open until 9pm at least 1 day a week.

Car Rentals   To rent a car in the Carolinas and Georgia, you need a major credit or charge card and a valid driver's license. Sometimes a passport or an international driver's license is also required if your driver's license is in a language other than English. You often need to be at least 25 years of age, although some companies rent to younger people (they may add a daily surcharge).

Drinking Laws   The legal age for purchase and consumption of alcoholic beverages is 21; proof of age is required and often requested at bars, nightclubs, and restaurants, so it's always a good idea to carry ID when you go out. Although local laws can vary, in general, no alcohol is served at bars, restaurants, or nightclubs between 4am and 12:30pm on Sunday. In addition, alcoholic beverages are not sold on Sunday in liquor stores, convenience stores, or grocery stores. Do not carry open containers of alcohol in your car or any public area that isn't zoned for alcohol consumption. The police can fine you on the spot. And nothing will ruin your trip faster than getting a citation for DUI (driving under the influence), so don't even think about driving while intoxicated.

Driving Rules   Speed limits are posted on tri-state highways. In addition, the law requires the driver and front-seat passenger to wear seat belts while the car is in motion. Children 4 and under must be buckled into safety seats in the back seat; those 5 to 12 must sit in the back seat if the front seat is equipped with air bags.

Electricity   Like Canada, the United States uses 110–120 volts AC (60 cycles), compared to 220–240 volts AC (50 cycles) in most of Europe, Australia, and New Zealand. Downward converters that change 220–240 volts to 110–120 volts are difficult to find in the United States, so bring one with you.

Embassies & Consulates   All embassies are in the nation's capital, Washington, D.C. Some consulates are located in major U.S. cities, and most nations have a mission to the United Nations in New York City. If your country isn't listed below, call for directory information in Washington, D.C. (✆ **202/555-1212**) or check **www.embassy.org/embassies**.

The embassy of **Australia** is at 1601 Massachusetts Ave. NW, Washington, DC 20036 (✆ **202/797-3000;** www.austemb.org). There are consulates in New York, Honolulu, Houston, Los Angeles, and San Francisco.

The embassy of **Canada** is at 501 Pennsylvania Ave. NW, Washington, DC 20001 (✆ **202/682-1740;** www.canadianembassy.org). Other Canadian consulates are in Buffalo (New York), Detroit, Los Angeles, New York, and Seattle.

The embassy of **Ireland** is at 2234 Massachusetts Ave. NW, Washington, DC 20008 (✆ **202/462-3939;** www.irelandemb.org). Irish consulates are in Boston, Chicago, New York, San Francisco, and other cities. See the website for a complete listing.

The embassy of **New Zealand** is at 37 Observatory Circle NW, Washington, DC 20008 (✆ **202/328-4800;** www.nzembassy.com). New Zealand consulates are in Los Angeles, Salt Lake City, San Francisco, and Seattle.

The embassy of the **United Kingdom** is at 3100 Massachusetts Ave. NW, Washington, DC 20008 (✆ **202/588-6500**). Other British consulates are in Atlanta, Boston, Chicago, Cleveland, Houston, Los Angeles, New York, San Francisco, and Seattle.

Emergencies   Dial ✆ **911** to report a fire, call the police, or get an ambulance. This is a nationwide toll-free call (no coins are required at a public telephone).

If theft or an accident has left you stranded, check the local telephone directory for a nearby office of the **Traveler's Aid Society** (www.travelersaid.org), a nationwide, not-for-profit social service organization that is geared to helping travelers in distress. If you're in trouble, seek it out.

In Georgia, the **Council for International Visitors,** 34 Peachtree St., Ste. 1200, Atlanta, GA 30303 (✆ **404/832-5560**), can provide a wide variety of help to international visitors in more than 42 languages. Offices are also located in North Carolina (322 Hawthorne Lane, Charlotte, NC 28204; © **704/342-2248**) and South Carolina (1 Poston Rd., Ste. 103, Charleston, SC 29407).

Gasoline   At press time, in the U.S., the cost of gasoline (also known as gas, but never petrol), is abnormally high. Taxes are already included in the printed price. One U.S. gallon equals 3.8 liters or .85 imperial gallons. Fill-up locations are known as gas or service stations.

Holidays   Banks, government offices, post offices, and many stores, restaurants, and museums are closed on the following legal national holidays: January 1 (New Year's Day), the third Monday in January (Martin Luther King, Jr., Day), the third Monday in February (Presidents' Day), the last Monday in May (Memorial Day), July 4 (Independence Day), the first Monday in September (Labor Day), the second Monday in October (Columbus Day), November 11 (Veterans Day/Armistice Day), the fourth Thursday in November (Thanksgiving Day), and December 25 (Christmas Day). The Tuesday after the first Monday in November is Election Day, a federal government holiday in presidential-election years (held every 4 years, and next in 2012).

For more information on holidays see "Calendar of Events" for each state in chapter 3.

Hospitals & Medical Centers   No matter where you go, you will rarely be far from a hospital, medical center, or emergency clinic. The major hospital facilities in the Carolinas and Georgia include the following: **Children's Healthcare of Atlanta,** 1600 Tullie Circle NE, Atlanta, GA (www.choa.org); **Duke University Medical Center,** Erwin Road, Durham, NC (www.mc.duke.edu); **Mission Hospitals,** 509 Biltmore Ave., Asheville, NC (www.missionhospitals.org); **Medical University of South Carolina,** 171 Ashley Ave., Charleston, SC (www.musc.edu); **Pitt County Memorial Hospital,** 2100 Stantonsburg Rd., Greenville, NC (www.uhseast.com); **St. Joseph's Hospital of Atlanta,** 5665 Peachtree Dunwoody Rd. NE, Atlanta, GA (www.stjosephsatlanta.org); **University of North Carolina Hospitals,** 101 Manning Dr., Chapel Hill, NC (www.unchealthcare.org); and **Wake Forest University Baptist Medical Center,** Medical Center Boulevard, Winston-Salem, NC (www.wfubmc.edu).

Insurance   Although it's not required of travelers, **health insurance** is highly recommended. Most health insurance policies cover you if you get sick away from home—but check your coverage before you leave.

International visitors to the U.S. should note that unlike many European countries, the United States does not usually offer free or low-cost medical care to its citizens or visitors. Doctors and hospitals are expensive, and in most cases will require advance payment or proof of coverage before they render their services. Good policies will cover the costs of an accident, repatriation, or death. Packages such as **Europ Assistance's Worldwide Healthcare Plan** are sold by European automobile clubs and travel agencies at attractive rates. **Worldwide Assistance Services, Inc.** (© **800/777-8710;** www.worldwideassistance.com) is the agent for Europ Assistance in the United States.

If you're ever hospitalized more than 150 miles from home, **MedjetAssist** (© **800/527-7478;** www.medjetassistance.com) will pick you up and fly you to the hospital of your choice in a medically equipped and staffed aircraft 24 hours day, 7 days a week. Annual memberships are $225 per individual and $350 per family; you can also purchase short-term memberships.

Canadians should check with their provincial health plan offices or call **Health Canada** (✆ **866/225-0709** or 613/957-2991; www.hc-sc.gc.ca) to find out the extent of their coverage and what documentation and receipts they must take home in case they are treated in the United States.

Travelers from the U.K. should carry their European Health Insurance Card (EHIC), which replaced the E111 form as proof of entitlement to free/reduced cost medical treatment abroad (✆ **0845 605 2030;** www.ehic.org.uk). Note that the EHIC only covers "necessary medical treatment." For repatriation costs, lost money, baggage, or cancellation, seek travel insurance from a reputable company, such as **Travel Insurance Web** (✆ **0870 890 3641;** www.travelinsuranceweb.com).

The cost of travel insurance varies widely, depending on the destination, the cost and length of your trip, your age and health, and the type of trip you're taking, but expect to pay between 5% and 8% of the vacation itself. You can get estimates from various providers through **InsureMyTrip.com.**

U.K. citizens and their families who make more than one trip abroad per year may find an annual travel insurance policy works out cheaper. Check **www.moneysupermarket. com**, which compares prices across a wide range of providers for single- and multitrip policies.

Most big travel agents offer their own insurance and will probably try to sell you their package when you book a holiday. Think before you sign. **Britain's Consumers' Association** recommends that you insist on seeing the policy and reading the fine print before buying travel insurance. The **Association of British Insurers** (✆ **020/7600-3333;** www. abi.org.uk) gives advice by phone and publishes *Holiday Insurance,* a free guide to policy provisions and prices. You might also shop around for better deals: Try **Columbus Direct** (✆ **0870/033-9988;** www.columbusdirect.net).

Trip-cancellation insurance will help retrieve your money if you have to back out of a trip or depart early, or if your travel supplier goes bankrupt. Trip cancellation traditionally covers such events as sickness, natural disasters, and State Department advisories. The latest news in trip-cancellation insurance is the availability of **expanded hurricane coverage** and the **"any-reason"** cancellation coverage—which costs more but covers cancellations made for any reason. You won't get back 100% of your prepaid trip cost, but you'll be refunded a substantial portion. **TravelSafe** (✆ **888/885-7233;** www.travelsafe.com) offers both types of coverage. Expedia also offers any-reason cancellation coverage for its air-hotel packages. For details, contact one of the following recommended insurers: **Access America** (✆ **866/807-3982;** www.accessamerica.com); **Travel Guard International** (✆ **800/826-4919;** www.travelguard.com); **Travel Insured International** (✆ **800/243-3174;** www.travelinsured.com); and **Travelex Insurance Services** (✆ **888/457-4602;** www. travelex-insurance.com).

On flights within the U.S., checked baggage is covered up to $2,500 per ticketed passenger. On flights outside the U.S. (and on U.S. portions of international trips), baggage coverage is limited to approximately $9.07 per pound, up to approximately $635 per checked bag. If you plan to check items more valuable than what's covered by the standard liability, see if your homeowner's policy covers your valuables. If it doesn't, get baggage insurance as part of your comprehensive travel-insurance package.

Internet Access Most hotels in the tri-state area provide Internet access. Cybercafes are found in large cities such as Atlanta or Charlotte. Rural areas are not as well connected, of course. To find a cybercafe in your destination, try www.cybercafe.com.

Legal Aid   If you are "pulled over" for a minor infraction (such as speeding), never attempt to pay the fine directly to a police officer; this could be construed as attempted bribery, a much more serious crime. Pay fines by mail, or directly into the hands of the clerk of the court. If accused of a more serious offense, say and do nothing before consulting a lawyer. Here the burden is on the state to prove a person's guilt, and everyone has the right to remain silent, whether he or she is suspected of a crime or actually arrested. Once arrested, a person can make one telephone call to a party of his or her choice. International visitors should call their embassy or consulate.

Lost & Found   Be sure to tell all of your credit card companies immediately if you discover your wallet has been lost or stolen and file a report at the nearest police precinct. Your credit card company or insurer may require a police report number or record of the loss. Most credit card companies have an emergency toll-free number to call if your card is lost or stolen; they may be able to wire you a cash advance immediately or deliver an emergency credit card in a day or two. Visa's U.S. emergency numbers are ℂ **800/847-2911** and 410/581-9994. American Express cardholders and traveler's check holders should call ℂ **800/221-7282.** MasterCard holders should call ℂ **800/307-7309** or 636/722-7111. For other credit cards, call the toll-free number directory at ℂ **800/555-1212.**

If you need emergency cash over the weekend when all banks and American Express offices are closed, you can have money wired to you via **Western Union** (ℂ **800/325-6000;** www.westernunion.com).

Mail   At press time, domestic postage rates were 28¢ for a postcard and 44¢ for a letter. For international mail, a first-class letter of up to 1 ounce costs 98¢ (75¢ to Canada and 79¢ Mexico); a first-class postcard costs the same as a letter. For more information go to **www.usps.com** and click on "Calculate Postage."

If you aren't sure what your address will be in the United States, mail can be sent to you, in your name, c/o General Delivery at the main post office of the city or region where you expect to be. (Call ℂ **800/275-8777** for information on the nearest post office.) The addressee must pick up mail in person and must produce proof of identity (such as a driver's license or passport). Most post offices will hold your mail for up to 1 month, and are open Monday to Friday from 8am to 6pm, and Saturday from 9am to 3pm.

Medical Conditions   If you have a medical condition that requires **syringe-administered medications,** carry a valid signed prescription from your physician; syringes in carry-on baggage will be inspected. Insulin in any form should have the proper pharmaceutical documentation. If you have a disease that requires treatment with **narcotics,** you should also carry documented proof with you—smuggling narcotics aboard a plane carries severe penalties in the U.S.

For **HIV-positive international visitors,** requirements for entering the United States are somewhat vague and change frequently. For up-to-the-minute information, contact **AIDSinfo** (ℂ **800/448-0440** or 301/315-2816 outside the U.S.; www.aidsinfo.nih.gov) or the **Gay Men's Health Crisis** (ℂ **212/367-1000;** www.gmhc.org).

Newspapers & Magazines   National newspapers include the *New York Times, USA Today,* and the *Wall Street Journal.* National newsweeklies include *Newsweek, Time,* and *U.S. News & World Report.* In large cities, most newsstands offer a small selection of the most popular foreign periodicals and newspapers.

North Carolina: Newspapers & Magazines

North Carolina's major dailies are the *News & Observer* (Raleigh) and the *Charlotte Observer* (Charlotte). There are also local papers in Asheville, Durham, Fayetteville, Greensboro, and Winston-Salem. The *North Carolina Folklore Journal* is available by subscription. (Contact the North Carolina Folklore Society, Department of English, Appalachian State University, Boone, NC 28608, for publication schedule and subscription rates.)

Passports   The websites listed below provide downloadable passport applications as well as the current fees for processing applications. For an up-to-date, country-by-country listing of passport requirements around the world, go to the "International Travel" tab of the U.S. State Department at **http://travel.state.gov**. International visitors to the U.S. can obtain a visa application from the same website. *Note:* Children are required to present a passport when entering the United States at airports. More information on obtaining a passport for a minor can be found at http://travel.state.gov. Allow plenty of time before your trip to apply for a passport; processing normally takes 4 to 6 weeks (3 weeks for expedited service) but can take longer during busy periods (especially spring). And keep in mind that if you need a passport in a hurry, you'll pay a higher processing fee.

For Residents of Australia   You can pick up an application from your local post office or any branch of Passports Australia, but you must schedule an interview at the passport office to present your application materials. Call the **Australian Passport Information Service** at © **131-232,** or visit the government website at www.passports.gov.au.

For Residents of Canada   Passport applications are available at travel agencies throughout Canada or from the central **Passport Office,** Department of Foreign Affairs and International Trade, Ottawa, ON K1A 0G3 (© **800/567-6868;** www.ppt.gc.ca). *Note:* Canadian children who travel must have their own passport. However, if you hold a valid Canadian passport issued before December 11, 2001, that bears the name of your child, the passport remains valid for you and your child until it expires.

For Residents of Ireland   You can apply for a 10-year passport at the **Passport Office,** Setanta Centre, Molesworth Street, Dublin 2 (© **01/478-0822;** www.irlgov.ie/iveagh). Those 17 and under and 66 and over must apply for a 3-year passport. You can also apply at 1A South Mall, Cork (© **21/494-4700**), or at most main post offices.

For Residents of New Zealand   You can pick up a passport application at any New Zealand Passports Office or download it from their website. Contact the **Passports Office** at © **0800/225-050** in New Zealand or 04/474-8100, or log on to www.passports.govt.nz.

For Residents of the United Kingdom   To pick up an application for a standard 10-year passport (5-year passport for children 15 and under), visit your nearest passport office, major post office, or travel agency or contact the **United Kingdom Passport Service** at © **0845/603-7788** or search its website at www.ukpa.gov.uk.

Police   Call © **911.**

Taxes   The United States has no value-added tax (VAT) or other indirect tax at the national level. Every state, county, and city may levy its own local tax on all purchases, including hotel and restaurant checks and airline tickets. These taxes do not appear on price tags.

Telegraph, Telex & Fax   **Telegraph and telex services** are provided primarily by **Western Union** (© **800/325-6000;** www.westernunion.com). You can telegraph (wire) money, or have it telegraphed to you, very quickly over the Western Union system, but this service can cost as much as 15% to 20% of the amount sent.

Most hotels have **fax machines** available for guest use (be sure to ask about the charge to use it). Many hotel rooms are wired for guests' fax machines. A less expensive way to send and receive faxes may be at stores such as the **UPS Store.**

Telephones   Many convenience groceries and packaging services sell **prepaid calling cards** in denominations up to $50; for international visitors these can be the least expensive way to call home. Many public pay phones at airports now accept American Express, MasterCard, and Visa credit cards. **Local calls** made from pay phones in most locales cost either 25¢ or 35¢ (no pennies, please). Most long-distance and international calls can be dialed directly from any phone. **For calls within the United States and to Canada,** dial 1 followed by the area code and the seven-digit number. **For other international calls,** dial 011 followed by the country code, city code, and the number you are calling.

Calls to area codes **800, 888, 877,** and **866** are toll-free. However, calls to area codes **700** and **900** (chat lines, bulletin boards, "dating" services, and so on) can be very expensive—usually a charge of 95¢ to $3 or more per minute, and they sometimes have minimum charges that can run as high as $15 or more.

For **reversed-charge or collect calls,** and for person-to-person calls, dial the number 0 then the area code and number; an operator will come on the line, and you should specify whether you are calling collect, person-to-person, or both. If your operator-assisted call is international, ask for the overseas operator.

For **local directory assistance** ("information"), dial 📞 411; for long-distance information, dial 1, then the appropriate area code and 555-1212.

Time   The continental United States is divided into **four time zones:** Eastern Standard Time (EST), Central Standard Time (CST), Mountain Standard Time (MST), and Pacific Standard Time (PST). Alaska and Hawaii have their own zones. For example, when it's 9am in Los Angeles (PST), it's 7am in Honolulu (Hawaii Standard Time, or HST), 10am in Denver (MST), 11am in Chicago (CST), noon in New York City (EST), 5pm in London (Greenwich Mean Time, or GMT), and 2am the next day in Sydney.

Daylight saving time is in effect from 1am on the second Sunday in March to 1am on the first Sunday in November, except in Arizona, Hawaii, the U.S. Virgin Islands, and Puerto Rico. Daylight saving time moves the clock 1 hour ahead of standard time.

Tipping   Tips are a very important part of certain workers' income, and gratuities are the standard way of showing appreciation for services provided. (Tipping is certainly not compulsory if the service is poor!) In hotels, tip **bellhops** at least $1 per bag ($2–$3 if you have a lot of luggage) and tip the **chamber staff** $1 to $2 per day (more if you've left a disaster area for him or her to clean up). Tip the **doorman** or **concierge** only if he or she has provided you with some specific service (for example, calling a cab for you or obtaining difficult-to-get theater tickets). Tip the **valet-parking attendant** $1 every time you get your car.

In restaurants, bars, and nightclubs, tip **service staff** 15% to 20% of the check, tip **bartenders** 10% to 15%, tip **checkroom attendants** $1 per garment, and tip **valet-parking attendants** $1 per vehicle.

As for other service personnel, tip **cabdrivers** 15% of the fare; tip **skycaps** at airports at least $1 per bag ($2–$3 if you have a lot of luggage); and tip **hairdressers** and **barbers** 15% to 20%.

Toilets   You won't find public toilets or "restrooms" on the streets in most U.S. cities but they can be found in hotel lobbies, bars, restaurants, museums, department stores, railway and bus stations, and service stations. Large hotels and fast-food restaurants are often the best bet for clean facilities. Restaurants and bars in resorts or heavily visited areas may reserve their restrooms for patrons.

Useful Phone Numbers   U.S. Department of State Travel Advisory ℂ **202/647-5225** (manned 24 hr.)

U.S. Passport Agency ℂ **202/647-0518**

U.S. Centers for Disease Control and Prevention International Traveler's Hot Line ℂ **888/232-6348.**

Visas   For information about U.S. visas go to **http://travel.state.gov** and click on "Visas." Or go to one of the websites listed below:

Australian citizens can obtain up-to-date visa information from the **U.S. Embassy Canberra,** Moonah Place, Yarralumla, ACT 2600 (ℂ **02/6214-5600**), or by checking the U.S. Diplomatic Mission's website at **http://Canberra.usembassy.gov/consular**.

British subjects can obtain up-to-date visa information by calling the **U.S. Embassy Visa Information Line** (ℂ **20/7499-9000**) or by visiting the "Visas to the U.S." section of the American Embassy London's website at **www.usembassy.org.uk**.

Irish citizens can obtain up-to-date visa information through the **Embassy of the USA Dublin,** 42 Elgin Rd., Dublin 4, Ireland (ℂ **353/1-668-8777**), or by checking the "Consular Services" section of the website at **http://dublin.usembassy.gov**.

Citizens of **New Zealand** can obtain up-to-date visa information by contacting the **U.S. Embassy New Zealand,** 29 Fitzherbert Terrace, Thorndon, Wellington (ℂ **644/462-6000**), or get the information directly from the website at **http://newzealand.usembassy.gov**.

Visitor Information   For information, contact the **North Carolina Division of Tourism, Film and Sports Development,** 301 N. Wilmington St., Raleigh, NC 27626-2825 (ℂ **800/VISIT-NC** [847-4862] or 919/733-8372; www.visitnc.com). Excellent visitor centers at the state borders on most major highways can also furnish detailed tourist information.

SOUTH CAROLINA

For general information, see the "North Carolina" section, earlier in this chapter. Also, for more specific information, see "Fast Facts: Charleston," in chapter 11.

American Express   Services in South Carolina are provided through **Abbott & Hill Travel,** 10 Carriage Lane, Charleston (ℂ **843/566-9051;** www.abbottandhilltravel.com).

Area Codes   It's **803** for Columbia and environs; **843** for Charleston and the South Carolina coast; and **864** for Greenville, Anderson, Spartanburg, and the Upstate area.

Emergencies   Dial ℂ **911** for police, ambulance, paramedics, and the fire department. You can also dial ℂ 0 (zero, *not* the letter O) and ask the operator to connect you to emergency services.

Fishing   A **fishing hot line** (ℂ **800/ASK-FISH** [275-3474]) gives you an up-to-date fishing report on South Carolina's major lakes, as well as information on fishing regulations. For more information, contact the **South Carolina Department of Natural Resources,** PO Box 167, Columbia, SC 29202 (ℂ **803/734-3886;** www.dnr.state.sc.us).

Liquor Laws The minimum drinking age is 21. Some restaurants are licensed to serve only beer and wine, but many offer those plus liquor in minibottles, which can be added to cocktail mixers. Beer and wine are sold in grocery stores Monday to Saturday. All package liquor is offered through local government-controlled stores, commonly called "ABC" (Alcoholic Beverage Control Commission) stores, which are closed on Sunday.

Newspapers & Magazines The major papers are the *State* (Columbia), the *Greenville News,* and the *Charleston Post and Courier.*

Taxes South Carolina has a 6% sales tax. Cities often tack an accommodations tax (an occupancy tax) on to your hotel bill. Counties also have the option of adding an extra .5% to 3% use tax.

Time Zone South Carolina is in the Eastern Standard Time zone and goes on daylight saving time in summer.

Visitor Information Before leaving home, write or call ahead for specific information on sports and sightseeing. Contact **South Carolina Division of Tourism,** 1205 Pendleton St. (PO Box 71), Columbia, SC 29201 (✆ **866/224-9339** or 803/734-1700; www.discoversouthcarolina.com). It can also furnish *South Carolina: Smiling Faces, Beautiful Places,* a detailed booklet with photos that cover each region of the state.

When you enter South Carolina, look for one of the nine **welcome centers** located on virtually every major highway near the border with neighboring states. Information sources for specific destinations in the state are listed in the individual chapters of this guide.

Weather Phone ✆ **803/822-8135** for an update.

GEORGIA

For more information, see the "North Carolina" section, earlier in this chapter. Also, for more specific information, see "Fast Facts: Atlanta," in chapter 16, and "Fast Facts: Savannah," in chapter 20.

Area Codes In metro Atlanta, you must dial the area code (**404, 770,** or **678**) and the seven-digit telephone number, even if you are calling a number within the same area code. It is not necessary to dial 1 before the area code when calling between communities within the Atlanta local calling area, even if they have different area codes. Other important area codes in Georgia include **912** for Savannah and **706** for Athens and Augusta.

Emergencies Dial ✆ **911** for police, an ambulance, paramedics, or the fire department.

Liquor Laws If you're 21 or over, you can buy alcoholic beverages in package stores between 8am and midnight (except on Sun, election days, Thanksgiving, and Christmas).

Newspapers & Magazines The *Atlanta Journal-Constitution* is the state's leading daily newspaper.

Taxes Georgia has a 7% sales tax, and an accommodations tax (an occupancy tax) is often tacked onto your hotel bill. Counties also have the option of adding an extra .5% to 3% use tax.

Time Zone   Georgia is in the Eastern Standard Time zone and goes on daylight saving time in summer.

Visitor Information   Contact the **Division of Tourism,** Georgia Department of Industry, Trade and Tourism, 75 5th St., Technology Square, Atlanta, GA 30308 (*✆* **800/VISIT-GA** [847-4842] or 404/962-4000; www.exploregeorgia.org), for information, a calendar of events (Jan–June or July–Dec), and the location of the visitor centers, which are open Monday to Saturday 9am to 6pm and Sunday noon to 6pm.

Index

North Carolina

A

AARP, 60
Abrams Falls Trail, 230
Accommodations, best, 4–6
Active vacations, 64–67
African American Arts Festival (Greensboro), 39
African Americans, 11–19, 20–21, 34
Airlie Gardens (Wilmington), 115
Air travel, 51–52
Alamance Battleground State Historic Site (Burlington), 170
Allanstand Craft Shop (near Asheville), 206, 219
Alum Cave Bluffs Trail, 230
American Automobile Association (AAA), 513
American Dance Festival (Durham), 40, 145
American Tobacco Company (Durham), 150
Amtrak, 52, 59
The Andy Griffith Show, 162
Annual Mountain Dance and Folk Festival (Asheville), 193–194
Annual Star Fiddlers Convention, 39
Antiques at Five Points (Raleigh), 143
Appalachian Craft Center (Asheville), 204
Appalachian Ski Mountain (Blowing Rock), 215
Appalachian Trail, 197, 230
Aquatic Safaris & Divers Emporium (Wilmington), 117
Architecture, 21–30
Area codes, 513
Art, 26–28, 30
Arts Center (Chapel Hill), 159
Arts Council of Moore County (Southern Pines), 189
Asheboro, 185
Asheville, 192–207
    accommodations, 198–200
    attractions, 194–196
    nightlife, 205
    outdoor pursuits, 196–197
    restaurants, 201–203
    shopping, 203–205
    side trips from, 206–207
    special events, 193–194
    traveling to, 192–193
    visitor information, 193
Asheville Wine Market, 204
Atlantic Beach, 127
ATMs, 55–56
Avon, 105

B

Backpacking, 66, 229
Bald Head Island, 122
Banner Elk, 210–213
Barbecue, 156
Barley's (Asheville), 205
Barn Dinner Theatre (Greensboro), 173
Barrier Island Kayaks, 63
Baseball, Durham, 147
Bath, 132–133
Beaches, 4, 96, 117
Bear Island, 128
Beaufort, 123–125
Beaufort Historic Site, 123
Beech Mountain, 213
Bele Chere (Asheville), 41, 194
Benjamin Vineyards (Graham), 219
Berkeley Cafe (Raleigh), 144
Biking and mountain biking, 64
    Asheville, 196
    Charlotte, 176
    Great Smoky Mountains, 229
    Pinehurst, 183
    Raleigh, 138
Biltmore Estate (Asheville), 193, 196
Biltmore Estate Winery (Asheville), 219
Biltmore Village (Asheville), 194, 195, 204
Birding, 64, 105, 111, 176, 229
Birthplace of Pepsi-Cola Store (New Bern), 130
Blowing Rock, 214–217
Blue Ridge Mountains, 61
Blue Ridge Parkway, 71–72, 190, 217–221
Blue Spiral 1 (Asheville), 204
Blumental Performing Arts Center (Charlotte), 179
Bodie Island Lighthouse, 105
The Bogue Banks, 127–129
Bonner House (Bath), 133
Books, recommended, 31–33
Bookshop, Inc. (Chapel Hill), 158
Boone, 207–210
Botanical Gardens (Charlotte), 174
Boulevard Trail, 230
Brevard Music Center, 194
Brevard Music Festival, 40
British Graveyard (Ocracoke Island), 107
Bryan Park Complex (Greensboro), 170–171
Buckridge Coastal Reserve, 61–62
Burgwin-Wright House (Wilmington), 114–115
Burlington, 169
Business hours, 513
Bus travel, 52–53

C

Cable Mill (Cades Cove), 228
Cades Cove, 228

Cades Cove Loop, 229
Cades Cove Visitor Center, 226
Café Zen (Durham), 150
Calendar of events, 39–42
Calhoun, John C., 15
Calico Jack's Marina (Beaufort), 125
Cameron, 189
Cameron Indoor Stadium (Durham), 146
Campbell House (Southern Pines), 186
Camping, 65, 138, 232
Canadian Hole, 106
Cape Fear Museum (Wilmington), 115–116
Cape Hatteras Lighthouse, 105
Cape Hatteras National Seashore, 104–106
Capital Area Visitor Services (Raleigh), 136
Car ferries, 53
Carolina Beach State Park, 117
Carolina Carriage Classic in the Pines (Pinehurst), 186
Carolina Hurricanes (Raleigh), 144
Carolina Panthers (Charlotte), 179
Carolina Theatre (Greensboro), 173
Car rentals, 513–514
Car travel, 52
Cataloochee Valley, 229
Cat's Cradle (Chapel Hill), 159
Cedar Island, 110–111
Cellphones, 70
Centers for Disease Control and Prevention, 57
Chapel Hill, 151–159
Charlies Bunion Trail, 230
Charlotte, 173–179
Charlotte Bobcats, 179
Charlotte Symphony Orchestra, 179
Cherokee, 72, 221–226
Chili Championship (Winston-Salem), 160
Chimney Rock Park (near Asheville), 206
Chimney Tops, 228
The Chocolate Fetish (Asheville), 204
Christmas at the Biltmore Estate (Asheville), 42
Civil rights movement, 20–21
Civil War, 16–19, 30, 110
Climate, 38–39
Clingmans Dome, 228
Club at Longleaf (Pinehurst), 182
Club Hairspray (Asheville), 205
Club Odyssey (Winston-Salem), 168
Coca-Cola 600 (Charlotte), 40
Coker Arboretum (Chapel Hill), 152
Colonial architecture, 22–23
Colonial era, 9–14

Georgia